medieval studies

SECOND EDITION

medieval studies

❧ An Introduction ❧

Edited by
JAMES M. POWELL

SYRACUSE UNIVERSITY PRESS

Copyright © 1992 by SYRACUSE UNIVERSITY PRESS
Syracuse, New York 13244-5160

Second Edition 1992
92 93 94 95 96 97 98 99   6 5 4 3 2 1

The paper used in this publication meets the minimum requirements of American National Standard for Information Sciences — Permanence of Paper for Printed Library Materials, ANSI Z39.48-1984. ∞™

Library of Congress Cataloging-in-Publication Data

Medieval studies : an introduction / edited by James M. Powell. — 2nd ed.
    p.   cm.
    Includes bibliographical references and index.
    ISBN 0-8156-2555-3. — ISBN 0-8156-2556-1 (pbk.)
    1. Middle Ages — Historiography.   I. Powell, James M.
D116.M4   1992
940.1′072 — dc20   91-31160

Manufactured in the United States of America

To the Memory of

သာ **DAVID HERLIHY** ၏

Whose Contributions to Medieval Studies
Opened New Pathways of Research
and Provided New Meaning to Our Teaching

Contents

⌒∽⌒ ⌒∽⌒

Illustrations

CHART

FIGURES

Preface

THE FIRST EDITION of *Medieval Studies: An Introduction* was well received and has proven useful to numerous medieval students and scholars during the last fifteen years. It has now been out of print for several years. The present edition is a substantial revision, enlarged by the inclusion of three new chapters on archeology, law, and science. We are grateful to our original contributors for their efforts and thank our new authors for their effort to help serve a broader audience.

Syracuse, New York
October 1991

JAMES M. POWELL

చరా రథ

Preface to the First Edition

THE PURPOSE of this volume is to provide the beginner in medieval studies, whether undergraduate or graduate student, with a convenient orientation to the field. Insofar as possible within the limits of the book, each contributor has attempted to lay a firm foundation for further study, not only through a discussion of the development and structure of his field, but also by giving valuable advice regarding further reading. To the degree that our efforts have been successful, it should be possible for students to use this volume both in an introductory course on medieval studies and as a ready reference companion to their research. Further, we have tried to take account of some of the more recent methodological developments in medieval studies, without neglecting traditional elements essential to the training of the medievalist.

The first two chapters, dealing with Latin paleography and diplomatics, introduce students to the use of manuscript materials. The accessibility of facsimiles and microfilms now makes possible extensive use of nonprinted sources in the early training of students. The practical advice given here by James J. John and Leonard Boyle will enable students to proceed with greater certainty in these difficult fields. Although not all medievalists have the same need for numismatics, Philip Grierson has made us aware of the significance of his field to other areas of research, and has illuminated the way for the uninitiated through his discussion of a wide range of problems extending from dating and cataloging of coins to values, weights, and overstrikes. George Beech has discussed the new uses being made of genealogical materials and other sources in social history by re-searchers employing prosopographical techniques to study the careers of officials, family histories, and the lives of lesser-known individuals. David Herlihy tells how medieval social and economic historians can make most effective use of the computer. A reading of his chapter should prepare the student adequately for a visit to a computer center and the preparation of a pilot project, undertaken with professional supervision. Given the in-tricacies of medieval chronology, Dean Ware gives especially useful help to the student reading medieval documents in their original language for the first time. The last four chapters are chiefly bibliographical introduc-tions to literature, philosophy, art and architecture, and music, though the reader will learn much in reading them about the principal research prob-lems to which scholars in these fields have devoted themselves. The au-thors have also made some effort to indicate the present state of research in their fields.

There are many other subjects that should have been included in this volume. In part, limitation of space has dictated some restrictions, but more important has been the difficulty in securing contributors with the proper qualifications and the time to devote to the project. It is our hope that the response to the present edition will be such that it will be possible to expand it in the future. In the meantime, the important contributions con-tained here will make a substantial impact on the training of medievalists.

Our field has reached a most important stage in its development. It currently enjoys considerable popularity, but we must be concerned be-cause the decline of study of classical languages in the schools may im-pede the continued growth of medieval studies. Although there is no lack of material for training medievalists, it has often been widely scattered and not easily adapted to convenient use. We hope that this volume will help to stimulate efforts to ensure that medieval studies will meet the challenge rising from the complex preparation required for its pursuit.

The planning for this volume has tried to emphasize medieval studies, rather than a single discipline. The editor has felt that students need handy but authoritative access to research in disciplines other than their own as a basis for interdisciplinary study. The selected bibliographies following specific chapters are intended as reading guides.

We would like to thank all those who have aided and encouraged this project, and we dedicate this book to our students, without whom it would be unnecessary.

Syracuse, New York
Spring 1976

Contributors

GEORGE BEECH is Professor of Medieval History and a member of the Medieval Institute at Western Michigan University. He received the Ph.D. degree from the Johns Hopkins University in 1960 and has taught at the University of Massachusetts and Swarthmore College. He is cofounder and coeditor of the journal *Medieval Prosopography,* 1980-. His publications include *A Rural Society in Medieval France: The Gatine of Poitou in the 11th and 12th Centuries* (1965), *A World Unto Itself: Life in a Medieval Village* (1975), and articles on Aquitanian aristocracy, William IX the Troubadour, personal names, and relations between England and Aquitaine around the time of the Conquest.

LEONARD E. BOYLE was Professor of Palaeography and Diplomatics at the Pontifical Institute of Mediaeval Studies, University of Toronto, 1961-84. Educated in Ireland and England (D.Phil. Oxford, 1956), he taught at the University of St. Thomas, Rome, 1956-61. He is the author of *A Survey of the Vatican Archives and of Its Medieval Holdings* (1972), *Pastoral Care, Clerical Education and Canon Law, 1200-1400* (1981), *Medieval Latin Palaeography: A Bibliographical Introduction* (1984), and articles on paleography, diplomatics, medieval universities, and the history of canon law in *Archivum Fratrum Praedicatorum, Bulletin of Medieval Canon Law, Mediaeval Studies,* and *Speculum.* He is a Fellow of the Royal Historical Society (London), of the Medieval Academy of America, and of the British Academy. He is also President of the Comité Internationale de Paléographie and, since 1984, Prefect of the Vatican Library.

WAYNE DYNES is Professor of Art History at Hunter College of the City University of New York. He has taught at Vassar College and Columbia University, and he received his doctorate at the Institute of Fine Arts, New York University. He is the author of *Palaces of Europe* (1969) and various articles on medieval art. From 1970 to 1973 he edited *Gesta,* published by the International Center of Medieval Art. He is Editor-in-Chief of the *Encyclopedia of Homosexuality* (1990) and co-author, with Marshall Myers, of *Hieronymus Bosch and the Canticle of Isaiah* (1987).

EDWARD GRANT is Distinguished Professor of History and Philosophy of Science and Professor of History at Indiana University, Bloomington. He is the author or editor of eight books and over fifty articles on medieval science, including *Physical Science in the Middle Ages* (1971), *A Source Book in Medieval Science* (1974), and *Much Ado About Nothing: Theories of Space and Vacuum from the Middle Ages to the Scientific Revolution* (1981). He has recently completed a volume on *The Medieval Cosmos, 1200-1687.* He is the recipient of research grants from the Program in History and Philosophy of Science of the National Science Foundation, as well as Fellowships from the Guggenheim Foundation (1965–66) and American Council of Learned Societies (1974–75). During 1965–66 and 1983–84, he was a Visiting Member of the Institute for Advanced Study, Princeton, New Jersey. Elective honors include Fellow of the American Academy of Arts and Sciences, Fellow of the Medieval Academy of America, *Membre effectif* of the Académie Internationale d'Histoire des Sciences and President of the History of Science Society (1985–86).

PHILIP GRIERSON is Professor Emeritus of Numismatics at the Universities of Cambridge and Brussels. He is the author of *Numismatics* (1975), *Bibliographie numismatique* (1966), editor and part author of the *Catalogue of Byzantine Coins in the Dumbarton Oaks Collection and in the Whittemore Collection* (1966–.), and part author of *Medieval European Coinage* (1986–.). He has at various times been Literary Director of the Royal Historical Society and President of the Royal Numismatic Society. He is presently Honorary Keeper of the Coins of the Fitzwilliam Museum, Cambridge, England, and Advisor in Byzantine Coins to the Dumbarton Oaks Center of Byzantine Studies, Washington, D.C.

The late DAVID HERLIHY was Mary Critchfield and Barnaby Keeney Professor of History at Brown University. After receiving his doctorate from Yale in 1956, he taught at Bryn Mawr, Wisconsin, and Harvard, where he was Lea Professor from 1973 to 1986. He was the author of *Pisa in the Early Renaissance: A Study of Urban Growth* (1958), *Medieval and Renaissance Pistoia: The Social History of an Italian Town* (1967), *Les Toscans et leurs familles* (1978; with Christiane Klapisch-Zuber; English trans. 1985), *Medieval Households* (1985; Italian trans., 1987) and *Opera Muliebra: Women and Work in Medieval Europe* (1990). Among his numerous honors were his Presidency of the American Historical Association in 1990, of the Society for Italian Historical Studies from 1981 to 1983, of the Medieval Academy of America in 1981, and the American Catholic Historical Association in 1972. He also received the John Gilmary Shea Prize for *Medieval Households,* and held a Guggenheim Fellowship in 1963–64. In 1985, the University of San Francisco awarded him a D.Litt. honoris causa. This volume has been dedicated to him.

JAMES J. JOHN is Professor of Paleography and Medieval History at Cornell University. He received his doctorate from the Medieval Institute at the University of Notre Dame in 1959. As a research assistant and associate at the Institute for Advanced Study, he collaborated on the last seven volumes of E. A. Lowe's *Codices Latini Antiquiores* (1953–71). He has been a Fellow at the Institute for Research in the Humanities at the University of Wisconsin and a member of the Institute for Advanced Study, Princeton.

THEODORE KARP is Professor of Music History and Literature at the School of Music at Northwestern University. He received the Ph.D. degree at New York University under Gustave Reese and Curt Sachs, and taught at the University of California, Davis. He is the author of a monograph and edition, *The Polyphony of St. Martial and Santiago de Compostela,* a *Dictionary of Music,* and articles on *trouvère chansons,* Gregorian chant, Notre Dame polyphony, and Johannes Martini in *Acta Musicologica, Journal of the American Musicological Society, Medievalia et Humanistica, Musical Quarterly,* and various *Festschriften.* He has been a Fellow of the National Endowment for the Humanities and a member of the Council of the American Musicological Society.

KENNETH PENNINGTON is Professor of Medieval History at Syracuse University. He completed his dissertation at Cornell University under Brian Tierney in 1972. He is the editor of the *Bulletin of Medieval Canon Law* and, along with Wilfried Hartmann, the editor of a new history of medieval canon law to be published in four volumes. His publications included *Pope and Bishops: The Papal Monarchy in the Twelfth and Thirteenth Centuries,* an edition of Johannes Teutonicus's *Apparatus ad Compilationem Tertiam,* and a number of articles.

JAMES M. POWELL is Professor of Medieval History at Syracuse University. In 1989–90, he was a Visiting Member of the Institute for Advanced Study, Princeton. His book, *Anatomy of a Crusade, 1213–1221,* won the John Gilmary Shea Prize of the American Catholic Historical Association in 1987. His most recent work is *Albertanus of Brescia: The Pursuit of Happiness in the Early Thirteenth Century.*

EDWARD A. SYNAN, former President of the Pontifical Institute of Mediaeval Studies and Professor emeritus of the University of Toronto, teaches the history of mediaeval philosophy in the Institute and University; a Fellow of the Royal Society of Canada, he holds a Ph.D. from the University of Toronto; his publications include books and articles on medieval thought and on Jewish-Christian relations; he is a Prelate of Honor, has been named for the 1991 Aquinas Medal of the American Catholic Philosophical Association, and has been awarded three honorary doctorates, LL.D. (Seton Hall University), Th.D. (Darlington Seminary), and D.Litt. (University of Dallas).

PAUL THEINER is Professor of English at Syracuse University. He did his undergraduate work at the University of Connecticut and took his advanced degrees at Harvard, where he studied under Magoun, B. J. Whiting, and William Alfred. He edited and translated *The Contra Amatores Mundi of Richard Rolle of Hampole,* and has written numerous essays, papers, and reviews, mainly on medieval English, Latin and French Literature, comparative studies, and the theory of literary history. He has taught at the University of California at Berkeley, and was a Fellow of the Institute for Research in the Humanities at the University of Wisconsin, 1965–66.

R. DEAN WARE is Professor of History at the University of Massachusetts, Amherst. He earned his doctoral degree at the University of Wisconsin, Madison. During 1970–71, he was Fulbright Professor of Medieval History at Trinity College, Dublin. In 1989–90, he served as President of the Midwest Medieval History Conference. His essays, articles, and reviews have appeared in the *Journal of Economic History, American Historical Review, Speculum, Isis, New Catholic Encyclopedia, Handbook of World History, Studies in Medieval Culture,* and other publications.

DAVID WHITEHOUSE is deputy director of The Corning Museum of Glass. Dr. Whitehouse studied archaeology at Cambridge University. From 1966 to 1973, as Wainwright Fellow at Oxford, he directed excavations at Siraf in the Persian Gulf. Subsequently, he was director of the British Institute of Afghan Studies in Kabul (1973–74) and of the British School at Rome (1974–84). His books include (with Ruth Whitehouse) *Archaeological Atlas of the World, Siraf III: The Congregational Mosque,* (with David Andrews and John Osborne) *Aspects of Medieval Lazio,* (with Richard Hodges) *Mohammed, Charlemagne and the Origins of Europe,* (with Donald B. Harden, Hansgerd Hellenkemper and Kenneth Painter) *Glass of the Caesars,* and *Glass of the Roman Empire.* David Whitehouse is an elected member of numerous professional associations, including the Royal Geographical Society and the Pontificia accademia romana di archeologia.

medieval studies

෴ 1 ෴

Latin Paleography

JAMES J. JOHN

ROM ANTIQUITY ONWARD authors have been reflecting on the fact that writing, by translating intelligible but fleeting sounds into enduring visual symbols, has enabled humans to overcome the feebleness of their memory and transcend the limits of both time and place, thus rendering possible the accumulation and dissemination of experience, knowledge, and wisdom that constitute civilization. Even universal recognition of the importance of writing, however, need not have resulted in any organized study of either the origins or the later history of writing. If the learned discipline of paleography now claims to be this organized study aiming at the production of a history of scripts from their beginnings down to the present, it still is far from totally accomplishing its basic task, and it actually came to a full realization of this task only rather slowly and indirectly.

Paleography's own history, which cannot be pursued in detail here (cf. Traube 1909–20, 1:1–80; Brown 1959–63; Petrucci and Pratesi 1988), reveals its development to have been fundamentally determined by its practical role as an auxiliary historical science, teaching how to read and date and place scripts, and much of this development took place under the aegis of other learned disciplines. It was in fact the field of diplomatics that first acutely felt the need to use the evidence of script as one of its criteria for determining the genuineness of charters. The magnificent response to this need provided by Jean Mabillon's *De re diplomatica,* published in Paris in 1681, actually constitutes, in its sections devoted to scripts, the first study

3

to which the word *paleography* could have been deservedly applied. The word itself, however, does not seem to have come into common use until 1708, when Bernard de Montfaucon published his study of Greek scripts and entitled it *Palaeographia Graeca.*

Because so many of paleography's tasks were long entrusted to, or claimed by, scholars whose primary allegiance was to diplomatics, epigraphy, numismatics, sigillography, or papyrology—none of which treats scripts for their own sake—paleographers proper long tended to concentrate their attention on the largely unclaimed scripts found in manuscript books. Today, however, there is rather general agreement that paleography should concern itself with the history of scripts wherever they are found, perhaps even with those frozen into type fonts. The vast expansion of paleography's field of concern that results from this attempted unification of interests previously so scattered does not eliminate, rather it reinforces, the need for divisions of labor on the basis of alphabets, time periods, etc. Now, however, the divisions can be based on factors more intrinsic to scripts themselves, and the laborers in the field can be more aware of, and hence more able to profit by, what their colleagues are doing in other corners of the same field. The focus in the present instance will be on scripts using the Latin alphabet and practised during the Middle Ages. For general introductions to other alphabetic, syllabic, and pictographic forms of writing, cf. Jensen (1969) and Diringer (1953, 1968).

Although paleography is claiming with growing insistence to be a full-fledged historical discipline, explanatory as well as descriptive, and seeking after knowledge interesting for its own sake, it continues to serve the practical purposes that presided over its birth and that constituted it as one of the most fundamental of the auxiliary historical sciences. The emphasis here will actually be on these practical purposes, in particular on the problems of describing the characteristics of scripts and of circumscribing the times and places of their use, since such an emphasis seems best suited to the needs of the beginner for whom this chapter is primarily intended. It is hardly necessary to add that these same problems are also intimately involved in any full-fledged historical approach to scripts.

The assignment of an approximate date and place of origin to a manuscript on the basis of its script—what can be called applied paleography—depends for its success on the prior establishment or ascertainment of some rules of scribal behavior peculiar to different times and places—what can be called theoretical paleography. The possibilities of pursuing theoretical paleographical studies have been extraordinarily enhanced in recent years by the publication, under the aegis of the Comité International de Paléographie Latine, of numerous illustrated national catalogues of dated manuscripts (cf. *CMD* and *Les manuscrits datés* 1985). The exact nature of the argumentation used by theoretical and applied paleography cannot be discussed here (cf. John 1987, 337–41; Autenrieth 1978; also Gilissen 1973 and in *Techniques* 1974, 25–40; Poulle 1974). It is important to remember, however, that the conclusions that applied paleography reaches with respect to the date and place of origin of a given manuscript may be true in the abstract or stylistically without necessarily being true concretely or factually. The scribe who learned the writing style peculiar to a given place may in fact have copied the manuscript in question elsewhere. It is also possible that a scribe may have learned to imitate a much earlier script, or anticipated a script that would become popular only later. For another kind of problem, namely that of determining whether more than one scribe was responsible for a piece of writing that is all in the same species of script, cf. Gilissen (1973) and also Poulle (1974). Macrophotography can be helpful here (cf. ibid.; also Fink-Errera 1962; Garand and Etcheverry 1975).

Just as paleography is itself an auxiliary science, so it has its own auxiliary sciences in turn, some of which may well be independent disciplines in their own right. There is perhaps no discipline that can a priori be excluded from potential service to paleography, but in a narrower and more proper sense its auxiliary sciences are those that provide knowledge about matters having a close and regular relationship to scripts, that is to say, the materials that receive and preserve them, the instruments by which they are made, and the fluid or other medium with which they are made. The paleographer may be forced to become his own auxiliary scientist by default, but if so, he still does not pursue these auxiliary sciences for their own sakes but only insofar as they may throw light on scripts.

Rather recently many of the auxiliary sciences have been drafted into the service of what is called codicology (cf. Masai 1950a; Delaissé 1959; Gruijs 1972; *Codicologica* 1976–; Gilissen 1977; Turner 1977; Canart 1979; Bozzolo and Ornato 1980; Muzerelle 1985; Lemaire and Van Balberghe 1985; Lemaire 1989; Martin and Vezin 1990), a name based on the Latin word for the book in the familiar form consisting of pages within a binding (*codex;* cf. below, pp. 55–57). Codicology, sometimes also called the archaeology of the book, makes the book, as such, the formal object of attention. All the elements, both material and intellectual, and all the techniques that combine in the production of a book are of interest to the codicologist, and this includes not only the script and any decoration that the book may contain but also the content itself, at least insofar as the latter affects the book's external form. The term "codicology" will actually be used here in a more limited sense for the study of the material support systems of the script, as if codicology were concerned with the body, and paleography with the soul.

The subjects that will now be addressed and the order of treatment are as follows: terminology, medieval scripts, abbreviations, numerals, punctuation, on reading, transcribing, and describing manuscripts, writing materials, ink, writing instruments, the external form of manuscripts, bindings, modern collections of medieval manuscripts, medieval libraries, and bibliography.

TERMINOLOGY

A long-term project is under way to supply paleography with a new and uniform nomenclature, not only for the genera and species of scripts but also for the elements and techniques that go into the making of letters (cf. *Nomenclature* 1954, 4; Gasparri 1976). Until this very complicated task has been accomplished—and its accomplishment is a long way off—it would be presumptuous to claim more for the terminology used than that it usually reflects common usage.

Most of the names employed for the various straight and curved strokes that combine to form letters are self-explanatory. The most basic stroke, the simple vertical or *i*-stroke, is called an *upright* or a *minim,* this latter name being a word that in Gothic script would be formed of nothing but a series of ten almost identical *i*-strokes. If minims or other vertical strokes are extended above or below the level of the shortest letters, the projecting portions are called *ascenders* or *descenders,* respectively. If the minim or upright, with or without an ascender or descender, supports another part of a letter, it is usually called the *stem.* The horizontal line connecting the obliques of *A* and the uprights of *H* is called a *bar.* Other horizontals may be called *arms* or *hastas* (e.g., in *E, F, L*) or *head-* or *top-strokes* (e.g., in *T*). The *body* of a letter is either the entire letter, as in the case of *a, c, e, i,* etc., or that portion of it that is not an ascender or descender, as in the case of *b, d, f, g, h, j,* etc. The connective line that may join one letter to the next is often called a *ligature,* but some authorities would prefer to reserve this term for describing two or more letters connected in such a way as to modify the form of one or more of them (e.g., & for *et*) (cf. Loew 1914, 140–41).

Of curved strokes, some are named from the letters they form, e.g., the *c*- or *s-curve. Bow* or *lobe* is the name given to the curves appended to a stem to form *b, d, p,* and *q.* The curved stroke attached to the upright of *h* is called a *limb.*

The *serif* or *finial* is the finishing stroke at the beginning or end of letters. Although not absolutely essential to the existence of letters, serifs or finials are nevertheless necessary to the well-being of any letters produced with a somewhat frayed writing edge or with a writing fluid of which the flow is not instantly responsive to pressure.

Scripts as a whole have been classified and named in various ways. A classification emphasizing the process by which they are produced divides them into *lettering* and *writing*. *Lettering* uses more than one stroke for each running segment of a letter, whether the method is that of building up or filling in or chiseling out the outline of a letter, while *writing* uses no more than one stroke for each part of a letter. Writing, in turn, has been subdivided into *cursive* and *noncursive*. In purely *noncursive* writing each part of each letter is made in a separate stroke. A *cursive* tendency is evident as soon as more than one part of a letter is made in one stroke. In a purely cursive script not only would all the parts of each letter be made in one stroke but each letter would, in turn, be connected to its neighbors without the writing instrument being lifted from the writing surface. In practice, of course, scripts can be only more or less, not absolutely, cursive.

Because the modified form that a letter can assume as a result of being written cursively may gain acceptance as the, or at least as a, new standard form of that letter and thereafter become written in non-cursive fashion, a distinction has been proposed between cursive on the one hand and current on the other (cf. Lieftinck 1954, 18–21; 1964, xiv–xv). *Cursive* would designate letter forms that were the result of having been originally written without the writing instrument being lifted from the surface (e.g., *d* with its ascender looped), even though they may in fact later be written in noncursive fashion, while *current* would designate letters that were actually written without the writing instrument being lifted from the surface.

From an esthetic or calligraphic viewpoint taking both process and appearance into account, scripts have been divided into *formal* and *informal*. *Formal* ones are carefully and deliberately produced, with the pleasure of the reading eye of more concern than the convenience of the writing hand. *Informal* or "everyday" scripts, produced with dispatch, cater more to the convenience of the writing hand than to the pleasure of the reading eye. In between these extremes there is room for various shades of *semiformal* scripts. Formal scripts tend to be non-cursive and informal ones tend to be current, but the correspondence is not exact.

Another classification, based mainly on appearance, has divided scripts into *majuscule* and *minuscule*. *Majuscule* designates an alphabet of which the letters are all of the same height (the printer's uppercase letters or capitals), while *minuscule* designates an alphabet of which some letters have ascenders or descenders (the printer's lowercase letters). Making a distinction that may not have been in the medieval scribe's mind, modern scholars have often defined majuscule scripts as those written or lettered between two real or imaginary parallel lines and minuscule scripts as those between four parallel lines of which the inner two contain the bodies of the letters and the outer two contain the ascenders and descenders (for a critique of this distinction cf. Mallon 1952, 102–103).

Finally, from the viewpoint of their content, scripts have been divided into *book* or *literary* on the one hand and *charter* or *documentary* on the other. The content need not, of course, have any effect on the intrinsic nature of the script, but in fact book scripts tend to be more formal and less cursive than charter scripts, and charter scripts in turn are more apt to cultivate idiosyncrasies that render forgery more difficult.

Shading means that a script has contrasting thick and thin strokes. It results, at least in writing as distinguished from lettering, either from a change of direction in the path of a broad-nibbed writing instrument or from a change in pressure on a flexible writing instrument. Shading caused by a broad nib produces a measurable *script* or *writing angle,* that is, the angle formed by the intersection of the thickest stroke with the horizontal writing line, the measurement being made in a clockwise direction from nine o'clock. This angle, the result of several variables, should be distinguished from a script's *slant,* which refers to the departure from the vertical, either to the left or to the right, of a script's minims and especially of its ascenders and descenders.

Ductus usually means the number, sequence, and direction of the strokes used in forming each letter of the script's alphabet, although the term is sometimes extended to include shading and pressure as well. A knowledge of ductus, which is more concerned with the dynamic than with the static aspect of letters, can be helpful in reading, dating, and placing scripts, but its most important service comes in explaining changes in the appearance of letters. It is largely ductus that determines where the inertial forces and strains generated by rapid writing will express themselves. But if ductus can help generate changes in appearance, changes in appearance can also generate and have generated changes in ductus. Gumbert (1974, 216–17), who uses the word *structure* for ductus, distinguishes two kinds of change: *metamorphosis* when the form changes but the ductus or structure remains the same, and *metanalysis* when the form remains the same but the ductus changes.

Because the names of particular canonical scripts will be discussed in the following section, they need not be mentioned here, but something should be said about the term *canonical* itself. A *canonical,* or *canonized,* script is of course a standard, widely used one, but more specifically it is one that has a well-defined and regular morphology with respect to all its structural elements and that possesses a recognized unity setting it apart from all other scripts, whether canonized or not (cf. Cencetti 1954–56, 55–56).

Provenance sometimes designates a manuscript's place of origin and sometimes any place where a manuscript has been preserved, but it serves best to designate a manuscript's earliest documented place of preservation. When place of origin is known, it is identical with provenance; when it is not known, provenance offers probable evidence for place of origin, the degree of probability declining as the time between the estimated date of origin and the date of attested provenance increases.

Finally, a word should be said about the names of individual manuscripts and scribes. The problems of identification that arise from the custom in scholarly literature of citing individual manuscripts by names derived (and frequently turned into Latin) from former or current owners and places of preservation can mostly be solved with the aid of the chapter on "The Nomenclature of Greek and Latin Mss." in Hall (1913, 286–357). The best guide to Latin place names is Graesse-Benedict-Plechl (1972). As for the names of medieval scribes, the most comprehensive collection is contained in *Colophons* (1965–82). (Cf. Catich 1968, 3–20; Cencetti 1954–56, 51–57; *CLA,* 6:xi–xii; Gasparri 1976; Mallon 1952, 100–104; Meyer and Klauser 1962; *Nomenclature* 1954; Parkes 1969, xxvi; Valentine 1965; Weijers 1989. An exhaustive codicological nomenclature in French is provided by Muzerelle 1985.)

A SKETCH OF MEDIEVAL SCRIPTS

The following survey, because of limitations of space, presents only a succinct description of the more common medieval scripts, along with some delineation of their temporal and geographical boundaries. Historical explanations of the origin, development, spread, contraction, and disintegration or disappearance of these scripts, which would present a more fascinating, if less certain, side of paleography, have not been emphasized. However, even if it were possible to arrive at definitive answers to the explanatory questions, these answers would still be less relevant than the descriptive ones to paleography's role as an auxiliary science. A small selection of facsimiles with transcriptions is inserted to aid in identifying the scripts being discussed.

The history of Latin script in the Middle Ages can be divided into at least three periods: (1) early medieval or pre-Caroline, (2) Caroline, and (3) Gothic. Each will be treated in turn. But, for reasons to be supplied below, some attention must also be directed first to the preceding Roman period and later to the succeeding humanistic and modern periods. The resultant sixfold periodization of the history of Latin script is certainly open to further refinement, but so long as the individual scripts within each period can be satisfactorily defined, dated, and placed, the main objectives of paleography as auxiliary science can be attained.

Roman Scripts

The Roman scripts, the history of which can itself be further periodized, naturally provide the background for the medieval scripts, but the slighting of historical explanation here would justify their being overlooked if it were not for the fact that some of them overlapped into, and some were revived during, the Middle Ages. The archaic script seen on the Lapis Niger and the Praenestine brooch (cf. Steffens 1909, pl. 1; Degering 1929, pl. 1; Diehl 1912, pl. 1 and figure on p. vii; Jensen 1969, figs. 510–11), ascribed to the sixth or fifth century B.C., was not used in the Middle Ages. But of the scripts that achieved a certain canonical status among the various types competing for favor in the late republican and early imperial periods, namely rustic and square capital and the earlier Roman cursive, only the cursive failed to enjoy some medieval usage. Of the canonical scripts developing from the second to the fourth or fifth century after Christ, namely the primitive minuscule or early half-uncial, the later Roman cursive, uncial, and half-uncial, all but the primitive minuscule overlapped into the Middle Ages. (Cf. *ChLA* passim; *CLA* passim; Mallon 1952, 1961; Mallon, Marichal, and Perrat 1939; Marichal 1948; Schiaparelli 1921; Seider 1972–81; Zangemeister and Wattenbach 1876–79.)

Rustic Capital

The rather inappropriate name "rustic" has been applied to this script because it seemed less formal and elegant than the square capital (see below). Rustic, which was *the* formal bookscript of the Romans, got its characteristic appearance from its pronounced shading, its finials, and the uniform height of nearly all its letters. Only *F* and *L* exceed the majuscule uniform-height rule with any frequency, though *B, G,* and *Q* also do so in some examples of the script. The thickest strokes tend to run at an angle about 45° above the horizontal writing line. Vertical strokes or strokes leaning to the right, which naturally are thin, have thick nearly horizontal finials at the foot, unless (as the third strokes of *M* and *N* and the second stroke of *V*) they are joined there to another part of the letter (see fig. 1.1). The script was full-fledged in the first century after Christ and it continued in use as a deluxe text script through the sixth century and for centuries longer as a script for titles and other special purposes, being especially popular in Spain. It was revived for prefatory texts in England in the eighth century (*CLA,* vol. 2, no. 193; vol. 5, no. 526; Lowe 1960, 21, 22, and pls. XXVII, XXX) and in France in the Carolingian period. The Utrecht Psalter (cf. *Codices Selecti,* vol. 75, 1982, for a complete facsimile edition) is the most famous example of the script in its ninth-century French revived form. Strangely enough, rustic capital was not revived by the humanists. (Cf. Pratesi 1964; Autenrieth 1988; Bischoff 1990, 55–61.)

Fig. 1.1. Rustic capital. Probably Italy. Ca. A.D. 400. Bibliotheca Vaticana MS. Palat. Lat. 1631, fol. 20v. Alphabet from Ehrle and Liebaert (1932), pl. 3b.

Square Capital

The name *square* or *elegant* or *monumental* capital has been given to very formal Roman majuscule scripts akin to the Roman upper case letters in modern printing fonts. Square capital shared the essential letter forms and ductus of rustic capital, but its thickest strokes were more vertical, running at an angle about 60° above the horizontal writing line, and a different principle governed the use of serifs. The writing was not always entirely "natural," since it could call for or allow a conscious change of script angle for certain strokes and sometimes it could pass over the border from writing to lettering, even when it was not executed with a chisel. Actually all the oldest extant examples, going back in less elegant forms to the third century B.C., are inscriptions, and with a few exceptions all the later and medieval ones are also either inscriptions or titles in manuscripts. In inscriptions the acme of perfection was reached in the second century after Christ (see fig. 1.2). As a script for the text of books in the Roman period square capital survives only in three fragmentary copies of

Vergil made between the fourth and sixth centuries (cf. *CLA,* vols. 1, 8, no. 13; vol. 7, no. 977; vol. 10, no. 1569). The letter forms in the three examples are by no means identical. Most authorities now doubt that this script was used for book texts either before or after the period of these Vergil manuscripts, but for titles and other special purposes it continued in use for centuries, undergoing a purifying reform in the Carolingian period. Then, after several centuries of hibernation, it was revived by the humanists of the fifteenth century and has remained in use ever since. (Cf. Autenrieth 1988; Bischoff 1990, 59–61; Meiss 1960.)

Fig. 1.2. Square capital. Rome. A.D. 112–13. Inscription on the Trajan column. E. M. Catich's spliced photograph reproduced with permission.

Imp(eratori). Caesari. divi. Nervae. f(ilio). Nervae | Trainao. Aug(usto). Germ(anico). Dacico. Pontif(ici)

Uncial

The letters of which the forms especially distinguish uncial from rustic capital are *A D E G H M Q* (see fig. 1.3). Rustic's characteristic finial at the foot of vertical strokes is lacking in uncial. This script is only imperfectly majuscule, since it always has letters projecting above the headline and below the base-line, especially *D H L* above and *F G P Q Y* below, but in the earliest examples of the script the projections are slight. The script is also roundish, but less so earlier than later. Although no extant example can be dated with certainty before the second half of the fourth century (cf. *CLA,* vol. 4, no. 467), uncial probably developed in the third or even second century. Extant remains, which are probably not perfectly representative, suggest that uncial was the most popular script for copying the text of books from the fifth century until well into the eighth. Of about 1,800 Latin literary manuscripts surviving from before the ninth century almost a third have at least a part of their text copied in uncial. As a text script uncial had a continuous existence into the ninth century and was revived in the tenth in the Ottonian realm (cf. Lowe 1972, 2:399–416, and pls. 80–87). For titles and other special purposes its continuous existence

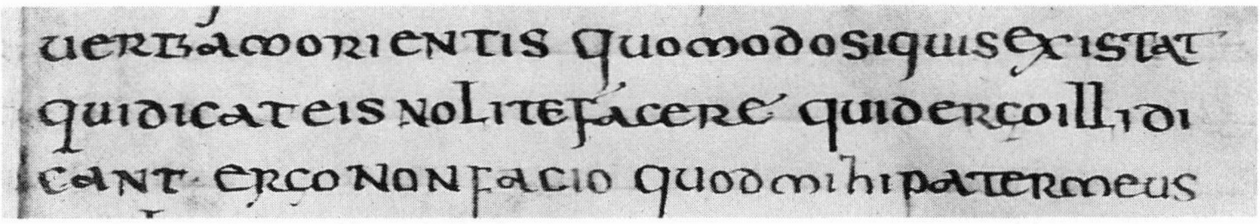

Fig. 1.3. Uncial. Luxeuil, France. A.D. 669. New York, The Pierpont Morgan Libr. MS. M. 334, fol. 132r. Reproduced with permission.

uerba morientis quomodo si quis existat | qui dicat eis nolite facere quid ergo illi di|cant, ergo non facio quod mihi pater meus

extended several centuries beyond this. A very early variety of the script used minuscule forms of *b* and *d,* which may suggest an original connection of uncial with primitive minuscule or early half-uncial. A group of fifth- and sixth-century uncial manuscripts with a characteristic form of *B* and *R* and mostly of legal content seems to have originated in Constantinople (cf. Lowe 1972, 2:466–74, and pls. 108–13). No example of uncial is known to survive from Ireland, and it shared rustic capital's neglect by the humanists. (Cf. Chatelain 1901–2; Lowe 1960; Lowe 1972, 1:103–26, 277–88, and pls. 8–21, 31–36; Petrucci 1971; Tjäder 1974; Bischoff 1990, 66–72.)

Half-uncial

This script, which has its thickest strokes almost perpendicular to the writing line, is uncial's nearest rival in popularity for the copying of books during the fifth, sixth, and seventh centuries. *CLA* assigns about one third as many half-uncial manuscripts (127) to these three centuries as uncial ones (380), with the ratio about one to four in the fifth (30:113) and seventh (37:144) centuries and about one to two in the sixth (60:123). The reason often given for the name that has been applied to this script since the eighteenth century at latest, namely its supposed devolution from uncial, is no longer accepted, but the name itself can still usefully serve to designate a rather well-defined species. Of the canonical form of half-uncial (see fig. 1.4), which was used well into the Middle Ages and which differs basically from uncial in its *a b d g m r s* and from rustic capital also in its *e f h q,* the earliest surviving dated examples come from shortly before A.D. 486 and 509/510 respectively (*CLA,* vol. 4, no. 508; vol. 1, no. 1a). However, the fully developed form of half-uncial seen in these manuscripts was prob-

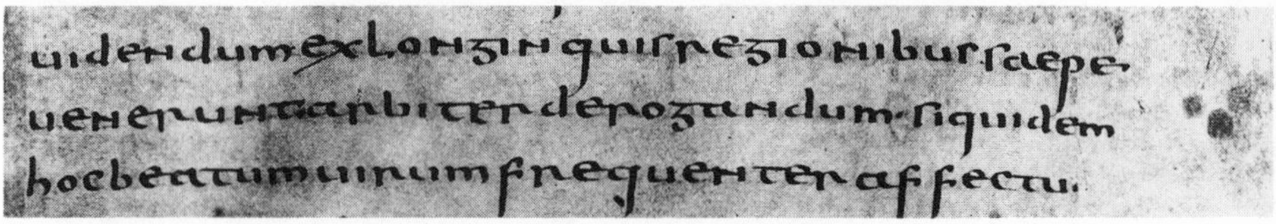

Fig. 1.4. Half-uncial. Verona, Italy. A.D. 517. Verona, Bibl. Capitolare Ms. XXXVIII (36), fol. 88r. Reproduced from *CLA,* vol. 4, no. 494.

uidendum ex longinquis regionibus saepe | uenerunt, arbitrer [*corrected from* arbiter] derogandum, siquidem | hoc beatum uirum frequenter affectu,

ably already in existence by the beginning of the fifth century or earlier (cf. *CLA,* vol. 3, no. 286; vol. 7, no. 984). The use of canonical half-uncial for the body of texts became less frequent in the eighth century, though it did not entirely cease until the ninth.

A somewhat similar and older script, to which the names "early half-uncial" and "primitive minuscule" have been applied, may be the product of an unrelated development taking place in the eastern Mediterranean (Bischoff 1990, 72–75) and hardly surviving the fifth century. This early half-uncial has more features in common with uncial, especially its *a g s,* and probably goes back to a period before uncial itself had attained its canonical form. The best known representative of this type is the Epitome of Livy, ascribed to the first half of the third century (Mallon 1961, 576–77; *CLA,* vol. 2, 2d ed., no. 208).

For more on half-uncial, see below under Insular, Visigothic, and Caroline scripts. (Cf. Chatelain 1901–02, pls. 61–100; Lowe 1972, 1:139–41, 303–14, and pls. 39–42; Bischoff 1990, 72–78.)

Roman Cursives

The earlier or older Roman cursive (cf. Steffens 1909, pl. 4; *CLA,* vol. 8, no. 1038), known also as majuscule or capital cursive and what Mallon (1952) and others now call the "classical common" (or "everyday") script, did not survive into the Middle Ages except in a bizarrely elaborated and hardly recognizable form used from the fourth to the seventh century for the first line of *Gesta municipalia* (cf. Tjäder 1954–82, 1:122, and pls. 43–45, 85). The later or newer Roman cursive, known also as minuscule cursive and what since Mallon is often called the "new common" (or "everyday") script (see fig. 1.5), took form no later than the second half of the third century and continued in use in some places as late as the eighth century. In the chancery at Naples it actually survived in not very altered form for several centuries longer (cf. Mazzoleni 1972, pls. IV–V). In certain areas and at different times between the sixth and eighth centuries this cursive was transformed, almost imperceptibly, into a number of book and documentary scripts with certain regional or "national" variations (cf. following section). Not only were two or more parts of a letter often made in one stroke, by means of loops and other connective strokes, but ligatures of two or more letters were frequent, sometimes even of letters from adjacent words. The uprights in this cursive often inclined somewhat to the right and strokes were normally not very shaded. In the well-known example shown in fig. 1.5 the *b* still has the form with its bow on the left, as in the older Toman cursive (cf. Mallon 1952, 32–35; Mallon 1961, 553–54, on the derivation of this form). (Cf. also Bischoff 1990, 61–66; Tjäder 1985.)

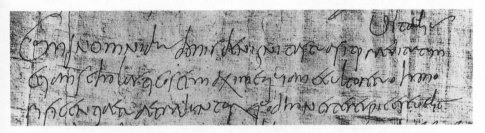

Fig. 1.5. Later Roman cursive. Egypt. A.D. 317–24. Strasbourg, Bibl. Nat. et Univ. Pap. Lat. 1 B. Reproduced from Garcia Villada (1923), pl. IV.

Cum in omnibus bonis benignitas tua sit praedita tum | etiam scholasticos et maxime qui a me cultore tuo hono|rificentiae tuae traduntur quod honeste respicere uelit

Early Medieval or Pre-Caroline Scripts

The disappearance by the later fifth century of effective imperial authority in most of the Latin-speaking half of the Roman Empire did not, of course, entail the disappearance of the Latin scripts heretofore used in these regions. On the contrary, the continuity in script was so pronounced that one cannot regard the later fifth century as the beginning of a new period, namely that of the early medieval or pre-Caroline scripts, except insofar as it introduced conditions that would allow the various provinces of the

West gradually to drift apart in their writing habits. The unconscious drifting apart was already underway in the sixth century, but that it had gone far enough to constitute a new era by the seventh or even by the eighth century would be hard to establish if the further "natural" aging of some of the traditional scripts had not been accompanied, starting in the sixth century but particularly in the seventh and eighth centuries, by clearcut and conscious transformations of half-uncial and the later Roman cursive. The Irish would be transforming a variant version of half-uncial by the late sixth century. A series of transformations, for book purposes, of the cursive documentary script that had grown out of the later Roman cursive would get under way in France by the mid-seventh century. In Spain half-uncial and cursive would both be transformed into a new script, the Visigothic minuscule, no later than the early eighth century. And in Italy by the mid-eighth century the inherited documentary script would be forged into one of the longest lasting of medieval book scripts, the Beneventan minuscule. These transformations, which will now be treated in brief detail, were only the more successful among many. A welter of other less popular examples, the full range of which can be seen in the facsimiles in *CLA* and *ChLA,* contributes to the picture of this period as one of increasing disunity in script. Most of these scripts would be swept away by the Caroline minuscule during the eighth century and the first half of the ninth, but those used on the newly contracted southern periphery and on the newly expanded northwestern periphery of the Latin-writing world would endure for at least several centuries longer. In addition, certain documentary scripts that developed out of the later Roman cursive, in particular the scripts of the Merovingian royal chanceries (cf. Lauer and Samaran 1908; Lot and Lauer 1936–49) and of the papal curia (cf. Rabikauskas 1958; Battelli 1965), would survive for several more centuries in the very heartland of the Latin-writing world. (Cf. *ChLA* and *CLA* passim; Lowe 1972, 1:2–65, and pls. 1–7; Bischoff 1990, 83–111.)

Insular Scripts

Perhaps the most distinctive and significant scripts to develop between the Roman and Carolingian periods are the Insular ones, so called because of their origin in Ireland and their long dominance throughout the British Isles. Among the extant manuscripts in these scripts are such unrivaled monuments of calligraphic skill as the Lindisfarne Gospels and the *Book of Kells* (cf. *CLA,* vol. 2, 2d ed., nos. 187, 274), both available in complete facsimile editions, the latter also entirely in color.

Two main types of Insular script developed, one called half-uncial or round or (by Lowe in *CLA*) majuscule, the other called minuscule or pointed. Each type was subject to variation with respect to formality or currentness as well as to individual letter forms, and one type also sometimes verged on the other. To cover these variations T. Julian Brown (1982, 101–2, and in his 1977 Lyell Lectures being prepared for posthumous publication) has proposed a fivefold classification of Insular scripts: half-uncial, current, cursive, and set minuscule, and hybrid minuscule incorporating various borrowings from half-uncial. The Insular round, a broad script with its thickest strokes almost perpendicular, tended to have most of its curved strokes formed according to the same symmetrical pattern and to be more circular than oval. The *a* looking like contiguous *oc* is characteristic. Even *l* and the upright of *b* have the form of shallow, reverse *s* curves. Ascenders and descenders do not project far beyond the body of the letter, the majuscule principle being observed about as faithfully as in uncial. Uprights have characteristic wedge-shaped finials. Ligatures are rare. The basic forms of all the half-uncial letters are usually found in this Insular script, but if a half-uncial alphabet provided the raw material, it must have been a half-uncial of a pre- or uncanonical type (cf., e.g., *CLA,* vol. 3, no. 395), because the script normally uses non-half-uncial as well as half-uncial forms of *d n r s* (see fig 1.6, where, however, only the half-uncial form of *d* occurs).

The minuscule or pointed type of Insular script (see fig. 1.7) has its thickest strokes sometimes running at an angle of 30° or less clockwise from the horizontal writing line. This angle facilitates ending the feet of descenders in a point. Letters are much more compressed laterally, with

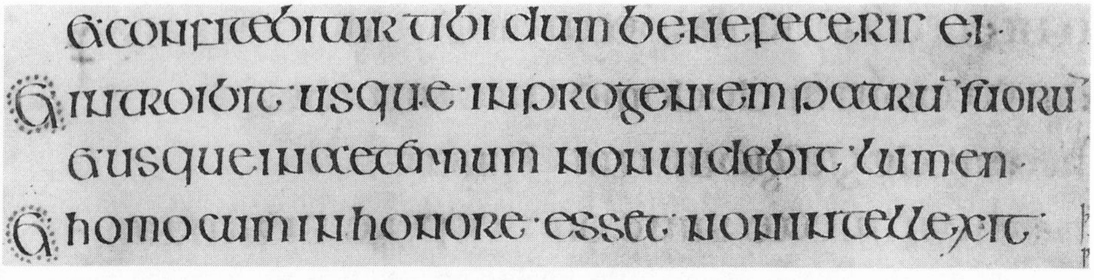

Fig. 1.6. Insular round. England. Mid 8th cent. New York, Morgan Libr. MS. M. 776, fol. 15r. Reproduced with permission.

> et confitebitur tibi dum benefeceris ei. | Et introibit usque in progeniem patru(m) suoru(m) | et usque in aeternum non uidebit lumen. | Et homo cum in honore esset non intellexit

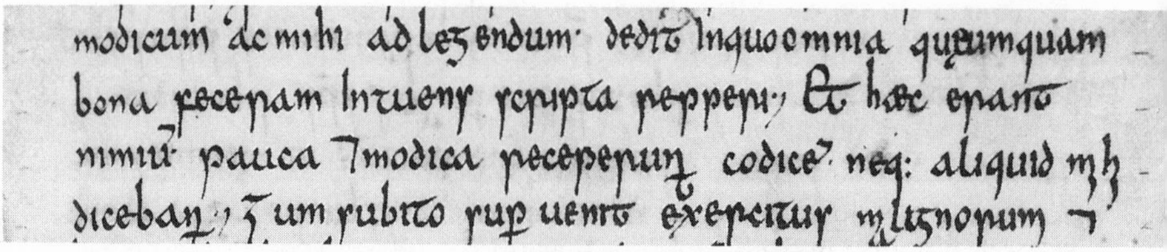

Fig. 1.7. Insular cursive minuscule. Probably Germany. Early 9th cent. Bloomington, Indiana Univ., Lilly Libr., MSS. Dept., Ricketts MS. 177, recto. Reproduced
with permission.

> modicum ac mihi ad legendum dedit in quo omnia quę umquam | bona
> feceram intuens scripta repperi. Et haec erant | nimiu(m) pauca (et) mo-
> dica receperunt codice(m) neq(ue) aliquid mihi | dicebant. Tum subito
> sup(er)uenit exercitus malignorum (et)

ovals and angles instead of circles and semicircles. An angular compressed
form of *a,* used along with an open *cc* form, is characteristic. More letters
have ascenders or descenders and these project further beyond the head-
or base-line. Apart from *a,* usually only *d* has alternate forms. Ligatures
are much more numerous than in the round script and in some cases the
pointed script becomes almost a full-fledged current cursive (cf. *CLA,* vol.
2, nos. 270, 275, 276).

Which of these scripts has temporal priority and the causal relationship between them, complicated by numerous mixtures of the two types,
are matters still under discussion. The round script must have been well
along in its development by the late sixth century in Ireland, even if the
Psalter in this script traditionally regarded as the handiwork of St. Columba (d. A.D. 597) was not really copied until the first half of the next
century (cf. *CLA,* vol. 2, 2d ed., no. 266). The earliest surviving dated example of the pointed script is an Antiphonary copied at Bangor, Ireland,
between A.D. 680 and 691 (cf. *CLA,* vol. 3, no. 311).

The Irish early brought their writing to Great Britain, probably no
later than Columba's settlement on Iona off the Scottish coast in the 560s,
and more effectively with the foundation of Lindisfarne in 635. The earliest dated examples extant of the English pointed type are from the 730s
and 740s (cf. *CLA,* vol. 2, no. 139; vol. 11, no. 1621). The Insular scripts
were also brought to the Continent (on the Irish cf. Bischoff, 1966–81,
3:39–54), where the earliest results still visible come from the monastery
that St. Columban founded at Bobbio in North Italy ca. A.D. 613. Anglo-
Saxon missionaries were particularly effective in establishing the new scripts

in Germany. Noticeable differences eventually developed between the Irish and English ways of writing, but in the early period they are hard to distinguish. Because of the Irish propensity for traveling, it may be hazardous to regard a documented actual place of origin as a stylistic place of origin.

The use of the round script was declining already in the ninth century, but a version of Anglo-Saxon minuscule called "square" and widely used in the tenth century south of the Humber shows some round influence (cf. Dumville 1987; Steffens 1909, pl. 71a). Irish examples of round used for special purposes survive in Gaelic texts from as late as the fifteenth century. The pointed script died out in Germany by the mid-ninth century, in England for Latin texts during the tenth and eleventh centuries, and for vernacular texts by the thirteenth, and in Ireland for Latin texts in the thirteenth, but for Gaelic texts a modified version of it has never completely died out down to the present day. (Cf. Bieler 1949; Bischoff 1966–81, 3:39–54; Bischoff 1990, 83–95; T. J. Brown 1972, 1982, 1984; *CLA*, vol. 2, x–xvi [2d ed., xiv–xx]; Gneuss 1981; Lindsay 1910, 1912; Lowe 1972, 2:441–58, and pls. 95–102; Morrish 1988; O Cróinín 1984; O'Neill 1984; O'Sullivan 1985; Spilling 1978.)

Visigothic Minuscule

This script, which was called *littera Toletana* (i.e., the Toledo script) in the Middle Ages, developed in Spain and in the adjacent regions of what is now France at latest early in the eighth century and probably by the late seventh. The modern name receives its justification from the fact that the script took shape during Visigothic rule of this region, even though this rule was about to be ended by Moslem conquest and even though the elements of the new script were of Roman, not Visigothic, origin. This script may resemble as well the kind of script that must have continued to be used in Latin-speaking communities in Africa after the Moslem conquest, if one may judge by several Latin manuscripts preserved at St. Catherine's monastery on Mt. Sinai (cf. Lowe, 1972, 2:417–40, 520–74, and pls. 88–94, 120–28).

All the letters of the half-uncial alphabet except *g* and *N* are found in the Visigothic alphabet and the breadth of the script, especially in its first centuries of existence, is also reminiscent of half-uncial. Even the characteristic uncial *g* may come from a variant version of half-uncial (cf. *CLA*, vol. 4, nos. 410a, 474; vol. 11, no. 1636). But the script also incorporates numerous elements from the later Roman cursive, particularly ligatures

of *e* with a following *c m n r s* or *x* and of *t* with a following *e i* or *r*.
Other characteristics include the regular use of a tall *i* at the beginning
of words (though not always before another tall letter) and in mid-word
for the semiconsonantal sound (as in *eius*), a *t* with its horizontal stroke
extending further and further down to the left, eventually touching the
stem at the base-line, and a tall, thin *y* (see fig. 1.8).

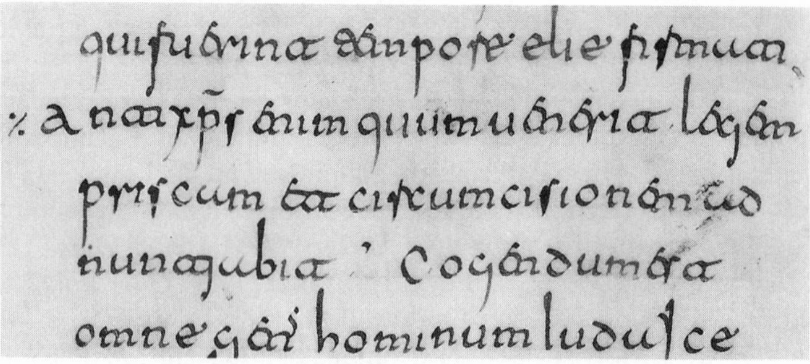

Fig. 1.8. Visigothic minuscule. Spain. A.D. 926. New York, Morgan Libr. MS. M.
644, fol. 172r. Reproduced with permission.

> qui fuerint tempore elie firmati. | Antichr(istu)s enim quum uenerit le-
> gem | priscam et circumcisionem ad|nuntiabit. Cogendum est | omne
> gen(us) hominum iudayce.

The Visigothic minuscule had assumed a rather mannered form by
the late eleventh century, when it was beginning to be supplanted by Caroline minuscule. It has been claimed by Mundó (1965) not to have died out
until the early fourteenth century, but Millares Carlo and Ruiz Asencio
(1983, 1:179–81) still defend the traditional view that it disappeared in the
twelfth century. Various criteria have been discovered for the dating of
Visigothic minuscule. The most useful, perhaps, at least for manuscripts
produced in the northern, non-Moslem regions, is a graphic distinction
introduced into literary manuscripts by the mid-tenth century between the
assibilated and unassibilated sounds of *ti* (cf. Lowe 1972, 1:40–64; Robinson 1939, 26). From this period onward the *i* for the assibilated sound was
extended below the base-line (see fig. 1.8, line 4). In general the script in
the earlier period tends to lean to the left and its ascending strokes are
club-shaped. In the later period ascenders have horizontal or oblique hair-
line approach strokes from the left. (Cf. also *Actas* passim; Arribas Arranz 1965; Avelino de Jesus da Costa 1990; Bischoff 1990, 96–100; Burnam

1912–25; Canellas 1974, vol. 2; Ewald and Lowe 1883; García Villada 1923; Millares Carlo and Ruiz Asencio 1983; Millares Carlo 1963, 1973; Nunes 1969– .)

Beneventan Minuscule

This script, named from the duchy in which it developed, is one of the most distinctive and enduring of the entire Middle Ages. The Benedictine abbey of Monte Cassino was the chief center for the production of Beneventan manuscripts, but the script was widely used in the surrounding regions of South Italy, and from the tenth to the twelfth century or later it was also used in Dalmatia. The earliest extant example seems to date from the mid-eighth century (cf. *CLA,* vol. 3, no. 381) and the latest date from the fifteenth and even early sixteenth (cf. V. Brown 1988; Kirchner 1955, pl. 28b). Examples of Beneventan minuscule have been identified in far more than a thousand extant, often fragmentary, manuscripts (cf. Loew and Brown 1980, vol. 2; V. Brown 1988).

The script derived most of its elements directly or indirectly from the later Roman cursive (as this was practiced in the eighth century) and during seven centuries of development it never lost the traces of its cursive origin, even though it gradually became one of the most formal and deliberate of all medieval scripts. In its mature phase, which it attained in the eleventh and twelfth centuries, the script shows regular and pronounced shading, with the thickest stroke running at an angle about 45° or less above the horizontal writing line (see fig. 1.9). The minim or *i*-stroke was broken into three segments, with the original body of the stroke reduced to an oblique hair-line connecting two enlarged lozenge-shaped finials. The most characteristic individual letters are *a* and *t* (distinguishable, once the top of *t* has begun to curve down on the left to touch the vertical at the base-line, only by a difference in the direction of their final strokes at the upper right) and tall *i* (used regularly both at the beginning of a word, except when followed by a letter with an ascender, and in mid-word for the semiconsonantal sound). Other characteristic features are obligatory ligatures of *ei, fi, gi, li, ri,* and *ti,* with the last having two forms according as the sound of *ti* is assibilated (see fig. 1.9, col. b, lines 2, 5) or unassibilated (see col. a, line 2). Still another feature characteristic from the mature period onward is the union of facing bows (see, e.g., the uncial *d* and *o* on fig. 1.9, col. b, line 4), achieved usually by juxtaposition rather than by overlapping. A variant type of Beneventan, rounder and less shaded, developed in Southeast Italy around Bari and in Dalmatia (cf. Loew and

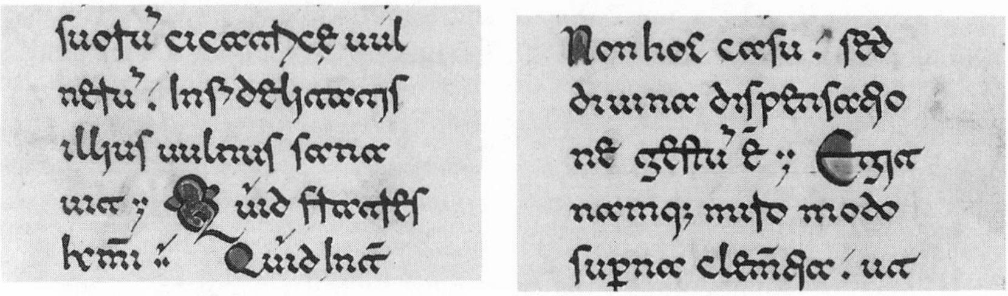

Fig. 1.9. Beneventan minuscule. South Italy. Ca. A.D. 1100. New York, Morgan Libr. MS. M. 642, fol. 135r. Reproduced with permission.

suoru(m) cicatricẹ uul|neru(m), infidelitatis | illius uulnus sana|uit. Quid fratres | k(arissi)mi? Quid int(er) | . . . Non hoc casu, sed | diuina dispensatio|ne gestu(m) e(st). Egit | namq(ue) miro modo | sup(er)na clem(en)tia, ut

Brown 1980, 1:150–52, and pls. VI–VIII). (Cf. also Bischoff 1990, 109–11, and fig. 22; Cavallo 1970; Lowe 1929; Lowe 1972, 2:477–79.)

Merovingian Scripts

If a script very much like the Beneventan might have come to prevail throughout the whole of Italy and in Southern Switzerland as well, the possibility was cut short by the triumph of Caroline minuscule. So too in the Merovingian lands, by which are meant here most of modern France and adjacent parts of the Lowlands, Germany, and Switzerland, candidates for the role played in South Italy by the Beneventan minuscule and in Spain by the Visigothic could not establish their dominance before they too, except for the Merovingian chancery script, were all swept aside by the same Caroline minuscule. Some of these Merovingian scripts are calligraphically and culturally very interesting, but because they survive in relatively few examples from rather brief spans of time, they cannot be given more than cursory attention here (cf. Bischoff 1990, 100–109).

The same Roman script models — particularly uncial, half-uncial, and the later cursive — were available for imitation and further development in Merovingian lands as were available in Italy and Spain. Uncial and half-uncial, in fact, continued to be used both for texts and for titles and other special purposes. The script named after Abbot Leutchar of Corbie (fl. ca. A.D. 765), for example, is basically half-uncial (cf. *CLA,* vol. 6:xxiii–xxiv; vol. 8, no. 1,067a; vol. 11, nos. 1,601–2). Uncial and half-uncial were also subject to mixing with each other and with descendants of the later

Roman cursive. An example of the latter process is furnished by another script used and probably developed at Corbie in the latter half of the eighth century and called *eN* because its *N* invariably has the capital form and its *e* ligates with a following *m r s t x* and possibly other letters but not with *N* (cf. *CLA,* 6:xxiv–xxv, and no. 711; vol. 5, nos. 638, 647, 655–57; Kirchner 1955, pl. 33; Stiennon 1973, 208–9). This script combines elements of a small and rapid form of half-uncial with ligatures derived from the later Roman cursive. Both the Leutchar and *eN* developments may well have begun after Pepin's coronation had put an official end to the Merovingian dynasty. Long before this, however, and certainly by the beginning of the seventh century, the later Roman cursive had acquired, whether by design or by gradual and unconscious transformation, a characteristic form (see fig. 1.10) that would maintain recognizable continuity in royal charters through the Carolingian and into the Capetian dynasty until the early eleventh century (cf. Lauer and Samaran 1908; Lot and Lauer 1936–49; Prou 1924, pl. X, 1; Steffens 1909, pl. 28; Mallon, Marichal, and Perrat 1939, pl. XXVII, 38). The name Merovingian has been most appropriately applied to this script, since all the earliest extant examples occur in charters issued by the Merovingian kings, but the name can justifiably be extended to other scripts evolving or devised in the same area during the pre-Caroline period and in particular to a series of new book scripts that are conscious, calligraphic stylizations of the Merovingian charter script, even though some of them did not actually come into existence until after the Merovingian dynasty had disappeared.

The earliest of these calligraphic stylizations, and one of two surviv-

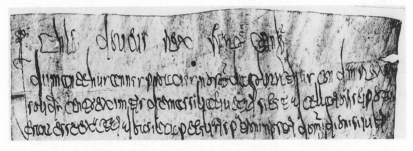

Fig. 1.10. Merovingian cursive. Nogent-sur-Marne, France. A.D. 692. Paris, Archives Nationales K 3, no. 5. Reproduced from Lauer and Samaran (1908), pl. 22.

xp [= chrismon] Chlodoueus rex franc(orum) u(iris) inl(ustribus) | Dum ante hus annus proauus nost(er) dagobercthus condam rex | solid(u)s cento eximtis de massilia ciuetati sicut ad cellario fisci potu|erant esse exactati ad basileca peculiaris patroni nostri dom(n)i dionisii ubi

ing in thirty or more examples, is called Luxeuil from the monastery where
it was most likely designed and employed (see fig. 1.11). Various kinds of
evidence argue for its use in the second half of the seventh century and
in the first half of the eighth (cf. *CLA,* vol. 6:xv–xvii; vol. 5, no. 579; Lowe
1972, 2:389–98, and pls. 74–79; Kirchner 1955, pl. 31; Lowe 1969, pl. X;
Mallon, Marichal, and Perrat 1939, pl. XLV, 66; Steffens 1909, pl. 25a).
The eighth-century script called *az* from its two characteristic letter forms
is a variant of the Luxeuil type, which had already made some, but not
regular, use of these same forms (cf. *CLA,* vol. 6:xviii, nos. 752, 765, 766;
Kirchner 1955, pl. 32, lines 7, 11 for *z;* Mallon, Marichal, and Perrat 1939,
pl. XLVII, 69).

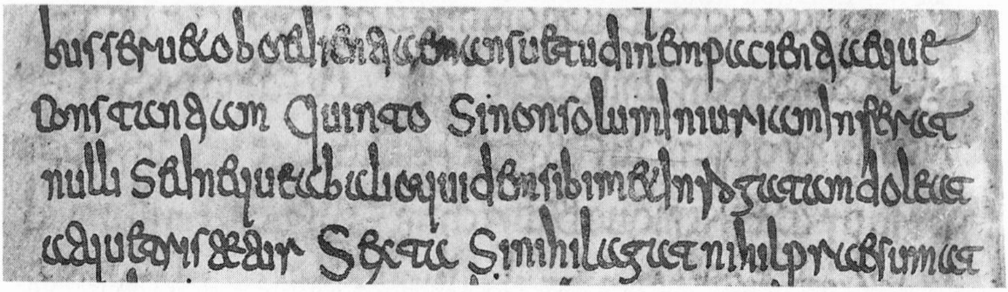

Fig. 1.11. Luxeuil minuscule. France, probably Luxeuil. Early 8th cent. New York,
Morgan Libr. MS. M. 17, fol. 37v. Reproduced with permission.

[omni]bus seruet oboedientiae mansuetudinem pacientiaeque | constan-
tiam Quinto Si non solum iniuriam inferat | nulli sed neque ab alio qui-
dem sibimet inrogatam doleat | atque tristetur Sexta Si nihil agat nihil
praesumat

Another, very graceful stylization of the Merovingian charter script,
retaining much of its rapid quality, is the *b* script, so named because its
b usually has a connective stroke to the right even when it is not ligated
with the following letter. This type was probably developed in the middle
or second half of the eighth century and perhaps in the nunnery of Chelles
near Paris (cf. Bischoff 1966–81, 1:16–34; *CLA,* vol. 6:xxi–xxii, nos. 719, 791).

Sharing the *b* with the vestigial connective stroke and surviving in even
greater numbers than the Luxeuil type is the stylization known as the Corbie *ab* script. Its characteristic *a,* like contiguous *ic,* represents a freezing
of the form the *cc*-like *a* sometimes assumed in ligature with a preceding
letter. A combination of evidence connects the origin of this script with
Corbie in the last decades of the eighth century; it would not entirely dis-

appear before ca. A.D. 830. (Cf. *CLA,* vol. 5, no. 554; vol. 6:xxv–xxvi, nos. 743, 767, 792; Kirchner 1955, pl. 34; Mallon, Marichal, and Perrat 1939, pl. XLVI, 67; Steffens 1909, pl. 29a; and Bischoff 1990, 106, for references to articles ascribing the script to a nunnery near Corbie.)

The special attention accorded to the foregoing Merovingian scripts because they represent conscious styles surviving in multiple examples should not hide the fact that these types not only account for far less than a majority of the seventh- and eighth-century Merovingian manuscripts written in other than pure Roman scripts, but they do not even constitute the paleographically most significant ones. There existed a seemingly endless variety of scripts (illustrated passim in *CLA*), some representing simply careless and unconscious departures from previous norms, some representing eclectic fusions of elements from earlier scripts, and some representing groping attempts to fashion a minuscule script smaller and more economical than the Roman scripts and more legible than even the stylized Merovingian ones. These last efforts eventually culminated, perhaps beyond anyone's intention, in the Caroline minuscule.

The Caroline Script

The Caroline Minuscule lasted more than four centuries in its original incarnation and then, largely as the result of its introduction into printing as the roman type font in the 1460s, has lasted almost six more centuries since it was revived by the Renaissance humanists around 1400. Optimists may regard it as one of humanity's permanent acquisitions. Other Latin scripts may have lasted even longer, but no other has so long been so widely used. The earliest dated surviving examples of the script are found in a Bible copied at Corbie in the 770s at the order of Abbot Maurdramn and in some dedicatory verses added to an Evangelistary copied in the entourage of Charlemagne between A.D. 781 and 783 (cf. *CLA,* vol. 6, no. 707; vol. 5, no. 681). From North France and the contiguous areas of Germany, where Caroline minuscule may have emerged in several places independently, the script rapidly spread over all but the southern extremes of the Carolingian Empire early in the ninth century. By the mid-ninth century it had almost totally supplanted all other text scripts within this area, including the Anglo-Saxon pointed script in Germany, for the copying of books. The abbey of Tours, whatever its role in the original development of Caroline minuscule, played an important part in this rapid dissemination. Surviving examples from the ninth century, which will be the subject of a much-awaited publication (cf. Bischoff 1963), approach 7,000, a quantum jump beyond the number of Latin manuscripts surviving from all previous centuries combined. In the second half of the tenth century Caroline minuscule began to supplant the Anglo-Saxon script in England for Latin texts. In the late eleventh century it started to take the place of Visigothic minuscule in Spain. And it of course accompanied Western Christendom as it expanded into Northern Germany, Eastern Europe, and Scandinavia from the ninth century onward. On another front it was also replacing the pre-Caroline charter scripts that had descended from the later Roman cursive. The German royal chancery adopted the Caroline in the ninth century, the French adopted it in the early eleventh, and the papal chancery did the same in the early twelfth. Private charters in these regions were naturally using Caroline minuscule, though not exclusively, much sooner. The Caroline in charters, in contrast to that in books, was distinguished by longer ascenders often ending in fancy curlicues, by fancy abbreviation strokes, and sometimes by ligatures of *ct, rt,* and *st* exaggerated in breadth. Finally, starting late in the eleventh century or early in the twelfth, the Caroline minuscule of North France gradually began to turn into Gothic, and by the early thirteenth century the same transformation had taken, or was taking, place almost everywhere in Europe.

The predominant forms of the Caroline alphabet throughout its history are all, except for its long *s,* substantially the same as those of the modern roman type font. With respect to earlier scripts, they are most like those of half-uncial, differing only in *a, g,* and *n* (see fig. 1.12). Caroline minuscule's internal unity does not mean, however, total uniformity in its appearance either through the centuries or throughout Western Europe at any one time. There were general, if minor, differences in size, in the ratio of breadth to height, in shading, and in slant, and particular differences in the forms of individual letters. Many of these differences do not, or only with difficulty, fit within any overall plan of development. In general, however, the Caroline letters over the centuries, at least outside Italy, underwent some lateral compression and as a result seem taller, they were written more compactly, and some of their curves gave way to angles. Caroline, in other words, was on the way to Gothic. The ductus of ascenders also changed. Instead of being formed, as they were in the ninth and much of the tenth centuries, by an overlapping looping stroke that began about mid-height and gave the ascender a club-shaped appearance, the ascenders were more and more being started at the top with a horizontal hair-line approach stroke which then turned downward.

In terms of individual letters Caroline minuscule had variant forms at both the beginning and the end of its original life span, forms that help to tie its history to both the preceding Merovingian and the succeeding

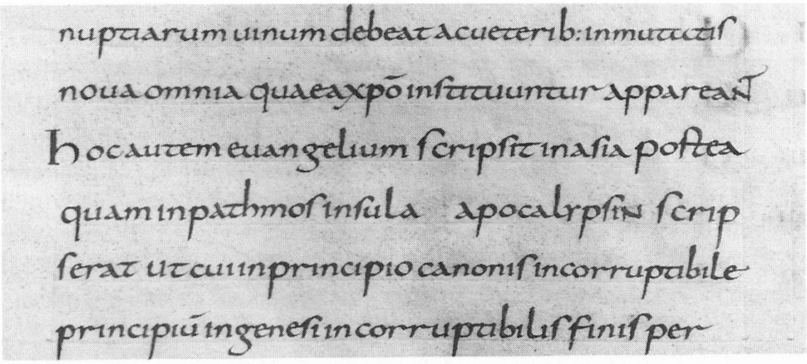

Fig. 1.12 Caroline minuscule. Tours. Early 9th cent. New York, Morgan Libr. MS.
M. 191, fol. 169r. Reproduced with permission.

nuptiarum uinum debeat ac ueterib(us) inmutatis | noua omnia quae a
chr(ist)o instituuntur appareant | Hoc autem euangelium scripsit in asia
postea|quam in pathmos insula apocalypsin scrip|serat ut cui in principio
canonis incorruptibile | principiu(m) in genesi | incorruptibilis finis per

Gothic scripts. In its early phase the variants included the *cc* form of *a*
rather frequently, the uncial *d* (i.e., with its ascender leaning or curved to
the left), and capital *N*. In its late phase the variants included the round
s at the end of words, *v*-shaped *u* particularly at the beginning of words,
an oblique hair-line over certain *i*'s, and again the uncial *d*. In the eleventh
century the letter *w* began to make its appearance. Changes in the treatment of the *ae* diphthong are also worth noting. In the ninth century the
two letters were usually written out in full, though the *e* with cedilla, which
is what remains of the *a* in an *ae* ligature, continued in use from pre-Caroline
times. The use of the *e* with cedilla increased in the tenth century and it
prevailed in the eleventh. Then in the course of the twelfth century the
cedilla began to be more and more often dropped in favor of simple *e,*
and in the early thirteenth century it completely disappeared.

Caroline minuscule's chief difference from the preceding Merovingian
scripts was its elimination of most of the latter's ligatures. The process
of elimination was gradual and the point at which a script can qualify in
this respect as Caroline is somewhat arbitrary. A few ligatures, in particular *et, ct, rt,* and *st,* were never completely eliminated from the Caroline
canon, although in the twelfth century the ampersand began to be replaced
by the *7*-like *nota tironiana* which Insular scribes had long been using.

At the same time that Caroline minuscule was being perfected, the old Roman scripts were undergoing refurbishment, mostly for use in titles and colophons but some of them also for use in texts themselves. Particularly noteworthy is the increased use of half-uncial for the first line or two of a new book or chapter in the important scriptoria at St. Amand, Tours, and other places under their influence. (Cf. Bischoff 1954; Bischoff 1966–81, 3:1–38; Bischoff 1974–80; Bischoff 1990, 112–27, 247–50, and pls. 12, 14; Autenrieth 1978; Bishop 1971; Cencetti 1954–56, 166–205 with a bibliographical survey; *CLA,* vol. 6:xii–xxx passim; 10:viii–xix; Dufour 1972; D. Ganz 1987; Garand 1980; Jones 1932; Ker 1960; Lowe 1969, 27–33; Marichal 1948, 63–64, 97–99; Rand 1929, 1934; Supino Martini 1987; Vezin 1974.)

Gothic Scripts

The geometric increase in manuscript production that accompanied the development of Caroline minuscule was repeated with the development of the scripts called Gothic, a name used in its current meaning since the eighteenth century and originally coined by the Italian humanists as a term of opprobrium for scripts that they considered barbaric. The decisive factor in bringing about the new explosion in book production — the vast majority of extant medieval Latin books, to say nothing about documents, are in Gothic writing — was the educational revival of the twelfth century that issued into the first universities. By the year 1500 almost eighty of these institutions of higher education had been founded in Western Europe. The enormous appetite for books that they generated led, by the thirteenth century, to a more efficient method of book production. This was the *pecia* or piece system (cf. Destrez 1935; Bataillon et al. 1988; and fig. 1.16 for a marginal *pecia* indication) that enabled multiple copies to be made directly and simultaneously from a single authoritative or corrected exemplar of a book, thus promoting a combination of accuracy and speed. In the fifteenth century the universities contributed greatly to the economic viability of the new printing industry.

The transition from Caroline minuscule to Gothic was so gradual and continuous a process, allowing for coexistence of the two species and of intermediate approximations, that the resemblance between the late Caroline and the early Gothic can seem to be much closer than that between the early and late Caroline on the one hand or between the early and late Gothic on the other (cf., e.g., *CMD-NL,* vol. 1, pls. 26, 92, 94, and 295). If Gothic prefers angularity to curves, height to width, and more rather than less shading, with the thickest stroke often almost perpendicular to the horizontal writing line, and if it prefers uncial *d* to Caroline *d*, round *s* to the tall *s* at the end of words, and *7* to the ampersand for *et*, then late Caroline was showing more and more of all these characteristics and sometimes more than some scripts that deserve to be called early Gothic. Even the breaking of shafts or minims to form angular or rectangular finials (see fig. 1.14) — which is usually considered the most characteristic feature of formal Gothic — is not entirely foreign to late Caroline. So obvious are the continuities that there has been a reluctance and sometimes even a refusal, from the time of Mabillon onward, to regard Gothic as a new type of script.

Whether or not Gothic is an essentially new script is a question of esthetic philosophy that can be left aside here. There is no question, however, that Gothic introduced something new, beyond increasing the number of letter parts by its angles and beyond the changes that late Caroline minuscule was already anticipating. These latter changes were all elements contributing to the formation of Gothic, but by themselves they did not constitute Gothic, nor did they obviously and necessarily lead to the formation of Gothic. For this, an esthetic leap was necessary, a conscious determination to tie the various elements at hand together in a comprehensive and systematic way. Conscious, comprehensive system and symmetry, which have more of the abstract and the mathematical than of the vital about them, may be said, though not without a touch of paradox, to be the very life of Gothic script. This emphasis upon the consciously systematic character of Gothic, without denying the importance of its angularity, verticality, etc., makes particularly useful as a practical test for separating beginning Gothic from ending Caroline the uniform treatment of the feet of all strokes standing on the base-line, including the feet of *f* and long *s* that had previously descended below the base-line (see fig. 1.13 and cf. Bischoff 1954, 11–14). This uniformity is more a sign of the self-consciousness essential to Gothic than it is itself an essential part of Gothic, since, as will be seen, there are scripts that receive the name Gothic and nevertheless do not observe this uniformity.

Uniformity in the feet of its minims by itself, however, qualifies a script only as early or primitive Gothic. Full-fledged Gothic must manifest more of the consequences of Gothic's angular esthetic. One easily recognizable sign of this, though its regular presence, too, cannot be made an absolutely essential part of full-fledged Gothic script, is the practice of fusing facing bows (now often become half hexagons), such as occur in contiguous uncial *d* and *e* (see fig. 1.14 and cf. Meyer 1897). When the rule was observed with complete consistency, every time *b*, uncial *d*, *h*, *o*, *p*, Gothic *v* and *y*, or the reversed-*c* abbreviation for *con* was followed within the

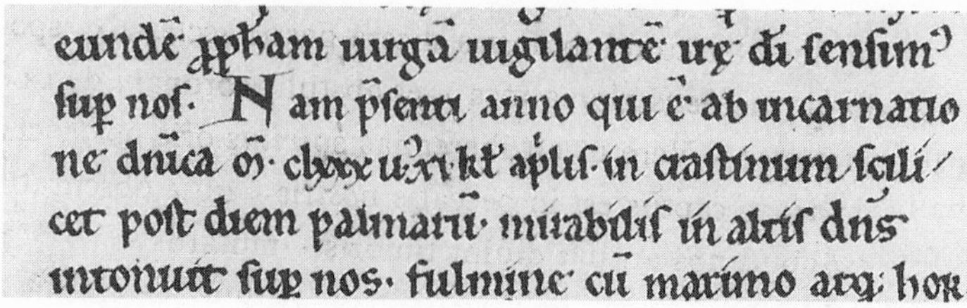

Fig. 1.13. Early Gothic textual. Liège. A.D. 1182. Louvain, Bibl. de la Univ., MS. VI (destroyed). Reproduced from Reusens (1899), pl. XXVII.

eunde(m) p(ro)ph(et)am uirga(m) uigilante(m) irẹ d(e)i sensim(us) | sup(er) nos. Nam p(re)senti anno qui e(st) ab incarnatio|ne d(omi)nica mclxxxii[(us)], xi k(a)l(endas) ap(r)ilis, in crastinum scili- | cet post diem palmaru(m), mirabilis in altis d(omi)n(u)s | intonuit sup(er) nos, fulmine cu(m) maximo atq(ue) hor[ribili]

same word by *c, d, e, g, o,* or *q,* the facing bows overlapped and usually shared a common stroke. The vast majority of Gothic scribes observed this rule from the thirteenth to the fifteenth century and beyond, but only a small minority of them did so with complete consistency. Examples of its observance can actually be found as early as 1146 (cf. Gasparri 1973, 115) and 1162 (cf. *CMD-F,* vol. 2, pl. XXa).

Hand in hand with the fusion of facing bows in Gothic went the development of a ligature of *r* with a preceding letter ending in a bow, namely, *b,* uncial *d, h, o, p, v,* and *y* (see figs. 1.14, 1.15, 1.19). This development was a systematic extension of a ligature of *R* with a preceding *O* that was occasionally used at the end of lines in uncial script (cf. facs. in *CLA,* vol. 2, nos. 126, 193) and that was taken over by Caroline minuscule. The 2-like part of the *R* that did not overlap the preceding bow eventually began, starting sporadically in the later thirteenth century, to be regarded as a complete *r* by itself, so that it could be used independently of a preceding bow (cf. fig. 1.22, where it is carried over into humanistic cursive).

Recently (cf. Zamponi 1988) attention has been called, on the basis of a study of various volumes of CMD, to still another characteristic of the more formal Gothic script. This is a tendency, sometimes a rule, starting in the twelfth century and continuing into the sixteenth and especially in Italy, to elide the angular or rectangular finial of the first minim or upright of a letter (i.e., in *i m n p r t u*) with the final horizontal stroke of a preceding *f g r t* (sometimes also *c e* and *x*) (see figs. 1.14, 1.15, 1.16).

Despite rather general agreement that the graphic features just discussed are basic to Gothic script, it remains true that the name Gothic

Fig. 1.14. Formal Gothic textual. Flanders, probably the Ghent-Bruges school, early 16th century. The author's collection.

Genuisti qui te fecit et in eternu(m) | permanes uirgo Iube domi|ne bene-
dicere. V(ersiculus) Per uirgine(m) | matrem concedat nobis domin(us) |
salutem et pacem a(men). L(e)c(ci)o tercia. | Quasi cedrus exaltat su(m) |
in lybano, et quasi cy|pressus in monte syon. Quasi | palma exaltata sum
in cades (et) | quasi plantacio rose in iherico.

is commonly applied to scripts that not only lack some of these features, but also possess others at odds with them. Because this situation leads to confusion about the nature of Gothic and the ways in which it is possible to share in that nature, there is a clear need for a comprehensive reconsideration of the whole problem. Until this is done, however, there is much practical value, despite the objections that scholars have raised (Gumbert 1974, 199–214, has answered them), in the classification and nomenclature of Gothic book scripts proposed by Lieftinck in 1954 as a result of his study of the scripts used in the Lowlands. He suggested a first division, on the basis of objective criteria, into three types: *textual, bastard,* and *cursive.* The term *hybrid* was later substituted for bastard (cf. *CMD-NL,* 1:xv–xvii). Within each of these types he then proposed a further threefold subdivision, depending on whether it was formal (*formata*), current or rapid (*currens*), or midway between these two extremes. These further subdivisions, which Gumbert (1974, 205, 215–33) would prefer to call levels (*niveaux*) with qualitative elements, are based on more subjective criteria. The final result is nine subdivisions of Gothic book scripts describable as follows: (1) formal or calligraphic textual, (2) (ordinary) textual, (3) current textual, (4) formal hybrid, (5) (ordinary or what Lieftinck would call textual) hybrid, (6) current hybrid, (7) formal cursive, (8) (ordinary or what Lieftinck would call textual) cursive, (9) current cursive. Among the three main divisions the textual enjoys a privileged position, both by virtue of its more thoroughgoing realization of the Gothic esthetic ideal and by virtue of its priority in time. And among the subdivisions of the textual type the formal enjoys a privileged position (see fig. 1.14). This is Gothic par excellence, the kind that the mere mention of the word Gothic evokes in the imaginations of those who have seen the deluxe manuscripts of the later Middle Ages, and it is also the kind to which what has so far been said here about Gothic primarily applies. The formal textual, which evolved out of the ordinary textual, reached its acme, both in stylistic perfection and in frequency of use, in the thirteenth and fourteenth centuries. Its contemporary names, *littera psalterialis* or *missalis,* indicate that even in this period it was used primarily for sumptuous liturgical books. By the fifteenth century its use was being reduced by the development of new formal scripts, but it was not extinct even in the sixteenth century. In fact, thanks to its adoption as the model for the first printing fonts, it is still in use today for the printing of vernacular German literature and of newspaper titles.

The ordinary Gothic textual (cf. Lieftinck 1954, figs. 14, 15, 18, 29b, 30) has a greater range of variation than the formal. In general it includes scripts that were written with more speed and less care than the formal, or with less thoroughness and consistency in observing the rules that the formal Gothic observed. Complete uniformity in the treatment of the feet of vertical strokes and in the angling of curves may not have been attempted, much less attained. Sometimes the difference between the formal and the ordinary may have been partly the result of the letters being written on such a small scale that the Gothic angles were inevitably slurred. This is true of a large group of manuscripts, mostly pocket-size Bibles produced in France in the thirteenth century, of which the miniature Gothic textual has been given the special name of pearl script (cf. facs. in Degering 1929, pl. 81; *CMD-F,* vol. 5, pl. XXIIIb; vol. 6, pl. XXa; Stiennon 1973, 247). Among other manuscripts in the ordinary textual category are many of those copied by professional scribes for various university communities (see figs. 1.15, 1.16), particularly the ones in the *littera Parisiensis* or Parisian script (cf. Destrez 1935, pls. 1–18; Kirchner 1966, pl. 18; Steffens 1909, pl. 98). By the mid-fifteenth century the ordinary textual, long used much more

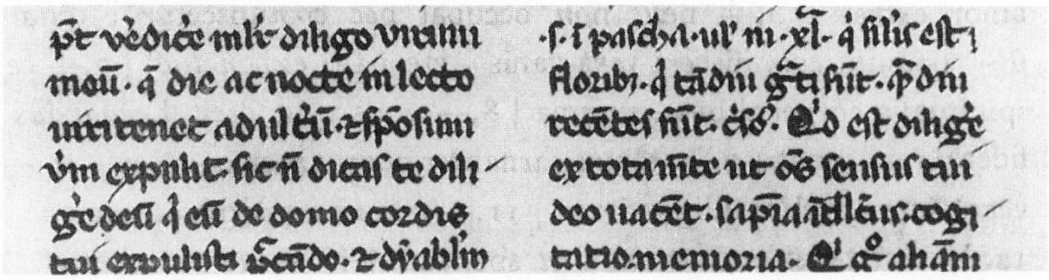

Fig. 1.15. Gothic textual Parisian script. Probably Paris. A.D. 1293. Louvain, Bibl. de l'Univ., MS. 46 (destroyed). Reproduced from Reusens (1899), pl. XXXIII.

[Non] p(otes)t v(er)edic(er)e m(u)l(ie)r diligo virum | meu(m), q(ue) die ac nocte in lecto | uiri tenet adult(er)u(m) (et) spo(n)sum | v(eru)m expulit. sic n(on) dicas te dili- | g(er)e deu(m) q(ui) eu(m) de domo cordis | tui expulisti p(e)cca(n)do (et) dyab(u)l(u)m | . . . . s(cilicet) i(n) pascha, u(e)l in (quadragesim)a, q(u)i si(mi)lis est [*expunctuated* i *used as a space filler*] | florib(us), q(u)i ta(m)diu g(r)ati su(n)t, q(u)a(m)diu | rece(n)tes su(n)t. c(r)iso(stomus). Q(u)id est dilig(er)e | ex tota m(en)te ut o(mne)s sensus tui | deo uace(n)t. sap(ienc)ia i(n)t(e)ll(e)c(t)us, cogi- | tatio, memoria. Q(u)i (er)go aliq(ue)m

frequently than the formal, was having more and more of its functions taken over by cursive and hybrid scripts to be treated below.

The third kind of textual, namely the current (cf. Lieftinck 1954, fig. 16), which was characterized by being written with more rapidity than the ordinary, had an even shorter life span. Its purposes were beginning to be

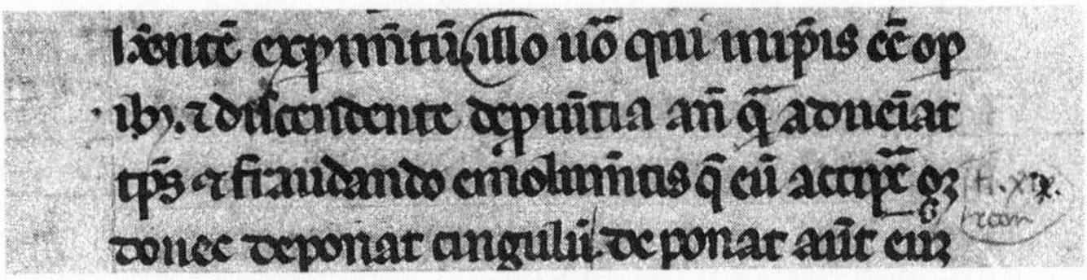

Fig. 1.16. Round Gothic textual Bolognese script. Probably Bologna. Ca. A.D. 1300. Princeton Univ. Libr. Taylor Collection of Fragments, AM 21140, Item 42. Reproduced with permission.

h(ab)ente(m) exp(er)im(en)tu(m), illo u(er)o qui in ip(s)is e(ss)e op(er)|ib(us), (et) discendente de p(ro)ui(n)tia an(te)q(u)a(m) adue(n)iat | t(em)p(u)s (et) fraudando emolum(en)tis q(ue) eu(m) accip(er)e o(portet) | [*in the margin a pecia reference:* fi(nit) xix (et) cor(recta)] donec deponat cingulu(m), deponat aut(em) eu(m) [*interlinearly a reference to side note* s] served by cursive scripts already in the late thirteenth and early fourteenth centuries.

Before these Gothic cursive scripts are discussed, however, a few words must be said about another kind of Gothic textual, namely the *rotunda* or round type characteristic of Italy, but also used in South France, Spain, and Portugal (see fig. 1.16, and cf. Canellas 1974, vol. 1, pl. XLIX; vol. 2, pls. XLVIII-LII; Kirchner 1955, pls. 43-44; Kirchner 1966, pls. 13, 23; Steffens 1909, pl. 106; Thomson 1969, pls. 75, 77). It is often referred to as the *littera Bononiensis* or Bolognese script, because its most characteristic form seems to have orginated at Bologna and it was certainly widely used there for making ordinary and deluxe copies of the legal texts needed for the studies at the university (cf. Pagnin 1933-34; Destrez 1935, pls. 19-26). A very formal version of the script continued to be used for liturgical manuscripts into the sixteenth and seventeenth centuries and for giant choral books even much later. This script, despite its name, does not lack angles, but because its letters are broader in relation to their height than they are in the more northern Gothic, the angles are softened, and by comparison the impression is roundish. Characteristic is the uncial *d* with a full bow and a short ascender lying almost horizontally to the left. The round Gothic also treats the feet of vertical strokes differently. In the more formal Italian examples of the script the feet of *f, h,* the first two strokes of *m,* the first stroke of *n, r,* and tall *s* are flat. The Gothic of more northern regions was also sometimes written with flat feet or *sine pedibus,* but the strokes so treated (cf. Kirchner 1966, pl. 11a) were not the same ones as in the round Gothic. A reversed *c* used as an abbreviation stroke for *-bus* and *-que* is another characteristic (see fig. 1.17, lines 1, 8).

Long before the Caroline minuscule was being transformed into the Gothic textual, it had already been adopted as a charter script (cf. preceding section). The charter features that it assumed in the process of adoption (cf. Steffens 1909, pls. 78b, 80-82, for twelfth-century examples) were superficial in terms of affecting the basic form and ductus of the letters, and they could be, and were, easily discarded. In the course of the thirteenth century, however, a more fundamental change ensued. The charter script was transformed into a new cursive unrelated to the later Roman cursive. The transformation, which took place everywhere but at different rates of speed, was well under way in an imperial register of 1240 and continued into the sixteenth century and later (cf. Steffens 1909, pls. 92, 96a, 97, 100, 105a, 107-8, 113b, 118b, 119-20, 123a), but rarely was it carried through with total thoroughness and consistency. The most characteristic among the new cursive features were the loops on the ascenders of *b, d, h,* and *l* and (less frequently) on the descenders of *f, p, q,* and long *s.*

Although the loops themselves often did not connect with the adjacent
letter or even facilitate the making of the strokes within the same letter,
it was becoming more and more common for several letters or even a whole
word to be written without the pen being lifted from the writing surface
and also for abbreviation strokes to be written the same way. Among individual letters that assumed characteristic forms with more or less regularity, attention should be called to *a, g, m, n, r, s,* and *u.* The *a* lost that
part of its stem that extended above the bow in the Caroline or uncial form.
The *g* had its ductus simplified, in comparison with the Gothic textual *g,*
by a reduction in the number of strokes. The *m, n, r,* and *u* began to have
the bottom of their first stroke (also the second in the case of *m*) continued
to the top of the following stroke by an oblique hair-line. The final stroke
of *m* and *n* at word-end was often extended below the base-line. The round
s at word-end, probably under the influence of the new appearance that
the letter was assuming in Gothic textual, frequently received a new and
simpler ductus that made it look like minuscule *b.* The *v*-shaped *u* at the
beginning of words often had the first stroke extended above the head-line

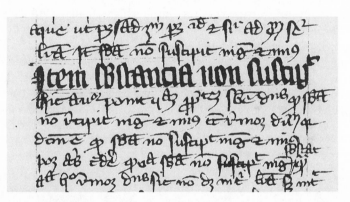

Fig. 1.17. Gothic textual (line 3) and current cursive (lines 1–2, 4–8). Germany.
14th cent. The author's collection.

aque ut p(atet) § ad 3^m p(atet) p(er) id(em) (et) si(milite)r ad 4^m se(qui-
tur) | l(itte)ra It(em) s(u)b(stanci)a no(n) suscipit m(a)g(is) (et) mi(nus) |
ITEM SUBSTANCIA NON SUSCIP(I)T | Hic au(ct)or ponit 5^am p(ro)-
p(r)i(eta)te(m) s(u)b(stanci)e d(ice)ns q(uod) s(u)b(stanci)a | no(n) r(e)-
cipit m(a)g(is) (et) mi(nus) t(un)c r(e)mo(vet) du(biu)m q(uia) | d(i)c(tu)m
e(st) q(uod) s(u)b(stanci)a no(n) suscip(i)t m(a)g(is) (et) mi(nus) | po(sse)t
a(liqu)is c(re)d(er)e q(uod) v(n)a s(u)b(stanci)a no(n) [suscip(i)t *can-
celled*] m(a)g(is) \s(u)bstat/ quam | a(li)a ho(c) r(e)mo(vet) d(ice)ns sic
no(n) d(ebet) int(ellig)i l(itte)ra s(ed) int(endi)t

and projecting or even looping to the right — so that it also resembled *b*.

If there is some difficulty, because of the variety and irregularity of this documentary script, in determining when it has been transformed enough to deserve the name cursive, there is likewise some difficulty in determining when, if ever, the cursive became Gothic. Because there is no room to discuss this latter difficulty here, it is simply being assumed that there is some way in which this cursive can validly qualify as Gothic, even though it clearly cannot do so in the same way as the textual does. Whether or not this assumption can be justified, the fact remains that the most important development in the history of Latin scripts in the fourteenth and fifteenth centuries, apart from the introduction of the humanistic ones, was the ever-increasing use of the new documentary cursive for the copying of books.

At first it was introduced with little modification and the results may be described as current Gothic cursive (see fig. 1.17, and cf. Lieftinck 1954, fig. 20) or, if more regularity and deliberation are evident, as ordinary or textual Gothic cursive (cf. Lieftinck 1954, figs. 19, 21, 23). An example of a characteristic English version of this Gothic cursive, which shows a number of Gothic textual features and to which the name *Anglicana* has recently been applied, survives in a book from the year 1291 (cf. Parkes 1969, xvi, pl. 4, i; Kirchner 1966, pl. 37a). The development of a formal or calligraphic Gothic cursive, for which the name *bastarda* has often been used, was already well under way in Italy in 1337 when the famous hundred copies of Dante's *Divine Comedy* were being made (cf. Steffens 1909, pl. 103; Lowe 1969, pl. XIX). Elsewhere the formal Gothic cursive emerged only towards the end of the fourteenth and the beginning of the fifteenth

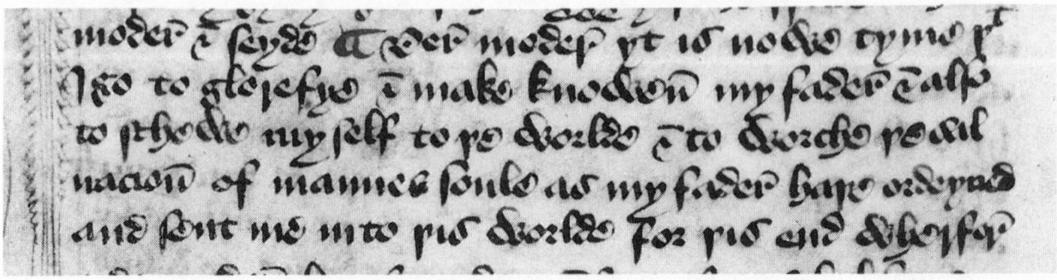

Fig. 1.18. Gothic cursive (mixed Anglicana and secretary). England. 15th cent. Department of Rare Books, Cornell University Library. MSS. B 41, fol. 1r.

moder (and) seyde ¶ Der moder yt is nowe tyme th(a)t | I go to glorefye (and) make knowen my fader (and) also | to schewe myself to the worlde (and) to worche the sal|uacion of mannes soule as my fader hathe ordeyned | and sent me into this worlde for this end wherfor century (cf. Lieftinck 1954, figs. 22, 24). A variety called the secretary script was very successfully introduced into England from France in the late fourteenth century, first for documents and then for books (cf. Parkes 1969, xix–xxii). Eventually it entered into mixtures with *Anglicana* (see fig. 1.18, where the Anglo-Saxon thorn occurs). In the formal Gothic cursive, curving strokes and in particular the characteristic loops on ascenders had an increasing tendency to become angular. That this formal script, which was employed for *de luxe* books commissioned by and for royalty, should have tolerated and even flaunted its loops—something totally unprecedented in the history of Latin book scripts—cries out for explanation.

Eventually the formalizing of the Gothic cursive went so far in the Lowlands and North France, probably under the influence of the formal textual, as to eliminate at least most of the cursive's characteristic loops. The change seems to have gotten under way around 1440 in the deluxe manuscripts copied under the patronage of the duke of Burgundy and the resulting script has recently been named Burgundian (see fig. 1.19, and cf. *CMD-NL*, 1:xv, xvi, and pls. 271, 274, etc.; also Lieftinck 1954, 23, 28–29, and fig. 25).

Fig. 1.19. Formal Gothic cursive (almost Burgundian). Clairvaux, France. A.D. 1485. Princeton Univ. Libr. MS. Garrett 91, fol. 178v. Reproduced with permission.

> Explicit Benedictus | deus qui inter tot | et varia impedime(n)- | ta dedit nobis hoc opus p(er)fice-|[re . . .] tuas in hoc laborioso op(er)e princi- | pal(ite)r suscepimus, et cui(us) adiutri- | ce gr(ati)a, opus ip(s)um co(n)- su(m)mauim(us), | tuis tuoru(m)q(ue) fratrum or(ati)onibus

While the Gothic cursive was becoming more formal, there was a corresponding movement of the Gothic textual towards the cursive. In terms of specific letter forms, this meant the adoption of the simplified forms of *a* and *g* and of round *s* at word-end and the abandonment of the angular feet on *f* and tall *s* which were then extended below the base-line. The resulting script, now known as Gothic hybrid, did not adopt loops on ascenders, but it often treated the bottoms of verticals as they were treated

in the Gothic cursive. this hybrid script was written with varying degrees
of formality, which may, like those of the Gothic textual and cursive, be
loosely classified under the three categories of formal (see fig. 1.20 and
cf. Lieftinck 1954, fig. 26, where the script is still called *bastarda;* and
CMD-NL, vol. 1, pls. 202–3), ordinary (cf. Lieftinck 1954, figs. 29a, 30;
and *CMD-NL,* vol. 1, pls. 207–8, 213–14, etc.), and current (cf. Lieftinck
1954, fig. 32, where the script is still called *bastarda currens;* and *CMD-NL,*
vol. 1, pls. 200, 205, 210–11, etc.). When the hybrid exempted other letters
besides *f* and tall *s* from observing the foot rule for Gothic textual, it can
be difficult to distinguish from Burgundian. The temporal and geographical limits of this hybrid Gothic have not yet been thoroughly studied. It
may have fourteenth-century Italian ancestry, and it was used in Catalonia
and in the southern half of France in the fifteenth century (cf. *CMD-F,*
vol. 1, pl. 88b; vol. 6, pl. 138c). Its center of gravity, however, seems to
have been in the lower Rhineland, where it was cultivated from the early
fifteenth century and whence it spread into neighboring regions of Germany, France, and the Lowlands. It continued in use well into the sixteenth
century. (Besides works already referred to, cf. Chaplais 1971; Dobiache
Rojdestvensky 1925; Heinemeyer 1982; Johnson and Jenkinson 1915; Mazal
1975; Newton 1971; Spilling 1978; Wright 1960.)

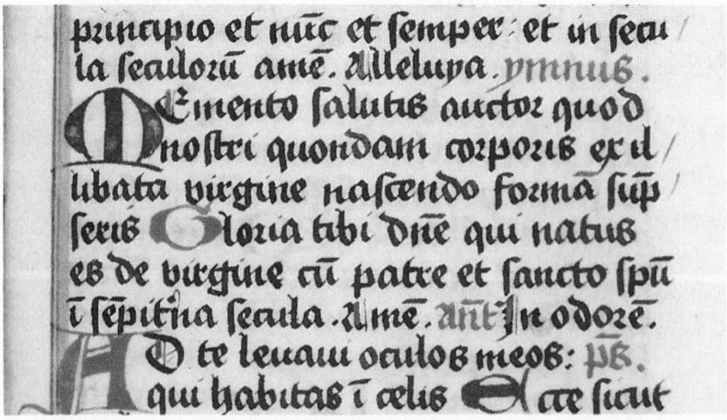

Fig. 1.20. Formal Gothic hybrid. Probably Flanders. A.D. 1528. Department of Rare
Books, Cornell University Library. MS. BX C36 H484, fol. 30r.

principio et nu(n)c et semper et in secu- | la seculoru(m) ame(n). Alle-
luya. *ymnus.* | MEmento salutis auctor quod | nostri quondam corpo-
ris ex il- | libata virgine nascendo forma(m) su(m)p- | seris Gloria tibi
d(omi)ne qui natus | es de virgine cu(m) patre et sancto sp(irit)u | i(n)
se(m)pit(er)na secula. Ame(n) *Ant(iphona).* In odore(m). | AD te leuaui
oculos meos. *PS(almus).* | qui habitas i(n) celis Ecce sicut

Humanistic Scripts

Because the humanistic scripts are in some sense the graphic expression of their inventors' and users' hostility to medieval culture, there might seem to be good reason, despite the considerable chronological overlap between the appearance of these new scripts and the disappearance of the Middle Ages, for not treating these scripts within an introduction to medieval paleography. They will, in fact, not be treated here at any length, but it is impossible to ignore them completely and for at least three reasons: (1) because many of the texts copied in these scripts were as "medieval" as they were "post-medieval"; (2) because an adequate practical command of the original Caroline minuscule demands that one be able to distinguish it from the form revived by the humanists; and (3) because an understanding of the later history of the Gothic scripts requires some understanding of the competing scripts that contributed to their decline. In a practical approach to paleography the third reason is insufficient, but the first two reasons easily suffice by themselves.

Of the two main humanistic scripts, one more formal and the other more cursive, the more formal takes precedence in time, if not necessarily in lasting effect. This script (see fig. 1.21), which has often been called without further qualification the Renaissance or humanistic script, which is today more frequently called the humanistic round or textual script or the formal humanistic, and which the humanists themselves called the *antiqua* or the new *antiqua* (cf. Battelli 1954), is none other than a revival of the Caroline minuscule. The invention, or revival, of the script is now regarded as the accomplishment of Poggio Bracciolini (1380–1459) and

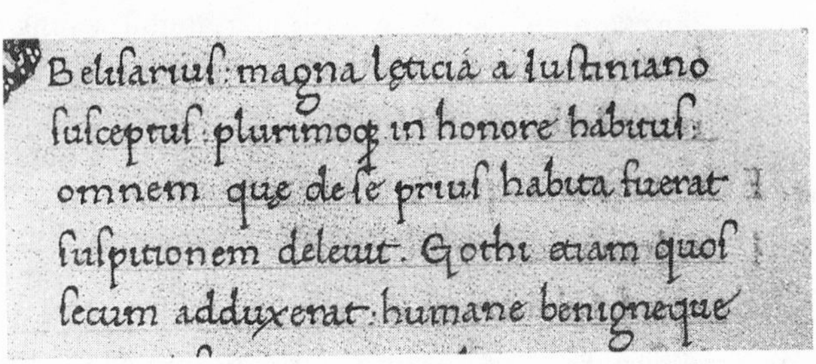

Fig. 1.21. Humanistic round. Italy. A.D. 1456. Princeton Univ. Libr. MS. Grenville Kane 55, fol. 78r. Reproduced with permission.

Belisarius, magna lęticia a Iustiniano | susceptus, plurimoq(ue) in honore habitus, | omnem quę de se prius habita fuerat | suspitionem deleuit. Gothi etiam quos | secum adduxerat, humane benigneque perhaps Niccolò Niccoli, achieved in Florence in the very last years of the fourteenth century (cf. Billanovich 1981; de la Mare 1977; also Ullman 1960, 21–57, and figs. 13–27, who argued for 1402). Poggio, a Florentine notary who became a papal secretary, had predecessors in expressing dissatisfaction with the legibility of the Gothic script, most notably Petrarch, who himself used a rather clear Italian form of Gothic textual (cf. Petrucci 1967; Ehrle and Liebaert 1932, pl. 45, where it is called *fere humanistica;* Foerster 1963, pl. 21; Kirchner 1955, pl. 48; Kirchner 1966, pl. 27; Steffens 1909, pl. 101; Thomson 1969, pl. 71), and he may also have profited from the inspiration of Coluccio Salutati (cf. Ullman 1960, 11–19). It is somewhat ironic that the earliest and strongest reaction against the Gothic should have come in Italy where its illegible possibilities were far less cultivated than in northern Europe. The specific Caroline manuscripts serving as models for Poggio's revival, insofar as there were specific models, have not been identified, but the elements of his script can be found in Italian manuscripts of the tenth to twelfth centuries (cf. Ullman 1960, 54, and pls. 1, 18; de la Mare 1969, xxii; de la Mare 1977; *CMD-IT,* vol. 1, passim). Long neglected by scholars, the humanistic round has become the subject of intense and very fruitful investigations by Ullman, de la Mare, and others, but much more study is still needed on the further development and spread of Poggio's invention before the patterns of development will be wholly clarified. It is already clear that there was more than one pattern.

The practical problem of distinguishing the humanistic round from the original Caroline of the tenth to twelfth centuries is often eased by a considerable difference in shading and proportions. When this is not the case, the presence in a Caroline-like manuscript of codicological features introduced in the Gothic period or at least widely used only from the Gothic period onward, for example, paper for writing material, ruling with ink, etc., can be very convincing evidence that one is dealing with the humanistic round and if the manuscript contains a text not composed before the later thirteenth century the evidence is of course foolproof. But even when the general impression given by the script is somewhat different from that of the later Caroline, it is still reassuring to find individual graphic elements that reveal, either inadvertently or by design, a touch of Gothic in the script's past. Among the Gothic elements occasionally carried over into the humanistic round, and not only at the beginning of the fifteenth century, are fusions of facing bows, uncial *d,* plain *e* instead of *e* with cedilla for the *ae* diphthong, *f* and tall *s* standing on the base-line rather than extending below, *i* with dot above, *R* in ligature with a preceding bow in letters besides *o* or the *2*-shaped part of the *R* in ligature used as an independent letter, round *s* regularly at word-end, *t* with its vertical stroke projecting well above the horizontal, and *v*-shaped *u* regularly at word-beginning. Some of these elements have to be used with caution, of course, since although they are characteristic of Gothic they were already beginning to appear in late Caroline and hence their presence may suggest an anticipation as well as a remembrance of Gothic. At least two of these elements, however, namely the dotted *i* and the *2*-shaped *r* used as an independent letter, did not occur at all in the original Caroline minuscule.

Added assurance that one is not dealing with a manuscript in later Caroline minuscule can be derived from the presence of Roman capitals, particularly square capitals, modeled on ancient inscriptions (see fig. 1.2) in titles and colophons. These ancient capitals were introduced by Poggio (cf. Ullman 1960, 54–56) and their use was continued by others (cf. Meiss 1960).

Much of the significance of Poggio's invention accrued to it as a result of its unforeseen adoption as a model for printing fonts, starting with Conrad Sweynheim and Arnold Pannartz, the Germans who introduced printing to Italy in 1465. By the mid-sixteenth century this roman type, as it is called, had replaced the Gothic fonts not only in Italy and Spain but also in France, and it had done the same in England and the Netherlands by the end of the sixteenth century and in Scandinavia in the course of the nineteenth. In the twentieth century almost the only exception to the universal sway of the roman type wherever the Latin alphabet is used is in German-speaking lands where the Gothic fonts continue to serve for printing belles lettres, school and devotional books, newspapers, etc.

The other kind of script widely cultivated by the humanists, what is usually called the humanistic cursive (see fig. 1.22, and cf. Battelli 1954, 40, and figs. 38–41; Ullman 1960, 59–77, and figs. 29–39, 50, 66; Wardrop 1963), tolerated a wider margin of variation than the round. In part this was because it did not have an authoritative canonized ancestor, such as the round had in Caroline minuscule, to impose limits on variation. But

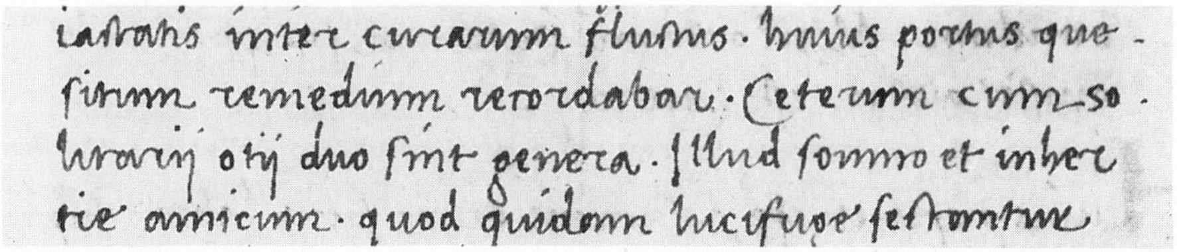

Fig. 1.22. Humanistic cursive. Italy. Ca. A.D. 1500. Department of Rare Books, Cornell University Library. MSS. Bd. Petrarch P P49 R4++, fol. 2r.

iactatis inter curarum fluctus, huius portus que- | situm remedium recordabar. Ceterum cum so- | litarii otii duo sint genera, Illud somno et inher- | tie amicum, quod quidam lucifuge sectantur it was also the result of the fact that this cursive was used for a wider variety of purposes, namely for documents (where the results have been called the humanistic chancery script) and for scholars' correspondence, notes, and private writing, as well as for books copied with varying degrees of formality.

The forms of many of the letters seem to result from speedier copying than was used in writing the round, for example, the form of *m* is conducive to, and doubtless results from, being written in one continuous movement of the pen. But the script does not have the loops on ascenders and descenders that are characteristic of cursive, and in books the connecting of one letter to another, aside from some common ligatures (*ct, et, st*), is perhaps more often the exception than the rule (cf. fig. 1.22 and Fairbank and Wolpe 1960, pl. 11, for exceptions). For these reasons some would prefer to call this script italic — the name applied to its printed version (cf. Cencetti 1963, 85; de la Mare 1969, xxix–xxxi). The humanistic cursive used little shading, it normally leaned to the right, and by comparison with the round it was angular. With regard to individual letters, characteristic ones besides the cursive *m* (and *n*) were the simplified *a,* Caroline *d,* and *f* and long *s* descending below the base-line.

The invention of the script is now dated in the 1420s and is ascribed to the Florentine humanist Niccolò Niccoli (1364–1437) (cf. Ullman 1960, 59–77). The hand that has been identified as Niccoli's (cf. Ullman 1960, figs. 29–39; Fairbank and Wolpe 1960, pl. 2c) was succeeded, starting in the 1430s, by far more formal examples (cf. de la Mare 1969, xxvii).

Although the humanistic cursive got started later than the round and was introduced into printing, where it would become known as the italic font, only in 1501 (cf. Wardrop 1963, 35), its influence on modern handwriting in contrast to modern printing has probably been much greater than that of the round. It gradually became the dominant script in the lands that adopted the round for their printing. By the mid-sixteenth century it was predominant in Spain, by the early seventeenth in France, by the mid-seventeenth in England and the Lowlands, and during the nineteenth in Scandinavia. Only German-speaking lands had not succumbed to its charms by the twentieth century (cf. Steffens 1909, pp. XXIV–XXV). (Cf. also Bischoff 1990, 145–49, and pls. 22–23; Derolez 1984; Fairbank and Hunt 1960.)

Modern Scripts

The continuations, further developments, and transformations to which Gothic and humanistic scripts were subject in modern times should be of almost as much interest to medievalists as the original development of these scripts. Medieval documents are sometimes preserved only in modern copies, and these copies are often not easy to read. Indications of medieval influence on later thought can sometimes be found in the annotations entered in medieval manuscripts by modern scholars. The evidence needed for tracing the provenance and later history of medieval manuscripts is often available only in ownership marks or other notes entered in modern scripts. But if it is easy to demonstrate the importance to a medievalist of a knowledge of modern scripts, it is far less easy to supply the needed knowledge. The field is vast and much of the ground has still to be cleared. Paleography may embrace all writing up to the present day, but paleographers have been slow and reluctant to face up to their duty. All that can be offered here, therefore, is a short list of works containing facsimiles, and preferably also transcriptions, of these modern scripts.

Among the paleographical works of general interest, there are valuable sections on modern scripts in Degering (1929); Prou (1924); Reusens (1899); Steffens (1909); and Thompson (1912). The various series of dated manuscripts will all eventually deal with manuscripts into or through the sixteenth century, though they do not provide transcriptions for their numerous plates (cf. *CMD*). Among works of interest for individual countries, cf. for France: Poulle (1966); Samaran (1922); for Germany; Dulfer and Korn (1967); and Mentz (1912); for Great Britain: Dawson and Kennedy-Skipton (1966); Hector (1966); Jenkinson (1927); Petti (1977); and Simpson (1973); for Ireland: O'Neill (1984); for Italy: Battelli (1965); and Federici (1934); for the Netherlands: Horsman et al. (1984); and for Spain and Portugal: Avelino de Jesus da Costa (1990); Arribas Arranz (1965); Canellas (1974, vol. 2); Millares Carlo with Ruiz Asencio (1983) and with Mantecon (1955); and Nunes (1969).

ABBREVIATIONS

According to a frequently cited admission of Ludwig Traube, one of the giants in the history of paleography, whenever he wanted to know the date of a manuscript the first thing he turned to was its abbreviations. Abbreviations can also be helpful in determining a manuscript's place of origin. But regardless of their usefulness in these respects, there is no question that the most important knowledge one can have about abbreviations is how to expand them correctly.

Abbreviations make paleography's interrelationship with philology particularly clear, since in the final analysis how an abbreviation ought to be expanded depends on what the context calls for in the way of meaning. Expanding abbreviations is not a totally exact science, but it is far from being an arbitrary exercise. Rules, of which a systematic exposition has been given by Schiaparelli (1926) (cf. also Laurent 1939 and Bischoff 1990, 150–68), presided over the formation of abbreviations, and a knowledge of the history of these rules can greatly aid both in correctly expanding abbreviations and in using them for dating and placing purposes, even though it cannot eliminate all need for memorizing individual abbreviations and for understanding the context in which they occur.

Most abbreviations consist of one or more of the letters of the word being abbreviated and a sign of some kind indicating the omission of the others. Some abbreviations, however, consist of a conventional symbol unlike any letter in the word being abbreviated, though perhaps originally deriving from a shorthand version of one or more of the letters involved (cf. the 7-like sign for *et* in fig. 1.7). Of the alphabetic kind of abbreviations, most are either suspensions (i.e., they consist of the first letter or letters of the word being abbreviated, with a subtype called syllabic suspensions consisting of the first letter of each syllable) or contractions (i.e., they consist of the first and last letter or letters and possibly others in between), although other variations are not unusual. The fact of abbreviation is usually indicated by a point or line or by variations of each or by combinations of both. It may also be indicated by one or more letters, usually the final ones, being placed above and slightly to the right of the beginning ones (see figs. 1.15, 1.17). More extreme forms of abbreviation, known as *notae tironianae* from Cicero's secretary Tiro, one of the reputed inventors of this ancient system of shorthand, were used as late as the eleventh century. The 13,000 or so Tironian notes can be studied in the works of Kopp (1965), Chatelain (1900), Schmitz (1893), and Ruess (1914) (cf. also Steffens 1909, pl. 56, and Bischoff 1990, 80–82).

The most useful guide to the expansion of abbreviations, a vade mecum for every student of paleography and every editor of ancient and medieval texts, has been provided by Cappelli (1929). However, even though this handy and invaluable repertory contains facsimiles and expansions of more than 14,000 abbreviations, besides numerous conventional symbols and epigraphical *sigla,* the student will still find it far from containing every abbreviation that he encounters. Some supplementary material is available in Pelzer (1966), Martin (1910), and Prou (1924).

The date that Cappelli supplies with each abbreviation is not a dependable criterion for dating the manuscript in which it is found. The abbreviation was undoubtedly used at the date assigned, but it may have been used centuries earlier or later as well. For dating and placing purposes in the earlier Middle Ages one must consult Traube (1907; 1909–20, 1:129–56), the pioneering works in this area, Lindsay (1915), Bains (1936), and Paap (1959). For the later Middle Ages the preliminary studies have yet to be made and their accomplishment is hindered by the vastness of the material to be surveyed and by the migrancy of scribes and of manuscript models (cf. Bozzolo et al. in *Actas* 1990, 17–27). In any event it is important to remember, when interpreting the evidence of abbreviations, that nothing prevents an abbreviation, of which the origin can be dated fairly closely, from remaining in use for centuries or from being revived after a period of disuse. Normally, therefore, an abbreviation form with a known date of origin can provide no more than a *terminus ante quem non.* Thus the presence of the *2*-shaped symbol instead of the apostrophe for the *ur*-ending argues that the manuscript was not copied before the end of the eighth century, but any time thereafter is possible. It is worth noting, however, that the form of this *2*-shaped sign changed with time and place and these changes may themselves be revealing. (Cf. similar differences in the form of the *7*-shaped symbol for *et* and *and* in figs. 1.14–18.) Also, nothing prevents abbreviations that originated in and were characteristic of one region from being transplanted to another region. Finally, one must remember that the absence of abbreviations need not mean ignorance of them. A scribe's full repertory may emerge only when space is extremely short.

NUMERALS

Numerals may be regarded as conventional nonalphabetic abbreviation symbols, like the division sign for *est.* Not even the Roman numerals, except for *C* and *M,* have any Latin alphabetical connection despite the eventual coincidence of their forms with the letters *I, V, X, L, D.* The dates of invention or introduction of the Roman and Arabic numerals provide *termini ante quos non* and a knowledge of the varying forms these numerals assumed over the centuries can be helpful for dating and placing as well as indispensable for correctly transcribing. The tables in Hill (1915) are especially useful. (Cf. Cappelli 1929, 413–28; Steffens 1909, XXXV–XXXVI, XL, with references to his plates; Bischoff 1990, 176–77; and fig. 1.17 for Arabic *3, 4,* and *5*).

PUNCTUATION

Although punctuation consists mainly of minutiae, it is far from being a small subject. Not only does it include signs establishing the author's real or presumed meaning (the equivalents of the period, colon, semicolon, comma, question mark, etc.) as well as corrector's signs bringing what the scribe (or author) actually wrote into line with what the author had intended (i.e., the equivalents of signs for deletion, omission, insertion, transposition, etc.), but it may also include signs expressing a reader's reactions to what he has read (attention, approval, disapproval, etc.). The subject is both vast and important, but nevertheless has received relatively little paleographical attention. The literature has been surveyed by Moreau-Marichal (1968) and Rafti (1968) (cf. also Bischoff 1990, 169–73). The neglect of this subject has been encouraged by the overwhelming profusion of material and also by the complications introduced when punctuation was supplied or modified by later readers, complications which photography, especially black-and-white, sometimes compounds rather than resolves. The interest that editors of texts might be expected to show in the study of punctuation tends to be undermined by the fact that successive copies of a work are more and more likely to reflect the scribe's system or lack of system rather than the author's (if there is a difference between the two). What is a discouragement to the editor, however, ought to be an encouragement to the paleographer.

In "reading" or determining the meaning of punctuation so it can be transcribed into its modern equivalents, the context must be consulted even if the scribe was using signs prescribed by the grammarians, since he may not have been using these signs with their recommended meaning. The most famous of the grammarians' prescriptions, namely those found in Isidore of Seville's *Etymologiae* (Bk. I, chap. 20; cf. also chaps. 18–19, 21, and II, chap. 18), called for a point at the base-line for the modern comma, at mid-height for something like the semicolon, and at the head-line for the period.

In the oldest Latin writings punctuation was hardly used, except for a point to separate words. Even in manuscripts of the fifth and sixth centuries punctuation consisted of little more than indentation, blank spaces, and occasional points (cf. Müller 1964; Wingo 1972). Blank space, though it is hardly mentioned in the grammarians' theories, was used for punctuation or in lieu of punctuation in all periods. St. Jerome introduced a system of spacing and indentation to separate *cola et commata* in his translation of the Bible (cf., *CLA,* vol. 2, no. 141, for a facsimile). The separation of words by blank space was encouraged by those, such as the Irish and English, for whom Latin was not a native tongue. Nevertheless, prepositions were often not separated from the noun they governed well into the twelfth and thirteenth centuries. An increasing use of punctuation, in an almost bewildering variety of combinations, occurred in the seventh and eighth centuries. The rules handed on by Isidore, already used for some deluxe copies of classical texts in the fifth and sixth centuries, were observed in various scriptoria in Germany and France in the ninth century and for deluxe liturgical manuscripts in the tenth and eleventh centuries (cf. Bischoff 1990, 169). A new system of punctuation was adopted in the twelfth century by the Cistercians for their table reading and later by the Carthusians, Dominicans, and Brothers of the Common Life for their liturgical books. It called for a 7-like sign over a point (*punctus circumflexus* or simply *flexus*) after incomplete meanings, a tick or reversed comma over a point (*punctus elevatus* or *metrum*) after fairly complete meanings to which something could still be added, and a comma below a point (*versus*) after complete sentences (cf. Hubert 1970, 160–65; Ker 1960, 58–59; Gumbert 1974, 159–69; Bischoff 1990, 170–71). The simple point sometimes served for the *circumflexus* or *versus.* It may be worth noting that a manuscript copied entirely in one style of script may reveal more than one system of punctuation or even the lack of any system at all.

If the invention of a given punctuation mark can be exactly or even approximately dated, its presence in a manuscript can furnish at least a rough *terminus ante quem non.* No exactly dated original question mark, for example, has been documented before the 770s (*CLA,* vol. 6, no. 707, provides a facsimile; cf. also Steffens 1909, pl. 46, col. 2, lines 27, 40; Vezin 1980). The hyphen began to come into common use only in the eleventh century, though some stray examples survive from as early as the eighth century in England (cf. *CLA,* Suppl., nos. 1,679, 1,703; Vezin in *Scriptorium* 19 [1965]: 86. The use of parentheses is attested in the fifteenth century and probably does not antedate the late fourteenth (cf. Roncaglia 1941).

Although the mere presence of a mark of which the invention goes back to Antiquity — such as paragraph signs and citation marks — is of little value to the medievalist as a *terminus ante quem non,* the varying forms these marks, as well as those invented later, assumed over the course of centuries can be of considerable help in both dating and placing, as preliminary studies of some of them have already shown. On paragraph marks cf. Lehmann (1959–62, 4:9–11, and facs. on p. 21); Sorbelli (1944); on citation marks cf. McGurk (1961a); and on omission and insertion marks cf. Lowe (1972, 2:349–80 and pls. 61–70).

ON READING, TRANSCRIBING, AND DESCRIBING MANUSCRIPTS

A paleographer need not make a transcription of a text in order to come to an opinion about the nature and origin of its script, but an opinion usually implies that the text has been read, entirely in the case of short ones and in at least extended representative sections in the case of long ones. Reading, in turn, implies that the paleographer ought *to be able* to transliterate the writing of the manuscript into the current alphabet and to show others how to do the same. Even though reading may be dismissed as merely a preliminary, and transcribing as an incidental, paleographical operation, they still may be very difficult ones and not only in the case of palimpsests (see below under Writing Materials) and shredded papyri but even in the case of manuscripts that are wholly intact. It has been said that paleography has essentially solved all its reading problems, but if this is true it is so only in principle, not in practice, even for the most experienced paleographers. And each student must of course gradually master both the principles and their application anew. Because of real difficulties in some texts, beginners can become justifiably discouraged, but they should not become discouraged too easily and regard as insuperable even those problems that can certainly be overcome with simple patience and persistence, together with a command of the language, subject matter, and abbreviations in question. Several cursory attempts at transcription, perhaps separated by enough time to give one a fresh perspective and in which only familiar letters and words are noted, will usually provide a sufficient command of the scribe's habits—his letter forms, ductus, ligatures, and other idiosyncrasies—to make possible the decipherment of what was not immediately apparent. Because facsimiles and transcriptions of similar scripts can be of the greatest help here, the accompanying bibliography emphasizes comparative material of this kind and calls special attention to it. For texts that must be eked out letter by letter, a work like Grandenwitz (1904) may be useful.

Because transcribing is sometimes rendered more complicated by the revisions that a manuscript has undergone, a system of conventional symbols has been devised to simplify recording and distinguishing both the primitive readings and the revisions they received before leaving the original scriptorium (cf. Masai 1950b). The application of a revised version of these symbols may be observed in Vanderhoven and Masai (1953) and in *CMD-B*. The system, which employs square brackets for deletions, various combinations of oblique lines for additions, a combination of deletion and addition signs for substitutions, and parentheses or underlining or italics for letters expanding abbreviations, was originally intended to facilitate the publication of diplomatic editions (on these cf. also Falconi 1969), but it can be useful as well both for recording transcriptions of texts to be used in constituting a critical edition and simply as a way of accurately preserving a text for (later) personal consultation, particularly if angular or other kinds of brackets are introduced for recording later alterations and the transcriber's own comments. For the conventions recommended to be followed in the making of critical editions of classical and medieval texts, cf. Bidez and Drachmann (1932) and Dondaine (1960) respectively.

Often one cannot stop with transcribing a text, but must go on to describe (in effect catalog) the manuscript containing the text. A competent description of a manuscript must naturally identify its literary contents as well as take account of its script or scripts, but it must also deal with all sorts of features that one may call codicological, to say nothing of its decorative features, if they are present, and its later history. What has been said above and what follows in the sections below can be of assistance in this descriptive work, but it would be advisable to consult some model catalogs, to which references may be found in Kristeller (1965). Many guidelines have been proposed for this work, which has a long history (cf. Wilson 1956; Petrucci 1984); especially useful in terms of current requirements for descriptions of manuscripts of various sorts are *Richtlinien* (1985) and Mazal (1975b, 133-72), and also, because they bring the computer into play, Gruijs and Holager (1981) and Jemolo and Morelli (1990).

WRITING MATERIALS

Assertions have sometimes been made that certain kinds of writing materials necessitate certain kinds of script. The facts, however, do not bear out this supposed necessity even where it would seem most likely to hold, namely in the case of inscriptions chiseled on stone (cf. Catich 1968, 90–97, 283–84). Nevertheless there are certain factual correlations between writing materials and scripts that may be more or less helpful in dating and localizing.

Papyrus was the predominant writing material of Antiquity even though it is probable that more extant Latin writing from before the fourth or fifth century after Christ survives on stone than on papyrus because of the latter's fragility. The vast majority of extant papyri owe their survival to the happy accident of having been buried in the favorable soil of Upper Egypt; it is no surprise, therefore, that no Latin papyri are known from before the first century B.C., when the Romans conquered Egypt (cf. Marichal 1950). Of a handful of extant Latin literary manuscripts on papyrus neither copied nor preserved in Egypt, the latest may date from the early eighth century (cf. *CLA,* vol. 5, no. 614; Tjäder 1954–82, 1:37–42). Surviving Latin documents on papyrus from Ravenna and the Merovingian chanceries are fairly numerous from the sixth and seventh centuries and an example from the papal chancery can be dated as late as the mid-eleventh century (cf. Tjäder 1954-82, 1:35-37, 42-48; Santifaller 1953, 52-76).

The earliest surviving example of parchment — the predominant writing material of the Middle Ages (cf. Reed 1972; Santifaller 1953, 77-115; Wattenbach 1896, 113-39; also Kenyon 1951, 87-120) — contains a sale contract in Greek dating from as early as 195-189 B.C. Animal skins in the form of leather rather than parchment had of course already been in use for writing for several millennia. The Roman world encountered parchment no later than the first century after Christ, but only a few Latin examples survive from before the fourth century. Only with the fifth century do extant Latin literary texts on parchment clearly begin to exceed those on papyrus, but because of the latter's poor survival prospects one may not be absolutely sure of the predominance of parchment until the seventh and eighth centuries, when the percentage of extant Latin literary texts written on papyrus approaches zero. Parchment has, of course, remained in use ever since, but during the fifteenth century its predominant position for the copying of books was taken over by paper.

Much more helpful for dating and placing purposes than the mere use of parchment, however, are the methods and quality of its preparation. Wattenbach (1896, 113-39) records some of the variations in time and place. As an example one may cite the kind of writing material developed by Irish and English artisans in the seventh and eighth centuries — velvet-like in appearance, somewhat rough to the touch, and showing little difference between the hair and flesh sides of the skins — which enables direct or indirect Insular influence to be inferred when it is encountered in manuscripts of Continental origin. This Insular material is called vellum in *CLA* (cf. vol. 1:xi; vol. 2:viii [2d ed., p. xii), but in current general usage vellum simply designates the finer kind of parchment.

Palimpsests are not limited to parchment, but it is appropriate to mention them here because papyrus palimpsests have not survived and even if they did would not offer the same possibility of being read. Etymologically the word palimpsest simply means something that has been rubbed or scraped off for rewriting, but the word has taken on the meaning of something that has actually been written on two or more times and that has usually had the ink of its previous writing washed off rather than scraped or rubbed. Even when palimpsests do not contain texts previously considered lost (e.g, Cicero's *De re publica,* which was found under St. Augustine's *Enarrationes in Psalmos*), and most do not, they can nevertheless be useful sources for economic, cultural, and intellectual history. The oldest palimpsests have been rather well catalogued (cf. Lowe 1972,

2:480-519, and pls. 114-19, for those of which the lower script antedates the ninth century), but many later ones still remain to be discovered or studied. What has greatly facilitated their exploitation for both paleographical and textual purposes (cf. Dold 1950) has been the invention of fluorescent photography, which depends on the fact that ink with metallic content, even if only a residue remains, does not fluoresce, while parchment (unlike papyrus) does so very well. Previously used chemical reagents often had the long-range effect of rendering both upper and lower scripts less legible than they were before (cf. facs. in *CLA*, vol. 4, nos. 486-87, 500), but newer chemical methods have been proposed and used (cf. Ouy 1958). Digital image-processing is perhaps an even more promising recent invention for reading not only palimpsests but also faded or disfigured texts of any kind (cf. Benton 1978; Benton and Soha 1979).

The invention of paper in China coincides roughly with the date of the earliest preserved parchment, but the appearance of paper in the Latin world and the beginning of its manufacture there occur much later (in general cf. Santifaller 1953, 116-52; Wattenbach 1896, 139-49). The oldest extant Latin literary text on paper may date from the tenth century (cf. Lowe 1972, 2:547, 557-58, 561, and pls. 120, 126-27). Paper was known in Moslem Spain by the ninth century and a document of the year 1009 and a liturgical text copied before the year 1036 still survive in Spain. In Sicily the Norman rulers were using paper for some documentary purposes by the early twelfth century and an extant Genoese cartulary on paper was begun in 1154. Literary evidence of about this same time shows an awareness in France and Germany of at least the existence of paper, although extant samples survive only from the thirteenth century onward. Paper was used in England too in the thirteenth century, but no extant examples seems to antedate the early fourteenth.

The first paper documents and books copied in the West used paper either from the East or from Spain where paper mills certainly existed in the twelfth century and possibly already in the eleventh or even tenth century. The use of paper in the Latin West did not become widespread, however, until after paper mills began to be established in Italy in the first half of the thirteenth century, apparently first at Fabriano in the province of Ancona and then in many other cities. France got paper mills in the first half of the fourteenth century, Germany certainly by the late fourteenth century, and England, strangely enough, not until the last decade of the fifteenth century.

Paper is made of various animal or vegetable materials that can be converted into pulp which, when drained through a screen or sieve, leaves a residue that dries out to form a sheet of paper. Paper of Eastern manufacture can be distinguished from the earliest Western products by differences in surface, color, texture, format, and the screen pattern that is reflected on the paper (cf. Irigoin 1950, 194-204). Among Western products themselves some rough dating possibilities are offered by changes in the screen patterns over the centuries (cf. Irigoin 1950, 201, 202; Briquet 1905, 22-29). Much more precise dates, however, can often be determined from the wire designs — monograms, animals, or other figures — that papermakers attached to their screens as an identifying label or trade mark for their products. Although the screen pattern as a whole could properly be called the watermark or *filigrane,* this name has been applied more specifically to these identifying designs (cf. Briquet 1907, the classic work on this subject; Mosin and Traljic 1957; Piccard 1961-; Irigoin 1980; and Zerdoun Bat-Yehouda 1989). The custom of using watermarks began in the Fabriano region in the last quarter of the thirteenth century (cf. Briquet 1907, no. 5,410, dated in 1282) and spread rapidly from there. In establishing dates for these marks, Briquet examined thousands and thousands of dated and placed documents, tracing the watermarks and recording the places and earliest dates they were used. Because this approach only establishes a *terminus post quem non* for the making of the particular sample of paper observed, it does not exclude an earlier or — since a watermark could remain in use for some years — even a later date of manufacture for other samples showing an identical watermark. Stevenson (1961; 1967, 26-127, 248-52) suggests some conditions and techniques that can narrow the possible leeway (for a more cautious approach cf. Bühler 1973, 257-65). The places of copying recorded by Briquet do not, of course, exclude still other places. Another difficulty with Briquet, namely the inaccuracies inherent in his method of tracing watermarks by hand from pages where they are often obscured by writing, can now be overcome through D. P. Erastov's beta-radiographic method of reproduction (cf. Irigoin 1980, 19, and fig. 5; *Techniques* 1974, 159-76).

INK

Of the many coloring materials, both dry and liquid, used in the making of letters — chalk, graphite, lead, crayons, paint, ink, etc. — only ink will be discussed here (for recipes cf. Zerdoun Bat-Yehouda, 1983; also Wattenbach 1896, 233-61; Diringer 1953, 544-53; and especially for chemical aspects Barrow 1972, 8-28). Cases in which a script's visual contrast from its background was achieved not by the positive application of color but rather by rearranging or removing some of the writing surface, as with incised inscriptions, can be left for treatment below under writing instruments.

Inks were made with a coloring substance, a solvent (rainwater, vinegar, or wine), and a gummy substance (such as gum arabic) that supplied emulsifying, viscous, suspensive, and adhesive properties for the coloring. A carbon base (soot, lampblack, or charcoal) provided the color for the oldest known inks. But by the first century after Christ a metallic gall ink — in which a combination of ferrous or possibly copper sulfate (green or blue vitriol respectively) and gall (a source of tannic acid) serves as a substitute for the carbon — was beginning to be experimented with, and eventually it became the most widely used of all writing fluids, in part because it was less likely to clog the pen than the carbon ink was. The special interest of metallic gall ink for dating and placing scripts is that the color of the ink varies according to the ratio of gall to vitriol. A ratio of three to one makes for a black ink. Lesser proportions of gall result in the ink turning to various shades of brown. Because different colors have in fact prevailed in different eras and regions (cf. Bischoff 1990, 16–18), ink color may be usable as corroborative evidence to establish a given period or place or origin. The evidence can usually be no more than corroborative, however, because the eventual color of metallic gall ink can also be affected not only by the chemical nature of the writing surface but by the circumstances of preservation as well. It is possible, however, that iron-based inks, especially when used on paper, may eventually become a feasible source of much more positive dating evidence. McNeil (1984) has developed a technique that enables him to date inks of this sort with an accuracy of ±30 years. The technique is based on the secondary ion migration that gradually and uniformly takes place from the ink and that can be measured by means of scanning auger microscopy (SAM).

WRITING INSTRUMENTS

While writing instruments have had a greater impact than writing materials on the form of scripts, somewhat paradoxically they are less useful for purposes of dating and placing and hence can be dealt with rather summarily. By writing instruments here are meant only those directly used to produce the letter forms, not such auxiliary scribal equipment as penknife, eraser, sponge, ruler, awl, inkpot, etc. (on these cf. Wattenbach 1896, 203–19, 228–32; Jones 1946; Diringer 1953, 559–61 and figs. XI, 1–2).

In terms of impact, writing instruments can clearly affect the appearance of letters. For one thing, through their flexibility or the breadth of their nibs they can facilitate or even necessitate shaded writing. For another, through the angle of the nib cut — if one assumes that the other factors in play here, namely the angle of the writing line and the angle of the pen, remain the same — they can determine the orientation of the thick and thin strokes on the writing surface and thereby facilitate the writing of one kind of script and obstruct another (cf. Hurm 1928, 8–12; and on the position of the writing surface Metzger 1968). Beneventan minuscule, for example, is more easily written with a broad nip cut so it is shorter on the left (from the scribe's perspective), while formal Gothic textual is more easily written with a nib cut so it is shorter on the right. One must remember, however, that nib width and angle are factors within the scribe's control and therefore cannot be given completely independent explanatory value. It is much more likely that the desired shape of the stroke determined how the nib was cut rather than vice versa. Furthermore, scribes were not completely at the mercy of the nib angle, as one can see when hair-lines run at right angles to each other or when parallel strokes are sometimes thick and sometimes thin. The limitations on the usefulness of writing instruments for dating purposes arise from ignorance about when many of the instruments first came into use, from the vastness of the periods during which they were used, and sometimes from difficulty in determining just which instrument was being used. Scribal portraits and literary evidence must be interpreted with some caution.

The variety of instruments used for making letters is very large (cf. Wattenbach 1896, 203–32; Diringer 1953, 553–63 with facs.; Hunger 1961, 40–43 with facs.; Bischoff 1990, 18–19). Even the naked hand can serve, as when one uses a finger to write in wet sand or on a dusty window. Historically most important in the Middle Ages, however, were the chisel and stylus among instruments that accomplish their task by removing or rearranging some of the writing surface, and the brush, reed, and quill among those that accomplish their task by applying coloring matter to the writing surface. The chisel, responsible for the stone inscriptions of Antiquity and the Middle Ages, is technically a lettering rather than a writing instrument (although the designs guiding the chisel were themselves probably made with a brush or other writing instrument). The chisel does not seem to favor rectilinear letter forms over rounded ones (cf. Catich 1968, 90–96). The stylus, made of iron, silver, bronze, ivory, etc., and particularly suited for writing on wax tablets, was used from Antiquity through the Middle Ages for school exercises, first drafts, letters, business records, etc. In the earlier Middle Ages it was also used in parchment manuscripts particularly for entering interlinear vernacular glosses (cf. Bischoff 1966–81, 1:

88–92). Of the color-applying instruments the most flexible is the brush, which can run and turn in every direction. It was used in Antiquity for wall writing and for the designs followed by the sculptors of inscriptions in stone, and in the Middle Ages also for initials. Because of the raggedness of an unserifed brushstroke ending, Catich (1968) has argued that the brush originally inspired the invention of the serif. Although metal pens were not unknown in Antiquity, the chief writing instrument in use then for literary texts was the reed (*calamus* or *canna*), which, if its nib is frayed or shredded, can almost take on the characteristics of the brush. It has been claimed, though this seems to be more of a possibility than a necessity, that its main characteristic is the absence of any strong contrast between thick and thin strokes. When, if ever, the reed went completely out of use is unknown—in any event it enjoyed a minor revival among some humanists in the fifteenth century—but there is no question that it was superseded sometime during the Middle Ages by the quill, made usually from a goose feather but also from feathers of swans, peacocks, crows, and turkeys. There is testimony to the use of the quill at latest by the sixth century, and Isidore of Seville in the early seventh century mentions it alongside the reed (*Etymologiae* 6:14). This early use would seem to dispose of the argument by Dobiache Rojdestvensky (1925) that the introduction of the quill brought about the development of Gothic script. Illustrated instructions for making reed and quill pens are given by Johnston (1939, 17–26).

THE EXTERNAL FORM OF MANUSCRIPTS

Neither the roll nor the codex—historically the two chief ways of attaching multiple pieces of writing material together for better preserving the integrity of texts—had any necessary influence on the form or ductus of scripts, and the particular ways in which the elements or parts of the roll and codex were disposed for writing did not have such influence either. Nevertheless, because external dimensions, column sizes, number of lines per column, and methods of quire formation, ruling, and pricking can be extremely various, with the differences or constellations of differences easily recognizable and often subject to exact measurement or enumeration, these external features—each a matter of direct interest to codicology—can sometimes furnish the most helpful of all evidence for attributing manuscripts to individual workshops or scriptoria. It must be remembered, of course, that material techniques can be transferred to new areas or revived from the past quite independently of the scripts with which they were first developed.

Because the roll — much older than the codex — was rapidly going out of fashion for Latin literary texts by the fourth century after Christ, it can be treated very summarily here. For details about its process of manufacture, its sizes — which rarely exceeded 10 to 11 meters — the dimensions of its writing columns, the number of lines per column, its labels and containers, cf. especially Schubart (1962, 37–99) and Kenyon (1951, 40–86); also Diringer (1953, chap. 4), Hunger (1961, 43–47), and Wattenbach (1896, 150–74). Although rolls can be made of parchment (cf. Santifaller 1965) or paper, ancient ones were normally made of papyrus. The writing was done in columns of which the axis was at right angles to the direction in which the rolling was done. Only exceptionally was the roll written on both sides (opisthograph). The roll had most of the inconveniences of the modern microfilm besides a few others of its own. In the parchment or paper rolls used in the Middle Ages for documentary, genealogical, or liturgical purposes (cf. Bischoff 1990, 32–33), often only one piece of material was involved and the column of writing ran in the same direction as the rolling process.

The form par excellence of the medieval book was not the roll, of course, but the codex, which has been defined in a fundamental study (Roberts and Skeat 1987, 1; cf. also Turner 1977) as "a collection of sheets of any material, folded double and fastened together at the back or spine, and usually protected by covers." The advantage of the codex over the roll with respect to convenience of use is so great that the invention of the codex may almost rival the invention of printing in terms of social and intellectual significance. There were other advantages that the codex enjoyed over the roll, such as greater compactness, durability (if the codex was made of parchment and the roll of papyrus), and economy (if both were made of the same material because the codex used both sides of the sheet). These advantages clearly had something to do with the invention of the papyrus or parchment codex in the first century after Christ by the Romans, who were simply extending a principle already in being when multiple wooden tablets covered with a recessed layer of wax for writing on were fastened together (cf. *CLA,* Suppl., no. 1,684, for a facsimile of a waxed tablet). The most important factor in popularizing the codex seems to have been its adoption by the Christians, probably from the very beginning, for their Scriptures. The codex did not become the predominant form for the pagan book before the fourth century.

While the *terminus ante quem non* provided by the mere use of the codex form is too early to be helpful to the medievalist, the methods used

in preparing and disposing the parts of the codex are potentially very helpful in determining both dates and places of origin. The quires or gather-
ings, that is, the groups of folded sheets or bifolia that were sewn together
to form the codex, have varied in size from one to more than fifty bifolia,
though the norm in most times and places has been four or five. Bifolia
within a parchment quire were usually arranged to avoid having flesh side
face hair side; the latter is normally darker than flesh side and often shows
traces of follicles. Flesh side would naturally face flesh side and hair side
would face hair side if the quire was formed by three successive folds of
a single piece of parchment or by two successive folds of two pieces of
parchment then properly united. There is evidence that quires constituted
by folding in this way, paper as well as parchment ones, may sometimes
have been copied before the leaves were folded and cut, that is, in an un-
natural sequence akin to the method of "imposition" used in printing. (Cf.
Gilissen 1977, pt. 1; Bozzolo and Ornato 1983, 123–212, 379–84.)

The bifolia composing the quire were ruled in some way to guide the
scribe's lines of script. Practice varied with respect to (1) the number of
bifolia ruled at one time, (2) whether they were ruled before or, as was
the earlier Insular practice, after folding, (3) whether the hair or flesh side
received the direct impression of the ruling instrument, and (4) the kind
of instrument used to make the impressions (the dry point or stylus from
the earliest period onward, lead starting only from the eleventh century,
and pen and ink starting only from the thirteenth century). When several
bifolia were ruled at one time with a stylus before they were folded, they
were often then rearranged to make groove face groove and ridge face ridge.
This would happen naturally if an entire sheet was ruled before it was folded
into bifolia. The practice of copying the first line on a page *below* the top
ruled line instead of above it has been shown by Ker (1985, 70–74) to provide, at least in England, a *terminus ante quem non* in the late twelfth
century for glossed books of the Bible and in the thirteenth century for
other texts. Some scribes, however, will continue to write above the top
ruled line.

The ruler that guided the path of the ruling instrument was itself usually guided by two parallel rows of minute holes pricked at regular intervals down the portion of the page intended for writing (cf. Jones 1946).
These prickings were of varying shapes and the rows of them were inserted
either within the area intended for writing (the practice in the oldest manuscripts) or on the edge of it or within the marginal area (where, if they
were close to the outer edge, they often have been cut off by binders). When

the ruling was done after the bifolia were folded, long the Insular practice, a row of holes can usually be seen towards both the inner and outer edges of each folio rather than only towards the outer edge.

Dimensions offer innumerable opportunities for codices to differ from one another, with the differences expressible in quantitative terms. Absolute dimensions as well as ratios of height to width varied with respect to both the page and the written area. Scriptoria often had favored proportions between script area and marginal area, though the original dimensions of the page have often been obscured by later trimming of the margins. On format or *mise en page* cf. Martin and Vezin (1990), Gilissen (1977, pt. 2), and Bühler (1973, 100–108). The number of columns and of lines per column also varies. The combination of choices that a given scriptorium made among all these variables in quire formation, ruling, pricking, and format, may turn out to be uniquely identifying of its products (cf. Gilissen 1969).

Differing methods of distinguishing and identifying the parts of a codex in order to facilitate consultation can provide further grounds for dating and localizing. Foliation, pagination, and column numbering were rather slow to become popular, since they had only limited reference value until printing produced a multitude of identical copies (cf. Lehmann 1959–62, 3:1–59). But quire marks or signatures, intended for the aid of the binder, were widely used throughout the Middle Ages (though many have been cut off in successive rebindings). They could vary according to (1) type of symbol used (letters or Roman or Arabic numerals), (2) location (usually on the last, occasionally on the first, page of the quire; in the middle or right half of the lower margin), (3) kind of script used, (4) the abbreviation for *quire* (*quaternio*), and (5) the decoration sometimes enclosing the mark. The practice of writing in the lower right margin of the last page of the quire the first word or words of the next quire (called catchwords or *reclamantes* or *custodes*), of which stray examples survive from the ninth and tenth centuries, began to be more widely observed in the eleventh century, with the earliest impulse apparently coming from Spain (cf. Vezin 1967). (On codicological questions see also Canart 1979; *Codicologica* 1976–; Delaissé 1959; Gruijs 1972; Lemaire 1989; Masai 1950a; Parkes 1976; Vezin 1978.)

BINDINGS

The pasting together of pieces of papyrus to form a roll and the provision of a container to hold and protect the roll might be regarded as a form of binding, but this term is more properly used to describe the process in which the separate quires of a codex are sewn together and provided with a permanently attached protective cover. By extension, the term is often applied primarily to the cover alone. Writing, by itself, does not imply binding, but most writing that has survived, apart from that found in documents, coins, and monuments, is in bound form and has survived because it was bound. What can be said, therefore, about the date and place of origin of bindings may throw light on the scripts that they protect and preserve.

Deluxe bindings have always attracted attention as a valuable, even if minor, form of art. But in recent decades scholarly attention has begun to be equally devoted to the systematic and historical study of less elaborate forms of binding decoration (cf. Kyriss 1951–58), as well as of the humble techniques used in making even totally unadorned bindings (cf. van Regemorter 1948, 1955; Pollard 1976; also Bischoff 1966–81, 1:93–100; and McGurk 1956). The history of bookbinding is thus claiming a more and more important place among the branches of codicology.

Unless the binding is original, however (and the older the manuscript the less likely this will be), it naturally furnishes better clues to a manuscript's later history than to its origin. But even when the binding is not the original one, it still constitutes a *terminus post quem non* for the script, except when it has been salvaged from an earlier book and reused or when the writing was entered after the book was already rebound.

Because rebinding and the consequent retrimming of the edges of the pages have frequently resulted in the removal of pricking holes, quire marks, catchwords, and other marginal notations, one cannot, of course, argue from the mere absence of these features now to their absence at the start. (Cf. also Helwig 1953–55; Diehl 1946; Wattenbach 1896, 386–408; Needham 1979; Gilissen 1983; Bischoff 1990, 30–32.)

MODERN REPOSITORIES OF MEDIEVAL WRITING; MEDIEVAL LIBRARIES

Where is script evidence to be found and how can one get at it? In general one may say that the great bulk of the evidence is preserved in public and ecclesiastical archives, libraries, and museums. Because the emphasis in this chapter has been more on books than on charters or inscriptions, only libraries will be discussed here. For help in keeping up with manuscripts in transit between libraries, see the section on "Manuscripts at Auction" in *English Manuscript Studies* (1989–).

The presence of medieval script material can be verified in some libraries only by direct communication with the library itself and sometimes only by an on-the-spot inspection. Usually, however, there are published catalogs of a library's manuscript holdings and an excellent bibliographical guide to these catalogs has been provided by Kristeller (1965). Microfilm copies of the many unpublished catalogs to which Kristeller also refers are now available on 348 reels from the Renaissance Society of America (cf. Cranz 1987). Kristeller's book also has a section devoted to general library guides, such as the *Jahrbuch der deutschen Bibliotheken* (1989) and the *Répertoire des bibliothèques et organismes de documentation* in France (1971). These guides, which are continually in need of revision, provide extremely useful information about library holiday schedules, daily hours, conditions for use, photographic facilities, etc. They are an indispensable help in preparing an *iter paleographicum*.

The need for many paleographical *itinera* has, of course, been lessened, if by no means eliminated, by the possibilities of photography. One can order microfilms directly from most larger libraries. In libraries with no photographic facilities the Institut de Recherche et d'Histoire des Textes in Paris may be able to arrange to make microfilms on commission for use on loan. The manuscript holdings of more and more libraries are being microfilmed in their entirety for use elsewhere. Thus microfilms of the Vatican Library manuscripts are available for use at St. Louis University and those of the Ambrosian Library in Milan are available for both use at and loan from the University of Notre Dame. The Hill Monastic Manuscript Library (HMML) at St. John's University in Collegeville, Minnesota, has microfilms of over 73,000 volumes and over 120,000 papyri including most of the manuscripts in Austria and those of various libraries in England, Ethiopia, Germany, Italy, Malta, Poland, Portugal, and Spain, and is ever acquiring more (cf. Plante 1967–74; *Annals of HMML*). HMML can usually arrange to have positive copies made by University Microfilms in Ann Arbor, Michigan, for purchase. Copies of thousands of manuscripts on microfilm from England and Wales, filling 2,652 reels, can be purchased from the Library of Congress (cf. Born 1955). Many other libraries, such as those of the Pontifical Institute of Mediaeval Studies in Toronto, the University of Pennsylvania, the Grabmann-Institut in Munich, have substantial microfilm collections. (Cf. also Sharpe 1971.)

Although access to modern libraries is a more immediate concern of the paleographer, he cannot ignore the medieval libraries and the manifold ways in which their holdings were transferred or dispersed and finally resettled in the modern ones. A scholar, for example, attempting to determine the exact place of origin of a manuscript lacking a localizing subscription by the scribe would greatly welcome a mark of early library ownership. Someone attempting to date a manuscript of which the place of origin is known would want to compare it, if possible, with exactly or approximately dated manuscripts from the same scriptorium. More often than not these latter, if they ever existed, would be manuscripts that were preserved in the same medieval library. Library history (cf. Christ 1984; Thompson 1939 for introductions) can often enable one to master the vicissitudes leading both back to a manuscript's earliest home and forward to the present homes of other books from the same library. A model study in this genre was made by Delisle (1868–81). The most solid foundations for library history of this kind are the library catalogs that were produced in the Middle Ages themselves. Gottlieb (1890) and Beddie (1930, 17–20) provide guides, now somewhat antiquated, to the extant catalogs (cf. also Derolez 1979). Editions of many of the texts can be found in Becker (1885), *MBKÖ* (1915–71), *MBKDS* (1918–), Derolez (1966–), and also Delisle (1868–81). Sometimes these catalogs are detailed enough, particularly when they supply the first words of the second folio (*dictio probatoria* — cf. Williman and Dziedzic 1978), to leave no doubt that the manuscript they are describing is identical with one in hand. When they are less detailed, however, the medieval home of an extant volume may be able to be established by other means. For an extraordinary "reconstruction" of the medieval libraries of Great Britain on the basis of ex libris, bindings, shelfmarks, etc., as well as catalog references, cf. Ker (1964 and Watson's *Supplement*). A similar work is now available for Germany (Krämer and Bernhard 1989–90).

BIBLIOGRAPHY

The following bibliography naturally concentrates more on the medieval than on the ancient or modern Latin scripts, and it emphasizes, although it does not limit itself to, easily accessible works. Because it also emphasizes works with facsimiles and particularly those with transcriptions (indicated here by an asterisk after the plate or facsimile reference), works with obsolescent texts could not always be excluded. References to complete facsimile editions of manuscripts include only a few recent series not listed in Omont (1935) and extending beyond Zotter (1976). References to journals and other serial publications have been limited to the most directly relevant; many other pertinent journals may be found in listings for articles. Current publications can be kept up with through the "Bulletin codicologique" in *Scriptorium* and through the *Gazette du livre médiéval,* a clearinghouse for the exchange of ideas and a bulletin board for announcing new publications, conferences, seminars, exhibitions, research projects, and library and university personnel changes. One may also consult *Codices manuscripti: Zeitschrift für Handschriftenkunde* and *Scrittura e civiltà*. The advantages of classification that had to be sacrificed for the convenience of having one alphabetical list are partially restored through the references to this list made in the various sections of the text above. All of the various series of dated manuscripts are listed here under the conventional *siglum* "CMD" followed by an abbreviation (usually the postal one) for the respective countries. Many of the works listed below contain further bibliography, but see Boyle in particular as well as Braswell, Mateu Ibars, and Tjäder (1977-). Occasional annotations are provided, especially for the handbooks. The latest of these handbooks, that of Bischoff (1990), by providing a critical evaluation and synthesis of the abundant paleographical scholarship of the last fifteen years, is itself an excellent bibliography.

Actas = *Actas del VIII Coloquio del Comité Internacional de Paleografía Latina: Madrid-Toledo 29 setiembre-1 octubre 1987* [= *Estudios y Ensayos* 6]. 1990. Edited by Manuel C. Díaz y Díaz. Madrid: Joyas Bibliográficas.

Archiv für Diplomatik, Schriftgeschichte, Siegel- und Wappenkunde. 1955-. Cologne.

Archivio paleografico Italiano. 1882-. Edited by E. Monaci, L. Schiaparelli, et al. Rome. 75 fascicles to 1984, with hundreds of pls., some of which are transcribed in *Bullettino*.

Aris, Rutherford. See *CLA*.

Armarium codicum insignium. 1980-. Turnhout: Brepols. Complete facsimile eds. 3 vols. to 1984.

Arribas Arranz, Filemón. 1965. *Paleografía Documental Hispanica*. 2 vols. Valladolid: Sever-Cuesta. 129 pls.* from A.D. 812 to 1641.

Autenrieth, Johanne. 1978. "Probleme der Lokalisierung und Datierung von spätkarolingischen Schriften (10. und 11. Jahrhundert)," *Codicologica* 4:67-74.

———. 1988. *"Litterae Virgilianae": Vom Fortleben einer römischen Schrift* [= *Schriften des Historischen Kollegs* 14]. Munich: Stiftung Historisches Kolleg. 21 figs.

Avelino de Jesus da Costa, P. 1990. *Album de paleografia e diplomática portuguesas*. Vol. 1. 5th ed. Coimbra. 312 facs., 189 B.C.-A.D. 1815.

Bains, Doris. 1936. *A Supplement to Notae Latinae: Abbreviations in Latin MSS. of 850 to 1050 A.D.* Cambridge: Cambridge Univ. Press. See also under Lindsay 1915.

Barrow, W. J. 1972. *Manuscripts and Documents: Their Deterioration and Restoration*. 2d ed. Charlottesville: Univ. Press of Virginia.

Bataillon, Louis J., Bertrand G. Guyot, and Richard H. Rouse, eds. 1988. *La production du livre universitaire au moyen âge: Exemplar et pecia*. Paris: Éditions du CNRS. 19 pls.

Battelli, Giulio. 1965. *Acta pontificum* [= *Exempla scripturarum* 3]. 2d ed. Vatican City: Bibliotheca Vaticana. 50 pls.* from the ninth to the nineteenth centuries.

―――. 1949, 1968. *Lezioni di paleografia.* 3d ed. Vatican City: Scuola Vaticana di Paleografia e Diplomatica. Reprint. 45 figs.* Needs another revision, but still very useful.

―――. 1954. "Nomenclature des écritures humanistiques." *Nomenclature* (q.v.), 35–44. With figs. 35–44.

―――. 1975. *Scritti scelti: codici, documenti, archivi.* Rome: Multigrafica editrice. 13 pls.

BEC = *Bibliothèque de l'École des Chartes.* 1839–. Paris.

Becker, Gustav. 1885. *Catalogi bibliothecarum antiqui.* Bonn.

Beddie, James S. 1930. "The Ancient Classics in the Mediaeval Libraries." *Speculum* 5:3–20.

Benediktsson, Hreinn. 1965. *Early Icelandic Script as Illustrated in Vernacular Texts from the Twelfth and Thirteenth Centuries.* Reykjavik: Manuscript Institute of Iceland. 78 pls.*

Benton, John F. 1978–79. "Nouvelles recherches sur le déchiffrement des textes effacés grattés ou lavés." Académie des Inscriptions & Belles-Lettres. *Comptes rendus des séances de l'année 1978,* 580–94. With 8 figs.

Benton, John F., Alan R. Gillespie, and James M. Soha. 1979. "Digital Image-Processing Applied to the Photography of Manuscripts, with Examples Drawn from the Pincus MS of Arnald of Villanova." In *Scriptorium* 33:40–55, and pls. 9–13.

[Bidez, J., and Drachmann, A. B.]. 1932. *Emploi des signes critiques, disposition de l'apparat dans les éditions savantes de textes grecs et latins: conseils et recommandations.* Paris; 2d ed. by A. Delatte & A. Severyns, Brussels-Paris: L'Union académique internationale, 1938.

Bieler, Ludwig. 1949. "Insular Palaeography: Present State and Problems." *Scriptorium* 3:267–94.

Billanovich, Giuseppe. 1981. "Alle origini della scrittura umanistica: Padova 1261 e Firenze 1397." In *Miscellanea Augusto Campana* [= *Medioevo e umanesimo* 44]. Padua: Antenore, 1:125–40, and pls. II–IV.

Bischoff, Bernhard. 1954. "La Nomenclature des écritures livresques du IXe au XIIIe siècle." In *Nomenclature* (q.v.) 7–14, with figs. 1–12.

―――. 1963. "Über den Plan eines paläographischen Gesamtkatalogs der festländischen Handschriften des neunten Jahrhunderts." *Archivalische Zeitschrift* 59:166–67.

―――. 1966–81. *Mittelalterliche Studien: Ausgewählte Aufsätze zur Schriftkunde und Literaturgeschichte.* 3 vols. Stuttgart: A Hiersemann. 46 pls.

―――. 1974–80. *Die südostdeutschen Schreibschulen und Bibliotheken in der Karolingerzeit.* Vol. 1, 3d ed., *Die bayrischen Diözesen.* Vol. 2, *Die vorwiegend österreichischen Diözesen.* Wiesbaden: O. Harrassowitz. 57 facs.

―――. 1990. *Latin Palaeography: Antiquity and the Middle Ages.* Cambridge-New York: Cambridge Univ. Press. 23 pls.* Translated by Dáibhí O Cróinín and David Ganz from the 2d rev. ed. of *Paläographie des römischen Altertums und des abendländischen Mittelalters.* Berlin: Erich Schmidt, 1986. French trans. by H. Atsma and J. Vezin, *Paléographie de l'antiquité romaine et du* *moyen âge occidental.* Paris: Picard, 1985. The best and most up-to-date treatment of the subject.

Bischoff, Bernhard and Virginia Brown. 1985. "Addenda to *Codices Latini Antiquiores,*" *Mediaeval Studies* 47:317–66. 18 pls., 54 new items, and new *membra disiecta* for 39 others.

Bishop, T. A. M. 1961. *Scriptores Regis: Facsimiles to Identify and Illustrate the Hands of Royal Scribes in Original Charters of Henry I, Stephen, and Henry II.* Oxford: Clarendon Press. 40 pls.

———. 1971. *English Caroline Minuscule.* Oxford: Clarendon Press. 24 pls.*

Bishop, T. A. M. and P. Chaplais. 1957. *Facsimiles of English Royal Writs to A.D. 1100 Presented to Vivian Hunter Galbraith.* Oxford: Clarendon Press. 30 pls.*

Born, Lester K. 1955. *British Manuscripts Project: A Checklist of the Microfilms Prepared in England and Wales for the American Council of Learned Societies 1941–1945.* Washington: The Library of Congress.

Boyle, Leonard E., O. P. 1984. *Medieval Latin Palaeography: A Bibliographical Introduction.* Toronto: Univ. of Toronto Press.

Bozzolo, Carla, and Ezio Ornato. 1980. *Pour une histoire du livre manuscrit au moyen âge: Trois essais de codicologie quantitative.* Paris: CNRS. Reprinted with supplement, 1983.

Braswell, Laurel Nichols. 1981. *Western Manuscripts from Classical Antiquity to the Renaissance: A Handbook.* New York: Garland.

Briquet, Charles M. 1905. "Notions pratiques sur le papier." *Le bibliographe moderne* 9:5–36. Reprinted in *Briquet's Opuscula = Monumenta Chartae Papyraceae Historiam Illustrantia* 4, Hilversum (1955): 310–20, and pls. LXXXII–LXXXV.

———. 1907. *Les Filigranes: Dictionnaire historique des marques du papier dès leur apparition vers 1282 jusqu'en 1600 avec 39 figures dans le texte et 16,112 fac-similés de filigranes.* 4 vols. Paris: Picard; 1968 reprinted ed. by Allan Stevenson brings the bibliography up to date.

Brown, Michelle P. 1990. *A Guide to Western Historical Scripts from Antiquity to 1600.* London: The British Library, and Toronto: Univ. of Toronto Press. 52 pls.*

Brown, T. J. 1959–63. "Latin Palaeography Since Traube." *Transactions of the Cambridge Bibliographical Society* 3:361–81; rev. ed. in *Codicologica* 1 (1976): 58–74.

———. 1972. "Northumbria and the Book of Kells." *Anglo-Saxon England* 1:219–46, and pls. II–VI.

———. 1982. "The Irish Element in the Insular System of Scripts to circa A.D. 850." In *Die Iren und Europa im früheren Mittelalter,* 2 vols., edited by Heinz Löwe, 1:101–19. Stuttgart: Klett-Cotta.

Brown, Virginia. 1988. "A Second New List of Beneventan Manuscripts (II)." *Mediaeval Studies* 50:584–625. See also Bischoff 1985 and Loew 1914.

Bruckner, Albert. 1935–78. *Scriptoria medii aevi Helvetica: Denkmäler schweizerischer Schreibkunst des Mittelalters.* 14 vols. Geneva: Roto-Sadag. Hundreds of pls. Vol. 14: *Indices.* See also under *ChLA.*

Bühler, Curt F. 1960. *The Fifteenth-Century Book: The Scribes, the Printers, the Decorators.* Philadelphia: Univ. of Pennsylvania Press. 8 pls.

————. 1973. *Early Books and Manuscripts: Forty Years of Research.* New York: Grolier Club.

Bullettino dell' "Archivio Paleografico Italiano": Rivista italiana di paleografia, diplomatica e scienze ausiliarie della storia. 1908-64. First series, Rome, 1908-19; new series, 1955-59; third series, 1962-64.

Burnam, John M. 1912-25. *Palaeographia Iberica: Fac-Similés de manuscrits Espagnols et Portugais (IXᵉ-XVᵉ siècles).* 3 Fascicles. Paris: Champion. 60 pls.*

Canart, Paul. 1979. "Nouvelles recherches et nouveaux instruments de travail dans le domaine de la codicologie." *Scrittura e Civiltà* 3:267-307.

Canellas, Angel. 1974. *Exempla scripturarum latinarum in usum scholarum.* 2 vols., 2d ed. Saragossa: Libreria General. 157 pls.* (those in vol. 2 devoted exclusively to Spanish manuscripts).

Cappelli, Adriano. 1929. *Lexicon abbreviaturarum: Dizionario di abbreviature latine ed italiane.* Rev. ed. Milan: Hoepli; later reprints.

Casamassima, Emanuele. 1988. *Tradizione corsiva e tradizione libraria nella scrittura latina del Medioevo.* Rome: Gela editrice. 30 pls.

Catich, Edward M. 1968. *The Origin of the Serif: Brush Writing & Roman Letters.* Davenport, Iowa: Catfish Press. 235 figs.

Cavallo, Guglielmo. 1970. "Struttura e articolazione della minuscola beneventana libraria tra i secoli X-XII." *Studi Medievali,* 3d series, 11:343-68.

Cencetti, Giorgio. 1954-56. *Lineamenti di storia della scrittura latina.* Bologna: Patron. Particularly useful for its lengthy surveys of the literature on various paleographical questions as well as for its penetrating insights.

————. 1963. *Compendio di paleografia latina per le scuole universitarie e archivistiche.* Naples: Istituto editoriale del Mezzogiorno. 36 facs.* A summary of the author's *Lineamenti.*

Chaplais, Pierre. 1971. *English Royal Documents: King John—Henry VI, 1199-1461.* Oxford: Clarendon Press. 27 pls.*

Chatelain, Émile. 1900. *Introduction à la lecture des Notes Tironiennes.* Paris: Author. 18 pls.

————. 1884-1900. *Paléographie des classiques latins.* 2 vols. Paris: Hachette. 195 pls.*

————. 1901-2. *Uncialis scriptura codicum latinorum novis exemplis illustrata.* Paris: Welter. 100 pls.*

ChLA = Chartae latinae antiquiores: Facsimile-Edition of the Latin Charters Prior to the Ninth Century. 1954-. Edited by Albert Bruckner, Robert Marichal, et al. Olten-Lausanne (from vol. 5, Dietikon-Zurich): Urs Graf. 39 vols. (except for 27, 29) by 1991. 1,155 items with complete facs.*

Christ, Karl. 1984. *The Handbook of Medieval Library History.* Translated by Theophil M. Otto from Milkau and Leyh (q.v.), vol. 3, chap. 5. Metuchen, N.J.: Scarecrow Press.

Chroust, Anton. 1902-40. *Monumenta palaeographica: Denkmäler der Schreib-*

kunst des Mittelalters. 1st and 2d series, Munich: Bruckmann, 1902–17; 3d series, Leipzig: Harrassowitz, 1931–40 (left incomplete). 690 pls.*

CLA = Codices latini antiquiores: A Palaeographical Guide to Latin Manuscripts Prior to the Ninth Century. 1934–71. Edited by E. A. Lowe. 11 vols. and Supplement. Oxford: Clarendon Press. Vols. 1, 3–11 reprinted, Osnabrück: Otto Zeller. 1982. Over 2,000 facs. of 1,811 MSS. See also Bischoff and Brown for Addenda; Rutherford Aris, *An Index of Scripts for E. A. Lowe's CLA* (Osnabrück: Zeller, 1982). The present writer is preparing a volume of indexes.

CMD = Catalogue des manuscrits datés.

CMD-A [A = Austria]. 1969–88. *Katalog der datierten Handschriften in lateinischer Schrift in Österreich.* Edited by Franz Unterkircher et al. 8 vols. Vienna: Verlag der österreichischen Akademie der Wissenschaften. 3,559 facs.

CMD-B [B = Belgium]. 1968–. *Manuscrits datés conservés en Belgique.* Edited by François Masai, Martin Wittek, et al. Brussels-Ghent: Story-Scientia. 5 vols. by 1987. 1,234 pls.

CMD-CH [CH = Switzerland]. 1977–. *Katalog der datierten Handschriften in der Schweiz in lateinischer Schrift vom Anfang des Mittelalters bis 1550.* Edited by Max Burckhardt, Pascal Ladner, Martin Steinmann, Beat Matthias von Scarpatetti, et al. Dietikon-Zurich: Urs Graf. 2 vols. by 1983. 1,471 facs.

CMD-D [D = Germany]. 1984–. *Datierte Handschriften in Bibliotheken der Bundesrepublik Deutschland* [up to 1550]. Edited by Johanne Autenrieth et al. Stuttgart: Anton Hiersemann. 3 vols. by 1991, dealing wtih Frankfurt am Main, Freiburg im Breisgau, and Stuttgart. 895 facs.

CMD-F [F = France]. 1959–. *Catalogue des manuscrits en écriture latine portant des indications de date, de lieu ou de copiste.* Edited by Charles Samaran, Robert Marichal, et al. Paris: Centre National de la Recherche Scientifique. 7 vols. by 1984. 1,442 pls.

CMD-GB [GB = Great Britain]. 1979–, [Vol. 1:] *Catalogue of Dated and Datable Manuscripts c. 700–1600 in The Department of Manuscripts, The British Library.* Edited by Andrew G. Watson. London: The British Library. Facs. of 915 MSS. [Vol. 2:] *Catalogue of Dated and Datable Manuscripts c. 435–1600 in Oxford Libraries.* Edited by Andrew G. Watson. Oxford: Clarendon, 1984. 878 facs. of 818 MSS. [Vol. 3:] *Catalogue of Dated and Datable Manuscripts c. 737–1600 in Cambridge Libraries.* Edited by P. R. Robinson. Cambridge: D. S. Brewer, 1988. 412 facs.

CMD-IT [IT = Italy]. 1971–. *Catalogo dei manoscritti in scrittura latina datati o databili per indicazione di anno, di luogo o di copista.* Turin: Bottega d'Erasmo. Vol. 1: *Biblioteca Nazionale Centrale di Roma.* Edited by Viviana Jemolo. 215 pls. Vol. 2: *Biblioteca Angelica di Roma.* Edited by Francesca Di Cesare. 1982. 222 pls.

CMD-NL [NL = Holland]. 1964–88. *Manuscrits datés conservés dans les Pays-Bas: Catalogue paléographique des manuscrits en écriture latine portant des indications de date.* 2 vols. Vol. 1: *Les manuscrits d'origine étrangère,* by G. I. Lieftinck, Amsterdam: North Holland Publishing Company. Vol. 2: *Les manu-*

scrits d'origine néerlandaise (XIVe-XVIe siècles) et supplément au tome premier, by J. P. Gumbert, Leyden: E. J. Brill, 963 pls.

CMD-S [S = Sweden]. 1977-80. *Katalog der datierten Handschriften in lateinischer Schrift vor 1600 in Schweden.* Edited by Monica Hedlund under the direction of Gert Hornwall and Jan-Olaf Tjäder. 2 vols. Stockholm: Almquist & Wiksell International. 397 facs.

CMD-V [V = Vatican City]. 1989-. *I manoscritti datati della Biblioteca Apostolica Vaticana.* Vol. 1: *Fondi Archivio di S. Pietro, Barberini, Boncampagni, Borghese, Borgia, Capponi, Chigi, Ferrajoli, Ottoboni.* Edited by J. Ruysschaert, Adriana Marucchi, and Albinia de la Mare. Vatican City.

Codices manuscripti: Zeitschrift für Handschriftenkunde. 1975-. Vienna.

Codices selecti phototypice impressi. 1960-. Edited by F. Sauer and J. Stummvoll. Graz: Akademische Druck- und Verlagsanstalt. 85 vols. by 1989, not all in the Latin alphabet.

Codicologica: Towards a Science of Handwritten Books. 1976-. Edited by A. Gruys and J. P. Gumbert. In *Litterae Textuales* (q.v.). Leyden: E. J. Brill. 5 vols. by 1980.

Colophons de manuscrits occidentaux des origines au XVIe siècle. 1965-82. Edited by the Bénédictins du Bouveret. 6 vols. Fribourg: Éditions Universitaires. 23,774 items arranged alphabetically by scribes' names.

Corbin, Solange. 1965-. *Répertoire de manuscrits médiévaux contenant des notations musicales.* Paris: Éditions du CNRS, 3 vols. until 1974. 94 pls. dealing with Parisian libraries.

———. 1977. *Die Neumen.* In *Palaeographie der Musik,* edited by Wulf Arlt, vol. 1, pt. 3. Cologne: Arno Volk-Verlag. 41 pls.

Cranz, F. Edward. 1987. *A Microfilm Corpus of Unpublished Inventories of Latin Manuscripts through 1600 A.D.* Vol. 1: *Catalogue of the Microfilm Corpus.* New London, Conn.

Dain, A. 1964. *Les manuscrits.* 2d ed. Paris: Les belles-lettres.

Dawson, Giles E., and Laetitia Kennedy-Skipton. 1966. *Elizabethan Handwriting 1500-1650: A Manual.* New York: Norton. 50 pls.*

Degering, Hermann. 1929. *Die Schrift: Atlas der Schriftformen des Abendlandes vom Altertum bis zum Ausgang des 18. Jahrhunderts.* Berlin: Wasmuth; English trans.: *Lettering.* London: Benn. Reprinted, New York: Universe Books, 1965. 240 pls., including inscriptions and vernacular languages.

[Delaissé, L. M. J.]. 1959. *Le siècle d'or de la miniature flamande: Le mécénat de Philippe le Bon.* Brussels: Bibliothèque royale de Belgique. 64 pls. Illustrates the codicological approach to deluxe books.

de la Mare, A. C. 1969. "Humanistic Script." In *The Italian Manuscripts in the Library of Major J. R. Abbey.* Edited by J. J. G. Alexander and A. C. de la Mare. New York-Washington: Praeger. Numerous pls.

———. 1973-. *The Handwriting of Italian Humanists.* Oxford: Oxford Univ. Press. Vol. 1, fascicle 1, 25 pls.

———. 1977. "Humanistic Script: the First Ten Years." In *Das Verhältnis der Humanisten zum Buch,* edited by Fritz Krafft and Dieter Wuttke [= Deutsche

Forschungsgemeinschaft, Kommission für Humanismusforschung, *Mitteilung* 4]. Boppard: Harald Boldt, 89–110, and 12 figs.

Delisle, Léopold. 1868–81. *Le Cabinet des manuscrits de la Bibliothèque Impériale [Nationale]*. 3 vols. and atlas. Paris.

Delitsch, Hermann. 1928. *Geschichte der abendländischen Schreibschriftformen*. Leipzig: Hiersemann. 104 pls.

Denholm-Young, N. 1954. *Handwriting in England and Wales*. Cardiff: Univ. of Wales Press. 31 pls.

Derolez, Albert. 1966–. *Corpus catalogorum Belgii: De middeleeuwse bibliotheekscatalogi der Zuidelijke Nederlanden*. Vol. 1: *Provincie West-Vlaanderen*. Brussels: Paleis der Academiën.

―――. 1979. *Les catalogues de bibliothèques* [= *Typologie des sources du moyen âge occidental* 31]. Turnhout: Brepols.

―――. 1984. *Codicologie des manuscrits en écriture humanistique sur parchemin*. Turnhout: Brepols.

Destrez, Jean. 1935. *La pecia dans les manuscrits universitaires du XIIIᵉ et du XIVᵉ siècle*. Paris: Editions J. Vautrain. 36 pls.

Diehl, Edith. 1946. *Bookbinding: Its Background and Technique*. 2 vols. New York: Rinehart.

Diehl, Ernst. 1912. *Inscriptiones latinae*. Bonn: Marcus and Weber. 50 pls., up to the 15th cent.

Diringer, David. 1953. *The Hand-Produced Book*. London: Hutchinson. 185 figs.

―――. 1968. *The Alphabet: A Key to the History of Mankind*. 3d ed. 2 vols. London: Hutchinson. 452 pls.

Dobiache Rojdestvensky, Olga. 1925. "Quelques considérations sur les origines de l'écriture dite 'gothique.'" In *Mélanges d'histoire du moyen âge offerts à M. Ferdinand Lot*. Paris: Champion.

Dold, Alban. 1950. "Palimpsest-Handschriften: Ihre Erschliessung einst und jetzt; ihre Bedeutung." In *Gutenberg-Jahrbuch*, 16–24. 5 facs.

Dondaine, Antoine. 1960. "Abréviations latines et signes recommandés pour l'apparat critique des éditions de textes médiévaux." *Bulletin de la Société Internationale pour l'Étude de la Philosophie Médiévale* 2:142–49.

Drogin, Marc. 1980. *Medieval Calligraphy: Its History and Technique*. Montclair, N.J.: Allanheld & Schram; London: George Prior. 42 figs. and 145 facs.

Dülfer, Kurt, and Hans-Enno Korn. 1967. *Schrifttafeln zur deutschen Paläographie des 16.–20. Jahrhunderts*. 2d ed. 2 vols. Marburg: Marburg-Institut für Archivwissenschaft. 50 pls.*

Dufour, Jean. 1972. *La bibliothèque et le scriptorium de Moissac*. Geneva: Librairie Droz. 78 facs.

Dumville, David. 1987. "English Square Minuscule Script: The Background and Earliest Phases." *Anglo-Saxon England* 16:147–79, and 7 pls.

Early English Manuscripts in Facsimile. 1951–. Copenhagen: Rosenkilde & Bagger. 22 vols. to 1988.

Ehrle, Franz, and Paul Liebaert. 1932. *Specimina codicum latinorum vaticanorum*. 2d ed. Berlin: Walter De Gruyter. Reprinted, Berlin, 1968. 50 pls.*

English Manuscript Studies 1100-1700. 1989-. Edited by Peter Beal and Jeremy Griffiths. Oxford: B. Blackwell.

Escudier, Denis. 1980. "Les manuscrits musicaux du Moyen Age (du IXe au XIIe siècle): Essai de typologie." *Codicologica* 3:34-45.

Ewald, P., and G. Loewe. 1883. *Exempla scripturae visigoticae.* Heidelberg. 40 pls.*

Fairbank, A. J., and Berthold Wolpe. 1960. *Renaissance Handwriting.* London: Faber. 96 pls.

Fairbank, A. J., and R. W. Hunt. 1960. *Humanistic Script of the Fifteenth and Sixteenth Centuries. Bodleian Picture Book,* no. 12. Oxford: Bodleian Library. 24 pls.

Falconi, Ettore. 1969. *L'Edizione diplomatica del documento e del manoscritto.* Parma: La Nazionale Tipographia Editrice. 26 pls.*

Favreau, Robert. 1979. *Les inscriptions médiévales* [= *Typologie des sources du moyen âge occidental,* 35]. Pp. 49-60: "L'écriture." Turnhout: Brepols.

Federici, Vincenzo. 1934. *La scrittura delle cancellerie Italiane dal secolo XII al XVII.* 2 vols. Rome: Sansaini. Reprinted, Turin, 1964. 114 pls.*, with 31 showing book and charter scripts copied prior to the twelfth century.

Fichtenau, Heinrich. 1946. *Mensch und Schrift im Mittelalter.* Vienna: Universum. 16 pls.*. Deals with handwriting and intellectual history.

Fink-Errera, Guy. 1962. "Contribution de la macrophotographie à la conception d'une paléographie générale." *Bulletin de la Société Internationale pour l'Étude de la Philosophie Médiévale* 4:100-18, and 5 pls.

Fischer, Hanns. 1966. *Schrifttafeln zum althochdeutschen Lesebuch.* Tübingen: Max Niemeyer Verlag. 24 pls., with selected transcriptions.

Foerster, Hans. 1946. *Mittelalterliche Buch- und Urkundenschriften.* Berne: P. Haupt. 50 pls.*

———. 1951. *Urkundenlehre in Abbildungen.* Berne: Haupt. 40 pls.*

———. 1963. *Abriss der lateinischen Paläographie.* 2d ed. Stuttgart: Hiersemann. 39 facs.* Especially useful for its surveys of the literature and frequent citations of texts.

Ganz, David. 1987. "The Preconditions for Caroline Minuscule." *Viator: Medieval and Renaissance Studies* 18:23-44, with 1 fig.

Ganz, Peter, ed. 1986. *The Role of the Book in Medieval Culture: Proceedings of the Oxford International Symposium 26 September-1 October 1982.* 2 vols. [= *Bibliologia* 3-4]. Turnhout: Brepols.

Garand, Monique-Cécile. 1980. "Manuscrits monastiques et scriptoria aux XIe et XIIe siècles." *Codicologica* 3:8-33, with 6 pls.

Garand, Monique-Cécile, and François Etcheverry. 1975. "Analyse d'écritures et macrophotographie." *Codices manuscripti* 4:112-22, with 7 pls.

García Villada, Zacarías. 1923. *Paleografía española, precedida de una introduccion sobre la paleografía latina.* 2 vols. Madrid: Revista de Filologia Española. 116 facs. on 67 pls.*

Gasparri, Françoise. 1973. *L'écriture des actes de Louis VI, Louis VII et Philippe Auguste.* Geneva: Droz. 138 pls.

————. 1976. "Pour une terminologie des écritures latines: doctrines et méthodes." *Codices manuscripti* 2:16–25.

Gazette = *Gazette du livre médiéval.* 1982–. Paris. Genevois, A.-M., J.-F. Genest, and A. Chalandon, with M.-J. Beaud and A. Guillaumont. 1987. *Bibliothèques de manuscrits médiévaux en France: Relevé des inventaires du VIIIe au XVIIIe siècles.* Paris: Éditions du CNRS.

Gilissen, Léon. 1973. *L'expertise des écritures médiévales: Recherche d'une méthode avec application à un manuscrit du XIe siècle: Le lectionnaire de Lobbes Codex Bruxellensis 18018* [= *Les Publications de Scriptorium* 6]. Ghent: Story-Scientia. 132 figs. and 44 pls.

————. 1977. *Prolégomènes à la codicologie: Recherches sur la construction des cahiers et la mise en page des manuscrits médiévaux* [= *Les Publications de Scriptorium* 7]. Ghent: Story-Scientia. 63 figs. and 95 pls.

————. 1969. "Un élément codicologique trop peu exploité: La réglure." *Scriptorium* 23:150–66.

————. 1983. *La reliure occidentale antérieure à 1400, d'après les manuscrits de la Bibliothèque Royale Albert Ier à Bruxelles.* Turnhout: Brepols. 75 pls.

Gneuss, Helmut. 1981. "A Preliminary List of Manuscripts Written or Owned in England up to 1100." *Anglo-Saxon England* 9:1–60 (947 items).

Gottlieb, Theodor. 1890. *Ueber mittelalterliche Bibliotheken.* Leipzig. Reprinted, Graz, 1955.

Gradenwitz, Otto. 1904. *Laterculi vocum latinarum: voces latinas et a fronte et a tergo ordinandas curavit O. G.* Leipzig: Hirzel. Reprinted, Hildesheim: G. Olms, 1966.

Graesse-Benedict-Plechl. 1972. *Orbis latinus: Lexikon lateinischer geographischer Namen des Mittelalters und der Neuzeit.* 3 vols. 3d ed. Edited by Helmut Plechl. Brunswick: Klinkhardt & Biermann.

Gruijs, Albert. 1972. "Codicology or the Archaeology of the Book? A False Dilemma." *Quaerendo* 2:87–108.

Gruijs, Albert, and Per Holager. 1981. "A Plan for Computer Assisted Codicography of Medieval Manuscripts." *Quaerendo* 11:95–127.

Gumbert, J. P. 1974. *Die Utrechter Kartäuser und ihre Bücher im frühen fünfzehnten Jahrhundert.* Leyden: E. J. Brill. 165 facs.

Hajnal, István. 1959. *L'enseignement de l'écriture aux universités médiévales.* 2d ed. Edited by L. Mezey. Budapest: Académie des sciences de Hongrie, 150 facs. on 50 pls., showing mostly thirteenth-century documents from Eastern Europe. The book's main thesis is questionable.

Hall, F. W. 1913. *A Companion to Classical Texts.* Oxford: Clarendon Press. Reprinted, Hildesheim, 1968.

Haselden, Reginald B. 1935. *Scientific Aids for the Study of Manuscripts.* London: Oxford Univ. Press, for the Bibliographical Society.

Hector, L. C. 1966. *The Handwriting of English Documents.* 2d ed. London: Arnold. 36 pls.*, to the nineteenth century.

Heinemeyer, Walter. 1982. *Studien zur Geschichte der gotischen Urkundenschrift.* 2d ed. Cologne: Böhlau-Verlag. With tables.

Helwig, Hellmuth. 1953–55. *Handbuch der Einbandkunde.* 3 vols. Hamburg: Maximilian-Gesellschaft.

Higounet, Charles. 1964. *L'écriture* [= *"Que sais-je?",* no. 653]. 3d ed. Paris: Presses universitaires de France. 45 figs.

Hill, G. F. 1915. *The Development of Arabic Numerals in Europe.* Oxford: Clarendon Press. 64 tables.

Horsman, P. J., Th. J. Poelstra, and J. P. Sigmond, [1984]. *Schriftspiegel: Nederlandse paleografische teksten van de 13de tot de 18de eeuw.* Terra Zutphen, 127 pls.*

Hubert, M. 1970–74. "Corpus stigmatologicum minus." *Bulletin du Cange* 37:5–171 and 39:55–84.

———. 1972. "Le vocabulaire de la 'ponctuation' aux temps médiévaux: Un cas d'incertitude lexicale." *Bulletin du Cange* 38:57–167.

Hulákovsky, Joannes M. 1852. *Abbreviaturae vocabulorum usitatae in scripturis praecipue latinis medii aevi, tum etiam slavicis et germanicis.* Prague: M. A. Vitek. Reprinted, Munich: Otto Sagner, 1988.

Hunger, Herbert. 1961. "Antikes und mittelalterliches Buch- und Schriftwesen." In *Geschichte der Textüberlieferung der antiken und mittelalterlichen Literatur.* Vol. 1. Edited by Hunger et al. Zurich: Atlantis Verlag. 46 facs. Deals with Greek as well as Latin scripts.

Hurm, Otto. 1928. *Schriftform und Schreibwerkzeug: Die Handhabung der Schreibwerkzeuge und ihr formbildender Einfluss auf die Antiqua bis zum Einsetzen der Gotik.* Vienna: Staatsdruckerei.

Irigoin, Jean. 1950. "Les premiers manuscrits grecs écrits sur papier et le problème du bombycin." *Scriptorium* 4:194–204.

———. 1980. "La datation par les filigranes du papier." *Codicologica* 5:9–36.

Jemolo, Viviana, and Mirella Morelli. 1990. *Guida a una descrizione uniforme dei manoscritti e al loro censimento.* Rome: Istituto Centrale per il Catalogo Unico delle Biblioteche Italiane e per le Informazioni Bibliografiche. 2 figs., many forms, and 39 pls.

Jenkinson, Hilary. 1927. *The Later Court Hands in England from the 15th to the 17th Century.* Cambridge: Cambridge Univ. Press. 44 pls.*

Jensen, Hans. 1969. *Sign, Symbol and Script: An Account of Man's Efforts to Write.* New York: Putnam. Translated from *Die Schrift in Vergangenheit und Gegenwart.* 3d ed. Berlin: Deutscher Verlag der Wissenschaften, 1969. 588 figs.

John, James J. 1987. "Paleography, Western European." In *Dictionary of the Middle Ages,* edited by Joseph R. Strayer, 9:334–51. New York: Charles Scribner's. 17 facs.*

Johnson, Charles, and Hilary Jenkinson. 1915. *English Court Hand* A.D. *1066 to 1500.* 2 vols. Oxford: Clarendon Press. Reprinted, New York, 1967. 44 pls.*

Johnston, Edward. 1939. *Writing & Illuminating, & Lettering.* Rev. ed. London: Pitman; later reprints. 25 pls.

Jones, Leslie W. 1932. *The Script of Cologne from Hildebald to Hermann.* Cambridge, Mass.: Mediaeval Academy of America. 100 pls., from eighth to early tenth century.

————. 1946. "Pricking Manuscripts: The Instruments and Their Significance." *Speculum* 21:389–403. 3 pls.

Journal of the Society for Italic Handwriting. 1962–. London.

Kenyon, Frederic G. 1951. *Books and Readers in Ancient Greece and Rome.* 2d ed. Oxford: Clarendon Press. 7 pls. and 2 figs.

Ker, Neil R. 1960. *English Manuscripts in the Century after the Norman Conquest.* Oxford: Clarendon Press. 29 pls.

————. 1964. *Medieval Libraries of Great Britain: A List of Surviving Books.* 2d ed. London: Royal Historical Society. *Supplement,* edited by Andrew G. Watson, London: Royal Historical Society, 1987.

————. [1985]. *Books, Collectors and Libraries: Studies in the Medieval Heritage.* Edited by Andrew G. Watson. London: Hambledon Press. 33 pls.

Kirchner, Joachim. 1955. *Scriptura latina libraria a saeculo primo usque ad finem medii aevi* Munich: Oldenbourg; 2d ed., 1970. 77 facs.*

————. 1966. *Scriptura gothica libraria a saeculo XII usque ad finem medii aevi.* Munich: Oldenbourg. 87 facs.*

————. 1967. *Germanistische Handschriftenpraxis: Ein Lehrbuch für die Studierenden der deutschen Philologie.* 2d ed. Munich: Beck. 12 facs.

Knight, Stan. 1984. *Historical Scripts: A Handbook for Calligraphers.* London: Adam & Charles Black. 115 facs., showing scripts in both original and enlarged size.

Kopp, Ulrich Friedrich. 1965. *Lexicon Tironianum: Nachdruck aus Kopps "Palaeographia critica" von 1817 mit Nachwort und einem Alphabetum Tironianum von Bernhard Bischoff.* Osnabrück: Zeller.

Krämer, Sigrid, and (vol. 3) Michael Bernhard. 1989–90. *Handschriftenerbe des deutschen Mittelalters* [= *MBKDS,* Ergänzungsband 1]. 3 vols. Munich: Beck.

Kristeller, Paul Oskar. 1965. *Latin Manuscript Books before 1600: A List of the Printed Catalogues and Unpublished Inventories of Extant Collections.* 3d ed. New York: Fordham Univ. Press. A new edition is imminent.

Kyriss, Ernst. 1951–58. *Verzierte gotische Einbände im alten deutschen Sprachgebiet.* Stuttgart: Hettler. 3 vols. of pls.

Lamb, Cecil M., ed. *The Calligrapher's Handbook.* 1968. 2d ed. London: Faber.

Lauer, Ph., and Ch. Samaran. 1908. *Les diplômes originaux des Mérovingiens.* Paris: E. Leroux. 48 pls.*

Laurent, M.-H. 1939. *De abbreviationibus et signis scripturae gothicae.* Rome: Apud Institutum "Angelicum."

Lehmann, Paul. 1959–62. *Erforschung des Mittelalters: Ausgewählte Abhandlungen und Aufsätze.* 5 vols. 2d ed. of vol. 1. Stuttgart: Hiersemann.

Lemaire, Jacques. 1989. *Introduction à la codicologie.* Louvain-la-Neuve: Institut d'Études Médiévales. 49 figs. and 24 and XLIII pls.

Lemaire, Jacques, and Émile Van Balberghe, eds. 1985. *Calames et cahiers: Mélanges de codicologie et de paléographie offerts à Léon Gilissen.* Brussels: Centre d'Étude des Manuscrits. 22 pls.

Lesne, Émile. 1938. *Les livres, "scriptoria" et bibliothèques du commencement du VIIIe à la fin du XIe siècle.* Lille: Facultés Catholiques.

Lewis, Naphtali. 1974. *Papyrus in Classical Antiquity.* Oxford: Clarendon Press. *A Supplement.* Brussels: Fondation Égyptologique Reine Élisabeth, 1989.

Lieftinck, G. I. 1954. "Pour une nomenclature de l'écriture livresque de la période dite gothique." In *Nomenclature* (q.v.), 15–34, with figs. 13–34.

Lindsay, W. M. 1910. *Early Irish Minuscule Script.* Oxford: Parker. 12 pls.

———. 1912. *Early Welsh Script.* Oxford: Parker. 17 pls.*

———. 1915. *Notae latinae: An Account of Abbreviations in Latin MSS. of the Early Minuscule Period (c. 700–850).* Cambridge: Cambridge Univ. Press. Reprinted, Hildesheim: Olms, 1963, with Doris Bains, q.v.

Litterae Textuales: A Series on Manuscripts and Their Texts. 1972-. Edited by J. P. Gumbert and M. J. M. De Haan. Amsterdam: Van Gendt. Includes *Codicologica.*

Loew (Lowe), E. A. 1914. *The Beneventan Script: A History of the South Italian Minuscule.* Oxford: Clarendon Press. 2d ed., 2 vols., Rome: Edizioni di Storia e Letteratura, 1980, revised by Virginia Brown. With a vastly expanded and annotated "Hand List of Beneventan MSS." 9 pls.

Lot, Ferdinand, and Philippe Lauer (with Georges Tessier for fascs. III–V). 1936–49. *Diplomata Karolinorum: Recueil de reproductions en fac-similé des actes originaux des souverains carolingiens conservés dans les archives et bibliothèques de France.* Fascs. II–IX. Toulouse: H. Didier. 273 pls.

Lowe, E. A. (see also Loew and under *CLA*). 1929. *Scriptura Beneventana: Facsimiles of South Italian and Dalmatian Manuscripts from the Eighth to the Fourteenth Century.* 2 vols. Oxford: Clarendon Press. 100 pls.*

———. 1960. *English Uncial.* Oxford: Clarendon Press. 40 pls.

———. 1969. *Handwriting: Our Medieval Legacy.* Rome: Edizioni di storia e letteratura. Transcriptions of facsimiles by W. Braxton Ross, Jr. 22 pls.* Slightly revised text, with larger plates and transcriptions, of "Handwriting." In *The Legacy of the Middle Ages,* edited by C. G. Crump and E. F. Jacob, 197–226, and pls. 25–40. Oxford: Clarendon Press, 1926. Emphasizes the Caroline script and its origins.

———. 1972. *Palaeographical Papers 1907–1965.* 2 vols. Edited by Ludwig Bieler. Oxford: Clarendon Press. 150 pls.

Mallon, Jean. 1952. *Paléographie romaine.* Madrid: Instituto Antonio de Nebrija de Filologia. 87 facs. on 32 pls.

———. 1961. "Paléographie romaine." In Samaran (1961), 553–84. 14 figs.

———. 1982. *De l'écriture: Recueil d'études publiées de 1937 à 1981.* Paris: Éditions du CNRS, Numerous pls.

Mallon, Jean, Robert Marichal, and Charles Perrat. 1939. *L'écriture latine de la capitale romaine à la minuscule.* Paris: Arts et métiers graphiques. 85 facs. on 54 pls.*

Manuscripta. 1957-. St. Louis.

Les manuscrits datés: Premier bilan et perspectives/Die datierten Handschriften: Erste Bilanz und Perspektiven, Neuchâtel/Neuenburg, 1983. 1985. Paris: Éditions CEMI. Critical reflections on *CMD* (q.v.) by the editors.

Marichal, Robert. 1948. "De la capitale romaine à la minuscule." In M. Audin, *Somme typographique*. Paris: Audin éditeur. 2 pls.

――――. 1963. "L'écriture latine et la civilisation occidentale du Ier au XVIe siècle." In *L'écriture et la psychologie des peuples*. Edited by Marcel Cohen et al. Paris: A. Colin. 14 figs.

――――. 1950. "Paléographie précaroline et papyrologie, II, l'écriture latine du Ier au VIIe siècle: Les sources." *Scriptorium* 4:116–42.

Martin, Charles Trice. 1910. *The Record Interpreter: A Collection of Abbreviations, Latin Words and Names Used in English Historical Manuscripts and Records*. 2d ed. London: Stevens & Sons. Reprinted, Hildesheim, 1969.

Martin, Henri-Jean, and Jean Vezin, eds. 1990. *Mise en page et mise en texte du livre manuscrit*. [Paris:] Cercle de la Librairie-Promodis. 445 figs.

Masai, François. 1950a. "Paléographie et codicologie." *Scriptorium* 4:279–93.

――――. 1950b. "Principes et conventions de l'édition diplomatique." *Scriptorium* 4:177–93.

――――. 1956. "La Paléographie gréco-latine, ses tâches, ses méthodes." *Scriptorium* 10:281–302. Also in *Codicologica* 1 (1976): 34–57, with a "Post-Scriptum" by Albert Derolez.

Mateu Ibars, Josefina, and Maria Dolores. 1974. *Bibliografía paleográfica*. Barcelona: Universidad de Barcelona. 17 pls.

Mazal, Otto. 1975a. *Buchkunst der Gotik*. Graz: Akademische Druck- und Verlagsanstalt. 169 figs. 1–40 devoted to Gothic scripts.

――――. 1975b. *Handschriftenbeschreibung in Österreich: Referate, Beratungen und Ergebnisse der Arbeitstagungen in Kremsmünster (1973) und Zwettl (1974)*. Vienna.

Mazzoleni, Jole. 1972. *Esempi di scritture cancelleresche, curiali e minuscole* [in Italy]. Naples: Libreria scientifica editrice. 30 pls.*

MBKDS = Mittelalterliche Bibliothekskataloge Deutschlands und der Schweiz. 1918–. Edited by Paul Lehmann, Paul Ruf, Bernhard Bischoff et al. Munich: Beck. 4 vols. to 1979.

MBKÖ = Mittelalterliche Bibliothekskataloge Österreichs. 1915–71. 5 vols. Edited by Th. Gottlieb et al. Vienna: Holzhausen.

McGurk, Patrick. 1956. "The Irish Pocket Gospel Book." *Sacris Erudiri* 8:249–70.

――――. 1961a. "Citation Marks in Early Latin Manuscripts (with a List of Citation Marks in Manuscripts Earlier than A.D. 800 in English and Irish Libraries." *Scriptorium* 15:3–13, and pls. 1–4.

――――. 1961b. *Latin Gospel Books from A.D. 400 to A.D. 800* [= Les Publications de Scriptorium 5]. Paris: Érasme.

McNeil, Roderick J. 1984. "Scanning Auger Microscopy for Dating of Manuscript Inks." In *Archaeological Chemistry—III*, edited by Joseph B. Lambert, 255–69. Washington: American Chemical Society.

Meiss, Millard. 1960. "Toward a More Comprehensive Renaissance Palaeography." *The Art Bulletin* 42:97–112, with 36 figs.

Mentz, Georg. 1912. *Handschriften der Reformationszeit*. Bonn: Marcus and Weber. 94 facs. on 50 pls.*

Merkelbach, Reinhold, and Helmut van Thiel. 1969. *Lateinisches Leseheft zur Einführung in Paläographie und Textkritik.* Göttingen: Vandenhoeck and Ruprecht. 111 pls.

Metzger, Bruce M. 1968. "When Did Scribes Begin to Use Writing Desks?" In his *Historical and Literary Studies: Pagan, Jewish, and Christian.* Leyden: E. J. Bill. Pls. III–XIX.

Meyer, Otto, and Renate Klauser. 1962. *Clavis mediaevalis: Kleines Wörterbuch der Mittelalterforschung.* Wiesbaden: Otto Harrassowitz. 8 pls. and numerous figs.

Meyer, Wilhelm. 1897. "Die Buchstaben-Verbindungen der sogenannten gothischen Schrift." *Abhandlungen der Königlichen Gesellschaft der Wissenschaften zu Göttingen,* philol.-hist. Kl., N. F. Vol. 1, no. 6. Berlin. 5 pls.

Milkau, Fritz, and Georg Leyh. 1952–57. *Handbuch der Bibliothekswissenschaft.* 2d ed. Wiesbaden: Otto Harrassowitz. Vols. 1, 3. See also under Christ.

Millares Carlo, Agustín. 1963. *Manuscritos visigóticos: Notas bibliográficas.* Barcelona: Consejo Superior de Investigaciones Científicas. 16 facs.*

———. 1973. *Consideraciones sobre la escritura visigotica cursiva.* Leon: Centro de Estudios e Investigacion "San Isidoro." 41 figs.*

Millares Carlo, Agustín, and J. I. Mantecon. 1955. *Album de paleografía hispanoamericana de los siglos XVI y XVII.* 3 vols. Mexico: Instituto panamericano de Geografía e Historia. 93 facs.*, from 1176 to 1643.

Millares Carlo, Agustín, and José Manuel Ruiz Asencio. 1983. *Tratado de paleografía española.* 3d ed. 3 vols. Madrid: Espasa-Calpe. More than 466 figs.*

Moreau-Marichal, J. 1968. "Recherches sur la ponctuation." *Scriptorium* 22:56–66.

Morrish, Jennifer. 1988. "Dated and Datable Manuscripts Copied in England during the Ninth Century: A Preliminary List." *Mediaeval Studies,* 50:512–38, and 9 pls.

Mosin, Vladimir A., and Seid M. Traljic. 1957. *Filigranes des XIIIe et XIVe ss.* 2 vols. Zagreb: Académie yougoslave des sciences et des beaux-arts. 852 pls., with 7,271 watermarks, including many overlooked by Briquet.

Müller, Rudolf W. 1964. *Rhetorische und syntaktische Interpunktion: Untersuchungen zur Pausenbezeichnung im antiken Latein.* Tübingen. With pls.

Mundó, Anscari M. 1965. "La Datación de los códices liturgicos visigóticos toledanos." *Hispania sacra* 18:1–25, and pls. i–xvi.

Muzerelle, Denis. 1985. *Vocabulaire codicologique: Répertoire méthodique des termes français relatifs aux manuscrits.* Paris: Éditions CEMI.

Needham, Paul. 1979. *Twelve Centuries of Bookbindings, 400–1600.* New York: P. Morgan Library/London: Oxford Univ. Press.

The New Palaeographical Society: Facsimiles of Ancient Manuscripts. 1903–30. Edited by E. M. Thompson, G. F. Warner, et al. 2 series. London: Oxford Univ. Press. 452 pls.*. *Indices,* by F. Wormald. 1932.

Newton, K. C. 1971. *Medieval Local Records: A Reading Aid* Helps for Students of History, no. 83. London: Historical Association. 12 pls.* Documents of English origin from ca. 1185 to 1498.

Nomenclature = Nomenclature des écritures livresques du IXe au XVIe siècle: Pre-

mier colloque international de paléographie latine, Paris, 28-30 avril 1953.
1954. Paris: Centre National de la Recherche Scientifique. 44 figs.

Nunes, Eduardo. 1969-. *Album de paleografia portuguesa.* Vol. 1. Lisbon: Instituto de alta cultura. 170 facs. on 60 pls* mostly of documents, A.D. 999-1712.

Ó Cróinín, Dáibhí. 1984. "Rath Melsigi, Willibrord, and the Earliest Echternach Manuscripts." *Peritia* 3:17-42, with 3 pls.

Omont, Henri. 1935. *Listes des recueils de fac-similés et des reproductions de manuscrits conservés à la Bibliothèque Nationale.* 3d ed. Edited by Ph. Lauer. Paris: Éditions des Bibliothèques Nationales de France.

O'Neill, Timothy. 1984. *The Irish Hand: Scribes and Their Manuscripts from the Earliest Times to the Seventeenth Century with an Exemplar of Irish Scripts.* Mountrath, Portlaoise: Dolmen Press. XXVI pls., 5 figs., and 53 facs.*

O'Sullivan, William. 1985. "Insular Calligraphy: Current State and Problems." *Peritia* 4:346-59.

Ouy, Gilbert. 1958. "Histoire 'visible' et histoire 'cachée' d'un manuscrit." *Le Moyen Age* 64:115-38, and 2 pls.

Paap, A. H. R. E. 1959. *Nomina sacra in the Greek Papyri of the First Five Centuries A.D.: The Sources and Some Deductions.* Leyden: Brill.

Pagnin, B. 1933-34. "La 'littera bononiensis', studio paleografico." *Atti del Reale Istituto Veneto di Scienze, Lettere ed Arti* 93:1,593-665 (also separately paginated 1-73), and pls. XVIII-XX.

Palaeographia latina. 1922-29. Edited by W. M. Lindsay. 6 pts. London: Oxford Univ. Press. Reprinted, 1974.

The Palaeographical Society: Facsimiles of Manuscripts and Inscriptions. 1873-94. Edited by E. A. Bond, E. M. Thompson, et al. 2 series. London: W. Clowes. 465 pls* *Indices,* 1901. Cf. also L. R. Dean. *An Index to Facsimiles in the Palaeographical Society Publications.* Princeton, 1914. Covers the *Palaeographical Society* and the first series of the *New Palaeographical Society.*

Parkes, M. B. 1969. *English Cursive Book Hands, 1250-1500.* Oxford: Clarendon Press. 24 pls.*

———. 1976. "The Influence of the Concepts of *Ordinatio* and *Compilatio* on the Development of the Book." In *Medieval Learning and Literature: Essays Presented to Richard William Hunt,* edited by J. J. G. Alexander and M. T. Gibson, 115-41, and pls. VIII-XVII. Oxford: Clarendon Press.

Pellegrin, Élisabeth. 1988. *Bibliothèques retrouvées: Manuscrits, bibliothèques et bibliophiles du Moyen Age et de la Renaissance. Recueil d'études publiés de 1938 à 1985.* Paris: Éditions du CNRS. 24 pls.

Pelzer, Auguste. 1966. *Abbréviations latines médiévales: Supplément au Dizionario di abbreviature latine ed italiane de Adriano Cappelli.* 2d ed. Louvain: Publications universitaires/Paris: Béatrice-Nauwelaerts.

Petrucci, Armando. 1967. *La scrittura di Francesco Petrarca* [= *Studi e Testi* 248]. Vatican City. 38 pls.

———. 1971. "L'onciale romana: Origini, sviluppo e diffusione di una stilizzazione grafica altomedievale (sec. VI-IX)." *Studi Medievali* (3d series) 12:75-134, and 20 pls.

————. 1984. *La descrizione del manoscritto: Storia, problemi, modelli.* Rome: La Nuova Italia Scientifica.

Petrucci, Armando and Alessandro Pratesí, eds. 1988. *Un secolo di paleografia e diplomatica (1887-1986): Per il centenario dell'Istituto di Paleografia dell'Università di Roma.* Rome: Gela editrice.

Petti, Anthony G. 1977. *English Literary Hands from Chaucer to Dryden.* Cambridge, Mass. 67 pls.*

Piccard, Gerhard. 1961-. *Die Wasserzeichenkartei Piccard im Hauptstaatsarchiv Stuttgart: Findbuch.* Stuttgart: Kohlhammer. 15 vols. by 1987.

Plante, Julian G. 1967-74. *Checklist of Manuscripts Microfilmed for the Monastic Manuscript Microfilm Library, Saint John's University, Collegeville, Minnesota* Vol. 1: *Austrian Monasteries,* 1-2. Collegeville: St. John's University.

Pollard, Graham. 1976. "Describing Medieval Bookbindings." In *Medieval Learning and Literature: Essays Presented to Richard William Hunt,* edited by J. J. G. Alexander and M. T. Gibson, 50-65. Oxford: Clarendon Press.

Poulle, Emmanuel. 1966. *Paléographie des écritures cursives en France du XVe au XVIIe siècle: Recueil de fac-similés de documents parisiens.* Geneva: Droz. 30 pls.*

————. 1974. "Paléographie et méthodologie: Vers l'analyse scientifique des écritures médiévales." *BEC* 132:101-10.

Pratesi, Alessandro. 1964. "Considerazioni su alcuni codici in capitale della Biblioteca Apostolica Vaticana." In *Mélanges Eugène Tisserant* 7 [= *Studi e Testi* 237]. Vatican City. 5 pls.

Prou, Maurice. 1924. *Manuel de paléographie latine et française.* 4th ed. Edited by Alain de Boüard. Paris: Picard. 55 facs.* Still valuable for its pls. and for its list of French abbreviations.

Questa, Cesare, and Renato Raffaelli, eds. 1984. *Il libro e il testo: Atti del convegno internazionale Urbino, 20-23 settembre 1982.* Urbino: Università di Studi. 150 pls.

Rabikauskas, Paul. 1958. *Die römische Kuriale in der päpstlichen Kanzlei.* Rome: Pontificia Universitas Gregoriana. 37 figs.

Rafti, Patrizia. 1988. "L'interpunzione nel libro manoscritto: Mezzo secolo di studi." *Scrittura e Civiltà* 12:239-98.

Rand, E. K. 1929. *A Survey of the Manuscripts of Tours* [= *Studies in the Script of Tours* 1]. Cambridge, Mass.: Mediaeval Academy of America. 200 pls.

Rand, E. K., and L. W. Jones. 1934. *The Earliest Book of Tours* [= *Studies in the Script of Tours* 2]. Cambridge, Mass.: Mediaeval Academy of America. 60 pls.

Randall, Lilian M. C. 1966. *Images in the Margins of Gothic Manuscripts.* Berkeley: Univ. of California Press. 739 figs. on 158 pls.

Reed, Ronald. [1972]. *Ancient Skins, Parchments and Leathers.* London: Seminar Press.

Reusens, Edmond. 1899. *Éléments de paléographie.* Louvain: The Author. Reprinted, Brussels, 1963. 60 pls.* and numerous figs.* Valuable for its facs. of scripts from the Lowlands.

Revue d'histoire des textes. 1971–. Paris. Continues the *Bulletin* of the Institut de Recherche et d'Histoire des Textes.

Reynolds, L. D., ed. 1983. *Texts and Transmission: A Survey of the Latin Classics.* Oxford: Clarendon Press.

Reynolds, L. D., and N. G. Wilson. 1974. *Scribes and Scholars: A Guide to the Transmission of Greek and Latin Literature.* 2d ed. Oxford: Oxford Univ. Press. 16 Greek and Latin pls.

Richtlinien Handschriftenkatalogisierung. 1985. 4th ed. Bonn: Deutsche Forschungsgemeinschaft.

Roberts, Colin H., and T. C. Skeat. 1987. *The Birth of the Codex.* London: Oxford Univ. Press. 6 pls.

Robinson, Rodney P. 1939. *Manuscripts 27 (S. 29) and 107 (S. 129) of the Municipal Library of Autun: A Study of Spanish Half-Uncial and Early Visigothic Minuscule and Cursive Scripts* [= *Memoirs of the American Academy in Rome* 16]. New York. 73 pls.*

Roncaglia, Aurelio. 1941. "Note sulla punteggiatura medievale e il segno di parentesi." *Lingua nostra* 3:6–9.

Ruess, Ferdinand. 1914. *Die Kasseler Handschrift der Tironischen Noten samt Ergänzungen aus der Wolfenbüttler Handschrift.* Leipzig: Teubner. 150 pls.

Samaran, Charles. 1922. "Note pour servir au déchiffrement de la cursive gothique de la fin du XVᵉ à la fin du XVIIᵉ siècle." *Le Moyen Age* (2d series) 24:95–106, and 3 pls.*

———, ed. 1961. *L'histoire et ses méthodes.* Paris: Gallimard.

Santifaller, Leo. 1953. *Beiträge zur Geschichte der Beschreibstoffe im Mittelalter, mit besonderer Berücksichtigung der päpstlichen Kanzlei.* Vol. 1: *Untersuchungen* [= *Mitteilungen des Instituts für österreichische Geschichtsforschung,* Erg.-bd. XVI, Heft 1]. Graz: Böhlau.

———. 1965. "Über späte Papyrusrollen und frühe Pergamentrollen." In *Speculum historiale: Geschichte im Spiegel von Geschichtsschreibung und Geschichtsdeutung.* Edited by Cl. Bauer, L. Boehm, and M. Müller. Freiburg: Alber.

Schiaparelli, Luigi. 1921. *La scrittura latina nell' età romana.* Como: Ostinelli. 11 facs.*

———. 1926. *Avviamento allo studio delle abbreviature latine nel medioevo.* Florence: Olschki. 4 pls.

Schmitz, Wilhelm. 1893. *Commentarii Notarum Tironianarum cum prolegomenis adnotationibus criticis et exegeticis notarumque indice alphabetico.* Leipzig. 132 pls.*

Schubart, Wilhelm. 1962. *Das Buch bei den Griechen und Römern.* 3d ed. Edited by Eberhard Paul. Heidelberg: Schneider. 31 facs.

Scriptorium: International Review of Manuscript Studies. 1946–. Antwerp (since 1969, Ghent).

Scrittura e Civiltà. 1977–. Rome (since 1990, Florence). Vol. 11 contains an index for the first 10 vols.

Seider, Richard. 1972–81. *Paläographie der lateinischen Papyri.* 2 vols. in 3 pts. Stuttgart: A. Hiersemann. 120 pls.*

Shailor, Barbara A. 1988. *The Medieval Book: Catalogue of an Exhibition at the Beinecke Rare Book & Manuscript Library, Yale University.* New Haven: Yale Univ. Reprinted, Toronto: Univ. of Toronto Press, 1991. 97 facs. and numerous hand drawings.

Sharpe, John L. 1971. "A Checklist of Collections of Biblical and Related Manuscripts on Microfilm in the United States and Canada." *Scriptorium* 25:97–109.

Salagi, Gabriel, ed. 1982. *Paläographie 1981: Colloquium des Comité International de Paléographie* [= *Münchener Beiträge zur Mediävistik und Renaissance-Forschung* 32]. Munich. 38 pls.

Simpson, Grant G. 1973. *Scottish Handwriting, 1150–1650: An Introduction to the Reading of Documents.* Edinburgh: Bratton. Corrected reprint, Aberdeen Univ. Press, 1986. 30 pls.*

Sirat, Colette. 1981. *L'examen des écritures: l'oeil et la machine: Essai de méthodologie.* Paris: Éditions du CNRS. 31 pls.

Sorbelli, Albano. 1944. "Dalla scrittura alla stampa: Il segno di paragrafo." In *Scritti di paleografia e diplomatica in onore di Vincenzo Federici.* Florence: Olschki.

Spilling, Herrad. 1978a. "Angelsächsische Schrift in Fulda." In *Von der Klosterbibliothek zur Landesbibliothek,* edited by Artur Brall, 47–98, with figs. 13–20. Stuttgart: A. Hiersemann.

———. 1978b. "Schreibkünste des späten Mittelalters." *Codices manuscripti* 4: 97–117.

Steffens, Franz. 1909. *Lateinische Paläographie.* 2d ed. Trier. 3d unaltered ed., Berlin: Walter de Gruyter, 1929. Reprinted, Berlin, 1964. Also a French trans. by R. Coulon, Paris, 1910. 125 pls.* Still the best general collection of facs. in terms of paleographical scope and the quality of the accompanying information.

Stevenson, Allan. 1961. *Observations on Paper as Evidence.* Lawrence: Univ. of Kansas Libraries.

———. 1967. *The Problem of the Missale Speciale.* London: Bibliographical Society.

Stiennon, Jacques, and Genevieve Hasenohr. 1973. *Paléographie du Moyen Age.* Paris: Colin. 51 pls.*

Supino Martini, Paola. 1987. *Roma e l'area grafica romanesca (secoli X–XII).* Alessandria: Edizioni dell'Orso. 80 pls.

Svensson, Lars. 1974. *Nordisk paleografi: Handbok med transkriberade och kommenterade skriftprov.* Lund: Studentlitteratur. 85 facs.* numbered 1–64.

Techniques = Les Techniques de laboratoire dans l'étude des manuscrits [= Colloques internationaux du Centre National de la Recherche Scientifique, no. 548]. 1974. Paris: Éditions du CNRS. Many illustrations.

Thompson, Edward Maunde. 1912. *An Introduction to Greek and Latin Palaeography.* Oxford: Clarendon Press. Reprinted, New York, 1973. 250 facs.* Being replaced by Bishop (1971), Parkes (1969), Wright (1960), etc., but still valuable for its facs. of Greek and Latin, literary and documentary texts from Antiquity to modern times.

Thompson, James Westfall. 1939. *The Medieval Library.* Chicago: Univ. of Chicago Press. Reprinted, New York, 1957, with a supplement by Blanche Boyer.

Thomson, S. Harrison. 1969. *Latin Bookhands of the Later Middle Ages: 1100–1500.* Cambridge: Cambridge Univ. Press. 132 pls.*

Tjäder, Jan-Olof. 1954–82. *Die nichtliterarischen lateinischen Papyri Italiens aus der Zeit 445–700* [= *Skrifter utgivna av Svenska Institutet i Rom,* 4°, XIX: 1–3]. Plates and pt. 1, Lund: Gleerup, 1954–55. Pt. 2, Stockholm: Åström, 1982. 160 pls.*

———. 1974. "Der Ursprung der Unzialschrift." *Basler Zeitschrift für Geschichte und Altertumskunde* 74:9–40.

———. 1977. "Latin Palaeography." *Eranos: Acta philologica suecana* 75 (1977): 131–61; 78 (1980): 65–97; 80 (1982): 63–92; 82 (1984): 66–95. Annotated bibliographical surveys.

———. 1985. "Later Roman (Common) Script." In Lemaire and Van Balberghe, 187–99 with 2 pls.

Traube, Ludwig. 1907. *Nomina sacra: Versuch einer Geschichte der christlichen Kürzung.* Munich: Beck.

———. 1909–20. *Vorlesungen und Abhandlungen.* 3 vols. Edited by Franz Boll. Munich: Beck. Reprinted, Munich, 1965.

Turner, Eric G. 1977. *The Typology of the Early Codex.* Philadelphia: Univ. of Pennsylvania Press. 9 pls. and 13 figs.

Ullman, Berthold L. 1932. *Ancient Writing and Its Influence.* New York: Longmans. Reprinted with Introduction and Supplementary Bibliography by Julian Brown, Cambridge, Mass.: MIT Press, 1969, and Toronto: Univ. of Toronto Press, 1982. 47 Greek and Latin facs.* Still useful, despite inevitable aging.

———. 1960. *The Origin and Development of Humanistic Script.* Rome: Edizioni di storia e letteratura, 70 facs. Groundbreaking.

Umbrae codicum occidentalium. 1960–. Amsterdam: North Holland. 10 vols. to 1966. Complete facs. eds.

Valentine, Lucia N. 1965. *Ornament in Medieval Manuscripts: A Glossary.* London: Faber. Numerous figs.

Van Regemorter, Berthe. 1948. "Evolution de la technique de la reliure du VIIIᵉ au XIIᵉ siècle." *Scriptorium* 2:275–85, and 4 pls.

———. 1955. "Le Codex relié depuis son origine jusqu'au Haut Moyen-Age." *Le Moyen Age* 61:1–26.

Vanderhoven, H., and F. Masai. 1953. *La Règle du Maître: Édition diplomatique des manuscrits latins 12,205 et 12,634 de Paris* [= *Les Publications de Scriptorium* 3]. Brussels: Érasme.

Vezin, Jean. 1967. "Observations sur l'emploi des réclames dans les manuscrits latins." *BEC* 125:5–33.

———. 1974. *Les scriptoria d'Angers au XIᵉ siècle.* Paris: H. Champion. 53 pls.

———. 1978. "La réalisation matérielle des manuscrits latins pendant le haut Moyen Age." *Codicologica* 2:15–51, with 8 figs. and 12 pls.

———. 1980. "Le point d'interrogation, un élément de datation et de localisation des manuscrits. L'exemple de Saint-Denis au IXᵉ siècle." *Scriptorium* 34:181–96, and pl. 13.

Visible Language: The Journal for Research on the Visual Media of Language Expression. 1967–. Cleveland.

Wardrop, James. 1963. *The Script of Humanism: Some Aspects of Humanistic Script, 1460–1560.* Oxford: Clarendon Press. 58 pls.

Wattenbach, Wilhelm. 1896. *Das Schriftwesen im Mittelalter.* 3d ed. Leipzig. Reprinted, Graz, 1958.

Weijers, Olga, ed. 1989. *Vocabulaire du livre et de l'écriture au moyen âge: Actes de la table ronde, Paris 24–26 septembre 1987.* Turnhout: Brepols.

Williman, Daniel, and Margarita Dziedzic. 1978. *"Dictio probatoria* as Fingerprint: Computer Discovery of Manuscript Provenances." *Computers and the Humanities* 12:89–92.

Wilson, William J. 1956. "Manuscript Cataloging." *Traditio* 12:457–555.

Wingo, E. Otha. 1972. *Latin Punctuation in the Classical Age.* The Hague: Mouton.

Wright, C. E. 1960. *English Vernacular Hands from the Twelfth to the Fifteenth Centuries.* Oxford: Clarendon Press. 24 pls.*

Zamponi, Stefano. 1988. "Elisione e sovrapposizione nella littera textualis." *Scrittura e civiltà* 12:135–76, and 4 pls. An abbreviated version of this essay appears in *Actas,* 229–37.

Zangemeister, Karl, and Wilhelm Wattenbach. 1876–79. *Exempla codicum latinorum litteris maiusculis scriptorum* and *Supplementum.* Heidelberg. 62 pls., with selected transcriptions.

Zerdoun Bat-Yehouda, Monique. 1983. *Les encres noires au moyen âge (jusqu'à 1600).* Paris: Éditions du CNRS.

———. 1989. *Les papiers filigranés médiévaux: Essai de méthodologie descriptive.* 2 vols. [= *Bibliologia* 7–8]. Turnhout: Brepols.

Ziegler, Ernst, and Jost Hochuli. 1985–. *Hefte zur Paläographie des 13. bis 20. Jahrhunderts aus dem Stadtarchiv (Vadiana) St. Gallen.* Rorschach: E. Löpfe-Benz. 5 Hefte to 1987, with 49 pls.* containing documentary scripts, 1228–1698, mostly in German.

Zotter, Hans. 1976. *Bibliographie faksimilierter Handschriften.* Graz: Akademische Druck- und Verlagsanstalt.

cx/ン 2 c&じ

Diplomatics

LEONARD E. BOYLE

IPLOMATICS, or in Mabillon's terminology, *Res diplomatica,* is a form of literary criticism that is based on a detailed exami- nation of documentary records in order to understand what they say and to see if what they say is consistent with what is known of fact. The art was not unknown to early times and to the Middle Ages, but it only acquired polish and accuracy in the seventeenth century. Popes, bishops, and jurists of the Middle Ages were always concerned about the interpretation and authenticity of documents, and Innocent III (1198–1216) issued a celebrated, if far from watertight, decretal on the detection of false *bullae* (Boyle 1967). The Humanists, too, were on their guard, the most famous case being the recognition by Lorenzo Valla in 1440 of the Donation of Constantine for what it was, a forgery.

In the sixteenth century, both Reformers and Counter-Reformers gave an impetus to the publication and critical study of historical documents: the Protestants, for example, with the *Ecclesiastica historia* of the Magde- burg Centuriators (13 vols., Basle, 1559–74), the Catholics with the *An- nales ecclesiastici* of C. Baronius (12 vols., Rome, 1588–1607). These were followed in the next century by such critical or semi-critical enterprises as the *Gallia christiana* of C. Robert (Paris, 1626; later expanded from one volume to four by C. Scévole and L. de Sainte-Marthe in 1656), the *Italia sacra* of the Cistercian F. Ughelli (9 vols., Rome, 1644–62), and the *Sacrosancta concilia* of the Jesuits F. Labbe and G. Cossart (17 vols., Paris, 1671–73).

By this time two centers of exact scholarship were in full swing: the Abbey of St.-Germain-des Près in Paris (Benedictines of the Congregation of St. Maur: hence "Maurists"), where Luc D'Achery (1609-85), the editor of the works of St. Bernard, the *Acta Sanctorum Ordinis S. Benedicti,* and the *Veterum aliquot Scriptorum Spicilegium,* had formed a small band of disciples; and the Institute founded at Antwerp by the Jesuit Jean Bolland (1596-1665) for the publication of critical *Acta Sanctorum.* It is to these two centers, not all that far apart, that diplomatics and its by-product paleography owe their origin.

Although it was Jean Mabillon of St.-Germain-des-Près in Paris who founded the art of *Res diplomatica* or diplomatics, the spur came from Antwerp and the Bollandists (Delehaye 1959; Knowles 1964). In 1675, the second volume of the *Acta Sanctorum* for April carried an introductory fifty-page essay in double columns entitled "Propylaeum antiquarium circa veri et falsi discrimen in vetustis membranis" (Van Papenbroeck 1675), the first part of which (pp. i-xxxiii) bore the heading "De Diplomatis" and was, in the words of the writer of the essay, Daniel van Papenbroeck ("Papebrochius," as he signs himself), expressly concerned with diplomata, "quae ante nongentis vel mille annos a primis Francorum Regibus signata dicuntur."

He and other scholars, Papenbroeck went on, had had misgivings for some time about reproductions of early "instrumenta fundationum, donationum et privilegiorum" which had appeared in some recent publications and were reputedly from originals in the archives of various monasteries. Now, and on a basis, roughly, of "Who? What? How? Why?," Papenbroeck proposed to document these suspicions, taking as a test case an alleged diploma of Dagobert I in 638 and comparing it from the points of view of authorship, content, style, formulae, monograms, and handwriting, with undoubted diplomata of the same Dagobert. To clinch his point and make it visually telling, he added reproductions of the monograms of the period and, interestingly, of the handwriting of the diplomata he was comparing and of some other contemporary writings. He then went on to voice his general distrust of early diplomata in the possession of certain monasteries in France and elsewhere, and in the second and third parts of the "Propylaeum" to discuss some Carmelite and other pretensions.

As soon as this volume of the *Acta Sanctorum* reached Paris, Jean Mabillon, who was already a seasoned scholar after years of work with D'Achery, set a small *équipe* of fellow Benedictines to comb the libraries and archives of Paris and environs in an effort to meet Papenbroeck's arguments and to pick holes in his criteria for the "discrimen veri et falsi." Six short years after the appearance of the "Propylaeum" came the monumental *De re diplomatica libri sex* (Mabillon 1681). He demolished or refined most of the criteria advanced by Papenbroeck and, as Papenbroeck later generously allowed, placed documentary criticism on a firm footing once for all.

If Papenbroeck (1628–1714) is the father of the critical study of diplomata, Mabillon (1632–1707) is the founder of the wider *Res diplomatica* or diplomatics of today. His approach to diplomata as such and to *instrumenta* in general was more measured and systematic and far less shrill than that of Papenbroeck; and he had the advantage over Papenbroeck of seeing beyond while building on another's foundations, and of being in a position to devote a long and exhaustive volume to what he called the "novum antiquariae artis genus," where his adversary had to be content with a short if pregnant essay. Above all else, Mabillon formulated a more comprehensive and compelling statement of documentary criticism than Papenbroeck, when he argued that any proper evaluation of the character, content, and authenticity of a given document must take account of internal as well as external criteria; of the changing fashions of composition, handwriting, and style from area to area and from age to age; and of the history, personnel, and usages of chanceries, notarial offices, and scriptoria from place to place and from period to period.

Mabillon's prodigious scholarship and his advocacy of "the new antiquarian art" of *Res diplomatica* soon prompted works of a similar studied approach to documentation. The *Dissertationes ecclesiasticae de re diplomatica* of the Spanish Benedictine Juan Perez came out in 1688, the influential *Formulare anglicanum* of Thomas Madox in 1702, the *Istoria diplomatica* of Scipione Maffei in 1727. Mabillon's own work was continued, and to some extent improved upon, by his fellow-Maurists Tassin and Toustain in a massive *Nouveau traité de diplomatique* which was spread over the years 1750 to 1765. This, too, had a wide influence. It was published in a German translation in nine volumes at Erfurt from 1759 to 1769, and as a result, diplomatics began to be taught in German universities and even in the law faculties there, producing a rich harvest of scholars in the next century. In France a précis of the *Traité* was published in two volumes in 1838 by Noël de Wailly of the École des chartes under the title *Éléments de paléographie pour servir à l'étude des documents inédits sur l'histoire de la France.*

By 1838, however, because of the French Revolution, the Maurists were only a respected memory, and other collaborative ventures had begun to fill the void left by their departure. As Europe settled down after the Congress of Vienna, France and Germany, two nations which had been on opposite sides, began, not without some stirrings of cultural pride, to take steps to exploit their respective documentary deposits, now considerably swelled by material that had accumulated after the suppression of so many monasteries (Knowles 1953). At Paris the École des chartes, founded in 1821 for the express purpose of providing a training in paleography, diplomatics, and chronology, the better to explore and publish the archival riches of the realm, soon became a force under diplomatists and paleographers such as J.-N. de Wailly (1805–86), Léopold Delisle (1826–1910), and Arthur Giry (1848–99), and in 1839 began to issue an authoritative house chronicle, the *Bibliothèque de l'École des chartes* (*BEC*). In Germany, some two years after the foundation of the École at Paris, the Gesellschaft für ältere deutsche Geschichtskunde or Societas pro aperiendis fontibus rerum Germanicarum was set up in Frankfurt, beginning the *Monumenta Germaniae Historica* (*MGH*) in 1824. The first, and long-lived, editor of the *Monumenta* was the talented G. H. Pertz (1795–1876). With the aid of Leopold von Ranke and others, he attracted a band of able collaborators to the *MGH*, among them the gifted Georg Waitz (1813–86), who, in turn, recruited scholars such as O. Holder-Egger, Harry Bresslau, and Ludwig Traube. The secretary of the fledgling enterprise, which also began to publish a periodical *Archiv* (later *Neues Archiv*, now *Deutsches Archiv*), was J. H. Böhmer. In 1831, independently of the *MGH*, he published the first part of an original and ambitious *Regesta chronologico-diplomatica regum atque imperatorum romanorum*, which in time inspired critical *Regesta* of papal letters by Jaffé (1851), Potthast (1874), and Kehr (1906).

Other countries, too, were beginning to take an interest in their archival deposits. With these two great institutions in Germany and France there may be noted, among others, the setting up of the Public Record Office in London by Act of Parliament in 1838, the inauguration some twenty years later of the Rolls series of English historical sources, and the foundation at Vienna in 1854 by Theodor von Sickel (1826–1908) of the Oesterreichisches Institut für Geschichtsforschung, on the model of the École des chartes, where he had studied. From this Austrian school there came in 1880 the third, with the *BEC* and the (*Neues*) *Archiv*, of the more influential of diplomatic periodicals, the *Mitteilungen des Instituts für österreichische Geschichtsforschung* (*MIöG*).

Revered though he is as the founder of diplomatics, Mabillon has been reproached for never defining what he meant when he coined the term *diploma* and for leaving his subject too vague. In point of fact, the term *diploma*, if it be a coinage at all in this context, was introduced not by Mabillon but by Papenbroeck. And Papenbroeck had at least some idea of what he personally wanted the term to mean. For although he uses the very wide term "old membranes" in the title, it is clear from the opening paragraph of his essay that the "old membranes" are, in this case, diplomata of Merovingian and other rulers of France before the year 1000, and that the diplomata in question are "instrumenta fundationum, donationum et privilegiorum."

What Mabillon really coined was the term "diplomatic," but only as an adjective. Answering Papenbroeck's attack on alleged Dagobertain and other diplomata, Mabillon wrote a book, *De re diplomatica,* "of this business of diplomata." Papenbroeck was simply Mabillon's springboard. Instead of taking Papenbroeck up and arguing "De diplomatis," as Papenbroeck had done, Mabillon went far beyond him to a *Res diplomatica.* He was opening up a new area: "Novum antiquariae artis genus aggredior." And although it had been occasioned by "this whole business of diplomata" raised by Papenbroeck, it was not at all confined to diplomata. Significantly, the *Res diplomatica* is never described by Mabillon in terms of diplomata but of the more elastic and comprehensive *instrumenta* (which, incidentally, was also used by Papenbroeck, but less widely): "Novum antiquariae artis genus aggredior, quo de veterum instrumentorum ratione, formulis et auctoritate agitur."

Instrumenta not diplomata were the stuff of the new art of the *Res diplomatica* upon which Mabillon was so conscious he was embarking. And if he did not state exactly what was to be understood by *instrumenta,* he did not fall far short of a definition of the *Res diplomatica,* itself, that is as descriptive as it is revealing. On the title page of his book *De re diplomatica libri sex,* the title says, "in which is explained and illustrated whatever pertains to the antiquity, matter, handwriting and style of old instruments; to seals, monograms, subscriptions, and dating; and to antiquarian, legal, and historical disciplines" (see bibliography for the full Latin title). A broad description, indeed, of the scope of the *Res diplomatica,* but one which Mabillon followed up in practice in the body of his book, where any and every type of written document is considered to belong to diplomatics, from *instrumenta* in their most formal sense, *Acta,* both public and private, and "chartae regales sive diplomata," to "testamenta, litterae, epistolae, chirographa, archiva, gesta . . . descriptiones."

In this all-embracing concept of the *Res diplomatica* which he had constructed from the "De diplomatis" of Papenbroeck, Mabillon was followed faithfully by his Maurist successors, Tassin and Toustain, who, in theory if not in practice, considered the object of diplomatics to be synonymous with archival material in general—letters, notes, charters, juridical and legislative documents, legal agreements, wills, briefs, schedules, registers, rolls, daybooks, inventories, etc.

With the emergence, however, of a strong and original school of German practitioners of the new antiquarian art in the nineteenth century, and particularly through the writings of Julius Ficker (1877–78) and Theodor von Sickel (1861–82), the *Res diplomatica* began to be narrowed to the *instrumenta* of the first part of Mabillon's title, and the *instrumenta* to be taken in the strict sense of *Urkunden* or original probative juridical documents, as may be seen very explicitly on the opening page of the diplomatist's indispensable companion, the *Handbuch* (1889) of Harry Bresslau, where Bresslau defines the object of diplomatics as "a written witness which is drawn up in a certain determined form and serves as proof of some action or fact of a juridical nature."

This restriction of Mabillon's *Instrumenta,* not to speak of his *Res diplomatica,* to probative juridical acts is at its strongest, perhaps, in the work of O. Redlich, who in 1907 argued that documents of nonjuridical bearing (reports, inquiries, protocols, administrative correspondence, accounts, and the like) had no place in diplomatics. The same point of view is to be found in Thommen (1905) and Steinacker (1927), and, above all, in Alain de Boüard, who in a highly regarded *Manuel de diplomatique* of 1925 defined the field of diplomatics as "charters and acts which have juridical effects and are drawn up according to a set form."

To A. Dumas, first in a review of de Boüard (1930), then in a series of articles in *Le moyen âge* from 1932 to 1934, this conception of diplomatics was much too confined. While allowing that the proper object of diplomatics is indeed the *instrumentum,* Dumas argued all the same that the notion of *instrumentum* included not only the written juridical instrumentum which declared the will and disposition of an agent, but also everything which had a juridical connection with that act, before or afterwards: verbal processes, for example, or reports, inventories, and burial registers.

By and large, this point of view was supported by Georges Tessier in his inaugural address as professor of diplomatics at the École des chartes in 1930, and by Robert Bautier in his address of 1961. If the former defined diplomatics as "the science of those rules which from age to age have governed the elaboration and production of instrumental acts as sources of history," the latter saw "no reason whatever" for confining diplomatics to "acts in the strict sense," to the exclusion of the generality of "administrative acts." For Bautier, all administrative documents, the strictly juridical with the nonjuridical, have this much in common at least: all are part of archival deposits. In short, it is not the fact that a document has a juridical character that qualifies it to be the object of diplomatics, but the simple fact that it is found in an archive. Not that, Bautier hastened to add, diplomatics is the same as archivistics. There is a difference. Where the latter is the studied organization and classification of archival material, the former is the discipline of the scientific exploitation of these deposits as sources of history.

By 1961, when Bautier succeeded Tessier, the position taken by Mabillon and reiterated forcefully by Dumas had regained much ground. This was chiefly due to Tessier, who in a well-known *Que sais-je?* paperback on diplomatics in 1952, and particularly in an essay on the same subject in the *Encyclopédia de la Pléiade* in 1960, had made a clear breakaway from the tight, juridical concept of diplomatics, presenting diplomatics, instead, as the description and explanation of any and every form of written act, legal, notarial, or commercial, from Babylonian tablets and Greco-Roman papyri to medieval charters and modern business papers.

But even this seemingly liberal view of diplomatics never ventures beyond the bounds of the juridical and quasijuridical. To keep on defining diplomatics in terms solely of acts of a juridical or quasijuridical nature is to bypass the fact that many, many documentary sources are far from juridical in character and yet have all the antiquarian stuff of history. An abbatial register containing nonjuridical records of letters, books, illnesses and deaths, visitors, and liturgical celebrations can as readily be the object of the "veri et falsi discrimen" of Papenbroeck and of Mabillon's new art of *Res diplomatica* as a batch of charters from a medieval lord or a bundle of commercial transactions from merchants in Marseilles. And what of letters of very public persons which have not the faintest whiff of the juridical—a letter from a bishop inviting a fellow-bishop to his consecration, a note from a ruler to a distant cousin congratulating her on her marriage, a cheerful greeting from a pope to another public person recovering from an illness?

Given the variegated wealth of written documentary remains from all ages, occupations, and jurisdictions, from the earliest records in writing to present-day consumer reports, it seems much more realistic and far less precious and selective to describe diplomatics as the scholarly investigation of any and every written documentary source, juridical, quasijuridical, or nonjuridical. This at least has the merit of retaining the openness of the "quidquid" of Mabillon's description of the *Res diplomatica,* and it has the advantage of embracing every possible form of written documentary evidence, from a charter of the most solemn kind to a scribbled commemoration in a flyleaf of a psalter, and from a record in elegant Rustic of the components of a Roman fire brigade to the patchy diary of an emigré during the French Revolution.

If the art of diplomatics came into being because there were records in writing which had to be scrupulously deciphered, examined, evaluated, and deployed in the interests of truth, and out of a respect for what was past, these records themselves owe their existence to the fact that there were people at one time or another who had felt the need to communicate in writing with their fellows, or to preserve in writing the memory of a transaction or event, formally or informally: "ob incertum futuri temporis eventum, quoniam saepe ex ignorantia sive etiam ex improbitate contingit ut denegatio rerum vere gestarum nascatur," as a donation of Offa put it in 785. Public persons (emperors, kings, popes, bishops, governments, local rulers) wanted to communicate authoritatively and unambiguously with their officials and subjects, and, as well, to have records kept of these communications and of the exercise of their jurisdiction or benevolence. Private persons (all those not possessing the quality that merited *fides publica,* and ordinary people in general) wished to make certain that their property was held by good title, that they could protect their businesses and investments, recover their loans and debts, enforce contracts, or dispose of their goods after death. Many, both public and private, were just as anxious to have detailed or "promemoria" records of income and expenses, engagements, correspondence, births, deaths, marriages, and burials.

The records that survive because of these demands of office, desires, and anxieties, therefore cover the whole gamut of public and private acts (charters, privileges, bulls, mandates, writs, legislation, leases, constitutions, contracts, conveyances, wills), as well as documents which precede or are posterior to these juridical acts (preparatory notes, protocols, drafts, formularies, registers, notarial notebooks, memoranda, and *imbreviaturae*), and those which have some juridical bearing or none at all (diaries, chapbooks, daybooks, ledgers, book loans, court rolls, mortuary rolls, rent rolls). In spite of the range of these sources, some with fixed rules of composition, some not, the act of judgment on the content and meaning, the truth or falsity, the credibility or implausibility, of the document in question depends on exactly the same rhetorical principles in each case: Who wrote it? What does it say? How is it written? Why, when, and where was it written? Who were involved in it besides the principal agent?

In a word, diplomatics is simply a straightforward application of the basic principles of literary criticism to documentary sources. The critical examination of any record, whether literary or documentary, and whether in an authentic form or in a copy, or as reported, must take a full and firm account of the substance of the document and of all the circumstances surrounding that document. Only when a document has been examined with all thoroughness, externally as well as internally, can its witness be evaluated properly, circumstantially, and fully.

The end, then, of the "antiquarian art" of diplomatics is to establish as unequivocally as possible just what a document is and what precisely it says. The question of authenticity is, from this point of view, incidental. When Lorenzo Valla tackled the Donation of Constantine, what he eventually established was what the document was, not what it was not. To many of the German school, however, diplomatics is a matter of the authenticity of documents as historical witnesses. To some, such as Bresslau, the interpretation of documents is only a secondary, if useful, aspect of the discipline.

While this approach may seem to be in line materially with Dom Mabillon's description of the *Res diplomatica* as that art which deals with "veterum instrumentorum ratione, formulis et auctoritate," it is far more limited than anything Mabillon had in mind. By this standard, the "pure" diplomatist is the counterpart of the "pure" paleographer, and is concerned only with forms and formulae and not with what they convey. Mabillon, the father of both diplomatists and paleographers, was more down-to-earth. His "new kind of antiquarian art" and his study of handwriting were simply ways of opening up and understanding the written records of the past. They were not ends in themselves.

The records which are the material object of the discipline of diplomatics were devised, composed, and written for purposes of entering into communication. And it is because they communicate something that they were and are preserved, whether they be contracts in double chirograph or examination grades in triplicate. And it is because they are still capable of communication that they are examined, transcribed, edited, studied, and subjected to critical scrutiny by researchers, scholars, and editors. Since documents were made for communication, then the first task of anyone reading them, whether professional diplomatist or not, is to make them communicate once again, resonantly and unmistakably. To profess to be concerned only with forms and formulae is to deny their nature. The forms and formulae were designed the better to preserve the burden of the document. They cannot be divorced from that central reality without losing their identity, though, of course, they may profitably be considered in their own right for a better understanding of the whole.

Arengae (introductory flourishes), for example, play a prominent role in acts and letters of ecclesiastical and secular rulers and often betray the preoccupations, and, perhaps, the pretensions of the ruler whose chancery employs them. One can plot, chart and analyze these, as Fichtenau (1957) and Fink (1964) have done so usefully, and the results may well prove invaluable to the diplomatist when studying kindred documents. But if one simply takes an *arenga* at its face value in a given document and is unaware that many *arengae* have been borrowed or adapted from books of *dictamen,* patristic sources, or even neighboring chanceries, then there is a danger of concluding that a sentiment expressed in that *arenga* is characteristic of the ruler who is the principal of the document or of the chancery that issued it, when, in fact, it is merely a commonplace. The preamble to the Lambeth constitutions of John Pecham in 1281 may seem to reflect a contemporary condition of the English clergy ("Ignorantia sacerdotum populum praecipitat in foveam erroris"), but it cannot be evaluated in isolation from its ultimate source, the Fourth Council of Toledo in 633, nor, for that matter, from the general, unexcited tone of the constitution as a whole.

And if, on the other hand, and out of a purist devotion to forms, an *arenga* is approached as though it were a thing apart from, and with almost no relationship to, the content of the document it introduces, the results are often at a remove or two from reality and can seriously impede the "discrimen veri et falsi." If, for example, one were to print the *arenga* of a certain letter of Innocent III in 1198 as it stands today in one of his registers of letters, there would be a distinct illogicality in that letter as a whole, since the point made rhetorically in the *arenga,* as it stands now, is not at all that of the body of the letter. The illogicality is due to the simple fact that the *arenga,* as it stands now in the register, is not at all the original *arenga.* From erasures and substitutions in the register the original *arenga* can easily be discerned and is wholly consistent with the body of the letter. What seems to have happened, therefore, is that the original *arenga* was modified some time after the total letter was registered in order to serve as a model to preface letters of a quite different tenor to that which it originally prefaced. Hence, what should be printed is not the *arenga* exactly as it stands now in the register but as it was before it was modified (Boyle 1967).

The *Res diplomatica* is, then, an art by which written records from any age and of any kind are made to speak again with a full, distinct voice. Whether one is dealing with printed documents or is editing unpublished materials, there is no escaping the fact that, if a document is not to speak with a muffled voice but to be as communicative as it was originally intended to be, it must be approached with all scholarly patience, discretion and sensitivity. Many documents will end up in gibberish if, for example, one is not aware that "usque ad" in a papal register of letters is the equivalent of modern omission points, and that "reverence points" are not.

Like any form of literary criticism, diplomatics is an exacting discipline. It demands a thorough competence in the language of the document under scrutiny and, in the case of written records, of the handwriting, scribal practices, and abbreviations of the period. It presumes a knowledge of chronology, monetary systems, and legal terminology, and of local usages, conventions, and modes of address. It relies on an easy familiarity with the methods, formulae, and practices of the chanceries, government bureaus, and notarial studios of the period and region.

All of this involves an appreciable expertise and a considerable general knowledge. From this point of view, Arthur Giry was in the best tradition of Mabillon and the Maurists when he attempted in his celebrated *Manuel* to include everything, or almost everything, that could possibly persuade documents to speak with all their original vigor: paleography, chronology, onomastics, philology, toponymics, style.

A recent scholar (Bautier 1961) has assured us that this approach is "bien depassée." Yet it has much to be said for it and is, I suspect, outmoded only in theory. Bresslau's *Handbuch,* while professing a narrower view of diplomatics, is in fact as much a mine of general diplomatic information as the manual of Giry. But although one will pick up from most manuals the basic notions of diplomatics and be made aware of distinctions between *actor* and *destinatarius,* public and private acts, *notarius* and *rogatarius,* the possibilities of the *Res diplomatica* are so vast that no manual, not even Giry or Bresslau, can be expected to cover them all.

If one is fortunate enough never to have to move far from one category of historical records, there will not be any great difficulty. The range will be familiar, the formulae second nature. But if one has to cross from one category to another, fresh formulae will have to be learned, new usages to be mastered. To pass from papal *bullae* and registers, with their predictable *clausulae,* comminations, and cadences, to royal charters, or imperial diplomata is no great step. But to move from these areas to manorial accounts, hordarian rolls, consistory court proceedings, *catasto* records, or the *imbreviaturae* of notaries, is, in each case, to enter another world of vocabulary, usages, and conventions.

There is always the possibility, of course, after nearly three hundred years of the pursuit of the *Res diplomatica,* that someone will have been there before and that one can therefore turn to matter already in print from an unfamiliar area and thus ease oneself in without too much strain. Just as one can be conveniently introduced to the mainstream of *chartae, epistolae,* diplomata, and *bullae* through the hundred and more examples in Foerster's *Urkundenlesebuch* (1947) and *Urkundenlehre in Abbildungen*

(1951), or to the span of South Italian chancery production through Mazzoleni's *Esempi* (1958), or to the diversity of English administration through the *English Royal Documents* of Chaplais (1961), so, too, one will find examples and texts from many of the more recondite classes of records in Johnson and Jenkinson (1915) or in the 450 facsimiles of the Paleographical Society and New Paleographical Society for England, in Prou's *Recueil* for France (1904), or in Federici's *Scritture* for Italy (1934).

But even with these collections of facsimiles and transcripts at one's back, and a battery of dictionaries, manuals, and aids at the ready, there are still certain basic questions which must be put to each new document, if it is to answer fully and without reticence as a witness to history. The set of questions proposed here is one that is a commonplace in law schools, courses in journalism, and the like. It reaches back in origin to Aristotle's *Ethics* (Book 3), where the subject is human, deliberate acts, and to the *De inventione rhetorica* (1:24-27) of Cicero, where lawyers are instructed how best to describe and present a client in court. The wording here of the set, though not the order, of the questions, is, however, that of a widely known *versus* and list of the *topoi* of circumstances which was much used by scholastics of the Middle Ages as a comprehensive framework for the discussion of the circumstances of human acts: *Quis, Quid, Quomodo, Quibus auxiliis, Cur, Ubi, Quando?*

Since any document of whatever kind is at some point the product of a human or responsible act, it is essential to inform oneself of its circumstances, if one is to view the act that it embodies in all its integrity. The circumstances enumerated in the above *versus* cover any and every category of circumstance, from Who? to When?, but they are not mutually exclusive. Rather, each throws light on the other, and all combine together to allow the diplomatist to form a secure and unblinkered judgment of the nature, intent, and purport of the deliberate act of will that is expressed in the production of a document, and which determined its contents.

QUIS?

Some person or other—a principal—is always at the center of, or at least behind, every written document. Once that person had confided his thoughts to writing or has expressed his will juridically or symbolically in a written document, then an ever-widening circle of persons is involved, unless the record is so private that the person wrote it himself and it was never copied by anyone else. A scribe makes a fair copy from notes or from an autograph, and others copy from that or from one another. Each scribe, in turn, becomes a part of the copy he makes, becoming a *Quis* or principal with respect to that copy at least. Scribes, notaries, and witnesses are part and parcel of juridical acts, each being, in one way or another, responsible for the making of the act and for the drafting, composing, witnessing, or writing that went with it.

To fully comprehend the circumstances of any document, juridical or nonjuridical, all persons connected with it, internally or externally, before, during, and after its composition, should therefore be identified if possible, and questioned about it as far as possible. Since all of these are cooperators rather than principals with respect to the act or document as such, they are more aptly considered under the heading *Quibus auxiliis?* Here the questioning is confined to the principal or principals, and particularly to those in records of juridical acts, private as well as public.

The identity of the principal or principals is of prime importance, for without such an identification the document or record falls flat. In juridical acts there are at least two persons or principals at the center of the act: an *actor* or originator of the act (a ruler, a merchant, a landowner, a moral person such as a cathedral chapter), and a *destinatarius* or the one to whom the act is directed (a subject, a tenant, a buyer). In private acts it may not be possible to identify the parties beyond their names, occupations, and localities, unless one is dealing with an area where local records are plentiful, with a cartulary or manorial pledge book in which there is a continuity over a number of generations, or with a series of notarial registers from a closely knit area.

In public acts, the *actor* at least will be a *persona authentica* or a person meriting *fides publica* — kings, emperors, popes, bishops, local rulers, etc., and moral persons such as chapters or communes. Usually these are not too hard to identify. There are such helps as *The Handbook of British Chronology* for rulers and bishops in Great Britain and Ireland (Powicke and Fryde 1961) and Cappelli's *Cronologia* (1906, 1929) which covers most of the rulers of continental Europe of the Middle Ages, as well as of other periods. But where the *Handbook* includes episcopal succession, the *Cronologia* gives only that of popes, so for bishops outside the British Isles one has to turn to Gams (1885) for the period up to 1198 (where at times it is quite uncritical), and to Eubel for bishops from 1198 onwards. The *destinatarius* in public acts is frequently a public or at least some well-known person and can readily be checked or identified, but more often than not (as in papal letters of provision, dispensation, indulgence) identification will require much local research, in unpublished episcopal registers, diocesan court records, and faculty office registers, for example.

The quality or title which is assigned to the parties or persons in records of all kinds is of particular importance, since it must accurately reflect the known condition of these persons at the time of the purported action, or be at least possible at that time. On the other hand, a document without any indication of time may well prove to be datable with some precision because of the way one or other of the persons in the document is styled. The honorific or rhetorical titles with which an *actor* endows himself may sometimes have social or political overtones and should be looked at closely. It has been suggested (Levillain 1930), for example, that the papal tendency from the ninth century onwards of describing the pope as "servus servorum Dei" probably represents a growing sense of primacy based on a rather unabashed exegesis of Mark 10:44, "Qui voluerit . . . primus esse . . . erit omnium servus."

Without a full and careful attempt at the identification of the parties or persons in an act or record, the questions that remain to be asked of the document will be less forceful and less productive. And if, in the first instance, the question *Quis?* is put all too perfunctorily, there may be cases of mistaken identification and of later embarrassment. Thus, Thomas Bradwardine of Canterbury (d. 1349) has for years been credited in various publications with the ownership of a thirteenth-century Parisian bible, which is now in the Royal Ontario Museum, Toronto, and all because someone once mistook a letter drafted on an endleaf to the archbishop for a letter drafted by him.

QUID?

In Aristotle and Cicero and in the medieval *versus,* the point of this query is to find out what exactly was done by the given person. From the viewpoint of diplomatics, what that person, or *actor,* did was to cause a record to be made of some event or an *instrumentum* to be drawn up that recorded a voluntary act of the *actor.* Since it is only through this written record or legal instrumentum that we are enabled to know just what was the intention of the given person or *actor* (and which will be considered properly under *Cur?*), the quality, features and the physical makeup of each document are of prime importance.

The range of documents is, of course, vast, and each class of document will have its own conventions and its own rules of style and production: charters, privileges, *bullae,* chirographs, final concords, writs of various kinds, letters of credence, letters close, letters patent, letters revocatory, mandates, transcripts, inquisitions; registers of popes, kings, abbots, bishops, notaries, treasurers, librarians; rent rolls, minutes, quittances, bills of exchange, cartularies, etc. All these documents do not possess the same credentials. Some, for example, are authentic (signed by witnesses, validated by seals, corroborated by a public authority or a *manus publica,* a notary); some are not. And all do not have the same quality. Authentic documents carry more weight than registered or loose copies; copies which are certified have priority over casual copies; copies in a notarial cartulary take on the quality of the notary.

If it is important to classify a document properly, it is likewise important to subject it to as full a physical examination as possible. In an authentic document the quality of the ink and the physical characteristics (how the seals are attached, for example) may be as revealing as the exact documentary genre to which it belongs, and may, in fact, help to identify the area of production or the actual chancery in which it was written. Like any other document, an authentic document should be scrutinized thoroughly. The *dorse,* or back, of the document should be examined for receipt marks, summaries, or notarial comments that might betray the origin or provenance of the document, and the face should be examined for any irregularities or peculiarities. Erasures deserve special attention, because of the possibility of forgery, but before any judgment is passed on them it would be wise to see if there exists any contemporary registered copy of the document. For, as in the case of the privilege of foundation of the Dominican Order (Koudelka 1958), a comparison of the authentic document with the document as it was registered may show that in fact the erasure had been authorized by the *actor* or his official.

The nature and makeup of documents which are nonauthentic though original — copies, registers, monastic cartularies, notarial notebooks, etc. — are just as important. A cartulary, for example, is not quite the same as a register. Where a register is often a simple collection of copies of outgoing documents commissioned or, on occasion, composed by the *actor* (bishop, pope, king, commune, etc.), a cartulary is generally a deliberate record of matter which a *destinatarius* (e.g., a monastery, a landowner, a merchant) had had made for the protection of his interests: grants, contracts, donations, for example. Cartularies, of course, should not always be accepted at their face value, but the chances are good that their copies were made from the original, authentic documents. This is not invariably true of registers (whether registers of authentic documents or of routine business and correspondence), where copies are often based on drafts or notes, or are highly abbreviated.

QUOMODO?

In diplomatics, this question bears on the form or manner in which a document is drawn up, on the formulae used in the document, and on the style in which it is written. The general question *Quomodo?* therefore, has to be divided into at least three basic questions, particularly when public and private acts are under examination. These questions, of course, should be asked of any written document, but only the more elaborate classes of documents such as *instrumenta* that embody public and private acts will be considered here. For the sake of convenience the term *instrumentum* will be used indifferently of anything from a royal charter or papal privilege to common papal letters or notarial instruments.

Form

Like everything else, *instrumenta* have a beginning (*protocol*), a middle (*corpus* or *contextus*) and an end (*eschatocol*). And like the generality of literary productions, a business letter, for example, they begin with an identification of the author and the addressee (generally preceded in public and private acts by a symbol or invocation or both) and with a greeting or formal statement from the author or writer ("Salutem in domino," for example; but a statement of place and date in a notarial instrument). Then, after some preliminaries (an *arenga* or rhetorical preparation for the burden of the communication, a *captatio benevolentiae* or flourish to disarm the addressee), the *instrumenta* get down to the nub of the matter in the *contextus* or *corpus* (narration or statement of the case, actual decision or mandate or act, qualifying clauses). Finally, they wind up in a fashion (greetings or warnings, date clause, completion) that leaves the addressee in no doubt that the communication is over, and the public at large, that the act is done.

But there are differences between the layout of *instrumenta* that transmit the acts of public persons and those in which the principals are private persons, just as there are variations in each depending on the solemnity of the act. By and large the layouts are somewhat as follows:

		PUBLIC	PRIVATE
P R O T O C O L	*Invocatio*	symbolic; verbal	symbolic, notarial sign
	Intitulatio	addressee	general: "Omnibus. . . ."
	Inscriptio	principal	name of notary; year, place, indiction
	Salutatio	greeting	
C O R P U S	*Arenga*	exordium, proem	rarely present
	Promulgatio	notification	sometimes present
	Narratio	background	on occasion combined
	Dispositio	act, decision	with disposition
	Clausulae	qualifiers: preceptive, prohibitive, derogative, or obligatory	clause of obligation is often an oath. Many clauses are legal *exceptiones*
	Sanctio	blessing; spiritual or temporal threat	mostly pecuniary, rarely spiritual
E S C H A T O C O L	*Subscriptio*	of principal	(repetition of date)
		of witnesses	listed only
		of officials: notaries, etc.	of notary, together with notarial sign: "Et ego . . . notarius rogatus. . . ." Known formally as the *Completio.*
	Datum	Day, month, year, place	
	Appreciatio	solemn ending: *Fiat. Fiat.*	
		Papal comma or period	notarial comma or period

As may be seen from the many samples of Roman *acta* in the *Chartae Latinae antiquiores,* especially in volumes 3 and 4, both the public and private *instrumenta* of the Middle Ages owe their forms and their conventions to the products of the later Roman chanceries. The private act, and notably the notarial instrument, derives directly from the private written act of the late Empire. The notary (or *Tabellio,* as he sometimes liked to call himself) of the twelfth and thirteenth centuries will spell out (generally at the beginning) the date, place, and circumstances of the act exactly as the late Roman *Tabelliones* did, and he will describe himself as *Rogatus* and label the whole formalities of the act a *Rogatio,* just as they did. At the behest of the parties to the contract (or perhaps of his own accord) he will load the *clausulae* with various *exceptiones* from classic Roman law (for which see Berger 1958 in bibliography), although their relevance is not always obvious at first glance.

There is, however, one crucial difference to be noted between the old Roman *actum* and the *instrumentum* of the medieval notary. The private written act of the Late Roman Empire had a dispositive force: of itself, it founded an obligation. The notarial instrument of the Middle Ages did not. Although the dispositive force of the *actum* endured for a time in Visigothic and Burgundian regions, it was gradually whittled away under the influence of Germanic forms of symbolical contract in neighboring parts (a rod (*festuca*); a ring; a joining of hands). Even in Lombardy, where the dispositive force had a very long run, it eventually merged into the probative. However, as the Notariat developed in Lombardy in the twelfth century out of the old *Tabellionatus,* notaries became public authorities or *manus publicae* with the quality and function of judges. As a result, the written private act recovered some of the force it once had, becoming *authenticum,* or indubitably probative, of itself, and independently of the signatures of the parties. But it never became dispositive again.

Formulae

The formulae used in instruments of all kinds were highly stylized and stereotyped. Even the more sincere and seemingly special formulae in public acts were often culled from all over the place or were repeated unblushingly from act to act. If a pope in the fifteenth century speaks of some cleric to whom he is granting a benefice as "well known for his piety, zeal, and virtue," this must not be taken too literally or cited as proof of the sanctity of that cleric, since the formula was centuries old by then, and was nothing more than pure form. Chanceries tended to be traditional and conservative. But how much of a document as a whole, apart from the worn formulae, was the work of the chancery is not always clear. Often the *narratio* in a grace or grant or privilege is simply a repetition, with appropriate clauses plucked from some formulary, of the text submitted by the petitioner.

Style

As in any age, the basic style of writing employed by medieval chanceries and notaries came out of an *Ars dictaminis,* or manual of correct usage.

In general, therefore, the only thing that a chancery or the odd notary did which was in any way original was to polish a period here, clean up a grammatical infelicity there, and make the petitioner's prose conform to the *stilus curiae* and to the rules of the *cursus* (di Capua 1941). But many chanceries and notaries had their own flourishes; and there is usually enough that is singular in the productions of chanceries and notarial studios to allow one to distinguish one product from another, to form a fair impression of their several styles, and to provide a basis for an evaluation of documents that profess to have been issued by them or that could have come from them.

QUIBUS AUXILIIS?

The question of what persons assisted in the action ("Quibus adminiculis?," as a more elegant version of the *topos* has it) brings up the subject of the drafting and engrossing of documents in general (scribes, notaries, chanceries) and of the ratification of juridical acts (witnesses, seals, notarial instruments).

Public acts of popes, bishops, and rulers were usually drafted and then formally written out (engrossed) in their chanceries. So when the hands of the clerks of a chancery are known and well documented, they can be used as a check on the authenticity of documents that purport to have been issued by that chancery. Other public acts and most private acts were composed and written by a clerk or notary engaged for the purpose. The latter usually displayed his own personal sign (Purvis 1954) on the *instrumentum,* but in the case of more prosperous notaries, who might have many scribes in their employ, this does not always mean that the notary, himself, engrossed the instrument from his notes and draft of the agreement or action. Sometimes he simply traced his personal sign and wrote the final formula known as the *completio.*

Private acts could be validated at any time and become public through ratification by any public authority. However, the chief means of ratification of such acts in continental Europe was the *instrumentum publicum,* one, that is, which was drawn up in form by a *manus publica* or notary who had delegation from some public authority. In England, where notaries were not employed until the late thirteenth century, and then only fitfully (Cheney 1972), contracts and conveyances were validated from the eleventh century onwards through chirographs (bipartite documents) or through writ charters which were authenticated by seals.

The use of seals was, of course, widespread, but because of difficulties encountered in the use of private or little-known seals (forgery was all too easy; see *A Guide to Seals in the Public Record Office* in bibliography), the practice grew up in Europe, and particularly in England, whereby private persons were enabled to have contracts drawn up in the form of a judicial decision and then authenticated in court through what was termed *jurisdiction gracieuse* or "noncontentious jurisdiction."

Witnesses have a prominent place in both public and private acts, whether to add solemnity to the occasion or to validate an act by their presence, their signatures, or their seals. The social status of the witnesses is usually noted with care, yielding valuable information for the historian on rank and occupations. The presence of autographs provides useful pointers to literacy at any given period, although a great deal of care has to be exercised in this regard (Galbraith 1948, 1966). A list of witnesses may often be helpful in the detection of forgery. Forgers at a distance of time from the period of their forgery will generally be careful to designate the *actor* correctly, but may often overreach themselves by including impossible or incorrectly styled witnesses (Hector 1959).

CUR?

According to Aristotle, the 'Why?' or, as medieval rhetorical writers glossed it, the *causa faciendi,* is the most important question of all. In the present context of diplomatics, its aim is to ascertain the precise purpose and therefore the point — the *res* — of a document. Since the question bears directly on the content of the document as a whole (and this applies to any kind of document), a scrupulous transcription of a manuscript document is a sine qua non, as is a command of the language of any document, printed or in manuscript, not to speak of a sensitivity to syntax.

In a printed account of the roofing of a monastery church by the monks themselves, the point of the edifying narrative will be blunted if the phrase, "fratres qui fabricae operam dabant," meaning," the monks who were in charge of the work on the roof," is carelessly read as "fratres qui fabricae operum dabant" and then even more wildly understood to mean, "the brothers who gave out jobs on the roof." And a nice legal point will be vitiated in a case to which authentic instruments (*vera*) were essential, if the technical phrase, "instrumentis pro veris ostensis," is rendered as "instruments having been presented as though they were true ones." Again, if when editing the entry, "Pro expensis O. Thome cellerarii," in a monastic accountbook, one prints the "O." as "Odonis" or, foxily, leaves it unexpanded, social historians and the world in general will have been denied the pleasant information that a sum of money was expended for the Name Day (*Onomasticon*) of Thomas the Cellarer.

The handwriting of local records and of private acts all too often presents a barrier to the understanding of the *res,* or point of a document, but a reasonable security may be achieved if one first masters the principles of abbreviation in the introduction of Cappelli's celebrated *Dizionario* (1906 and 1929) or in any general manual of paleography and diplomatics such as that of Stiennon (1973), and then goes on to study the facsimiles in Prou's *Recueil* (1904), Johnson and Jenkinson's *English Court Hand* (1915), or Federici's *Scritture* (1934).

The Latin, too, of these acts and records is not always elegant and easy, but it is none the less intelligible when given a respectful hearing. Gooder's *Latin for Local History* (1961) and some judicious pages of Hector (1966) will be of help by way of introduction, as will special studies such as those of Stenton (1955) and Vieillard (1927). Du Cange's *Glossarium* (1937) is very useful for the vocabulary of diplomatic documents in general; so also is the *Revised Medieval Latin Word-List* for that of British documents (Latham 1965). But, it hardly need be said, vocabulary goes so much better with syntax. No amount of vocabulary will offset a lack of an easy familiarity with basic Latin usage and construction.

UBI?

The circumstance of place has always enjoyed an important position in documents. Justinian, when regulating the office of the *Tabellionatus,* insisted that the *Tabelliones* should be specific not only about the date, but also about the place when drawing up a document. The medieval notaries, the successors of the Roman *Tabelliones,* were very conscious of this, noting, for example, that a contract was established "in officina mea," "in camera episcopi," "apud Novum Templum, Lond." Popes, bishops, and rulers were just as careful to state where exactly a document was issued: "apud S. Petrum," "apud Westmonasterium," "in manerio meo apud. . . ." This circumstance can be of great value when determining the authenticity or the credibility of a document. A comparison with other records (with, for example, the known itinerary of a pope, bishop, or king) will soon show whether or not the principal or the subject of the document was, or could have been, in the place recorded in the document at that time.

Place-names in Latin often cause difficulties. Some of these have been removed by the recently enlarged *Orbis latinus* (Graesse 1972), and quite detailed lists for some areas are to be found incidentally in some sources that are not as widely known as they should be: for Italy in the volumes of the *Rationes decimarum Italiae* (12 vols., Vatican City, 1932–52), for Spain in the *Rationes decimarum Hispaniae* (2 vols., Madrid, 1949), for Belgium in various volumes of the *Analecta Vaticano-Belgica,* first series (Rome-Brussels, 1906–), and for France and many other countries in vols. 14–16 of the *Lettres communes de Jean XXII* of G. Mollat (Paris, 1947).

Names of dioceses, monasteries, and churches can often be a source of frustration. Some dioceses have several names, or the names have several variants; monasteries are sometimes listed by their local or unofficial names; many churches are named after one and the same saint. There is a good list of the Latin names of monasteries in Migne's *Patrologia Latina* (PL 220, cols. 1009–1256) and in Cottineau's *Répertoire* (1935–37); there is a useful if restricted list in H. Hoberg's *Taxae pro servitiis communibus* (Vatican City 1949). Church names are a different matter, particularly if only the title is given without any further specification. Before plumping for the first location that comes to hand with a church of the title one is trying to locate, the other categories of circumstance should first be brought to bear on the problem, to see, for example, if there are any pointers to location in any other parts of the manuscript or instrument. Thus, the date in a psalter of the consecration of a church ("sancti Clementis") of unspecified location was for long accepted by art historians as the date of consecration of a Roman church of that name which possesses important frescoes, and the date became a key date in the history of the development of certain Italian art forms. However, when the psalter was finally examined as a whole with a thorough attention to all the circumstances of that date entry, the date proved, in fact, to be that of the consecration of an artistically unimportant church miles away from Rome (Boyle 1960).

QUANDO?

As Papenbroeck, Mabillon, and the Maurists were well aware, a grasp of chronology is vital for the understanding as well as the evaluation of any document. For the British Isles, Cheney's *Handbook of Dates* (1955), with its comprehensive and clear introduction on the various reckonings of time and with its chronological tables, is essential, as is, but in a less general way, the *Handbook of British Chronology* (Powicke 1961). For the continent of Europe and for chanceries which employed the indication or fiscal reckoning, Capelli's *Cronologia* (1929) is very helpful, and particularly for the line of succession in the various kingdoms, duchies, and principalities of Italy and other areas. Here and there, it is necessary to draw on special studies such as that of Lane Poole for chronology in general (1934) or that of Higounet for the Pisan reckoning of time (1952).

Since many private acts, local records, ecclesiastical courts, etc., more often than not use church festivals and saints' days to date events, some acquaintance with the medieval liturgical year is a great asset. Cheney, Cappelli, Grotefend (1948), and others provide useful lists of these feasts. Often, however, local records are dated by feasts of saints who had only a very limited or local cult, so one has to turn to some comprehensive dictionary of the saints, a good, up-to-date example of which is the *Bibliotheca sanctorum* (13 vols., Rome, 1961–71).

This classic set of circumstances is rarely given a mention in manuals of diplomatics. Yet if one keeps it in mind, not much that is essential will be missed when documents of any kind are being evaluated. Certainly a recourse to these circumstances should foster those habits of caution, circumspection, and respect of sources that mark the prudent historian.

BIBLIOGRAPHY

Manuals

Adelung, J. C., and A. Rudolph. 1759–69. *Neues Lehrgebäude der Diplomatik.* 9 vols. Erfurt.

Bonenfant, P. 1947. *Cours de diplomatique.* 2d ed. Liège: Desoer.

Boüard, A. de. 1925. *Manuel de diplomatique française et pontificale.* Vol. 1, *Diplomatique générale.* Avec un album de 54 planches en phototypie. Paris: A. Picard; Transcription et explication des planches de l'album. Paris: Picard, 1929. Vol. 2, *L'acte privé.* Paris: Picard, 1948; 34 plates; Transcription et explication des planches de l'album. Paris, Picard, 1952.

Bresslau, H. 1889. *Handbuch der Urkundenlehre für Deutschland und Italien:* Berlin: Veit; 2d ed. in 2 vols.—vol. 1, Leipzig: Veit, 1912; vol. 2, edited by H. W. Klewitz, Leipzig: Veit, 1931; index by H. Schulze, Berlin: W. de Gruyter, 1960; the so-called third edition, Berlin, 1958, is a simple reprint of the second.

Delehaye, H. 1959. *L'oeuvre des Bollandistes.* Rev. ed. Brussels: Société des Bollandistes.

De Wailly, N. 1838. *Éléments de paléographie pour servir a l'étude des documents inédits sur l'historie de France*. Par l'ordre du Roi et par les soins du ministre de l'instruction publique. 2 vols. Paris: Imprimerie royale.

Dölger, F. 1956. *Byzantinische Diplomatik*. Ettal: Buch-Kunstverlag Ettal.

Foerster, Hans Philipp. 1951. *Urkundenlehre*. Berne: Haupt.

Fumagalli, A. 1802. *Istituzioni diplomatiche*. Milan: Dalla stamperia e fonderia al genio tipografico.

Gatterer, S. 1765. *Elementa artis diplomaticae universalis*. Göttingen: N.p.

Giry, A. 1894. *Manuel de diplomatique*. Diplômes et chartes — chronologie technique — eléments critiques et parties constitutives de la teneur des chartes — les chancelleries — les actes privés. Paris: Hachette; reprinted, Paris: Alcan, 1925.

Knowles, M. D. 1953. *Medieval Religious Houses, England and Wales*. London: Longmans.

———. 1963. *The Historian and Character and Other Essays*. Cambridge: Cambridge Univ. Press.

———. 1964. *Great Historical Enterprises*. London: Nelson. "The Bollandists," pp. 1–32; "The Maurists," pp. 33–56; "The *Monumenta Germaniae Historica*," pp. 63–96; "The Rolls Series," pp. 99–134.

Leclercq, H. 1953–57. *Jean Mabillon, Vie et Oeuvres*. 2 vols. Paris: Letouzey et Ané.

Mabillon, J. 1681. *De re diplomatica libri sex in quibus quidquid ad veterum instrumentorum antiquitatem, materiam, scripturam et stilum; quidquid ad sigilla, monogrammata, subscriptiones ac notas chronologicas; quidquid inde ad antiquariam, historicam, jorensemque disciplinam pertinet, explicatur et illustratur*. Paris: L. Billaine. A supplement was added by Mabillon in 1704, and a new edition was put out in Paris: Robustel, 1709, in which various parts of the supplement were incorporated in their proper places.

Madox, T. 1702. *Formulare Anglicanum*. London: Tonson and Knaplock. A classic introduction to the diplomatics of royal and private charters, it separated the study of diplomatics from that of paleography.

Maffei, F. S. 1727. *Istoria diplomatica che serve d'introduzione all'arte critica in tal materia*. Mantua: A. Tumermani.

Manuel d'Archivistique. 1973. Brussels: Ministère des Affaires culturelles.

Mazzoleni, J. 1970. *Paleografia: Diplomatica e Scienze ausiliarie*. Naples: Libreria scientifica editrice.

Meisner, H.-O. 1935. *Aktenkunde: Ein Handbuch für Archivbenutzer*. Berlin: Mittler.

———. 1952. *Urkunden- und Aktenlehre der Neuzeit*. 2d ed. Leipzig: Koehler und Amelang.

Paoli, B. C. 1889. *Diplomatica*. Florence: N.p.; new ed., edited by G. C. Bascapé. N.p., 1942.

Papenbroeck, D. van. 1675. "Propylaeum antiquarium circa veri et falsi discrimen in yetustis membranis." In *Acta Sanctorum Aprilis* 2. Antwerp: Meursium.

Perez, J. 1688. *Dissertationes ecclesiasticae de re diplomatica*. Madrid: L. Perez.

Redlich, Oswald. 1970. *Urkundenlehre: Einleitung*. Munich: R. Oldenbourg.

Santifaller, L. 1967. *Urkundenforschung: Methoden, Ziele, Ergebnisse.* Weimar: Böhlau Nachf; 2d ed., Cologne: Böhlau Verlag.

Schönemann, C. T. C. 1801-2. *Versuch eines vollständigen Systems der allgemeinen, besonders älteren Diplomatik.* 2 vols. Hamburg: Bohn; reissued in a second edition as *Lehrbuch der allgemeinen, besonders älteren Diplomatik, zum Gebrauch akademische Vorlesungen.* 2 vols. Leipzig: Vogel, 1818.

Tassin, R. P., and C. Toustain. 1750-65. *Nouveau traité de diplomatique où l'on examine les fondaments de cel art par deux religieux bénédictins de la congregation de Saint-Maur.* 6 vols. Paris: Desprez.

Tessier, G. 1962. *Diplomatique royale française.* Paris: Picard.

——. 1952. *La diplomatique.* Que sais-je? no. 536. Paris: Picard.

——. 1961. "Diplomatique." In *L'histoire et ses méthodes.* Edited by Ch. Samaran. *Encyclopédia de la Pléiade* 11. Paris: Gallimard.

Thommen, R. 1905. *Diplomatik. Die Lehre von den Königs- und Kaiserurkunden.* Leipzig: Teubner; 2d ed., 1913.

Valenti, F. 1961. *Il documento medioevale: Nozioni di diplomatica generale e di cronologia, con 30 tavole.* Modena: Editrice modenese.

Von Sickel, Th. 1861-82. *Beiträge zur Diplomatik 1-8.* In *Sitzungsberichte der Wiener Akademie.* Vienna: Gerold.

Facsimiles

Bishop, T. A. M. 1961. *Scriptores Regis: Facsimiles to identify and illustrate the hands of royal scribes in original charters of Henry I., Stephen, and Henry II.* Oxford: Oxford Univ. Press.

——, and P. Chaplais. 1957. *Facsimiles of English Royal Writs to A.D. 1100 presented to V. H. Galbraith.* Oxford: Oxford Univ. Press.

Chaplais, P. 1961. *English Royal Documents, King John–Henry VI, 1199-1461.* Oxford: Oxford Univ. Press.

Chartae Latinae Antiquiores: Facsimile edition of the Latin Charters prior to the Ninth Century. 1954-. Edited by A. T. Bruckner and R. Marichal. Olten and Lausanne: U. Graf:

    1. *Switzerland: Basel–St. Gall,* 1954.

    2. *Switzerland: St. Gall–Zürich,* 1956.

    3. *British Museum, London,* 1963.

    4. *Great Britain (without B.M., London),* 1967.

The series, cited as *CHLA,* parallels the *Codices Latini Antiquiores* of E. A. Lowe. 12 vols. Oxford: Clarendon Press, 1934-72, cited as *CLA.*

Exampla scripturarum edita consilio et opera procuratorum Bibliothecae et Tabularii Vaticani, 1930-:

    2. *Epistolae et Instrumenta saeculi XIII.* Edited by B. Katterbach and C. Silva-Tarouca. Vatican City: Bibliotheca Apostolica Vaticana, 1930.

    3. *Acta pontificum.* Edited by C. Battelli. 2d ed. Vatican City: Bibliotheca Apostolica Vaticana, 1965.

Federici, V. 1934. *Le scritture delle cancellerie italiane dal sec. XII al XVII.* Rome: P Sansaini.

Grieve, H. E. P. 1959. *Examples of English Handwriting.* 2d ed. Chelmsford, England: Essex Education Committee.

Jenkinson, H. 1927. *The later Court Hands in England.* 2 vols. Cambridge: Cambridge Univ. Press.

Johnson, C., and H. Jenkinson. 1915. *English Court Hand, A.D. 1066 to 1500, illustrated chiefly from the Public Records.* 2 vols. Oxford: Oxford Univ. Press. Text plates.

Katterbach, B. 1927. *Specimina supplicationum ex registris vaticanis.* Rome: Bibliotheca Apostolica Vaticana.

Lauer, Ph., and Ch. Samaran. 1908. *Les diplômes originaux des Mérovingiens: Facsimiles phototypiques avec notices et transcriptions.* Paris: Leroux.

Mazzoleni, J. 1958. *Esempi di scritture cancelleresche, curiali e minuscole.* Naples: Libreria Scientifica editrice. 30 facsimiles, mostly of S. Italian chanceries, 819–1493.

Michaud, H. 1969. *La grande chancellerie et les écritures royales au XVIe siècle (1515–1589).* Paris: Presses Universitaires de France.

The New Palaeographical Society Facsimiles of Ancient Manuscripts. 1903–32. Edited by E. M. Thompson, G. F. Warner, F. G. Kenyon, and J. P. Gilson. First series. London: Oxford Univ. Press, 1903–12; index volume, 1914. Second series. London: Oxford Univ. Press, 1913–30; index volume, 1932.

The Palaeographical Society. Facsimiles of Manuscripts and Inscriptions. 1873–1901. Edited by E. A. Bond, E. M. Thompson, and G. F. Warner. 2 vols. London: Clowes, 1873–83, 1884–94; index volume, 1901.

Poulle, E. 1966. *Paléographie des écritures cursives en France du 15e au 17e siècle.* Geneva: Droz.

Prou, M. 1904. *Manuel de Paléographie Recueil de facsimiles d'écritures du Ve au XVIIe siècles . . . accompagnés de transcriptions.* Paris: Picard. This pendant to his *Manuel de paléographie* is almost exclusively given over to diplomatic records.

Rycraft, A. 1973. *English Mediaeval Handwriting.* 2d ed. York: Borthwick Institute. *Sixteenth and Seventeenth Century Handwriting.* 1972. Series 1. 3d ed. Series 2. 3d ed. York: St. Anthony's Press.

Warner, G. F., and H. J. Ellis. 1898. *Facsimiles of Royal and Other Autographs in . . . the British Museum.* Vol. 1: *William I–Richard I.* London: British Museum.

Aids

L'art de vérifier les dates et les faits historiques, par un religieux de la congrégation de St.-Maur. 1818–44. 4th ed. Edited by N. V. de St. Allais et al. 44 vols. Paris: Moreau. Still very useful.

Berger, A. 1958. *Encyclopedic Dictionary of Roman Law.* Philadelphia: American Philosophical Society.

Cappelli, A. 1906. *Cronologia, Cronografia e Calendario perpetuo dal principio dell'Era Cristiana ai giorni nostri.* Milan. 6th ed., Milan: Hoepli, 1929.

————. 1929. *Lexicon abbreviaturarum: Dizionario di abbreviature latine ed italiane.* Milan: Hoepli. Numerous reprintings.

Cheney, C. R. 1955. *Handbook of Dates for Students of English History.* 3d ed. London: Office of the Royal Historical Society.

Chevalier, U. 1905–7. *Répertoire des sources historiques du moyen âge: Topobibliographie.* 2 vols. Paris: Picard.

Cottineau, L. H. 1935–37. *Répertoire topo-bibliographique des abbayes et prieurés.* 2 vols. Macon: Protat frères.

Davis, G. R. C. 1958. *Medieval Cartularies of Great Britain: A Short Catalogue.* London: Longmans.

Di Capua, F. 1941. *Fonti ed esempi per lo studio dello "Stilus curiae romanae" medioevale.* Rome: Maglione.

Du Cange, C. D. 1968. *Glossarium ad scriptores mediae et infimae Latinitatis.* Paris: N.p. The standard edition is *Glossarium mediae et infimae Latinitatis,* edited by F. Favre. 10 vols. Niort: L. Favre, 1883–87; reprinted, Paris: Librairie des sciences et d'art, 1937.

Eubel, C. 1960. *See Hierarchia . . .*

Favier, J. 1958. *Les archives.* Que sais-je? no. 805. Paris: Presses Universitaires de France. A general survey of French archives and those of some other countries.

Foerster, H. 1947. *Urkundenlesebuch für den akademischen Gebrauch.* Berne: Haupt. 100 samples of diplomatic documents.

————. 1951. *Urkundenlehre in Abbildungen mit Erläuterungen und Transkriptionen.* Berne: Haupt.

Gams, B. 1885. *Series episcoporum Ecclesiae Catholicae.* 2d ed. Leipzig: Hiersemann.

Gooder, E. A. 1961. *Latin for Local History. An Introduction.* London: Longmans.

Graesse, J. G. Th. 1972. *Orbis latinus, oder Verzeichnis der wichtigsten lateinischen Ortsund Ländernahmen.* Re-edited in 3 vols. by H. Plechl and S.-C. Plechl as *Orbis Latinus. Lexikon lateinischer geographischer Namen des Mittelalters und der Neuzeit.* Brunswick: Klinkhardt und Biermann. Also available in a one-volume handbook: *Orbis Latinus Handausgabe.* Brunswick: Klinkhardt und Biermann, 1971.

Grotefend, H. 1891–98. *Zeitrechnung des deutschen Mittelalters und der Neuzeit.* 2 vols. Hanover: Hahnsche Buchhandlung.

————, and O. Grotefend. 1948. *Taschenbuch der Zeitrechnung des deutschen Mittelalters und der Neuzeit.* 8th ed. Hanover: Hahn.

A Guide to Seals in the Public Record Office. 1964. London: Public Record Office. Valuable pages on the study, composition, and forgery of seals.

Hall, H. 1908–9. *A Formula Book of English Official Historical Documents.* Vol. 1, *Diplomatic Documents.* Cambridge: Cambridge Univ. Press, 1908. Vol. 2, *Ministerial and Juridical Records.* Cambridge: Cambridge Univ. Press, 1909.

Hector, L. C. 1966. *The Handwriting of English Documents.* 2d ed. London: Edward Arnold.

Hierarchia Catholica medii et recentioris aevi [1198–1903]. 1913–58. Edited by C. Eubel. 6 vols. Regensburg: Monasterii, sumptibus et typis librariae; reprint, 1960.

Jaffe, P. 1851. *Regesta Pontificum Romanorum* ad a. post Christumnatum 1198. 2 vols. Berlin: Veit; 2d ed. Leipzig: Veit, 1885–88.

Kehr, Paul F. 1906–75. *Italia Pontificia.* 10 vols. Berlin: Weidmann.

Latham, R. E. 1965. *Revised Medieval Latin Word-List from British and Irish Sources.* London: Oxford Univ. Press.

Martin, C. T. 1912. *The Record Interpreter: A Collection of Abbreviations, Latin Words and Names Used in English Historical Manuscripts and Records.* 2d ed. London: Stevens; reprint, 1949.

Meyer, O., and R. Klauser. 1962. *Clavis mediaevalis. Kleines Wörterbuch der Mittelalterforschung.* Wiesbaden: Harrasowitz.

Mullins, E. 1958. *Texts and Calendars: An Analytical Guide to Serial Publications.* London: Royal Historical Society.

Potthast, A. 1862. *Bibliotheca historica medii aevi: Wegweiser durch die Geschichtswerke des europäischen Mittelalters bis 1500.* Berlin: Weber; 2d ed. in 2 vols., 1896. Now slowly being replaced by the *Repertorium fontium historiae medii aevi.* Rome: Istituto storico italiano per il medio evo, 1962–.

————. 1874–75. *Regesta Pontificum Romanorum inde ab a. post Christumnatum 1198 ad a. 1304.* 2 vols. Leipzig: Veit.

Powicke, F. M., and E. B. Fryde. 1961. *A Handbook of British Chronology.* 2d ed. London: Royal Historical Society.

Record Repositories in Great Britain. 1971. 4th ed. London: H. M. Stationery Office.

Stein, H. 1907. *Bibliographie générale des cartulaires français où relatifs à l'histoire de France.* Paris: Picard.

Stiennon, J., and G. Hasenohr. 1973. *Paléographie du Moyen Age.* Paris: Colin.

Thomas, D. H., and L. M. Case. 1959. *Guide to the Diplomatic Archives of Western Europe.* 2d ed. Philadelphia: Univ. of Pennsylvania Press, 1959, 1975. A good survey of archival deposits, though *diplomatic* has a political connotation.

Walther, J. L. 1751. *Lexicon diplomaticum.* Leipzig: N.p.; 2d ed., Ulm: Sumptibus Gaumanis, 1756. The first influential dictionary of abbreviations.

Wright, A. 1776. *Court-hand Restored, or the Student's Assistant in Reading Old Deeds, Charters, Records, etc.* London: B. White; 10th ed., edited by C. T. Martin. Stevens, 1912.

Select Topics

Barraclough, G. 1934. *Public Notaries and the Papal Curia.* London: Macmillan.

Bartoloni, F. 1953. "Paleografia e diplomatica. Conquiste di ieri. Prospettive per il domani." *Notizie degli Archivi di Stato* 13:119–29.

Bautier, R. H. 1961. "Leçon d'ouverture du cours de Diplomatique à l'École des chartes (26 Octobre 1961)." *Bibliothèque de l'École des chartes [BEC]* 119:194–

225. See also A. Petrucci. "Diplomatica vecchia e nuova." *Studi medievali,* 3d series, 4 (1963): 785–98.

———. 1964. "Recherches sur la chancellerie royale au temps du Philippe IV," *BEC* 122:89–174.

Blok, D. P. 1967. "Les formules de droit romain dans les actes privés au haut moyen âge." In *Miscellanea Mediaevalia in memoriam J. F. Niermeyer.* Groningen: Walters.

Bock, F. 1941. *Einführung in das Registerwesen des avignonesischen Papsttums.* Rome: Quellen und Forschungen aus italienischen Archiven und Bibliotheken. With an album of 39 plates.

Boyle, L. E. 1960. "The Date of the Consecration of San Clemente, Rome." *Archivum Fratrum Praedicatorum* 30:417–27.

———. 1967. Review of O. Hageneder and A. Haidacher, *Die Register Innocenz' III,* I, vol. 1, *Pontifikatsjahr 1198–1199: Texte.* Graz: Böhlan, 1964. *Speculum* 42:153–62.

———. 1972. *A Survey of the Vatican Archives and of Its Medieval Holdings.* Toronto: Pontifical Institute of Medieval Studies.

Von Brandt, A. 1963. *Werkzeug des Historikers.* 3d ed. Stuttgart: Kohlhammer; esp. pp. 97–142.

Brooke, C. N. L. 1971. "Approaches to Medieval Forgery." In *Medieval Church and Society: Collected Essays.* London: Sidgwick and Jackson.

Chaplais, P., ed. 1964. *Diplomatic Documents Preserved in the Public Record Office, 1101–1272.* London: H. M. Stationery Office.

———. 1965. "The Origin and Authenticity of the Royal Anglo-Saxon Diploma." *Journal of the Society of Archivists* 3:48–60.

———. 1966. "The Anglo-Saxon Chancery: From the Diploma to the Writ." *Journal of the Society of Archivists* 4:160–76.

Cheney, C. R. 1950. *English Bishops' Chanceries, 1100–1250.* Manchester: Manchester Univ. Press.

———. 1966. *The Study of the Medieval Papal Chancery.* Glasgow: Jackson.

———. 1972. *Notaries Public in England in the Thirteenth and Fourteenth Centuries.* Oxford: Clarendon Press.

———, and M. G. Cheney. 1967. *The Letters of Pope Innocent III (1198–1216) Concerning England and Wales: A Calendar with an Appendix of Texts.* Oxford: Clarendon Press. With a valuable introduction on papal diplomatics.

Classen, P. 1955. "Kaiserreskript und Königsurkunden. Diplomatische Studien zum römisch-germanischen Kontinuätsproblem." *Archiv für Diplomatik* 1:1–87; 2 (1956): 1–115.

Clémencet, S. 1967. "Les archives de l'officialité de Paris." In *Huitième Centenaire de Notre Dame de Paris.* Paris: J. Vrin.

La Critica del Testo: Atti del secondo congresso intermazionale della Società italiana di Storia del Diritto. 1971. 2 vols. Florence: N.p. Various articles of diplomatic import.

Denholm-Young, N. 1946. "The Cursus in England." In *Collected Papers in Medieval Subjects.* Oxford: Blackwell.

Dumas, A. 1930. Review of de Boüard. *Manuel de diplomatique*. *Le moyen âge* 40:104-22.

———. 1932. "La diplomatique et la forme des actes." *Le moyen âge* 42:5-31.

———. 1933-34. "Études sur le classement des formes des actes." *Le moyen âge* 43 (1933): 81-97, 145-82, 251-64; 44 (1934): 17-41.

Fichtenau, H. 1957. *Arenga. Spätantike und Mittelalter im Spiegel von Urkundenformeln*. Graz: Böhlaus Nachf.

Ficker, J. 1877-78. *Beiträge zur Urkundenlehre*. Innsbruck: Wagner.

Fink, K. A. 1964. "Arengen spätmittelalterlichen Papsturkunden." In *Mélanges Eugène Tisserant* 4. Studi e Testi 234. Vatican City: Typis Vaticanis.

Fuhrmann, H. 1963. "Die Fälschungen im Mittelalter. Ueberlegungen zum mittelalterlichen Wahrheitsbegriff." *Historische Zeitschrift* 197:529-54, 555-79 (discussion); 550-81 (reply).

Galbraith, V. H. 1934a. "Monastic Foundation Charters of the Eleventh and Twelfth Centuries." *Cambridge Historical Journal* 4:205-22, 296-98.

———. 1934b. *An Introduction to the Use of Public Records*. Oxford: Oxford Univ. Press.

———. 1948a. *Studies in the Public Records*. London: Nelson.

———. 1948b. "The Literacy of the Medieval English Kings." *Proceedings of the British Academy* 21:201-38. Reprinted in *Studies in British History: British Academy Lectures*, edited by L. S. Sutherland. London: Oxford Univ. Press, 1966.

Genicot, L. 1972. *Les actes publics*. Typologie des sources du moyen âge. Fasc. 3. Turnhout: Brepols.

Hector, L. C. 1959. *Palaeography and Forgery*. London: St. Anthony's Press.

Higounet, C. 1952. "Le style pisan. Son emploi. Sa diffusion géographique." *Le moyen âge* 68:31-42.

Hill, R. 1951. "Bishop Sutton and His Archives: A Study in the Keeping of Records in the Thirteenth Century." *Journal of Ecclesiastical History* 2:43-80.

Jacob, E. F. 1953. *The Medieval Registers of Canterbury and York*. London: St. Anthony's Press.

Koudelka, V. 1958. "Note sur le Cartulaire de S. Dominique." *Archivum Fratrum Praedicatorum* 28:92-114.

Levillain, L. 1930. *"Servus servorum Dei." Le moyen âge* 40:5-7.

Major, K. 1968. "The Teaching and Study of Diplomatic in England." *Archives* 8:114-18.

Neuss, E. 1954-56. *Die Aktenkunde der Wirtschaft*. 2 vols. Berlin: Rütten und Loening. The diplomatics of modern commerce.

Ourliac, P., and J. de Malafosse. 1961. *Histoire du droit privé*. Paris: Presses Universitaires de France.

Petrucci, A. 1958. *Notarii. Documenti per la storia del notariato italiano*. Milan: Giuffrè.

———. 1963. "L'edizione delle fonti documentarie è un problema sempre aperto." *Rivista storica italiana* 75:69-80.

Poole, R. L. 1915. *Lectures in the History of the Papal Chancery down to the Time of Innocent III*. Cambridge: Cambridge Univ. Press.

———. 1934. *Studies in Chronology and History.* Oxford: Oxford Univ. Press.

Prevenier, W. 1967. "La chancellerie des comtes de Flandre dans le cadre européen à la fin du XIIe siècle." *BEC* 125:54–95.

Purvis, J. S. 1954. *Notarial Signs from York Archiepiscopal Records.* London: St. Anthony's Press.

Quirin, H. 1964. *Einführung in das Studium der mittelalterlichen Geschichte.* 3d ed. Brunswick: G. Westermann; esp. pp. 65–93, 133–53.

Redlich, O. 1911. *Die Privaturkunden des Mittelalters.* Berlin: Oldenbourg.

Riedmann, J. 1967–68. "Studien über die Reichskanzlei unter Friedrich Barbarossa in den Jahren 1156–1166." *Mitteilungen des Instituts für österreichische Geschichtsforschung* 75 (1967): 322–402; 76 (1968): 23–105.

Santifaller, L. 1958. *Neuere Editionen mittelalterlicher Königs- und Papsturkunden.* Vienna: Böhlaus Nachf.

Steinacker, H. 1927. *Die antiken Grundlagen der frühmittelalterlichen Privaturkunden.* Leipzig: Teubner.

Stenton, F. M. 1922. *Transcripts of Charters Relating to Gilbertine Houses.* Horncastle: W. Morton for Lincoln Record Society. Valuable note in introduction on private charters.

———. 1929. "Acta episcoporum." *Cambridge Historical Journal* 3:1–14.

———. 1955. *Latin Charters of the Anglo-Saxon Period.* Oxford: Clarendon Press.

Stiennon, J. 1960. *L'écriture diplomatique dans le diocèse de Liège du XIe au milieu du XIIIe siècle: Réflet d'une civilisation.* Paris: Colin.

Tessier, G. 1930. "Leçon d'ouverture du cours de diplomatique de l'École des chartes, 8 décembre 1930." *BEC* 91:241–63.

Valois, N. 1881. "Étude sur le rhythme des bulles pontificales." *BEC* 42:161–98, 257–72.

Van Caenegem, R. C. 1959. *Royal Writs in England from the Conquest to Glanvill.* London: Quaritch. Valuable introduction.

Vieillard, J. 1927. *La latin des diplômes royaux et chartes privées de l'époque mérovingienne.* Paris: Champion.

Walker, D. 1971. "The Organization of Material in Medieval Cartularies." In *The Study of Medieval Records: Essays in Honour of Kathleen Major.* Edited by D. A. Bullough and R. L. Storey. Oxford: Clarendon Press.

Periodicals

AD   *Archiv für Diplomatik, Schriftgeschichte, Siegel- und Wappenkunde.* Cologne 1955–.

AfU   *Archiv für Urkundenforschung.* Berlin, 1908–1942.

AHP   *Archivum historiae pontificiae.* Rome, 1965–.

AntAnn *Anthologica Annua.* Rome, 1955–.

Arch.   *Archives. The Journal of the British Records Association.* London, 1956–.

ASI   *Archivio storico italiano.* Florence, 1842–.

ASRSP	*Archivio della Società Romana di Storia Patria.* Rome, 1878–.
AST	*Analecta sacra tarraconensia.* Barcelona, 1925–.
AZ	*Archivalische Zeitschrift.* Stuttgart, 1876–.
BAH	*Boletín de la Real Academia de la História.* Madrid, 1877–.
BAPI	*Bullettino dell'Archivio paleografico italiano.* Rome, 1908–.
BCRH	*Bulletin de la Commission royale d'histoire.* Brussels, 1854–.
BEC	*Bibliothèque de l'École des chartes.* Paris. 1839–.
BIHBR	*Bulletin de l'Institut historique belge de Rome.* Brussels, 1919–.
BIHR	*Bulletin of the Institute of Historical Research.* London, 1927–.
BISIAM	*Bullettino dell'Istituto storico italiano per il medio evo e Archivio Muratoriano.* Rome, 1886–.
DA	*Deutsches Archiv für Erforschung des Mittelalters.* Marburg, 1937–.
EHR	*English Historical Review.* London, 1886–.
HS	*Hispania sacra.* Madrid, 1948–.
JSA	*Journal of the Society of Archivists.* London, 1964–.
LMA	*Le moyen âge.* Brussels-Paris, 1888–.
MAH	*Mélanges d'archéologie et d'histoire,* Rome-Paris, 1881–.
MIöG	*Mitteilungen des Instituts für österreichische Geschichtsforschung.* Vienna, 1880–.
NA	*Neues Archiv der Gesellschaft für ältere deutsche Geschichtskunde.* Frankfurt-am-Main, 1876-1935.
QFIAB	*Quellen und Forschungen aus italienischen Archiven und Bibliotheken.* Rome, 1898–.
RABM	*Revista de archivos, biblotecas y museos.* Madrid, 1871–.
RHDFE	*Revue historique de droit français et étranger.* Paris, 1855–.
RHE	*Revue d'histoire ecclésiastique.* Louvain, 1900–.
RHM	*Römische historische Mitteilungen.* Rome-Graz-Vienna, 1956–.
RM	*Revue Mabillon.* Ligugé, 1905–.
RPDSA	*Rivista italiana di paleografia, diplomatica e scienze ausiliarie della storia.* Rome, 1955–.
RQ	*Römische Quartalschrift für christliche Altertumskunde und Kirchengeschichte.* Freiburg-im-Breisgau, 1887–.
RQH	*Revue des questions historiques.* Paris, 1866-1959.
SZG	*Schweizerische Zeitschrift für Geschichte.* Zürich 1951–. Formerly *Jahrbuch für schweizerische Geschichte,* 1876-1920; *Zeitschrift für schweizerische Geschichte,* 1921-1950.
ZRGKA	*Zeitschrift der Savigny-Stiftung für Rechtsgeschichte, kanonistische Abteilung.* Weimar, 1911–.

⟡ 3 ⟡

Numismatics

PHILIP GRIERSON

UMISMATICS differs from other auxiliary sciences of history in several respects. In the first place, it is concerned with a particular type of archeological object and not basically, as are paleography, diplomatics, and indirectly sigillography, with written documents, though when these are available they greatly simplify the numismatist's task. Second, the objects with which it is concerned are of great interest to collectors. Many of them are consequently in private possession and not, like manuscripts and archival material, for the most part in public depositories. Their study and consultation can, therefore, often present problems. Third, arising out of this last, much numismatic research is carried on by persons whom the historian tends to regard as amateurs. Often they have had little or no training in how to evaluate evidence or handle documents, and they lack an understanding of the background to the coinages with which they deal. As collectors they are tempted to exaggerate the value of their possessions, and, even when not collectors, they may attach undue importance to their observations and discoveries. They forget that minting and its organization form relatively minor activities of governments, and that the precise mint of a coin or its exact date is not always of much historical consequence.

Medieval numismatics started as a poor relation of classical numismatics, partly because scholars in the sixteenth century were less interested in the history of the Middle Ages than in that of Greece and Rome, partly because medieval coins tend to be intrinsically less beautiful than classical ones and thus less attractive to collectors. They are occasionally illustrated in numismatic works of the sixteenth century, but usually in a quite grotesque fashion. The head of St. Paul on a coin of Münster, for example, will be transformed into one of Charlemagne by the simple process of changing the inscription surrounding it from *Scs Paulus* to *Carolus Magnus*. Even a hundred years later, the only completely useless pages in the *Familiae Byzantinae* (1680) of the great Ducange are those dealing with coins, a high proportion of which are wrongly identified, to say nothing of being enlarged to the same uniform diameter and having their designs reproduced in the conventional idiom of the day. Virtually the only seventeenth-century work on medieval numismatics which the scholar still regularly consults is François Leblanc's *Traité historique des monnoyes de France,* first published in 1690. It owes its usefulness to its frequent reliance on mint documents and not to its coin illustrations and descriptions, which are little if at all superior to those of Ducange.

Substantial advances were made in many countries in the eighteenth century, notably in Italy, where a long series of monographs on the coinages of separate states and cities was collected in the six volumes of Filippo Argelati's *De monetis Italiae variorum illustrium dissertationes* (Milan, 1750–59) and its five-volume continuation, G. A. Zanetti's *Nuova raccolta delle monete e zecche d'Italia* (Bologna, 1775–89). Both are publications which the modern scholar still regularly consults, although, as in the case of Leblanc, mainly for the written documents which they use or reproduce. The same is largely true of Rogers Ruding's *Annals of the Coinage of Great Britain* (London, 1816; 3d ed., 1840), although its plates are of much higher quality than those in Argelati and Zanetti and often faithful enough to allow identifications with specimens in collections today.

A great step forward was made with the appearance of Joachim Lelewel's *Numismatique du moyen-âge, considérée sous le rapport de type* (Paris, 1836), the three volumes of which were accompanied by an *Atlas* illustrating nearly 1,000 coins or significant details of their designs, all meticulously drawn by the author. It was the first comprehensive work on medieval coinage ever published. Although its details are now out of date, and its use of written records inadequate even by the standards of the time, it is a work whose pages can still be studied with profit, for the great Polish scholar was one of the first to see the need for studying the paleography of coin inscriptions and to divine and illustrate the process by which types and monograms are transformed in the process of repeated copying. The year 1836 was indeed an *annus mirabilis* in the history of numismatics, for it also saw the publication at Metz of Felicien de Saulcy's *Essai de classification des suites monétaires byzantines,* the earliest monograph on

Byzantine coinage; the formation of the Numismatic Society of London, later the Royal Numismatic Society, and the first issue of its journal, later the *Numismatic Chronicle;* the foundation of the *Revue de la numismatique française,* later the *Revue numismatique;* and the publication at Leipzig of the first issue of the *Blätter für Münzkunde* of Hermann Grote, one of the greatest and most prolific of German scholars in the field of medieval numismatics.

The next decade saw the founding of further societies and journals, notably Bernhard Koehne's *Zeitschrift fur Münz-, Siegel-, und Wappenkunde* at Berlin and the *Revue de la numismatique belge* (later the *Revue belge de numismatique*) at Tirlemont (later at Brussels), and the publication of monographs of solid worth. F. de Saulcy's *Recherches sur les monnaies des ducs héréditaires de Lorraine* and Domenico Promis's *Monete dei Reali di Savoia,* still standard works, were both published in 1841, in Metz and Turin, respectively. The remainder of the century was a period of intense numismatic activity. Thousands of new coin types were published and classified, and monographs were produced on virtually all the mints and coinages, even the most obscure, of medieval and modern Europe. Photographic illustration came into general use in the 1880s, supplementing or replacing the line drawings which, up to then, had been in general use and had indeed attained a remarkable degree of perfection. Descriptive numismatics in the medieval field reached its climax in a great work of synthesis, Arthur Engel and Raymond Serrure's *Traité de numismatique du moyen âge* (3 vols., Paris, 1891–1905), written jointly by a distinguished amateur and a scholar-dealer who died at the age of thirty-six after a prodigious numismatic output of the highest quality. Even today, a hundred years after the publication of its first volume, "Engel and Serrure" remains the standard *Historia Numorum* of the Middle Ages.

The work of scholars in the present century has in part been devoted to refining the conclusions of their nineteenth-century predecessors, particularly in regard to the dating of coins, and in part to developing new lines of enquiry, notably in the study of metrology, coin circulation, and mint output, which were formerly neglected or believed to be either irrelevant or impossible. Some of the consequent research may seem at first sight to involve unprofitable and irrelevant minutiae, but detailed studies of letter forms and typological changes are essential preliminaries to proper hoard description and coin dating; they are not, as the historian is sometimes inclined to suspect, and as indeed does occur in the modern period, simply intended to produce new varieties for the collector. The historian must be in a position to evaluate the results of such research. This is the more important in that he will normally expect to do most of his work at second hand, using catalogs, monographs, and periodical literature but not attempting to draw conclusions from the coins themselves. It is true that he will be unwise to write about these unless he has actually handled some specimens to see at least what they are like, but he will usually leave the actual research to specialists.

MATERIALS: COINS

Medieval coins are found by the thousand every year. Their subsequent fate depends partly on the circumstances of their finding, partly on the legislation of the country where they are found, and partly on the degree to which such legislation is observed. Coins brought to light in regular excavations are normally preserved as part of the archeological record, and in fortunate cases are published. Hoards found by chance are in some countries claimed by public authorities and find their way to museums, but their fate is much influenced by the precise terms of the local law of treasure trove and the way it is administered. Where the law is too exigent and compensations to finders are known or believed to be inadequate, coins tend to be clandestinely sold and eventually reach the coin market without reliable record of provenance; in extreme cases they are melted down. Where easier conditions prevail there is usually some hope that hoards will be declared and properly recorded before being, as a rule, broken up, important items being retained for museums after full compensation has been paid, and the remainder handed back to the finders to be disposed of as their owners see fit. There are some countries which have virtually no law of treasure trove at all, so that hoards are simply divided between finders and the owners of the land where they are found. In virtually all countries, single coins found by chance end up on the coin market, though often after a considerable interval during which they are retained as curios or ornaments by their finders.

The coins with which the scholar has to deal may therefore exist in any of three possible contexts: in that of their deposit, in museums, or in circulation amongst collectors. These categories are neither mutually exclusive nor permanent: coins from hoards will usually pass to museums or collectors, collectors' coins are often acquired by museums, and coins in museums, through the sale or exchange of duplicates, sometimes pass back to collectors. But the classification corresponds broadly to different kinds of material as the scholar sees it, and it brings out some of the problems that confront him in his work.

COIN FINDS

Coins as found can be classed as hoards, area finds, cumulative finds, and casual finds, though fundamentally more important than the circumstance of their finding is that of their "loss," for coins casually lost are usually different in character from those deliberately hidden and for some reason not recovered. Few coins are deliberately abandoned, though Charon's obol, grave goods which may include coins, and the contents of wishing wells are exceptions to the rule.

Hoards are the most important form in which coins come to light. They are by definition groups of coins, sometimes with other valuables as well, which were deposited as single entities, usually by their legitimate owners, who had accumulated them as savings or had to conceal what they possessed in time of danger. Sometimes, however, they belonged to pirates or robbers who hid them with other loot. They are on occasion very large. The Brussels hoard of 1908, found during repairs to a house in the rue d'Assaut, contained over 140,000 thirteenth-century silver pennies of the British Isles and the Low Countries. Hoards are useful to numismatists primarily as sources of coin — they supply most of what now exists — but secondarily for establishing the chronology of coin issues, usually through the comparison of a number of hoards whose contents overlap. They can sometimes also be used for studying fluctuations in mint output, or the age- and geographical structure of the currency at particular times.

The evidence of single hoards has to be used with caution, since, if they chanced to belong to merchants, or to pilgrims far from home, their contents will not be typical of the region where they were found. Hoards are known for all periods of the Middle Ages, but are naturally most abundant in times of general unrest, the most important groups being those of Scandinavia and eastern Europe in the Viking period. It was reckoned a few years ago that over 62,000 Muslim coins of the ninth and tenth centuries have been found in Scandinavia, while the numbers of German and English coins of the tenth and eleventh centuries from the same area were put at over 70,000 and 10,000 respectively (Sawyer 1971, 88). The figures would now have to be substantially expanded — the English element was in 1981 put at 57,000 (Blackburn and Metcalf 1981, 149) — and over and above the coins there is also a vast quantity of silver in the form of jewelry and bullion produced by melting imported coins. Hoards of the late Roman period, buried at the time of the barbarian invasions, are also numerous, often providing crucial evidence regarding the dates at which particular provinces were lost and the incidence and routes of Germanic raids.

The coins found in the excavation of limited sites often provide valuable dating information for the archeologist, but only where a substantial area is systematically excavated does enough material come to light to allow us to compare the coin populations of different periods. So far as the Middle Ages are concerned, such area finds are only useful to the Byzantinist, partly because more sites in the Near East have been systematically excavated, partly because Byzantium had coins of low denominations whose owners seem to have accepted their loss more casually than their opposite numbers in the West. Isolated coin finds, on the other hand, are better recorded for the West than for former Byzantine lands, and form important guides to the areas over which particular coins circulated. Cumulative finds, that is, coins lost or abandoned singly but found together, are unusual but always of interest. Medieval examples are the coins that came to light during the excavation of the shrine of St. Peter at Rome in 1940–49 (Serafini in Ghetti and others 1951, 1:224–44), those of the ninth–twelfth centuries found in three offering places in Swedish Lapland (Rasmusson and others in Serning 1956, 183–322) and the curious accumulations of late medieval and early modern small change found in 1919 in clearing the stream that used to flush the latrines of Crossraguel Abbey in Ayrshire (Macdonald 1919), and more recently under church floors in the Scandinavian countries (Jensen 1977). Isolated finds, when adequately recorded, are particularly helpful for identifying mints and showing the patterns of coin circulation.

The literature on coin finds is unsatisfactory in a number of respects. Only hoards which are exceptionally large, or are important because of their particular contents, tend to be published in separate works: the Crondall hoard of early Anglo-Saxon gold coins, the Fécamp hoard of late tenth-century French deniers, the Seega hoard of late twelfth- and early thirteenth-century German bracteates. The same is true of excavation material, though there are exceptions (Corinth, Athens, Sardis). Otherwise, accounts of finds tend to be scattered through the periodical literature, and can only be traced from references in secondary works or, in a few cases, with the help of specialized bibliographies. Medieval British hoards, but not finds of single coins, have been inventoried by J. D. A. Thompson (1956). There is an excellent bibliography for Czechoslovakia, and partial ones, covering either particular regions (e.g., Thuringia) or particular series (e.g., Arabic coins, Byzantine coins, coins of the Avar period) for other countries in Central and Eastern Europe. There is an immense summary by Gert Hatz of German coins in tenth- and eleventh-century finds in Sweden which is a model of its kind, and a systematic corpus of Swedish hoards of the Viking age began to appear in 1975. A survey for France has recently started publication (Duplessy 1985), and there are important regional studies, such as for Languedoc and Gascony (Depeyrot 1987). But the literature on coin finds, despite their importance, is one in which it is not easy to find one's way, the only periodical specially devoted to the subject (*Coin Hoards,* London: Royal Numismatic Society, 1975ff.) being uneven in both coverage and quality. Nor are hoard descriptions, when located, always as complete as one could wish. Many of them may fail to record the weights of the coins, or the precise issues or numbers involved.

Coins in Museums

With public collections, we move from natural accumulations of coins in the hands of contemporary users to artificial ones put together for scientific purposes in modern times. A hoard will often consist largely or even entirely of duplicates, since it represents the circulating medium at a particular point in time. Museum curators, on the other hand, are primarily interested in sequences of issues, and try to build up collections which will illustrate the coinage changes of the past. This may involve some duplicates, and many near-duplicates, but museum authorities will in the main try to avoid cluttering up their trays with identical specimens of the same coin. When duplicates from hoards have to be retained, whether because of the local law of treasure trove or because of the conditions attached to a gift, the hoards are usually kept as separate entities apart from the main collection.

Museum material is best studied by personal examination, and most museums are ready to allow serious students access to their holdings. For more prolonged study, and in any case where material has to be compared from a number of collections, numismatists have traditionally made use of plaster casts, but these have now been largely replaced by polaroids. Ideally, of course, museum collections should be published, but this has been done very insufficiently, and catalogs in course of time become out of date, partly because of advances in knowledge and partly because of the subsequent growth of collections. In most great museums the cataloging of medieval series had been neglected in favor of that of their classical rivals. The two volumes of the catalog of Anglo-Saxon coins in the British Museum date from 1887 and 1893 respectively, thus giving a very incomplete view of present holdings, and though there are more modern catalogs of the Anglo-Norman coins (1916) and the "Tealby" coinage of Henry II (1951), the later medieval series, from 1180 onwards, is uncataloged. In France the royal coinage in the Cabinet des Médailles is well cataloged, with volumes on the Merovingian (1892), Carolingian (1896), and Capetian and Valois kings down to 1515 (1923–32), but nothing has been done on the feudal coinage, and the Merovingian and Carolingian volumes are in need of extensive revision. Berlin is in a more deplorable state, with no published catalog of its huge medieval German collection at all.

In the early 1930s a new type of catalog, known as a *Sylloge,* in which all coins are illustrated but descriptive text is cut to a minimum, was devised for the study of die relationships in ancient Greek coinage. In the 1950s the same plan, but with volumes of a smaller and more convenient format, was adopted by a Committee of the British Academy for publishing the coins of the British Isles. The bulk of Anglo-Saxon coins in British provincial museums, as well as those in the Danish national collection, have now been published in sylloge form, and the publication of the British Museum Anglo-Saxon collection in this fashion is now under way. But although such volumes represent an immense boon to the experienced numismatist, they cannot be easily used by the historian unless he has already familiarized himself with the coinages through less austere forms of publication.

The main coin collections in most countries are those of their national museums or sometimes, for historical reasons, their national libraries: the British Museum, the Bibliothèque Nationale, the Staatliche Museen at Berlin, the Hermitage at Leningrad. The best collection of medieval European coins in the United States is in the Museum of the American Numismatic Society in New York, though that of the Smithsonian Institution is also of importance. The collection of Byzantine coins at the Dumbarton Oaks Center of Byzantine Studies in Washington is the largest and for some periods the most important in the world. Below these national collections are those of universities and important civic and private museums, and below these again are many collections of varying importance in local museums. The last sometimes present the student with problems, for they are often too small to have anyone on their staff with sufficient knowledge to answer queries satisfactorily, or supply the student with casts or photographs, or even provide access to the coins. This is the more unfortunate when they are custodians of important hoard material or have been given or left specialized private collections which they lack the resources or interest to look after properly.

Coins in Private Collections

Private collectors are not usually reluctant to show their coins to serious enquirers, or to provide information about them, but knowledge of what is in private hands is almost inevitably limited to the relatively small circle of the owner's friends, or to students of particular coin series. For practical purposes coins currently in private hands are inaccessible to the general historian except for individual specimens or series which may have been published in specialist studies. Private collections as a whole are rarely published during the lifetimes of their owners, who live in the hope of obtaining particular rarities they do not yet possess and are reluctant to see their collection published in what they regard as an "imperfect" form. When they die, however, their collections frequently come up for public auction, and it occasionally happens that a scholar's interest will change or he falls on hard times, and so is led to dispose of parts of his collection during his lifetime. Auction catalogs are for the most part extremely well illustrated, since this is likely to enhance the prices of the coins, and the descriptions are often executed in a wholly professional manner. Such sale catalogs are therefore an essential part of every numismatist's library. Those of the English sections of the R. C. Lockett collection, sold at Glendining's (London) over the years 1955–61, are essential for the study of English coinage from the Anglo-Saxon period to the Restoration; that of the Arthur Löbbecke collection, sold by Riechmann (Halle) in 1925, is one of the best guides to German bracteates; and the three volumes of the Marchéville sale catalog, sold in Paris by Florange and Ciani over the years 1927–29, rank with the catalogs of the Bibliothèque Nationale as the best guide to French royal coinage from Hugh Capet to the death of Henry IV.

Sale catalogs, apart from a few extremely well-known ones, are not easy to trace or consult. The only classified guide of reasonable proportions is that in my *Bibliographie numismatique* (1979), for the much longer list forming vol. 7 of the *Dictionary Catalogue of the Library of the American Numismatic Society* (Boston, 1962, and supplements) is an alphabetical list by dealers and owners. A further complication is that many sales are not of single collections with easily classifiable contents but of large numbers of coins brought together by dealers and auctioneers from different sources, so that one can never predict what will not turn up in them: a gold solidus of Louis the Pious, a unique tremissis of the Suevi, a new coin of some obscure German or Italian mint. Their contents may perhaps in the future be put on a computer from reference purposes, but that day is not yet. Nor is the consultation of sale catalogs easy, for they are not regarded as "books" by librarians and usually do not form part of the holdings of even national libraries. They have to be seen in coin cabinets or by the courtesy of coin dealers, who find the more important ones essential for the identification and cataloging of the material daily passing through their hands. Since they often turn up in coin sales, however, they are things of which every numismatist tries to form a library for himself.

MATERIALS: WRITTEN SOURCES

The student of medieval numismatics is more fortunate than his classical counterpart in that written sources regarding the coinage have survived in some quantity from the Carolingian period onwards, and, for the last three centuries of the Middle Ages, exist in abundance. Prior to the Carolingian age, however, there are only scraps: a reference here to the existence of a mint, there to the name of a denomination, in the barbarian law codes to penalties for false coining, and so on. But the Carolingians brought Frankish coinage under royal control, and their capitularies tell us a fair amount regarding the conditions of minting in the ninth century. For the tenth and eleventh centuries there is little beyond grants of minting rights, especially by German sovereigns, but with the twelfth century mint documents proper survive in a few centers and with the thirteenth century they become abundant in a number of countries. Byzantium, although a highly organized state with efficiently run central institutions, remains the great exception. As a result of the breach in administrative continuity caused by the Turkish conquest, we have from it no mint documents whatsoever, and indeed few written sources relating to its coinage.

What survives in the West can be conveniently considered under the four headings of minting records, taxation and related records, coin lists and exchange rates, and commercial records. There are inevitably many documents useful to numismatists that do not come under any of these headings — formal "advices" to governments by merchants and others on monetary policy, notably those given to Philip the Fair in the early fourteenth century (Guilhiermoz 1922–26) and to Charles V by Nicole Oresme in the 1360s (Johnson 1956), casual references to money and coins in noncommercial correspondence and conversation manuals, accounts of coinage changes or financial crises in the pages of chroniclers — but it is impossible to try to cover everything here. An excellent selection of material, showing the kind of document that may be expected to be useful, is available in Wilhelm Jesse's *Quellenbuch zur Münz- und Geldgeschichte des Mittelalters* (Halle, 1924; reprinted, Aalen, 1968). Coin references in written sources, however, particularly when made the basis of statistical analysis, must be employed with prudence (Balaguer 1986).

Mint Documents

The most important of these form three classes: (1) mint contracts, (2) mint ordinances and related documents, and (3) mint returns.

Mint contracts vary greatly in detail, some of them simply confiding minting operations to a contractor for a term of years, others setting out the range of denominations to be struck and prescribing their weights and fineness. Occasionally they contain instructions on the designs of the coins and the privy marks to be used to distinguish them from other issues. They often lay down the price to be paid for bullion, this being thought necessary because of the assumption that the master's profit should depend on the volume of coin struck, not on his being able to buy bullion cheap and pocket the difference between what he had paid and the face value of the resulting coin. Late medieval contracts sometimes lay down the proportions of different denominations, for moneyers preferred to strike high denominations to low ones—the labor costs were proportionally smaller, since it took twelve times as long to strike twelve pennies as one shilling—and if left to their own devices the mints were apt to leave the public desperately short of small change.

The category of mint ordinances and related documents covers virtually all records relation to the working of the mint other than its accounts. Mint ordinances do not differ in any important particular from guild ordinances of the Middle Ages. They lay down, often in great detail, the rights and privileges of moneyers, how they shall carry out their duties, their hours of work and entitlement to holidays, and so on. Good examples are the *Constitutum artis monetariorum* of the Florentine mint (Conti 1939) and the *Capitulare Massariarum monete* of that of Venice (Papadopoli 1893–1919, 1:311–38). Another type of mint record, unfortunately very rare, is represented by the so-called *Libro della Zecca* of Florence, which records the names of the magistrates appointed each spring and fall to take charge of the mint for six months and the privy marks used on the coins during their periods of office. The old edition of this (Orsini 1760), used by generations of scholars, is now superseded by one with valuable notes and supplementary matters (Bernocchi 1974–85, vol. 1). The Florentine *Libro* was begun at the instance of the historian Giovanni Villani when he was one of the magistrates in 1317, and was carried on regularly down to the end of the Republic in 1533. Mint records also sometimes include lists of personnel and documents relating to their appointment, and occasional inventories of mint equipment, usually made at the changeover of one official or mint master to another. A good example of the latter is an inventory of the equipment of the mint of Namur in 1407 printed in Jesse's *Quellenbuch,* Doc. No. 350.

Much more important to the economic historian are records of mint output. Daily accounts of the numbers of coins struck, or at least of their value, were often kept in the later Middle Ages, but these "journals" have rarely survived. Much commoner, and existing in some countries from the thirteenth century onwards, are returns of the totals struck during particular periods of time—a year, two years, the period of a particular mint master's *bail*—for these were usually incorporated in treasury records after the payments due as seigniorage to the ruler had been calculated. Usually, to the numismatist's vexation, totals are given as sums of money, without being broken down into particular denominations, but occasionally the figures for each denomination are given also. Mint output can sometimes be reckoned from the numbers of coins put aside as samples for checking weight and fineness—in English parlance, called the Trial of the Pyx—if the exact prescriptions for these are known (e.g., one coin in every £10 struck) and there is reason to suppose that they were observed. But mints were often casual over such matters, and the totals based on such calculations cannot always be accepted with confidence.

Taxation and Related Records

Public financial records which are of permanent usefulness to governments, have an inbuilt survival factor, but since they deal with sums of money rather than coins they are not always useful to numismatists. There are exceptions, however, especially in the case of an international institution like the papacy, whose agents had to cope with coinage from many different countries. One of the most revealing sources on late twelfth-century coinage is the *Liber Censuum,* a list compiled in 1180 of payments made to the Holy See by ecclesiastical establishments from all over Europe (Fabre and Duchesne, 1889–1905, with useful notes on the coins). The denominations it lists—a substantial number consist of Muslim gold coins, which were more stable in value than local silver or billon pennies and enjoyed the prestige attached to payments in gold—can be interpreted in the light of detailed collectors' returns of later times. The payments of Crusader Tenths, ordered by the Council of Lyon in 1274 and prolonged on various pretexts over a period of thirty years, throw a flood of light on local Italian coinages of the late thirteenth century. When the information in them has been finally digested by numismatists it will be found that almost every detail of the accepted chronology of city coinages in that period will have to be revised (cf. Day 1968). The summary of receipts of the Apostolic Camera during the pontificate of John XXII (1316–34) brings out the over-

whelming importance of the gold florin in international payments in the
early fourteenth century, for the gigantic total of over 3.5 million such coins
completely eclipses the next largest figures, 272,000 French agnels and
150,000 doubles, while the rest, down to one solitary Hungarian florin,
are virtually nowhere (Göller 1910, 15–16). It is not surprising that Schäfer's
great study of fourteenth-century papal finance includes an excursus on
the coins and their values which is quite exceptional in its range and usefulness (Schäfer 1911, 38*–151*).

National records, however, should not be overlooked. The Liberate
and Patent Rolls of thirteenth-century England show Henry III regularly
buying gold, usually in the form of Muslim coins, to be used as alms at
the great festivals of the Church, and from the sums paid for them we can
ascertain what they were and how their values changed (Grierson 1951,
1974). The accounts of the Lord High Treasurer of Scotland, which unfortunately exist continuously only from 1488 onwards, are a mine of information on European gold coinage of the late fifteenth century, partly
because they detail the contents of the various "kists" of treasure checked
after the death of James III in 1488, and partly because they list the extraordinarily varied selection of coins paid out daily to James IV for his
personal needs (mainly for gambling in the evenings) with their equivalents in Scottish money (Dickson 1877, 1:79 and passim).

Coin Lists and Tables of Exchange Rates

One of the earliest known coinage tables is that in Pegolotti's *La Pratica
della Mercatura,* which records the fineness of over 150 coins of gold, silver
and billon met with by merchants in western Europe and the Mediterranean world (Evans 1936, 287–92). Although Pegolotti's text in its final form
dates from ca. 1340, internal evidence shows that the basis of the coin list
must have been put together in the 1270s or 1280s, and that it was added
to subsequently from time to time (Grierson 1957b). A Datini document
of the late fourteenth century also includes a list containing elements going back over a century and related to that employed by Pegolotti (Ciano
1964, 86–90). It was the coming of the grosso and the revival of gold coinage in the thirteenth century that induced merchants to systematize their
information on such matters. Further lists are to be found in Italian manuals of arithmetic of the fourteenth century, which were usually compiled
with the interests of merchants in mind. Pegolotti accompanies his account
of hyperpyra with small drawings of the details that characterize types of
differing fineness. This feature was to be developed in the future, as in the

elaborate drawings of hundreds of privy marks in the mid-fifteenth century work, known rather inconsequently from the title of a former owner as the "Manuscript of the Bishop of Chartres," in the Bibliothèque Nationale. This has unfortunately never been published in its entirety, but sections from it, with some of the drawings, are reproduced in Chalon (1852, 51–66) and F. de Saulcy (1879–92, 1:70–82).

Pegolotti's list of coin finenesses is unofficial in character, but governments as well as merchants had to interest themselves in rates of exchange. Two monetary ordinances of St. Louis already fix the rates at which the sterling and a few feudal issues were to pass in France (Saulcy 1879–92, 1:132), and from the fourteenth century onward, official proclamations, known usually as *gride* in Italy and *evaluacies* or *placaarts* in the Low Countries, became common. No general collection of them exists, though many are reproduced amongst the *pièces justificatives* of numismatic monographs of the last century, for example, in those of P. O. Van der Chijs on the coinages of the Low Countries. At the end of the fifteenth century printed proclamations began to appear, illustrated in due course with engravings of the coins referred to (Van Gelder 1958), till in time the engravings swallowed up the text and there emerged the lavishly illustrated money books so characteristic of the hundred years from the mid-sixteenth to the mid-seventeenth century.

Although coin lists in all their forms are a most valuable source for the numismatist, there is need for caution in their use. Their figures for coin finenesses, though sometimes basd on analyses carried out by or on behalf of merchants or mints, are not always reliable, more particularly since the possibility of subsequent miscopying has to be allowed for. Coins were retained in the lists long after they had disappeared from circulation, and compilers were sometimes surprisingly ill-informed on political geography. The "Manuscript of the Bishop of Chartres" attributes a florin of Albert I of Austria (1350–58), identified by its having as privy mark the Austrian Bindenschild, to the Wittelsbach Count Albert of Hainault (1389–1404), and a French merchant's book of the early sixteenth century supposes a florin of Lucca, having *Luca* in its inscription and the Volto Santo as type, to have been struck by "Luke, duke of Milan" (Blanchet 1891, 169).

Commercial Records

The usefulness of commercial records to the numismatist is unpredictable. Some deal almost entirely with sums of money, or only with domestic trade, and tell us little about actual coins. Where foreign trade and money changing are involved we can hope to learn a good deal. One of the earliest large commercial archives to have survived, a huge group of contracts and related records of a Marseilles business firm which fell afoul of Charles of Anjou, so that its records were confiscated and are now in the Archives départementales des Bouches-du-Rhône, is full of information on thirteenth-century exchange notes throughout the Mediterranean area, though since the exchanges are apt to include concealed interest they cannot always be taken at their face value (Blancard 1884–85). The so-called Runtingerbuch, the account book of the Regensburg partnership of Matthäus and Wilhelm Runtinger covering the years 1383–1407, is a mine of information on south German coinage and exchange rates, since the trading connections of the firm extended from Bohemia, Austria, and Venice to the Rhineland and the Low Countries (Bastian 1935–44). The account books, and still more the incidental letters, of members of the Cely family, English wool exporters dealing with the Low Countries, are a most valuable source for exchange rates in the late fifteenth century, since they often note exactly the figure at which each coin was reckoned in a transaction (Grierson 1967). On the other hand, the immense account book of the Venetian Giacomo Badoer (Dorini and Bertelè 1956), recording innumerable trading transactions at Constantinople and elsewhere in the Near East over the years 1436–40, is of great value to the economic historian through its recording of the prices of goods and commodities, but tells the numismatist little that he did not already know and is extremely difficult to use in the absence of explanatory notes or index. Commercial records are potentially numismatic sources of great value, but whether they will be so in any particular case can only be discovered by inspection.

PROBLEMS AND METHODS

The study of medieval numismatics in the twentieth century has been basically concerned with five main topics, one purely numismatic and the others merging into monetary history. The purely specialist subject is numismatic chronology, the effort to date and localize coins more precisely than can be done by the simple reading of their inscriptions. Two of the others, coin metrology and metallic fineness, represent extensions of what we can learn about coins from superficial examination through the study of those features which mainly determined their value. The third and fourth, mint output and the behavior of coins in circulation, are extensions of our knowledge of coinage as distinct from our knowledge of coins.

Dating and Localization

Medieval coins, by and large, are undated, though there are exceptions. Many Byzantine copper coins, from the twelfth year of Justinian (A.D. 538/39) to the early eighth century, are dated by the regnal year of the reigning emperor, and a fair number of late medieval coins of the Lower Rhineland, beginning with Aachen in 1372, are dated by the Year of the Incarnation. There are also isolated cases of dating in between, and there are occasional coins which can be dated, either precisely or approximately, by references in type or inscription. But in general, if we have a coin bearing the name of a medieval sovereign, there is nothing about it to show at what point in his reign it was struck, and his reign may have been a long one. The problem can be aggravated by a variety of circumstances: when several rulers of the same name succeeded each other, as with William I and II of England (1066–1100), Edward I–III of England (1272– 1377), John I–III of Brabant (1268–1355); when the name of a ruler is immobilized on coins for many years after his death, as happened to those of Carolingian kings in many feudal mints in France; when there is no reference to a ruler but only the name or symbol of a city or other minting authority, which may be carried on unchanged not merely over decades but over centuries; when the type bears no formal identification of ruler or mint at all, as was the case with most Anglo-Saxon and Frisian coins of the late seventh and early eighth centuries. Since the dates and mints of coins are matters with which the numismatist is directly concerned, he has in such cases to resort to other ways of ascertaining them.

The means that are used depend on circumstances. Mints have occasionally indulged in the bad practice of what is known as overstriking, that is, of using old coins as blanks instead of melting them down and preparing fresh flans. When the impression of an earlier striking can be identified with certainty, the scholar is provided with an easy and certain method of determining the chronological order of the types. It was in this fashion that Alfred R. Bellinger in the 1920s, on the basis of the huge numbers of such coins found in the American excavations at Corinth, determined the relative chronology of the so-called Anonymous folles struck in the Byzantine Empire from 970 to 1092, something done only very inadequately by Warwick Wroth in his catalog of the Byzantine coins in the British Museum (Bellinger 1928). The evidence of overstriking has also been used to disprove Arthur Sambon's elaborate attribution of Salernitan folles to a series of princes from Gisulf I (946–77) to Gisulf II (1052–77), since the relative chronology of the coins can be established by their mutual overstriking, and the earliest of them are found overstruck on Byzantine folles of the 1050s. Therefore the entire series must have been struck by, or be contemporary with, Gisulf II and Robert Guiscard (1077–85) (Grierson 1956, 1972).

A more generally useful guide to dating is the evidence of hoards. The order of issue of the eleven coin types of Edward the Confessor and the thirteen of William the Conqueror and William Rufus has basically been determined by a comparison of the contents of overlapping hoards. It is indeed a tribute to advancing technique that while H. A. Grueber in vol. 2 of the catalog of Anglo-Saxon coins in the British Museum, which dates from 1893, arranged Edward the Confessor's coins in no very rational sequence nor always properly distinguished the issues, G. C. Brooke found no difficulty in determining the order of the coins of the two Williams when he published the corresponding catalog of those of the Norman kings in 1916. The evidence for the reign of Edward the Confessor is of particular interest, since it shows how easily a priori reasoning can mislead. The early coins of the king weigh on an average ca. 16 grains, like those of his predecessors, while the coins of his later years weigh about 20 grains apart from one issue, which for some unknown reason reverted to ca. 16 grains. If it were not for the evidence of the hoards, and one had only metrological considerations to guide one, this late class would almost certainly have been put with the other light coins early in the reign, despite the problems over the sequence of moneyers this would involve. It is true that hoard evidence cannot always be accepted at its face value and has to be critically evaluated, for individual hoards may, by their original owners' choice, have only included heavy or light coins, or coins of some particular type, or they may have become accidentally or even deliberately salted with material they did not originally contain, but in this case there is sufficient evidence from a number of hoards to prove the case.

Dating and localization on the evidence of style is also common. If a group of coins of the same or related types is examined carefully, it is often possible to divide them into distinct stylistic groups, and within each group it may be found that several coins were struck by the same obverse or reverse die. In the past century the possibility of die linkages was not always realized, partly because many fewer coins were available for study and partly because of the difficulty of comparing material in different collections; it was indeed at one time widely assumed that all die-linked coins must be modern counterfeits. Scholars therefore tended to stop short at the level of style. Stylistic arguments, however, usually involving assumptions about stylistic evolution which may be true over long periods but are not always so over short ones, proved an irresistible attraction. The principles were set out by Barclay Head, one of the most distinguished numismatists of his generation, in an epoch-making article (Head 1874), and were most conspicuously used in the study of ancient Greek coins, partly because information about hoards or other circumstances of finding was rarely available in this series, and partly because classical scholars with a penchant for art history rarely suffered from any lack of confidence in the reliability of their *Stilgefühl*. The weakness of reliance on style alone became apparent when it came to be tested against the more objective evidence of die study. It was revealed, for example, how in some Greek series two or more obverses markedly different in style, and "therefore" dated several decades apart, might on occasion share the same reverse die or vice versa, for die linkages of this kind are usually good evidence of coins having been struck at about the same time (Ravel 1945).

Stylistic reasoning, just when it was becoming discredited, or at least going out of fashion, elsewhere, has in recent years enjoyed a rather odd vogue amongst students of medieval coinage. It is, within its limits, a perfectly legitimate technique. Many coin issues are stylistically extremely uniform, for in a well-organized mint the dies would probably all be made by the same workman, and uniformity would result from frequent repetition. But breaches of continuity can occur — a die-sinker may vary his work because of illness or to relieve boredom or because he is told to do so, or he may be temporarily replaced, or dies may be imported from outside — and the obvious conclusions to be drawn from die similarities or differences are not necessarily the correct ones (Stewart 1969). The pseudo-imperial tremisses struck by the Visigoths in the sixth century can be broken down into a number of well-marked stylistic groups, which on a meager basis of find records, lavishly reinforced by conjecture, have been attributed to different regions and even mints in Spain (Tomasini 1964). But if one applied the same reasoning to a number of Merovingian coins of the seventh century bearing a royal bust of a very distinctive type and style, all or most of these would be assigned to a single mint, when in fact we know from the inscriptions on the coins that they were struck by different moneyers at nearly twenty localities in northeastern Gaul, from Maastricht and Cologne in the north to Strasbourg in the southeast (Bauer 1951). The explanation here is probably that the dies were cut by an itinerant die-sinker who worked for the moneyers in a number of places, but in other circumstances it might be different. The stylistic groupings found in late tenth-century Anglo-Saxon coins, for example, are better explained on the supposition that the dies were made at one place, or at a few places, and distributed on a regional basis. In both cases, if the coins had been without inscriptions, stylistic considerations alone would have resulted in quite incorrect ideas on their mint attributions.

The study of die relationships is in fact greatly to be preferred to that of style in the grouping of coins, but for many medieval series it is possible to go further, and study punches and letter forms as well. The reason is that the lettering and design on medieval dies were in varying degrees made by punches, while ancient dies were cut almost entirely by graving tools. Medieval coins struck by different dies can therefore have elements in their designs which not merely resemble but are identical with each other, and since the punches used would wear out or break at different intervals and have to be replaced, it is sometimes possible to follow, on a series of coins, the sequence of replacements and the ways in which the new punches differed from the old.

The result is, in favourable circumstances, a wonderful tool for the study of virtually uniform coin series. Its value was perhaps most successfully displayed by the Fox brothers' and Lawrence's studies of the coinage of the three Edwards struck between 1279 and 1377 (Fox and Shirley-Fox 1909–13; Shirley-Fox 1928; Lawrence 1926–33), and, though not quite so satisfactorily, in Lawrence's analysis of the "short-cross" coinage struck in England in the name of *Henricus rex* from 1180 to 1247 (Lawrence 1915). The latter, for example, can be divided into eight classes following each other chronologically, each class having certain stylistic features but the main identifications being based on the gradual evolution of letter forms, with six forms of the lowercase H, seven of E, seven of R, six of C, and so on. The same method can be applied to the analysis of coin series over shorter periods, as for example in the so-called Tealby coinage of Henry II, struck over the two decades 1158–80, with a series of slightly changing designs of the royal bust which can be divided into six main classes distinguished by the changing forms of the crown, the different details of the royal mantle, the initial absense of hair and the subsequent introduction and growing complexity of a curl over the king's left ear, and so on, the order being determined partly by typological considerations and partly by hoard evidence (Allen 1951, xxi–xli, lx–lxxiv).

To establish the order of issue without any uniform coin series is a very considerable achievement, but it cannot be credibly transformed into precise dating without the use of other kinds of evidence. These may take various forms, such as the existence of hoards containing firmly dated coins in other series, or the copying of details elsewhere, or written records, of which the last is by far the most valuable. Five of the six varieties in the "Tealby" series seems to represent consecutive issues, but they can only be dated approximately, mainly to three- or four-year periods (1158–ca. 1161, ca. 1161–ca. 1165, etc.). The dating of the short-cross series consists equally of such approximations except for Class V, where a sudden transition from extremely rough work, with a grotesque royal head, to a new coinage neater in workmanship and altogether superior in style, can be attributed to a recoinage which is known from the Patent Rolls to have been ordered by King John in 1205. Approximations in uniform series are in any case all that we can expect, for there would have been no precise dates; the small changes involved did not normally come about through the withdrawal of the dies of one variety and their replacement by those of another, but rather with the gradual wearing out of dies and punches and their replacement by others sufficiently different, in the numismatist's eye, to constitute a new variety. Where changes in type are involved, however, there should be precise dates, for the changes will usually have been made in response to instructions from higher authority, but what the dates were may be difficult to ascertain. Those of the issues of Ethelred II, for example, depend on assumptions regarding the periods for which each issue was allowed to run, a matter which at the time of writing cannot be regarded as certain. When regular periodicity was not the rule we are often in great doubt, since minting, where it is documented, is known to have been highly irregular, with huge fluctuations from one year to another, and the factors governing these are still imperfectly understood. There are also some coin series in which the stylistic and typological changes are so slight that precise dating appears a hopeless enterprise, though this is a conclusion which numismatists are naturally reluctant to accept.

Metrology

The value of coins to contemporary users depended mainly on their metallic content, which is in turn a function of their weight and fineness. Nineteenth-century numismatic monographs normally, and rightly, devoted considerable attention to weights, but coin catalog and hoard descriptions frequently omitted those of individual specimens. This was partly because the weights of worn coins were thought to be of no interest or value, and partly because of the time and labour involved in weighing hundreds and even thousands of coins at a time when weights had to be manipulated manually. Today, in any well-equipped coin room, electric balances with efficient dampers are in general use, so that coin weights can be ascertained quickly and accurately. Small museums and private collectors, however, still often find themselves in difficulties. Hoards, though not usually collections, often continue to be published without any recording of the weights, since, at least when theoretical weights are known from documents, those of individual specimens may not seem greatly to matter.

This is sometimes true, as for example in the case of badly corroded coins from excavation finds, but the weights of worn coins in hoards may help to determine the date of burial, and the weights of unworn ones have a role to play in determining the theoretical weights to which coins were originally struck. It is true that wear can at best provide only a rough guide to dating, since researches carried out by modern mints show that its rate varies in a quite unpredictable manner, not being directly correlated to either the sizes of the coins or the relative relief of their designs, but depending on the extent to which particular denominations are used (Grierson 1963). An average figure, for a coin in active circulation, would seem to be about 0.2 percent of its weight per annum, but since for some denominations it will be half or double this, the occasional attempts by scholars to date hoards precisely on the evidence of wear (e.g., Dolley and Seaby 1968) do not carry conviction.

For periods earlier than the late thirteenth century, in any case, the absence of mint documents leaves the weights of actual specimens our only guide to the theoretical weights to which they were struck. When the coins are rare their weights can serve as nothing more than a rough indication, but where the coins are plentiful their weights can be plotted in a frequency table, which will normally show whether or not they form a homogeneous group and where the theoretical weight is likely to fall. Correspondence with the theoretical weight will be much closer for gold coins and the higher denominations of silver, which were normally struck *al pezzo,* that is, with the weights of individual coins checked before issue, than for lower denominations, which were often struck *al marco,* that is, so many pieces to the mark or pound, with a substantial tolerance of variation on either side of the average. But while the mode of the weights of any group of coins ascertained in this fashion is likely to approach the theoretical weight, it will not be identical with it, since allowance for wear has to be made. As this can be only roughly estimated and not precisely computed, it is not worth analyzing the frequency curve in too recondite a fashion in the hope of arriving at a highly precise figure, as mathematically minded numismatists are somewhat prone to do. Comparisons of figures derived from the actual specimens of late medieval English gold coins with their theoretical weights as known from documents show a discrepancy of about 1 percent. This may seem high in the light of an annual loss for wear of about 0.2 percent or less, but there will always have been a tendency for heavy specimens to be withdrawn for melting, and although the coins probably came mainly from hoards, they will nonetheless have been slightly worn. Allowances for silver would be larger, but it is impossible to propose any exact figure. The numismatist has to make the best estimate he can in the light of the type and quality of the material with which he is working.

Coin Fineness

The study of coin fineness is a necessary complement to that of metrology, but it is a subject that nineteenth-century numismatists tended to sidestep. Coins could not be analyzed as easily as they could be weighed. For gold coins there was the touchstone, but this had already fallen out of common use, and although a practiced operator could get very accurate results with it, numismatists were in general suspicious of its reliability. There was also the specific gravity method, but this required very accurate balances and some degree of skill, besides giving limiting figures and not precise ones if copper as well as silver was believed to be present in the alloy. Neither method could be applied to silver coins, since the "streaks" of different silver alloys on the touchstone are not clearly distinguishable and the specific gravities of silver and copper are very close to each other, instead of being widely separated as are those of silver and gold. Chemical analysis was only rarely attempted, since it likewise involved specialized knowledge and apparatus. Coin owners were also naturally reluctant to accept the damage it involved to often quite valuable objects. The inability to measure the fineness of silver was particularly unfortunate, for debasement of the penny was normal in many countries between the eleventh and the thirteenth centuries and information about it was highly desirable. Such knowledge was also sometimes necessary for the correct identification of denominations from the later Middle Ages, for there were mints which preferred to differentiate between these by changes in fineness, which are often imperceptible to the eye, than by changes in weight. The double briquet, a large silver coin of Charles the Bold, weighed 3.06 g., exactly the same as the simple briquet worth half as much, but it was twice as fine, 798/1000 as against 399/1000.

This is a field in which much progress has been made in recent years. It was the subject of a conference held in London in December 1970, under the auspices of the Royal Numismatic Society, and the substantial volume containing its proceedings included not merely a number of important papers on individual topics but also a comprehensive survey, by D. M. Metcalf, of all analyses of medieval coins published up to that time. The touchstone has by now dropped out completely, but the specific gravity method, using refined techniques and methods of calculation, is regularly used for gold and has been applied to several medieval series: to pseudoimperial coinages struck by the Germanic invaders of the Roman Empire in the fifth and sixth centuries; to the Frankish coinage of the seventh and Lombard coinage of the seventh–ninth centuries; to a study of the debasement of the Byzantine nomisma in the eleventh century; to the history of the hyperpyron and other denominations from 1092 onwards; to the Sicilian tari of the Normans and Hohenstaufen. Other nondestructive methods have been devised, such as X-ray crystallography, X-ray spectrometry, and neutron activation analysis, while methods which would be regarded as unacceptable for modern coins, notably microchemical analysis and ocular spectrometry, have been refined to the point at which for many medieval coins they can be admitted. Although they do some damage to a coin, it is usually possible to find points on the edge, or in the interior of cracks, where the cleaning of the surface and the subsequent sparking, or the removal of small quantities of material from the interior by a milliprobe, will leave barely perceptible traces.

Nearly all of these new methods suffer some disadvantages. Since they involve a high degree of technical skill and knowledge, and access to specialized and costly apparatus, they require the collaboration of scientists with numismatists who both know what information they want and can make available the coins whose analysis is needed. Nondestructive methods other than specific gravity determinations and neutron activation analysis take account only of samples of the surface, and these are not likely to be representative of the composition of the coin as a whole. Thus results given by different methods do not always coincide, and numismatists, one suspects, have sometimes put their money on the wrong horse, either because particular results fitted in better with their preconceptions or because they were impressed by the more precise figures resulting from some particular method, forgetting that precision and accuracy are not interchangeable terms and that not every result can be usefully expressed to several places of decimals. Relatively few systematic studies of silver and billon coins, apart from one of outstanding merit on royal and feudal deniers in the time of Philip Augustus (Dumas and Barrandon 1982), have as yet been undertaken. But the field is one in which more progress has been made in the last few decades than in the whole of the preceding century, and great advances in our methods and knowledge can be expected in the future.

Mint Output

Calculations of varying reliability regarding mint output now proliferate in numismatic publications. When they are trustworthy they are of considerable interest to the historian, though more by throwing light on the resources of governments than through any contribution they can make to economic history, since the absence of reliable figures for population and for incomes and their distribution, and information on velocity of circulation, makes it difficult to know how to interpret them. Up to quite recent times it was assumed that no such calculations would ever be possible, and that except for such happy survivals as that of a treasury inscription at Delphi that includes minting figures we would forever remain ignorant of coin output prior to the beginning of mint records in the thirteenth century. Now they are deduced from estimates of the numbers of dies used in minting, and in some circumstances result in figures that the historian is likely to accept as trustworthy.

Probable totals for the numbers of dies used for any coin issue can be reckoned, often within a rather large margin of error, from the number of observed die duplicates in any random sample of a coinage. This is a matter for the statistician, and various formulae have been devised for working it out. The most useful is a formula and table prepared by C. S. S. Lyon (1965), a numismatist who is by training a mathematician and by profession an actuary, but a number of different formulae exist of varying applicability and use (Esty 1986). Observation of the number of die duplicates gives one the number of dies represented in the sample, and from this one can calculate the limits within which there is a 95 percent chance that the total of dies used in the issue — or, if the sample comes from a hoard, from as much of the issue as was struck before its burial — should fall. Where one is dealing with the output of a single moneyer and issue in an Anglo-Saxon mint the total number of dies will be quite small and can be fairly closely calculated, but where a large mint is involved one can expect to find only a few die-links in a sample, which will result in the limiting figures being very wide apart indeed.

Figures arrived at in this way will provide some idea of the relative sizes of different issues. To convert them into mint output, they have to be multiplied by the average number of coins which an obverse or reverse die is likely to have struck. The most generally used multiple, for reverse dies, is 10,000, for which there seems to be good evidence. A London scholar has shown the possibility, by actual experiment, of striking at least 8,000 heavy silver coins in high relief with a modern replica of a pair of ancient Greek dies (Sellwood 1963). His first upper die broke after striking 116 coins, his second after 1,490 coins, and his third became unusable, through shortening, after 7,786 coins. Figures for die capacity in English mints in the late thirteenth and early fourteenth century, where we know the number of dies supplied and the value and approximate numbers of coins struck in given periods of time, work out at 10,000/15,000 or about twice this, and occasionally even larger figures, for the obverse dies (Stewart 1963, 1964; Mate 1969). Where one is dealing with a large mint of the later Middle Ages, working with adequate supplies of bullion and striking silver coins in low relief about 17 mm. in diameter, a figure of 10,000 is probably the best one to use.

It is here that the difficulty comes, for neither this nor any other "average" can properly be applied to other historical periods without taking account of different circumstances. D. M. Metcalf, who has written extensively in this field, has at various times ascribed to Offa of Mercia a mint output of 40 million pennies (Metcalf 1963, with subsequent controversy in *NCirc* 71 (1963): 114–15, 165–77; 72 (1964): 23, to the Byzantine Emperor Leo V an output of between 2 and 13 million copper folles (Metcalf 1967), and so on. That mint output of this order of magnitude is not in itself impossible is shown by some late medieval figures known from mint documents: e.g., over 28 million coins struck at the two mints of London and Canterbury in the two years between Sept. 1281 and Oct. 1283, and over 15 million between Oct. 1283 and May 1285. But modern mint reports show that die/coin ratios are greatly affected by the size, weight, and metal of the coins, and this must have been even more true when coins were struck by hand with dies of much more variable quality. Figures valid for English thirteenth-century pennies are quite inapplicable to Byzantine folles, sometimes ten times as heavy, three times as large in area, struck in substantially higher relief, and of copper and not silver. Minting conditions in thirteenth-century England, where large numbers of dies were striking the same types and one can reasonably assume that each was used to capacity, must also have been quite different from those in the workshops of Offa's moneyers, each disposing of only small quantities of silver and changing their coin designs frequently, so that there is no presumption that a die remained in use till it was worn out and only then replaced by another. One must also ask why Offa's coinage is not commoner today if it was once so plentiful, and why there are no recorded Offa hoards. Statistics cut both ways, and if late medieval English coins have managed to survive in large numbers, the same should be true of eighth-century ones.

Quite apart from the uncertainty of the multiplier, the conclusions of scholars working in this field must be treated with reserve if the material involved is of such a nature as to make die identification exceptionally difficult, as is the case with badly struck or poorly preserved coins, and indeed with extremely uniform ones, for even small errors in die identification will be enormously magnified when probable totals come to be worked out. An Italian scholar, on the basis of a large hoard published in 1937 by Bertelè, has reckoned that during the minority of the Emperor John

V (1341–47) the Byzantine mint struck just over 5 million silver coins bearing the name of the Empress-Regent Anna of Savoy (Brunetti 1963). If his initial die observations were correct his total would be much too small, as he supposed that an obverse die would strike only 2,800 coins, and, since the coins are the same size as English sterlings and would have been struck under much the same conditions, one can fairly assume a multiplier of 15,000 per obverse die and put the total issue at between 30 and 40 million. In this case, once again, one must ask why only some 250 specimens, most if not all from a single hoard, have managed to survive. The error here lies in the initial estimate of 197 obverse and 200 reverse dies out of a total of 206 legible coins. Brunetti worked from photographs, not from the original coins, and an examination of the latter, now at Dumbarton Oaks, makes it clear that the number of die duplicates is far larger, and consequently the total of dies used for the coinage far smaller, than he believed.

Coins in Circulation

The study of coinage in circulation involves a number of topics: the variations in its volume, its distribution through different classes in society, the particular functions it served, its longevity, its relationships to the coinages of other countries, its area of circulation, and so on. Some of these topics can be handled better by economic historians than by numismatists, but to virtually all of them numismatics has substantial contributions to make.

Variations in the volume of coinage are determined partly by levels of mint output and partly by losses through export or hoarding, phenomena not unrelated to each other. The monetary literature of the later Middle Ages is full of the laments of merchants on the dearth of coin, and scholars have recently developed a lively interest in this and related phenomena. Before it is possible to advance further, however, some study must be devoted to the factors governing mint output. It is often assumed that a large and regular mint output is normal, and any decline a symptom of economic malaise. One may doubt if this is really the case. Coins are neither consumed like food nor quickly worn out like clothing; once made, they will normally remain in use for considerable periods of time. The model of minting activity, in a closed and stable economy, would, one imagines, involve three phases: (1) a phase of intense mint output, in which an old coinage was withdrawn and a new one put into circulation; (2) a phase of virtual stagnation, when the amount already struck remained sufficient for the needs of commerce and little or no renewal was required, and (3) a period of limited but steady activity, as more and more coins were lost or became worn to the point of unacceptability and had to be replaced. Finally it would be thought necessary to scrap the "new" coinage altogether and replace it by a fresh one. No doubt the limited reminting in the third phase, and some presumably in the second, would proceed by fits and starts, as reluctant moneyers, profitably engaged in other activities, were from time to time recalled to their duties.

Economies, however, to adapt an epigram of Oscar Wilde, are rarely closed and never stable, and figures for mint output, when they are available, usually show only the initial phase of intense minting that one would expect. Thereafter they fluctuate greatly from year to year, as mint output does today. Loss of coin was in many cases important, though the contention of C. C. Patterson (1972) that silver coin is at all periods irrecoverably "lost" at an annual rate of 2 percent, so that coin stocks have a half-life of only 35 years, is certainly unproven and indeed altogether improbable. Mint supplies, coming partly from newly mined ores, partly from domestic plate and bullion, partly from imported metal, coined or otherwise, and partly from old domestic coin, vary greatly according to circumstances. Fresh metal may suddenly become available in quantity through new discoveries; warfare and the taxation that accompanies it result in the melting of plate and other forms of dethesaurization; economic and, even more, political events — subventions to allies, payments of tributes or ransoms (Richard Coeur de Lion, John II of France) — affect the flow of metal across political frontiers. The high level of English mint activity in the years 1300–1301, which supplied us with some of the die-capacity figures discussed above, was due to a sustained attempt to rid the country of debased continental imitations of the sterling by converting them into regular coin. There is a large range of potential factors, but how they will affect mint output and the circulating medium under varying conditions has still to be worked out.

The distribution of coin, in the sense of its ownership and use amongst different social classes, can never be precisely known, but something of its function in society can be inferred from the denominations struck. One can usefully speculate on the role of gift exchange in early medieval society, when for a time only gold was minted and no silver or copper coins existed; on the significance of the introduction of the silver penny (Grierson 1959, 1961b, 69–70; Duby 1974, 48ff.; *contra,* Metcalf 1967); on the roles of "petty" and large coins in the later Middle Ages; on that of copper or lead tokens, which were effectively sub-coinages, in the same period (Courtenay 1972–73, and for a recent discovery Dolley and Seaby 1971). Coin longevity is particularly important in view of the widespread practice of regular *renovationes monetae* in many parts of Europe. This involved the reminting of the whole of the coinage at regular intervals, such as six or three years, or even one year—there is one particularly flagrant case of six months—and was customary over large areas of Germany and neighboring countries in the twelfth and thirteenth centuries and in England from the reign of Ethelred II to that of Stephen (Suchodolski 1961). Its mechanism and its economic implications are still imperfectly explored, as are some of its occasional vagaries, for example, the practice at Merseburg in the thirteenth century of gradually reducing the weights of the pennies struck in the course of each year, apparently in anticipation of their recall on the Nativity of the Virgin (8 Sept.). Between this festival and Martinmas (11 Nov.) 300 pennies were to be struck to the mark, between Martinmas and Christmas 312, between Christmas and Candlemas (2 Feb.) 324, and so on. The dies were to be broken on 15 August, but the old pennies could still be used up to 8 September (Jesse 1924, no. 127). All of these are aspects of medieval numismatics on which work is being done, or is likely to be done in the future.

A topic which interested few nineteenth-century scholars but in recent years has been much studied is the distribution of coinage. The new interest is oddly parallel to the similar development in natural history, where ecology and attendant disciplines now preempt the roles played in the nineteenth century by descriptive morphology and by the search for and classification of new species. It was recognized, of course, that certain coins, like the English sterling and the Florentine florin, had an international circulation, and the imitations to which these gave rise were carefully listed and studied, but the domestic circulation of coin, and the economic implications of international coinages, were neglected. Now these have come to the fore. One may instance the studies to which the great coin finds of Scandinavia, ranging from late Roman gold solidi of the fifth and sixth centuries (Fagerlie 1967; Kyhberg 1986) to Muslim, German, and English silver coins of the tenth and eleventh, have given rise. The late N. L. Rasmusson, curator of the Swedish National Collection, inaugurated a series of detailed papers under the title of *Commentationes de nummis saeculorum IX–XI in Suecia repertis* (Stockholm, 1961ff.) intended to prepare the way for their eventual publication and later study. In addition to innumerable studies of detail, which have involved the rewriting of much of the numismatic history of Germany and England during these centuries, this field of research has resulted in one stupendous monograph, Gert Hatz's *Handel und Verkehr zwischen dem Deutschen Reich und Schweden in der späten Wikingerzeit* (Lund, 1974), one of the most impressive works on the borderland between numismatics and economic history to have appeared in the last half-century. Other scholars in similar fields have allowed their enthusiasm to outrun their judgment. One may instance Maurice Lombard's essay (1947) on the use of Muslim coinage in Latin Christendom based on virtually no evidence at all, for while Muslim coins sometimes reached the West (Duplessy 1956) they never played more than a marginal role in its economy. More valuable has been the study in Germany of the regional pennies of the feudal period. Scholars prior to the 1930s had produced a number of important regional studies – Julius Cahn's monographs on the Rappenmünzbund (1901) and the coinage of the lands around Lake Constance (1911), and Wilhelm Jesse's on the Wendische Münzverein (1928) in the north – but a new era opened with the publication of Walter Hävernick's study (1931) of the Cologne penny in the twelfth and thirteenth centuries, the first of a series making full use of hoard material and records of single coin finds as well as of written documents, and integrating the results in their geographical and economic settings. Circumstances postponed the exploitation of these new techniques until the postwar period, when the publication of a long series of monographs and shorter studies by such scholars as Peter Berghaus, Gert Hatz, Vera Hatz, Wolfgang Hess, and others, most of them Hävernick's pupils, have provided models which one hopes will in due course be followed elsewhere.

NUMISMATICS AND THE HISTORIAN

Numismatics is a legitimate branch of study in its own right, but it is also an auxiliary science of history, and the preceding section has indicated some of the services it can render to the economic historian. Its possible usefulness to other historians is no less important. Since the minting of coin is an activity of the state, the way it is organized, and the types and inscriptions employed are all potentially of interest to the student of political institutions. The reestablishment of royal control over Frankish coinage by Pepin and Charlemagne is one aspect of the re-creation of effective government in western Europe in the eighth century; the discovery of how efficiently minting was organized in the late Anglo-Saxon period contributed greatly to a very necessary reassessment of the quality of government in pre-Conquest England. Nor are its services confined to general themes. The form of the fluttering tails of the imperial diadem on solidi struck in the name of Julius Nepos enabled J. P. C. Kent to show that Odovacar complied with Zeno's injunction to recognize Nepos as Emperor in the West after the deposition of Romulus Augustulus, thus explaining the puzzling references in our literary sources to Odovacar having taken steps to avenge Nepos's murder (Kent 1966). The redating of some early papal coins, on the basis of hoard evidence, from Leo VIII (963–65) to Leo III (795–816) showed what denari the earlier pope was minting between 795 and 800, thus throwing new light on the constitutional consequences for the city of Rome of Charlemagne's coronation (Grierson 1952). Numismatics can aid the historian of art and literature partly because coins are often fairly closely dateable, which is not usually the case for statues or paintings nor sometimes for works of literature, and partly because many coins are themselves works of art. Even a cursory examination of the changing styles of the Byzantine nomisma from the reign of Michael III onwards is sufficient to convince one that the so-called Macedonian Renaissance is something more than a myth, as art historians have recently been tempted to suppose. The coin references in the English adaptation of a French-Flemish conversation manual published by Caxton in 1483 allow one to say with confidence that the translation was made nearly twenty years earlier, in the winter of 1465/66, when the future printer was governor of the "English Nation" at Bruges (Grierson 1957a). One can never, in short, predict when numismatic evidence will not be of use to the historian.

This does not mean that the historian is bound to accept all that the numismatist asserts. Specialists inevitably possess information unknown to the nonspecialist and have acquired skills to which he can lay no claim, but they are neither infallible nor always levelheaded. They may err through simple ignorance, as when a collector published a common Norman-Sicilian coin as an unknown tetarteron of Irene, wife of the Byzantine Emperor Alexius I, and made it the basis for farfetched speculations on the political role of this lady after her husband's death. Or they may err through lack of judgment, as I once did in absolving the Emperor Michael IV from starting the debasement of the nomisma in the eleventh century (Grierson 1961), or through an uncritical faith in the pronouncements of scientists on coin analyses, or in the infallibility of stylistic criteria for mint identification, or in the applicability of statistical methods to virtually anything. Statistics has indeed been much misused in the past few years, since coins, being objects that can be counted and measured in various ways, lend themselves better than many other types of historical material to the present vogue of cliometrics. The historian must in fact exercise his or her critical faculties by trying to understand how numismatists reach their conclusions, and be prepared to reject them if they do not measure up to standards of what is reliable and what is not. But it is equally the historian's duty to recognize that stylistic criteria and statistical methods have their place in numismatics, and that even when numismatists assert something that is not immediately obvious—that long-cross pennies of Henry III having *Henricus rex III* and a bust without a scepter (coins of Lawrence's Class III) can be dated 1248–50 or that a coin bearing the name of Ethelred and ostensibly struck by the moneyer Aescman at the mint of Lincoln was in fact struck in Dublin (Doley 1962)—they may well have good reasons for so doing.

BIBLIOGRAPHY

1. Works Cited in Abbreviated Form in Chapter
(For abbreviations of periodicals, see Section 3 below.)

Allen. 1951. See Section 7h. *Catalogue of English Coins in the British Museum.*

Balaguer, Anna M. 1986. "The use of documentary sources in monetary history." In *Problems of Medieval Coinage in the Iberian Area.* Aviles: N. p. 2:325–35.

Bastian, F. 1935–44. *Das Runtingerbuch 1383–1407 und verwandtes Material zum Regensburger-Südostdeutschen Handel und Münzwesen.* 3 vols. Regensburg: Bosse.

Bauer, Horst-Ulbo. 1951. "Der Triens des Rauchomaros." *Schweizer Münzblätter* 2:96–102.

Bellinger, Alfred R. 1928. *The Anonymous Byzantine Bronze Coinage.* Numismatic Notes and Monographs, No. 35. New York: American Numismatic Society.

Bernocchi, Mario. 1974–85. *Le monete della repubblica fiorentina.* 5 vols. Florence: Olschki.

Bisson. 1979. See Section 6a.

Blackburn and Metcalf. 1981. See Section 6c.

Blancard, Louis, ed. 1884–85. *Documents inédits sur le commerce de Marseille au moyen-âge,* 2 vols. Marseilles. N.p.

Blanchet, Adrien. 1891. "Le Livre du changeur Duhamel," *Revue numismatique³* 9:60–86, 165–202.

Brunetti, L. 1963. "Sulla quantità di monete d'argento emesse sotto Anna di Savoia, imperatrice di Bisanzio (1341–1347)." *RIN* 65:143–68.

Chalon, Renier. 1852. *Recherches sur les monnaies des comtes de Hainaut. Suppléments.* Brussels: N.p., 1852.

Ciano, C., ed. 1964. *La "Practica della Mercatura" Datiniana.* Milan: Giuffré.

Cipolla. 1956. See Section 4.

Conti, P. Ginori, ed. 1939. *Constitutum artis monetariorum civitatis Florentie.* Florence: Olschki.

Courtenay, W. J. 1972–73. "Token Coinage in the Administration of Poor Relief During the Later Middle Ages." *Journal of Interdisciplinary History* 3:275–95.

Day, J. 1968. "Le circulation monétaire en Toscane en 1296." *Annales: Économies, Sociétés, Civilisations* 23:1054–66.

Depeyrot, Georges, ed. 1987. *Trésors monétaires du Languedoc et de Gascogne (XIIe et XIIIe siècles).* Toulouse: Association pour la promotion de l'archéologie.

Dickson, T., ed. 1877–1916. *Accounts of the Lord High Treasurer of Scotland* (A.D. 474–1498). 11 vols. Edinburgh: N.p.

Dolley, R. H. M. 1962. "Significant New Die-Links in the Hiberno-Norse Coinage of Dublin." *NCirc* 70:6.

Dolley, R. H. M., and Seaby, W. A. 1968. "A Parcel of Edwardian Shillings in the Ulster Museum," *SCMB:* 161–66.

Dolley, M., and Seaby, W. A. 1971. "A Find of Thirteenth-Century Pewter Tokens from the National Museum Excavations at Winetavern Street, Dublin." *NCirc* 79:446–48.

Dorini, U., and Bertelè, T., eds. 1956. *Il Libro dei Conti di Giacomo Badoer.* Rome: Libreria dello Stato.

Duby, Georges. 1974. *The Early Growth of the European Economy.* Ithaca: Cornell Univ. Press.

Dumas and Berrandon. 1982. See Section 7c.

Duplessy. 1956. See Section 6d.

————. 1985. See Section 7c.

Esty, Warren W. 1986. "Estimation of the Size of a Coinage: a Survey and Comparison of Methods," *NC* 146:185–215.

Evans, Allan, ed. 1936. Francesco Balducci Pegolotti, *La Practica della Mercatura.* Mediaeval Academy of America, Publication No. 24. Cambridge, Mass.

Fabre, P., and Duchesne, L. 1889–1905. *Le Liber Censuum de l'Église romaine.* 2 vols. Paris: N.p.

Fagerlie, Joan M. 1967. *Late Roman and Byzantine Solidi Found in Sweden and Denmark.* Num. Notes and Monographs, No. 157. New York: American Numismatic Society.

Fox, H. B. Earle, and Shirley-Fox, J. 1909–13. "Numismatic History of the Reigns of Edward I, II and III." *BNJ* 6 (1909): 197–212; 7 (1910): 91–142; 8 (1911): 137–48; 9 (1912): 181–206; 10 (1913): 95–123.

Ghetti, B. M. Apollonj, and others. 1951. *Esplorazioni sotto al Confessione di San Pietro in Vaticano seguite negli anni 1940–1949.* 2 vols. Città del Vaticano: N.p.

Göller, E. 1910. *Die Einnahmen der Apostolischen Kammer unter Johann XXII.* Paderborn: Schöningh.

Grierson, Philip. 1951. "'*Oboli de Musc.*'" *English Historical Review* 66:75–81.

————. 1952. "The Coronation of Charlemagne and the Coinage of Pope Leo III," *Revue belge de philologie et d'histoire* 30:825–32.

————. 1956. "The Salernitan Coinage of Gisulf II (1052–77) and Robert Guiscard (1077–85)," *Papers of the British School at Rome* 24:37–59.

————. 1957a. "The Date of the *Livre des Mestiers* and its Derivatives," *Revue belge de philologie et d'histoire* 35:778–83.

————. 1957b. "The Coin List of Pegolotti." In *Studi in onore di Armando Sapori* 1:483–92. Milan: Istituto editoriale cisalpino.

———. 1959. See Section 5b.

———. 1961a. "Notes on the Fineness of the Byzantine Solidus," *Byzantinische Zeitschrift* 54:91-7.

———. 1961b. "La fonction sociale de la monnaie en Angleterre aux VIIe et VIIIe siècles." In *Moneta e scambi nell'alto medioevo,* 341-62. Spoleto: Centro italiano di studi sull'altomedioevo.

———. 1963. "Coin Wear and the Frequency Table," *NC*[7] 13:v-xv.

———. 1967. "Coinage in the Cely Papers." In *Miscellanea mediaevalia in Memoriam Jan Frederik Niermeyer,* 379-404. Groningen: Wolters.

———. 1972. "La cronologia della monetazione salernitana nel secolo XI." *RIN* 74 (1972): 153-65.

———. 1974. "Muslim coins in thirteenth-century England." In *Near Eastern Numismatics, Iconography, Epigraphy and History. Studies in Honor of George C. Miles,* edited by D. K. Kouymjian, 387-91. Syracuse: Syracuse Univ. Press.

Guilhiermoz, P. 1922-26. "Avis sur la question monétaire donnés aux rois Philippe le Hardi, Philippe le Bel, Louis X et Charles IV le Bel." *RN*[4] 25 (1922): 73-80, 173-210; 27 (1924): 109-28; 28 (1925): 90-101, 217-37; 29 (1926): 91-101.

Hall, E. T., and Metcalf, D. M., eds. 1972. *Methods of Chemical and Metallurgical Investigation of Ancient Coinage.* London: Royal Numismatic Society.

Hävernick, Walter. 1931. *Der Kölner Pfennig in 12. and 13. Jahrhundert.* Stuttgart: Kahlhammer.

Head, Barclay V. 1874. "On the Chronological Sequence of the Coins of Syracuse." *NC*[2] 14:1-80.

Hill, David, and Metcalf, D. M. 1984. *Sceattas in England and on the Continent.* The Seventh Oxford Symposium on Coinage and Monetary History. Oxford: BAR British Series 128.

Jensen, J. Steen. 1977. "Kirkegulvsmønter," *Hikuin* 3:295-302.

Johnson, Charles. 1956. *The De Moneta of Nicholas Oresme and English Mint Documents.* Edinburgh: Nelson, 1956.

Kent, J. P. C. 1966. "Julius Nepos and the Fall of the Western Empire." In *Corolla Memoriae Erich Swoboda dedicata,* 146-50. Graz: Böhlaus.

Kyhlberg, Ola. 1986. "Late Roman and Byzantine solidi. An Archaeological Analysis of Coins and Hoards." In *Excavations at Helgö X. Coins, Iron and Gold,* 13-126. Stockholm: N.p.

Lawrence, L. A. 1915. "The Short Cross Coinage 1180-1247." *BNJ* 11:59-100.

———. 1926-33. "The Coinage of Edward III from 1351," *NC*[5] 6 (1926): 417-69; 9 (1929): 106-68; 12 (1932): 66-174; 13 (1933): 15-79.

Lombard. 1947. See Section 6d.

Lyon, C. S. S. 1965. "The Estimation of the Number of Dies Employed in a Coinage." *NCirc* 73:180-1.

Macdonald, George. 1919. "The Mint of Crossraguel Abbey." *NC*[4] 19:269-311.

Mate, Mavis. 1969. "Coin Dies under Edward I and II." *NC*[7] 9:208-18.

Metcalf, D. M. 1963. "Offa's Pence Reconsidered." *Cunobelin. The Yearbook of the British Association of Numismatic Societies,* 44-46, 50.

————. 1967. "How Extensive was the Issue of Folles during the Years 775–820[?]". *Byzantion* 37:302–30.

Orsini, Ignazio. 1760. *Storia delle monete della repubblica fiorentina.* Florence: N.p.

Papadopoli, Nicolò. 1893–1919. *Le Monete di Venezia.* 4 vols. Venice: N.p.

Patterson, C. C. 1972. "Silver Stocks and Losses in Ancient and Mediaeval Times." *Econ. Hist. Rev.* [2] 25:203–35.

Ravel, O. 1945. "The Classification of Greek Coins by Style." *NC*[6] 5:117–24.

Saulcy, Félicien de. 1879–92. *Recueil de documents relatifs à l'histoire des monnaies frappées par les rois de France depuis Philippe II jusqu'à François Ier.* 4 vols. Paris: N.p.

Sawyer. 1971. See Section 6c.

Schäfer, K. H. 1911. *Die Ausgaben der Apostolischen Kammer unter Johann XXII. nebst den Jahresbilanzen von 1316–1375.* Paderborn: Schöningh.

Sellwood, D. G. 1963. "Some Experiments in Greek Minting Techniques." *NC*[7] 3:217–31.

Serning, Inga. 1956. *Lappska offerplatsfynd från järnålder och medeltid i de Svenska Lappmarkerna.* Uppsala: Almqvist and Wiksell.

Shirley-Fox, J. 1928. "The Pennies and Halfpennies of 1344–51," *NC*[5] 8:16–46.

Stewart, I. H. 1963. "Medieval Die Output: Two Calculations for English Mints in the Fourteenth Century." *NC*[7] 3:98–106.

————. 1964. "Second Thoughts on Medieval Die Output." *NC*[7] 4:293–303.

Stewart, Ian H. 1969. "Style in Medieval Coinage." *NC*[7] 9:269–89.

Suchodolski. 1961. See Section 6a.

Thompson. 1956. See Section 7h.

Tomasini, Wallace J. 1964. *The Barbaric Tremissis in Spain and Southern France. Anastasius to Leovigild.* Numismatic Notes and Monographs, No. 152. New York: American Numismatic Society.

Van Gelder, H. Enno. 1958. "Les plus anciens tarifs monétaires illustrés des Pays-Bas," In *Centennial Publication of the American Numismatic Society,* edited by H. Ingholt, 239–72. New York.

2. General Bibliographical Works

Grierson, P. *Bibliographie numismatique.* 2d ed. Brussels: Cercle d'Études numismatiques, 1979.

Clain-Stefanelli, E. E. *Numismatic Bibliography.* Munich: Battenberg-Verlag, 1984.

Dictionary Catalogue of the Library of the American Numismatic Society. 7 vols. Boston: G. K. Hall, 1962. First and Second Supplements, 1962–67, 1968–72. Boston: G. K. Hall, 1968, 1973.

The first of the works listed above is the most useful introduction, since it includes critical notes and is arranged with the historian's interests in mind. The second is a greatly expanded version of the same author's *Select Numismatic Bibliography*

(New York: Stack's, 1965). The A.N.S. catalogue is the most comprehensive, but is without any commentary and can only be consulted in large libraries.

Current publications (books and articles) are listed, with brief summaries, in *Numismatic Literature* (New York: American Numismatic Society, 1947-), now appearing twice a year, but work of recent decades on particular regions and subjects can be more quickly traced in the bibliographical surveys produced for the last three International Numismatic Congresses, as follows:

A Survey of Numismatic Research, 1966-1971. Vol. 2. *Mediaeval and Oriental Numismatics.* Edited by J. Yvon and Helen W. Mitchell Brown. New York: International Numismatic Commission, produced for the New York-Washington congress of September 1973.

A Survey of Numismatic Research 1972-1977. Edited by Robert Carson, Peter Berghaus and Nicholas Lowick. Berne: International Numismatic Commission, produced for the Berne Congress of September 1979.

A Survey of Numismatic Research 1978-1984. Edited by Martin Price, Edward Besly, David MacDowall, Mark Jones and Andrew Oddy. Vol. 1. *Ancient, Mediaeval and Modern Numismatics.* London: International Numismatic Commission, produced for the London congress of September 1986.

A Survey of Numismatic Research 1985-1990. Edited by Tony Hackens, Paul Naster, Maurice Colaert, Raf van Laere, Ghislaine Moucharte, François de Callataÿ, and Véronique van Driessche. 2 vols. Brussels: International Numismatic Commission, produced for the Brussels Congress of September 1991.

3. Current Periodicals

The chief publications, containing what are substantial articles, are marked with an asterisk. The smaller ones are sometimes summaries of papers read to societies, sometimes supplements to dealers' lists, but the short articles and papers in them are often important. Dead periodicals, and periodicals containing little or no medieval material, are omitted. Details about these can be found in the bibliographies noted at the beginning of this bibliography. Standard abbreviations used in virtually all numismatic publications for those most usually cited are noted below.

        *Acta Numismatica. Barcelona, 1971-.
        *Annali (Istituto italiano di Numismatica). Rome, 1954-.
        Berliner Numismatische Zeitschrift. Berlin, 1949-.
        Bollettino del Circolo Numismatico Napoletano. Naples, 1916-.
        *Bollettino di Numismatica. Rome, 1983-.
BNJ   **British Numismatic Journal.* London, 1905-.
BCEN   *Bulletin [du] Cercle d'Études numismatiques.* Brussels, 1964-.
BSFN   *Bulletin de la Société française de numismatique.* Paris, 1946-.
        *Gazette numismatique suisse: alternative title to the *Schweizer Münzblätter* (q.v.).

HBN   *Hamburger Beiträge zur Numismatik. Hamburg, 1947–.
JMP   *Jaarboek [van het Koninklijk Nederlandsch Genootschap] voor Munt-
         en Penningkunde. Amsterdam, 1914–. Continues the Tijdschrift
         of the same society.
JNG   *Jahrbuch für Numismatik und Geldgeschichte. Munich, 1949–.
MN   *Museum Notes (of the American Numismatic Society). New York,
         1945–.
NNA   *Nordisk Numismatisk Arsskrift. Copenhagen, 1936–.
         *Numisma. Madrid, 1951–.
NC   *Numismatic Chronicle. London, 1838–.
NCirc   Numismatic Circular. London, 1892/93–. Originally entitled Spink's
         Numismatic Circular
NNM   *Numismatic Notes and Monographs. New York, 1920–. Separate
         monographs, published by the American Numismatic Society.
         *Numismatický Sborník. Prague, 1953–. Continuation of *Numis-
         maticky Časopis Československý Prague, 1925–52.
NZ   *Numismatische Zeitschrift. Vienna, 1870–.
         Numismatist, The. Wichita, 1888–.
         *Numizmaticheskii Sbornik. Moscow, 1960–.
         *Numizmatikai Közlöny. Budapest, 1902–.
         *Numizmatika i sfragistika. Kiev, 1963–.
         *Nummus. Oporto, 1952–.
RBN   *Revue belge de numismatique. Brussels (originally Tirlemont), 1842–.
RN   *Revue numismatique. Paris, 1836–.
         Revue suisse de numismatique: alternative title to the Schweizerische
         Numismatische Rundschau (q.v.).
RIN   *Rivista italiana di numismatica. Milan, 1888–.
         *Schweizer Münzblätter. Basel, 1949–.
RSN   *Schweizerische Numismatische Rundschau. Berne (originally Geneva),
         1891–.
SCMB   Seaby's Coin and Medal Bulletin. London, 1945–.
         Spink's Numismatic Circular. See Numismatic Circular.
SCN   *Studi şi cercetari de numismatica. Bucharest, 1951–.
         *Travaux [du] Cercle d'Études numismatiques. Brussels, 1964–. Sepa-
         rate monographs.
         *Trudy Gosudarstvennogo Ermitazha. Leningrad, 1945–. Only some
         volumes in this series are devoted to numismatics.
WN   *Wiadomosci Numizmatyczne. Warsaw, 1957–.

4. General Works

Bloch, M. Esquisse d'une histoire monétaire de l'Europe. Paris: Armand Colin,
    1954. Put together from the author's notes after his death.
Carson, R. A. G. Coins, Ancient, Mediaeval and Modern. 2d ed. London: Hutchin-

son, 1970. Large descriptive work, without references. The three-volume paperback printing of 1971 allows one to have European coinage (medieval and
modern) separately.

Cipolla, C. M. *Money, Prices and Civilization in the Mediterranean World from
the 5th to the 17th Century.* Princeton: Princeton Univ. Press, 1956. Brief,
penetrating sketch.

Engel, A., and Serrure, R. *Traité de numismatique du moyen âge.* 3 vols. Paris,
1891–1905. Standard work of reference.

Friedensburg, F. *Münzkunde und Geldgeschichte der Einzelstaaten.* Munich: Oldenbourg, 1928. Brief histories of national coinages.

Grierson, P. *The Coins of Medieval Europe.* London: Seaby, 1991. Outline sketch,
very fully illustrated (enlargements).

———. *Numismatics.* London: Oxford University Press, 1975. General introduction to the subject.

Grierson, P., and M. Blackburn. *Medieval European Coinage, with a Catalogue
of the Coins in the Fitzwilliam Museum Cambridge.* Vol. 1–. Cambridge: Cambridge Univ. Press, 1986–. A projected survey in 13 vols., of which only vol. 1
(see below, Section 7b) has so far appeared.

Jesse, W. *Quellenbuch zur Münz- und Geldgeschichte des Mittelalters.* Brunswick:
Klinkhardt and Biermann, [1968]. Reprint of 1924 ed., with valuable updating.

Porteous, J. *Coins in History. A Survey of Coinage from the Reform of Diocletian
to the Latin Monetary Union.* London: Weidenfeld and Nicolson, 1969. Good
general history, without references.

Spufford, P. "Coinage and Currency." In *Cambridge Economic History of Europe.*
Vol. 3: *Economic Organization and Policies in the Middle Ages,* 576–602. Cambridge: Cambridge Univ. Press, 1963.

———. *Money and its Use in Medieval Europe.* Cambridge: Cambridge Univ.
Press, 1988.

5. Works of Reference

Luschin von Ebengreuth, A. *Allgemeine Münzkunde und Geldgeschichte.* 2d ed.
Munich: Oldenbourg, 1924. Immensely valuable reference book, where one
can find, for example, the weights of the various marks and pounds used in
the Middle Ages set out in tabular form.

Martinori, E. *La Moneta.* Rome: Istituto italiano di numismatica, 1915. General
encyclopaedia, often useful.

Mateu y Llopis, F. *Glosario hispánico di numismatica.* Barcelona: Consejo superior de investigaciones cientificas, 1946. Particularly useful for its references
to coin names in medieval documents, especially those of the Iberian Peninsula and other Mediterranean countries.

Rentzmann, W. *Numismatisches Legenden-Lexicon des Mittelalters und der Neuzeit.* Berlin: N.p., 1865/66. Reprinted, Osnabrück: Biblio, 1969. More useful
for the early Modern period than for the Middle Ages, but the only work where

one can look up a personal name or a place name and find, for example, all rulers named *Johannes* listed together.

――――. *Numismatisches Wappen-Lexicon des Mittelalters und der Neuzeit.* Berlin: N.p., 1876. Reprinted, Düsseldorf: Auktion Schenk, 1965. Useful for the last centuries of the Middle Ages.

Schrötter, F. von, ed. *Wörterbuch der Münzkunde.* Berlin: Walter de Gruyter, 1930. The best encyclopedia of the subject.

6. Topics

Various important aspects of medieval numismatics cannot be fitted into the regional pattern of subsequent sections. The most important are as follows:

a. Minting Activity

Balog, P. "Études numismatiques de l'Egypte musulmane. Périodes fatimite et ayoubite. Nouvelles observations sur la technique du monnayage." *Bull. de l'Institut d'Égypte* 33 (1951): 1–40. Also an earlier article by the same author in ibid. 31 (1949): 95–105.

Bisson, Thomas N. *Conservation of Coinage. Monetary Exploitation and its Restraint in France, Catalonia and Aragon (c.A.D.1000–c.1225).* Oxford: Clarendon Press, 1979.

Cipolla, C. M. "Currency depreciation in Medieval Europe." *Econ. Hist. Rev.*[2] 15 (1963): 413–22.

Lopez, R. S. "An Aristocracy of Money in the Early Middle Ages." *Speculum* 28 (1953): 1–43.

――――. "Continuità e adattamento nel medio evo: un millenio di storia delle associazioni di monetieri nell'Europa meridionale." In *Studi in onore di Gino Luzzatto,* 74–117. Milan: Giuffrè, 1949. Good bibliographical notes.

Sellwood, D. G. "Medieval Monetary Techniques." *BNJ* 31 (1962): 57–65.

Suchodolski, S. "*Renovatio monetae* in Poland in the 12th Century." *Polish Numismatic News* (Supplement to *WM* 5 [1961]: 55–75). Covers more ground than the title suggests.

――――. "Some Problems of the Techniques of Coining in Early Medieval Poland." *WN* 3 (1959): 23–40. In Polish, with English summary.

b. Means of Exchange

Bloch, M. "Economie-nature et économie-argent: un pseudo-dilemme." *Ann. d'hist. écon. et sociale* 5 (1933): 7–16. Repr. in his *Mélanges historiques* (Paris: SEVPEN, 1963), II:868–77.

Dopsch, A. *Naturalwirtschaft und Geldwirtschaft in der Weltgeschichte.* Vienna: Schroll, 1930.

Grierson, P. "Commerce in the Dark Ages: A Critique of the Evidence." *Trans. Roy. Hist. Soc.*[5] 9 (1959): 123-40. Reprinted in *Studies in Economic Anthropology*, edited by G. Dalton, 74-83. New York: Doubleday, 1971.

Sayous, E. *L'Origine de la lettre de change, les procédés de crédit et de paiement dans les pays chrétiens de la Méditerranée occidentale entre le milieu du XIIe et le XIIIe siècle.* Paris: Librairie du Recueil Sirey, 1933.

Spufford, Peter. *Handbook of Medieval Exchange.* London: Royal Historical Society, Guides and Handbooks, no. 13, 1986.

Van Werveke, H. "Monnaies, lingots ou marchandises? Les instruments d'échange au XIe et au XIIe siècle." *Ann. d'hist. écon. et sociale* 4 (1932): 452-68.

————. "Monnaie de compte et monnaie réelle." *Rev. belge de philol. et d'hist.* 13 (1934): 123-52.

c. Viking-Age Hoards

Blackburn, M. A. S., and Metcalf, D. M., eds. *Viking-Age Coinage in the Northern Lands.* The Sixth Oxford Symposium on Coinage and Monetary History. Oxford: BAR International Series 122, 1981.

Commentationes de nummis saeculorum IX-XI in Suecia repertis. Pars I-. Edited by N. L. Rasmusson and L. O. Lagerqvist. Stockholm: Almqvist and Wiksell, 1961-. Studies preparatory to the eventual publication of a *Corpus* (see next entry); two volumes have appeared to date; vol. 1 includes a brief introductory survey by Rasmusson.

Corpus nummorum saeculorum IX-XI qui in Suecia reperti sunt. Vol. I-. Edited by B. Malmer and N. L. Rasmusson. Stockholm: Almqvist & Wiksell, 1975-. Planned for about 30 vols.

Hatz, G. *Handel und Verkehr zwischen dem Deutschen Reich und Schweden in der späten Wikingerzeit.* Die deutschen Münzen des 10. und 11. Jahrhunderts in Schweden. Lund: Kungl. Vitterhets Historie och Antikvitets-akademien, 1974. Contains the fullest bibliography of the further surveys by E. Person (Swedish hoards), M. Stenberger (Gotland hoards), R. Skovmand (Danish hoards), C. A. Nordman (Finnish hoards), H. Holst (Norwegian hoards), and others.

Polskie skarby wczesnosredniowieczne. 4 vols. and index. Warsaw and Wroclaw: Polskie Badania Archeologiczne, vols. 1 (1959), 4 (1959), 10 (1965), 12 (1966): *Atlas:* Polskie Towarzystwo Archeologiczne i Numizmatyczne, 1982.

Sawyer, P. H. *The Age of the Vikings.* 2d ed. London: Arnold, 1971. Contains (pp. 86-119) the best introduction in English.

d. The Role of Muslim Coinage in Europe

Cahen, C. "Quelques problèmes concernant l'expansion économique musulmane au haut moyen âge." *L'Occidente e l'Islam nell'alto medioevo* (Spoleto: Centro di studi sull'alto medioevo, 1965), 391-432, and discussion on pp. 487ff.

Includes bibliographical references to earlier literature by Lombard, Bolin, Grierson, Perroy, Himly, and others.

Duplessy, J. "La circulation des monnaies arabes en Europe occidentale du VIIIe au XIIIe siècle." *RN*⁵ 18 (1956): 101–64. List of finds, showing how few there are prior to the twelfth century.

Lombard, M. "Les bases monétaires d'une suprématie économique: l'or musulman du VIIe au XIIe siècle." *Annales: Écon., Soc., Civil.* 2 (1947): 143–60. Reprinted in his *Espaces et réseaux du haut moyen âge*, 7–29. Paris: Mouton, 1972.

e. Gold and Silver Coinages in the Thirteenth Century

Bloch, M. "Le problème de l'or au moyen-âge." *Ann. d'hist. écon. et sociale* 5 (1933): 1–34. Reprinted in his *Mélanges historiques* 2:839–67. Paris: SEVPEN, 1963.

Grierson, P. "The Origins of the Grosso and of Gold Coinage in Italy." *Numismaticky Sbornik* 12 (1971–72): 33–48. This whole volume, the report of a symposium held in Czechoslovakia in 1970, is relevant.

Lopez, R. S. *Settecento anni fà: il ritorno all'oro nel occidente ducentesco.* Naples: Edizioni scientifiche italiane, 1955. Summarized in "Back to Gold, 1252." *Econ. Hist. Rev.*² 9 (1956): 219–40.

Watson, A. M. "Back to Gold—and Silver." *Econ. Hist. Rev.*² 20 (1967): 1–34.

f. International Coinages

Berghaus, P. "Die Perioden des Sterlings in Westfalen, dem Rheinland und in den Niederlanden." *HBN* 1 (1947): 34–53.

———. "Umlauf und Nachprägung des Florentiner Guldens nördilich der Alpen." In *Congresso internazionale di Numismatica, Roma, 1961* 2 (*Atti*): 595–607. Rome, 1965.

Chautard, J. *Imitations des monnaies au type esterlin frappées en Europe pendant le XIIIe et le XIVe siècles.* 2 pts. Nancy: N.p., 1872.

Dannenberg, H. "Die Goldgulden vom Florentiner Gepräge." *NZ* 12 (1880): 146–85.

Mayhew, N. J. *Sterling Imitations of Edwardian Type.* London: Royal Numismatic Society, 1983.

Nagl, A. "Die Goldwährung und die handelsmässige Geldrechnung im Mittelalter." *NZ* 26 (1894): 41–258.

Rigold, S. E. "The Trail of the Easterlings." *BNJ* 26 (1949): 31–55.

g. Currency Problems

Braudel, F. "Monnaies et civilisations. De l'or du Soudan à l'argent d'Amérique." *Annales: Econ., Soc., Civil.* 1 (1946): 9–22. Largely reproduced in his book, *The Mediterranean and the Ancient World in the Age of Philip II,* 1:462–542.

English translation, London: Collins, 1972. Mainly sixteenth century, but important for the end of medieval conditions.

Cipolla, C. M. "Currency Depreciation in Medieval Europe." *Econ. Hist. Rev.*[2] 15 (1963): 413–22.

Nef, J. U. "Silver production in Central Europe, 1450–1518." *Journal of Political Economy* 49 (1941): 575–91.

Perroy, E. "À l'origine d'une économie contractée: les crises du XIVe siècle." *Annales: Écon., Soc., Civil.* 4 (1949): 167–82.

h. Monetary Theory

Babelon, J. "La théorie féodale de la monnaie." *Mém. de l'Acad. des Inscriptions* 28(i) (1908): 279–347.

Bridrey, M. *La théorie de la monnaie au XIVe siècle. Nicole Oresme.* Paris: Giard et Brière, 1906. With the long, critical review by A. Landry in *Le Moyen Age* 22 (1909): 145–78.

Johnson, C. *The De Moneta of Nicholas Oresme and English Mint Documents.* Edinburgh: Nelson, 1956. Text and translation.

Langholm, Odd. *Wealth and Money in the Aristotelian Tradition: A Study in Scholastic Economic Sources.* Bergen: Universitetsforlaget, 1983.

7. Countries and Regions

This section lists the standard works used for purposes of reference, though it has to be recognized that these are no longer always up to date. It takes account only exceptionally of collectors' handbooks, since while the information in these is often more correct than that in the older works, the explanatory matter that would make them useful to historians is usually lacking. The coinage of Byzantium and of the Dark Ages is most conveniently treated apart from the main regional headings. For each section a much fuller list will be found in my *Bibliographie numismatique,* but this contains nothing later than 1978. It should be noted that even standard works vary substantially in quality from country to country. In some the coinages have been studied in depth, with extensive reference to die analysis and coin distribution, while in others there has been no progress beyond the nineteenth century.

a. Byzantium

Bellinger, A. R., and Grierson, P. *Catalogue of Byzantine Coins in the Dumbarton Oaks Collection and in the Whittemore Collection.* Washington: Dumbarton Oaks Center for Byzantine Studies, 1966–. Vol. 1 (1966) covers 491–602; vol. 2 (1968), 602–717; and vol. 3 (1973), 717–1081. The latter two each contain lengthy introductions. Two further volumes are expected.

Grierson, P. *Byzantine Coins*. London, Berkeley, and Los Angeles: Methuen and Univ. of California Press, 1982. General survey, very fully illustrated.

Hahn, W. *Moneta Imperii Byzantini. Rekonstruktion des Prägeaufbaues auf Synoptisch-tabellarischer Grundlage*. 3 vols. Vienna: Österreichische Akademie der Wissenschaften, 1973–81. Essential work of reference, but covers only 491–720.

Hendy, M. F. *Coinage and Money in the Byzantine Empire 1081–1261*. Washington: Dumbarton Oaks Center for Byzantine Studies, 1969. Supersedes earlier publications for the period it covers.

————. *Studies in the Byzantine Monetary Economy c.300–1450*. Cambridge: Cambridge Univ. Press, 1985.

Morrisson, C. *Catalogue des monnaies byzantines de la Bibliothèque Nationale*. 2 vols. Paris: Bibliothèque nationale, 1970. Ends at 1204; excellent introduction sections.

Morrisson, Cécile, and others. *L'or monnayé. I. Purifications et altérations de Rome à Byzance*. Cahiers Ernest Babelon 2. Paris: Éditions du C.N.R.S., 1985.

Sabatier, J. *Description générale des monnaies byzantines*. 2 vols. Paris: N.p., 1862 (and later reprints).

Wroth, W. *Catalogue of the Imperial Byzantine Coins in the British Museum*. 2 vols. London: British Museum, 1908.

b. Dark Ages

Belfort, A. de *Description générale des monnaies mérovingiennes*. 5 vols. Paris, 1892–95.

Bernareggi, E. *Il sistema economico e la monetazione dei Longobardi nell'Italia superiore*. Milan: Ratto, 1960.

————. "Le monete dei Longobardi nell'Italia Padana e nella Tuscia." *RIN* 65 (1963): 35–142.

Gariel, E. *Les monnaies royales de France sous la race carolingienne*. 2 vols. Strasbourg: N.p., 1883–84.

Grierson, P., and Blackburn, M. *Medieval European Coinage, with a Catalogue of the Coins in the Fitzwilliam Museum, Cambridge*. Vol. 1: *The Early Middle Ages (5th–10th Centuries)*. Cambridge: Cambridge Univ. Press, 1986.

Hill, David, and Metcalf, D. M. *Sceattas in England and on the Continent*. The Seventh Oxford Symposium on Coinage and Monetary History. Oxford: BAR British Series 128, 1984.

Lafaurie, J. "Monnaie en argent trouvée à Fleury-sur-Orne: Essai sur le monnayage d'argent franc des Ve et VIe siècles." *Annales de Normandie* 14 (1964): 173–222. Essential for the silver coinage, which apart from the Cimiez hoard was virtually unknown in the nineteenth century.

Miles, G. C. *The coinage of the Visigoths of Spain: Leovigild to Achila II*. New York: American Numismatic Society, 1952.

Moneta e scambi nell'alto medioevo. Settimane di studi del centro italiano di studi sull'alto medioevo, VIII. Spoleto: Centro di sull'alto medioevo, 1961. Essential collection of studies.

Morrison, K. F., and Grunthal, H. *Carolingian Coinage. NNM* No. 158. New York: American Numismatic Society, 1967.

Prou, M. *Les monnaies carolingiennes.* Cat. des monnaies françaises de la Bibliothèque Nationale. Paris, 1896.

—————. *Les monnaies mérovingiennes.* Cat. des monnaies françaises de la Bibliothèque Nationale. Paris, 1892.

Sutherland, C. H. V. *Anglo-Saxon gold coinage in the light of the Crondall Hoard.* London: Oxford Univ. Press, 1948.

Tomasini, W. H. *The Barbaric Tremissis in Spain and Southern France. Anastasius to Leovigild. NNM* No. 152. New York: American Numismatic Society, 1964.

Wroth, W. *Catalogue of the Coins of the Vandals, Ostrogoths and Lombards . . . in the British Museum.* London: British Museum, 1911.

c. France

Blanchet, A., and Dieudonné, A. *Manuel de numismatique française.* 4 vols. Paris: Picard, 1912–36. Standard work. Vol. 1 covers the Gaulish, Roman, Merovingian, and Carolingian periods; vol. 2, the royal coinage; vol. 3, jettons, tokens, and medals; and vol. 4, feudal coins.

Caron, E. *Monnaies féodales françaises.* Paris: N.p., 1882. Supplement to Poey d'Avant.

Dieudonné. A. *Catalogue des monnaies françaises de la Bibliothèque Nationale. Les monnaies capétiennes.* 2 vols. Paris: Leroux, 1923–32. To 1515.

Dumas, F. "Le debut de l'époque féodale en France d'après les monnaies." *BCEN* 10 (1973): 65–77. Most recent survey of its origins.

Dumas, Françoise, and Barrandon, Jean-Noël. *Le titre et le poids de fin des monnaies sous le règne de Philippe-Auguste (1180–1223).* Cahiers Ernest Babelon 1. Paris: Éditions du C.N.R.S., 1982.

Duplessy, Jean. *Les monnaies françaises royales de Hugues Capet à Louis XVI (987–1793).* Vol. 1 (Hugues Capet – Louis XII). Paris: Platt; Maastricht: Van der Dussen, 1988.

—————. *Les trésors monétaires médiévaux et modernes decouverts en France.* Vol. 1:*751–1223.* Paris: Bibliothèque nationale, 1985.

Lafaurie, J. *Les monnaies des rois de France.* Vol. 1, *Hugues Capet à Louis XII.* Paris: Bourgey and Monnaies et Médailles, S.A., 1951.

Poey d'Avant, F. *Les monnaies féodales de la France.* 3 vols. Paris, 1858–62.

d. Low Countries

There is no work covering the Low Countries as a whole, though they will be the subject of the next volume to appear of Grierson and Blackburn's *Medieval*

European Coinage (above, Section 4). An Oxford Symposium volume, *Coinage in the Low Countries (880–1500),* edited by N. J. Mayhew (BAR International Series 54. Oxford, 1979), is uneven and necessarily selective. The standard works on the principal fiefs are as follows:

Bernays, E., and Vannérus, J. *Histoire monétaire du comté puis duché de Luxembourg et de ses fiefs.* Brussels: Académie royale de Belgique, 1910; supplement 1934.

Chalon, R. *Recherches sur les monnaies des comtes de Hainaut.* Brussels: N.p., 1848; supplements 1852, 1854, 1857, and by A. de Witte in 1891.

Chestret de Haneffe, J. de. *Numismatique de la principauté de Liège.* Brussels: N.p., 1890; supplement Liège, 1900.

Gaillard, V. *Recherches sur les monnaies des comtes de Flandre.* 2d ed. Ghent, 1857. Ends with 1384; it is continued in a series of articles by L. Deschamps de Pas in *RN* (1861, 1862, 1866, 1869, 1874) and *RBN* (1876).

Ghyssens, J. *Les petits deniers de Flandre du XIIe et XIIIe siècles.* Brussels: Cercle d'Études numismatiques, 1971.

Van der Chijs, P. O. *De munten der Nederlanden ven de vroegste tijden tot aan de Pacificatie van Gend '1576).* 9 vols. Haarlem: N.p., 1851–66. The most important vols. are 2 (Guelders), 6 (Holland), and 7 (Utrecht).

Van Gelder, H. F. *De Nederlandse munten.* 7th ed. Utrecht: Aula Boeken, 1980. Brief but authoritative survey.

Van Gelder, H. E., and Hoc, M. *Les monnaies des Pays-Bas bourguignons et espagnols, 1434–1713.* Amsterdam: J. Schulman, 1960.

Weiller, R. *Les monnaies luxembourgeoises.* Numismatica Lovaniensia 2. Louvain-la-Neuve: N.p., 1977.

Witte, A. de. *Histoire monétaire des comtes de Louvain, ducs de Brabant.* 3 vols. Antwerp: N.p., 1894–99.

e. Germany and Austria

No general reference work exists save for the earliest period (Dannenberg). For the coinages and monetary history of individual fiefs, which it is impossible to cover here, see my *Bibliographie,* pp. 138–59.

Berghaus, P. "Die Münzpolitik der deutschen Städte im Mittelalter." In *Finances et comptabilités urbaines du XIIIe au XIVe siècle,* 75–85. Brussels: Pro Civitate, 1964.

Dannenberg, H. *Die deutschen Münzen der sächsischen und fränkischen Kaiserzeit.* 4 vols. and plates. Berlin: N.p., 1876–1905.

Förschner, Gisela. *Deutsche Münzen.* Münzkabinett, Historisches Museum, Frankfurt am Main. Vol. 1. Melsungen: Verlag Gutenberg, 1984–. Only the first volume (Aachen-Augsburg) of the catalogue of this important collection has appeared at the time of writing.

Gaettens, R. *Die Wirtschaftsgebiete und der Wirtschaftsgebietspfennig der Hohen-staufenzeit.* Lübeck: Riechmann, 1963.

Joseph, P. *Goldmünzen des 14. und 15. Jahrhunderts (Disibodenberger Fund).* Frankfurt: N.p., 1882.

Metcalf, D. M. *The Coinage of South Germany in the 13th Century.* London: Spink, 1961.

Suhle, A. *Hohenstaufenzeit im Münzbild.* Munich: Hiersemann, 1963.

———. *Deutsche Münz- und Geldgeschichte von den Anfängen bis zum 15. Jahrhundert.* 2d ed. Munich: Battenberg, 1964. Brief general history, with notes and references.

f. Italy

For Italy, as for Germany, it is impossible to cover individual states; see my *Bibliographie,* pp. 159–69.

Cipolla, C. M. *Le avventure della lira.* Milan: Edizioni di Communità, 1958. Outline history.

Corpus Nummorum Italicorum. Vol. I–XX. Rome: N.p., 1910. Huge reference work, arranged regionally, without explanatory text.

Sambon, G. *Repertorio generale della monete coniate in Italia.* Part 1 (all published). Paris: The Author, 1912. Tabular analysis, requiring revision in detail, but gives a good picture of Italian coinage to the thirteenth century.

g. Spain and Portugal

Batalha Reis, P. *Preçario das moedas portuguesas da 1140 a 1640.* Lisbon: The Author, 1956. Fully illustrated list for collectors, but useful as a guide.

Botet y Sisó, J. *Les monedes catalanes.* 3 vols. Barcelona: Istitut d'Estudis catalans, 1908–11.

Crusafont i Sabater, M. *Numismatica de la Corona Catalano-Aragonesa medieval (795–1516).* Madrid: Editorial Vico, 1982.

Gil Farres, O. *Historia de la moneda española.* 2d ed. Madrid: The Author, 1975.

Heiss, A. *Descripcion general de las monedas hispano-cristianas desde la invasion de los Arabes.* 3 vols. Madrid: N.p., 1865–69. Huge reference work, parts of which are superseded by Botet y Sisó and Mateu y Llopis.

Mateu y Llopis, F. *La ceca di Valencia y las acuñaciones valencianas de los siglos XIII al XVIII.* Valencia: The Author, 1929.

Teixeira de Aragão, A. C. *Descripçao geral e historica das moedas cunhadas em nome dos reis, regentes e governadores de Portugal.* 3 vols. Lisbon: N.p., 1874–80.

Vaz, J. Ferraro. *Numaria medieval portuguesa, 1128–1383.* 2 vols. Lisbon: The Author, 1960. Extravagantly produced but essential commentary.

h. British Isles

Blackburn, M. A. S., ed. *Anglo-Saxon Monetary History. Essays in Memory of Michael Dolley.* Leicester: Leicester Univ. Press, 1986.

Brooke, G. C. *English Coins.* 3d ed., revised by C. A. Whitton. London: Methuen, 1950. Standard reference work.

Catalogue of English Coins in the British Museum:
Keary, C. F., and Grueber, H. A. *Anglo-Saxon Series.* 2 vols. 1887–93.
Brooke, G. C. *The Norman Kings.* 2 vols. 1916.

Allen, D. F. *The Cross-and-Crosslets ("Tealby") Type of Henry II.* 1951.

Cochran-Patrick, R. W. *Records of the Coinage of Scotland.* 2 vols. Edinburgh: N.p., 1876. Archival material.

Dolley, R. H. M. *The Hiberno-Norse Coins in the British Museum.* London: British Museum, 1966. Basic work on the earliest coinage.

———. *Mediaeval Anglo-Irish Coins.* London: Seaby, 1969.

Dowle, A., and Finn, P. *The Guide-Book to the Coinage of Ireland from 995 A.D. to the Present Day.* London: Spink, 1969. For collectors, but with explanatory text and bibliography.

Feavearyear, A. E. *The Pound Sterling. A History of English Money.* 2d ed. London: Oxford Univ. Press, 1963.

Mayhew, N. J., ed. *Edwardian Monetary Affairs (1279-1344).* BAR British Series 36. Oxford, 1977.

North, J. J. *English Hammered Coinage.* 2 vols. 2d ed. London: Spink, 1980, 1975 Excellent work of reference, fully illustrated, but concerned essentially with classification and dating.

Oman, C. *The Coinage of England.* Oxford: Oxford Univ. Press, 1931. Unreliable in detail, but the best general history.

Ruding, R. *Annals of the Coinage.* 3d ed. 3 vols. London: N.p., 1840. Essential references to archive material.

Stewart, I. H. *The Scottish Coinage.* 2d ed. London: Spink, 1967.

Sylloge of Coins of the British Isles. London: British Academy, 1958–. Summary catalogs, technical in character, of material, mainly Anglo-Saxon, in various museums. 40 vols. have been published up to time of writing, and the series continues.

Thompson, J. D. A. *Inventory of British Coin Hoards, A.D. 600-1500,* London: N.p., 1956.

i. Scandinavia

Bendixen, K. *Denmark's Money.* Copenhagen: National Museum of Denmark, 1967; short history in English.

Lagerqvist, L. O. *Svenska mynt under Vikingtid och Medeltid (ca.995-1521) samt Gotländska mynt (ca.1140-1565).* Stockholm: Numismatiska Bokförlaget, 1969. Best descriptive work on Swedish coins.

Mønt. Edited by S. Aakjaer. Nordisk Kultur, 29. Stockholm: Bonniers Förlag, 1936.

Standard work by B. Thordeman, H. Holst, and G. Galster, covering the coinages of Sweden, Norway, and Denmark, respectively.

Schive, C. J. *Norges mynter i middelalderen.* Christiania: N.p., 1865. Standard reference book.

Skaare, K. *Moneta Norwei. Norsk mynt i tusen ar.* Oslo: N.p., 1966. Short history of Norwegian coinage.

j. Eastern and Central Europe

Cach, F. *Nejstaršičeske mincé.* 3 vols. Prague: Ceská Numismatická Spolecnost, 1970–74. Intended to supersede the old standard work of Fiala (1895–98).

Castelin, K. *Grossus Pragensis. Der Prager Groschen und seine Teilstücke, 1300–1547.* 2d ed. Brunswick: Klinghardt and Biermann, 1973. Covers the last two centuries of the Middle Ages, after Turnwald ends.

Gumowski, M. *Handbuch der polnischen Numismatik.* Graz: Akademische Druck- und Verlagsanstalt, 1960. Adaptation of a work published in Polish in 1914, with updated bibliographies and partially revised text.

Kiersnowski, R. *Wstęp do numizmatyki polskiej wieków średnich* (Introduction to medieval Polish numismatics). Warsaw: Panstwowe Wydawnictwo Naukowe, 1964. Standard work in Polish.

Spasskij, I. G. *The Russian Monetary System.* Amsterdam: Schulman, 1967. General history, translated from Russian.

Turnwald, K. *Ceské a moravske denáry a brakteaty.* Československá Spolecnost Prátel Drobné Plastiky, 1949. Reproduces the plates that originally accompanied the standard work of E. Fiala, with corrected attributions and new text, in Czech.

k. Hungary and the Balkans

Ljubić, S. *Opis jugoslavenskih novaca.* Zagreb: N.p., 1875. Many sections are now superseded.

Metcalf, D. M. *Coinage in South-Eastern Europe 820–1396.* London: Royal Numismatic Society, 1979.

Mouchmov, N. A. *Numismatique et sigillographie bulgares.* Sofia: National Museum, 1924.

Réthy, L. *Corpus nummorum Hungariae.* German translation from Hungarian edition of 1899–1907, by G. Probszt. Graz: Akademische Druck- und Verlagsanstalt, 1958.

l. Crusader States

Bates, M. L., and Metcalf, D. M. "Crusader Coinage with Arabic Inscriptions." In *A History of the Crusades,* edited by Kenneth M. Setton, 6:421–82 (Madison: Univ. of Wisconsin Press, 1989.

Metcalf, D. M. *Coinage of the Crusades and the Latin East in the Ashmolean Museum, Oxford.* Royal Numismatic Society, Special Publications, No. 15. London, 1983.

Porteous, J. "Crusader Coinage with Greek or Latin Inscriptions." In *A History of the Crusades,* edited by Kenneth M. Setton, 6:354–420 (Madison: Univ. of Wisconsin Press, 1989.

Schlumberger, G. *Numismatique de l'Orient latin.* Paris: N.p., 1878; supplement, 1882.

m. Other Christian States in the Orient

Bedoukian, P. Z. *Coinage of Cilician Armenia. NNM* No. 147. New York: American Numismatic Society, 1962.

Lang, D. M. *Studies in the Numismatic History of Georgia in Transcaucasia. NNM* No. 130. New York: American Numismatic Society, 1955.

n. Muslim Coins

No general work exists, but those most likely to concern the Western medievalist are as follows:

Balog, P. *The Coinage of the Mamlouk Sultans of Egypt and Syria.* New York: American Numismatic Society, 1964.

Hazard, H. W. *The Numismatic History of Late Medieval North Africa.* New York: American Numismatic Society, 1952.

Hinz, W. *Islamische Masse und Gewichte umgerechnet ins metrische System.* Leyden: Brill, 1955.

Lane-Poole, S. *Catalogue of Oriental Coins in the British Museum.* 10 vols. London, 1875–90. This and Lavoix are the standard works of reference.

Lavoix, H. *Catalogue des monnaies musulmanes de la Bibliothèque nationale.* 3 vols., unfinished. Paris: N.p., 1887–96. Covers the Caliphate (1), Spain and Africa (2), and Egypt and Syria (3).

Sauvaire, H. *Matériaux pour servir à l'histoire de la numismatique et de la métrologie musulmanes.* Paris: N.p., 1882. Very full guide to the written material.

Walker, J. *A Catalogue of the Arab-Byzantine and Post-Reform Umaiyad Coins.* London: British Museum, 1956.

∽ 4 ∾

Archaeology

DAVID WHITEHOUSE

HE LEXICON WEBSTER DICTIONARY defines archaeology as "the science of antiquity, especially prehistoric antiquities, which investigates the history of peoples by the remains belonging to the earliest periods of their existence." Today, most archaeologists describe their discipline more specifically. It is indeed the systematic recovery and study of remains, but of remains in context. Here, "context" has cultural, spatial, chronological, and environmental implications, and in the field the archaeologist is part of a team, which in any given project may include, in addition to the excavators and those responsible for recording what is uncovered (such as surveyors, architects and photographers), geomorphologists and specialists in a dozen laboratory sciences, from radiometric dating to the identification of pollen and microfauna. Similarly, after an excavation, archaeologists studying the artifacts and other finds work with conservators and experts in the analysis and identification of materials as diverse as leather, earthenware and metals.

Medieval archaeology is the application of archaeological techniques to the period which, in the western Mediterranean and Europe, began when the Roman Empire disintegrated. Thus, the statute of the British Society for Medieval Archaeology describes its objective as the "study of unwritten evidences of British history since the Roman period". Few medieval archaeologists, however, would claim that their discipline extends to the present day or even to the end of the preindustrial period; for the majority, as for historians, the Middle Ages ended in, or not long after, the fifteenth century.

This chapter discusses the archaeology of Europe and the western Mediterranean between about 500 and 1500. It pays particular attention to the United Kingdom, and most of the publications cited in the bibliography are in English. However, it also refers to medieval archaeology in other parts of Europe, notably Italy, where the discipline has developed rapidly in the last twenty years.

THE DEVELOPMENT OF MEDIEVAL ARCHAEOLOGY

The roots of all European archaeology lie in the antiquarian studies of Renaissance humanists. In the sixteenth century, popes and other members of aristocratic families in Italy began to collect ancient art and to sponsor excavations to enrich their collections. In the eighteenth century the rediscovery and exploration of the buried cities of Pompeii and Herculaneum led to a more systematic search for classical antiquities. In the following century, classical (and biblical) archaeology was put on a more or less scientific basis by Heinrich Schliemann (1822-90; he excavated at Troy and Mycenae in the 1870s), by Bilotti, Curtius, and Conze, and by Sir Arthur Evans (1851-1941), who began his excavations at Knossos in 1900.

In the same general period, antiquarians also turned their attention to the remains of early Christianity. The first serious study of the Roman catacombs was made by Panvinius, who published *De ritu sepeliendi mortuos apud veteres christianos et de eorumdem coemeteriis* in 1512. Later, Bosio (1576-1629) devoted a lifetime of research to the catacombs; his monumental *Roma sotterranea* was published posthumously in 1632. Meanwhile, in France, de Peiresc assembled a large collection of antiquities, including early Christian sarcophagi from Arles. The first public display of Christian antiquities, the Museo Sacro in the Vatican, opened in 1766. The true founder of early Christian archaeology, however, was G. B. de Rossi (1822-94), who established the journal *Bullettino di Archeologia Cristiana* and published two massive works: *Roma Sotterranea* (1864-77) and *Inscriptiones christianae urbis Romae* (1857-85).

Meanwhile, in northern Europe, which was never part of the Roman Empire and consequently lacked the monumental classical ruins and the marble statuary that attracted the Italian humanists, antiquarians had begun to investigate the remains of their prehistoric and early historical past (chiefly megalithic tombs and medieval rune stones). Among the first Scandinavian antiquarians was Ole Worm (1588-1654), who worked under the patronage of King Christian IV of Denmark. In 1666, the first laws to protect antiquities were enacted in the kingdom of Sweden and Finland. In about 1682, the Danish royal collection of antiquities was installed in a museum at Slotsholm, Copenhagen. Just as classical archaeology came of age in the nineteenth century, so too did the archaeology of northern Europe. In 1836, C. J. Thomsen (1788-1865) devised the "Three Age" system, which divided Scandinavian prehistory into ages of stone, bronze and iron, and J. J. A. Worsaae began to excavate carefully—and to make detailed records of his excavations. Typological analysis was further refined by the British archaeologist General Pitt-Rivers (1827-1900) and by the Swede Oscar Montelius (1843-1921), both of whom interpreted typological change in an evolutionary manner akin to Darwinism. At the same time, Pitt-Rivers brought the techniques of archaeological excavation and recording to a new level of competence.

This was the background against which medieval archaeology began. In the United Kingdom the first investigations of medieval sites were concerned with the cemeteries of the pagan Anglo-Saxons. The earliest "excavations," conducted with little regard for associations of objects and none for stratigraphy, were carried out in Kent by Bryan Fausset, between 1757 and 1773. Fausset supposed that the cemeteries belonged to the Roman period and credit for recognising their real identity goes to James Douglas, who published *Nenia Britannica* in 1779. In the early nineteenth century, numerous Anglo-Saxon cemeteries came to light, usually as a result of agriculture or construction of roads, railroads, and canals. By the 1850s, the corpus of material was very large indeed, and in 1855 John Yonge Akerman produced the first true synthesis of early medieval antiquities, *The Remains of Pagan Saxondom.*

The first important applications of the typological approach to medieval archaeology were those of E. Salin, who published *Der altgermanisch Thierornamentik* in 1904, and E. T. Leeds, whose *The Archaeology of the Anglo-Saxon Settlements* appeared in 1913. In both cases, the authors used rigorous analyses of form and and ornament to establish relative chronologies for the brooches and other items of personal adornment that are found in very large numbers in the cemeteries of the Migration Period. After studying the distribution of particular types they also attributed them to ethnic groups described in the written sources.

The Archaeology of the Anglo-Saxon Settlements was a milestone in the development of medieval archaeology in the United Kingdom. Ten years later, in *The Archaeology of the Cambridge Region,* Cyril Fox (1882-1967) took another step forward by demonstrating the relationship between settlement and the environment in his study of the distribution of artifacts (including Anglo-Saxon brooches) in the context of physical geography. Other ground-breaking studies were to follow, notably by T. D. Kendrick, who worked on Anglo-Saxon and Viking material. The culmination of this formative period was the discovery and excavation in 1939 of the seventh-century ship burial (or cenotaph) at Sutton Hoo in Essex—the richest assemblage of artifacts ever discovered in the United Kingdom.

In the postwar period, medieval archaeology developed rapidly and it is now practiced in all parts of Europe. New field techniques were evolved. The work of Axel Steensberg in Sweden and the publication, in 1954, of the brilliant excavation of the remains of a seventh- to ninth-century settlement at Warendorf in Westphalia stimulated the study and careful excavation of the buried remains of rural settlements, which hitherto had been largely neglected. The excavation by Brian Hope-Taylor of the residence of the Anglian kings at Old Yeavering in 1953–57 was an archaeological tour-de-force, which showed for the first time in the United Kingdom how the ephemeral remains of long-decayed timber buildings can be detected, excavated, and interpreted. At the same time, excavation in the centers of bomb-damaged cities such as Canterbury (by S. S. Frere) and London (by W. F. Grimes) provided a glimpse of the enormous potential or urban archaeology. By 1957, the time was ripe in the United Kingdom for the creation of a professional association of archaeologists and others interested in the material remains of the Middle Ages, and the Society for Medieval Archaeology was founded.

This review of the development of medieval archaeology in the period between 1900 and 1960 in one country—the United Kingdom—is not intended to suggest that the United Kingdom played a preeminent role in the development of the discipline; one could have written an equally relevant case history of northwestern Europe, Scandinavia—or France, where Michel de Boüard established the *Centre de recherches archéologiques médiévale* at Caen University in 1955 and the journal *Archéologie Médiévale* began publication in 1971.

Medieval archaeology in the sense of a systematic study arrived in the Mediterranean in the 1960s. Before this date, in Italy for example, the overwhelming thrust of medieval studies was historical and art-historical. "Major" buildings (such as churches, palaces and fortifications) were considered to be the legitimate field of the architectural historian, and "minor" domestic buildings were ignored. The only medieval remains to be treated in an "archaeological" manner were early Christian churches and catacombs, and the objects recovered from them, and the cemeteries of "Germanic" tradition. In Italy, any movement that may have existed toward enlarging the scope of medieval archaeology died in the Fascist era, when most of the resources of the state archaeological service were devoted to the clearance of the major public monuments of the Roman period.

Although the first medieval field projects in Italy were carried out by non-Italians, the encouragement of Gian Piero Bognetti and other Italian scholars was crucial to their success. By the mid-1960s, there was a widespread awareness of the neglect of post-classical archaeology and remedies began to be applied. The first university course in medieval archaeology was offered in Milan, in 1966–67. The Museo dell'Alto Medioevo in Rome opened its doors in 1967. The first multi-period urban excavation in Italy began in 1968, at Genoa. At the same time, the government-appointed Franceschini commission published its far-reaching report, *Per la salvatezza dei beni culturali in Italia* (1967), in which the eminent Etruscologist Massimo Pallottino noted that the dichotomy between archaeology and the history of art, reflected in the existence of separate *Soprintendenze alle Antichità* (Superintendencies of Antiquities) and *Soprintendenze ai Monumenti* (Superintendencies of Monuments), no longer met the requirements. The former were responsible for Roman and earlier monuments and sites, and the latter for medieval and later monuments. Archaeological techniques, Pallottino argues, are as applicable to post-Roman sites as to sites of earlier periods. Pallottino concluded that responsibility for all archaeological sites should be assigned to the *Soprintendenze alle Antichità*. This came about with the creation of the new Ministero dei Beni Culturali (Ministry of Cultural Properties) and of the *Soprintendenze Archeologiche* (Archaeological Superintendencies).

In the last fifteen years, medieval archaeology has developed rapidly in Italy. The first conference of medieval archaeologists was held in 1972 and the first volume of the journal *Archeologia Medievale* appeared in 1974. In volume two of *Archeologia Medievale,* Riccardo Francovich, the protagonist of medieval archaeology in Italy, noted that the discipline was still an orphan without an institutional home. Consequently, some of the most promising initiatives came from outside the *Soprintendenze.* These included the establishment of the multidisciplinary *Centro per lo Studio delle Civiltà Barbariche* (Center for the Study of Barbarian [i.e., Migration period] Cultures) in the University of Florence and of the *Centro per il Collegamento degli Studi Medievali e Umanistici* (Center for the Connection of Medieval and Humanist Studies) in the University of Perugia. Three years later, Tiziano Mannoni presented the first critical survey of medieval archaeology in Italy. He noted that four of the professors of medieval archaeology were specialists in classical art and archaeology, two in the history of medieval and modern art and architecture, two in medieval history and one in European protohistoric and medieval archaeology. Clearly, Italian medieval archaeologists were still a rare species—hence the continuing collaboration in joint projects with specialists from Poland, France, and the United Kingdom. Nevertheless, the orphan was about to be adopted, for in 1979 the *Soprintendenze* announced the first openings for "medieval" inspectors.

ARTIFACT STUDIES

Traditionally, interest in the material culture of the Middle Ages was to a great extent restricted to the study of art and architecture. It focused on paintings, sculpture, textiles, and portable *objets de luxe:* the kinds of objects that are generally regarded as fine or decorative art (and which very rarely occur in archaeological excavations), or are relegated to the category of minor arts. The principal exceptions were early medieval metalwork and numismatics, for many European countries have a centuries-long tradition of numismatic studies.

The growth of medieval archaeology has played the leading role in changing this situation. For the archaeologist, artifacts are one of the principal sources of information, and today there is hardly a category of medieval manmade object that does not receive the specialist's attention.

Ceramics, for example, are one of the richest sources of archaeological information on the Middle Ages. In most regions, they occur in such quantities (especially in the later Middle Ages) that they can be used to study chronological, social, and economic relations between peoples and places to an extent that is seldom possible with other, scarcer materials. In the past, medieval pottery was studied for two main purposes: to use changes in form, decoration, or technique to establish chronologies, and (especially in the Migration Period) to identify cultural or ethnic groups. Pottery studies, however, also contribute towards evaluating social and economic status. Comparison of the range and quantity of ceramics found on sites of similar date helps the archaeologist to assess the relative positions of their occupants. A wider range and greater quantity of luxury tableware, for example, occurs in excavations at major ports with affluent merchant communities (such as London, Southampton, Genoa, and Naples) than at rural sites occupied by peasants. Similarly, the repeated occurrence of ceramics made in one area at sites in other regions provides an insight into patterns of production and exchange. Thus, the discovery in the United Kingdom, the Netherlands, and Scandinavia of fragments of seventh- to eleventh-century amphorae made at Badorf in Germany probably reflects trade in Rhenish wine, and the widespread occurrence of thirteenth-century "polychrome ware" pitchers made in the Saintonge region of France probably reflects trade in the wines of Gascony.

Pottery, therefore, can be used as an indicator of several social activities. Its usefulness increases remarkably when the archaeologist invokes the assistance of the laboratory scientist. Indeed, the analysis of clays and glazes has opened up new fields of inquiry. The examination of a thin section reveals many of the minerals contained in the clay from which a pot was formed, and these often indicate the region in which it was made. Thus, even if the exact location of the kiln is unknown, the archaeologist can sometimes determine the source of a particular type of pottery. When this information is used in conjunction with the pattern of distribution, it becomes possible to investigate questions of production and exchange. At the same time, the chemical analysis of glazes provides information on the history of technology.

The result of all this activity is that we know more now than ever before about the production, distribution, and use of pottery in the Middle Ages. Needless to say, some countries are better known than others, but on balance progress has been impressive. We know now that in most areas of Europe and the Western Mediterranean manufacturing and long-range distribution ceased at the end of the Roman period; that in the early Middle Ages production was workshop- or home-based; that professional or semiprofessional production reemerged in or after the ninth century; and that the range of quantity of pottery in urban communities grew rapidly in the twelfth century. By the thirteenth century, professional workshops were providing table and kitchen wares, together with vessels for industrial purposes, transportation, and storage.

CHRONOLOGY

Archaeology, I claimed earlier, is the study of material remains *in context*. Generally speaking, the first kind of context that archaeologists attempt to establish for the remains they discover is chronological.

For the medieval archaeologist, the most obvious source of information on chronology is coins. Although most medieval coins do not bear the date of issue, they usually have rulers' names and sometimes the year of the reigns in which they were struck. Further information on the dates of particular issues can be obtained from studying the composition of hoards, especially those whose contents overlap (see chap. 3). Coins, therefore, are generally the most closely datable artifacts found in excavations, and for this reason they are potentially very valuable indicators of the dates of excavated features. However, given that the archaeologist has little or no knowledge of the length of time that elapsed between a coin being minted and its inclusion in the context in which it was found, the information it contains must be treated with caution. In fact, frequently all that can be deduced about the date of a deposit containing a coin is that it was laid down in or after the year in which the coin was struck.

In many areas, the neglect (until fairly recently) of the material remains of daily life meant that, coins apart, the medieval archaeologist lacked the type-fossils — indicators of activity, status, or date — that other branches of archaeology had taken for granted for decades. Pottery (which was hardly ever recycled and is virtually indestructible) is the most abundant artifact on the vast majority of sites of the Middle Ages, and in all countries considerable efforts have been devoted to establishing datable typologies. These typologies, whether they are of ceramics, glass, metal objects, or some other commonly occurring artifact, are used to establish the approximate date of the structure or deposit with which the objects are associated.

In addition to dated type-series of artifacts, medieval archaeologists also make use of dating by thermoluminescence and archaeomagnetism, radiocarbon dating, and dendrochronology. Probably, the best-known technique of estimating the date of archaeological remains is radiocarbon dating. This exploits the fact that there are three main isotopes of carbon (^{12}C, ^{13}C and ^{14}C) and that two of these (^{12}C and ^{13}C) are stable, whereas ^{14}C decays at a known rate. The continuous decay of ^{14}C is balanced by its continuous production in the upper atmosphere. This means that the ratio of ^{12}C to ^{14}C remains approximately the same. Carbon is passed between the environment and living things in a process known as the carbon cycle, and the ratio of ^{12}C to ^{14}C found in the atmosphere also occurs in plants and animals. As far as living things are concerned, however, the cycle ceases with death, after which the stable isotope ^{12}C remains unchanged in whatever parts of the plant or animal survive, but the unstable isotope ^{14}C continues to decay. Since the rate of decay is known, it is possible to calculate how long ago the plant or animal died from the ratio of the two isotopes.

Radiocarbon dating is not without problems. Although the production of ^{14}C in the atmosphere is continuous, it does not occur at a constant rate. Variations in the production rate over the last 7,000 years, however, have been calculated by reference to samples dated by dendrochronology (see below), and calibration tables exist for the conversion of "radiocarbon years" into "calendar years." Moreover, all dates are accompanied by a probable error due to the random decay of the ^{14}C isotope. This probable error reduces the usefulness of radiocarbon dating for the later medieval period, when artifacts (such as pottery) are frequently more closely datable than ^{14}C samples. However, the value of radiocarbon dating for early medieval sites that lack distinctive artifacts and for isolated objects (such as the remains of ships) should not be underestimated.

Dendrochronology, or tree-ring dating, is a method of dating wood based on measurements of variations in the width of the annual growth rings of the trees from which it was cut. The technique was developed at the beginning of this century by A. W. Douglass as a means of studying long-term changes in climate. Since the 1960s, dendrochronology has been used by archaeologists and historians of art and architecture to date wooden artifacts and buildings that contain structural timbers.

The principles of dendrochronology depend on the fact that the widths of the annual growth rings of trees vary according to the amount of moisture received during the growing season. Over the years, the pattern of annual variations becomes increasingly distinctive and characteristic of the time and place in which the tree was growing. The dendrochronologist first compiles a continuous dated sequence (known as the master chronology) of measured tree-ring widths for a specific region, working backwards from the present. Undated sequences may then be compared year by year with the master chronology. When the sequences match exactly, the dates of the hitherto undated sequences are established. The most useful trees for dendrochronology are oaks and conifers. In theory, dendrochronology is an extraordinarily precise method of dating since it is year-specific. In practice, however, the theoretical degree of accuracy is rarely attainable because of gaps or uncertainties in the sequence or errors of counting. Nevertheless, where samples and master chronologies are available, dendrochronology is a more accurate method of dating objects and structures of the medieval period than any other technique.

RURAL ARCHAEOLOGY

"Rural archaeology" here means the archaeology of landscapes, land use, and rural settlements. Some of the earliest rural archaeology in Europe was practiced in the United Kingdom. The excavation of a moated homestead at Llysworney, Glamorgan, was published in 1865, and in 1908 Hadrian Allcroft produced (in *Earthwork of England*) one of the first accounts of one of the most distinctive relics of the late medieval countryside; the "deserted medieval village" (DMV). In the 1940s, W. A. Hoskins made a detailed survey of the DMVs in the country of Leicester, using parish registers, Domesday Book, and other documents to identify sites and discover when, and why, they were abandoned. The study of British DMVs gained momentum in the postwar period. In 1952, the Deserted Medieval Village Research Group was founded; in 1953, excavations began at the deserted site of Wharram Percy with the objective of excavating totally the entire settlement (the project is still in progress); and, in 1954, Maurice Beresford published the first synthetic study, *The Lost Villages of England*. In 1972, The Moated Sites Research Group was established.

Rural archaeologists employ a number of techniques to study the evolution of the landscape and of the communities that it supported, from analysis of place names to field survey and "shovel testing," which is an attempt to assess the extent of settlement by collecting samples of earth and noting the presence or absence of artifacts. Area surveys, which began on the ground as "field walking" (systematic exploration, in which ruins, remains of field boundaries and buried structures, and concentrations of artifacts and other debris are investigated and recorded), are greatly assisted by aerial photography, which has the enormous merit of documenting sites in their topographical settings.

Among the scientific techniques that aid the archaeologist in the reconstruction of ancient landscapes is pollen analysis. This is the study of pollen grains preserved in archaeological deposits. Flowers release pollen grains in immense quantities. The grains have extremely durable skins, which in favorable conditions may survive for thousands of years. The skins are distinctive and can be identified: occasionally to the level of individual species, but more often to the level of genera. After identifying the grains in a sample, the botanist constructs a quantitative analysis of species whose pollen is present. This provides information on the character of local vegetation in the period to which the sample belongs. Problems of interpretation exist — pollen is extremely light and can be carried by the wind for many miles before it falls to earth — but the cumulative evidence of many samples from the same region in the same general period provides a valuable insight into the natural and cultivated environment.

Three of the most common remnants of the medieval landscape in the lowlands of the United Kingdom are DMVs, moated sites, and areas of "ridge and furrow." DMVs are the remains of villages and hamlets, and frequently consist of low earthworks which conceal the buried remains of the manor house, the church, dwellings, and other features. Even without excavation, the topography of the settlement can often be mapped in detail, especially when work on the ground is accompanied by aerial photography. Moated sites are homesteads protected by a ditch, which gave protection and (in marshy areas) sometimes provided a form of drainage. Ridge and furrow, which consists of areas of long, parallel ridges separated by narrow depressions, is the remains of ploughed fields. The great majority of ridge and furrow is medieval, but a few examples may possibly be earlier, and others are certainly later.

The popular image of rural settlements in many parts of the Mediterranean is that of the compact village perched on a position of natural defense, often a promontory at the confluence of two ravines or valleys. In Italy, for example, the most common type of nucleated settlement is the *castello*. Some of the earliest archaeological surveys in the Mediterranean were carried out in the countryside immediately north of Rome, and these suggested that the Roman pattern of dispersed settlement survived until the ninth century, after which the population established itself in *castelli*. Archival research supported this view, for the move to such sites (a process known as *incastellamento*) was well documented in regions in the tenth and eleventh centuries. Recent discoveries, however, have revealed that the history of rural settlement is far more complex, and far less uniform, than had been supposed. While it is true that the tenth and eleventh centuries *did* see the establishment of *castelli* in many areas, it is equally true that a similar process occurred in some regions at much earlier dates. One of the most impressive achievements of medieval archaeology in France is the total excavation of just such a settlement, at Rougiers (Var). This fifteen-year project, completed in 1976, is the subject of an exemplary monograph by the excavator, Gabrielle Démians D'Archimbaud.

URBAN ARCHAEOLOGY

One of the pioneer examples of urban archaeology is the excavation of Novgorod, on the River Volkhov in the Soviet Union, where excavations began in 1929. The city was founded in the ninth century. The subsoil is compact clay which impedes drainage and so tended to remain waterlogged. This determined the character of construction and of the preservation of archaeological features. Deep foundations and cellars (the digging of which destroys archaeological deposits) did not exist, and there was a rapid buildup of cultural debris. In places, the archaeological features are 30 feet deep. They include the remains of numerous timber houses, some 140 workshops, and corduroy roads made of logs, some of which have 30 superimposed surfaces. The almost ubiquitous use of timber provided the raw material for an unusually detailed dendrochronological sequence (see p. 170). Among the vast number of artifacts recovered in the course of half a century of excavation are 700 documents written on birch bark (*beresta,* pl. *beresty*) and evidence for trade with both Scandinavia and western Asia.

The archaeology of the city underwent a revolution in western Europe, in the aftermath of World War II. Traditionally, archaeologists investigated cities that died (such as Ostia, Leptis Magna, and Ephesus) and are not, therefore, covered by modern buildings; the excavation of a significant slice of a living city, like Athens, was exceptional. Beginning in the 1950s, however, archaeologists in a number of European countries took advantage of the clearance of war-devastated areas to investigate the origins and development of present-day cities. The accelerating pace of urban renewal focused attention on the urgent need to excavate city centers before archaeological deposits were removed by the builders of progressively deeper foundations, basements, and underground parking facilities. The destruction of this finite archaeological resource was the subject of *The Future of London's Past,* a landmark publication which appeared in 1973.

Extensive urban archaeology, however, is a phenomenon of the 1970s and 80s. It requires special skills: the ability to work quickly in difficult conditions, to record and interpret complex and fragmentary stratigraphies, to integrate the activities of personnel and earth-moving machines, and to process efficiently artifacts and other finds that sometimes occur in prodigious quantities.

It is important to note that urban archaeology is concerned comprehensively with the development of cities, rather than their character at a given moment. One of its essential characteristics, therefore, is that it deals with all periods represented in the archaeological record. Urban excavations, therefore, should be multi-period projects, in which no one type of monument, activity, or period is accorded special priority. If this ideal is not always realized, it is because urban archaeology is often a race against time and excavations are compelled to make difficult decisions about the investigation or sacrifice of individual features.

Urban archaeology is taking place in almost every European country. In the United Kingdom, large-scale projects have been completed, or are under way, in London, Winchester, York, Exeter, Lincoln, King's Lynn, Southampton, Tamworth, Hereford, and elsewhere. In Eire, excavations in Dublin revealed extensive remains of the Viking settlement. In Scandinavia, urban excavations include long-term projects at Bergen and Trondheim. In the Soviet Union, in addition to the excavations at Novgorod, work has taken place in Moscow and Kiev. In Germany, the excavations at Hamburg (between 1947 and 1959) and Lübeck are particularly note-worthy. In France, urban excavations include work in Paris (notably in the Cour Napoléon at the Louvre), Tours, and Marseilles. In Italy, five urban projects deserve particular attention: at Pavia, which led to an excellent survey and policy, modelled on the London document and published in 1981; Verona; Milan, where excavations in advance of subway construction were sponsored jointly in 1982–83 by the *Soprintendeza Archeologica* and *Metropolitana Milanese* (the subway contractors); excavations at the Crypta Balbi in the heart of Rome, which promises to tell us more about the evolution of the city between about 500 and 1000 than a century and a half of excavations in the Forum; and at Naples, where work by the *Soprintendenza* and the *Istituto Universitario Orientale* holds out equally exciting possibilities.

SUBSISTENCE

Another aspect, currently the subject of debate between historians and ar-chaeologists, is the contribution of archaeozoology (the study of animal remains from archaeological sites) to our understanding of the economic basis of medieval society. More efficient excavation has led to the recovery of large samples of animal remains from sites of all kinds and periods. Such remains are capable of yielding a wide range of information: on stock rearing and butchery practices, on the relative consumption of different domestic and wild animals — all of which has direct implications for systems of land use and hence the study of territory. A striking aspect of this information is the way in which it corroborates, or at times is in conflict with, the information extracted from the archive. Archaeobotany (the study of plant remains) plays a similar role, although in most circumstances plant remains are far less durable than bones and consequently large samples are much less common.

FORTIFICATION

The study of castles and other forms of fortification is almost a self-contained discipline, which combines archival research with the documen-tation of standing remains and excavation. Several journals are devoted exclusively to the history of fortification, notably the French publication

Château Gaillard, and readers should consult this and the several volumes listed on page 183.

ECCLESIASTICAL SITES

Here, too, investigations often involve both standing and buried remains, and a synthesis of written and material evidence. Excavations beneath the floors of existing buildings (such as York Minster, the cathedral in Florence, and Cologne cathedral) have revealed the stages in the structural history of the buildings, despite the practical difficulties inherent in elucidating features that had been damaged by the construction of foundations and burial vaults. (Indeed, the study of burials both inside churches and in associated graveyards is an important source of information on medieval demography, nutrition, and health.) Another noteworthy aspect of "ecclesiastical" archaeology is the current study of several of the great landowning abbeys of the early Middle Ages, including Farfa and San Vincenzo al Volturno in Italy.

ARCHAEOLOGY AND THE HISTORIAN

Here, as in many other areas, the archaeologist has much to learn from the historian, and vice versa. Indeed, the most impressive exercises in medieval archaeology are those in which the historian is an integral part of the project; I am thinking of the massive program of urban archaeology undertaken at Winchester in England, the excavation of a rural settlement at Brucato in Sicily, recently published in two handsome volumes, and the ongoing project at San Vincenzo al Volturno.

Despite its rapid progress and widespread acceptance among historians, medieval archaeology has not yet convinced all historians that it is a legitimate means of investigating historical periods. Even in the United Kingdom, where medieval archaeology has a relatively long history, J. L. Bolton was able, in 1980, to publish *The Medieval English Economy, 1150–1500* without a single reference to archaeological data. And in (of all places!) *25 Years of Medieval Archaeology,* P. H. Sawyer wrote that "archaeologists should concentrate on being archaeologists and resist the temptation to draw heavily on other kinds of evidence, historical or linguistic. Many texts that archaeologists cite with great confidence are the subject of debate. The date of Gildas is uncertain and may well be much earlier than is commonly supposed, the significance of the Tribal Hidage is not as straightforward as some comments on it imply, and Domesday Book rarely answers the questions that are asked of it. The Anglo-Saxon Chronicle is naturally used a great deal, but more care should be taken to get the dates right. The Ordnance Survey's *Map of the United Kingdom before the Norman Conquest* has Edward the Elder's fortifications three years late. Such an error may be of no consequence to the archaeologist but it does matter to historians trying to understand what happened in those years."

Fortunately, the number of historians (and archaeologists) who regard documentary information and archaeological data as fundamentally incompatible diminishes from year to year. The benefits to be gained from a multidisciplinary approach are simply too great to be ignored. Thus, the study of rural settlement, and in particular the so-called deserted medieval villages has benefitted enormously from pooling the information recovered by historians and archaeologists (not to mention geographers and students of place-names). The study of urban history, and in particular the survival or revival of city life in the early Middle Ages, has been transformed by the concerted efforts (as at Winchester and, recently, Ferrara and other Italian cities) of archivists and archaeologists – and of architectural historians, particularly those concerned with vernacular architecture. The study of production and distribution, again in particular for the early medieval period, has been rejuvenated by the study of pottery and other products such as *pietra ollare* in and around the Alps. In a sense, therefore, writing about "medieval archaeology" conceals two of its basic characteristics: that, especially in the case of urban and landscape studies, it is often part of a diachronic investigation extending from prehistoric times to the present day, and that, to be most effective, it functions as an integral part of a multidisciplinary inquiry that embraces the archives with one hand and the natural sciences with the other.

BIBLIOGRAPHY

A. Periodicals and Serial Publications

Anglo-Saxon England (United Kingdom).
Archeologia Medievale (Italy).
Archéologie du Midi Médiéval (France).
Archéologie Médiévale (France).

British Archaeological Abstracts (United Kingdom).
Château Gaillard. Études de castelologie médiévale (France).
Frühmittelalterliche Studien (Germany).
Lübecker Schriften zur Archäologie und Kulturgeschichte (Germany).
Medieval Archaeology (United Kingdom).
Medieval Ceramics (United Kingdom).
Nordic Archaeological Abstracts (Denmark).
Notiziario di Archeologia Medievale (Italy).
Rotterdam Papers (The Netherlands).
Zeitschrift für Archäologie des Mittelalters (Germany).

B. General

Barker, P. 1977. *Techniques of Archaeological Excavation.* London: Batsford.

Berger, R., ed. 1970. *Scientific Methods in Medieval Archaeology.* Los Angeles: California Univ. Press.

Biddick, K., ed. 1984. *Archaeological Approaches to Medieval Europe.* Kalamazoo: Western Michigan Univ. Medieval Institute Publications.

Biek, L. 1963. *Archaeology and the Microscope.* London: Lutterworth Press.

Bouard, M. De. 1975. *Manuel d'archéologie médiévale de la fouille à l'histoire.* Paris: Société d'Édition d'Enseignment Supérieur.

Bruce-Mitford, R., ed. 1975. *Recent Archaeological Excavations in Europe.* London: Routledge.

Francovich, R., ed. 1987. *Archeologia e storia del Medioevo italiano,* Florence: La Nuova Italia Scientifica.

Grierson, P. 1975. *Numismatics.* London: Academic Press.

Redman, C. L., ed. 1989. *Medieval Archaeology.* Binghamton: State Univ. of New York.

Riley, D. 1980. *Early Landscapes from Air.* Sheffield: Univ. of Sheffield, Department of Prehistory and Archaeology.

Sherratt, A., ed. 1980. *The Cambridge Encyclopaedia of Archaeology.* Cambridge: Cambridge Univ. Press.

Tite, M. S. 1972. *Methods of Physical Examination in Archaeology.* London: Seminar Press.

Wainwright, F. T. 1962. *Archaeology and Place-names in History: An Essay on Problems of Co-ordination.* London: Routledge.

Wilson, D. R., ed. 1975. *Aerial Reconnaissance for Archaeology.* London: Council for British Archaeology.

C. Regional and Period Studies

Beresford, M. W., and J. K. St. Joseph. *Medieval England: An Aerial Survey.* 2d ed. Cambridge: Cambridge Univ. Press.

Bruce-Mitford, R. 1975–1983. *The Sutton Hoo Ship Burial.* 3 vols. London: British Museum Publications.

Campbell, J., E. John, and P. Wormald. *The Anglo-Saxons.* Oxford: Phaidon.

Clarke, H. 1984. *The Archaeology of Medieval England.* London: British Museum Publications.

Colvin, H. M., ed 1963. *The History of the King's Works. The Middle Ages.* London: Her Majesty's Stationery Office.

Dannheimer, H. 1962. *Die germanischen Funde der späten Kaiserzeit und des frühen Mittelalters in Mittelfranken.* Berlin: Walter de Gruyter.

Evison, V. I., ed. 1981. *Angles, Saxons and Jutes. Essays presented to J. N. L. Myres.* Oxford, Oxford Univ. Press.

Farrell, R. T., ed. 1982. *The Vikings.* London: Phillimore.

Harden, D. B., ed. 1956. *Dark Age the United Kingdom: Studies Presented to E. T. Leeds.* London: Methuen.

Hill, D. 1981. *An Atlas of Anglo-Saxon England 700–1066.* Toronto: Univ. of Toronto Press.

Hinton, D. A., ed. *25 Years of Medieval Archaeology.* Sheffield: Univ. of Sheffield. Department of Prehistory and Archaeology.

Hodges, R. 1982. *Dark Age Economics. The Origins of Towns and Trade A.D. 600–1000.* London: Duckworth.

Hodges, R., and D. Whitehouse. 1983. *Mohammed, Charlemagne and the Origins of Europe.* London: Duckworth; Ithaca, N.Y.: Cornell Univ. Press.

Kramer, W., ed. 1958. *Neue Ausgrabungen in Deutschland.* Berlin: Verlag Gebr. Mann.

Lamm, J. P., and H.-A. Nordström, ed. 1983. *Vendel Period Studies: Transactions of the Boat-grave Symposium, Stockholm, 1981.* Stockholm: Statens Historiska Museum.

Milne, G., and B. Hobley. 1981. *Waterfront Archaeology in the United Kingdom and Northern Europe.* London: Council for British Archaeology.

Myres, J. N. L. 1969. *Anglo-Saxon Pottery and the Settlement of England.* Oxford: Clarendon Press.

Platt, C. 1989. *Medieval England: A Social History and Archaeology from the Conquest to 1600 A.D.* London: Routledge.

Randsborg, K. 1980. *The Viking Age in Denmark: The Formation of a State.* London: Duckworth.

———. 1990. *The First Millennium in Europe and the Mediterranean: An Archaeological Essay,* Cambridge: Cambridge Univ. Press.

Roesdahl, E. 1982. *Viking Age Denmark.* London: Colonnade Books for British Museum Publications.

Sawyer, P. H. 1962. *The Age of the Vikings.* London: Edward Arnold.

Thomas C. 1986. *Celtic the United Kingdom.* London: Thames and Hudson.

Von Uslar, R. 1964. *Studien zu frühgeschichtlichen Befestigungen zwischen Nordsee und Alpen* (Beihefte der Bonner Jahrbücher 11). Cologne: Rheinland-Verlag.

White, L., Jr. 1962. *Medieval Technology and Social Change.* Oxford: Clarendon Press.

Wilson, D. M., ed. 1976. *The Archaeology of Anglo-Saxon England.* London: Methuen.

——. 1980. *The Northern World.* London: Thames and Hudson.

Withold, H. 1965. *Die Slawen im frühen Mittelalter.* Berlin: Akademie Verlag.

D. Artifact Studies

Allan, J. P. 1984. *Medieval and Post-Medieval Finds from Exeter, 1971–1980.* Exeter: Exeter City Council and Univ. of Exeter.

Anon. [Ward Perkins, J. B.]. 1967. *London Museum Medieval Catalogue* Reprint. London: Her Majesty's Stationery Office.

Anon. 1977. *Die Zeit der Staufer* (exhibition catalogue). 3 vols. Stuttgart: Württembergisches Landesmuseum.

Anon. 1987. *Age of Chivalry: Art in Plantagenet England 1200–1400* (exhibition catalogue). London: Royal Academy of Arts.

Ardwison, G., ed. 1984. *Birka II.I. Systematische Analysen der Gräberfunde.* Stockholm: Kungl. Vitterhets Historie och Atikvitets Akademien.

Backhouse, J., D. H. Turner, and L. Webster, eds. *The Golden Age of Anglo-Saxon Art, 966–1066* (exhibition catalogue). London: British Museum Publications.

Baumgartner, I., and I. Krueger, 1988. *Phönix aus Sand und Asche: Glas des Mittelalters.* Munich: Klinkhardt and Biermann.

Clain-Steffanelli, E. E. 1984. *Numismatic Bibliography.* New York: Stack's.

Cowgill, J., M. De Neergaard, and N. Griffiths. 1987. *Knives and Scabbards* (Medieval Finds from Excavations in London 1). London: Her Majesty's Stationery Office.

Deroche, V., and J. M. Spieser, eds. 1989. *Recherches sur la céramique byzantine* (*Bulletin de Correspondence Hellénique, Supplément* 18). Paris: Brocard.

Foy, D. 1988. *Le verre médiéval et son artisanat en France méditerranéenne.* Paris: Centre National de la Recherche Scientifique.

Foy, D., and G. Sennequier, G. 1989. *A travers le verre du moyen âge à la renaissance.* Rouen: Musées et Monuments départmentaux de la Seine-Maritime.

Graham-Campbell, J. 1980. *Viking Artefacts. A Select Catalogue.* London: British Museum Publications.

Grew, F., and M. De Neergaard. 1988. *Shoes and Pattens* (Medieval Finds from Excavations in London 2). London: Her Majesty's Stationery Office.

Grierson, P. 1979. *Bibliographie Numismatique,* 101–211. Brussels: Cercle d'études numismatiques.

Grierson, P., and M. Blackburn. *Medieval European Coins, with a Catalogue of the Coins in the Fitzwilliam Museum, Cambridge.* Vol. 1: *The Early Middle Ages.* Cambridge: Cambridge Univ. Press.

Hinton, D. 1974. *A Catalogue of the Anglo-Saxon Ornamental Metalwork, 700–1100, in the Department of Antiquities, Ashmolean Museum.* Oxford: Clarendon Press.

Hurst, J. G., D. S. Neal, and H. E. J. Van Beuningen. 1986. *Pottery Produced and*

Traded in North-West Europe 1350-1650 (Rotterdam Papers 6). Rotterdam: Stichting 'Het Nederlandse Gebruiksvoorwerp.'

Llubia, L. M. 1967. *Cerámica medieval española*. Barcelona: Editorial Labor.

Lobedey, U. 1968. *Untersuchungen Mittelalterlicher Keramik*. Berlin: W. De Gruyter.

McCarthy, M. R., and C. M. Brooks. 1988. *Medieval pottery in Britain* A.D. *900-1600*. Leicester: Leicester Univ. Press.

Naumann, J., and others. 1988. *Keramik vom Niederrhein: Die Irdenware der Düppen-und Pottbäcker zwischen Köln und Kleve*. Cologne: Kölnisches Stadtmuseum.

Peacock, D. P. S., ed. 1977. *Pottery and Early Commerce: Characterization and Trade in Roman and Later Ceramics*. London: Academic Press.

Platt, C., and R. Coleman-Smith. 1975. *Excavations in Medieval Southampton, 1953-1969*. Leicester: Leicester Univ. Press.

Renaud, J. G. N. 1975. *Rotterdam Papers 2: A Contribution to Medieval Archaeology*. Rotterdam: Stichting 'Het Nederlandse Gebruiksvoorwerp.'

Ryan, M., ed. 1987. *Ireland and Insular Art*, A.D. *500-1200*. Dublin: Royal Irish Academy.

Stenberger, M. 1947-58. *Die Schatzfunde Gotlands der Wikingerzeit*. Stockholm: H. Ohlssons boktryckeri.

Tylecote, R. F. 1986. *The Prehistory of Metallurgy in the United Kingdom*. London: The Institute of Metals.

White, L., Jr. 1962. *Medieval Technology and Social Change*. Oxford: Oxford Univ. Press.

Wilson, D.M. 1964. *Anglo-Saxon Ornamental Metalwork, 700-1100, in the British Museum*. London: Trustees of The British Museum.

Zarnecki, G., J. Holt, and T. Holland, eds. 1984. *English Romanesque Art 1066-1200* (exhibition catalogue). London: Arts Council of Great the United Kingdom.

E. Chronology

Baillie, M. G. L. 1982. *Tree-Ring Dating and Archaeology*. Chicago: Univ. of Chicago Press.

Eckstein, D. 1984. *Dendrochronological Dating* (Handbooks for Archaeologists 2). Strasbourg: European Science Foundation.

Striker, C. L. 1988. *What is Dendrochronology?* Philadelphia: Author, Univ. of Pennsylvania, Department of History of Art.

F. Rural Archaeology

Anon., ed. 1970. *Archéologie du Village Déserté*. Paris: Librairie Armand Colin (École Pratique des Hautes Etudes, VIe Section, et Institut d'Histoire de la Culture Materielle de l'Academie Polonaise des Sciences).

Astill, G., and A. Grant, eds. 1988. *The Countryside of Medieval England*. Oxford: Basil Blackwell.

Barker, G. 1986. "L'archeologia del paessaggio italiano." *Archeologia Medievale* 13: 7–30.

Barker, G., and R. Hodges. 1981. "Archaeology in Italy, 1980: New Directions and Mis-directions." In G. Barker and R. Hodges, eds. *Archaeology and Italian Society,* 1–16. Oxford: British Archaeological Reports.

Bazzana, A., P. Guichard, and J. M. Poisson, eds. 1983. *Habitats fortifiés et organization de l'espace en Méditerranée médiévale.* Lyon: Maison de l'Orient.

Beresford, M. 1963. *The Lost Villages of England.* London: Lutterworth Press.

Beresford, M. W., and J. G. Hurst, eds. 1971. *Deserted Medieval Village Studies.* London: St. Martin's Press.

Bradford, J. S. P. 1957. *Ancient Landscapes.* London: Bell.

Chapelot, J., and R. Fossier, 1980. *Le village et la maison au moyen âge.* Paris: Gallimard.

Cherry, J. 1983. "Frogs Around the Pond: Perspectives on Current Archaeological Survey Projects in the Mediterranean Region." In D. R. Keller and D. W. Rupp, eds. *Archaeological Survey in the Mediterranean Area,* 375–416. Oxford: British Archaeological Reports.

Demians D'Archimbaud, G. 1981. *Les fouilles de Rougiers: Contribution à l'archéologie de l'habitat rural médiéval en pays méditerranéen.* Paris: Centre National de la Recherche Scientifique.

Demolon, P. 1972. *Le village merovingien de Brebières (VIᵉ-VIIᵉ siècles), avec une étude de sa faune.* Arras: Imprimerie Centrale de l'Artois (Mémoires de la Commission Départmentale des Monuments Historiques du Pas-de-Calais).

Duby, G. 1968. *Rural Economy and Country Life in the Medieval West.* London: Edward Arnold.

Fowler, P. J., ed. 1972. *Archaeology and the Landscape.* London: John Baker.

Fox, C. F. 1932. *The Personality of the United Kingdom.* Cardiff: National Museum of Wales.

Hamilton, J. R. C. 1956. *Excavations at Jarlshof, Shetland.* Edinburgh: Her Majesty's Stationery Office.

Heidinga, H. A. 1987. *Medieval Settlement and Economy North of the Lower Rhine,* Assen/Maastricht: Van Gorwin.

Holmqvist, W., ed. 1961. *Excavations at Helgö.* Vol. 1: *Report for 1954–1956.* Stockholm: Kungl. Vitterhets Historie och Antikvitets Akademien.

Hope-Taylor, B. 1977. *Yeavering: An Anglo-British Centre of Early Northumbria.* London: Her Majesty's Stationery Office.

Hoskins, W. G. 1955. *The Making of the English Landscape.* London: Hodder and Stoughton.

Hurst, J. G., ed. 1979. *Wharram: A Study of Settlement on the Yorkshire Wolds.* London: Society for Medieval Archaeology.

Jahnkuhn, H. 1976. *Haithabu: Ein Handelsplatz der Wikingerzeit.* 6th ed. Neumünster: Karl Wachholtz.

Janssen, W. 1975. *Studien zur Wüstungsfrage im fränkischen Altsiedelland zwischen Rhein, Mosel und Eifelnordrand* (Beihefte der Bonner Jahrbücher 35). Cologne: Rheinland-Verlag.

Maxwell, G. S. 1983. *The Impact of Aerial Reconnaissance on Archaeology*. London: Council for British Archaeology.

Orwin, C. S. and C. S. 1967. *The Open Fields* 3d ed. Oxford: Clarendon Press.

Pesez, J. M., ed. 1987. *Brucato: Histoire et archéologie d'un habitat médiévale en Sicile*. Rome: École Française de Rome.

Plog, S., F. Plog, W. Wait. 1978. "Decision making in modern surveys." In M. B. Schiffer, ed., *Advances in Archaeological Method and Theory* 1:383–421. New York: Academic Press.

Rowley, T., ed. 1974. *Anglo-Saxon Settlement and Landscape*. Oxford: British Archaeological Reports.

Taylor, C. 1974. *Fieldwork in Medieval Archaeology*. London: Batsford.

Taylor, C. 1983. *Village and farmstead: A History of Rural Settlement in England*. London: George Philip.

G. Urban Archaeology

Barley, M. W., ed. 1977. *European Towns: Their Archaeology and Early History*. London: Academic Press for *British Archaeology*.

Biddle, M. and C. Heighway. 1973. *The Future of London's Past: A Survey of the Archaeological Implications of Planning and Development in the Nation's Capital*. Worcester: Rescue Publications.

Carver, M. O. 1987. *Underneath English Towns: Interpreting Urban Archaeology*. London: Batsford.

Clarke, H., and A. Carter. 1977. *Excavations in King's Lynn, 1963–1970*. London: Society for Medieval Archaeology.

Fevrier, P. A. 1980. *Histoire de la France urbaine*. Vol. 1: *La ville antique*. Paris: Seuil.

Galinie, H., and B. Randoin. 1979. *Les archives du sol à Tours et l'avenir de l'archéologie de la ville*. Tours: L.A.U.

Gerevich, L. 1971. *The Art of Buda and Pest in the Middle Ages*. Budapest: Académiai Kiadó.

Hall, A. R., and H. K. Kenward, eds. 1982. *Environmental Archaeology in the Urban Context*. London: Council for British Archaeology.

Hodges, R., and B. Hobley, eds. 1988. *The Rebirth of Towns in the West*. London: Council for British Archaeology.

Hudson, P. 1981. *Archeologia urbana e programmazione della ricerca: L'esempio di Pavia*. Florence: All'Insegna del Giglio.

Horsman, V., C. Milne, and G. Milne. 1989. *Aspects of Saxon-Norman London*. Vol. 1: *Building and Street Development*. London: Middlesex Archaeological Society.

Kargar, M. K. 1958–61. *Drevnii Kiev: Ocherki po Istorii Materialnoi Kultury Drevnerusskogo Goroda* (Ancient Kiev: An Outline History of the Material Culture of the Medieval Russian Town). 2 vols. Leningrad: Institut Arkheologii Akademii Nauk SSSR.

Kolchin, B. A., ed. 1985. *Drevnyaya Rus: Gorod, Zamok, Selo* (Ancient Rus: Town, Castle, Village). Moscow: Nauka.

Kolchin, B. A., and V. L. Yanin, 1982. *Novogorodski I Sbornik: 50 let raskopok Novgoroda,* Moscow: Izd-vo "Nauka."

Odelberg, M. 1974. *Birka.* Stockholm: Riksantikvarie ambetet.

Platt, C. 1975. *The English Medieval Town.* London: Secker and Warburg.

Schofield, J., and R. Leech, eds. 1988. *Urban Archaeology in the United Kingdom.* London: Council for British Archaeology.

Vince, A., ed. 1991. *Aspects of Saxon-Norman London.* vol. 2: *Finds and Environmental Evidence.* London: London and Middlesex Archaeological Society.

H. Subsistence

Aston, M., ed. 1988. *Medieval Fish, Fisheries and Fishponds in England.* Oxford: British Archaeological Reports.

Clark, G. 1989. "Animals and Animal Products in Mediaeval Italy: A Discussion of Archaeological and Historical Methodology." *Papers of The British School at Rome* 57: 152–71.

Clark, G., and others. 1989. "The Food Refuse of an Affluent Urban Household in the Late Fourteenth Century: Faunal and Botanical Remains from the Palazzo Vitelleschi, Tarquinia (Viterbo)." *Papers of The British School at Rome* 57:200–321.

Chaplin, R. 1971. *The Study of Animal Bones from Archaeological Sites.* London: Seminar Press.

Maltby, M. 1979. *Faunal Studies on Urban Sites: The Animal Bones from Exeter 1971-1975.* Sheffield: Sheffield Univ., Department of Prehistory and Archaeology.

Renfrew, J. 1973. *Palaeoethnobotany.* London: Methuen.

I. Fortification

Herrnbrodt, A. 1958. *Der Husterknupp: Eine niederrheinische Burganlage des frühen Mittelalters.* Cologne: Böhlau.

Kenyon, J. R. 1978-1984. *Castles, Town Defences and Artillery Fortification in the United Kingdom and Ireland.* 2 vols. London: Council for British Archaeology.

King, D. J. C., 1983. *Castellarium Anglicanum: An Index and Bibliography of the Castles in England, Wales and the Islands,* Millwood, NY, Kraus International Publications.

O'Neil, B. H. St. J. 1960. *Castles and Cannon: A Study of Early Artillery Fortifications in England.* Westport, Conn.: Greenwood Press.

Thompson, M. W. 1987. *The Decline of the Castle.* Cambridge: Cambridge Univ. Press.

J. Ecclesiastical Sites

Addyman, P., and R. Morris, eds. 1976. *The Archaeological Study of Churches.* London: Council for British Archaeology.

Butler, L. A. S., and R. K. Morris. 1986. *The Anglo-Saxon Church: Papers on History, Architecture and Archaeology in Honour of Dr H. M. Taylor.* London: Council for British Archaeology.

Doppelfeld, O., and W. Weyres. 1980. *Die ausgrabungen im Dom zu Köln.* Mainz: Philipp von Zabern.

Horn, W., and E. Born. 1979. *The Plan of St. Gall.* Berkeley: California Univ. Press.

Rodwell, W. J., and K. Rodwell, 1977. *Historic Churches—A Wasting Asset.* London: Council for British Archaeology.

K. Archaeology and History

Dymond, D. P. 1974. *Archaeology and History: A Plea for Reconciliation.* London: Thames and Hudson.

Prosopography

GEORGE BEECH

ROSOPOGRAPHY is a form of historical inquiry which attracted considerable attention from historians of Antiquity and the Modern Era earlier in the century and has now firmly established itself in medieval studies. Its object is the identification and study of the influential people of a given period, the people who held the positions of power in their society. More specifically, it seeks biographical data about their place and family of origin, their social status, their friends, acquaintances, and other personal contacts, and about their careers. It then attempts to assess the importance of family and personal relationships in their achievement of rank and office or function, and in influencing the courses of action they followed in their adult careers. In so doing, prosopographers hope to acquire a better understanding of the power structure of medieval society.[1]

Prosopography thus proceeds from two assumptions which it constantly attempts to verify or disprove in individual cases. The first of these is that, without discounting factors such as chance and individual merit, family ties usually counted for a great deal in personal advancement. Detailed studies of any number of individual families have borne this out time and again and leave no doubt as to its general validity. The second assumption, closely related to the first, is the belief that personal relationships played a vital, perhaps decisive, role in the internal working of any medieval institutional structure, especially in the earlier Middle Ages when the institutions of secular and ecclesiastical government had reached only a relatively rudimentary state of development.[2] A close relationship with the dominant figure in any group of people wielding power — be it king, count, bishop, or some other — was liable to be more important as a source of authority, wealth, or prestige than the holding of an office. The people controlling such groups, the king or his counterpart, tended to rely more on those linked to them either by family, vassalage, or some other relationship of dependence than on those who were not, and whenever the opportunity presented itself they would seek to install men of the first type as their officials. In other words, it is not so much a constitutional or legal description of the powers of any office or group of offices in a power structure which will explain its workings as it is the personal relationships between those holding the offices. To understand the institution one must understand those relationships. A number of recent studies of the Carolingian kings and their followers have lent credence in this assumption by showing that a large percentage of the men holding the highest offices of their day were also attached to the royal family by some kind of close personal bonds or marriage. Suspecting that some such network of personal relationships may have bound together the members of other institutions or power elites, the prosopographer attempts to uncover and describe them, and finally to evaluate their importance.

Contemporary German medievalists often refer to prosopography as *Historische Personenforschung* or *Personengeschichte* and thus emphasize its aspect of individual biography, with the goal of finding out as much as possible about the family and personal relationships of the individual in question. In calling it collective or multi-biography, other historians have laid stress on its concern with the groups of people, rather than isolated individuals, who control, shape, or otherwise influence the affairs of their society. Regardless of this difference, prosopographers proceed in the same way, starting with a chosen group as the focal point. The first step is the compilation of data for the biographies of the individuals of the group; the second is their comparison for the purpose of noting what qualities or characteristics they shared and in what respects they differed.

Prosopographers have usually concentrated their attention on the most powerful or influential people in a society, but their methods can perfectly well be extended to take into account individuals of lesser importance. This can include virtually any social group or group of individuals who have in common an office, a function, a specific kind of work, or status. Parish priests in Germany in the eleventh century could serve as the object of study just as well as royal advisors in France in the fourteenth century. It is clear that parish priests from an entire country constituted a social group in a different way than did royal advisors who knew one another personally and frequently met for purposes of designing policy, but the same questions can be asked of both. Who were they, from what kinds of families did they come, from what kinds of communities and where, how did they acquire their positions, to what degree was theirs a stable group, how many rose to higher posts, how many dropped out, and so on? The farther down the social scale this approach is carried, for instance into the world of peasant society, the scarcer the information about individual members of the group, simply because they appear less often in the documents, and answers to these questions accordingly lose depth and precision. That is to be anticipated, however, and does not alter the fact that prosopography is a tool for social as well as political historians.

It is perhaps appropriate here to point out that prosopography would not have been necessary in medieval history if gaps in the sources, and the peculiar character of those which do survive, had not deprived us of biographical information about the influential people of that time. With a few exceptions, scribes of medieval documents usually give very little if any explicit information about a person's family background, friends, and career, doubtless because in most cases that was unnecessary or irrelevant to the events or transactions being recorded at the time. Consequently, many of the most influential men in the world of medieval politics, both lay and clerical, appear for the first time in surviving documents already vested with authority and prestige. Since little is said of family ties and other personal affiliations, there is a natural inclination to assume either that these mattered little or that these people had emerged, as it were, from obscurity, and probably from humble backgrounds, to push their way up to prominence. But previous experience has shown repeatedly that this happened rarely in the stratified society of medieval Europe and warns against such assumptions.

A clearer conception of what prosopography is all about can be conveyed by pointing out what it is not. It differs from historical biography in that it usually leads to "biographies" which have a fragmentary, highly incomplete character, especially in periods like the early Middle Ages where the paucity of source materials sometimes forces the historian to be satisfied with knowing nothing more than the name of a prominent individual and the approximate time and place of his life. The conventional biographer would not even bother with such a subject, but information of this kind, when correlated with that about other similar people may well be exceedingly informative to the prosopographer.

Prosopography differs from institutional history, to which it is otherwise closely akin, in that the institutional historian is interested in the institution and its functioning, whereas the prosopographer is concerned with the persons who control it. For instance, the historian of the episcopacy in the eleventh century strives on the basis of many specific examples to generalize about the office of bishop, describing matters such as mode of election, the theoretical and actual powers of the incumbent, the income he enjoyed, the prestige attendant upon the office, and other similar things. The prosopographer, bearing all of this in mind, focuses his attention on the men who occupied the office, the families from which they came, their careers prior to becoming bishop, the ways in which they acquired the office, the people with whom they associated, and the policies they followed once in power. An illustration of this is the recent study of the higher clergy (bishop, archdeacons, *prévôt,* and dean of the chapter) of the diocese at Liège from the eleventh to the fifteenth century.[3] The author sought to ascertain the social status of each official's family, his region of origin, his position prior to occupying his office, and the persons and circumstances responsible for his coming to power. Having compiled this information for each official, the author combined and compared the results and found that although all came from the aristocracy, the bishops tended to belong to families of higher rank than the *prévôts,* the *prévôts* to more illustrious families than the deans, and so forth.

Credit for conceiving and carrying out the first prosopographical study belongs to a German classicist, O. Seeck, at the end of the nineteenth century.[4] Ideally suited to a period documented by fragmentary references in inscriptions and papyrus texts to thousands of prominent people, this approach has continued to flourish in Roman studies without break until the present day. Several prosopographical dictionaries of important people have been published for the Republican and Imperial periods with the most recent, 1971 and 1980, covering the period A.D. 266–527, and a continuation is projected.[5] Within a few years of Seeck's first work, modern historians, both American and European, borrowed and adapted the techniques of prosopography to their respective fields, and the volume of their studies has grown steadily ever since. In the view of Lawrence Stone, a variety of factors or conditions have contributed to the ready response it has found among twentieth century historians.[6] On the one hand, dissatisfaction with traditional institutional history along with an increasing skepticism about the motives of political leaders put historians in a mood to look beyond institutional structures or ideologies for the explanation of policies or programs, stimulated a search for those relatives, friends, and interests. On the other hand, the development of the social sciences supplied historians with new questions to be posed and new approaches to social and political analysis. Anthropology, for instance, drew attention to the importance of family and kinship ties in human behavior, sociology to social groups in general, and economics insisted on the economic interests behind men's actions. Finally, Stone sees the development of new techniques of quantification associated with computers as encouraging attempts, which formerly would have been inconceivable, to analyze masses of data about members of large social groups.

Given the chronological proximity and the similarly sparse documentation of the ancient and medieval worlds, it is not surprising that medievalists soon appropriated the techniques of Roman historians for their period. But prosopographical investigations were far and few between prior to World War II.[7] Interest picked up in the late 1940s and 50s but it was not until the decades of the 60s and 70s that the prosopographical approach began to be applied by significant numbers of medievalists. Then the publication of a number of important new studies employing this approach demonstrated its utility and persuaded scholars who had hitherto wondered what the name meant that it could be carried out successfully in widely diverse domains. As new publications multiplied so did the need for some sort of bibliographical control for the convenience of interested scholars. Thus in the late 1970s the editors of *Francia: Forschungen zur Westeuropäischen Geschichte* began to publish an occasional series of essays and review articles under the heading *Prosopographia*, and in 1980, *Medieval Prosopography*, the first journal was created. Two of its contributing editors organized an international conference on medieval prosopography in Bielefeld in December 1982.[8] Two more followed this in Paris in October 1984, the first *Prosopographie et la Genèse de l'État Moderne* and the second, *Informatique et Prosopographie*.[9]

A survey of the published research over the past fifteen to twenty years brings out that the great bulk of this work has concentrated on the study of various elite groups in medieval society. As might have been expected, politically and socially influential people, including nobility, governmental officials at differing levels, and members of representative assemblies, have attracted more attention than other groups. But there have also been many studies of ecclesiastical dignitaries, particularly bishops and cathedral chapters, as well as of monastic communities. Nor have students and masters at the universities been neglected. On the other hand relatively few studies have been made of urban elites and even fewer have focused on peasants. Of all of the research in question most has come from individual scholars working alone; nonetheless, several large scale collaborative ventures involving teams of scholars are currently underway and have produced impressive results.

German scholars have led the way in the application of prosopography to medieval history for the past three decades both in their development of new methods for extracting information from previously neglected sources and in the volume and variety of their published work. Noted already in 1939 for his *Königtum und Stämme in der Werdezeit des Deutschen Reiches,* Gerd Tellenbach left an indelible mark on the first generation of German prosopographers, many of whom studied under him as part of the Freiburger Arbeitskreis. In his twenty years at Freiburg, 1944–64, he directed the dissertations, many of them in prosopography, of no less than sixty doctoral students.[10] A number of these latter now occupy chairs of medieval history in the German Universities where they have continued their research and publication in addition to training students of their own.

In the late 1960s two of his students, Karl Schmid, who replaced him at Freiburg, and Joachim Wollasch of Münster, collaborated to found what has become easily the largest prosopographical undertaking in medieval studies in the past two decades. The goal of their project—called *Societas et Fraternitas. Begründung eines kommentierten Quellenwerkes zur Erforschung der Personen und Personengruppen des Mittelalters*—was the prosopography of prominent people, lay, clerical, and monastic, from the ninth through twelfth centuries in the Holy Roman Empire, France, and Italy.[11] Their sources were monastic necrologies, obituaries, confraternity agreements, and other documents including charters commemorating the living and the dead. These documents, which exist in relative abundance for otherwise poorly documented periods such as the ninth and tenth centuries, name great masses of people, high into the thousands, including many of the most eminent individuals of the day but historians had previously made almost no use of them. The reasons for this include (1) lack of published editions for some, (2) inadequate editions for others, and, finally and most decisively, (3) scholars' inability to identify most of the people involved because they took only the single name customary to the period and were thus usually indistinguishable from others similarly named. The problem then was to work out a method which would break through the anonymity of these lists and permit personal identification. The key to this has proved to be focusing first on the groups of which most persons named in these sources are a part, rather than on isolated individuals, and seeking to identify the groups through repeated appearances in different documents. Prominent individuals can then be identified through membership in given groups of relatives, friends, or vassals. Schmid and Wollasch have insisted from the beginning that the project should start by placing fundamental emphasis on the publication of these various memorial records in editions of the highest quality which preserve as nearly as possible the appearance of the originals. In fact they have favored photo-facsimile editions which are of exceptional quality and depart from the originals only in not reproducing colors.[12]

In 1967 a continuing grant from the German government (Deutsche Forschungsgemeinschaft) enabled the project, called "Personen und Gemeinschaften," to be housed at Münster as part of a large interdisciplinary program for research into early medieval society (*Mittelalterforschung*) called the "Sonderforschungsbereich 7." With this came the founding of *Frühmittelalterstudien* (*FMS*) which has become an outstanding journal for early medieval studies in general as well as for publishing many of the monographs of members of this project. The annual reports (*Berichte*) published in *FMS* during the life of the governmental grant (1967–85) provide the fullest account of the activities and publications of Societas et Fraternitas and are invaluable for keeping up with project as well as gaining an idea of its scope. In addition to *FMS*, the Sonderforschungsbereich 7 also created a monograph series *Münstersche Mittelalterschriften*, which has published nearly fifty separate works since 1970, a number of which were authored by members of Societas et Fraternitas.

In the twenty years of their existence the members of this group have published necrologies, confraternity books, *libri memoriales*, and other memorial texts from about a dozen different monastic houses from the eighth through twelfth century (see the following works in the Bibliography: Althoff, 1978; Klostergemeinschaft von Fulda, 1978; Liber Memorialis von Remiremont, 1970; Liber Vitae von Corvey, 1983; Materialien, 1986; Neiske, 1979; Synopse, 1982; Totenbücher, 1983; Verbrüderungsbuch, 1972). Two of these stand out above the others in scope and in importance, Fulda and Cluny. The 1978 edition of Fulda necrological materials in five volumes was a combination of original sources along with essays on the abbey's history and prosopographical investigations into the identity of several hundred of the many thousands of individuals named in the documents. Ten different scholars collaborated on this monumental edition. The synopsis of Cluniac necrologies of 1982 in two volumes was a reconstitution of the lost necrology of the abbey of Cluny on the basis of extant necrologies from seven Cluniac dependencies—Limoges, Moissac, etc.—in the form of a parallel edition of entries from each. Separate facsimile editions of each of these seven, along with prosopographical essays on prominent people, are planned for the future.

In addition to these editions of texts, the directors of Societas et Fraternitas saw their project as calling for a whole series of accompanying studies on specialized topics such as manuscript tradition, codicology and paleography, personal names, and most importantly, prosopographical investigations into the individuals and groups encountered in the documents. At the time of the issuing of a summary account of accomplishments and perspectives of the project in 1981, the separate monographs in these categories numbered nearly 150 with well over twenty scholars having participated.[13]

Even though not formally part of the Sonderforschungsbereich 7, another group of German scholars at Freiburg has been working closely with the Münster school under the direction of Karl Schmid. With a research project entitled "Gruppenbildung und Gruppenbewusstsein," the Freiburg scholars have compiled a computerized data bank of names (some 400,000 by 1983) taken from all sorts of memorial documents which can be drawn upon for prosopographical research.[14]

Even before the Münster project was getting underway a group of British scholars was launching a major collective project, the Prosopography of the Later Roman Empire. The British Academy sponsored this undertaking which has been carried out by Cambridge classicists and led, until his death in 1970, by A. H. M. Jones, then most recently by J. R. Martindale. This group has as its goal the publishing of biographical notices accompanied by references to original sources for all distinguished lay people in the empire in the period in question and has thus far brought out two volumes of nearly 2,500 pages, both of which are of interest to medievalists. Volume 1 deals with the years A.D. 260–395 and volume 2 with the period A.D. 395–527. See *Prosopography* I (1971), II (1980) in the Bibliography. A third and final volume will cover the years A.D. 527–640 (on this project see Mathisen 1986; Heinzelmann 1982).

At the same time a team of French scholars directed by H.-I. Marrou and J.-R. Palanque at the University of Paris–Sorbonne, and with the backing of the Académie des Inscriptions et Belles Lettres, was preparing *Prosopographie chrétienne* for the same period, to treat the religious figures omitted by the British. With André Mandouze as principal author, they published their first volume of biographical notices for Africa during the period A.D. 303–533 in 1983 and their undertaking promises to be one of long term. (*Prosopographie Chrétienne*, 1983, Bibliography). Even though both of these projects are still incomplete scholars already have at their disposal incomparable biographical registers for the study of late Roman and early medieval society which will stand as models for medievalists seeking to create comparable repertories for the later period.

Alongside these projects can be set that of the German Historical Institute in Paris directed by K.F. Werner and named the PROL – Prosopographia regnorum orbis latini. Begun in the late 1960s, it has as its objective the creation of a register (it is not computerized) of biographical notices on prominent people in the western Latin kingdoms from later Rome to the twelfth century. By 1979, the members of this group had made entries on more than 300,000 individuals and were envisaging the time when they could claim to have a complete documentation on all persons mentioned in texts for a single century (Werner 1977).

Each of the aforementioned undertakings is explicitly prosopographical in its objectives in contrast to several others currently underway which serve different ends but which are still of interest to prosopographers. Into this category falls the German project "Series episcoporum," which began in 1976 with the objective of reworking, expanding, and completing the work of the same name by P. B. Gams (1873–86). Instead of the bare listing of names and dates of all bishops in the Latin church from the beginnings to 1198, the codirectors of the new project, S. Weinfurter of Eichstätt and O. Engels of Cologne, along with their nearly one hundred coworkers, propose to give much more in the way of vital biographical and career data for each bishop when available (Weinfurter 1986). Two volumes have appeared in the series which, when completed, will provide a magnificent working tool for every medievalist in need of information about given bishops (*Series episcoporum* 1982, 1984).

The British History of Parliament is another project of large dimensions which will provide valuable information for prosopographers of later medieval English government and society. The medieval segment of this enterprise has proceeded more slowly than the modern and in 1983 plans called for the first phase to cover Parliament's meeting during the years 1386–1422. This alone involves the preparation of some 3,200 biographical notices (Rawcliffe and Clark 1983). In the meantime, a recent study of more limited scope addresses itself to the question of the representatives of the lower clergy in Parliament from 1295–1340 (Denton and Dooley 1987).

Even though collective scholarly projects such as these stand out through their scope and chronological coverage most recent prosopographical research has been carried out by individual scholars. A good case in point is recent publication on social and political elites of the early medieval period. using more or less the same format as the authors of the PLRE, German scholars have brought out lists of biographical notices of prominent people for several of the early Germanic kingdoms. Examples include officials in the Merovingian kingdom (Ebling 1974; Selle-Hosbach 1974), in Lombard Italy (Jarnut 1972; Hlawitschka 1960), and in Visigothic and Suevi Spain (Garcia Moreno 1974; Claude 1978).[15] In some cases analysis accompanies and elucidates the interrelationships of those named (Althoff 1984), in others (Werner 1965) there is analysis alone without biographical lists. The aforementioned work of the Münster-Freiburg schools has been a highpoint of prosopographical research on leading lay, ecclesiastical, and monastic groups in the Empire, France, and Italy in the ninth through eleventh centuries.

Crusader historians have begun recently to apply the prosopographical approach to their subject as seen in the monographs of J. Longnon on the fourth (1978) and J. M. Powell on the fifth crusade (1986). On a related topic there is D. Wojtecki's study of the thirteenth-century Teutonic Knights (1971).

A growing number of English and American scholars have been concentrating their efforts recently on the late Anglo-Saxon and Anglo-Norman periods. Most of their publication has been scattered in short articles but there have also been longer monographs such as those of Kealey (1981) and Turner (1985, 1988).[16] An important work for another part of the Norman world was the list of Norman and French families who settled in South Italy and Sicily in the eleventh and twelfth centuries (Ménagier 1981). By 1984, the Anglo-Norman research had progressed to such a point that one group of scholars proposed the compiling of an Anglo-Norman biographical dictionary (Chandler, Newman, and Spear 1984). Of potentially great value to prosopographers of this period is the computerization of Domesday Book by a team of scholars from the University of California, Santa Barbara, which makes easily available the names of the many thousands of people named in this text (Fleming 1986).[17]

With regard to studies of political elites in the thirteenth to fifteenth centuries, a host of new monographs has appeared in the past decade. These include T. Evergates' study of aristocracy in the Troyes region (1975), W. M. Newman's detailed monograph on the lords of Nesle in Picardy (1971), A. Demurger's examination of royal *baillis* and *sénéchaux* in early fifteenth-century France (1978), J. Rogozinski's book on fourteenth-century Montpellier (1982), and, above all, Fr. Autrand's important thesis on the leading members (678 in all) of the Parlement of Paris from the mid-fourteenth to the mid-fifteenth century (1981).[18] On the English scene two examples of significant research are the books of K. B. McFarlane (1973) on the later English nobility and N. Saul's on the gentry in fourteenth-century Gloucestershire (1981).

When one turns to the ecclesiastical and monastic world of medieval Europe, he encounters a large number of new works from the past two decades. Only the most significant can be mentioned here beginning with the episcopate. Reference has already been made to the vast project to rework the *Series Episcoporum* of Gams (see above, p. 193). The Institute of Historical Research in London has similarly been engaged in a reedition of the eighteenth-century *Fasti Ecclesiae Anglie* of John Le Neve, a work in many volumes listing, with references to sources, bishops, chapter dignitaries, and canons of English and Welsh cathedrals (see Greenway 1980). N. Kamp's three-volume prosopography of the bishops in the kingdom of Sicily, 1194–1266, is a monumental one (1973–75). H. Zielinski has published (1984) the first volume of an analysis of imperial German bishops of the eleventh century, with the biographical notices to follow in a second. A number of scholars examined medieval cathedral chapters in efforts to answer such questions as how one became a canon, what kinds of men rose to that office, etc. H. Millet's study of approximately 800 canons of the chapter at Laon from 1272–1412 is the most extensive of these monographs (1982). Similar attempts at identification have been directed at monastic communities most notably in a number of the monographs of the Münster school referred to earlier such as the detailed studies of Fulda and Cluny. O. Dexle's prosopography of eighth- and ninth-century communities of monks and canons in France is another example (1978), as is W. R. Thomson's 1975 monograph on some fifty Franciscan friars who became bishops in the period 1226–61. A group of American scholars has announced a large scale project to gather biographical information on medieval nuns (McLaughlin 1987). Still another sector of the ecclesiastical world under investigation is the papal curia of the thirteenth century (Paravicini-Bagliani 1986).

A good deal of attention has also been paid to students and masters in the schools and universities of the later Middle Ages. In 1955 and 1960, S. Stelling-Michaud identified and followed the careers of Swiss students of law at the University of Bologna in the thirteenth and fourteenth centuries. In 1982, Ch. Renardy compiled a list of biographies of nearly 800 masters resident in the diocese of Liège between 1140 and 1350. In a four-volume work published between 1971 and 1985, C. M. Ridderikhoff and H. de Ridder-Symoens made available the Procurator's Register of students of the German nation at the University of Orleans, 1444–1556 and accompanied it with biographical notices for nearly 1,300 students of that period. The painstaking research of A. B. Emden in compiling biographical dictionaries of students at medieval Oxford and Cambridge (1957–59, 1963) led to a new interest in prosopographical studies of students at those universities. In the 1970s, a group of Cambridge scholars computerized the indices of Emden's two registers, and these have served as the basis for a number of new studies, including the first volumes in a new history of Oxford.[19] Questions taken up include the social and geographical origins of students, the percentages of those of lay and monastic status, careers subsequent to the university, etc. At the end of the medieval period comes J. Farge's biographical register of doctors of theology at the University of Paris in the first part of the sixteenth century (1980) and his study of stands taken by those men on the question of the Reformation (1985).

Urban populations have been a natural target for prosopographers intent on identifying various occupational, social, and political elements among medieval townspeople. Under other headings reference has already been made to studies of a number of these such as students, masters, governmental officials, bishops, and canons of cathedral chapters, all of whom usually formed part of urban communities. An interest in the history of medicine has also resulted in the compilation of two biographical dictionaries of medieval physicians (Talbot 1965; Wickersheimer 1936) and very recently studies based on these have begun to appear (Jacquart 1979; Gottfried 1983, 1984). J. Harvey has compiled a biographical dictionary of medieval English architects (2d ed., 1979) and S. Thrupp wrote an important monograph on merchants in later medieval London (1948). A number of shorter studies have been made of late medieval urban officials, town council members and the like (Wried 1986; Esch 1986; Hammer 1978), and the anatomy of town rebellion in fourteenth-century Germany has been investigated (Rotz 1974, 1976). S. Reynolds has studied the identity of the rulers of twelfth-century London (1972). A computerized edition of a Freiburg (Switzerland) *Bürgerbuch* of the period 1341–1416 was being prepared in 1979 (see Bachler 1984).

Medieval peasant populations present problems for the prosopographer in that given their lack of prominence, as well as the nature of the surviving records, peasants rarely stand out as anything more than vast numbers of largely undifferentiated, virtually anonymous individuals. Nonetheless, a number of historians of medieval English villagers have recently been seeking to draw up biographical lists of identifiable peasants (usually as members of families) in given villages at given times and to base their generalizations on analyses of groups of people rather than on random sampling. Examples of this approach are the works of J. A. Raftis (1974, 1982), E. Britton, (1977), and A. R. and E. B. DeWindt (1981). The DeWindts, for instance, published a biographical register of hundreds of Huntingdonshire peasants in their 1981 edition of various courts records from Huntingdonshire in the 1280s. Still, one recent critic spoke of peasant prosopography as being only in its infancy (Poos 1986).

No matter what the subject or group of people under investigation, the success of historians in carrying out prosopographical research depends on their perusing the widest possible range of original sources for biographical information and on their refining to the highest degree their techniques or methods for extracting this information. The remainder of this chapter will be devoted to a discussion of the original sources most useful for prosopography, then of the methods which have been developed to exploit them. No form of evidence can be overlooked in the quest for data about influential people, but not all are equally valuable. Up to the present, archaeological remains have offered little and, barring spectacular new finds, are not likely to be productive for some time to come. Inscribed tombstones have been useful for establishing death dates, family ties, and social rank, but unfortunately very little of this survives prior to the thirteenth and fourteenth centuries. Funerary inscriptions do exist in substantial numbers in European churches and museums, but the published accounts of them when such exist, are hopelessly scattered in the journals of local historical societies. To remedy this in the case of France, a group of scholars at the Center of Medieval Studies in Poitiers began in 1974 the gathering of medieval inscriptions on a regional basis and has now published twelve volumes in a series entitled *Corpus des inscriptions de la France médiévale.*[20] Numismatics can occasionally offer assistance when coin finds reveal who was striking money at a given time, but this type of evidence is too fragmentary and incomplete to be consistently useful. Seals and heraldic emblems may give clues to family origins and social status, but not before the thirteenth century.

In quantity, explicitness, and coverage of periods when numismatics, sigillography, and heraldry offer little or nothing, written documents remain the most valuable source of information for prosopography. Narrative sources vary considerably in value for studies of this kind. Annals and chronicles often name the powerful people of a region, and even though some chroniclers manifested little interest in the identification of the men who figure in their accounts, a few like Adémar of Chabannes were acutely conscious of questions of family origin. Adémar's chronicle, for instance, contains a great deal of unique biographical and genealogical information about the aristocracy of northern Aquitaine in his day.[21] Hagiographical literature generally contains little more than background information about the saint or holy man in question, although the author sometimes mentions his circle of friends and acquaintances. Few literary forms are more explicit in naming a person's friends and family than his personal letters, but far too few of these survive to be of much help to the historian. Another category of documents is that of ecclesiastical obituaries or calendars listing the death dates of people whose names churchmen saw fit to enter and whom they commemorated, either because of their fame or because they had some kind of connection or relationship with the church. Somewhat similar are the rolls of the dead (*rotuli mortuorum*) which monks carried on circuits between certain chosen abbeys and in which they announced the death of some famous person or of members of their own community.[22] Another source of a prodigious number of names of laity and clergy of the eighth through the eleventh centuries is the *libri memoriales,* or memorial books of abbeys from Italy, the Holy Roman Empire, and England. In these books scribes entered the names of individuals and groups of people with whom their monastery had some contact and for whom prayers were said. As with the obituaries, identification of people named in them is often very difficult. As mentioned earlier the Münster-Freiburg scholars have shown in magisterial fashion the utility of all these memorial documents for medieval prosopography.

Whatever the merits of the aforementioned sources, none comes close to rivaling in importance the documents which were drawn up to record specific transactions, such as charters, diplomas, notices, writs, and court rolls. Rare in the time of the barbarian kingdoms, these documents survive by the hundreds of thousands in virtually every part of western Europe after the ninth and tenth century and are a mine of information for the prosopographer. Issued mainly by kings, monasteries, and cathedral churches prior to the twelfth century, then also by the lay aristocracy, for the purpose of proving ownership or establishing some other right, each of these documents names anywhere from one to as many as a hundred people not only as principals to a transaction but also as witnesses. Because the witnesses sometimes came from the retinues of important men, the witness lists provide unparalleled opportunities for determining who associated with whom, and therefore for singling out the various social groupings of a given region at a given time. Furthermore, the custom of advising or requiring various members of the family to confirm actions of one of their own makes the charters easily the best source of genealogical information available about individuals of a certain time. Without them, very little medieval prosopography would be possible.

Nonetheless, certain problems hamper historians in their effort to extract the maximum of data from medieval charters. Accessibility is one, for huge quantities of them, especially those of the later Middle Ages, are unpublished and largely unknown due to being widely scattered and poorly or superficially inventoried in archival collections. For instance, no single French archive, provincial or national, appears to have a list of all the charters it possesses for the medieval period. Then many of the published editions of cartularies or collections of charters suffer from defects which detract seriously from their usefulness. Insufficient effort by the editor to date the undated charters, and to separate the authentic from the forged ones, lays traps for the unsuspecting historian unfamiliar with the edition. In many cases, the editor's failure to index comprehensively all the people appearing in his charters means that they are in effect lost to everyone save the researcher who takes the trouble to leaf through the volume page by page. In other instances, especially in cases where the original does not survive, but only later copies, the published version of a charter may not be the best one available. Working his way through seventeenth- and eighteenth-century manuscript copies of medieval charters in the Bibliothèque Nationale in Paris, the German historian K. F. Werner discovered a number of witness lists of ninth- to eleventh-century charters which had been omitted from nineteenth-century published editions because the editors failed to take the trouble to hunt down the best extant version. Just a handful of those missing witness lists enabled Werner, in a brilliant piece of detective work, to revise substantially the prevailing views about the history of the aristocracy of the provinces of Anjou, Maine, and the Touraine in Carolingian times.[23]

Since family membership usually played an extremely important role in determining at least where a person's career began, if not the later course it took, the identification of family and relatives is the starting point of all prosopography. "Family" here is taken in a broad, not restricted sense. On the one hand, it means all living relatives or kinsmen, both immediate — such as parents, grandparents, and children — and collateral — such as aunts, uncles, cousins, second cousins, and so forth. On the other hand, it takes into account ancestors on both sides of the family as far back as possible. Members of the immediate family normally exerted a greater influence over a person's life and career, but experience has shown that more distant relatives or ancestors — above all, those particularly distinguished in their own right — could also help explain some later preferment, advancement, or modification of status.

When compared with genealogical research in early modern and modern European history, medieval genealogy suffers from the serious handicap of the lack of enough evidence to permit the construction of precise and extended family trees for more than a relatively small number of families. Prior to the tenth century, only royalty and occasionally a noble lineage or two can be known with any accuracy, and then rarely for more than couple of generations. A good many aristocratic houses can be followed continuously from the eleventh and twelfth centuries, but uncertainty continues to plague the family trees of many others, especially families of the lesser aristocracy.

In many cases genealogists have had to be content with partial identifications, such as the case where only one of the parents is located, or with vague assertions to the effect that X is related to Y but in a way which cannot at present be known, or even with just the probability that X came from family Y. Progress beyond this point will often be impossible but this is not necessarily a worthless conclusion since an unspecified relationship, or even the probability of one, is almost always more worth knowing than nothing at all.

The foundation for most medieval genealogy has been laid by the research of the countless amateur and professional historians who have been attracted to the subject for centuries for various personal, social, and academic reasons. In France it was a number of sixteenth- and seventeenth-century scholars who elevated the subject from stories compounded of myth and fact to scientific accounts with a high degree of reliability. They accomplished this at the cost of prodigious labors in sifting through mountains of documents in search of genealogical data on the families of royalty and nobility of the Middle Ages. So thorough was the research of men like Ph. Labbe, E. Baluze, the Père Anselme, and above all the brothers Louis and Scévole Sainte-Marthe, that any modern genealogist in French history must begin with their works. Another early work of lasting value to the modern genealogist is the *Gallia Christiana*. Although its purpose is not family history but a survey of French bishoprics and abbeys, it supplies valuable biographical information about medieval French bishops, abbots, and other ecclesiastical dignitaries and thus renders a service to the genealogist. The same can be said for its English, Spanish, and Italian counterparts.

While acknowledging his debt to them, the modern medievalist can accept the results of earlier genealogists only after thorough checking. This is a natural consequence of the fact that modern scholars sometimes have access to documents which the earlier scholars missed. In addition, inadequate scholarship occasionally mars the work of earlier writers, especially when they were not professional historians but untrained laymen trying their hand at family history.[24]

As might well be imagined, personal names have proven to be the basic means for identifying a person as a member of a certain family, especially when, as is often the case, unequivocal proof of a blood relationship is missing. However the assumption that a person belonged to a certain family because he bore a name common to it is by no means always justified. This is due to peculiar features in medieval naming customs. After the eleventh century, the process of identification through names is less complicated than before, but even then it is not always a simple matter. From that time on, scribes increasingly identified the people in their charters by adding a second name, or surname, to the baptismal, or first name. People chose these surnames from a variety of sources but a common one was the patronymic or matronymic, that is, the father's or the mother's name. The scribe could render this in several ways, such as Geraldus filius Hugonis, Geraldus Hugonis, or Geraldus de Hugoni, but all meant the same thing — Gerald the son of Hugh. Patronymics obviously would solve the genealogist's problem, except for the fact that the aristocracy seldom took that kind of surname. Instead, they preferred to be known by the name of their principal residence or castle. The lords of Lusignan, a family of castellan rank in Poitou, called themselves variously Hugo de Liziniaco, Hugo Liziniacensis, and Hugo dominus de Lizianiaco. Without hesitation, one can consider any otherwise unidentified Hugo of Lusignan to be a member of that family, but this does not apply to just anyone who took the surname Lusignan. Other families might appropriate the name of the village, castle, or town as a surname and the chances of this occurring increase as the size of the community in question increases. Under those circumstances the first name becomes the key to identification.

Although in most cases surnames aid in identification, this is not always so, and, to be specific, lack of the same surname does not necessarily rule out family membership, since surnames were not initially hereditary family names. People sometimes changed surnames, and occasionally more than once in a lifetime. In the case of the aristocracy, this could happen when a son acquired a village or a castle different from his father's and took its placename as his surname. Once again, the first name is the decisive element in identification.

The difficulties increase and the reliability of conclusions decreases once the search turns back to the period prior to the eleventh century, when it was the Germanic custom to give single names only. Then it is often difficult, if not impossible, to distinguish between different people bearing the same name; to decide, for example, whether the William who appears in three or more contemporary charters from the same region is the same person, or two or three different ones. Only someone who knows like-named individuals well enough to distinguish between them on the basis of some other identifying characteristics can resolve the dilemmas arising from such a circumstance. Extraordinary variations in the spelling of the same name from region to region, and even within the same region, do not help either. Readings found for the name Conrad prior to the eleventh century range from Chonradus, Choanradus, Chuanradus, Chuonradus, Cuonradus, and Honratus in Bavaria and Swabia, to Guneradus in Italy, Conradus in Neustria, and Cohunradus, Cunrhadus, Gundradus and Gohuntdradus in Burgundy.[25] Nor did the tendency of some people to take a nickname entirely different from their baptismal name aid the scholar. Thus, in a charter of Cluny, a woman who called herself Richoara in the beginning of the act is listed as Deca at the end.[26]

When all of these complications have been taken into account, identity of names remains a vital factor in establishing the probability of family relationships, especially in the case of families which first appear in documents around the year A.D. 1000. One of the most familiar predicaments confronting historians of the Frankish aristocracy of the early Middle Ages is that of the prominent family of the eleventh and twelfth centuries which, because of its surname, can be followed back to the end of the tenth century, but whose trace is then lost in the earlier period of single names. Marc Bloch assumed that the first known member of the family was its founder, or at least the person who raised it to prominence, through control of the castle after which he named himself.[27] For a number of years this view had widespread acceptance, but then in the 1960s detailed monographs on French and Belgian aristocracy called it into question by showing that many important families of the eleventh century could indeed be traced further back and that, in fact, most descended from distinguished ancestors of Carolingian times.[28] The first family head to take a surname from a castle was not the founder but simply the first to preside over the family at a time when its wealth and power came to be centered around a fixed, fortified site. Leading names or the names preferred by the family in the eleventh and twelfth centuries, what the Germans call *Leitnamen,* provided the key to the identification of earlier ancestors who had no surnames. Having determined what those key names were, scholars looked for appearances of the name in earlier generations in the same and in neighboring regions. The finding of the desired names, often in unexpected places, did not in itself prove the existence of a family relationship but it did establish the possibility and, more often, the probability of one, which other evidence then confirmed. A monograph by J. Wollasch on the origins of the lords of Déols, a castellan family in Berry, illustrates this procedure. Unable to find the ancestors of Ebbo, the first known lord of Déols around A.D. 900, Wollasch consulted charters of abbeys of northern Aquitaine and ascertained that the name, in combination with two others common in the family, showed up frequently in the later ninth century in the area around Poitiers, more than 100 miles distant. While he could not identify a specific family from which this Ebbo might have descended, he established the likelihood that it was one near Poitiers, and such a hypothesis fits in well with the fact that Ebbo acknowledged as his lord the Duke of Aquitaine, who was also Count of Poitou and had his principal residence in Poitiers.[29]

Other forms of evidence often come to the aid of the genealogist who, through identity of personal names, has shown the probability of a family relationship between two people of different generations, but lacks definitive proof of it. Birth or residence in the same place obviously supports the possibility of a relationship and needs no further comment. The possession of adjacent properties or properties in the same village can also lend weight to the suspicion that two people or families may be related, since originally this may have been a single estate which was divided among heirs after the death of the parents. Precisely the same applies to office holding. With titles, like fiefs, tending to become hereditary in France in the tenth century, one may automatically suspect that any given official was related to the previous holders of the same office, although this alone does not have the force of certainty. After the discouragement of clerical marriage in the eleventh century, aristocratic families could maintain their hold on ecclesiastical offices by arranging for a title to pass from uncle to nephew in successive generations. The special ties which associated many leading families with a favored monastery which they had either founded or heavily endowed can also serve as an element in family identification. Thus, pronounced favoritism toward a specific house can link a person to those who had been its principal benefactors in earlier generations. One may also suspect that a person who requests burial at a certain monastery, and who perhaps takes the monastic cowl there in his old age, is related to others of his status who were buried there in earlier times.

It is the great merit of several recent German historians to have shown that a systematic coordination of all the indices to family relationship — that is, names, properties, offices, preferred monasteries, etc. — can refine the techniques of genealogical research to a high degree and lead to successes hitherto thought impossible. An example of this was K. F. Werner's monograph on the origins of the family of the counts of Anjou.[30] Refusing to accept the verdict of Louis Halphen that the family of the first known count, Fulk the Red (A.D. 886–942), simply could not be identified, Werner reattacked the problem and solved it by locating new and more complete charter copies in the Bibliothèque Nationale in Paris, and by looking further afield than Halphen for possible ancestors. Evidence of names supported by contiguous property holdings showed that Fulk's father belonged to a Frankish family in the Orléans region in the mid-ninth century, and that his mother was a relative of Adalard, *sénéschal* of Louis the Pious, and one of the most powerful advisors of Charles the Bald. By proving that one distinguished comital family of feudal times descended from high Carolingian aristocracy and was not self-made, Werner made an important contribution to the whole of later Carolingian history and demonstrated how genealogy could lead to results far more significant than ordinary family history.

Lack of clarity about names is closely related to another more basic problem for prosopography, namely uncertainty about the very structure of aristocratic families in the Middle Ages. Medieval documents continually speak of familial units, using Latin terms which we translate by clan, kindred, lineage, and family, yet the precise meaning of these terms is often obscure today. Questions arise concerning the *parentela,* clan or group of kinsmen; how many and which relatives it embraced and how meaningful

the relationship linking the members was. What obligations and respon-
sibilities did it impose on members, and what privileges did it confer? Which
collateral relatives did it group and what about affinal kin, that is, in-laws
or relatives by marriage?[31] Another question concerns the way in which
people traced their ancestry. After the tenth century, it was clearly through
the male line, but some recent studies have demonstrated that in the early
Middle Ages people calculated descent through both female and male lines.
A German historian who has studied this subject more thoroughly than
anyone else, Karl Schmid, argues that aristocratic family structure underwent basic changes in the unsettled years of the tenth and eleventh centuries, and that it was the "territorialization" of families of the aristocracy
which accounts for the development of the male-oriented lineage of the
later Middle Ages.[32] Settled on an hereditary estate dominated by a castle,
and no longer reliant on the favors of the king or a territorial prince for
its status or importance, the family came to depend more and more on
its male head to defend and administer wisely its possessions and to pass
them on intact to his heir. As his role in family affairs took on greater importance, particularly in matters of war, his children came increasingly to
trace their descent through his side of the family, and the ultimate result
was the male dominated lineage so well known for aristocratic society after
the eleventh century. Whatever may be the validity of Schmid's views, and
so far they have persuaded many, it is obvious that prosopographers can
only profit from a better awareness of what medieval aristocratic families
were like and what kind of an influence or hold they exerted over individual members.[33]

From its initial preoccupation with the genealogical question of family origin, prosopography next moves to a study of the individual's life and
career. The childhood and adolescence of most people normally remain
completely unknown, although an occasional reference sometimes reveals
where and with whom boys spent the customary several years as squires
while training for knighthood.[34] The friendships and acquaintances formed
as a result of such an apprenticeship may well contain the clue to later
associations, alliances, or favors. Likewise, in the case of those who received an education, mention of their mentor or of the school where they
studied may shed light on their circle of acquaintances. After knighthood,
the several years of travel which many young men of good families spent
in search of adventure, tournaments, and sometimes a wife, further enlarged the group of people they came to know and with whom they sometimes formed lasting ties of friendship.[35]

The way a person married, the type of partner chosen, can be a valuable guide to social standing. It has long been assumed that since aristo-

cratic marriage was a kind of business contract with benefits to both parties, people tended to avoid economic and social disparagement by marrying their social equals. However, recent studies have found evidence of not a few cases where men married into families of higher standing than their own.[36] The object of the historian with regard to marriage is to identify the wife and her family and its status: what kind of offices or functions her father held, how much property he had and where, what kinds of important people her family associated with, and all other similar indices to her family's rank are important.

An acquaintance with the children of an aristocratic marriage also contributes to the biographies of their parents. Something of the parents' social expectations and status can also be learned from the careers which they planned for their children, whether in the church or in some secular office. And of course, the same applies to the spouses they chose or approved for their children.

Marriage was also the occasion when many young men entered upon their inheritances or their share of the family patrimony. A family's status passed to its children at birth, but it was the inheritance which provided them with the means to live in the style of their equals. The nature and size of that patrimony can indeed be an excellent guide to social status, especially if information about the person's parents and ancestors is missing or incomplete. Consequently a vital segment of any aristocratic biography is what German scholars call *Besitzgeschichte,* that is, a description of the individual's inheritance, determining if possible its size, location, and composition. Very often the historian has to deal with highly fragmentary information, since wills or personal testaments rarely survive before the twelfth or thirteenth centuries, and frequently the only clue to a person's property comes at those moments when he or she parted with some of it to endow a church. Yet even those donations which happened to be recorded often contain valuable hints as to the character of the whole. For instance, lavish gifts suggest that much greater holdings lay in reserve since important families did not normally endanger their position by stripping themselves bare. Vast estates thus hint at a high-ranking family and, conversely, donations of small properties usually imply a more modest standing, although this is not an infallible guide, since the powerful sometimes restricted their gifts in order to avoid excessive dismemberment of their estates. Similarly, the dispersion of holdings over a large area, such as an entire county or more, probably identifies its owner as a person of more than local importance, whereas their concentration in a single district usually means the contrary. Likewise, when a patrimony included one or more castles it quite obviously marked out its holder as a member of the higher aristocracy. Ownership of parish churches and tithes furnished another source of income, but all levels of the aristocracy held them, so it is difficult to use them as a criterion for higher or lower rank. The same is true of income from rights over peasants, as opposed to income from land. These included labor services, tallage, marriage taxes, death taxes, military service, and, above all, rights of justice. Variations in the size of an estate over a period of time are of interest because they may indicate a change in rank. If a person increased his or her holdings in a dramatic fashion, the question becomes how, under what circumstances, by purchase or gift, and if the latter, from whom, and why? The same questions apply for the opposite case, that of the person whose holdings diminished in size or importance.

A person's life as a mature adult affords the greatest number of opportunities to observe his or her activities and to form an estimate of social status and influence in contemporary affairs. Central to the inquiry is a study of any office that may have been held in secular administration or the church or to the function exercised. An acquaintance with the person's office and its attributes—that is, with the authority it conferred, the prestige it enjoyed, and the income it bestowed—will tell a good deal about the status of its holder. In some cases, documents picture the individual in the act of exercising authority, making decisions, issuing instructions, or giving orders; in many others, one must infer this from a general knowledge of the office in question.

Proof that someone held a certain office almost always comes from the titles taken or given in documents. A careful study of titles, the customs governing their usage, and especially any variation in usage, may very well cast light on the status of the people who held the offices. To be sure, discrimination has to be used in interpreting this kind of evidence, since scribes from different chanceries—whether papal, royal, episcopal, comital, seigneurial, or monastic—sometimes attached slightly different meanings to the same terms. Then, regardless of who used it, the key title *dominus* could have a number of different meanings. Depending on the context and on the position of the word either before or after a personal name, *dominus* could identify its bearer as either the lord of a vassal or peasant, as a castellan or commander of a castle, as a husband, as a cleric or monk, or simply as a member of the aristocracy whether he be count, bishop, castellan, or abbot. Once these variations have been recognized, a study of the usage of this title can be revealing. For instance, in Poitou from the ninth to the mid-eleventh centuries, only counts, bishops, and abbots took the title *dominus* along with the title of their office, as in *dominus Guillelmus comes*. Then, after 1050, a new group of men identifiable as castellans began to use it, and finally, around 1100, knights (*milites*) appropriated it. What amounts to an extension or popularization of the title suggests a rise in the social prestige of the latter two groups of men, and, in fact, other evidence clearly supports such a conclusion.[37]

In addition to personal titles and titles of office, medieval scribes also employed another category of terms to single out people on the basis of their work or profession, place of residence, legal status, dependence on a lord, or some sort of personal distinction. Historians of the aristocracy have regularly relied on several terms in this last category, and especially *vir illuster, clarus, nobilis,* and *venerabilis,* to identify members of the aristocracy. But, again, caution is in order when evaluating such terms. A statistical study of thousands of personal titles, titles of office, and descriptive terms in Poitou has shown that scribes employed the term *vir nobilis* very rarely between the ninth and twelfth centuries, and then only to designate otherwise obscure men, and never counts, viscounts, bishops, abbots, or castellans.[38] In view of this it is difficult to avoid the conclusion that *nobilis vir* was not, as has been thought, a term which separated nobles from everyone else, but one which identified those whose status was obscure because their identity was not automatically known to any contemporary. In sum, the study of personal titles and other such terms is a vital part of prosopographical research and deserves the most detailed attention. It requires the broadest approach possible since, as is evident from some of the examples just cited, observation of individual cases out of context would result in a failure to see their actual meaning.

How an individual acquired an office is a matter of basic interest. One may have inherited it; it may have come through marriage; possibly it was a favor bestowed in recognition of services rendered. Whenever a man was the first in his family to hold the office, it obviously falls into one of the latter two categories and probably signified an improvement in rank or status. Occasionally a contemporary source states explicitly that so-and-so owed his office to this or that personage, but in many if not most instances, this, as well as the circumstances leading to the promotion, is obscure. Under these conditions, the approach which offers the greatest promise of explanation as to how a given individual acquired a new office is that of attempting to determine what contacts or connections he had with people in a position to confer such an office, and especially with the leading men of his region or province. In the case of the highest aristocracy, such as dukes and counts, this means the king; in the case of lesser men, it means the dominant figures in their province or county.

The best guide not only to the origin of a person's office but to his standing in society as a whole is to be found in the people with whom he associated. Their status as high, middle, or low level aristocracy is a gauge to his own, since, lacking evidence to the contrary, one usually assumes that he had approximately the same rank as those with whom he had regu.lar contact. A number of factors other than social status may also explain why someone kept company with certain people and thus help to clarify his relationships with them but in the final analysis all reduce to some sort of common interest or common bond. Family ties, relationships of lordship-vassalage, and office holding are among those encountered most often. As mentioned earlier, the charter witness lists are the best source of this type of information for long periods in the Middle Ages.

Greater precision on an individual's rank or importance with any given group of people may be inferred from several types of information. In the first place, the office alone conferred a certain status on its holder since some automatically ranked higher than others, as, for instance, the precedence of viscounts over vicars in Carolingian times. Another index to status was the order people took in the witness lists. Although this subject has not received extensive study, there are strong reasons for believing that, in many cases, the numerical order of witnesses corresponded to their rank in the particular assembly of which they were members. Thus, J. C. Russell found a clear and consistent order of precedence among the aristocracy, lay and ecclesiastical, who witnessed the charters of King John of England.[39] Whether the courts of lesser people, at the same or different times, observed the same kind of protocol with comparable consistency remains to be seen. Constant changing of the position of the same witnesses would tend to discourage such a conclusion, but a permanent change of rank for a single individual may well point to an enhancement or a disparagement of status.

A person's role or function in the charters in which he appears will also tell a good deal about him. Put in the most simple terms, people participated either passively as onlookers or witnesses to the actions of others, or actively as principals in a transaction in one of many capacities such as donor, seller, buyer, plaintiff, or defendant in a dispute. At first glance, those who initiated transactions seem to overshadow those who merely witness; but this conclusion depends on two variables—first, the object and the importance of the transaction, and second, the quality or rank of the other people present. Thus, just witnessing an act of a distinguished personage may label someone as having a higher rank than the individual who made a donation in the presence of simple villagers. In the same way, a donation of minor importance, such as a small field or an annual rent of a few pennies, may lead one to suspect that the donor had limited resources and perhaps low status. On the other hand, the man who granted huge estates, founded a monastery, or made some similar action, must be considered someone of high family, regardless of whether or not distinguished people witnessed his act.

Evidence about the geographical scope or range of a person's movements, personal contacts, and possessions can also contribute to determining that person's social importance. The man whose holdings were confined to a single small district and who is seldom, if ever, seen journeying beyond that district cannot have been comparable in status, other things being equal, to the individual whose possessions spread over an entire province or more, and whose travels carried him long distances from home. The frequency of a person's appearance in charters seems also to be a good, though not infallible, criterion of status. The most prestigious and powerful people generally turn up more often than others, and, conversely, rarity of appearance usually implies social insignificance.

An outstanding example of the way in which many of the aforementioned approaches for charter analysis can be combined to produce a rich harvest of information about a single family over an extended period of time is the study by J. F. Lemarignier on the eleventh-century Capetian kings.[40] He demonstrated how evidence from personal titles, witness lists, and subject and range of transactions converged to document much more thoroughly and exactly than could be done with chronicle evidence the decline in authority and prestige of the early Capetians, reign by reign and almost decade by decade, from A.D. 987 to 1077. During that ninety-year period, their charters came to deal with less and less important matters and the territorial range of their movements and activities became more and more restricted, to the point that a French king rarely traveled south of the Loire by mid-century. At the same time, they slowly abandoned the traditional method of appending just the royal signature to their diplomas and began to solicit the *signa* of their followers as witnesses, a clear sign that the older custom no longer sufficed to validate a royal act, and an equally clear sign of their declining prestige. The social standing of the people with whom the king appeared also steadily dropped and finally included ordinary knights and even burghers, a far cry from earlier times when only the most distinguished were admitted to his presence. What Lemarignier has accomplished with the Capetians can certainly be attempted on a broad scale with the aristocracy in general, and only the relative rarity of charters for the latter will somewhat limit its success.

At the conclusion of a survey like this, it is fitting to attempt to assess the importance of prosopographical studies in medieval history at the present time. There can be little doubt that the prosopographical approach has made exceptional advances in medieval research in the past fifteen years, appealing to an ever-larger number of scholars in widely differing fields. A comparison of the bibliography of the first version of this essay (1976) with the present one makes this clear. The earlier one had to be completely revamped with wholesale replacement of its titles by new ones reflecting the trends and accomplishments of the past fifteen years. The earlier one could hope to be reasonably comprehensive, something completely out of question for the present one, which aims, at best, at giving guidance to other works or bibliographies which themselves can provide fuller coverage. A veritable flood of new monographs and biographical lists in almost all major fields of medieval research has brought about this change and thus testifies to the spreading enthusiasm for the prosopographical approach. Many new projects are now underway, a few of great scope and collective in character, but most being carried out by individuals on a smaller scale. Some, most notably that of the Münster school, have been highly productive, many others have proceeded more slowly because of the time-consuming demands of assembling biographical data on given groups of people. Historians have begun to organize in order to better coordinate their labors—witness the international colloquia of the early 1980s and the beginning of a new journal in 1980. The very volume of new studies, scattered as they inevitably are in so many different journals and books, has magnified the difficulties facing the prosopographer now seeking to keep abreast of new publications, and points to the need for more effective bibliographical control than now exists. Yet this is a minor technical problem. These same studies have amply shown that the prosopographical approach has already led to a better understanding of almost every different social or occupational group in medieval society, and will doubtless continue to do so in the future.

NOTES

1. The term prosopography appears at least as early as the sixteenth century, a word coined by an as yet unknown author from the classical Greek *prosopon* (person), and referring to the description and the study of personal appearance. Historians began to employ it commonly with its currently accepted meaning by at least the later nineteenth century but possibly as early as the eighteenth century. How and when the change in meaning occurred is not yet clear. See Nicolet 1970, 210–11, and Werner 1979, 67–69.

2. G. Tellenbach, "Zur Bedeutung der Personenforschung für die Erkenntnis des früheren Mittelalters," *Freiburger Universitätsreden* (Freiburg: Hans Ferdinand Schulz Verlag, 1957), 10.

3. L. Génicot, "Haut clergé et noblesse dans le diocèse de Liège du XIᵉ au XVᵉ siècle,"

in *Adel und Kirche. Gerd Tellenbach zum 65. Geburtstag dargebracht von Freunden und Schülern* (Freiburg: Herder, 1968), 237–58.

4. For brief surveys of the history of prosopography in the twentieth century see Nicolet 1970; A. Chastagnol, "La prosopographie; méthode de recherche sur l'histoire du Bas-Empire," *Annales, Économies, Sociétés, Civilisations* 25 (1970): 1229–35; and Lawrence Stone, "Prosopography," in *Historical Studies Today,* edited by F. Gilbert and S. Graubard (New York: Norton, 1972), 107–40.

5. A. H. M. Jones, J. R. Martindale, and J. Morris, *The Prosopography of the Later Roman Empire* (Cambridge: Cambridge Univ. Press) 1(1971): 266–395, 2(1980): 395–527.

6. Stone, "Prosopography," 113–18.

7. G. Beech, "Prosopography," *Medieval Studies: An Introduction,* edited by J. M. Powell (Syracuse: Syracuse Univ. Press, 1976), 155.

8. N. Bulst and J.-Ph. Genet, eds., *Medieval Lives and the Historian: Studies in Medieval Prosopography, Proceedings of the 1st International Interdisciplinary Conference on Medieval Prosopography* (Kalamazoo: Medieval Institute Publications of Western Michigan University, 1986).

9. *Informatique et Prosopographie, Table Ronde CNRS,* edited by H. Millet, (Paris: 1985). *Prosopographie et la Genèse de l'État Moderne,* edited by Fr. Autrand, (Paris: Éditions du Centre National de la Recherche Scientifique, 1986).

10. K. Schmid, "Der 'Freiburger Arbeitskreis.' Gerd Tellenbach zum 70. Geburtstag," *Zeitschrift für die Geschichte des Oberrheins* 131(1974): 344–47. It is conceivable that through his students Tellenbach exercised a greater influence on the direction of medieval research in the next generation than any other medieval scholar in recent times.

11. K. Schmid and J. Wollasch, "Societas et Fraternitas," *FMH,* 9(1975): 1–48

12. One disadvantage of this, which is in no way a scholarly criticism, has been the resulting high cost of publication which, unfortunately, has probably limited their circulation in the scholarly world.

13. *Erträge und Perspektiven der Sonderforschungsbereich 7: "Mittelalterforschung" an der Westfälischen Wilhelms-Universität in Münster* (Münster: Wilhelms-Univ. Verlag, 1981).

14. G. Althoff, "Unerforschte Quellen aus Quellenarmer Zeit, IV. Zur Verflechtung der Führungschichten in den Gedenkquellen des frühen 10. Jahrhunderts," in *MLH,* 37, 39; and D. Geuenich, "Datenbank mittelalterlicher Personen," *MLH,* 405, 413.

15. On recent Lombard prosopography see Fanning, "A Review of Lombard Prosopography," 1981.

16. On this subject, see Hollister "Elite Prosopography in Saxon and Norman England," 1981.

17. For one of the first examples of results obtained from this database, see Fleming 1987.

18. For recent research on the French representative assemblies, see Bulst 1984, 1986.

19. For reviews of recent publications, see Burson 1982; Evans 1986.

20. The most recent volume is Vol. 12. *Aude-Herault* (Paris: Centre National de la Recherche Scientifique, 1988).

21. L. Levillain, "Adémar de Chabannes généalogiste," *Bulletin de la Société des Antiquaires de l'Ouest* (1934–35), 237–63.

22. L. Delisle, *Rouleaux des morts du IXe au XVe siècle* (Paris: Mme. Ve. J. Renouard, 1866).

23. K. F. Werner, "Untersuchungen zur Frühgeschichte des Französischen Fürstentums," *Die Welt als Geschichte* (1958), 18:256–89; (1959), 19:146–93; (1960), 20:87–119.

24. It must be recognized, however, that genealogists today enjoy a tremendous advantage over their predecessors of a century or more ago in having at their disposal a formidable

array of dictionaries, encyclopedias, and bibliographies which makes it possible for them to determine quickly what has already been written on this or that person or family. See the many works of this kind, too numerous to be cited individually here, in the Bibliography.

25. Maurice Chaume, *Recherches d'histoire chrétienne et médiévale: Mélanges publiés à la mémoire de l'historien avec une biographie* (Dijon: Academie des Sciences, Arts et Belles-lettres, 1947), 218.

26. Ibid. This is an early instance of the reduction of Richard to Dick, although here in the feminine form.

27. M. Bloch, *Feudal Society*, vol. 2, *Social Classes and Political Organization*, L. A. Manyon, trans. (Chicago: Univ. of Chicago Press, 1961), 283–92.

28. L. Génicot, "La noblesse au Moyen Age dans l'ancienne 'Francie,'" *Annales, Écono-mies, Sociétés, Civilisations* 17(1962): 1–22.

29. J. Wollasch, "Königtum, Adel und Kloster im Berry während des 10. Jahrhunderts," in *Neue Forschungen über Cluny und die Cluniacenser,* edited by G. Tellenbach (Freiburg: Herder, 1959), 17–165; app. 1: "Zur Verbreitung des Namens Abbo in Aquitanien bis zum Ende des 10. Jahrhunderts."

30. Werner, "Untersuchungen," *Die Welt als Geschichte* (1958), pt. 2, "Zu den Anfängen des Hauses Anjou," 264–79.

31. A. Murray, *Germanic Kinship Structure: Studies in Law and Society in Antiquity and the Early Middle Ages* (Toronto: Pontifical Institute of Mediaeval Studies, 1983).

32. K. Schmid, "Zur Problematik von Familie, Sippe und Geschlecht, Haus und Dynastie beim mittelalterlichen Adel," *Zeitschrift für die Geschichte des Oberrheins* 107(1957): 1–62.

33. On this see C. Bouchard 1986.

34. Sidney Painter, *William Marshal: Knight-errant, Baron and Regent of England* (Baltimore: Johns Hopkins Univ. Press, 1967), 16.

35. G. Duby, "Au XIIᵉ siècle: Les jeunes dans la société aristocratique dans la France du Nord-Ouest," *Annales, Économies, Sociétés, Civilisations* 19(1964): 835–47.

36. See essays in Settimane di studio del centro italiano di studi sull'alto medioevo, no. 24, *Il matrimonio nella societa altomedievale* (Spoleto: Presso de la sede del Centro, 1977).

37. G. Beech, "Personal Titles and Social Classes in Medieval France from the 9th to the 12th Century," paper delivered at the American Historical Association Convention, December 30, 1971, New York City. On the use of titles as a gauge of the social importance of the *milites* in France in the eleventh and twelfth centuries see J. Flori, *L'essor de la chevalerie XIᵉ-XIIᵉ siècles* (Genève: Droz, 1986), 120.

38. Ibid.

39. J. C. Russell, "Social Status at the Court of King John," *Speculum* 11(1937): 319–28. For a recent summary of the study of early medieval witness list rankings, see H. Fichtenau, "Die Reihung der Zeugen in Urkunden des frühen Mittelalters," *Mitteilungen des Instituts für Österreichische Geschichtsforschung* 87(1979): 301–15.

40. J. F. Lemarignier, *Le gouvernement royal aux premiers temps capétiens (987–1107)* (Paris: Picard, 1965), 128–30.

BIBLIOGRAPHY

The volume of new monographs in medieval prosopography since the 1970s has been so great as to preclude any possibility of a complete bibliography of recent publications. I have thus chosen to lay stress on listing, in part 1, works which contain bibliographies or give reviews of recent prosopographical publications in the various fields of medieval studies. Works which contain biographies and lists of officials and prominent people come in part 2. Part 3 lists recent monographs on methodological problems and part 4 deals with computers and medieval prosopography. Part 5 contains a highly selective listing of recent monographs in medieval prosopography. In its overall emphasis, this bibliography reflects the author's closer acquaintance with French and English history. This, in turn, explains the inevitable gaps in citation of works for other parts of Europe, Byzantium, and Islam.

Abbreviations

Francia   *Francia: Forschungen zur Westeuropäischen Geschichte.* 1972–. Paris.

FMH   *Frühmittelalterliche Studien.* 1967–. Münster.

HMO   *L'histoire médiévale et les ordinateurs.* 1981. Rapports d'une Table Ronde internationale. Documentations et recherches publiées par l'Institut Historique Allemand de Paris. Edited by K. F. Werner. Munich: K. G. Saur.

IP   *Informatique et Prosopographie.* 1985. Table Ronde CNRS. Edited by H. Millet. Paris: Centre National de la Recherche Scientifique.

MLH   *Medieval Lives and the Historian: Studies in Medieval Prosopography.* 1986. Proceedings of the 1st International Interdisciplinary Conference on Medieval Prosopography, University of Bielefeld, 3–5 December, 1982. Kalamazoo: Medieval Institute Publications.

MP   *Medieval Prosopography.* 1980–. Kalamazoo.

PGEM   *Prosopographie et la Genèse de l'État moderne.* 1986. Edited by Fr. Autrand. Paris: École Normale Superieure de jeune filles.

PLRE   A. H. M. Jones, J. R. Martindale, and J. Morris. *The Prosopography of the Later Roman Empire.* 1971–80. Cambridge: Cambridge Univ. Press. Vol. 1, 1971. Vol. 2, 1980.

PS   *Prosopographie als Sozialgeschichte?* 1978. Methoden personengeschichtlicher Erforschung des Mittelalters. Sektionsbeiträge zum 32. Deutschen Historikertag, Hamburg, 1978. Munich: W. Fink Verlag.

Bibliographies of Modern Works

There are many bibliographical guides, both general and specialized, to modern works on individuals or groups relevant to the interests of the prosopographer. For fuller information on these, see E. V. Crosby, C. J. Bishko, and R. L. Kellog, *Medieval Studies: A Bibliographical Guide* (New York: Garland, 1983).

Continuing (serial) Bibliographies

Bibliographies that appear at regular intervals and thus index new titles as they appear.

Annual Bibliography of British and Irish History. 1975–. London.
Bibliografia Storica Nazionale. 1939–. Rome.
Bibliographie annuelle de l'histoire de France. 1955–. Paris. See under heading *Généalogie et biographie collective.*
Bibliographie de l'histoire de Belgique. 1953–. Annually, in the *Revue Belge de Philologie et d'Histoire.*
Cahiers de Civilisation Médiévale. 1958–. Poitiers. The annual bibliographies of this periodical list current works on medieval people (for the ninth to the twelfth centuries) under their names, not in a special biographical section.
Indice Histórico Español: Bibliografía historica de España e hispanoamerica. 1953–. Barcelona.
International Medieval Bibliography. 1967. Minneapolis: Leeds. See under heading Genealogy and (since 1986) Prosopography, as well as under names of notable people in index.
Jahrbuch der Historischen Forschung in der Bundersrepublik Deutschlands. 1974–. Stuttgart.
Oesterreichische Historische Bibliographie. 1965–. Vienna.
Rouse, R. M. 1969. *Serial Bibliographies for Medieval Studies.* Berkeley: Univ. of California Press. A valuable list of indexes, bibliographies, and journals which have serial bibliographies of medieval studies.

Finished Bibliographies

Bibliographies listing modern works dealing specifically, if not exclusively, with prosopographical topics.

Bachrach, B., G. Beech, and J. Rosenthal. 1981. "Bibliography of U.S. Publications in Medieval Prosopography, 1970–79." Pt. 1, *MP* 2(1): 87–102. Pt. 2, *MP* 2(2): 55–69.
Bulst, Neithard. 1982. "Neuerscheinungen der Jahre 1979–80 zur Prosopographie des hohen und späten Mittelalters (11.–15. Jahrhundert)." *MP* 3(2): 73–100.
Bulst, Neithard. 1984. "Neuerscheinungen der Jahre 1981–82. zur Prosopographie des hohen und späten Mittelalters, 11.–15. Jahrhundert. *MP* 5(2): 53–100.
Genet, Jean-Philippe. 1982. "Recent Publications in Medieval Prosopography 11th–15th centuries. Articles in French language periodicals, 1979–80." *MP* 3(2): 53–71.
Griffiths, Ralph. 1983. "Bibliography of Studies in Medieval Prosopography: Wales, 1970–80." *MP* 4(1): 83–89.
Heinzelmann, M. 1982a. "Neuerscheinungen der Jahre 1979–80 zur Prosopographie

des Frühmittelalters (5.-10. Jahrhundert). Eine kommentierte Bibliographie zu Publikationen der Länder Benelux, Deutschland, Frankreich, Oesterreich, Schweiz." *MP* 3(1): 113-42.

————. 1982b. "Gallische Prosopographie, 260-527." *Prosopographica* IV. *Francia.* 10:531-718.

Nelson, Janet. 1982. "Anglo-Saxon England, 1970-81." *MP* 3(1): 109-12.

Rosenthal, J. 1983. "Bibliography of English Scholarship, 1970-81," Pt. 1:1066-1307. *MP* 4(1): 69-81. Pt. 2:1307-1509. *MP* 4(2): 47-61.

Van Caenegem, R. C. 1978. *Guide to the Sources of Medieval History,* 301-5. Amsterdam: North Holland.

Review articles evaluating previous prosopographical research in given medieval fields.

Baldwin, R. 1981. "Missing Persons: A Look at the Prosopography of the Later Roman Empire." *MP* 2(2): 1-8.

Burson, M. C. 1982. "Emden's Registers and the Prosopography of Medieval English Universities." *MP* 3(2): 35-51.

Day, G. 1983. "Genoese Prosopography, 12th to 13th Centuries: The State of the Question and Suggestions for Research." *MP* 4(1): 31-44.

de Ridder-Symoens, H. 1986. "Possibilités de carrière et de mobilité sociale des intellectuels-universitaires au moyen âge." In *MLH,* 343-57.

Dobson, R. B. 1986. "Recent Prosopographical Research in Late Medieval English History: University Graduates, Durham Monks, and York Canons." *MLH,* 181-99.

Evans, R. 1986. "The Analysis by Computer of A. B. Emden's Biographical Registers of the Universities of Oxford and Cambridge." In *MLH,* 343-57.

Fanning, S. 1981. "A Review of Lombard Prosopography." *MP* 2(1): 13-33.

Genet, J.-Ph. 1980. "Medieval Prosopographical Research at the University of Paris I." *MP* 1(2): 1-14.

Gillespie, J. 1980. "The Forest and the Trees: Prosopographical Studies and Richard II." *MP* 1(1): 9-14.

Hollister, C. W. 1981. "Elite Prosopography in Saxon and Norman England." *MP* 2(2): 11-20.

Jaritz, G., and A. Muller. 1986. "Medieval Prosopography in Austrian Historical Research: Religious and Urban Communities." *MP* 7(1): 57-86.

Mathisen, R. W. 1981. "Late Roman Prosopography in the West, A.D. 260-640: A Survey of Recent Work." *MP* 2(1): 1-12.

Reeves, A. C. 1980. "Histories of English Families in the 1970's." *MP* 1(2): 59-71.

Collections of Biographies and Lists of Officials, Dignitaries, and Prominent People

Included in this list are the most important of the dictionaries of use to the medieval prosopographer. For a complete list see the annotated reference to Slocum noted below. It should be noted that since the authors of these dictionaries intended their works for broader informational purposes and not specifically for prosopographical research, the historian following the latter line of inquiry will usually find them deficient in some kinds of information, most notably in their failure to cite all original sources on the people in question. Many of these dictionaries can serve as most useful guides, but medievalists still need prosopographical dictionaries modelled after those of the Roman historians such as that of the *PLRE* (1971, 1980).

Allgemeine Deutsche Biographie. 1967. 2d ed. 56 vols. Unchanged. Berlin: Duncker and Humblot.

Althoff, G. 1978. *Das Necrolog von Borghorst* (Veröffentlichungen der Historischen Kommission für Westfalen 40 = Westfälische Gedenkbücher und Nekrologien 1). Edition und Untersuchung. Münster: Aschendorfsche Verlagsbuchhandlung.

Anselme de Saint-Marie. 1967. *Histoire généalogique et chronologique de la maison royale de France et des grands officiers de la couronne.* New York: Johnson Reprint.

L'art de vérifier les dates. 1818–44. Edited by Saint-Allais. 42 vols. Paris: Moreau.

Borgolte, M. 1986. *Die Grafen Alemanniens in merowingischer und karolingischer Zeit. Eine Prosopographie.* Sigmaringen: J. Thorbecke.

Burke's Genealogical and Heraldic History of the Peerage, Baronetage, and Knightage. 1967. Edited by P. Townsend. 104th ed. London: Burke's Peerage.

Burke's Genealogical and Heraldic History of the Landed Gentry. Edited by P. Townsend. 1969. 18th ed. London: Burke's Peerage.

Cosenza, M., ed. *Biographical and Bibliographical Dictionary of the Italian Humanists and of the World of Classical Scholarship in Italy, 1300–1800.* 1967. 2d rev. ed. 5 vols. Boston: G. K. Hall.

Dictionary of the Middle Ages. 1982–88. Edited by J. R. Strayer. 12 vols. New York: Scribner's.

Dictionary of National Biography. 1921–22. 22 vols. London: Oxford Univ. Press.

Dictionnaire d'archéologie chrétienne et de liturgie. 1924–53. 15 vols. Paris: Letouzey.

Dictionnaire de biographie française. 1933–. 12 vols. to date. Paris: Letouzey.

Dictionnaire de Spiritualité. 1937–. 14 vols. to date. Paris: Beauchesne.

Dictionnaire de théologie catholique. 1902–50. 15 vols. Paris: Letouzey.

Dictionnaire d'histoire et de géographie écclésiastique. 1912–. 17 vols. Paris: Letouzey.

Duchesne, L. M. O. *Fastes épiscopaux de l'ancienne Gaule.* 3 vols. Paris: Fontemoing. 1900. 1915.

Dugdale, W. *Monasticon Anglicanum.* 1817–30. 6 vols. London: Longman, Hurst, Rees, Orme and Brown.

Dupont-Ferrier, G. *Gallia Regia ou État des officiers royaux des baillages et des sénéchausées de 1328–1515.* 1942–66. 6 vols. Paris: Imprimerie Nationale.

Emden, A. B. 1957–59. *A Biographical Dictionary of Members of the University of Oxford from A.D. 1176–1500.* 3 vols. Oxford: Clarendon Press.

———. 1963. *A Biographical Register of the University of Cambridge to 1500.* Cambridge: At the Univ. Press.

Enciclopedia Italiana. 1949–. Rome: Istitute della Enciclopedia Italiana.

Farge, J. K. 1980. *Biographical Register of Paris Doctors of Theology 1500–36.* Toronto: Pontifical Institute of Mediaeval Studies.

Fasti Ecclesiae Anglicanae. London: Institute of Historical Research, 1962–. A reedition of which many volumes have appeared. See D. E. Greenway, "Cathedral Clergy in England and Wales: Fasti Ecclesiae Anglicanae." *MP* 1(1): 15–22 (1980).

Gallia Christiana in provincias ecclesiasticas distributa. 1715–1865. 16 vols. Paris: V. Palme.

Gams, P. B. 1957. *Series Episcoporum Ecclesiae Catholicae.* Graz: Akademischer Druck.

Germania Sacra. 1962–. Historisch-statistische Beschreibung der Kirche des alten Reiches. Neue Folge. Berlin: de Gruyter. Many volumes have appeared.

Glorieux, P. 1934. *Répertoire des maitres en théologie de Paris au XIIIe siècle.* Paris: J. Vrin.

———. 1971. *La faculté des arts et ses maitres au XIIIe siècle.* Paris: J. Vrin.

Harvey, J. 1987. *English Medieval Architects: A Biographical Dictionary to 1500.* 2d ed. Gloucester: Sutton.

Houben, H. 1980. "Das Fragment des Necrologs von St. Blasien." *FMS* 14:274–98.

Index Biobibliographicus Notorum Hominum. 1973–. Edited by J.-P. Lobbes. Osnabrück: Biblio Verlag. This index the first fascicles of which are already in print, is the beginning of an enormous project aiming at publishing an alphabetical list of famous people of all times and countries with references to biographical works on them. Its value to the medievalist remains to be seen.

Index to Biographies of Englishmen, 1000–1485, Found in Dissertations and Theses. 1974. Edited by Jerome V. Reel, Jr. Westport, Conn.: Greenwood Press.

Die Klostergemeinschaft von Fulda im früheren Mittelalter. 1978. Unter Mitwirkung von Gerd Althoff, Eckhard Freise, Dieter Geuenich, Franz-Josef Jakobi, Hermann Kamp, Otto Gerhard Oexle, Mechthild Sandmann, Joachim Wollasch, Siegfried Zorkendorfer. Edited by Karl Schmid. Münstersche Mittelalter-Schriften 8/1, 2.1–3.3. Munich: W. Fink Verlag.

Knowles, D., C. N. Brooke and J. London. 1972. *The Heads of Religious Houses, England and Wales, 940–1216.* Cambridge: Cambridge Univ. Press.

Lexikon des Mittelalters. 1980–. 3 vols. to date. Munich: Artem's Verlag. Conceived at least in part from a prosopographical perspective, this is a work of great value containing many biographical notices of high quality.

Lexikon für Theologie und Kirche. 1930–38. 10 vols. Freiburg: Herder.

Liber memorialis von Remiremont (Monumenta Germaniae Historica, Libri memoriales 1). 1970. Edited by Eduard Hlawitschka, Karl Schmid and Gerd Tellenbach. Dublin: Weidmann.

Der Liber Vitae von Corvey (Veröffentlichungen der Historischen Kommission Westfalens). 1983. Edited by Karl Schmid and Joachim Wollasch. Wiesbaden: Dr. Ludwig Reichert Verlag.

Materialien und Untersuchungen zum Verbrüderungsbuch und zu den älteren Urkunden des Stiftsarchivs St. Gallen. Subsidia Sangallensia 1. 1986. St. Galler

Kultur und Geschichte 10. Edited by Michael Borgolte, Dieter Geuenich, and Karl Schmid. Sarganserländische Buchdruckerei.

Neiske, Franz. 1979. *Das ältere Necrolog des Klosters S. Savino in Piacenza.* Münstersche Mittelalter-Schriften 36. Edition und Untersuchung der Anlage. Munich: W. Fink Verlag.

The New Catholic Encyclopedia. 1967. New York: McGraw-Hill.

Poeck, D. 1983. *Longpont.* Vol. 1: *Ein cluniacensisches Priorat in der Ile-de-France.* Vol. 2: *Untersuchungen. Editions des Kartulars.* Münster: W. Fink Verlag.

Prosopographia Cartusiana Belgica, 1314-1796. Jan de Grauwe. 1976. Gand: De Backer.

Prosopographie chrétienne du Bas Empire. I. A. Mandouze. 1983. *Prosopographie de l'Afrique chrétienne 303-533.* Paris: Centre Nationale de la Recherche Scientifique.

The Prosopography of the Later Roman Empire. A. H. N. Jones, J. R. Martindale, and J. Morris. 1971-80. Vol. 1:260-395 (1971). Vol. 2:395-527 (1980). Cambridge: Cambridge Univ. Press.

Realencyclopädie für protestantische Theologie und Kirche. 1896-1913. 3d ed. 26 vols. Leipzig: Hinrichs.

Renardy, Chr. 1981. *Le monde universitaire du diocèse de Liège. Répertoire biographique, 1140-1350.* Paris: Les Belles Lettres.

Russell, J. C. 1936. *Dictionary of Writers of 13th Century England.* London: Longmans, Green.

Sanders, I. J. 1960. *English Baronies: A Study of their Origin and Descent.* Oxford: Clarendon Press.

Sandmann, M. 1984. *Studein zu langobardisch-italischen Herrscherverzeichnissen unter besonderer Berücksichtigung der Herrscherverzeichnisse im Codex 27 Scaff. I der Biblioteca Antoniana zu Padua und im Codex Ottobon. lat. 6 der Biblioteca Apostolica Vaticana zu Rom.* Münstersche Mittelalter-Schriften 41. Munich: W. Fink Verlag.

Series episcoporum ecclesiae catholicae occidentalis ab initio usque ad annum MCXCVIII. Series 5 Germania. The "new" Gams (see above under Gams). Edited by S. Weinfurter and Odilo Engels.

    I. *Archiepiscopatus Coloniensis.* 1982. With collaboration of H. Kluger and E. Pack. Stuttgart: A. Hiersemann.

    II. *Archiepiscopatus Hammaburgensis sive Bremensis.* 1984. With collaboration of H. Kluger, E. Pack, and R. Grosse. Stuttgart: A. Hiersemann.

Slocum, R. 1967. *Biographical Dictionaries and Related Works: An International Bibliography of Collective Biographies, Biobibliographies, Collections of Epitaphs, Selected Genealogical Works, Dictionaries of Anonyms and Pseudonyms, Historical and Specialized Dictionaries, Biographical Materials in Government Manuals, Bibliographies of Biography, Biographical Indexes, and Selected Portrait Catalogues.* Detroit: Gale Research. This work has value for the prosopographer in that it gives the only comprehensive view of all the various biographical dictionaries and other related works now available. The author separates these into three main categories of dictionaries — (1) universal biographies; (2) biographies by individual countries; and (3) biographies by vocation (e.g., arts, education, religion, including clergy, saints, theologians). Although he may have missed one or two, his list of dictionaries concerning the Middle Ages seems complete.

Die Synopse der cluniacensischen Necrologien. 1982. Münstersche Mittelalter-Schriften 39. Unter Mitarbeit von Wolf-D. Heim, J. Mehne, F. Neiske, D. Poeck. Edited by J. Wollasch. 2 vols. Munich: W. Fink Verlag.

Talbot, C. H., and E. A. Hammond. 1965. *The Medical Practitioners in Medieval England.* London: Wellcome Historical Medical Library.

Die Totenbücher von Merseburg und Magdeburg. 1983. Monumenta Germaniae Historica, Libri memoriales et necrologia. Nova Series 2. Anhang: Register zum Totenbuch von Lüneburg. Edited by G. Althoff and J. Wollasch. Hannover: Hahnsche Buchhandlung.

Das Verbrüderungsbuch der Abtei Reichenau. 1979. Monumenta Germaniae Historica, Libri memoriales et necrologia. Nova Series 1. Edited by Johanne Autenrieth, Dieter Geuenich, and Karl Schmid.

Vies des saints et des bienheureux selon l'ordre du calendrier avec l'historique des fêtes par les Bénédictins de Paris. 1935–39. 13 vols. Paris: Letouzey.

Wedgwood, J., ed. 1936. *History of Parliament.* Vol. 1: *Biographies of the Members of the Commons house, 1439–1509.* London: H. M. Stationery Office, 1936. Vol. 2: *Register of the Ministers and Members of both Houses 1439–1509.* London: H. M. Stationery Office, 1938.

Wickersheimer, E. 1936. *Dictionnaire biographique des médecins en France au Moyen Age.* 2 vols. Paris: Droz.

Methodology

Recent works discussing methodological problems including those touching on names and family structure.

Althoff, G. 1978. "Personenstatistik aus mittelalterlichen Quellen?" *PS,* 20–25.

Billot, Claudine. "Le migrant en France à la fin du Moyen Age: Problèmes et méthodes." 1986. *MLH,* 235–42.

Bouchard, C. 1986. "Family Structure and Family Consciousness among the Aristocracy in the 9th–11th Centuries." *Francia,* 14:639–58.

Bouchard, C. 1988. "Patterns of Women's Names in Royal Lineages, 9th–11th Centuries." *MP* 9(1): 1–32.

Bouchard, C. 1988. "Migration of Women's Names in the Upper Nobility, 9th–12th Centuries." *MP* 9(2): 1–20.

Bulst, N. 1986. "Zum Gegenstand und zur Methode von Prosopographie." In *MLH,* 1–16.

Carney, T. F. 1973. "Prosopography: Payoffs and Pitfalls." *Phoenix* 27:156–79.

Chastagnol, A. 1970. "La prosopographie, méthode de recherche sur l'histoire du Bas Empire." *Annales, Économies, Sociétés, Civilisations* 25:1229–1235.

Clark, C. 1987. "English Personal Names ca. 650–1300: Some Prosopographical Bearings." *MP,* 8(1): 31–60.

Ebling, H., J. Harnut, and G. Kampers. 1980. "Nomen et Gens. Untersuchungen zu den Führungsschichten des Franken-, Langobarden- und Westgotenreiches im 6. und 7. Jahrhundert." *Prosopographica* III. *Francia* 8:687–745.

Freed, J. "The Prosopography of Ecclesiastical Elites: Some Methodological Considerations from Salzburg." *MP* 9(1): 33–60.

Freise, E. 1978. "Wie repräsentativ ist die mittelalterliche 'Personenüber-lieferung'?" *PS,* 26–32.

Geuenich, D. 1986. "Eine Datenbank zur Erforschung mittelalterlicher Personen und Personengruppen." In *MLH,* 405–17.

Gillespie, J. L. 1978. "Medieval Multiple Biography: Richard II's Cheshire Archers." *The Historian* 40:675–85.

Klapisch-Zuber, Chr. 1986. "Quelques réflexions sur les rapports entre prosoprographie et démographie historique." In *MLH,* 29–35.

Mason, E. "Through a Glass Darkly: Sources and Problems in English Baronial Prosopography." *MP* 2(2): 21–31.

Mehne, J. "Personen als Funktionsträger in den mittelalterlichen Quellen." *PS,* 14–19.

Nicolet, C. 1970. "Prosopographie et histoire sociale: Rome et l'Italie a l'époque républicaine." *Annales, Économies, Sociétés, Civilisations* 25:1209–28.

Schmid, K. 1957. "Zur Problematik von Familie, Sippe und Geschlecht, Haus und Dynastie beim mittelalterlichen Adel." *Zeitschrift für die Geschichte des Oberrheins* 107:1–62.

———. 1959. "Uber die Struktur des Adels im Mittelalter." *Jahrbuch für Fränkische Landesforschung,* 1–24.

———. 1965. "Religiöses und Sippengebundenes Gemeinschaftsbewusstsein in Frühmittelalterlichen Gedenkbüchereintragen." *Deutsches Archiv für Erforschung des Mittelalters* 20:18–81.

———. 1967a. "Uber das Verhältnis von Person und Gemeinschaft im Früheren Mittelalter." *Frühmittelalterliche Studien* 1:225–49.

———. 1967b. "Probleme der Erforschung: Frühmittelalterliche Gedenksbücher." *Frühmittelalterliche Studien* 1:366–89.

———. 1970. "Die Mönchgemeinschaft von Fulda als sozialgeschichtliches Problem." *Frühmittelalterliche Studien* 4:172–300.

———. 1974. "Programmatisches zur Erforschung der mittelalterlichen Personen und Personengruppen." *Frühmittelalterliche Studien* 9(1974): 116–30.

———. 1978. "Überlieferung und Eigenart mittelalterlicher Personenbezeichnung." *PS,* 6–13.

———. 1981. "Prosopographische Forschungen zur Geschichte des Mittelalters." In *Aspekte der historischen Forschung in Deutschland und Frankreich,* 54–78. Vorträge auf dem deutschfranzösischen Historiker-Kolloquium Göttingen, 1979. Edited by G. A. Ritter and R. Vierhaus. Gottingen: Vendenhoeck and Ruprecht.

Schmid, K. and J. Wollasch. 1975. "*Societas et Fraternitas.* Begründung eines kommentierten Quellenwerkes zur Erforschung der Personen und Personengruppen des Mittelalters." *FMS* 9:1–48.

Stone, L. 1972. "Prosopography." In *Historical Studies Today.* Edited by F. Gilbert and S. Graubard. New York: Norton.

Tellenbach, G. 1957. "Zur Bedeutung der Personenforschung für die Erkenntnis des früheren Mittelalters." In *Freiburger Universitätsreden.* Freiburg: Hans Ferdinand Schulz Verlag.

Turner, R. 1982. "12th and 13th Century English Law and Government: Suggestions for Prosopographical Approaches." *MP* 3(2): 22–34.

Werner, K. F. 1977. "Problematik und erste Ergebnisse des Forschungsvorhabens PROL (Prosopographia Regnorum Orbis Latini). Zur Geschichte der west- und mitteleuropäischen Oberschichten bis zum 12. Jahrhundert." In *Quellen und Forschungungen aus italienischen Archiven und Bibliotheken* 57:69–87.

Wollasch, J. 1978. "Klösterliche Gemeinschaften als Träger sozialen Lebens vor der Zeit der Städte." *PS,* 39–43.

Computers and Medieval Prosopography

Journals

Computers and the Humanities. 1966–. Flushing, N.Y.

Computers and Medieval Data Processing (CAMDAP). 1970–. Montreal.

Le médiéviste et l'ordinateur, 1979–. Paris.

Proceedings of Colloquia Dedicated Wholly or in Part to This Subject

Informatique et Histoire Médiévale. 1977. Communications et débats de la Table Ronde du CNRS organisée par l'Ecole Française de Rome et l'Institut d'Histoire médiévale de Pise. Rome: École Française de Rome.

L'histoire médiévale et les ordinateurs. 1981. Rapports d'une Table Ronde internationale. Edited by K. F. Werner. Munich: K. G. Saur.

Computer Applications to Medieval Studies. 1984. Edited by A. Gilmour-Bryson. Kalamazoo: Medieval Institute Publications.

Informatique et Prosopographie. 1985. Table Ronde du CNRS Paris, 1984. Edited by H. Millet. Paris: Centre National de la Recherche Scientifique.

Review Article

Mathisen, R. 1988. "Medieval Prosopography and Computers: Theoretical and Methodological Considerations." *MP,* 9(2): 73–128. This may well contain the fullest (over 150 titles) and most recent bibliography published.

Recent Monographs in Medieval Prosopography

Althoff, G. 1984. *Adels und Königsfamilien im Spiegel ihrer Memorialüberlieferung. Studien zum Totengedenken der Billunger und Ottonen.* Munich: W. Fink Verlag.

Autrand, Fr. 1981. *Naissance d'un grand corps de l'État: Les gens du Parlement de Paris, 1345–54.* Paris: Université de Paris I, Panthéon Sorbonne.

Bachler, H. 1984. "The Use of a Relational Data Base Model for the Implementation of an Information System on the Medieval City of Freiburg." In *Computer Applications to Medieval Studies,* 89–106. Edited by A. Gilmour-Bryson. Kalamazoo: Medieval Institute Publications.

Bouchard, C. 1981. "The Origins of the French Nobility: A Reassessment." *The American Historical Review* 86:501–32.

Britton, E. 1977. *The Community of the Vill.: A Study in the History of the Family and Village Life in 14th Century England.* Toronto: MacMillan of Canada.

Bullock-Davies, C. 1978. *Menestrellorum Multitudo: Minstrels at a Royal Feast.* Cardiff: Univ. of Wales Press.

Bulst, N. 1984. "Deputies at the French Estates General of 1468 and 1484. A Prosopographical Approach." *MP* 5(1): 65–80.

Chandler, V., C. Newman, and D. Spear. 1984. "A Proposal for a Dictionary of Anglo-Norman Biography." *MP* 5(2): 33–40.

Chantraine, H. 1983. "Ein neues Hilfsmittel zur Erforschung der Spätantike: Die Prosopographie chrétienne du Bas Empire." *Prosopographia V. Francia* 11:697–712.

Clark, L., and C. Rawcliffe. 1983. "A History of Parliament, 1386–1422: A Progress Report." *MP* 4(2): 9–42.

Claude, D. 1978. "Prosopographie des Spanischen Suebenreiches." *Prosopographia II. Francia* 6:647–76.

Contreni, J. 1978. *The Cathedral School of Laon from 850–930: Its Manuscripts and Master.* Munich: Arbeo-Gesellschaft.

Demurger, A. 1978. "Guerre civile et changements du personnel administratif dans le royaume de France de 1400–18: L'exemple des baillis et sénéchaux." *Francia* 6:151–298.

———. 1986. "L'apport de la prosopographie à l'étude des mécanismes des pouvoirs XIII–XVᵉ siècles." In *PGEM,* 289–301.

Denton, J. H., and J. P. Dooley. 1987. *Representatives of the Lower Clergy in Parliament, 1295–1340.* Woodbridge: Boydell Press.

DeWindt, A. R., and E. B. DeWindt. 1974. *Royal Justice and the Medieval English Countryside.* 2 vols. Toronto: Pontifical Institute of Medieval Studies.

Dobson, R. B. 1973. *Durham Priory, 1400–1450.* Cambridge: Cambridge Univ. Press.

Dunbabin, J. 1984. "Careers and Vocations." In *The History of the University of Oxford.* Vol. 1, *The Early Oxford Schools,* 565–606. Edited by J. I. Catto and T. A. R. Evans. Oxford: Oxford Univ. Press.

Esch, A. 1986. "Zur Prosopographie von Führungsgruppen im spätmittelalterlichen Rom." *MLH,* 291–301.

Evergates, T. 1975. *Feudal Society in the Baillage of Troyes under the Counts of Champagne, 1152–1284.* Baltimore: Johns Hopkins Univ. Press.

Farge, J. 1985. *Orthodoxy and Reform in Early Reformation France: The Faculty of Theology, 1500–43.* Leiden: E. J. Brill.

Fleming, R. 1987. "Domesday Book and the Tenurial Revolution." In *Anglo-Norman Studies IX. Proceedings of the Battle Conference, 1986,* 87–102. Woodbridge: Boydell.

————. 1986. "A Report on the Domesday Book Database Project." *MP* 7(2): 55–62.

Freed, J. 1977. *The Friars and German Society in the 13th Century.* Cambridge, Mass.: Medieval Academy of America.

Friedlander, A. 1983. "Heresy, Inquisition, and the Crusader Nobility of Languedoc." *MP* 4(1): 45–67.

Garcia Moreno, L. A. 1974. *Prosopografía del reino visigodo de Toledo.* Salamanca: Universidad de Salamanca.

Genet, J.-Ph. 1986. "Entre statistique et documentation: Un système de programmes pour le traitement des données prosopographiques." In *MLH,* 359–79.

Gottfried, R. S. 1984. "English Medical Practitioners, 1340–1530." *Bulletin of the History of Medicine* 58:164–82.

Greenway, D. E. 1980. "Cathedral Clergy in England and Wales: Fasti Ecclesiae Anglicanae." *MP* 1(1): 15–22.

Griffiths, Q. 1970. "New Men Among the Lay Counselors of Saint Louis' Parlement." *Medieval Studies* 32:234–72.

Hammar, C. I., Jr. 1978. "Anatomy of an Oligarchy: The Oxford Town Council in the 15th and 16th Centuries." *Journal of British Studies.* 18:1–27.

Henneman, J. B. 1984. "Who were the Marmousets?" *MP* 5(1): 19–64.

Jacquart, D. 1981. *Le milieu médical en France du XIIe au XVe siècle.* Geneva: Droz.

Jarnut, J. 1979. *Bergamo, 568–1098. Verfassungs- Sozial- und Wirtschaftsgeschichte einer Lombardischen Stadt im Mittelalter.* Wiesbaden: Steiner.

Kamp, N. *Kirche und Monarchie im Staufischen Konigreich Sizilien.* Vol. 1, *Prosoprographische Grundlegung: Bistümer und Bischöfe des Königreichs, 1194– 1266.* 1973–75. 3 vols. Munich: W. Fink Verlag.

Kealey, E. 1981. *Medieval Medicus. A Social History of Anglo-Norman Medicine.* Baltimore: Johns Hopkins Univ. Press.

Kedar, B. 1972. "The Passenger List of a Crusader Ship 1250: Toward the History of the Popular Element on the 7th Crusade." *Studi Medievali* 13:267–79.

Keller, H. 1979. *Adelsherrschaft und städtische Gesellschaft in Oberitalien 9. bis 12. Jahrhundert.* Tübingen: M. Niemeyer Verlag.

Kerherve, J. 1986. "Prosopographie des officiers de finances: L'exemple des trésoriers de l'Épargne bretons du XVe siècle." In *MLH,* 367–89.

Keynes, S. 1980. *The Diplomas of King Aethelred the Unready, 978–1016: A Study in their Use as Historical Evidence.* Cambridge: Cambridge Univ. Press.

Leistad, G., F. L. Naeshagen, and P.-A. Wiktorson. 1984. "Online Prosopography: The Plan for Nordic Medieval Data Bases." *Francia* 12:699–722.

Lewis, P. 1986. "The Problems of Prosopography in Later Medieval France." *PGEM,* 281–88.

Longnon, J. 1978. *Les compagnons de Villehardouin. Recherches sur les croisés de la 4ᵉ croisade.* Geneva: Droz.

Mason, E. 1987. "The Donors of Westminster Abbey Charters, 1060–1240." *MP* 8(2): 23–39.

Mathisen, R. 1979. "Resistance and Reconciliation: Majorian and the Gallic Aristocracy after the Fall of Avitus." *Prosopographia* II. *Francia* 7:597–628.

McConica, J. K. 1972–73. "The Prosopography of the Tudor University." *Journal of Interdisciplinary History* 3:543–54.

McFarlane, K. 1973. *The Nobility of Later Medieval England.* Oxford: Clarendon Press.

McLaughlin, M. M. 1987. "Looking for Medieval Women: An Interim Report on the Project 'Women's Religious Life and Communities A.D. 500–1500." *MP* 8(1): 61–91.

Meisel, J. 1980. *Barons of the Welsh Frontier: The Corbet, Pantulf and Fitz Warin Families, 1066–1272.* Lincoln: Univ. of Nebraska Press.

Menagier, L.-R. 1981. "Inventaires des familles normandes et franques emigrées en Italie méridionale et en Sicile XIᵉ–XIIᵉ siècles." In *Hommes et Institutions de l'Italie normande.* London: Variorum Reprint.

Millet, H. 1982. *Les chanoines du chapitre cathédrale de Laon, 1272–1412.* Rome: École Française de Rome.

———. 1986. "Quels furent les bénéficiaires de la soustraction d'obédience de 1398 dans les chapitres cathédraux français?" In *MLH,* 123–37.

Mooers, S. 1986. "Networks of Power in Anglo-Norman England." *MP* 7(2): 25–54.

Mornet, E. 1978. "*Pauperes scholares:* Essai sur la condition matérielle des etudiants scandinaves dans les universités aux XIVᵉ et XVᵉ siècles." *Le Moyen Age.* 84:53–102.

———. 1986. "Préliminaires a une prosopographie du haut clergé scandinave: le chapitre cathédral de Roskilde, 1367–1493." In *MLH,* 139–62.

Newman, W. M. *Les seigneurs de Nesle en Picardie XIIᵉ–XIIIᵉ siècle: leurs chartes et leur histoire: Étude sur la noblesse régionale écclesiastique et laïque.* 1971. 2 vols. Philadelphia: American Philosophical Society.

———. 1972. *Le personnel de la cathédrale d'Amiens, 1066–1306, avec une note sur la famille des siegneurs de Heilly.* Paris: Picard.

Oexle, O. G. 1978. *Forschungen zu monastischen und geistlichen Gemeinschaften im Westfränkischen Bereich.* Munich: W. Fink Verlag.

Orme, N. 1986. "English Schoolmasters, 1000–1500." *MLH,* 303–12.

Paravicini Bagliani, A. 1986. "Pour une approche prosopographique de la cour pontificale du XIIIᵉ siècle. Problèmes de méthode." In *MLH,* 113–20.

Poos, L. R. 1986. "Peasant 'Biographies' from Medieval England." In *MLH,* 201–14.

Powell, J. M. 1986. *Anatomy of a Crusade, 1213–21.* Philadelphia: Univ. of Pennsylvania Press.

Radding, Ch. 1988. *Origins of Medieval Jurisprudence. Pavia and Bologna, 850–1150.* New Haven: Yale Univ. Press.

Raftis, J. A. 1974. *Warboys: 200 Years in the Life of an English Medieval Village.* Toronto: Pontifical Institute of Mediaeval Studies.

———. 1982. *A Small Town in Late Medieval England: Godmanchester, 1278–1400.* Toronto: Pontifical Institute of Mediaeval Studies.

Rosenthal, J. 1970. *The Training of an Elite Group: English Bishops in the 15th Century.* Philadelphia: American Philosophical Society.

Rogozinski, J. 1976. "Ennoblement by the Crown and Social Stratification in France, 1285–1322. A Prosopographical Survey." In *Order and Innovation in the Middle Ages: Essays in Honor of Joseph R. Strayer,* 273–92. Princeton: Princeton Univ. Press.

———. 1982. *Power, Caste, and Law: Social Conflict in 14th Century Montpellier.* Cambridge: Mediaeval Academy of America.

Rotz, R. 1975. "Urban Uprisings in Germany: Revolutionary or Reformist? The Case of Brunswick 1374." *Viator* 4:207–23.

———. 1976. "Investigating Urban Uprising with Examples from Hanseatic Towns, 1374–1416." In *Order and Innovation in the Middle Ages: Essays in Honor of Joseph R. Strayer,* 215–33. Princeton: Princeton Univ. Press.

Saul, N. 1981. *Knights and Esquires: The Gloucestershire Gentry in the 14th Century.* Oxford: Clarendon Press.

Schwinger, R. Ch. 1986. "Zur Prosopographie studentischer Reisegruppen im 15. Jahrhundert." In *MLH,* 333–41.

Selle-Hosbach, K. 1974. *Prosopographie merowingischer Amtsträger in der Zeit von 511 bis 613.* Bonn: Selle-Hosbach.

Stelling Michaud, S. 1960. *L'université de Bologne et la pénétration des droits romain et canonique en Suisse aux XIIIe et XIVe siècles.* Geneva: Droz.

Thomson, W. R. 1975. *Friars in the Cathedral: The First Franciscan Bishops, 1226–1261.* Toronto: Pontifical Institute of Mediaeval Studies.

Thrupp, S. 1948. *The Merchant Class of Medieval London, 1300–1500.* Chicago: Univ. of Chicago Press.

Turner, R. V. 1985. *The English Judiciary in the Age of Glanville and Bracton, ca. 1176–1239.* Cambridge: Cambridge Univ. Press.

———. 1988. *Men Raised up from the Dust: Administrative Service and Upward Mobility in Angevin England.* Philadelphia: Univ. of Pennsylvania Press.

Vale, M. 1986. "Mobility, Bureaucracy, and the State in English Gascony, 1250–1340." In *MLH,* 303–12.

Verger, J. 1986. "Prosopographie et cursus universitaires." In *MLH,* 313–32.

Wedemeyer, E. 1970. "Social Groupings at the Fair of St. Ives 1275–1302." *Medieval Studies* 76:27–59.

Weinfurter, S. 1986. "'Series episcoporum'—Probleme und Möglichkeiten einer Prosopographie des früh- und hochmittelalterlichen Episkopats." In *MLH,* 97–111.

Werner, K. F. 1979. "The Important Noble Families in the Kingdom of Charlemagne: A Prosopographical Study of the Relationship between King and Nobility in the Early Middle Ages." In *The Medieval Nobility: Studies on the Ruling Classes of France and Germany from the 6th to the 12th Century,* 137–202. Edited by T. Reuter. Amsterdam: North-Holland.

Wriedt, K. 1986. "Amtsträger in norddeutschen Städten des Spätmittelalters." In *MLH,* 227–34.

Zielinski, H. 1984. *Der Reichsepiskopat in spätottonischer und salischer Zeit 1000–1125.* Wiesbaden: F. Steiner Verlag.

cx/~> 6 <~o

Computer-assisted Analysis of the
Statistical Documents of Medieval Society

DAVID HERLIHY

N THE EARLY 1970s, when the first edition of this chapter was
written, the historian who wished to use a computer faced
many frustrations. The "computer" in those days meant a
big machine, a "mainframe." Computers were then housed in the inner
reaches of intimidating structures known as computer centers. The centers
themselves were filled with heavy, noisy, typewriter-like devices known as
keypunch machines. The machines crunched forth a continuous stream
of perforated cards, which were then the chief means of communicating
with the hidden jinni. The first edition of this chapter described in detail
the layout of the then ubiquitous eighty-column punch card. Today, the
punch card is a quaint fossil out of the early history of computing.

In those bygone days, the historian had usually to press through
throngs of users to deliver a box of cards, carrying instructions and data,
to those who attended the machine. The attendants submitted the historian's cards, or "job," with others in a batch, to be read by mechanical
card readers; the card readers in turn passed on what they read, the data
and the programs, to the computer. The computer processed the batch
jobs one by one, while the historian waited anxiously for the results. He
or she felt fortunate if "output" emerged in thirty minutes. More often
than not, the results were disappointing, either because of flaws in the
instructions or errors in the data. The failure was explained by cryptic
messages, sometimes by reference to numbers in an unknown code. Mistakes forced the humiliated historian to consult thick manuals of instruc-

tion in the center's library, written in unfamiliar and usually impene-
trable jargon. The historian then patiently made the corrections—this
too consumed much time—resubmitted the job, and awaited the results.
Hours, days slipped by in frustrating interactions with the remote, laconic
machine.

Since the early 1970s, the arts of computing have undergone a revolution, and most sections in the original edition of my chapter are now obsolete. I shall have to review here relevant innovations in the computing
arts and the ways they have made computing much more "user-friendly"
and much more amenable to the special needs of historians. Nonetheless,
while much has changed, much abides. To use computers in the analysis
of medieval data still requires effort and money. That work is, to be sure,
much lighter than in former years, and the costs have dramatically fallen.
But the use of the computer is not now, and will never be, entirely effort-
less and free.

Today as in the past, the historian who contemplates enlisting a computer in the analysis of statistical records from the Middle Ages must initially decide whether the added work and expense justify the benefits to
be expected from its use. To make that decision wisely and well, the historian must initially possess at least a rudimentary knowledge of what a
computer is; what it reads; how it reads; how it remembers and processes
data; how it returns the results of its work; what it does well and what
it does poorly. The historian must also have, it goes without saying, a close
familiarity with the medieval records to be analyzed, in order to judge
whether or not the analysis can be done cheaply and efficiently by machine processing.

In this essay, I can offer only the briefest and the most rudimentary characterization of the current state of the art in computing. On
this topic, historians now have at their disposal an abundant literature
and even several specialized journals.[1] It is, moreover, highly recommended that prospective users visit the computing centers on their campuses, talk with consultants available there, and also enroll in as many
introductory "short courses" as their time allows; those courses give instruction in computer use, in word processing, in statistical packages, in
"spreadsheets" and data base management systems, and in programming
languages.

The discussion here is limited to an examination of certain basic concepts that govern the computing arts. There is a risk that this essay may
fall between two stools: those who already know something about computers will find it superficial; and those who know nothing will find it
incomplete. I hope that the historian will at least acquire a list of ques-

tions that should be asked concerning computers and concerning the suitability of the historian's own records for machine processing. This chapter also includes some suggestions for the quick and efficient coding of records and some remarks about the various packages, programs, or applications now available for processsing the data. Finally, those historians who do not, themselves, intend to make use of computers may perhaps gain from these pages a better understanding of computer-assisted statistical analysis of medieval documents. The use of computers in medieval history is now already a generation old, and it undoubtedly has a long life to come.

WHAT COMPUTERS DO

The "computer" of everyday language is a logical machine designed to transform or manipulate symbols by effective procedures. The computer is not, in other words, simply a number cruncher, even though, when so directed, it can become a powerful mathematical calculator.[2] But the computer can also work easily with letters or other symbols. Word processing, now ubiquitous in modern scholarship, is the most evident example of the use of computers in the manipulation of symbols. Numbers are only one set of symbols with which computers can work, and arithmetical transformations are only a part of the procedures it can execute.

The computer recognizes and, if directed, transforms symbols according to "effective procedures." An effective procedure is in turn a sequence of logical commands, from which all ambiguity or uncertainty is excluded. In perhaps more familiar language, an "effective procedure" is an "application" (also called a "program") that directs the computer to recognize, transform, or interpret one, some, or all symbols in a given set in some prescribed fashion. To take a homely example out of word processing, the user might want to convert a text using the conventions of American spelling in place of English spelling. Among the directions would be the command: "change 'labour' to 'labor'." The computer finds all occurrences of the word "labour" in the text and replaces it with "labor." That is an effective (that is, unambiguous) procedure, and it does not involve numbers.

What is the basis of computer power? I would call it the resource of two infinities. As a machine, the computer can perform the same task over and over again in exactly the same way for as long as it is allowed to run and has records to process. The first infinity, in other words, is the unlimited number of records that the computer can read, transform, or interpret. Unlike human beings, it does not become tired or bored, and, barring some mechanical breakdown, it rarely makes mistakes. Like the broom directed to haul water by the magician's apprentice, it will go on hauling water for as long as there is water to haul.

The second infinity is the range of effective procedures — of applications or programs — that it can imitate and execute. The theoretical basis of computing was largely laid before World War II, and a principal figure in its development was the English logician Alan Turing. In 1936, he proved that a logical machine could be built that could execute any effective procedure transforming any set of symbols. Moreover, a universal machine — now called a universal Turing machine — could be made that would be able to imitate the operations of any other logical machine. In less abstract terms, by definition one computer can imitate in its operations any other computer; they are all Turing machines. Computers are the perfect mimics. This means, in turn, that the computer can replicate any human logical process, provided only that it not contain any ambiguous symbols or commands. Much of the theory in modern computing is devoted to proving what computers cannot do, what are the logical boundaries to their work.

These high speculations need not concern historians. In practical terms, whatever the historian does with the data, the computer can mimic exactly. In sum, the computer can process a limitless number of records in limitless ways. Its power is awesome. But it cannot make its own records, and it cannot speculate or hypothesize. It cannot replace, but it does stimulate and challenge, the historical imagination.

THE DECISION TO COMPUTERIZE

Armed with awareness of what a computer does and what its powers are, the historian must next weigh the costs and benefits deriving its use.

Data and Applications

The historian should be aware that there now exist many libraries of both medieval data and applications.[3] Especially notable here is the Medieval and Early Modern Data Bank (MEMDB), jointly sponsored in the

United States by Rutgers, the State University of New Jersey, and the Research Libraries Group, Inc.[4] In 1989–90, the MEMDB became an on-line system, available to subscribers through the Research Libraries Information Network. Medievalists, in other words, now need not necessarily generate their own machine-readable files or develop their own applications.

However, even to make efficient use of preexistent data sets, the historian should have some idea how they are created and organized. I therefore here assume that he or she is working with manuscript or printed records, deliberating whether or not a computer would be useful in their analysis, and then proceeding to convert them into forms that the machine can efficiently utilize.

Considerations

The decision to seek the assistance of a computer in analyzing medieval statistical documentation requires strongly affirmative answers to three questions:

1. Am I working with serial records? Does the documentation constitute a series of repeated answers to the same set of questions? Each set of answers in the series represents a "logical unit," or a "record" in more familiar language. The record may be as short and simple as a single name in a list, or as complex and lengthy as inventories of household possessions in a tax survey. But simple or complex, the records remain repetitive. The series or run of records may be distributed over time (as, for example, the citation of currency exchange rates over years at particular markets), or over space (as hearths or families in a survey or census), or by some other standard. But as answers to the same question or set of questions, the records possess a comparable structure and yield comparable information.

The computer's power derives significantly from iteration, from its power to execute tirelessly the same processes over and over again. It therefore works best with records conveying the same types of data, over and over again. On the other hand, if the documentation is not readily divisible into logical units or records, or if the units, themselves, are responding to different questions, possess different structures, and yield different information, then the effectiveness of computer processing greatly diminishes. Variations in the records, their content and their format, increase the difficulty of entering the data, complicate the processing, and weaken the results. As a machine, the computer does not handle the idiosyncratic or the irregular very well, and never the unexpected.

2. Is the series big and its constituent records numerous? The historian who utilizes a computer must face initial expenditures in effort and money. He or she must learn about computers, design a record layout, and develop or select analytical programs. But once these initial outlays have been made, the size of the file can be increased, or new and similar files processed, with consummate ease. The computer can analyze 100,000 records almost as easily as it can 100. Given these large "economies of scale," the costs of processing per record unit are substantially cheaper when the file is big than when it is small.

3. Do the records carry numerical data or information that can be converted easily and unambiguously into numeric form? The computer, as mentioned, works easily with the entire set of symbols it recognizes. It can sort nominal lists by whatever key the user selects: by first name, last name, by title, place of origin, or name of occupation when given, and so forth. At the same time, numerical data allow mathematical manipulations, which the computer can greatly facilitate. To calculate by pencil the average of several hundred citations of grain prices is a simple but still formidable task; it is quickly done by computer. And no human can match the computer's accuracy in making calculations.

Many sets of late ancient and medieval records fulfill these conditions. For example, numerous inscriptions have reached us from the period of late antiquity; many of them were placed on gravestones to honor a departed relative or loved one. The inscriptions are short, repetitive in layout, and also very numerous. They often contain data already in numeric form (as for example, age at death) and carry much other information which can be represented by unambiguous numeric symbols (location of the stone, sex of the decedent, sex and relationship of the one who raised the stone, titles, occupations, religion, and so forth).

Private acts from medieval chartularies and parchment collections, which multiply from the eighth century, also invite the application of automatic data processing, even if they have so far resisted the development of methods for editing their entire, usually complex texts into coded form. However, partial sets of information can still be coded from the charters, regarding names of persons and their titles, types of payments made, rents collected, and so forth. Several of the prosopographical data banks mentioned above are based on the personal names taken from early medieval charters. Household surveys, which similiarly date from the late eighth century and which become especially large and numerous from the thirteenth, are a third type of document which invites computer-assisted analysis.

Some years ago, with the collaboration of Dr. Larry Poos, I redacted the great polyptych of the abbey of St.-Germain-des-Prés near Paris into machine-readable form. The document, drawn up in the first quarter of the ninth century, is a survey of the abbey's estates in the neighborhood of Paris. The logical units in this survey are the entries describing the dependent farms; the entries give the names and juridic status of the persons resident upon the farms, describe the attached fields and their sizes, and stipulate the rents due from them. These entries number nearly 2,000; the machine-readable edition allows the user to return repeatedly to the document with new sets of questions, in search of patterns. If answers had to be painfully retrieved by manual counts and sorting, many of these questions would not be worth the asking.[5]

A similar example of a medieval document amenable to computer processing is the Florentine Catasto of 1427–1430. This vast survey of the lands then subject to the Florentine commune — nearly the whole of the modern province of Tuscany — includes data on more than 60,000 households and more than 260,000 people. The logical unit is the hearth or household, the heads of which responded to the same set of questions put to them by the surveyors. Curiously, the redactors themselves were never able to calculate the final totals — the sums of persons or of property values registered in the survey. The reach of the surveyors exceeded their grasp. From 1966, a team of workers from America and from France entered data from this great survey first onto cards and then onto tape. The computer, in 1978, added the numbers and produced the totals that the Florentine surveyors, for all their care and energy, were unable to calculate in 1427.[6]

Types of Data

To use a machine-readable data set well, the historian also needs some appreciation of the way in which different types of data are represented within the computer.

Computers work with symbols, and the symbols are represented internally by numeric values. The code of equivalence between symbol and numeric values differs according to different manufacturers, but today ASCII (American Standard Code for Information Interchange) codes have become very nearly the lingua franca of the computing arts. Extended ASCII codes now include as many as 256 characters, including "control" characters that cannot be printed or displayed unless transformed. (The old punch card could represent only 64 characters.) However, the historian in designing his records is well advised to use a much more limited set. A good rule is to use for coding or transcription only the set of numbers (including the decimal point and the plus and minus signs, if needed), the set of capital letters (lowercase letters would usually be redundant), and carriage returns to separate the records. Punctuation marks are best avoided. Marks, such as commas and brackets, have different meanings for different computers and different applications. An ASCII file that contains only numbers, letters, and carriage returns is the simplest type of file; it is also the type most easily transported, from one application to another and from one computer system to another. The files the historian converts into machine-readable form should be viewed as a kind of edition or publication; they should readily usable by other scholars besides the one who made them.

Data are represented in the computer in three basic modes: (1) alphanumeric characters, (2) real numbers (also called floating point), and (3) integer numbers.

"Alphanumeric characters," as the name suggests, include letters, numbers, punctuation marks, arithmetic signs — in sum, the entire set of characters that the computer recognizes. One alphanumeric character represents one "byte" of information. The byte, or its subdivision the "bit" (eight of which make a byte), are universal measures in the computer world, used to describe the size of memories or the rates of data processing or data transfer. The capacity of internal memories, diskettes, disks, and tapes is measured in "kilobytes" (units of 1,024 bytes, usually referred to as Ks), "megabytes" (MBs, more than a million bytes), and now even "gigabytes" (more than a billion bytes). Modems and hardwired communications systems are evaluated by the "baud rate," or bits transferred per second between terminal and computer.

Within the computer, alphanumeric characters can be compared, interpreted, changed, rearranged (as in alphabetical order), but are not usually subject to arithmetic manipulations or transformations. At all events, adding "Joseph" and "John" does not make much sense in the real world. Unless the historian is largely concerned with analyzing literary texts, the chief use of alphanumeric characters is to process names and to provide easily recognized labels, both for records and ultimately for printed output.

"Real numbers," or "floating-point numbers," include only the number set 1-9, 0, and plus and minus signs, and always possess a decimal point (a positive sign and the decimal point may be implied when the number is originally read into the machine). The real number in the computer's memory always contains a set count of significant digits, and the decimal point floats to the right or left within the register according to whether the value represented is large or small. Almost all the arithmetic operations performed by the computer are done in real numbers. The system of real numbers has, however, one principal deficiency. Floating-point numbers, particularly after manipulation, often carry infinitesimal fractional values, which do not significantly affect the calculations but do affect tests for equality. A "6" for example may, at one moment, be represented in a computer register as a tiny bit larger or less than the exact number six. When asked whether three times one-third equals three, the computer may well reply "no," as it cannot exactly represent one-third. Modern systems can correct for these minute deviations, but require time to do it. And the name of this game is speed.

The difficulty in reliably comparing real numbers for equality is one principal reason why computers work also with a second set of numbers, which are exclusively integers and never carry a decimal point and never a fractional value. "Integer numbers" may also be positive or negative, and can be transformed by the normal arithmetical operations. However, in the results, fractional values are always discarded. In integer arithmetic, the number ten divided by six, seven, eight, nine, or ten gives the same answer — one. Integer numbers can, however, be reliably tested for equality, and this quality is advantageous in all applications. Moreover, whenever the historian uses numbers to represent a particular quality, as, for example, a "1" for male and a "2" for female in the code book, those numbers must be treated as integer values, if they are to be reliably identified in the processing. The representation of discrete categories by numbers is the essence of coding, and here integer numbers find their widest application. In identifying categories, fractional values would normally be meaningless. If "1" signifies male and "2" female, what could be the sense of "1.5"?

Integer numbers have the further advantage that, in many systems, they can be stored more economically and retrieved more quickly than their alphanumeric equivalents. This is why most code books use numbers rather than letters or other symbols to code information. The "user-friendliness" of present applications has rather obscured these distinctions, especially between real and integer numbers, but they remain present in the inner workings of the computer. Data base management systems will usually require that the user classify data entered according to the types just described.

With a sense of the records and an appreciation of how the computer will represent them, the historian is now ready to consider the machines themselves.

COMPUTER SYSTEMS

The "computer" of everyday language may be more precisely described as a data-processing system. The system consists of several mechanical and electronic devices linked together, "on line" in the technical jargon. The physical components of computing systems are called, in the technical jargon, "hardware." Applications or programs presented to the system and data are called "software." They are so described since both applications and data usually change, and are meant to change, with each job or run executed by the system.

All computing systems include a minimum of three types of components: an electronic calculator or accumulator (now most commonly called the "central processing unit" or CPU), which actually does the calculations and comparisons; "memory," which directly delivers commands and data to the CPU and also retains data and applications, and sometimes results, from one job to another; and "input-output" devices (I/O) which carry applications and data to the CPU and which retrieve and display the results.

The Mainframe and the PC

From a historian's perspective, the most dramatic change in the computing arts has been the development over the last ten years of the small, micro- or "personal" computer, the PC. The advent of the microprocessor, a CPU on a chip that packs extraordinary speed and power into a small space, and high-capacity memory systems, shortly to be reviewed, give the PC the resources of the mainframes of two decades ago. The historian is now freed from dependency on the big computer center. There is even a certain satisfaction in owning, or at least enjoying personal and private access to, these amazing machines.

Though the PC is now the cheapest and most convenient computing tool, access to a mainframe is still advantageous. "Video display terminals" (VDTs) now provide the principal means of communicating with the mainframe. Most PCs, through a telephone link, or "modem," and appropriate software, can double as terminals and can converse with the big machines. Many college campuses now have networks, which permit a "hardwire" connection between the PC functioning as a terminal and the mainframe. With this connection, communications between the PC and the mainframe are nearly instantaneous, as fast as 60,000 bits per second. No longer must the historian carry boxes of cards to the computer center and wait around anxiously for the usually disappointing results. Now he or she can be disappointed almost instantaneously.

Access to a mainframe allows the historian to make use of devices not usually part of a PC system. The user can, for example, back up big or important files on magnetic tape through the tape drives that mainframe computers always support. The user might also want to print out large files on a high-speed line printer, rather than on the smaller, slower printers usually serving PCs. Finally, access to a mainframe can link the historian to communications networks, which permit users to learn what is happening in the art; to read bulletin boards; to send letters and files to other users, even outside one's home university, and even overseas; and to access a large variety of libraries or collections of machine-readable data. In the near future, data bases specifically designed for medievalists, such as those maintained by the MEMDB, will become available through these networks.

Though the mainframe serves useful purposes, the PC offers unique advantages. PCs can be located in convenient places, at home or office, and be readily accessible all hours of the day. Some "lap-top" computers are small and light and contain their own power supply; they can be carried directly into libraries and archives, for the direct entry of data. We assume in the rest of this essay that the medievalist will be doing his or her primary work on a PC.

Operating Systems

All computers, big and small, need an "operating system," software instructions which essentially monitor and coordinate all the attached devices and allow the user, through fairly simple commands, to direct the computer to perform various tasks: displaying, copying, or deleting files; finding records within them; sorting entries; or other operations. The most common operating systems for PCs are the aging MS-DOS (Microsoft Disk Operating System), used on IBM microcomputers and their many clones; Macintosh, a highly successful system oriented to the use of a pointer (a "mouse") and symbols ("icons") to point to; and UNIX (first designed for big computers) with its many cousins, a maze of an operating system that can do many things for the few who can master its intricacies.

Commands given directly to the operating system are the quickest of all commands that the user without special expertise can execute, but they are also not easily combined to do complicated tasks, at least not by those without special training. The medievalist, in processing data, should plan to use higher-level programming languages or statistical or data-management packages, about which more will be said presently.

Memory

The historian needs to know the capacity and speed of the PC system he or she is thinking of adopting, and a critical measurement here is memory. Memory serves several purposes and comes in several modes. The computer needs an internal memory called "RAM" (Random Access Memory). In it, the machine stores the programs it is executing and, in whole or in part, the data it is processing. This working memory is always volatile, that is, its contents change from job to job, and disappear entirely when the computer is turned off. The size of the memory, measured in bytes, determines what applications can be loaded into the computer, and also affects the speed with which the CPU can access and process data. The historian should now require in a PC at least one megabyte of RAM.

Some PCs also contain a permanent internal memory, called "ROM," for Read Only Memory, on which the operating system or special applications can be stored and loaded into RAM when needed.

Neither RAM nor ROM is designed to carry over data or applications from one job to another. Some "lap-top" computers include a battery-powered memory board, which can serve these functions, weighs little, and can substitute for an external disk drive. The board is, however, dependent on constant power, and if its battery wears down, its contents vanish. Though convenient, it is not a safe and secure place for the permanent storage of important programs or data.

For permanent storage of data and programs, PCs make primary use of magnetic disks, on which a drive records information by magnetizing particles on their specially prepared surfaces. A newer type of external storage is the "Compact Disk" (CD), based on laser optical technology. These latter disks, comparable to the compact disks used in audio recordings, can carry enormous amounts of data, but cannot be overwritten; they constitute, in other words, external ROM. In spite of their high capacity, they do not as yet match the magnetic disks for convenience.

The magnetic disks and the drives that serve them are of two principal types: "floppy" disks or diskettes, and fixed, or "hard," disks. The standard size of diskettes is now 5.25 or 3.25 inches in diameter; high-density versions of the 5.25-inch disk can hold 1.2 megabytes. They seem, however, destined to be replaced by the smaller, more convenient, and better packaged 3.25-inch diskettes. These latter diskettes, used in the newer IBM Personal System/2 family of PCs and in the Macintoshes, are capable of holding 0.72 MB or, in high-density format, 1.44 MB of data. Every PC needs at least one floppy disk (or diskette) drive. Since the diskette is easily transportable, it serves not only as external storage but also as the chief means by which new applications and new data can be entered and the results of processing retrieved in machine-readable form. Unless the PC is connected to a mainframe, the floppy drive will likely be the only means of reading in or reading out machine-readable information.

A hard, or fixed, disk cannot usually be removed and carried elsewhere, but it is able to hold texts and applications millions of characters in length. Reading and writing to and from a hard disk is also much faster than to or from diskettes. A hard disk is further required to store many large applications, such as spreadsheets or data base management systems. Most new computers include as standard equipment a hard disk drive of 20 megabyte capacity. This is already too small, if the historian is working with large data sets or applications. Today, even 80 MB of storage is not excessive.

Backup

High-capacity, hard disk systems work so well as to lull the user into a false sense of security. However, though wondrously helpful, the computer can also be wondrously destructive, and the historian must plan to back up all important files or applications. The risks are many, from "system crashes" to accidental erasures to "viruses" roaming through the system. The task of backing up files grows more difficult as the files grow larger. When files are small, floppies will serve. The user can also purchase an external tape drive, which can be used to dump at regular intervals the contents of the hard disk. If the system is connected with a mainframe, the critical files can be "uploaded" and then "downloaded" onto tape, as mentioned. Whatever the solution adopted, the rule holds: every file of value must be backed up. Otherwise, hours, days, weeks, and even years of labor are jeopardized.

I/O

Diskettes, as mentioned, are the chief means of entering data or retrieving results in machine-readable form. But for the historian who is working directly from records, the VDT is the principal device used to enter the data through its attached keyboard. The keyboard resembles a typewriter's, but allows the entry of a much larger number of characters: a full 256 in modern systems. Like the familiar shift key on the typewriter, certain other keys — labeled "control," "alternate," or "escape" — change the significance of other keys struck when they are depressed. To retrieve the results of an analysis, the historian can either display them on the video screen or have them printed in "hard," that is, permanent copy.

I shall now assume that the historian possesses a set of medieval serial records to process and has selected a suitable machine. The processing itself is divisible into two principal phrases: "data entry," or the translation of the records into machine-readable form; and "applications," or the use or the development of programs which will perform the actual analysis. The last part of this chapter looks at these two phases separately. Of the two, data entry is distinctly the more difficult, slower, and more expensive phase of the operation. Worlds of possibilities open once the data are rendered machine-readable, but the path thereto is steep and arduous.

DATA ENTRY

Data, and applications too, may either be keyed into the computer or "imported." To be imported, they must already exist in machine-readable form, stored on disk or tape, and accessed by a disk drive, tape drive, or communications network. The keying in of data, once done by keypunch machines, is now almost always done at a terminal, through which the data are entered onto a diskette or disk. Keying is slow and costly, and much of it today is done "offshore," that is, outside the continental United States by data entry personnel who may not even understand the texts they are copying.

Optical Scanners

A device that offers great promise for the future is the "optical scanner," which has the capability of translating a printed page into ASCII codes, thus converting it into machine readable form. For long the best-known scanners have been the Kurzweil Discoverer and the Kurzweil 4000. These scanners work very well in converting literary texts when they are printed in modern typeface. Nonetheless, careful proofreading is still required, as the scanners can easily confuse look-alike characters, such as an "8" and a "B." And their services are expensive. In 1988, a new optical scanner for the Macintosh Computer, called "OmniPage," was announced by Caere Corporation, Los Gatos, California. Its vendors claim that it can correctly interpret a wide range of type fonts. It requires special resources — such as four megabytes of internal memory — but seems to be much cheaper than the older machines.

While the powers of OmniPage still await evaluation, optical scanners have proved least satisfactory in interpreting the data presented in tables or in serial entries — exactly the kinds of material with which this chapter is concerned. Even when the text is correctly read, the entries will almost always have to be heavily edited, reformatted, and sometimes coded. The optical scanner, for example, may find it difficult to recognize where one record ends and the next begins. And medieval records present special problems, such as the frequent presentation of numeric values in Roman numerals. While, in theory, a computer could be instructed to interpret Roman numerals, this would require much complicated programming. For this kind of records, optical scanning only displaces the burden of work from keying to a later, but still indispensable, phase of editing.

Full-Text Entry

The historian has the option of entering the records in their full text, just as they appear in print or in manuscript, and just as a fully accurate optical scanner would read them. This strategy is appropriate and even advisable, if the primary goal of the enterprise is the retrieval of individual entries. The end user could call in and read the records in their original form, without the burden of deciphering coded information.

On the other hand, if the primary purpose of the data set is aggregate analysis, then coding has decisive advantages. It reduces the burden of data entry; it diminishes the size of the stored file and the amount of memory needed to hold it; and it increases the speed and efficiency of the final processing.

Coding

In coding his or her documentation, the researcher must respond to three questions:

1. What is the logical unit in the documentation, that is, what defines the record in the series? In a census, for example, the logical unit

might be the individual, the household, the parish, or the village. The best advice, here, is to select as the logical unit the one used by those who redacted the document: did the surveyors present their questionnaire to individuals, to household heads, to the parish priest, or to the village elders? This is consistent with the principle of "empirical," as opposed to "analytic," coding. The machine-readable record should reflect the logical units and the categories of the original documentation, not the analytic categories reflective of the historian's ultimate interests.

2. What kinds of information are carried on the record? The historian must identify exactly the categories of information represented and their constituent elements. Ideally, all categories should be carried on the machine-readable record, but this may not be feasible when the entries are particularly long and complex, as in the Florentine Catasto of 1427.[7]

The categories of information are assigned a certain number of spaces on the machine-readable record, and the spaces together constitute a data "field." Numeric values in the original are not coded but are directly transcribed; care, however, must be taken to assure that the field is large enough to accommodate the greatest possible value.

The principal work of coding is the assignment of a symbolic value, usually a number, to elements within a category. Categories in a census might be sex, marital status, residence, relationship to the head of household, occupation, and so forth. To identify both the categories of information and the elements within them requires that the historian have a close knowledge of the documentation even before composing the code book. The elements must be discrete and mutually exclusive. If two elements in a category—as for example, two occupations—can be applied to the same person, then a second data field would have to be assigned.

The layout of fields on the machine-readable record is called its "format." To accelerate coding, the data fields should be laid out in the same order in which the information appears on the original record. It is also advisable to include some redundant information for purposes of verifying accuracy. For example, in coding the Florentine Catasto, we included for each family the gross total of assessed wealth, the deductions allowed, and the net wealth after deductions. The last value was, in a strict sense, redundant, as it was easily calculated from the first two. Its inclusion nonetheless served as a check that all the values were correctly entered.

Besides data fields, the record should always include a reference back to the original document from whence the information was taken. Processing will almost always reveal errors, and the researcher must retain the ability to return to the original document for purposes of verification. The source reference may also provide a means of identifying the record uniquely within the set. Or the record might be numbered, to allow its quick retrieval for purposes of verification and editing.

Inconsistencies in spelling, notorious in medieval records, raise special problems. In coding the Catasto, we standardized all names, in order to facilitate the retrieval and sorting of records. If the set of names is limited, as for example, in regard to occupations or titles, a better strategy is the following. The occupational name can be entered as originally spelled, but the record can also carry the occupation in coded or numeric form which would not reflect spelling variations. For example, the variant French forms for the occupation "miller," *munier* or *musnier,* would be coded with the same number. For aggregate analysis, the computer uses the number, while the original spelling is preserved in an alphanumeric field on the same record. This will be further illustrated when we cite examples of coding in regard to the Paris *tailles,* or tax lists.

In former years, the researcher wrote in the fields on big code sheets. These were passed on to the keypunch operator, who punched the data onto cards. Usually, too, the cards had to be verified for accuracy on another machine, which involved keying in the codes a second time. Now that the VDT has replaced the keypunch, a second keying may still be advisable to assure accuracy. Operating systems such as MS-DOS usually include a "compare" command, which reads the two files and identifies any differences between them. This is the electronic equivalent to the older process of mechanical verification.

Data Base Management Systems

Certain prepackaged programs or applications now greatly facilitate the burden of entering data. All applications — word processing, data base management, spreadsheets, or statistical processing systems — make provision for data entry. "Data base management" (DBM) systems offer the most flexibility, as they are primarily designed for entering, retrieving, and sorting the records in seemingly limitless configurations.

In accepting data, DBM systems usually work in a conversational mode, that is, they present on screen a series of questions, to which the user types in appropriate answers. The entries can also be "menu driven," that is, the computer shows on screen a list of possible choices and asks the user to type in a number or letter identifying the one to be chosen. Under such systems, fields cannot be confused, and the data are stored in ways that allow marvelously quick retrieval or sorting. Some systems even allow pictures and visual materials to be kept on file.

There are, however, some disadvantages in DBM systems. The data are stored in ways that accelerate retrieval, but it may be difficult to export the file in simple ASCII codes for importation into a different application, or to a different computer. Moreover, when the records are relatively few, the conversational mode of entry serves very well, but it slows the entry of very long runs of records. The presentation of questions or menus on the screen takes time; they must be read, and the user must respond. Direct mode, in which the user simply enters the data, is obviously quicker.

Customized Data Entry Programs

An alternative to the use of a DBM system for entering data is to design a data entry program that will reflect the exact nature of the documentation. The program would be written in one of the "higher-level" programming languages. Even BASIC, the most common programming language available on PCs, can serve very well.

The goal of an entry program is to reduce to an absolute minimum the number of keystrokes needed to enter the record—to repackage, as it were, the original data in the most economical form possible. To accomplish this, a customized data entry program takes advantage of two characteristics of serial records: information on one record is often repeated on the next, and some common names, whether of persons or of occupations, can be entered in abbreviated form. The computer can be programmed to recognize abbreviations and to restore them automatically to the original spelling. This reconversion makes the record more comprehensible to the human user.

I shall illustrate this method by entries out of the *tailles,* or tax lists, of Paris.[8] The *tailles* of Paris, which date from 1292 to 1313, are almost a perfect example of medieval serial documentation. Seven survive, four of which are published. They are long (the earliest and largest, from 1292, contains nearly 15,000 entries). The entries give, for each district (*queste*) of the city and for streets or zones within it, the names, often the occupation, and the tax assessment of the residents. The entries are rigorously repetitive and contain in the tax assessments quantitative information. Typical entries randomly chosen from the *taille* of 1313 are the following:

LA SECONDE QUESTE SAINT-GERMAIN
SI COMMANCE DE LA PORTE SANT-HONORE DEDANZ LES MURS,
JUSQUES AU COING DEVANT LA CROIZ DU TIROUER

Aalis la liniere	VI s.p.
Pierre le pastaier	VI s.p.
Nicolas d'Avion	XXXVI s.p.

To transfer this information onto a machine-readable record, fields must be assigned for all the information represented; to facilitate coding, the data fields but not the name fields are also tagged as shown in the following listing:

Field Name	Columns	Tag
Series (arbitrarily identified as 1)	1–2	s
Year (1313)	3–6	y
Page (in Michaëlson's edition)	7–9	p
Queste (Parisian district, numbered in consecutive order)	10–11	q
Street (location in the queste, also in consecutive order under each queste)	12–13	r
Livres or pounds of assessment	14–17	l
Sous of assessment	18–19	s
Deniers of assessment	20–21	d
Comment on entry (the "p." in the entries means "paid," coded here as 1)	22–23	e
First occupation (when given)	24–26	o
Second occupation (when given)	27–29	j
Gender (1 = male, 2 = female)	30	g
Comments on names	31–32, 44–45, 57–58	-
Names	33–43, 46–56, 59–69	-
Comment on record	70	-
Record sequence numbers (e.g., 1 of 1)	71–72	-

The comment on the name, given in the form of a number essentially serves to distinguish family names and names of occupation from personal names. It is also used to identified articles and prepositions in the original record, for example, 06 = "de," and 07 = "le."

The program also recognizes abbreviations for common French names, "a" for ANTHOINE, "p" for PIERRE, "n" for NICOLAS, and so forth, and also for most occupations. Abbreviations for occupations are distinguished from other types of names by placing a "05" in front of the letter or letters, "05a" for "05AVOCAT," "05bg" for "05BOULENGIER," and so forth. When the program encounters an abbreviated occupation, it both resolves the abbreviation and looks up the occupation in a code listing; it then inserts the code number in the "o" field (or the "j" field if it is a second occupation). Variations in spelling can be introduced for occupational names by the use of an "=", thus, "05a = advocat" will enter "05ADVOCAT" in the name field, but the same code number in the "o" field. The automatic insertion of an occupation number saves the user the chore of looking up the code in a lengthy list and reduces the likelihood of mistakes. The abbreviated occupational names are mnemonic and more easily found, or even memorized, than code numbers.

Proper names are entered before the data fields, corresponding to the order they are presented on the record (in fact, the tags allow the data fields to be entered in any order, as the computer will rearrange them correctly). Names are separated by an "x," and a "/" is used to separate the nominal from the numeric data fields (otherwise the tags might be construed as abbreviated names). When more than three names are entered, the additional names are automatically carried forward to a second or third supplementary record, as needed. The place of each record in the set is shown by the sequence numbers in the last two columns.

The user would make the following entries on the keyboard and the computer would display on the screen the following resolutions, and then ask whether or not they are correct. If correct, they are added to the permanent file:

aalisx05li/s631g2
011313006010100000600014060002   AALIS   05LINIERE   011
px05pt/g1
011313006010100000600012020001   PIERRE   05PASTAIER   011
nx06avion/s36
011313006010100003600010000001   NICOLAS   06AVION   011

The names and the tagged fields are entered directly from the printed source; no code sheets are required. The entry program also checks the reconstituted record to make sure that letters and numbers are in their proper fields and all values within their proper ranges. By carrying forward information from one record to another and by the use of abbreviations, the coding of the data is greatly expedited. I have used variations of this program for other lengthy data sets based on nominal lists, and it works quite well. The disadvantage is that this method of entry requires "customized" programming. However, the time spent in developing the program is regained for large files by the reduced number of needed keystrokes and by enhanced speed.

APPLICATIONS

After generating the machine-readable file, the historian can proceed to its analysis. Here again, a choice exists between customized development of analytical programs or the use of commercially available applications, spreadsheets, and statistical packages. Both recourses have their own distinct advantages and disadvantages.

Languages

The preparation of a customized analytic program, like a data entry program, requires the command of a programming language such as BASIC. Customized programs can be designed to tell the historian exactly what he or she wants to know. They do, however, require time and labor in writing and debugging, and errors may inadvertently slip into the program, tainting the results. Historians need not reinvent the wheel, and for most purposes it is advisable to utilize the commercially available packages.

Nonetheless, even if the historian does not intend to write an analytical program, it is invaluable, nearly indispensable, that he or she have a knowledge of simple programming. On the assumption that the data file has been generated in simple ASCII codes, it will have to be modified in order to be imported into other applications. Most of them require that the fields be separated by some sort of marker, such as a "tab stop," and these separators will have to be inserted into the file. This is not a difficult task, but a simple program must still be written to accomplish it. So also, many tasks of file management — copying, correcting, reformatting, retrieving, or viewing the file in all or in part — are best done by simple programming.

Packages

Once the historian has learned how to import files, he or she has a wide choice of analytical packages. DBM systems can accomplish some aggregate analysis, sometimes referred to as "reports." But aggregate analysis is not their principal purpose. For fairly simple and straightforward numeric analysis, "spreadsheets" are perhaps the best choice. They calculate quickly and store the results in whatever form the user wants. Most now also have the capacity of drawing graphs in any number of styles.

For complex and powerful forms of statistical analysis, packages such as SPSS ("Statistical Package for the Social Sciences") may well be the appropriate application. Again, the historian must learn what they do from the thick manuals that accompany such packages, and also master the art of importing or converting the data into the form that the particular application requires.

It is impossible to give here an adequate introduction into the various statistical methods that can be usefully applied to historical or medieval data. The historian should make use of the statistical consulting services available at most universities and also read an elementary book on statistics. Here, I limit the discussion to certain broad observations.

Statistics serve various purposes, and one of the most fundamental is the description of collected data, the "statistical universe" or the "population" (not necessarily comprised of people). Strategies will differ, depending on whether the categories in the universe are distinct but not numerically related (as, for example, sex, residence, or occupation in the Parisian tax lists), or with values that can be regarded as numerically related and as forming points on an interval scale (prices, ages of persons, wealth assessments in a tax survey, and so forth). For the former type of data, the historian can calculate frequency distributions, in both absolute figures and in percentages, which illuminate the composition of the set and facilitate comparisons with other populations. Values distributed along an interval scale allow further the calculation of "measures of central tendency," which indicate certain central points on the scale of values. The three most common measures are the "mean" (the arithmetic average of all values), the "median" (the middle value when all values are arranged in ascending or descending order) and the "mode" (the most common single value). The researcher may also want to know how the values are scattered as well as concentrated; this is accomplished through "measures of dispersion." The most common are the "range" (the highest and lowest values present) and the "standard deviation," the exact nature of which is explained in all elementary statistical texts.

However, the historian will rarely be content with description alone, and will usually want to study statistical relationships. Here the appropriate strategy will again be determined by the character of the records and the nature of the data. If the historian is studying relations among categories, as for example, the number of men showing certain occupation as opposed to the number of women, the tests will be "non-parametric," since they can show the existence of a relationship, but do not measure its strength.

If the data represent values on a scale, then parametric measurements can be applied that will tell not only whether a relationship exists, but also its strength. Several methods of doing this are available. The most common is "regression analysis," which studies how one variable, considered to be dependent, varies when the values of a second variable, considered to be independent, change. For example, the historian might ask whether or how strong is the relationship between the wealth of a household and its size, as shown in a particular survey. This examination leads to the calculation of a "product-moment coefficient of correlation." This measure ranges from the value of "1.0" for perfect association of the two variables, to "0.0" for no relationship, to "-1.0" for perfect negative correlation. There are many implied assumptions concerning the data in making such calculations which cannot be discussed here, and the historian will find it well worth the time to read the chapters on regression and correlation in any text on statistics.

Still more sophisticated methods are "multivariate analysis" (which measures the relationship among a set of variables), "analysis of variance," and "factor analysis." These powerful methods assume very precise and clean data, which are often difficult to obtain from medieval sources. It must always be recalled that no statistical method can really compensate for crude or inaccurate data. But the historians should at least be aware of the existence and the purposes of these more advanced techniques, which may at some time help solve problems of which he or she is at present unaware.

Historians have always sought to control their documents and thus to develop a better understanding of them. But some documents, even out of the Middle Ages, are so big and boring that they have resisted full control and hence full understanding. The computer is not bothered by big and boring documents. It easily masters them when they are properly presented. It has already proved to be an invaluable help for medievalists, and its versatility and power are sure to expand in years to come.

NOTES

1. Of many general introductions to the history and principles of computing, I have found particularly enlightening Joseph Weizenbaum, *Computer Power and Human Reason: From Judgment to Calculations* (1976). Written specifically for historians though now also largely obsolete is Edward Shorter, *The Historian and the Computer: A Practical Guide* (Englewood Cliffs, New Jersey: Prentice-Hall, 1971). For journals, see *Computers and the Humanities* and *L'Ordinateur et le Médiéviste,* the latter a useful bulletin of information about medieval projects which, by fall 1987, had reached its eighteenth number. Peter Denley and Deian Hopkin, eds., *History and Computing* (1987), a collection of papers delivered at a conference in March 1986, presents a useful overview of computer-assisted research projects in history.

2. On the differentiation between numerical and formal analysis, see my further discussion in "Numerical and Formal Analysis in European History" (1981).

3. There are now many data banks of medieval data, at various stages of completion and accessibility. Most are prosopographical in nature, that is, they are repositories of refer-

ences to the same person. Some, such as the several efforts to render the Domesday Book of 1086 into machine-readable form, are actual editions of a major medieval document. The data banks relevant to the Middle Ages of which I am aware are the following: REAL (Institut für mittelalterliche Realienkunde Oesterreichs, Krems/Donau, Austria, information about daily life in medieval Austria taken largely from pictorial sources); Datenbank mittelalterlicher Personen und Personengruppen (Univ. of Freiburg, Germany, containing 400,000 names of Carolingian, Ottonian, and Salian royalty, nobility, and clergy, based on such sources as obituaries and charters); Migration in Austria, 1350–1600, a bank sponsored by the Ludwig-Boltzmann Institut für Historische Sozialwissenschaft and so far containing about 2,000 entries from the Bürgerbuch of Salzburg, 1441–1451; Prosopographische Datenbank zur Geschichte der südöstlichen Reichsgebiete bis 1250, sponsored by the Forschungsinstitut für historische Grundwissenschaften, Karl-Franzenz Universität, Graz, Austria; the Hull Domesday Project (Hull Univ., England, another project to put the Domesday Book into machine-readable form proceeds under the direction of Professor C. Warren Hollister of the Univ. of California, Santa Barbara); Parisian Tax Rolls from the Reign of Philip the Fair (Paris, sponsored by the Centre National de la Recherche Scientifique); the Women's Writers Project (Brown Univ., a data base containing prosopographical information and machine-readable editions of works in English by women, 1330–1830, directed by Suzanne Woods).

4. Information about the MEMDB, its data collections, and access to them may be procured by writing to the Medieval and Early Modern Data Bank, Dept. of History, CN 5059, Rutgers, the State Univ. of New Jersey, New Brunswick, NJ 08903 USA. For a brief description of the bank, see Carlin 1988.

5. See Herlihy 1985, 62–72.

6. See Herlihy and Klapisch-Zuber 1978, 1985.

7. In creating our machine-readable edition of the Catasto, we did not include the names of family members apart from the head nor the descriptions of the individual plots of land that the family owned.

8. The *taille* of 1313 is one of seven surviving tax lists from Paris during the reign of Philip IV the Fair. The earliest dates from 1292, and four of them have been published. The examples here are taken from Karl Michaëlson's edition (1951, 6) of the *taille* of 1313.

BIBLIOGRAPHY

Carlin, Martha. *The MEMBD Handbook.* Stanford: Research Libraries Group, 1988.

Computers for the Humanities: A Conference Sponsored by Yale University on a Grant from IBM, January 23–25, 1965. New Haven: The Conference, 1965.

Denley, Peter, and Deian Hopkin, eds. *History and Computing.* Manchester: Manchester Univ. Press. 1987.

Floud, Roderick. *An Introduction to Quantitative Methods for Historians.* 2d ed. London: Methuen, 1979.

Heffer, Jean. *Outils statistiques pour les historiens.* Paris: Publications de la Sorbonne 1971.

Herlihy, David. "Numerical and Formal Analysis in European History," *The Journal of Interdisciplinary History* 12 (1981): 115–36.

————. *Medieval Households.* Cambridge, Mass.: Harvard Univ. Press, 1985.

Herlihy, David, and Christiane Klapisch-Zuber. *Les Toscans et leurs familles.* Paris: N.p., 1978. English trans.: *Tuscans and Their Families.* New Haven, Conn.: Yale Univ. Press, 1985.

Histoire et Mesure. Paris, 1986–.

Le livre de la taille de Paris, l'an de grâce 1313. Edited by Karl Michaëlson. Acta Universitatis Gotoburgensis. Göteborgs Hogskolas Årsskrift 57. Göteborg: N.p., 1951.

Le Médiéviste et l'ordinateur. A bulletin published at the École des Hautes Études, 54 bd Raspail, 75006 Paris.

Ohlen, Norbert. *Quantitative Methoden für Historiker.* Munich: N.p., 1980.

Spufford, Peter. *Handbook of Medieval Exchange.* London: Royal Historical Society, 1986.

Weizenbaum, Joseph. *Computer Power and Human Reason: From Judgment to Calculations.* San Francisco: W. H. Freeman, 1976.

Ꙭ 7 Ꙭ

Medieval Chronology
Theory and Practice

R. DEAN WARE

O DEFINITION OF HISTORY can ignore its temporal dimension, and the historical practitioner is characteristically occupied with ordering and establishing events in time. It is apparent, however, that this work of arrangement and computation can only be carried on within the context of some chronological system. To describe position in a continuum or, in the case of history, to date an event, requires a reference point from which to measure and, of course, units of measurement. The system in use throughout the western world today, for example, utilizes a wide range of measuring units: seconds, minutes, hours, days, weeks, months, and years. Of these, the day, month, and year are natural astronomical periods: the rest are artificial. A further incongruity is that, while the minute is a multiple of the second — as is the hour of the minute, the day of the hour, and the week of the day — the week, month, and year are incommensurable. Our system also provides various reference points from which, as appropriate, time is measured: the day by hours from midnight and noon, the month by days from its commencement, and the year by months and days from its conventional beginning on 1 January. All historical time is arbitrarily divided into eras prior and subsequent to the birth of Christ.

In Europe during the Middle Ages, the chronological systems employed are so profuse and bewildering that a deliberate study of the methods of medieval time reckoning, and of the vocabulary in which these calculations are expressed, is prerequisite to an intelligent handling of historical

CHART TO ILLUSTRATE THE PATTERNS OF CHRONOLOGICAL DEVICES

A.D. (*Leap year)	Indiction	Metonic Cycle	Solar Cycle	Paschal Cycle	Epacts	Paschal Term	Golden Number	Dominical Letter	Weekday of Jan. 1	Concurrent	Key	Easter
528*	VI	13	5	529	15	21 Ma	XVI	BA	Sa	6	11	26 Ma
529	VII	14	6	530	26	9 Ap	XVII	G	M	7	30	15 Ap
530	VIII	15	7	531	7	29 Ma	XVIII	F	Tu	1	19	31 Ma
531	IX	16	8	532	18	17 Ap	XIX	E	W	2	38	20 Ap
532*	X	17	9	1	0	5 Ap	I	DC	Th	4	26	11 Ap
533	XI	18	10	2	11	25 Ma	II	B	Sa	5	15	27 Ma
534	XII	19	11	3	22	13 Ap	III	A	Su	6	34	16 Ap
535	XIII	1	12	4	3	2 Ap	IV	G	M	7	23	8 Ap
536*	XIV	2	13	5	14	22 Ma	V	FE	Tu	2	12	23 Ma
537	XV	3	14	6	25	10 Ap	VI	D	Th	3	31	12 Ap
538	I	4	15	7	6	30 Ma	VII	C	F	4	20	4 Ap
539	II	5	16	8	17	18 Ap	VIII	B	Sa	5	39	24 Ap
540*	III	6	17	9	28	7 Ap	IX	AG	Su	7	28	8 Ap
541	IV	7	18	10	9	27 Ma	X	F	Tu	1	17	31 Ma
542	V	8	19	11	20	15 Ap	XI	E	W	2	36	20 Ap
543	VI	9	20	12	1	4 Ap	XII	D	Th	3	25	5 Ap
544*	VII	10	21	13	12	24 Ma	XIII	CB	F	5	14	27 Ma
545	VIII	11	22	14	23	12 Ap	XIV	A	Su	6	33	16 Ap
546	IX	12	23	15	4	1 Ap	XV	G	M	7	22	8 Ap
547	X	13	24	16	15	21 Ma	XVI	F	Tu	1	11	24 Ma
548*	XI	14	25	17	26	9 Ap	XVII	ED	W	3	30	12 Ap
549	XII	15	26	18	7	29 Ma	XVIII	C	F	4	19	4 Ap
550	XIII	16	27	19	18	17 Ap	XIX	B	Sa	5	38	24 Ap
551	XIV	17	28	20	0	5 Ap	I	A	Su	6	26	9 Ap
552*	XV	18	1	21	11	25 Ma	II	GF	M	1	15	31 Ma
553	I	19	2	22	22	13 Ap	III	E	W	2	34	20 Ap
554	II	1	3	23	3	2 Ap	IV	D	Th	3	23	5 Ap
555	III	2	4	24	14	22 Ma	V	C	F	4	12	28 Ma

records. This department of knowledge is technical chronology, which is
not concerned with dates, per se, but rather with theoretical constructs
by which dating is effected. It is a subject that has attracted interest from
Antiquity to the present, and very substantial contributions to its literature were made in the Middle Ages, most conspicuously by Bede, but also
by Byrhtferth, Gerland, Ari Thorgilsson, Robert of Hereford, John of
Sacrobosco, and Robert Grosseteste, not to name another dozen obscure
figures, or to list the large number of mostly anonymous *computi*. The
foundations of the modern critical study of technical chronology are the
works of Joseph Scaliger, *De emendatione temporum* (1583), and Denis
Petau, *Opus de doctrina temporum* (1627), and continued activity since
that time has been abundantly productive in the form of minute analyses,
monumental surveys, and handbooks by the score. Nevertheless, no reliable and comprehensive account of medieval chronography and chronological practice has been written, though many individual topics have been
investigated exhaustively, and nearly definitive treatments of limited aspects of the general subject do exist. The essay on technical chronology
included in Giry's *Manuel de diplomatique,*[1] written at the close of the
last century, remains the best single dissertation; but in addition to being
untrustworthy in detail, it makes no attempt to explore the intellectual implications of chronological theory, and even the history of progress in this
branch of learning is ignored except for incidental allusion, though it is
a highly instructive chapter in the advancement of science.

   It should be emphasized that this present essay does not pretend to
meet the need for an up-to-date, complete, accurate, and intelligible volume on medieval chronology, a desideratum as obvious as any in medieval
studies today. Here the intent is merely to offer some brief explanation of
assorted chronological elements and practices in fashion during the Middle Ages, along with instruction for converting their data into modern
terms.[2] That there is need for some formal introduction into the subject
is made evident by the example of a dating clause from an Irish chronicle,
chosen not quite at random, which illustrates in a conceit of redundancy
some of the styles and mechanisms of time reckoning that were at once
the pride and the despair of the medieval computist.

> The Kalends of January on Sunday, and the twenty-sixth of the moon
> thereon. A.D. 1318; Dominical Letter A., and Tabular Letter O. (*post-
> punctata*); the second year after the bissextile; the eighth year of the De-
> cemnovennial Cycle; the fifth of the Lunar Cycle; the twenty-fifth of the
> Solar Cycle according to Gerlandus and the eleventh according to Dio-
> nysius; and the first Indiction; has six as the Concurrent, is an Embolismal
> year, has seventeen as epacts, and thirty-nine as Claves.[3]

THE CIVIL CALENDAR

The civil calendar of medieval Europe was that of Rome, as instituted by the authority of Julius Caesar and modified by Augustus at the end of the first century B.C. This Julian calendar supplanted one that had itself gone through several changes during the earlier Republic, but was originally a lunar calendar of ten months: March, April, May, June, *Quinctilis, Sextilis,* September, October, November, December.[4] At some undetermined date, but earlier than ca. 450 B.C., the months of January and February were created to fill in the previously undenominated period between December (the "tenth" month) and March. Then ca. 450 B.C. January was substituted for March as the beginning of the year, the names of the numbered months thereafter being meaningless. Probably at this same time the divisions of the month, earlier established by direct observation of the moon, the Kalends, Nones, and Ides, became fixed by formula and disconnected from the actual phases of the moon.[5] The calendar now was lunisolar, that is, the months were approximate lunations (four 31-day months: March, May, *Quinctilis,* October; seven of 29 days; February with 28), and a rough synchronization with the solar year was attained by periodic intercalation. The method of intercalation is the most puzzling feature of the pre-Julian calendar, and no convincing explanation of it has yet been offered. Since the twelve lunar months add up to 355 days, in every second year February was truncated at either the 23rd or 24th day and a month (*mensis intercalaris*) of 27 days was inserted. This net addition of 22 or 23 days every other year maintained some correspondence with the solar year, but the biennial error of a day or so was significant enough to disrupt the relation of the months to the seasons after a while.[6] On occasion, then, the intercalation was omitted in an attempt to restore this relationship, but the crudity, if not caprice, of the manipulation precluded satisfactory results of any duration. In 46 B.C., advised by the astronomer Sosigenes, Julius Caesar brought confusion to an end by having the year run 445 days to bring the seasons and months again into harmony, and he introduced a new calendar on 1 January 45 B.C. This was a solar calendar of 365.25 days, distributed among the months to achieve an alternation of 31 and 30 days, except for February with 29. The extra quarter-day was to accumulate to integer and be intercalated every fourth year in February, the traditional month of intercalation. It will be observed that, by the addition of this extra day, February's total is raised to thirty and there is a perfect alternating series of 31- and 30-day months in the intercalary year. Unfortunately the rule for intercalation was misunderstood and too frequently applied over the following years and the emperor Augustus was obliged to suspend intercalation for some years to rectify the blunder. Augustus also, for reasons unknown, altered the pattern of month lengths from that set down by Julius Caesar. February, September, and November were shortened by one day and *Sextilis* (now renamed August, as *Quinctilis* had been renamed July), October and December were lengthened by one day. The length of the year was thus unchanged, but the series of alternation was destroyed. The new arrangement, January (31), February (28), March (31), April (30), May (31), June (30), July (31), August (31), September (30), October (31), November (30), December (31), is that of today's calendar. Indeed, the Julian calendar in this Augustan form, except for a technical adjustment in the sixteenth century, has remained the same for nearly two thousand years and is the one most widely employed in the modern world.

There is, however, one feature of the Julian calendar as employed in Antiquity and in the Middle Ages that differs from present usage: the manner of designating the days of the month. For this purpose the three days called *Kalendae, Nonae,* and *Idus* provided the means of describing all the rest. From the Ides (the 13th day in eight months, the 15th in four)[7] to the end of the month the days were counted in anticipation of the Kalends of the following month. That is, 31 January is the day before the first day of February (*Pridie Kalendas Februarias*), 30 January is the third day, reckoned inclusively, before the first day of February (*ante diem III Kalendas Februarias,* usually abbreviated simply *III Kal. Feb.*), and so on. In like fashion, 12 January is *Pridie Idus Januarias,* 11 January is *III Id. Jan.,* etc., back to the Nones, the ninth day (again reckoning inclusively) before the Ides. Then 4 January is *Pridie Nonas Januarias,* etc., back to the Kalends. There are three potential traps in this system, not always avoided by medieval (or modern) writers: (1) the misleading appearance of the word February in the formulas of the latter half of January; (2) the reverse numeration; and (3) the inclusive reckoning. The intercalation of an extra day in February every four years involves a further complication. Today we do this by adding a day at the end of February. The ancient and medieval practice was to interpolate the additional day between the 23rd and 24th days[8] and to describe it as a "doubling" of the 24th. Since 24 February is designated *VI Kal. Mart.,* the sixth day before the Kalends of March, this doubling created a second (*bis*) *VI Kal. Mart.,* or a *dies bissextus,* and bissextile is still a synonym for leap year.

Medieval documents sometimes show deviations of one sort or another from the pure Roman system. The usage *Pridie,* for example, may be replaced with the number, as in *ante diem II Idus Januarias.* Also on occasion, the days following the Ides are counted in forward rather than reverse order, that is, 14 January might be described as *prima die kalendarum Februarii.* This latter, of course, foreshadows the modern mode of reckoning the days of the month in direct order, a method that enjoyed a premature vogue in the chancery of Pope Gregory I but was neglected during the next several centuries, except for isolated cases. A charter of King Ethelbert II of Kent, dated A.D. 732, *die vicesima februarii mensis,* is an example of forward count; and one of King Swaefred of Essex, dated A.D. 704, *tertia decima die mensis iunii quod est idus iunii,* combines it with the classic mode.[9] In the later Middle Ages the direct reckoning was increasingly common and became standard practice in the English chancery from the end of the twelfth century.

THE ECCLESIASTICAL CALENDAR

Particularly in the later Middle Ages, dating according to the feasts of the ecclesiastical calendar came to rival the Roman system of designation. While every day in the year has some religious association, only the greater celebrations were generally employed for dating purposes, though in the case of saints' days even minor figures might enjoy a local prominence. The final fifteen annals written by the first scribe of the Peterborough recension of the Anglo-Saxon Chronicle,[10] covering the years 1117–1131, provides a representative sampling of dating by reference to holy observances. In addition to frequent reference to Christmas and Easter, two holidays we still employ chronologically, there is also notice of days commemorating Saints John, Thomas, Luke, Andrew, Lawrence, Nicholas, and Peter, as well as those of the Nativity, Annunciation, and Assumption of St. Mary. Another ecclesiastical device illustrated in these same annals is dating by *Introitus,* which is the initial word or phrase of the psalm verse with which the Mass of a particular day is opened. For example, the annal for 1127 identifies a certain Sunday as that when *Exsurge quare obdormis Domine* is sung, the introit traditional to Sexagesima Sunday, which fell on 6 February in that year. The most familiar introits are those of the several Sundays preceding and following Easter: *Circumderunt* (Septuagesima, ninth Sunday before Easter),[11] *Exsurge* (Sexagesima), *Esto mihi* (Quinquagesima, or Shrove Sunday), *Invocavit me* (Quadragesima, or first Sunday in Lent), *Reminiscere* (second Sunday in Lent), *Oculi mei* (third Sunday in Lent), *Letare Hierusalem* (fourth Sunday in Lent), *Iudica mei* (fifth Sunday in Lent, or Passion Sunday), and *Domine ne longe* (sixth Sunday in Lent, or Palm Sunday). After Easter, the introits for the five succeeding Sundays are *Quasimodo geniti, Misericordia domini, Jubilate, Cantate domino,* and *Vocem jocunditatis.* [12] Of course, the Sundays themselves are frequently identified explicitly rather than inferentially by introit.

In addition to the Sundays cited, other significant feasts such as Shrove Tuesday, Ash Wednesday, Ascension Day, Pentecost, etc., are satellites of Easter and follow it as it moves in the calendar. As we shall see in the later discussion of the dating of Easter, the latitude of these movable feasts is 35 days, Septuagesima Sunday, for example, coming as early as 18 January or as late as 22 February (in the leap years A.D. 672 and 1204). For this reason dating by fixed feasts is more usual, and of these the principal ones are Christmas (25 December), Circumcision of Christ (1 January), Epiphany (6 January), Nativity of St. John the Baptist (Midsummer Day, 24 June), St. Michael's Day or "Michaelmas" (29 September), Exaltation of the Cross (14 September), All Saints' Day (1 November), as well as days honoring the Blessed Virgin Mary: Purification or "Candlemas" (2 February), Annunciation or "Lady Day" (25 March), Assumption (15 August), and Nativity (8 September). In connection with all these observances reference might also be to the vigil or eve of the feast, the day before it occurs; the morrow or day following; and the octave or *utas,* the eighth day subsequent. The famous cycle of six fairs in Champagne offers an interesting illustration of international economic activity regulated according to the ecclesiastical calendar, half the opening dates being fixed and half movable. The fair at Lagny began on 2 January, that at Bar-sur-Aube on Tuesday before mid-Lent, the first fair at Provins on Tuesday before Ascension Day, the "hot" fair at Troyes on Tuesday after the fortnight of St. John's Day, the second fair at Provins on the Day of the Exaltation of the Cross, and the "cold" fair at Troyes on the morrow of All Saints' Day. [13]

The designation of specific days of the week is infrequent in medieval records, but here, too, there is an ecclesiastical usage in opposition to the Roman names. The pagan names, *dies Solis, Lunae, Martis, Mercurii, Jovis, Veneris,* and *Saturni,* are still preserved in five of the seven French equivalents (*lundi, mardi, mercredi, jeudi, vendredi*) and in all the English names, though in Germanic dress. The Church adopted a classical Latin word, *feria,* "feast day," for day of the week, and numbered them *prima, secunda, tertia, quarta, quinta, sexta, septima.* For *feria prima,* however, *dies dominicus* or *dominica* (cf. French *dimanche*) was generally substituted, and for *feria septima,* the Hebrew-derived *sabbatum* or *dies sabbati* (cf. French *samedi*) was used. The week itself is *Septimana* or *Hebdomada,* though the phrase "in the octaves" (see octave above) conveys the meaning "within the week" following some specified day. The day continued to be divided, by immemorial custom, into periods of light (*dies*) and dark (*nox*), each period subdivided into twelve hours reckoned from dawn and dusk respectively. The length of these hours varied with the season, those at night becoming twice as long as daytime hours in the winter. Even after clocks began to be used in the later Middle Ages, they were often equipped with an adjusting mechanism so that they could be set to conform to variable hours. The ordinary method of indicating time in the Middle Ages, however, was not by the numbered hours of the day or night but by the hours of the Divine Office, the monastic *horarium*. The variability of these from summer to winter or for liturgical reasons was no less than that of the *horae vulgares;* but, in general, they marked obvious stages in the day: dawn (*Lauds*), daybreak (*Prime*), morning (*Terce*), midday (*Sext*), afternoon (*Nones*), evening (*Vespers*), nightfall (*Compline*), midnight (*Matins*). The chief meal normally followed *Nones,* perhaps about 2:00 P.M.; hunger ultimately drove *Nones* to an earlier hour, whence our noon. These canonical hours developed in different ways and at different times but all were in existence by the end of the fifth century. It was the provisions for celebrating the Divine Office contained in the Rule of St. Benedict (died ca. A.D. 550), however, that regularized and popularized their observance, and from the eighth century to the Second Vatican Council this liturgy of the hours remained essentially unchanged.

THE BEGINNING OF THE YEAR

Of all the features of medieval chronological practice that create confusion and error, the most pernicious is the absence of uniformity in reckoning the beginning of the year.[14] Gervase of Canterbury was not alone in his frustration at the computations of chroniclers, "some counting years from Christ's Annunciation, others from his Nativity, Circumcision, or Passion. Who is to be believed?"[15] Even today so fundamental a fact as the date employed by Bede, the most important chronographer in the Middle Ages, has not been conclusively established.[16] Five different beginnings of the year, two derived from Antiquity and three ecclesiastical importations, are to be discovered in medieval usage. I do not include a reckoning from 1 March, which, although the ancient Roman beginning, and sometimes regarded figuratively as a beginning because it is the month of the vernal equinox, was not, except uniquely at Venice, an official calculation.

The two Roman dates that were in use in the Middle Ages were 1 January and 1 September. The former was the first day of the civil year in the Julian calendar and has recovered that position in recent centuries. During the Middle Ages, however, except in the Iberian peninsula (see Era of Spain), 1 January was the least common reckoning; and yet, paradoxically, it was everywhere referred to as New Year's Day. It was apparently the Church's disinclination to accept this pagan date that explains its medieval eclipse, though an attempt was made to hallow it by declaring it the Feast of the Circumcision. Roman consuls continued to enter office on this day, as they had since 153 B.C., and when the emperors assumed the consulship after A.D. 567, the title was effective from 1 January following accession. Its convenience for some calendrical and astronomical purposes was recognized, however, and both Golden Numbers and Dominical Letters, to be discussed later, changed on 1 January. The other Roman date, 1 September, marked the start of the fiscal year and survived in the West in one form of indictional reckoning (see Indiction). The date remained in use in the Byzantine world and eventually it came also to be the date from which the civil year was calculated.

The other three beginnings of the year current in the Middle Ages were ecclesiastical in origin: 25 March, Annunciation Day; 25 December, Nativity of Christ; and Easter, the Day of Resurrection. This last enjoyed a limited vogue, especially in France (hence it is *mos Gallicanus*) in the thirteenth and fourteenth centuries, but the manifest inconvenience of a movable date precluded serious competition with the other two styles. Dating the year from Christmas, 25 December, which by the fifth century was generally celebrated as the date of Christ's birth, is not certainly attested before Bede (died A.D. 735); but it had become the ordinary calculation throughout Western Europe by the tenth century, and was only gradually supplanted in popularity by the reckoning from Annunciation, 25 March. This final usage, literally the year *ab incarnatione,* was dominant by the late Middle Ages and remained the beginning of the legal year in England, where it is called "Lady Day," until 1752. The calculation from 25 March means that the period from 1 January to 24 March is included in what we would call the previous year. A famous illustration is the inscription on King Henry VIII's tomb that says he died 28 January 1546, though we reckon the year 1547 to have begun on 1 January. A variant style of the Annunciation, more logical, perhaps, but less favored, was a calculation from 25 March before Christmas, which results in a date one year later than the other. This is better appreciated if we say that this variant mode, termed the *calculus Pisanus* from its long association with Pisa, is computed from 25 March 1 B.C.; whereas the ordinary computation, designated *calculus Florentinus* in contrast, is from 25 March A.D. 1.

THE CHRISTIAN AND OTHER ERAS

The modern system of numbering years from the birth of Christ was invented in the first half of the sixth century by a certain Dionysius Exiguus, who chose to calculate his Easter table *ab incarnatione domini nostri,* in preference to perpetuating the memory of the infamous persecutor Diocletian by employing the prevailing era of his name. This Era of Diocletian, also known as the Era of the Martyrs, was reckoned from 29 August A.D. 284, the year (though not the day) of his accession. It entered the West as an adjunct of Easter tables calculated in Egypt, where the era originated, but its rejection by Dionysius resulted in its becoming confined to the East, where, even today, it is used by the Coptic Church. The Dionysian or Christian Era does not appear to have attracted much notice until Bede adopted it as the chronological framework for his *Historia Ecclesiastica* (A.D. 731). It has been suggested that Bede accepted the *annus domini* as a practical way to deal with the diverse reckonings of his sources, but the appropriateness of the system to his subject must also have recommended it. Bede himself became the first writer to calculate years *before* the Incarnation when he specified the consulship of Julius Caesar as *ante vero incarnationis Dominicae tempus anno sexagesimo.*[17] In any event, its utilization by Bede in his immensely popular history gave prominence to the chronological system of Dionysius and within a century or so it was ubiquitous. Although there was controversy, almost from his own day, regarding the accuracy of the Dionysian calculation of A.D. 1, and the year of Christ's birth has yet to be determined conclusively, the functional value of the era, which does not depend upon its historicity, remains unimpaired. There is a fallibility, however, to which students need to be alert: the lack of a year zero, required when calculations involve a mix of B.C. and A.D. dates. For this reason astronomers conventionally count the year before 1 B.C. as 0, and compute 2 B.C. as −1, 3 B.C. as −2, and so on. Thus the interval, say, between the capture of Rome by the Gauls in 390 B.C. (−389) and its capture by the Visigoths in A.D. 410, is 799, not 800, years.

In addition to the Christian Era, and that of Diocletian in reaction to which it originated, the medievalist on occasion encounters dates according to several other eras. The ancient reckoning by olympiads, for example, though officially abolished after 293 cycles by the emperor Theodosius in A.D. 395, continued in use among Byzantine chronographers as an archaism. The word even appears in several western documents, but is patently exotic; it has lost all relation to the classical olympiad computed from 776 B.C. and seems merely to be a synonym for quadrennium.[18] The Era of Rome (A.U.C., *ab urbe condita*), usually calculated from 753 B.C., is another ancient device noted from time to time in the Middle Ages. Its use by Paulus Orosius, whose *Historia adversos Paganos* (A.D. 418) became a standard text, explains its appearance in later writers such as Bede. In the sixth century there existed a short-lived era calculated from A.D. 541, the year of the last annual consulship. Dating according to the consulship was, of course, usual in the Roman world; but the office was left vacant after the tenure of Flavius Basilius, Jr., for a quarter century, and during this interim years were reckoned *post consulatum Basilii.* It is a curiosity that when the office was resumed in A.D. 567, not by an annual magistrate but as an honor held for life by the emperor, the phrase *post consulatum* continued to be employed as a dating formula, although its literal meaning no longer applied. In a papal letter to St. Boniface, the date is given as *Kalendis Aprilis, imperante Domno Augusto Constantino a Deo coronato magno Imperatore vicesimo quarto, post consulatum eius anno secundo:* that is, 1 April A.D. 743. Constantine V was coruler with Leo III from A.D. 719, so it is the twenty-fourth year of his rule; he became sole emperor 19 June 741 and consul as of 1 January A.D. 742; hence it is the second year of, not after, his consulship.[19]

Unlike the foregoing, which are styles of dating that sooner or later every medievalist will encounter, but not with regularity, there are three other eras that are standard but peculiar each to its region, so that, depending upon his research interests, a student might deal with one or another of them habitually, or, perhaps, never at all. The Era of Byzantium, for example, often cited in the form *annus mundi,* is usual in the East from the seventh century and all but unknown in the West. The reference point is Creation, 1 September 5509 B.C., which may be compared with the mundane dates computed by Eusebius-Jerome (5198 B.C.), the Era of Alexandria (5502 B.C.), the Hippolytan Era (5500 B.C.), the Jewish Era (3761 B.C.), and the Vulgate date of 3952 B.C. calculated by Bede. The Byzantine Era survived the capture of Constantinople, and was still in use in Russia to the end of the seventeenth century.

Another era in common use in the Middle Ages, but only within a limited territory, is the Era of Spain. The origin of this style is unknown, but the date from which it is computed, 1 January 38 B.C., coincides with the Augustan subjugation of Spain. If this is indeed what the era commemorates, it is analogous to several other provincial eras, such as that of Macedonia (148 B.C.), Achaea (146 B.C.), Asia (85 B.C.), Mauretania (A.D. 40), etc., singular only in its survival. A different theory is that the date is not historical but calendrical, that it simply marks the start of four 84-year cycles projected back from one beginning 1 January 298 B.C. in order to include the year of incarnation. This conjecture, however, presumes inclusion of the nonexistent year zero in the calculation and is, moreover, refuted by the appearance of the era in slightly earlier inscriptions. In any event, this era was adopted by the Visigoths and employed in the Iberian peninsula, though never universally or exclusively, in adjacent parts of France, and in Vandal Africa. The dating formula of this style is distinctive in that the word *annus* never occurs, only *era;* and the 1 January beginning of the year is a further anomaly. The Spanish Era was abandoned for the Christian Era in most of the peninsula only during the fourteenth century, and by Portugal not until the fifteenth century. At the same time, a Christmas reckoning of the year's beginning was substituted for 1 January just as that date was starting to recover its ancient popularity elsewhere in Europe.

The final era is one with which the medievalist will have to contend if his study touches Islamic history: the Era of the Hegira. It was instituted by Caliph Omar a few years after the death of Mohammed and it supplanted a luni-solar calendar about which little is known. This era is reckoned from the beginning of the year (in the old calendar) in which Mohammed made his "migration," *hegira,* from Mecca to Medina, the first day of the first month Muharram A.H. 1 (*anno Hegirae*) corresponding to 16 July A.D. 622. The Moslem calendar, in accordance with Koranic prescript (Sura 9, verse 36), is strictly lunar, with 12 months that are very nearly true "moon-ths" of 30 and 29 days in alternation. Because an average lunation is some 43 minutes longer than the 29.5 days allowed by the calendar, an excess that accumulates at the rate of about one day in three years, an intercalary day is added to the last month eleven times in thirty years to preserve agreement between the observed moon and the calendar month. Since the Moslem lunar year of 354 (or 355) days is approximately 11 days shorter than the solar year, the result is that the months pass through all the seasons every 32 solar years. Therefore, 32 Christian years and 33 Moslem years are nearly coterminous, and 97 Christian years is only a week longer than 100 Moslem years. To illustrate: the year A.H. 100 ended on 23 July A.D. 719, but the Christian calendar advanced only 97 years and eight days during that first Islamic century. Again, A.H. 538 started on 16 July A.D. 1143, precisely 521 Christian years after the introduction of the era.

The equation of years of the Hegira with those of the Christian Era is not simple. There is no coincidence of years, months, or even days (the Moslem day starts at sunset) in the two calendars. Moreover, the relationship is continually shifting. Normally one year of either era falls into two of the other. On just two dozen occasions before A.D. 1500 has a Moslem year been fully contained in a Christian year; and in all but three of these cases (A.D. 868, 933, and 1454, when the Moslem year began on 1 January)

the Christian year also includes the end of the preceding and the beginning of the succeeding Moslem year. Example: In the year A.D. 672, the
year A.H. 51 ended on 7 January, A.H. 52 ran from 8 January till 26 December, and A.H. 53 began 27 December. A formula for discovering equivalence does exist but is overly complicated. Fortunately, nearly all handbooks
of chronology supply tables of conversion and these are best consulted.
If an approximation is sufficient, reduce the Hegira date by 3 percent (because 97 A.D. years = 100 A.H. years) and add the result of 621.5 (because
A.H. 1 starts in mid-A.D. 622). Example: When did the year A.H. 472 begin?
(472 − 14 + 621.5 = 1079.5). The date is actually 4 July A.D. 1079, and
though not all answers will be so close, none will be as much as a year off.

THE INDICTION

Of the various chronological devices employed during the Middle Ages,
the most characteristic is that of reckoning according to the Indiction. That
this practice prevailed throughout Europe is evidenced in every sort of
record — chronicle and diploma, lay and ecclesiastic, public and private.
Its time of vogue is that of the medieval world itself, the fourth to the
fourteenth century.

The Indiction was in origin a fiscal cycle, a period of years between
tax reassessments. Disregarding the controversy as to the date and place
of its initiation (probably Egypt at the end of the third century A.D.), the
indictional cycle was certainly fixed at 15 years by 312 and medieval computists took this as the base year in their calculations. Use of the Indiction
for dating purposes is attested from early in the fourth century, and by
the end of the century it was widespread, at least among ecclesiastical
writers. The earliest instance of its use by the imperial chancery seems to
be in an edict of Constantine II, dated A.D. 356;[20] from Justinian's reign,
dating by Indiction was prescribed by law (Corpus Iuris Civilis, *Novellae,*
47.i). The papal chancery began to utilize the system from the late fifth
century and employed it regularly from the end of the sixth century.

The word *Indictio* originally designated the 15-year fiscal cycle itself;
in its chronological usage Indictions are the individual years within a cycle, numbered I through XV, followed by the *Indictio prima* of the next
cycle. It is a peculiarity that it is the position of the year within the cycle
that is identified and only extraordinarily is the number of the cycle given.
Rarely does this create a problem, however, as the Indiction is usually associated with other chronological data that establish the cycle. An excep-

tion is a charter of King Wihtred of Kent (A.D. 690–725), dated simply *in mense Iulio Indictione XIIIma,* which may be assigned either to A.D. 700 or 715.[21] What does make for occasional confusion is the fact that the indictional year is not coterminous with the calendar year. Down to the eighth century in western Europe (and in the papal chancery until the eleventh century), the indictional year always commenced on 1 September, comprising, therefore, the last four months of one calendar year and the first eight months of the next. *Indictio I,* then, corresponds to the year 1 September A.D. 312–31 August A.D. 313 (as well as to the year 1 September A.D. 327–31 August A.D. 328 and every succeeding fifteenth year). The principle adopted in most tables of conversion, however, equates the Indiction with the year in which it chiefly falls, so that *Indictio I* is normally identified as A.D. 313, 328, and so forth, despite the fact that the final four months of every year are in the next Indiction.

The common rule for calculating the Indiction for any date is to subtract 312 from it and divide the result by 15. The remainder is the Indiction, and if there is no remainder the Indiction is XV. To illustrate: To find the Indiction for the year 1066, subtract 312, divide by 15, the remainder is 4. Therefore, 1066 is *Indictio IV;* but this is true only for the greater part of the year. The Battle of Hastings, 14 October 1066, is *Indictio V.* A simpler method of calculating the Indiction is to add 3 to the date and divide by 15. (The 3 is arrived at by projecting the indictional cycles back to the beginning of the Christian Era and noting that A.D. 1 would have been the fourth Indiction.) This method is especially convenient for dates in the fourth, seventh, tenth, and thirteenth centuries since the hundreds, being divisible by 15, can be ignored. Thus Pope Gregory I died in March A.D. 604, *Indictio VII* (drop 600, 4 + 3 = 7); Otto I died in May A.D. 972, *Indictio XV* (drop 900, 72 + 3 divided by 15 = 0); and Frederick II died in December 1250, *Indictio IX* (drop 1200, 50 + 3 divided by 15 = 8: but December falls into the next Indiction).

The indictional year commencing 1 September was the only one known until the early eighth century (except for a "vulgar" reckoning from 1 January, the start of the old Roman civil year, attested sporadically in Italy from an early date). Then, ironically, the greatest chronographer in the Middle Ages, Bede, confused subsequent chronology by giving currency to an Indiction calculated from the autumnal equinox (believed to be 24 September) and so created a new computistical year. So influential were his writings that this "Bedan" reckoning prevailed in England from his day and, passing to the continent at the time of Charlemagne, was followed in the chanceries of the later kings of France and Germany. The papal chancery, however, continued to employ the older reckoning until 1087, but, after a century of mixed practice, adopted the "Bedan" usage consistently from the pontificate of Alexander III (1159–81). In the Byzantine world, the 1 September reckoning was adhered to continuously.

In addition to these two indictional years, described variously as "Greek," "Byzantine," or "Constantinopolitan" (1 September), and "Bedan," "Imperial," "Western," or "Caesarean" (24 September), a third mode of calculation called "Papal," "Pontifical," or "Roman," made an appearance in the eleventh century. This indictional year started 25 December, to coincide with the year calculated from the Nativity. In spite of its name, the papal chancery employed this style only during the period of mixed practice between the abandonment of the "Greek" and the adoption of the "Bedan" usage, but it was occasionally used elsewhere. Since there is only a week between their initial dates, this "Papal" Indiction was frequently confused with the "vulgar" reckoning from 1 January.

There are also several Indictions of limited provenance, such as that peculiar to Genoa (*secundum cursum Janue*), whose idiosyncrasies can complicate the study of local records particularly. But the reckonings from 1 September, 24 September, and 25 December/1 January are the important styles, and failure to observe their difference can result in misdating by one year. As a dating element, the Indiction (of whatever sort) only became common in the West after Bede, and was fast disappearing by the fourteenth century. Public notaries, however, continued to date by the Indiction into the sixteenth century and isolated instances of its use may even be found to a later date. The importance of the Indiction in the ordinary dating clause is that it provides a check, by its agreement or not, on the other elements, and sometimes it permits greater precision. For example, suppose we have a document of King Henry I of England, dated 1115, sixteenth regnal year, *Indictio VIII*. Since Henry's sixteenth year starts 5 August 1115, this is the *terminus a quo* for the document; and the eighth Indiction fixes its *terminus ad quem* at 23 September because the balance of the year 1115 is *Indictio IX*. In a case of incompatibility, that is, if this same document were dated in Henry's fifteenth regnal year (which ends 4 August 1115), *Indictio IX* (which starts 24 September 1115), it is usually the Indiction that is incorrect. Quite aside from errors of transcription, which might affect either element equally, the presumptive rule is that the more pedantic the computation the more fallible. Calculation of the Indiction, which is not as esoteric as many chronological devices, was yet sufficiently taxing that some honest computists admitted their doubts by adding the phrase "more or less" to Indiction numbers. The incompetence of the computist who figured a sixteenth and a seventeenth Indiction, however, is quite extraordinary.[22]

THE REGNAL YEAR

Another very common dating device in the Middle Ages, carrying on a method familiar to the ancient world, is by regnal year. The awkwardness of this technique is that the principle of calculation varies from place to place and from one time to another. To avoid a discussion of specific usages, which is the province of diplomatics rather than chronology, it will suffice to observe that regnal years may be reckoned from actual moment of accession, from the first significant exercise of sovereignty, or from formal coronation, all without regard to the calendar year. Moreover, the year of accession itself may go unnumbered so that the first regnal year coincides with the ensuing calendar year; or the year of accession, whatever the date, is counted as the first regnal year, so that the second regnal year coincides with the ensuing calendar year. To cite the example of England, the present practice of dating a ruler's reign from the decease of the predecessor did not begin until the late thirteenth century, and only then because the heir was out of the country.[23] Prior practice, at least from the later tenth century, was to date the commencement of a reign from coronation day, which might follow election promptly or only after some lapse of time. The 14-year postponement of King Edgar's coronation (until 11 May A.D. 973) is certainly exceptional, but a delay of a few weeks or months is common. How the earlier Anglo-Saxon kings calculated their reigns cannot be determined although evidence of regnal dating does survive.[24] It is generally held that William the Conqueror dated his reign from his coronation on 25 December 1066, consistent with custom; but despite the inclusion of the regnal year in many documents, 5 January (death of Edward the "Confessor") and 14 October (Battle of Hastings) are alternative possibilities. A grant of William to the Abbey of Holy Trinity at Caen is typical in its ambiguity even while volunteering synchronism with other reigns. It is dated *Anno ab Incarnatione Domini MLXXXII, indictione V, apostolicae sedis cathedram possidente papa Gregorio VII, regni mei XVI anno, in Francia regnante Philippo, Romanis in partibus imperiali iure dominante Henrico.*[25] The regnal year of one of the contemporary rulers would have been helpful. Had the papal year of Gregory VII been noted, for instance, say, his tenth (which began 30 June 1082), not only would the document be dated more closely but a 5 January reckoning of William's regnal year would be excluded. The regnal year of King John involves a peculiar difficulty. His coronation was on Ascension Day, 27 May 1199, and the regnal years are calculated from the movable feast (it is Thursday, the fortieth day after Easter) rather than from the date. Thus, his years contain as few as 349 days and as many as 384 days, and consequently several regnal years include identical dates of two successive calendar years; for example, the dates from 3–22 May of both 1201 and 1202 occur in John's third regnal year.

THE DATE OF EASTER

The crucifixion of Christ was on the first day of the Hebrew feast Passover, which fell on a Friday in an undetermined year, and He arose two days later. These statements are commonly agreed upon; and to them we can add that Passover is observed on the 14th day of Nisan, the month of the vernal equinox, and that 14 Nisan is the day of the full moon. The controversy that grew up concerning the proper day to celebrate Easter, the commemoration of the Resurrection — whether on the day of Passover itself (Quartodecimanism), which might fall on any day of the week, or on the Sunday after Passover — is not germane to our subject. The concern of technical chronology is with the calendrical devices invented and employed to find the date after it was prescribed by the Council of Nicaea (A.D. 325) that Easter is the first Sunday after the full moon that occurs on or after the vernal equinox, itself defined as 21 March. The difficulty posed by this formulation, which links three disparate phenomena (a day of the week, a phase of the moon, and a position of the sun), stimulated the construction of a rich array of computistical mechanisms designed to provide infallible identification of future Easter dates. The enormity of the problem can be gathered from the fact that the range open to Easter by the Nicene definition is 35 days, just short of one-tenth of the year. The earliest possible date is 22 March, if the full moon comes on 21 March, the day of the equinox, and it is Saturday. The latest date is 25 April, but this only happens if the full moon comes on 20 March, just missing the equinox, and if the next full moon (18 April) falls on Sunday. Such coincidences are not frequent: Easter is on each of its extreme dates about once a century.

In an attempt to elucidate a certain guide to Easter Day, periodicity was the obvious factor to exploit and several cycles were produced that became permanent parts of the medieval chronological equipment. The numbers to be harmonized are 7, 29.5, and 365.25 (days in the week, month, and year). It has long been known that there are almost exactly 235 lunations in 19 years. This decemnovennial or Metonic cycle, named after Meton, the Athenian who discovered it, requires the distribution of seven half-days over the 235 lunations and the omission of one day (the moon's "skip," *saltus lunae*) at the end of the cycle to attain a perfect reconciliation of sun and moon; but at the start of each nineteenth year the moon is at precisely the same phase. The completed cycle contains twelve solar years of twelve new moons and seven solar years of thirteen new moons, these last being termed embolistic years. On occasion, the first eight years of the cycle are separately denominated *Ogdoas* and the final eleven are called *Hendecas,* but this has no computistical significance.

The Metonic cycle was employed in the construction of the Easter table, commencing in A.D. 532, by Dionysius Exiguus (hence it is sometimes misnamed Dionysian), the same person who, by reckoning *anni domini,* invented the Christian Era. The utility of the cycle is that the full moon controlling Easter, the so-called Paschal Term, is predicted by it. For example, A.D. 532, the first year in the Dionysian table, has a new moon on 22 March so the Paschal Term is the fourteenth day thereafter, Monday 5 April. Easter is, by definition, the following Sunday, in this year 11 April. Every nineteenth year after A.D. 532, for example, A.D. 551, 570, etc., has a new moon on 22 March and a Paschal Term of 5 April. Easter, of course, will vary from 6 April to 12 April, depending on the *day* of 5 April. In A.D. 551 the Paschal Term fell on Wednesday, so Easter was 9 April, while in A.D. 570 it fell on Saturday so Easter was the following day, 6 April. In the year 533, the moon is eleven days old on 22 March and the Paschal Term (the fourteenth day following the new moon) is 25 March: so also for A.D. 552, 571, etc. To facilitate tabulations, numbers I through XIX were assigned in repeating sequence to the years of the Christian Era. These Golden Numbers, as they are called, are thus a convenient index to both the phase of the moon on 22 March (or any other day, for that matter) and to the Paschal Term. To cite the year 532 again, it was I for its Golden Number, as do A.D. 551, 570, etc. Therefore, all years with Golden Number I have a new moon on 22 March and a Paschal Term of 5 April, and all years with Golden Number II have a moon eleven days old on 22 March and a Paschal Term of 25 March. The equation is reciprocal, of course: the age of the moon on 22 March can be used to find the Golden Number, as well as to fix the Paschal Term. This age of the moon expressed in days has the technical appellation "epacts," meaning "excess," and since twelve lunations fall short of a solar year by 11 days, the moon on 22 March (or on any date) will always be 11 days older than in the previous year, and after 19 years will be back to the original phase.

The chart supplies data for the epacts of 22 March, which is the common medieval practice. This date is recommended by the fact that it is the earliest possible Easter and the Paschal Term is always within the following lunation. But sequences of epacts can be drawn up for any fixed date, and the correspondence with Golden Numbers in the 19-year cycle permits the same easy determination of the Paschal Term. One less-common medieval alternative to 22 March is 1 January, and it is important to note that the Gregorian calendar routinely tabulates the epacts of that date. When consulting printed lists it is essential to confirm that the compiler has not converted medieval into modern epacts. To find the epacts of 22 March in any year, divide the year by 19 (to eject complete cycles), multiply the remainder by 11 (the annual increment), and divide by 30 (to eject complete lunations); the remainder is epacts. To find the Golden Number of any year, add 1 to the year (if the series are projected back, Golden Number I will fall on 1 B.C.) and divide by 19; the remainder is the Golden Number, or XIX if there is no remainder.

From a knowledge of either the epacts or the Golden Number, then, the Paschal Term, the full moon on or after the vernal equinox, can be determined. To fix the date of Easter, however, which is the Sunday next, the device named Dominical Letter is brought to bear. Letters A through G are assigned to the dates 1–7 January, and then A again to 8 January, and so on through the entire year, with recurring sequences of these seven letters. These letters are ferial, or day, letters, but the important one is the Dominical Letter, that which falls on the first Sunday. Every other Sunday on the calendar will have the same letter, of course, so the Dominical Letter immediately after the Paschal Term identifies Easter. If the Dominical Letter is known, and it is commonly supplied in dating clauses, the day of the week of every date in that year can be ascertained, in some cases at a glance, in others by simple arithmetic. The Dominical Letter for A.D. 539, for example, is B; so 1 January (A) is Saturday, as are 8, 15, 22, and 29 January. It follows that 1, 8, 15, and 22 February and 1, 8, 15, 22, and 29 March are Tuesdays, and so on through the year. For discovering weekdays in the last months of the year it is helpful to remember that in common years 1 October is the same day as 1 January, and 1 November is the same as 1 February. In leap years, the insertion of an extra day at the end of February pushes every subsequent date in the year one weekday later. Thus, in leap years 1 October is the same day as 2 January, and 1 November is the same as 2 February. The Dominical Letters are accommodated to leap year by having one serve for January and February and another for the remainder of the year. The year 540 is a leap year with Dominical Letter AG. This means that 1 January is Sunday and 1 March is Thursday, as it would be *in a common year* with Dominical Letter G. There is a pattern to the recurrence of Dominical Letters in a series of years. It is apparent that, 365 days being 52 weeks with one day left over, 1 January and 31 December will be the same weekday; or, to put it differently, each year will commence one weekday later than the previous year. In 534, 1 January is a Sunday: so 1 January A.D. 535 is Monday and 1 January A.D. 536 is Tuesday. This is why Dominical Letters run in retrograde order. Every fourth year, as we have seen, Dominical Letters are paired; but the reverse sequence is not interrupted: 534 is A, 535 is G, 536 is FE, 537 is D, and so on continuously. What does happen, however, is that the forward progression of weekdays takes a "leap" after every fourth year: 1 January A.D. 534 is Sunday, 1 January A.D. 535 is Monday, 1 January A.D. 536 is Tuesday, but 1 January A.D. 537 is *Thursday*—hence, the origin of the term "leap year," although the "leap" actually is at the outset of the year following the *annus bissextilis*.

A device parallel in function to that of the Dominical Letter is the Concurrent, a number that expresses the interval in days between the last Sunday in December and 1 January. If the year begins on Tuesday, as in A.D. 541, say, the Concurrent is 1, Wednesday 2, Thursday 3, Friday 4, Saturday 5, Sunday 6, Monday 7. Note that, in the last case, the Concurrent is 7, not 0, because it must describe a finite number of intervening days. It is apparent that there is correspondence between Concurrents and Dominical Letters, the numbers 1 to 7 equating with letters F to G (retrograde). In leap years, the Concurrent is that of the Dominical Letter following 29 February. The Concurrent is also used in conjunction with another series of numbers, called Solar Regulars, to find the weekday of the first of any month. The Solar Regulars are numbers permanently attached to the twelve months, in the following series starting with January: 2, 5, 5, 1, 3, 6, 1, 4, 7, 2, 5, 7. By adding the Concurrent of a particular year to the Solar Regular for the month in question, the weekday of the month's beginning is indicated by the sum (diminished by 7 if necessary). Example: what is the weekday of 1 June A.D. 534? The year 534 has Dominical Letter A and Concurrent 6: add the Concurrent to the Solar Regular for June (another 6), subtract 7, the result is 5; so 1 June is the fifth weekday, Thursday.

Yet another group of numbers, called *claves terminorum,* was available to the medieval computist in his calculations. These "keys" are numbers between 11 and 39, recurring in cycles of 19 like Golden Numbers, though unrelated to them, that establish the dates of movable feasts when added to their so-called fixed terms. The fixed term of Septuagesima Sunday, for example, is 7 January, for Easter it is 11 March, for Pentecost 29 April. Example: To find Septuagesima Sunday in the year 543, add the key 25 to 7 January. The answer is 1 February, and since it is a Sunday, it is the date. In the year 544, on the other hand, the key is 14, so the answer is 21 January; but that is a Thursday, so the following Sunday, 24 January, is Septuagesima.

The Metonic Cycle was but one of several cycles that recommended themselves to the task of determining Easter. We have seen that its chief feature is a decemnovennial reconciliation of the solar year and the lunar month, but the day of the week eludes its harmony. Since 365 days is 52 weeks and 1 day, each year commences 1 weekday later than the previous year. In 7 years a cycle would be completed, then, were it not for leap year. This disruption in the regular progression of days means that it is only after 28 years (4 × 7) that a recurring cycle is produced. It should be noted that the pattern of initial days during the 28-year cycle is coincident with that of Dominical Letters, which identify Sundays specifically; in short, the sequence of Dominical Letters is a manifestation of this 28-year cycle. To find the position of any year within the cycle, usually called the Solar Cycle, it is necessary to know that the first cycle is computed from 9 B.C. Therefore, the rule is to add 9 to the year and divide by 28: the remainder is the *annus circuli solis*.

We have seen that after 19 years the original relationship of the sun and moon returns, and that every 28 years there is a repetition of the weekday sequence. Obviously there remained the ambition to discover that repeating cycle of years in which the days of the week and the dates of the month would concur with the moon phase. Early in the Middle Ages there was some use of an 84-year cycle, made up of three Solar Cycles; but while the day and the year were in agreement, since the Solar Cycle alone harmonizes them, there was a small discrepancy with the moon that soon led to the abandonment of this cycle. It is a matter of some historical consequence, however, that during its brief vogue this 84-year cycle was transmitted to the Celtic Church, which persisted in employing it after it had been replaced elsewhere by a superior calculation. It was competition particularly between two modes of reckoning Easter that led to the celebrated Council of Whitby (A.D. 664). The Great Cycle (*Annus Magnus*), finally constructed to satisfy the several periodicities, was one of 532 years. This Great Cycle includes four internal cycles marred by one other defect: the 19-year Metonic Cycle has an integer number of lunations (235), but not days (6939.75); the 28-year Solar Cycle has an integer number of days, and in recurring sequence, but not a whole number of lunations; a 76-year cycle (19 × 4) contains an integer number of both days (27,759) and months (940), but the weekday at the beginning of one cycle is not the same as that of the following cycle. Therefore, the Great Cycle of 532 years (7 × 76), which reconciles the Solar Cycle with the Metonic Cycle (28 × 19), is the shortest that suffices to meet all requirements of congruency. Although all these cycles are pertinent to paschal computations, the Great Cycle is frequently called the Paschal Cycle, because it alone brings Easter back to the same day (always Sunday, of course) and date of the month in a year that commences on the same weekday with the moon at the same phase. In short, the pattern of Dominical Letters, epacts, Paschal Term, Golden Number, Concurrent, and Key of any year repeats every 532 years.

CONCLUSION

There are a great many more eras, peculiar calculations, and variant reckonings to be found in the Middle Ages than have been described in this essay. Indeed, an exhaustive list can hardly be drawn up. Even that Irish dating clause, to which this entire study has been but an extended exegesis, includes two elements about which nothing so far has been said. The reference to Tabular Letter O. (*postpunctata*), for example, invokes a curious system of identifying Easter by a letter between A and U (J excluded), *postpunctata*, reckoned from 21 March; or a letter of the same series, but *praepunctata*, reckoned from 10 April. In this passage the computist has blundered: Easter in 1318 is 23 April, hence it should be Tabular Letter .O (*praepunctata*). Likewise, the citation of the twenty-fifth year of the Solar Cycle according to Gerlandus refers to an eleventh-century chronographer who computed his 28-year cycle from the year A.D. 525, rather than the date A.D. 532 of Dionysius Exiguus; but here, too, there is confusion. The correct calculation is the eighteenth year according to Gerlandus, or the twenty-second year according to Gerlandus as misinterpreted by John of Sacrobosco, who was in turn misunderstood by the Irish computist.[26]

One very common dating practice that has been omitted from the discussion, of which abundant examples might be adduced, is by reference to comets, eclipses, plagues, and other phenomena making such impression on contemporaries that they became dating devices. Bede, for example, notes the deaths of an archbishop of Canterbury and a king of Kent as occurring on the same day, 14 July, *anno memorato praefatae eclypsis et mox sequentis pestilentiae;* but this is not technical chronology, strictly speaking, because it is neither theoretical nor systematic. It is also well to emphasize that this essay has dealt with medieval chronology, so no account has been taken of the so-called Gregorian reform of the calendar that so bedevils students of modern history. In 1582, Pope Gregory XIII ordered the suppression of 10 days, so that Thursday, 4 October, was succeeded by Friday, 15 October, to compensate for the slight inaccuracy of the Julian calendar that had accumulated to the point that the vernal equinox was now falling on 12 March in contrast to the calendar equinox

of 21 March, as established at Nicaea. Future error was guarded against
by a revised formula for intercalation, that is, omitting leap year in century years three of four times, with exceedingly remote exceptions. This
substantial calendrical dislocation, affecting each country as it adopted
the reform, involves discontinuity in series such as Dominical Letters,
epacts, etc. Therefore, the general statements made about cycles, patterns,
and sequences, as well as rules of conversion, are understood to apply
only to the Middle Ages and whatever postmedieval period there is before
the date of acceptance of the new calendar. England, for example, did not
subscribe until 1752, and Russia only in the twentieth century.

It is fitting that we close as we commenced with an example taken from
Irish materials, because the Irish are so very prominent in the history of
the *computus,* computistical elaboration, and chronological controversy.
We are told that, in the year 1096, a great panic fell upon the men of
Ireland, because the Feast of the Decollation of St. John the Baptist,
29 August, fell on Friday in this year. This alone is unexceptional; but,
in addition, it was an *annus bissextilis* and embolismal as well! Fortunately,
by extended fasting and other pious actions, Irishmen averted the fright-
ful consequences portended by the aforesaid calendrical concatenation.[27]
The anecdote amply testifies to the great significance attached to technical
chronology in the Middle Ages, and I trust that this essay has indicated
something of its importance to the student of medieval history.

NOTES

1. A. Giry, *Manuel de diplomatique* (Paris: Hachette, 1894), bk. 2.

2. The facts of provenance and the enumeration of records in which particular usages
are customary have been largely omitted as pertaining more to diplomatics than chronology.
Cf. Professor L. Boyle's chapter in this volume for a discussion of this discipline, with citation of guides.

3. S. MacAirt, ed., *The Annals of Innisfallen* (Dublin: Institute for Advanced Studies,
1951), *sub anno* 1318.

4. In some of the details of the early Roman calendar, I have accepted the reconstructions of A. K. Michels, *The Calendar of the Roman Republic* (Princeton: Princeton Univ.
Press, 1967).

5. *Kalendae,* the first day, when the appearance of the new moon was announced (calo,
"call"); *Nonae,* "nines" (though certainly not known by this name before fixed by formula),
at the moon's first quarter; *Idus* (perhaps from Etruscan *iduo,* "divide"), at full moon.

6. $(2 \times 355 + 22 = 732$, whereas $2 \times 365.25 = 730.5$) The evidence of eclipses indicates
that there was a 4-month discrepancy in 191 B.C. and one of 2.5 months in 168 B.C.

7. The Ides in the early lunar calendar was the time of full moon and so literally di-

vided the month. In the pre-Julian lunisolar calendar this ceased to be true, but it may be remarked that the months of the late Ides (15th day) were the long (31-day) months, March, May *Quinctilis,* October, and these remained the months of late Ides in the Julian calendar, as modified by Augustus.

8. It will be recalled that this is the point in the pre-Julian calendar where February was cut off and the *mensis intercalaris* inserted.

9. W. de Gray Birch, ed., *Cartularium Saxonicum* (London: Whiting, 1885-99), vol. 1, nos. 148, 111.

10. D. Whitelock, D. Douglas, and S. Tucker, eds., *The Anglo-Saxon Chronicle* (London: Eyre and Spottiswoode, 1961).

11. The name Septuagesima means "seventieth," but it is clearly not 70 days before Easter. Its designation and that of the following three Sundays have not been satisfactorily explained.

12. A full list of introits may be found in H. Grotefend, Zeitrechnung des deutschen Mittelalters und der Neuzeit, 2 vol. in 3 pts. (Hannover: Hahn, 1891-98) vol. I, 98-99; and Giry, *Manuel de diplomatique,* 275-314, offers an extensive list of saints.

13. R. D. Face, "Techniques of Business in the Trade between the Fairs of Champagne and the South of Europe in the Twelfth and Thirteenth Centuries," *Economic History Review,* 2d series, 10 (1957-58): 427.

14. R. L. Poole, "The Beginning of the Year in the Middle Ages," reprinted in *Studies in Chronology and History,* edited by A. L. Poole (Oxford: Oxford Univ. Press, 1934), 1-27.

15. W. Stubbs, ed., *The Historical Works of Gervase of Canterbury,* "Rolls Series" 73 (London: Longman, 1879-80) 1:88.

16. A recent discussion of Bede's practice is by K. Harrison, "The Beginning of the Year in England, c. 500-900," *Anglo-Saxon England* 2 (1973): 51-70.

17. B. Colgrave and R. A. B. Mynors, eds., *Bede's Ecclesiastical History of the English People* (Oxford: Clarendon Press, 1969), bk. 1, chap. 2.

18. Giry, *Manuel de diplomatique,* 96.

19. G. La Piana, "A Note on Chronology in the Letters of St. Boniface," *Speculum* 17 (1942): 270-72.

20. H. Leclercq, "Indiction," *Dictionnaire d'Archéologie Chrétienne et de Liturgie,* ed. F. Cabrol (Paris, 1907-53), vol. 7, pt. 1 (1926), col. 531.

21. Birch, *Cartularium Saxonicum,* vol. 1, no. 98.

22. A. M. Freeman, ed., *The Annals of Connacht* (Dublin: Institute for Advanced Studies, 1944), *sub annis* 1423-24.

23. Henry III died on 16 November 1272 while Edward was on Crusade. Although Edward did not return to England until early August 1274, and was not crowned until 19 August, he dated his reign from 20 November 1272, the date of his father's funeral and of his own proclamation. In future, a new reign was held to start when the old one stopped: "The king is dead, long live the king!"

24. Examples indubitably authentic from the eighth, ninth, and tenth centuries are nos. 23, 168, 190, 416, 618 in *Anglo-Saxon Charters: An Annotated List and Bibliography,* edited by P. H. Sawyer (London: Royal Historical Society Guides and Handbooks, No. 8, 1968).

25. H. W. C. Davis, ed., *Regesta Regum Anglo-Normannorum,* 1066-1154 (Oxford: Clarendon Press, 1913), vol. 1, no. 150.

26. MacAirt, *Annals of Innisfallen,* xlvi.

27. J. F. Kenney, *The Sources for the Early History of Ireland: Ecclesiastical* (New York: Columbia Univ. Press, 1929; slightly revised reprint, New York: Octagon Books, 1968), 749-50.

BIBLIOGRAPHY

Agustí y Casanovas, J., ed. *Manual de cronologia española y universal.* Estudios No. 25. Madrid; Escuela de Estudios Medievales, 1952.

Archer, P. *The Christian Calendar and the Gregorian Reform.* New York: Fordham Univ. Press, 1941.

Bond, J. J. *Handy-Book of Rules and Tables for Verifying Dates with the Christian Era.* London; N.p., 1866. 4th ed., 1889.

Britton, C. E. *A Meteorological Chronology to A.D. 1450.* Meteorological Office, Geophysical Memoirs no. 70. London: H. M. Stationery Office, 1937.

Burnaby, S. B. *Elements of the Jewish and Mohammedan Calendars.* London: G. Bell and Sons, 1901.

Butcher, S. *The Ecclesiastical Calendar: Its Theory and Construction.* Dublin: N.p. 1877.

Cappelli, A. *Cronologia, Cronografia e Calendario Perpetuo.* Milan: "Manuali Hoepli," 1906. 3d ed., 1969.

Cheney, C. R. *Handbook of Dates for Students of English History.* London: Office of the Royal Historical Society, 1945. Reprinted with corrections, 1978.

Colson, F. H. *The Week: An Essay on the Origin and Development of the Seven-Day Cycle.* Cambridge: Cambridge Univ. Press, 1926.

Coyne, G. V., M. A. Hoskins, and O. Pedersen, eds. *Gregorian Reform of the Calendar.* Vatican City: Specola Vaticana, 1983.

Del Piazzo, M. *Manuale di cronologia.* Fonti e studi di Corpus membranarum italicarum, vol. 4. Rome: Associazione Nazionale Archivistica Italiana, 1969.

Freeman-Grenville, G. S. P. *The Muslim and Christian Calendars.* London: Oxford Univ. Press, 1963. 2d ed., London: R. Collins, 1977.

Fotheringham, J. K. "The Calendar," in *The Nautical Almanac for the Year 1931.* London: H. M. Stationery Office, 1929.

Ginzel, F. K. *Handbuch der mathematischen und technischen Chronologie.* 3 vols. Leipzig: Heinrichs, 1906–14.

Giry, A. *Manuel de diplomatique.* Paris: Hachette, 1894.

Goldstine, H. H. *New and Full Moons 1001 B.C. to A.D. 1651.* American Philosophical Society Memoirs, vol. 94. Philadelphia: The Society, 1973.

Grotefend, H. *Zeitrechnung des deutschen Mittelalters und der Neuzeit.* 2 vols. in 3 pts. Hannover: Hahn, 1891–98.

Grotefend, H. *Taschenbuch der Zeitrechnung des deutschen Mittelalters und der Neuzeit.* Hannover, 1898. 10th ed., edited by Th. Ulrich, 1960.

Grumel, V. *Chronologie.* Traité d'études byzantines, no. 1. In *Bibliothèque byzantine.* Paris: Presses Universitaires de France, 1958.

Jones, C. W. *Bedae Opera de Temporibus.* Mediaeval Academy of America Publication no. 41. Cambridge, Mass.: The Academy, 1943.

Kubitschek, W. *Grundriss der antiken Zeitrechnung.* Handbuch der Altertumswissenschaft, vol. 1, pt. 7. Munich: C. H. Beck'sche Verlagsbuchhandlung, 1928.

Lietzmann, H. *Zeitrechnung der römischen Kaiserzeit, des Mittelalters und der*

Neuzeit für die Jahre 1-2000 nach Christus. Berlin: Walter de Gruyter, 1934. 3d ed., edited by K. Aland, 1956.

Mahler, E. *Handbuch der jüdischen Chronologie.* Leipzig, 1916.

Merzbach, U. C. "Calendar." In *Dictionary of the Middle Ages,* vol. 3, edited by J. Strayer. New York: Scribner, 1983.

Neugebauer, P. V. *Astronomische Chronologie.* 2 vols. Berlin: Walter de Gruyter, 1929.

Newton, R. R. *Medieval Chronicles and the Rotation of the Earth.* Baltimore: Johns Hopkins Univ. Press, 1972.

O'Neil, W. M. *Time and the Calendars.* Manchester: Manchester Univ. Press, 1975.

Oppolzer, T. von. *Kanon der Finsternisse.* Vienna: Kaiserlich-Königlichen Hof- und Staatsdruckerei, 1887. Translated as *Canon of Eclipses* by O. Gingerich. New York: Dover, 1962.

Poole, R. L. *Medieval Reckonings of Time.* Helps for Students of History, no. 3. London: Society for Promoting Christian Knowledge, 1918.

———. *Studies in Chronology and History.* Edited by A. L. Poole. Oxford: Oxford Univ. Press, 1934.

Richmond, B. *Time Measurement and Calendar Construction.* Leiden: Brill, 1956.

Samuel, A. E. *Greek and Roman Chronology.* Munich: Beck, 1972.

Schroeter, J. F. *Spezieller Kanon der zentralen Sonnen- und Mondfinsternisse.* Kristiana: Dybwad, 1923.

Spier, A. *The Comprehensive Hebrew Calendar.* New York: Bohrman House, 1952.

Stamp, A. E. *Methods of Chronology.* Historical Association Leaflet no. 92. London: Office of the Royal Historical Society, 1933.

Van Wijk, W. E. *Le nombre d'or, étude de chronologique technique.* The Hague: Nijhof, 1936.

familiar 8 familiar

Medieval English Literature

PAUL THEINER

EDIEVAL LITERATURE, taken as a whole, is a field so vast as to
defeat utterly the hope that it might be embraced, let alone
encompassed, by any single scholar, no matter how early he
or she began the task, how assiduously the task was pursued, or how long
a lifetime was devoted to it. But on the other hand, medieval literature,
as such, is not really a field at all; that is, not a single field. It is instead
a wide-ranging and loosely connected aggregation of fields, some closely
related, but others so remote from each other that quite competent practitioners of one may have only the vaguest of notions about what goes on
in the other, may indeed be only dimly aware that the other exists. In fact,
the aggregation is so loose that the fields themselves are defined along widely
diverging lines. A person who specializes in hagiography, for example, is
immersed in a field somewhat loosely characterized as a literary genre, but
which is spread across a vast extent of time, a broad geographical area,
and a confounding number of language boundaries as well. On the other
hand a Chaucer scholar occupies a space that is much shorter in time and
much more narrowly circumscribed geographically, and which has only
one primary language to deal with—though it must be remembered that
it is a language foreign to anyone now alive. Nevertheless, the Chaucerian's
study is complicated by the presence within the Chaucer canon of a vast
array of genres, by the chosen author's playful, ironic, and irreverent attitude toward just about all of them, by the need to cultivate other languages
and the materials of other cultures in order to situate the works of Chau-

cer among those of his medieval predecessors and contemporaries, by the presence of a good deal of (often tantalizing) biographical information about Chaucer, and so on.

Aside from an orientation to genre and subject matter, like hagiography, or to a single author like Chaucer, some students of medieval literature define their fields largely with respect to time and place — the literature of fourteenth-century England — or to language and place — Anglo-Norman literature — to types too broad to merit genuinely the term genre — medieval lyric — even, in some cases, to single works — the *Nibelungenlied* — which, unsurprisingly, will turn out to involve a great deal that is beyond the scope of that poem's text itself. To sum up, it will suffice to note that the medieval period extends over about a millennium — roughly from A.D. 500–1500 — and over a geographical area that reaches from Russia to Italy to Iceland, leaving very few empty spaces along the way. To put this vastness into perspective, we might observe that the medieval period is in time almost exactly twice as long as all subsequent historical eras put together, that the literature written in this period is recorded in a staggering array of different languages, and that these languages themselves vary significantly, as all languages do, over time. The result of this is that a student of medieval literature in general would need to command an extent and variety of cultural materials — languages obviously not the least among them — that would simply be impossible to survey, let alone master. To put this all into a more literary and figurative perspective, though admittedly a homely one, we medievalists are like the blind men in the traditional story: we are feeling our way around the elephant of medieval literature, each covering only a tiny part of the whole creature and each apt, as perhaps all people are, to extrapolate from that little part a confidently mapped projection of the whole. And we must remember one final thing: we do not have available to us an omniscient narrator to tell us that what is "really" there is an "elephant."

Still — before the tone of this chapter becomes too gloomy to bear — it is of course possible to embark on meaningful study of medieval literature without being able to see clearly the ultimate definition of the field as a whole, or to perceive in detail the most salient features that such a field would have. We are caught up in one version of the hermeneutic circle: one must know the individual works in order to define the whole, but one must know the whole to comprehend properly the individual works. But this circle, while it may bring grief to the seekers after perfection, is famously hospitable to entry; one need only choose the point at which one wishes to make the leap. I propose simply that we enter the field of medieval literature through an overall view of the English literature of the

Middle Ages, and that we go no farther for the present than to take note
of some small number of things outside of the immediate field of English
literature that are of particular concern to students of English literary history. Needless to say, the choice of English, rather than some other national
literature, is not meant in any way to suggest that the English tradition
is more central or more important than, say, French or German literature
in the overall scheme of medieval studies. My choice of English is clearly
ethnocentric (as would be the choice of any other single tradition), and
is not intended to make a statement about the overall shape of medieval
literature, but to provide ease of access to it for an audience of English-
speaking readers.

Even within this carefully selected and demarcated field, I make no
pretense to coverage; English medieval literature is, all by itself, much too
vast an area to permit that. The present chapter will instead attempt to
introduce the field in general, set some chronological boundaries, describe
major features, both literary and linguistic, and provide some guidance
in the most important bibliographical items for a person approaching the
literature of medieval England for the first time. The chapter will end with
some observations about influential trends in recent research and commentary. And to all of this is appended a bibliography which has two purposes. The first is to flesh out the bibliographical information for all titles
mentioned in the body of the text, and the second is to open up further
investigation to the intellectually curious. This bibliography is kept very
brief, not only in order to conserve space, but more importantly to discourage the belief that it contains everything of primary importance to
the field: it most emphatically does not. In the fields of Old and Middle
English literature alone — leaving aside crucially important adjacent fields —
there are currently published *every year* about ten times as many items
as are contained in my entire bibliography. In other words, the selectivity
of topics addressed in the text is clearly reflected in the apparatus; this is
not an outline of the field, but an introductory and propaedeutic guide.

The field of English medieval literature is in some ways admirably constructed for clarity. It is divided into Old English literature, which extends
from its beginnings in the seventh and eighth centuries on up to the middle of the eleventh century or so, and Middle English literature, which
finds its earliest texts in the twelfth century, but which survives in relatively few important pieces until the late thirteenth century, and does not
reach its peak of creativity until well into the second half of the fourteenth
century, which is of course the age of Chaucer, Langland, Gower, and the
Gawain-poet. The Old English literary tradition was effectively ended by
the Norman conquest of the eleventh century, which consisted not only

of a military triumph—as every schoolchild knows—but of a supplanting of the native stock and the native language in positions of power by the invaders and their friends and compatriots. And the emergence of the new Middle English tradition was not fully realized until the Norman hold on the literary and linguistic stock of the nation was gradually loosened and the new English vernacular took hold. This vernacular language, while it was obviously descended from Anglo-Saxon stock, naturally had much grafted onto it in the meantime, not only from the Norman and French languages and literatures, but from Scandinavian sources as well. The result of this for literary history is a rather neat division between Old and Middle English (certainly neater than between the corresponding Old and Middle periods of either French or German) with a gap of about a century between them, a period from which virtually no English texts survive at all. Thus, the distance in time between the most important Old English text, *Beowulf,* and *The Canterbury Tales* is approximately the same as the distance between the age of Chaucer and our own era. Consequently, a contemporary of Chaucer's would have found the text of *Beowulf* at least as incomprehensible as any modern reader would find the text of *The Canterbury Tales,* unless she had specific language training (which would have been simply unavailable).

There have of course been efforts to trace an unbroken tradition of English literature from the earliest Old English monuments right down through the Middle English period into the modern era: one thinks immediately of R. W. Chambers's *On the Continuity of English Prose from Alfred to More and His School,* and of Charles Leslie Wrenn's parallel "On the Continuity of English Poetry."[1] Nevertheless, though Chambers shows brilliantly how the prose rhythms of Old English are conveyed to the Renaissance through the mediation of such Middle English classics as the *Ancrene Riwle* and the English writings of the fourteenth-century mystic Richard Rolle of Hampole, and Wrenn argues convincingly for the artistic quality and integrity of Old English verse, neither really demonstrates the need to study subsequent literary periods as a whole in the light of the literary achievements of the Anglo-Saxons.[2] Modern university training has always kept the literature of the Old English and Middle English periods distinct, and it is not entirely unusual for Ph.D. candidates writing on Chaucer or *Sir Gawain and the Green Knight* to have no training in Old English at all. It may even be that the recent trend in American English studies to organize the curriculum along other than historical lines will further isolate the study of Old English language and culture, but it could just as well turn out that this one form of dehistoricization might cause some Old English works to be studied alongside works from other periods in courses organized along generic or topical lines, thereby effectively bridging a gap not entirely crossable by historicist means. And, in any event, the study of Old English remains eminently worthwhile in its own right, not only because the literature in question is as effectively moving as the verse of any other era, but because Old English literature is both the product and cause of a civilization that flourished for over half a millennium.

Naturally, one can make no serious attempt to confront Old English literature without making a careful and sustained effort to learn the language in which it is written. Fortunately, there are in print a number of good textbooks for the introductory course in Old English, and most of the better ones, like Cassidy and Ringler's update of *Bright's Old English Grammar and Reader,* will provide enough explanatory material, along with paradigms and reading selections, to permit self-instruction. Similarly, there are many grammars of Old English available. Serious and advanced students may want to own Alistair Campbell's *Old English Grammar,* which is heavily detailed and highly authoritative, but students nearer the beginning end of Old English studies may have to learn quite a bit of philology just to be able to read Campbell. A good short discussion, likely to provide all the grammatical information one is going to need for a long while, can be found in Quirk and Wrenn's *Old English Grammar.* This book is brief enough to serve as a kind of handbook, is written so as not to presume much prior familiarity with the technical language of Germanic philology, and has more readily usable information than can usually be found in an introductory grammar and reader.

Although any good text, like Cassidy and Ringler, will have its own glossary, the beginning student will find many occasions to consult a dictionary, and in Old English lexicography there is something of a gap. The first authoritative dictionary was Bosworth and Toller's *Anglo-Saxon Dictionary,* which first appeared nearly a century ago, and is by no means so obsolete that the beginning student cannot consult it to some profit, but it is apt to be unsatisfactory much too often to permit the student to rely very heavily upon it. There is currently under way an *Old English Dictionary* project at the University of Toronto, which when it is completed should prove to be definitive for generations to come, but which unfortunately is just beginning to see results into print. At any rate, the beginner will want something more accessible and compact for those first few trips through an Anglo-Saxon sermon or a poetic text. A good choice is Jess Bessinger's *Short Dictionary of Anglo-Saxon Poetry,* which has clear, concise, and unfudged definitions, and is available in both hard and soft covers. There are two main drawbacks, however. First of all, this dictionary covers only the poetic corpus, and it turns out that many words found in prose texts simply do not ever occur in the poetry, which consists of only about 30,000 or so lines of verse. Another possible drawback is that Bessinger has normalized the spelling of his entries in a way which may or may not conform to the normalization employed in the text one is reading; if your text is not normalized in harmony with the dictionary it will be annoying and frustrating to try to find some words that actually are included. At the very least, one should read thoroughly the prefatory material in which the normalization and alphabeticization are explained.

A somewhat fuller dictionary, also keyed to the poetic texts, but providing rather extensive treatment of compounds (and not a few citations from the poems themselves) is Grein's *Sprachschatz der angelsächsischen Dichter.* The beginner will find — no doubt with some shock — that Grein's definitions are usually given in Latin (and in German when they are not in Latin), but since the definitions are almost always simple lexical equivalents, this dictionary can be used profitably even by those with no real knowledge of Latin or German grammar. Another helpful tool is Ferdinand Holthausen's *Altenglisches etymologisches Wörterbuch,* which not only gives brief lexical equivalents (in German) for the Old English words, but also gives for each a list of cognates from other Germanic languages. The reason that this is helpful, rather than additionally encumbering, is that Old English words are often poorly attested; that is, a word may only occur once or twice in all of the poetry, which often makes guesswork out of trying to establish what it means. The listing of cognates helps the student to recreate the process by which the philologists themselves have decided to list a particular meaning for the word, and hence to appreciate both the artistry and the tentativeness inherent in such textual detective work.

The standard text for all Old English poetry is the six-volume Krapp-Dobbie edition called *The Anglo-Saxon Poetic Records.* This work is a masterpiece of textual scholarship and is the text most frequently cited in present-day secondary writings, but the neophyte will have to use other editions along with it, since *Records* provides no glossaries and very little commentary that is not confined to the establishment of the text itself and other linguistic matters. For *Beowulf,* the most widely read of the Old English poems, we have numerous editions besides the one found in *Records,* and many of them are filled with useful and interesting information, extensive commentaries, and very helpful glossaries. I, myself, never fail to buy any secondhand copy I can find; they are unfailingly interesting, not only as sources of information about the poem, but also as a kind of metacommentary on the changing interests and perspectives of literary scholars over the past century and more. Especially worthwhile is the great edition of Friedrich Klaeber, which, though ponderous in much of its commentary, is a gold mine of information and still often used as a classroom text. Also of great interest is the edition done by C. L. Wrenn and revised by Whitney Bolton.

And of course there are general introductions and studies of Old English literature, history, and culture. One of the giants in this field is R. W. Chambers, *Beowulf: An Introduction to the Study of the Poem,* which provides just the sort of background information that is required to begin serious consideration of the poem as a cultural entity. Along with Chambers — and with the introductions and commentary in the various good editions — Garmonsway and Simpson's translations of the analogues to the *Beowulf* story will allow the modern reader to come as close as we can to acquiring the knowledge of myth and narrative that came naturally to the audience of the original poem. Finally, because it is inexpensive and readily available, the Penguin translation of Beowulf by David Wright has within much useful information, and is an excellent trot as well. Its rendering of the poem into Modern English prose gives nothing of the cadenced flavor of the poem, of course, but it is a very straightforward guide to what one intelligent modern reader makes of the various cruxes in the text.

Apart from *Beowulf,* most of the better Old English poems — pieces like *The Wanderer, The Seafarer, The Dream of the Rood,* the *Battle of Maldon, Judith,* and the like — are quite widely anthologized. Most of the ones I have just named, for example, would be found in any introductory grammar and reader: Cassidy and Ringler has all of them. An inexpensive and convenient anthology is John C. Pope's *Seven Old English Poems,* which contains all of the above except *Judith* (which is a bit long for most anthologies), and which has the added feature of a forty-page essay on the versification of poetry in the Old English alliterative tradition, which makes an excellent introduction not only to the system of scansion proposed by Pope himself (in his important study, *The Rhythm of Beowulf*), but also to the older theory formulated by Edouard Sievers, which is still the one most students will want to cut their teeth on. Those who feel uneasy with either system may want to look at David Hoover's *New Theory of Old English Meter.*

The standard Old English poems are also to be found in many individual editions. The old series called *Methuen's Old English Library* is especially rich in this regard. These books naturally vary somewhat in quality and interest, but the least of them is very good indeed, and well worth picking up wherever they can be located in used-book stores and the like. Old English prose texts are rather more difficult to find, and apt, on the whole, to be rather less satisfactory on the average, when they are found. There is no standard collected edition that would correspond to the *Anglo-Saxon Poetic Records,* but in the sixties there were reissues (and updatings) of the volumes in the German series *Bibliothek der angelsächsischen Prosa,* originally put out under the general editorship of C. W. M. Grein and Richard Wülcker and issued over a sixty-year period beginning in the 1870s. Also, the many volumes of texts presented to the public by the Early English Text Society since it began issuing books in 1864 include a number of Old English prose works, many in reliable and attractive editions; some, like Sweet's versions of the King Alfred translations and Skeat's Aelfric series, are still the standard versions of the works they contain. Both of these, by the way, were also reissued in the sixties, a decade which also saw the first appearance, also under the E. E. T. S. name, of Pope's masterful edition of Aelfric's *Homilies* (1967). And of course there have also been important editions of Old English prose works that came out independently of either of these series; beginning students will want to look at Plummer's fine edition of the *Anglo-Saxon Chronicle,* which was completed in 1899, for example, and also at Dorothy Bethurum's *Homilies of Wulfstan* (1957). Finally, some prose texts are also available in the already mentioned *Methuen's Old English Library,* the most notable of which is Dorothy Whitelock's edition of Wulfstan's *Sermo Lupi ad Anglos,* possibly the best known of all pieces in Old English prose.

The student about to embark on the study of Old English literature will want also to get a reliable historical overview of the field as a whole, and perhaps, unless he is already well versed in the area, some general background in Anglo-Saxon history and culture. There are numerous books in both of these areas, to be sure, so my recommendations should be considered only as points of departure. Among the literary histories, try first Stanley Greenfield and Daniel Calder's *New Critical History of Old English Literature;* then, for a somewhat different slant, Barbara Raw, *The Art and Background of Old English Poetry.* And it should be remembered also that some books on rather narrower topics than all of Old English literary history will also provide useful insights into the historical contextualization of Anglo-Saxon verbal art. One might look, for example, at John Niles's *Beowulf: The Poem and Its Tradition.* Among other things, a newer critical book like Niles's (which came out in 1983) will supply much bibliographical guidance to the work of its predecessors. For a more general history of the period, look first at Stenton's *Anglo-Saxon England,* a volume in the Oxford history of England, and then at some recent collections of individual essays, like Woods and Pelteret, *The Anglo-Saxons: Synthesis and Achievement,* or Paul Szarmach, *Sources of Anglo-Saxon Culture.*

Much can also be learned from David Hill, *An Atlas of Anglo-Saxon England.*

Since one of the difficulties in embarking on a field of study nowadays is grappling with the current work of the most active minds in the field, some mention should be made of ways to keep up with the secondary literature. For literary scholars in all areas of study, a prime source of information is the MLA's annual *International Bibliography.* This is about as exhaustive as such a thing can be, and the entries in all fields of medieval literature are a tribute to the industry of medievalists the world over. Nevertheless, the very extent of this bibliography's coverage means that it does not appear as quickly as some other possible sources of bibliographical guidance. Hence, the student will want to become acquainted with *The Year's Work in English Studies* and the *International Medieval Bibliography.* Perhaps even more important are the annual bibliographical summaries available in the periodicals *Anglo-Saxon England* and the *Old English Newsletter.* The latter lists the previous year's work in the spring issue, where it also gives abstracts of conference papers, an excellent way to see what kinds of things are going on in the field, since such pieces are often trial runs of ideas and longer expositions which will subsequently turn into books and articles. In the fall issue, the *Old English Newsletter* publishes reviews and summaries. There are also bibliographical works published in book form, some of which are represented in the bibliography at the end of this chapter; their disadvantage is that they are usually by their very nature farther from up-to-date than any of the things I've mentioned so far, but on the other hand they are more compact and easier to handle.

All of this more or less brings us up to the question of what is current in Old English studies. It should be pointed out right at the outset that any pronouncements on such matters are heavily and notoriously contingent. What looks like a promising new trend to one scholar may be a blind alley to a second, nothing new at all to a third, and unsubstantiated nonsense to yet another. So be it; I plunge ahead nevertheless. First of all, I will use the term "current" to mean the work of the last decade or so; in other words since the appearance of the first edition of this book in 1976, where I characterized what I then considered to be current in the same field. At that time I chose first to speak of the offshoots of Magoun's importation of oral-formulaic theory from the classical realm, where Milman Parry had developed it to account for the art of the Homeric poems, into the field of Old English poetics. Magoun's seminal essay, "Oral-Formulaic Character of Anglo-Saxon Narrative Poetry," appeared in 1953, but it had made possible a new paradigm—in the Kuhnian sense—for the study of Anglo-Saxon poetic art, and its implications (and limitations) fueled discussion for at least a couple of decades thereafter. Such discussions have by no means come to an end. Indeed, a recent contribution, like John Miles Foley's 1983 essay, "Literary Art and Oral Tradition in Old English and Serbian Poetry," will often shed light on arguments that had been formulated and debated for years. But generally speaking, the work done now is apt to be more in the way of summarizing debate than initiating it, as in Dwight Conquergood's "Literary and Oral Performances in Anglo-Saxon England: Conflict and Confluence of Traditions," which also appeared in 1983. We are no longer in that heated period when oralists and anti-oralists were squared off and scoring debating points and sparks at the same time. By now the stunning contributions of oral-formulaic theory have been pretty much absorbed into the mainstream view of how these poems work, while the objections of its opponents have often already effected the corrections they originally sought to make.

Having said that, however, I must also add that one of the ways in which the developments that grew out of oral-formulaic theory have continued to contribute powerfully to the ongoing scholarly conversation is in their paving the way for and informing theoretical discussions of other sorts. One thing that the oral-formulaicists were able to do quite convincingly was to cast doubt upon our complacent ways of formulating such notions as how a poem actually works. Following on New Critical tenets, there was a tendency to talk about organic unity, poetic tension, and so forth, as if these elements were somehow essential constituents of poetry, rather than entities made in our own time by the very way in which we approached poetic texts. Oral-formulaic theory opened up our eyes to the obviously different ways of the oral performance and, indeed, by linking up with scholars in other fields, like the classicist Eric Havelock, to the basic differences between oral and lettered cultures. Many good things came out of this new perspective, but no doubt the most enduring has been, and will prove to be, the foregrounding of the "madness" of poems and of cultural artifacts in general. This awareness that poems are not *naturally* this or that, but are constructed out of a complex implication with all of our cultural artifacts taken together, remains an abiding and powerful influence in current critical approaches.

Another trend that contributed powerfully, and somewhat ironically, to the same set of realizations was the exegetical movement, which began to emerge and expand in the years following the 1950 paper, "Historical Criticism," by the Princeton Chaucerian, D. W. Robertson, Jr. By the end of the fifties, important interpretative works from this school were beginning to appear in Old English studies, such books as Bernard Huppé's *Doctrine and Poetry,* which came out in 1959. All during the sixties the critical debate raged between the exegetical school — usually called Robertsonians, in tribute to their intellectual leader — and their opposite notoriously conservative version of historicism to the typically, but not necessarily, leftleaning formulations of the New Historicism, an approach which seems to be filtering its way down from Renaissance studies, where it is flourishing mightily, to the medieval period.

In the meantime, while both oral-formulaic theory and exegetical tenets have contributed from within the field of medieval studies to what amounts to a foregrounding of theoretical problems in poetics and in cultural studies in general, there has been similar pressure in the very same directions from without, where literary theory in all of its various forms has continually occupied the energies of an increasingly large number of scholars over the past two decades, originally in Europe, mainly in France, but now all over the world of Western culture. The impact of this surge of interest has been much slower to be felt in medieval studies than elsewhere, and slower in early periods, like Old English, than in Chaucer studies. Not surprisingly, literary studies among medievalists have over the years been much slower to respond to new critical directions than the work of their colleagues in more modern fields. There seems to be a natural conservatism built into the fact that medievalists need to acquire painstakingly and over a long period of time a wide (and deep) assortment of historical and linguistic skills and attainments just to be able to begin to read medieval texts with any sort of sophistication at all. And with all of this time and effort invested, we have always been reluctant to move to new ways of looking at things, ways which almost inevitably involve the acquisition of even more knowledge, and what's worse, the numbers, usually, as would have been the case in any field of literature at the time, followers of the New Criticism. To oversimplify grossly, the Robertsonians tried to show that medieval artists had only one narrowly demarcated set of Augustinian concepts to demonstrate, and that all medieval poems were therefore to be read as versions of this doctrinal message. And the New Critics — perhaps I should say we New Critics — "knew" that poems just didn't work this way: poems were things that had ironies, complexities, ambiguities, but certainly never anything as simple and crass as messages. After all, one of the apostles of New Critical theory, I. A. Richards, had clearly shown that one of the things that most interfered with true critical response was the presence of what he called "doctrinal adhesions."

Again, as in the case of the oral-formulaic wars, the original terms and tensions of the debate have mellowed, but they have evolved into a continuing discussion of the now generally accepted place of the exegetical tenets in literary studies. In brief, the strictures that the more rabid Robertsonians would have placed upon critical inquiry—with their view that the discovery in the poem of anything other than the doctrinal was irrelevant at best, and at worst something very like sinful—these constraints have gone by the way, leaving the residue of an opening up of the critical mind, a willingness on the part of medievalists to consider seriously the relevance of the claims made on behalf of an alternative way of looking at the way poems operate, how they are generated, and how they are received by their respective publics. In this sense, there is a direct line—and not a very long one at that—from Robertson's pain of loss at the other end, where at least some of what we have so laboriously learned seems no longer relevant. Thus, medievalists were the last into the New Critical camp, barely getting there from the Old Philology before everyone else began to move in the direction of theory. And we are only in the last few years seeing any significant amount of work in Old English that owes much to theory as all other fields have known it.

This conservatism is somewhat ironic in that students of medieval literature have always been equipped with many of the tools that spurred others into theoretical pursuits, specifically knowledge of the ways of language and a bent toward what amount to interdisciplinary and cross-disciplinary study. Already by the early seventies, for example, there was a lively interest among medievalists in the intersections of literature and the other arts, especially painting, exemplified for instance by the translation into English in 1970 of Frederick Pickering's *Literature and Art in the Middle Ages,* and the appearance in 1972 of Annemarie Mahler's important essay, "Art and Visual Imagery: A Methodology for the Study of Medieval Styles," both of which were full of theoretical implications for students of medieval culture. And more recently, we can see how the influence of interdisciplinary studies and theoretical concerns have affected our field, with titles like Carol Edwards's 1983 essay, "The Parry-Lord Theory Meets Operational Structuralism." Except for the appearance of some works that have affinities with feminist theory, though, books like Jane Chance's *Woman as Hero in Old English Literature* and Pauline Stafford's *Queens, Concubines and Dowagers: The King's Wife in the Early Middle Ages,* the movement into theory has been slow. But this slowness, if the past is any indication, is not a sign that such studies are not relevant to medieval literature or to Old English in particular, but rather point to work yet to be done, to scholarly and critical opportunities. At any rate I would strongly advise beginning students of Old English to begin to look at theory. One could begin with a general book like Terry Eagleton's *Literary Theory: An Introduction,* which came out in 1983, or perhaps Jonathan Culler's 1982 book, *On Deconstruction: Theory and Criticism After*

Structuralism. A readily available and continually useful source of ideas and information along the same lines can be had by consulting the volumes of the *New Accents* series, edited by Terence Hawkes, which now runs to about thirty volumes and will introduce the reader to a wide variety of critical discourse.

Another new area in Old English studies can be described more by methodological affinity than by substantive areas in which it might appear to be useful, and that is computer applications, or the relevance of computer technology to the study of Old English literature. A 1974 report to the Medieval Academy by Vern Bullough, Serge Lusignan, and Thomas Ohlgren set out some of the areas in which computer technology had proved to be amenable to research efforts, areas like stylistics, linguistic analysis, and textual criticism, for example. So far, though, the main benefit of the computer for literary students has been in the compiling of things like concordances and dictionaries. The great new *Old English Dictionary,* mentioned already, is an outstanding example. Interested students will want to look at Roberta Frank's *Plan for the Dictionary of Old English,* which was issued in 1973, to see how the work is going to be carried out; they can also look at Cameron, Kingsmill, and Amos's 1983 book, *Old English Word Studies: A Preliminary Author and Word Index,* to see the first fruits of the effort. Aside from the fact that a large number of dictionaries, concordances, and bibliographies have been obviously fostered by the aid of the computer, there is little else at the moment that a person not involved directly can observe about this field. The student who is interested in the possibilities held forth by this technology should acquaint herself, though, with a periodical called the *Bulletin of the Association for Literary and Linguistic Computing.* In a field that moves as quickly as computer technology one cannot rely for long on "current" information.

Finally, what is currently being done in Old English also includes a heavy preponderance of what might be called straightforward scholarship and criticism: books and essays that establish new relationships, define new influences, chart new ways, but along very familiar lines. The sheer quantity of information and criticism is impressive; indeed, it is staggering. There is no way for the student to get a feel for this without the hard spadework of constantly consulting the bibliographical guides, constantly looking up and finding the pieces that interest him most, and in turn following their own bibliographical guidance. Even in what seems a fairly small field, like Old English studies, there will be more leads than can actually be followed.

As we move from the field of Old English to the next chronological period, Middle English, we are immediately struck by gross contrasts.

Whereas Old English texts themselves are written in a number of different dialects and at a number of different times—late Old English varies, as we would expect, from early Old English even within the same dialect— Middle English emerges, as it were from its Norman captivity, as a more or less totally different language. We are reminded once again that the composition of *Beowulf* and the composition of *The Canterbury Tales* are slightly farther apart in time than the composition of *The Canterbury Tales* and the composition of *Finnegan's Wake*. Similarly, there is a corresponding difference in the overall texture of the poetic language, since the great bulk of Middle English literature was written after the twelfth-century rise of romance had forever changed the European sensibility. And the historical sweep and scale of Middle English literature is much vaster than its Old English counterpart, with many more voices, many more, and more varied, genres, simply much more material: the *major* works of Chaucer alone—let alone his other writings—contain about the same number of lines of verse as all of the extant Old English poetry put together. And because of this relative density, the map of the literary terrain can be drawn with much greater thickness and precision than is the case in Old English, where the features to be accounted for are far fewer in number and much more widely scattered. Thus the literary history of the Middle English period is more likely to strike us as coherent than is Old English literary history—concepts of genre and of effects of contiguity, like the notion of influence, seems much more intelligible in the thicker context of the later period, though ironically the actual literary history of the period has proved as difficult to write as the history of Old English.

The student of medieval literature—an American student, at any rate— almost invariably begins with Chaucer, then moves on to other Middle English writers, and only later picks up the study of Old English and perhaps of other medieval vernaculars. This procedure makes good sense in many ways, in particular because both the language and the poetic idiom of the Chaucer canon, different as it will seem from literature of the more modern eras, is nevertheless much less foreign and hence much more accessible to present-day readers. Whereas the student of Old English has typically to work laboriously through grammar-and-reader texts for some time before being able to read the main literary monuments even at a very slow pace, the beginner in Middle English can go directly to a well-edited Chaucer text, spend a relatively short time on the introductory material, and then essentially learn to read the language by means of actual engagement with the poems themselves. Obviously mastery will not be so quickly attained, but pretty good comprehension, fair speed of reading, and a great deal of enjoyment can be had virtually from the start.

For about thirty years, from its publication in 1957, the standard Chaucer text was F. N. Robinson's second edition of *The Works of Geoffrey Chaucer,* and even the present-day student will find all but the most recent articles using this edition as the basis for citation and scholarly reference. Just last year, however, this text was supplanted by the *New Riverside Chaucer,* edited by Larry Benson. In effect, this new edition—from the same publisher as the Robinson text—is the direct successor to the old standard text, becoming, as it were, the third edition of Robinson that has been eagerly awaited for many years now. For all of this pedigree, this book may be less attractive to the beginning student than some other, simpler editions. Its very authoritativeness requires, after all, a formidable array or apparatus that could well daunt and impede the novice; and it is very expensive, even in the context of today's budget-crippling book prices. Some excellent alternatives for the beginner are the editions of the major poems by A. C. Baugh and E. Talbot Donaldson, or Robert Pratt's edition of *The Tales of Canterbury.* These books are all very convenient to use, with glosses and explanations of difficult passages readily accessible to the passing reader, and any of them can be used with confidence as an introduction to Middle English and to Chaucer.

While most students will, in effect, learn Middle English by learning to read the Chaucer texts, there is certainly more linguistic guidance available to those who want it, perhaps because they are more interested in language itself than the average student of literature, or maybe because they want to move on to other dialects and authors whose language is less accessible than Chaucer's. These students can turn to Karl Brunner's excellent guide, translated into English in 1963 as *An Outline of Middle English Grammar.* Or, if they have started with Chaucer and are gradually weaning themselves away from his relatively easy language, they might want first to look at David Burnley's *Guide to Chaucer's Language,* which came out in 1983, or the earlier and still vastly useful *Guide to Chaucer's Pronunciation,* by Helge Kokeritz. Students who are capable of handling the language will want also to consult Udo Fries's 1985 book, *Einführung in die Sprache Chaucers.* As one moves on from Chaucer, one becomes more deeply immersed in the question of Middle English dialects, and the subject will be found treated compactly, but, for students of literature at least, quite fully, in Moore and Marckwardt's *Historical Outlines of English Sounds and Inflections,* which will also offer the beginner some insight into the general field of diachronic linguistics. At the same time, many anthologies of Middle English literature put together for the introductory survey of that subject will cover the dialects and their characteristics in at least a rudimentary way. One widely used anthology, Fernand Mosse's

Handbook of Middle English is excellent in this regard, cramming a good deal of linguistic information into a small space.

Then, there is the matter of dictionary assistance. As in Old English literature, practically all texts edited for student use have glossaries, and although these vary considerably in detail and quality, they are almost always sufficient to get you through the text they gloss with a minimum of difficulty and confusion. All of the major Chaucer texts, for example, have very useful glossaries and linguistic guidance in general, and the Chaucer student can also consult Oxford's relatively new (1979) *Chaucer Glossary,* which goes beyond the scope of most other glossaries of any kind. Still, the student should be aware of general help, and the big item here is the vast and authoritative *Middle English Dictionary,* which got under way in the mid-thirties and now, several decades and editors later, has been issued in volumes and fascicles that take the entries up through the word *simile.* (For comparative purposes, in 1976, when the first edition of *Medieval Studies: An Introduction,* was issued, the entries stopped at the word *leten.*) Needless to say, this dictionary is absolutely invaluable as far as it goes, and should be consulted for all serious and complicated questions. In the meantime, readers whose lexicographical difficulties involve words at the very end of the alphabet will have to use shorter dictionaries — none of which is really satisfactory — glossaries to individual texts or authors, or such instruments as the monumental *Oxford English Dictionary.* This last was not of course intended to be a dictionary of Middle English, but the range of its historical coverage and citation makes it an eminently useful book for curious medievalists.

If acquiring a reading familiarity with Middle English is not terribly difficult — compared with learning Old English, at any rate — finding one's way around in the literature presents problems, both because of the sheer wealth of the original materials and also because of the enormous mass of secondary literature that has been built up over the years, particularly in recent times: there are now published annually well over 500 items relating to the study of Middle English language and literature, let alone studies in the culture that supported this literary output and the collateral studies in history, anthropology, literary theory, and the like, all of which are now considered crucial to the understanding of any textual material whatsoever. Some of the bibliographical guides already mentioned in connection with Old English literature, works like the *MLA International Bibliography, The Year's Work in English Studies,* and the *Cambridge Bibliography of English Literature,* are equally relevant to the student of Middle English. In addition both the *Chaucer Review* and *Neuphilogische Mitteilungen* publish bibliographies and other reports on research in progress that are now of increasing importance since the fullest of the guides, the MLA's, takes longer and longer to appear. More and more frequently also, no doubt due to computer-assisted compilation techniques, special topic bibliographies are appearing in book form. These, like all bibliographical books, are in a sense out of date as soon as they appear, but they are tremendously convenient up to a certain point in the historical record, after which they must be supplemented by periodical materials and the like. The topics covered will include things like Joanne Rice's *Middle English Romance: An Annotated Bibliography, 1955–1985,* or Malcolm Andrew's *The Gawain-Poet: An Annotated Bibliography, 1839–1977.* Sometimes also these specialized compilations will prove to be study guides of somewhat broader scope than most bibliographies proper, books like Frieda Penninger's *English Drama to 1660 (Excluding Shakespeare): A Guide to Information Sources,* which came out in 1976. It should be noted, by the way, that any such guide which takes the secondary literature back to a certain point in time—like the 1955 of Rice's book—will serve admirably for most scholarly purposes. Generally speaking, there is very little chance that an article published before that date will prove to be of much interest, unless it is often cited in more recent books and essays, in which case, of course, it will be readily recoverable from the footnotes and bibliographies of these works themselves.

Fortunately for students of Middle English literature, there is one authoritative guidebook that is absolutely indispensable and readily available in all college and university libraries. And that is the *Manual of the Writings in Middle English, 1050–1500,* under the general editorship of Albert E. Hartung. This monumental work was originally published in 1916, the work of John Edwin Wells, and is usually called Wells's *Manual,* even in its more recent revised versions. Wells's book covered the literature only up to 1400, but the fifteenth century—universally regarded as belonging to the Middle Ages, in any event—has been added to the coverage in the overhaul that has been going on for several years now, first under the editorial guidance of J. Burke Severs, and now under Hartung. Needless to say, whereas Wells put his work out in a single volume—followed by nine supplements over the next thirty years or so—the revision has been farmed out into individual volumes by individual editors. At any rate, the great value of the *Manual,* especially for the beginner, is not in its accounting of editions and secondary scholarship, valuable as that kind of guidance may be, but rather in its delineation of the whole field of Middle English literature. It is the place to which one goes simply to find out what there *is* in some particular area—how many romances there are from the thirteenth or fourteenth century, what they are called, where they can be found. Even if one finds the arrangement of materials or the commentary faulty—and this is much less likely to be the case with the revised and re-written volumes—nevertheless the information itself is the indispensable starting place from which new speculations and new arrangements can spring forth.

For all of these reasons, the *Manual* is the cherished instrument of all of those who wish to order the writings in Middle English for their own scholarly or critical purposes. For generations of scholars, in fact, the *Manual* stood in the stead of a comprehensive history of the period, even though, with its generic arrangement and chronological plodding, it was obviously a good deal less than a history. The fact is, though, that there were no other real literary histories of the period either. The most widely used one, the section called "The Middle English Period," in A. C. Baugh's *Literary History of England,* scarcely improved upon what an intelligent reader could put together for herself from the information that Wells had assembled. But at present we are somewhat better off. The *Manual* is, in itself, infinitely more comprehensive and more critically intelligent in its updated versions—by different hands for each of Wells's sections, with some new ones added—and the kind of expansion of knowledge which has made this possible has also allowed the historical narrative to take a more incisive shape. Therefore, virtually any student will find much to learn in J. A. W. Bennett and Douglas Gray's *Middle English Literature,* published in 1986 as part of the *Oxford History of English Literature,* and almost any scholar, much to admire. Similarly, for the broader context of medieval literature as a whole, as it is represented in *The Middle Ages,* edited by Whitney Bolton as part of *The New History of Literature,* which appeared in 1986. And there are now also numerous studies and guides to particular authors, genres, and periods, including not only the by now venerable *Ricardian Poetry,* by J. A. Burrow, but also more recent things, like A. S. G. Edwards's *Middle English Prose: A Critical Guide to Major Authors and Genres* (1984), Marion Glasscoe's *Medieval Mystical Tradition in English* (1984), and David Lawton's *Middle English Alliterative Poetry and Its Literary Background* (1982), to name only a few.

But to begin with, there is Chaucer. We are often told, especially by old-fashioned literary historians, that the greatest figure of an age is seldom the one on whom to model one's view of the era in historical perspective; somehow, the literary giants rise above their intellectual and cultural environments in such ways as to make their careers and contributions highly uncharacteristic, even eccentric. And it is certainly true that Chaucer is, in many ways, quite clearly not the "typical" Middle English poet that the guidebooks are supposed to encapsulate. In fact, the more often

I read *Troilus and Criseyde* or *The Canterbury Tales*, the more I come to believe that much of what I learned about Chaucer as a medieval poet was really all about John Gower, and not about Chaucer at all. Nevertheless, Chaucer is the magnet of Middle English studies: most students begin their study of the period in a Chaucer course, so they become familiar with the period through his eyes and ears, and most established medievalists working in the English tradition will come to a consideration of Chaucer at some point, often at many points, in their careers.

Similarly, the trajectory of modes of approaching medieval literature in English is most clearly traceable in Chaucer studies, where new notions are often first applied, and where the traditional overlay of tried-and-true methods is most clearly evident. Indeed, one could make a case for the study of critical scholarship in this area being most clearly mapped along the trail of footnotes in the *New Riverside Chaucer,* already mentioned above. It is more practical for the beginning student, though, to get some organized guidance, and fortunately, this is readily available. First of all, there is Beryl Rowland's *Companion to Chaucer Studies,* which came out in a revised edition in 1979. This is as good a guide, in small compass, to the questions that Chaucerians have posed over the years as can be had, and if some of the questions, about Chaucer the Man and the like, are less often posed nowadays, all the more reason for the student to have some summary way of at least glimpsing matters that she will seldom now see aired out in full-length treatments. After going through this book, which consists of a series of essays on various topics in Chaucer studies, each written by an expert in the field, the beginner could profitably turn to the first chapter of Lee Patterson's *Negotiating the Past: The Historical Understanding of Medieval Literature,* published in 1987, where the history of Chaucer criticism is not only organized, but admirably ordered and rationalized as well. Indeed, what follows here is strongly indebted to Patterson, although it also varies from him and expands on his treatment.

Basically, the history of Chaucer criticism is organized around the succession of critical eras, which are still fairly clearly discernible, in spite of their inevitable interpenetrations and entanglements. The first of these, the age of philological discovery, is as crucial to the overall enterprise as it is difficult to comment on. From the mid-nineteenth century on, extending to about the mid-twentieth, there was established, organized, codified, and dispersed an enormous—and enormously impressive—array of facts: facts about Chaucer's life, about the histories—political and economic, intellectual, cultural, and literary—of his time, about his language, about other works and traditions in medieval literature, both within and without the English tradition, facts about every conceivable aspect of his work, or anything relating to it. It goes without saying, of course, when the very notion of "facts" has been so visibly problematized, that these facts often bore a content, a meaning of their own (and Patterson is superb at elucidating this problem for us). This amassing of information was crucial in exactly the obvious way: it has provided every succeeding generation of medievalists with a solid foundation from which to assemble critical speculation. And it is difficult to comment on because so much of it is by now assumed, by now assimilated into the background and incorporated into the apparatus of current books and articles. In other words, the present-day student will have little call to look directly at very much of this philological spadework, but he will find it, in its effects of enablement, everywhere he looks.

The first clearly demarcated critical school in the study of Chaucer was the New Criticism, which flourished mightily during the fifties, as did the New Criticism in all other branches of literary study, and settled itself down into the sixties and seventies as the dominant mode of addressing literary texts of all kinds. Since, until very recently, no graduate students or young faculty members had been brought up in any other kind of critical environment, the tenets of the New Critics — the absolute importance of close reading, to the exclusion of any other kind of reading, most prominent among them — seemed simply and inevitably — "naturally," one is tempted to say — not just *a* way of looking at poems, but *the* way of approaching them. And, indeed, the advent of the New Criticism brought a tremendous vigor and delight to the critical study of the Chaucerian canon, as it had to English and American poetry generally when Cleanth Brooks and Robert Penn Warren, among others, brought this mode of analysis to a generation of students eager to find a new way of seeing and writing about poetry as an art form. And this, of course, was the key to the appeal of this new method; as its devotees always said, it was a way of seeing poems as poems, and not as so many documents for the storing of this fact or that. During the fifties there was much scoffing and some rather clever parody from those who had been raised in the philological tradition, but there proved to be more vitality and excitement in the New Critical work than in the scoffing, and the day was quickly and assuredly won.

And looking at some of the work of the New Critics in the field of Chaucer studies will still reveal much of what the excitement was about. In the work of Charles A. Owen, Jr., of Charles Muscatine, and of E. Talbot Donaldson, there is a presence of critical insight and sensitivity that is still impressive upon rereading, more than a generation after their work has been assimilated to the status of critical classics. In an essay like Owen's

"Crucial Passages in Five of the Canterbury Tales: A Study in Irony and Symbol," which dates back to 1953, we find an attention to the patterning of the poetic text that is at once powerful and powerfully suggestive. He will take small, generally unobtrusive elements in the text, like the grisly black rocks of *The Franklin's Tale,* and show how they operate on levels and in ways that the reader had not previously been aware of. They turn out to be more complex than we had previously imagined, and the complexity is of a sort that could never be approached or guessed at by the information-gathering methods of the older era critics and scholars. This subtlety turns out, as it always does in New Critical analyses, to be not merely an element in poetic excellence, but pretty close to the essence of poetic excellence, itself.

And over and over again, the best of the New Critics provide us with this kind of insightful analysis. I, myself, can date my initial resolve to pursue the study of medieval literature to the impression made upon me by Charles Muscatine's *Chaucer and the French Tradition* (1957), which came out while I was an undergraduate, taking my first course in Chaucer. Like Owen, Muscatine reveals in exquisite detail the internal patterning of the works he studies, most famously in the case of *The Knight's Tale.* At the same time, however, he derives Chaucer's sensitivity to certain tones and patterns in his own work — the Chaucerian style, in its essence — from his predecessors in both the high and low modes of late medieval French poetry. This mode of connecting the internal patterning of the poetry with patterns, tropisms, and tendencies resident in other genres, other traditions, and other ages marks many of the works that extend the domain of the new sensitivity to internal patterning to make a new historical criticism, a new form of inscribing the present work within the scope and context of some previously existing cultural pattern.

So it is, for example, with Robert O. Payne's *Key of Remembrance* (1963), which describes the Chaucerian poetic in terms of the complex tradition that the Middle Ages inherited from the rhetorical treatises of the ancients. In this case, as it happens, there was an older historical formulation to overthrow. When J. M. Manly first approached the question in 1926, with his lecture called "Chaucer and the Rhetoricians," his argument was that Chaucer had grown and developed as an artist by becoming progressively less and less dependent on rhetoric, and more and more open to experience and to his own unique genius. But Payne found the rhetorical tradition to be anything but a burden. He saw in it an organizational theme and a cultural matrix both, and saw also that, far from inhibiting Chaucer's artistic freedom and hamstringing his creativity, rhetoric provided precisely the means by which an artistic development could be formed and guided. He established, in other words, the historical relationship between a given cultural configuration, medieval rhetoric, which unfolded and developed in time, and the molds into which Chaucer chose to cast his own poetic conceptions. And this same kind of move, from internal patterning to recognitions of the reenactment of cultural patterns in the world at large, could be found in another influential book of the time, Robert M. Jordan's *Chaucer and the Shape of Creation: The Aesthetic Possibilities of Inorganic Structure,* which appeared in 1967, and which sought to derive a structural model for Chaucer's notion of form that is not anachronistically rooted in our own post-romantic notions of organic structure, a shape — or a model of shaping — that Chaucer is not likely, to put it gently, to have noted or formulated for himself. In the result, a model whose own imaginative roots can be traced all the way back to antiquity can, by analogy, render perfectly coherent on their own terms many Chaucerian structures whose internal logic had previously seemed flawed or unbalanced.

But generally speaking, the main thrust of the New Criticism was to move away from the historically grounded into the exploration of poetic configuration as a force in its own right. And this poetic configuration is always internal to the works studied and thus not accessible to historical methods that relied upon the notions of influence or development. This kind of New Criticism produced, in fact, dozens of powerful readings of poems and parts of poems, perhaps nowhere more brilliantly than in the essays of E. Talbot Donaldson, conveniently put together in his *Speaking of Chaucer* (1970), a book that all medievalists ought to be familiar with. The essays contained in *Speaking of Chaucer* had in their own way turned the sensibilities of a whole generation of scholars and critics away from the fact mongering that had come to characterize the end of the philological tradition, and tuned them in to the apprehension of ways of poetic patterning, tonal control, devices for securing paradox and irony, and the manipulation of point of view. The fact that all of these things constitute at present the very basis for going on in literary studies — constitute, that is, the very notion of how a poem is to be read — should not blind us to the fact that it was the New Critics who made of these things fact, who gave birth to our most basic notions of how to deal with a poetic text.

But there was also in all of this a grave danger, and it was a danger that was highlighted in the celebrated opposition between Donaldson, the champion of the New Critical close reading, and D. W. Robertson, who founded, along with Bernard Huppé, a school of interpretation that for a long time was usually just referred to as Robertsonianism — though the bumptious awkwardness of that appellation suggests that this term was most often used by those in the opposition — and is now usually called exe-

getical criticism, a designation that is both more accurate and more respectful of the intricacy and scholarly weight of the school's inventions and
contributions to medieval studies. The budding medievalist will want to
consult *Critical Approaches to Medieval Literature: Selected Papers from
the English Institute, 1958-59,* edited by Dorothy Bethurum, where the
main battle lines between the two camps are drawn with an incisiveness
and spirit that still commends these essays to interested readers thirty years
later. The occasion for the conflict was provided by the rise of the exegetical criticism, which is usually dated from a 1950 essay of Robertson's, entitled "Historical Criticism." With this paper, Robertson made a call for
a new kind of historical criticism of medieval literature, one that projected
a series of readings designed to demonstrate in detail that the primary
function of medieval literature was to expound a very limited set of Augustinian doctrines, mainly revolving around the concept of *caritas* in its
opposition to *cupiditas.* Robertson believed that no medieval poet could,
or would wish to, avoid serving this function, and that therefore no medieval poem could satisfactorily be read as conducing to any meaning other
than the serving of this doctrinal function. In a word, Robertson provided
the meaning that any medieval poem would have, and then projected a
research program that would flesh out the truth of this meaning in the
case of each individual poem. And in this way, he set out an absolutely
new paradigm for literary research in the medieval field, and one that understandably had the prevailing New Critical practitioners bristling with
anger and invective. To get the flavor of this debate, the student should
begin by consulting, in Bethurum's anthology, the Donaldson argument
contra exegesis and Robert Kaske's argument pro. If this whets the appetite sufficiently, then she may wish to go on to such things as Kaske's "Chaucer and Medieval Allegory," Francis Utley's "Robertsonianism Redivivus,"
A. Leigh DeNeef's "Robertson and the Critics," and my own "Robertsonianism and the Idea of Literary History." If the debate is, in the student's
mind, resolved in favor of the exegetes, there will be plenty of places to
turn to see the results, so far, of Robertson's projection; in particular, all
will want to look at the works of John Fleming, Robertson's most direct
heir, whose studies are filled with a subtlety and creative insight that any
founder would be proud to think he paved the way for, and the works of
Judson Allen cited in the bibliography.

     In all of this, the grave critical danger posed by the sharpest and clever-
est of the New Critics, and brought into sharp relief by the proposals of
the exegetical school, was that the New Critical program was dealing somehow with the essence of poetry. And an essence, of course, is a source in
opposition to the notion of historical genesis. Indeed, one of the New

Critical objections most frequently cited in regard to Robertson was that he just didn't understand how poems work. In the light of New Critical tenets, this was certainly true, but the lasting contribution of the exegetes has been in the vivid demonstration that how poems work, what a poem is, how to read a poem—these are all matters of historical configuration. In other words, our notion of what a poem is and how it works is a creation of cultural influences at work in our place and time, and it is this only. Whatever resemblances or congruences our notion of a poem may have with the one prevailing in Attic Greece, or in medieval Paris or London, have to be demonstrated, not simply assumed as "natural."

Ironically, this new historical consciousness is, in medieval studies, the main and most productive continuing influence of Robertson and his school. That is, the actual program he proposed, the precise definition of the new historicism that he envisioned and embodied in his own work, has always remained rather uneasily by the side of the interests and ambitions of most medievalists in the years between the fifties and the present time. It has resulted to be sure, as in the works of Fleming and Allen, in some enduring scholarship, but only with a relatively small minority of practitioners is the program bought on its own terms. Nevertheless, in its casting doubt on the legitimacy of the New Critical claim to absolute possession of the poetic essence, it has paved the way for many of the developments we can now see coming to the fore. The irony here is that, while the Robertsonian agenda was and essentially remains thoroughly conservative, often even reactionary in the way in which it wishes to pursue history only in the backward direction, freezing as it were the only right and proper meaning of a poem in one particular state—many would say a state that suits a particular socio-cultural agenda—it functioned, in dislodging the absolute grip of New Critical dogma upon the critical mind, as an invitation to other new historicisms, which in their turn, pursuing history both forward and backward in dialectical movement, are almost invariably left-leaning, or to use the word of their own practitioners (myself included), "progressive."

Where, then, does the newest work in the study of Middle English literature come down in its methodologies, its ideological orientations, its style and tone? One answer is that every trend that I have described is thriving, producing work that is intellectually fresh and lively in its own area. In a way, this would be hard to deny. If we look at an anthology like Julian Wasserman and Robert Blanch's *Chaucer in the Eighties,* we are struck not by the amount of cited work that could not have been produced before this decade, but by the continuities that the works of the eighties share with those of the previous two or three decades. But there is much that is utterly new, and practically nothing that could have been approached in exactly the same way in any earlier epoch. Even some of the titles alone have a vastly different flavor, in comparison to anything that has gone before, as in Sheila Delany's "Rewriting Women Good: Gender and the Anxiety of Influence in Two Late-Medieval Texts," or even Arlyn Diamond's simpler "Troilus and Criseyde: The Politics of Love." For it is perfectly evident that one mighty influence on literary studies at the present time, in all of its chronological divisions, is the presence and development of theory, which I have already mentioned in connection with the study of Old English. Therefore, we are witnessing a great influx of work that is oriented toward the methodologies and terminologies of feminist theory, of both Freudian and Lacanian psychoanalysis, or Foucault.

Thus, if we look at the panorama of work currently being offered as commentary on medieval literature, we will be seeing not only studies founded on the spadework of the great philologists, enabled by the development of the close-reading techniques of the New Criticism, and informed by the painstaking scholarship of the exegetes, but also work inspired by Marxist historicism, feminist theory, Derridean deconstruction, and the like. Indeed, since the enterprise called "Theory" embraces such large areas of the humanities and social sciences put together, one is apt to find citations to writers in what seems at first a bewildering array of fields: in contemporary criticism in general there is as likely to be a reference to Erving Goffman as to Kittredge, or Root, or Manly.

So then, what sorts of particular titles are we likely to encounter? Well, as I have suggested, much that is being done today follows closely on the work of predecessors in either the New Critical or exegetical line. At its least self-conscious, this body of scholarship and criticism would include such things as the late John Gardner's *Poetry of Chaucer,* or even his fleshing out of the *Life Records,* called *The Life and Times of Chaucer.* On a more sophisticated plane, we move to studies that are solidly mainstream, but in no way derivative, working an old field, but making it yield its fruits in interesting ways, books like Alfred David's *Strumpet Muse: Art and Morals in Chaucer's Poetry* (1976), or Robert Burlin's *Chaucerian Fiction* (1977), or perhaps Monica McAlpine's *Genre of Troilus and Criseyde* (1978). Following on the work of the original Robertsonians, we find on the one hand John Fleming's *Reason and the Lover* (1984), which is directed toward the *Roman de la Rose,* but in its search for Augustinian antecedents for the poem is especially instructive for students of English literature, and on the other the work of Judson Allen, both in *The Ethical Poetic of the Later Middle Ages* (1982), and, with Theresa Moritz, in *A Distinction of Stories: The Medieval Unity of Chaucer's Fair Chain of Narratives for*

Canterbury (1981). Allen's case is particularly interesting for students of the criticism of medieval literature, since, in his simultaneous embracing and holding off of the Robertsonian legacy, he illustrates vividly the positioning of that strand in the sociology of work in medieval studies.

Much of what is continuous in critical work can also be approached in various thematically oriented anthologies of essays, a form of dissemination of knowledge and opinion that seems to be growing in popularity. In this line, one might want to look at things like John J. Burke, Jr.'s *Signs and Symbols in Chaucer's Poetry* (1981), or David Jeffrey's *Chaucer and the Scriptural Tradition* (1984), both of which will prove invaluable to those curious about the exegetical heritage. But these anthologies abound, and they cover medieval literature and culture from almost every conceivable angle, with some of the most interesting of late being Thomas Heffernan's *Popular Literature of Medieval England* (1985) and Josie P. Campbell's *Popular Culture in the Middle Ages* (1986) — which show the rise in interest in the more broadly based notion of culture reflected in the study of the middle ages; the corresponding treatment of the putatively higher elements in Scattergood, Sherborne, and Burrow's *English Court Culture in the Later Middle Ages* (1983), and the topically oriented collections represented in Lawrence Roberts's *Approaches to Nature in the Middle Ages* (1982) and Lois Ebin's *Vernacular Poetics in the Middle Ages* (1984), along with a survey that should interest anyone trying to find an overview of current work, Thomas D. Cooke's *Present State of Scholarship in Fourteenth-Century Literature* (1982), which tells us much about the questions of current interest to medieval scholars, even though its focus is not on English literature.

Much of the bedrock work of scholarship continues, of course, and is represented by solid contributions, indeed, work that is often monumental, as in George Kane and E. Talbot Donaldson's edition of the B-text of *Piers Plowman,* which came out in 1975, or in J. A. Burrow's new edition of *Sir Gawain and the Green Knight* (1982). With our present-day interest in the intellectual issues behind such enterprises, one might also wish to read Paul Ruggiers's historical account, *Editing Chaucer: The Great Tradition* (1984), Charles Moorman's excellent *Editing the Middle English Manuscript* (1975), which will be instructive to all readers of medieval literature, whether they ever edit a single word or not, or Derek Pearsall's collection, *Manuscripts and Readers in Fifteenth-Century England: The Literary Implications of Manuscript Study* (1983). The same kind of scholarly solidity, often combined with new approaches and insights that would equally qualify the works to be listed under current trends include books as varied in their subject matter and angle of vision as David C. Fowler's

The Bible in Middle English Literature (1984), an indispensable guide, John Fyler's *Chaucer and Ovid* (1979), and Winthrop P. Wetherbee's *Chaucer and the Poets: An Essay on Troilus and Criseyde* (1984), both of which revivify the idea of source studies, so often in the past the last refuge of plodders, V. A. Kolve's *Chaucer and the Imagery of Narrative: The First Five Canterbury Tales* (1984), and Alastair Minnis's fascinating and provocative *Medieval Theory of Authorship: Scholastic Attitudes in the Later Middle Ages* (1984).

Indeed, the list of the last paragraph could be continued right on through an entire volume the size of the present one (and with profit to the reader, too), but an arbitrary halt must be called. If one mentions Minnis, how can one not also cite Janet Coleman's *Medieval Readers and Writers: 1350-1400* (1981), which, preceding Minnis's book, has an equal claim to being foundational? Well, there is room for nothing here but the reminder that this part of my essay — and the bibliography that follows — is necessarily arbitrary, and is intended to provoke further exploration, not pretend to guarantee coverage.

With that having been said, let me end this excursion with a brief — and, of course, arbitrary — dip into a few things that seem really to have changed greatly the face of medieval criticism in the decade or so since the appearance of the first edition of this book. The motivating impulses here are literary theory in general and feminist theory in particular. In the latter area any number of useful and provocative books and essays have come forth since the pioneering work of Joan Ferrante's *Woman as Image in Medieval Literature from the Twelfth Century to Dante,* which was published in 1975. As is usually the case in newer fields, much of the most interesting pieces are in essay form, things like Maureen Fries's "The 'Other' Voice: Woman's Song, Its Satire and Its Transcendence in Late Medieval British Literature," Susan Scribanoff's "Taking the Gold out of Egypt: The Art of Reading as a Woman," which appeared not in a medieval journal, but in an anthology on feminist theory called *Gender and Reading: Essays on Readers, Texts, and Contexts,* and even David Herlihy's "Did Women Have a Renaissance? A Reconsideration." But there are also books, like Richard J. Schrader's *God's Handiwork: Images of Women in Early Germanic Literature* (1983), and Peter Dronke's *Women Writers of the Middle Ages: A Critical Study of Texts from Perpetua (+203) to Marguerite Porete (+1310).*

In the more general area of theory, which, it should go without saying, embraces a wide variety of different intellectual enterprises, there are any number of tacks to take. An instructive sequence, to me at least, would be to go back just a bit, perhaps to an essay like Mark Amsler's "Literary

Theory and the Genres of Middle English Literature," which came out in 1980, or to Morton Bloomfield's piece, "Contemporary Literary Theory and Chaucer," which appeared in 1981 in an anthology entitled *New Perspectives on Chaucer,* and then to plunge forward into the work of Judith Ferster in *Chaucer on Interpretation* (1985), or perhaps R. A. Shoaf's *Dante, Chaucer, and the Currency of the Word: Money, Images, and Reference in Late Medieval Poetry* (1983), or to David Aers's *Chaucer, Langland, and the Creative Imagination* (1980), or to his anthology, called *Criticism, Ideology, and History,* which came out in 1986. Like all my other lists, this one could be expanded enormously, but looking into even this much theory-based criticism will illustrate both the variety of things that fall under that rubric and also the relative "mainstreamness" of the theoretical enterprise in the hands of medievalists.

There is, of course, no predicting where the critical turn will indeed turn next. In recent weeks I have heard eminent medievalists say both that anything even resembling the older criticism — meaning pre-theory — is dead and also that there will soon be a return to more "historical" (rather than "theoretical") forms of inquiry and writing on medieval subjects. But there is clearly a sense in which both of these views are sure to be wrong. In the first place, nothing of real value is ever really obliterated, but finds itself embedded in, and transformed by, newer modes or approaches as they, in turn, develop, flourish, and quiet down again. But in the second, nothing is ever merely returned to, either. Even as the more reactionary of the Robertsonians wished, in vain, to banish modern speculation from the view of medieval literature, freezing meaning, as it were, in its Augustinian forms, so anyone of any persuasion will wish, in vain, for the influence of the exegetes, or of the more contemporary theorists, to go away. Once *A Preface to Chaucer* has been recorded and assimilated, its traces will be forever present in subsequent critical thought, and the same thing will be true of the traces of Derrida, of Foucault, of Lacan, or of Jameson.

NOTES

1. Full citations for these and all subsequent materials mentioned in the text will be found in the bibliography located at the end of this chapter. In order to save space, the reference in the text will usually only be full enough to permit the location of the item in the bibliography.

2. A word on the terms "Anglo-Saxon" and "Old English": when applied attributively, the two are synonymous; Old English poetry and Anglo-Saxon poetry are the same entity. Most modern writers in English, however, follow the convention that "Old English" is used

to designate the language and literature of the period, while "Anglo-Saxon" is used for the people themselves and their nonlinguistic artifacts: Old English elegy, but Anglo-Saxon polity.

BIBLIOGRAPHY

Let me emphasize once again that this list has no pretensions whatsoever to completeness. It does include everything mentioned in the text and a few more relatively recent items that seem to me to be of a level of interest and importance similar to pieces mentioned in the text. It specifically *excludes* everything mentioned in the bibliography I included in the first edition of this guide, except for those items that are mentioned in the text in this edition. This exclusion is pursued solely to save space and avoid duplication and in no way implies that the dropped items are no longer of any interest. Far from it.

Aers, David. *Chaucer, Langland, and the Creative Imagination.* London: Routledge, 1980.
———, ed. *Medieval Literature: Criticism, Ideology, and History.* New York: St. Martin's, 1986.
Allen, Judson Boyce. *The Ethical Poetic of the Later Middle Ages.* Toronto: Univ. of Toronto Press, 1982.
———, and Theresa Anne Moritz. *A Distinction of Stories: The Medieval Unity of Chaucer's Fair Chain of Narratives for Canterbury.* Columbus: Ohio State Univ. Press, 1981.
Amsler, Mark E. "Literary Theory and the Genres of Middle English Literature," *Genre* 13 (1980): 389–96.
Andrew, Malcolm. *The Gawain-Poet: An Annotated Bibliography, 1839–1977.* New York: Garland, 1980.
———, and Ronald Waldron, eds. *The Poems of the Pearl Manuscript.* Berkeley: Univ. of California Press, 1979.
Baugh, Albert C., ed. *Chaucer's Major Poetry.* New York: Appleton-Century-Crofts, 1963.
———, ed. *A Literary History of England.* 2d. ed. New York: Appleton-Century-Crofts, 1967.
Beale, Walter H. *Old and Middle English Poetry to 1500: A Guide to Information Sources.* Detroit: Gale, 1976.
Bennett, J. A. W., and Douglas Gray. *Middle English Literature.* Oxford: Clarendon, 1986.
Benson, Larry D., ed. *The New Riverside Chaucer.* Boston: Houghton Mifflin, 1987.
Berkhout, Carl T., and Milton McGatch, eds. *Anglo-Saxon Scholarship: The First Three Centuries.* Boston: Hall, 1982.
Bessinger, Jess B., Jr. *A Concordance to the Anglo-Saxon Poetic Records.* Pro-

grammed by Philip H. Smith, Jr.; Index of Compounds compiled by Michael W. Twomey. Ithaca, N.Y.: Cornell Univ. Press, 1978.

———. *A Short Dictionary of Anglo-Saxon Poetry.* Toronto: Univ. of Toronto Press, 1960.

Bethurum, Dorothy, ed. *Critical Approaches to Medieval Literature: Selected Papers from the English Institute, 1958–1959.* New York: Columbia Univ. Press, 1960.

Bloomfield, Morton W. "Contemporary Literary Theory and Chaucer." In Donald Rose, ed., *New Perspectives on Chaucer,* 23–36. Norman, Okla.: Pilgrim, 1981.

Boitano, Piero, ed. *Chaucer and the Italian Trecento.* Cambridge: Cambridge Univ. Press, 1983.

———, and Anna Torti, eds. *Intellectuals and Writers in Fourteenth-Century Europe.* Cambridge: Brewer, 1986.

Bolton, Whitney F., ed. *The New History of Literature.* Vol. 1, *The Middle Ages.* New York: Peter Bedrick, 1986.

Borden, Arthur R., Jr. *A Comprehensive Old English Dictionary.* Washington, D.C.: Univ. Press of America, 1982.

Bosworth, Joseph, and T. Northcote Toller. *An Anglo-Saxon Dictionary.* London: Oxford Univ. Press, 1898. *Supplement,* edited by T. Northcote Toller, 1921.

Brewer, Derek. *Chaucer and His World.* New York: Dodd, Mead, 1978.

Brown, Phyllis Rugg, Georgia Ronan Crompton, and Fred C. Robinson, eds. *Modes of Interpretation in Old English Literature.* Toronto: Univ. of Toronto Press, 1986.

Brunner, Karl. *An Outline of Middle English Grammar.* Translated by Grahame Johnston. Cambridge, Mass.: Harvard Univ. Press, 1963.

Bullough, Vern L., Serge Lusignan, and Thomas H. Ohlgren. "Report: Computers and the Medievalist." *Speculum* 49 (1974): 392–402.

Burke, John J., Jr., ed. *Signs and Symbols in Chaucer's Poetry.* University: Univ. of Alabama Press, 1981.

Burlin, Robert B. *Chaucerian Fiction.* Princeton: Princeton Univ. Press, 1977.

Burnley, David. *A Guide to Chaucer's Language.* Norman: Univ. of Oklahoma Press, 1984.

Burrow, J. A. *Medieval Writers and Their Work: Middle English Literature and Its Background 1100–1500.* Oxford: Oxford Univ. Press, 1982.

———. *Ricardian Poetry: Chaucer, Gower, Langland, and the Gawain-Poet.* New Haven: Yale Univ. Press, 1971.

———, ed. *Sir Gawain and the Green Knight.* New Haven: Yale Univ. Press, 1982.

Cameron, Angus, Allison Kingsmill, and Ashley Crandall Amos. *Old English Word Studies: A Preliminary Author and Word Index.* Toronto: Univ. of Toronto Press, 1983.

Campbell, Alistair. *Old English Grammar.* Oxford: Oxford Univ. Press, 1959.

Campbell, Josie P., ed. *Popular Culture in the Middle Ages.* Bowling Green, Ohio: Popular Press, 1986.

Cassidy, Frederic G., and Richard N. Ringler, eds. *Bright's Old English Grammar and Reader.* 3d ed. New York: Holt, 1971.

Chambers, R. W. *Beowulf: An Introduction to the Study of the Poem, with a Discussion of the Stories of Offa and Finn.* 3d ed., with a supplement by C. L. Wrenn. Cambridge: Cambridge Univ. Press, 1959.

———. *On the Continuity of English Prose from Alfred to More and His School.* Includes extract from the introduction to *Nicholas Harpsfield's Life of Sir Thomas More*, edited by E. V. Hitchcock and R. W. Chambers. Oxford: Oxford Univ. Press, 1932.

Chance, Jane. *Woman as Hero in Old English Literature.* Syracuse: Syracuse Univ. Press, 1986.

Coleman, Janet. *Medieval Readers and Writers: 1350–1400.* New York: Columbia Univ. Press, 1981.

Conquergood, Dwight. "Literary and Oral Performance in Anglo-Saxon England: Conflict and Confluence of Traditions." In David W. Thompson, Wallace A. Bacon, Eugene Bahn, Lee Hudson, and Alethea Mattingly, eds., *The Performance of Literature in Historical Perspective.* Lanham, Md.: Univ. Press of America, 1983.

Cooke, Thomas D., ed. *The Present State of Scholarship in Fourteenth-Century Literature.* Columbia: Univ. of Missouri Press, 1982.

Culler, Jonathan. *On Deconstruction: Theory and Criticism after Structuralism.* Ithaca, N.Y.: Cornell Univ. Press, 1982.

David, Alfred. *The Strumpet Muse: Art and Morals in Chaucer's Poetry.* Bloomington: Indiana Univ. Press, 1976.

Davis, Norman, Douglas Gray, Patricia Ingham, and Anne Wallace-Hadrill, comps. *A Chaucer Glossary.* Oxford: Clarendon, 1979.

Delany, Sheila. "Rewriting Women Good: Gender and the Anxiety of Influence in Two Late-Medieval Texts." In Julian Wasserman and Robert Blanch, eds. *Chaucer in the Eighties,* 75–92. Syracuse: Syracuse Univ. Press, 1986.

DeNeef, A. Leigh. "Robertson and the Critics." *Chaucer Review* 2 (1967): 205–34.

Diamond, Arlyn. "*Troilus and Criseyde:* The Politics of Love." In Julian Wasserman and Robert Blanch, eds., *Chaucer in the Eighties,* 93–103. Syracuse: Syracuse Univ. Press, 1986.

Donaldson, E. Talbot, ed. *Chaucer's Poetry: An Anthology for the Modern Reader.* New York: Ronald Press, 1958.

———. *Speaking of Chaucer.* New York: Norton, 1970.

Dronke, Peter. *Women Writers of the Middle Ages: A Critical Study of Texts from Perpetua (+203) to Marguerite Porete (+1310).* Cambridge: Cambridge Univ. Press, 1984.

Eagleton, Terry. *Literary Theory: An Introduction.* Minneapolis: Univ. of Minnesota Press, 1983.

Ebin, Lois, ed. *Vernacular Poetics in the Middle Ages.* Kalamazoo, Mich.: Medieval Institute Publications, Western Michigan Univ., 1984.

Edwards, A. S. O., ed. *Middle English Prose: A Critical Guide to Major Authors and Genres.* New Brunswick, N.J.: Rutgers Univ. Press, 1984.

Edwards, Carol. "The Parry-Lord Theory Meets Operational Structuralism." *Journal of American Folklore* 96 (1983): 151–69.

Ferrante, Joan. *Woman as Image in Medieval Literature from the Twelfth Century to Dante.* New York: Columbia Univ. Press, 1975.

Ferster, Judith. *Chaucer on Interpretation.* Cambridge: Cambridge Univ. Press, 1985.

Fleming, John V. *Reason and the Lover.* Princeton: Princeton, Univ. Press, 1984.

Flynn, Elizabeth A., and Patrocinio P. Schweikert, eds. *Gender and Reading: Essays on Readers, Texts, and Contexts.* Baltimore: Johns Hopkins Univ. Press, 1986.

Foley, John Miles. "Literary Art and Oral Tradition in Old English and Serbian Poetry." *Anglo-Saxon England* 12 (1983): 183–214.

Ford, Patrick K., and Karen G. Borst, eds. *Connections Between Old English and Medieval Celtic Literature.* Lanham, Md.: Univ. Press of America, 1985.

Fowler, David C. *The Bible in Middle English Literature.* Seattle: Univ. of Washington Press, 1984.

Frank, Roberta. *Plan for the Dictionary of Old English.* Toronto: Univ. of Toronto Press, 1973.

Fries, Maureen. "The 'Other' Voice: Women's Song, Its Satire and Its Transcendence in Late Medieval British Literature." *Studies in Medieval Culture* 15 (1981): 155–78.

Fries, Udo. *Einführung in die Sprache Chaucers: Phonologie, Metrik und Morphologie.* Tübingen: Niemayer, 1985.

Fyler, John M. *Chaucer and Ovid.* New Haven: Yale University Press, 1979.

Gardner, John C. *The Life and Times of Chaucer.* New York: Knopf, 1976.

———. *The Poetry of Chaucer.* Carbondale: Southern Illinois Univ. Press, 1977.

Glasscoe, Marion, ed. *The Medieval Mystical Tradition.* Cambridge: Brewer, 1984.

Green, Martin, ed. *The Old English Elegies: New Essays in Criticism and Research.* Rutherford, N.J.: Fairleigh Dickinson Univ. Press, 1983.

Green, Richard Firth. *Poets and Princepleasers: Literature and the English Court in the Late Middle Ages.* Toronto: Univ. of Toronto Press, 1980.

Greenfield, Stanley B., and Daniel G. Calder. *A New Critical History of Old English Literature.* New York: New York Univ. Press, 1986.

Greenfield, Stanley B., and Fred C. Robinson, eds. *A Bibliography of Publications on Old English Literature to the End of 1979.* Toronto: Univ. of Toronto Press, 1980.

Grein, C. W. M. *Sprachschatz der angelsächsischen Dichter.* In collaboration with Ferdinand Holthausen. Revised by J. J. Köhler. Heidelberg: Carl Winters Universitätsbuchhandlung, 1912.

———, and R. P. Wülcker, eds. *Bibliothek der angelsächsischen Prosa.* 13 vols. Kassel: G. H. Wigand, 1872–1900, and continued by H. Hecht, ed., Hamburg: Henri Grand, 1901–1933.

Heffernan, Thomas J., ed. *The Popular Literature of Medieval England.* Knoxville: Univ. of Tennessee Press, 1985.

Herlihy, David. "Did Women Have a Renaissance? A Reconsideration." *Medievalia et Humanistica* 13 (1985): 1–22.

Hill, David. *An Atlas of Anglo-Saxon England.* Oxford: Blackwell, 1981.

Holthausen, Ferdinand. *Altenglisches etymologisches Wörterbuch.* Heidelberg: Carl Winters Universitätsbuchhandlung, 1934.

Hoover, David L. *A New Theory of Old English Meter.* New York: Peter Lang, 1985.

Huppé, Bernard F. *Doctrine and Poetry: Augustine's Influence on Old English Poetry.* Albany: State Univ. of New York, 1959.

————. *The Hero in the Earthly City: A Reading of Beowulf.* Medieval and Renaissance Texts and Studies, vol. 33. Albany: State Univ. of New York Press, 1984.

Jeffrey, David Lyle, ed. *Chaucer and Scriptural Tradition.* Ottawa: Univ. of Ottawa Press, 1984.

Jordan, Robert M. *Chaucer and the Shape of Creation: The Aesthetic Possibilities of Inorganic Structure.* Cambridge, Mass.: Harvard Univ. Press, 1967.

————. *Chaucer's Poetics and The Modern Reader.* Berkeley: Univ. of California Press, 1987.

Kane, George, and E. Talbot Donaldson, eds. *Piers Plowman: The B Version.* London: Athlone, 1975.

Kaske, Robert E. "Chaucer and Medieval Allegory." *ELH* 30 (1963): 175–92.

Klaeber, Friedrich, ed. *Beowulf and the Fight at Finnsburg.* 3d ed., with two supplements. Boston: Heath, 1950.

Kökeritz, Helge. *A Guide to Chaucer's Pronunciation.* New Haven, Conn.: Whitlock, 1954.

Kolve, V. A. *Chaucer and the Imagery of Narrative: The First Five Canterbury Tales.* Stanford, Calif.: Stanford Univ. Press, 1984.

Krapp, George P., and Elliott V. K. Dobbie, eds. *The Anglo-Saxon Poetic Records.* 6 vols. New York: Columbia University Press, 1931–53.

Lawton, David, ed. *Middle English Alliterative Poetry and Its Literary Background: Seven Essays.* Cambridge: Brewer, 1982.

Magoun, F. P., Jr. "Oral-Formulaic Character of Anglo-Saxon Narrative Poetry." *Speculum* 28 (1953): 446–67.

Mahler, Annemarie. "Art and Visual Imagery: A Methodology for the Study of Medieval Styles." *Yearbook of Comparative and General Literature* 21 (1972): 7–14.

Manly, J. M. "Chaucer and the Rhetoricians." In Richard J. Schoeck and Jerome Taylor, eds., *Chaucer Criticism.* Vol. 1, *The Canterbury Tales,* 268–90. Notre Dame, Ind.: Univ. of Notre Dame, 1960.

Mann, Jill. *Chaucer and Medieval Estates Satire: The Literature of Social Classes and the "General Prologue."* Cambridge: Cambridge Univ. Press, 1973.

A Manual of the Writings in Middle English, 1050–1500. Albert E. Hartung, general editor. New Haven: The Connecticut Academy of Arts and Sciences, 1967–present.

McAlpine, Monica E. *The Genre of Troilus and Criseyde.* Ithaca: Cornell Univ. Press, 1978.

Middle English Dictionary. Edited by Hans Kurath and his successors. Ann Arbor: Univ. of Michigan Press, 1952–.

Middleton, Anne. "The Idea of Public Poetry in the Reign of Richard II." *Speculum* 53 (1978): 94–114.

Minnis, Alastair J. *Medieval Theory of Authorship: Literary Attitudes in the Later Middle Ages.* London: Scolar Press, 1984.

Moore, Samuel. *Historical Outlines of English Sounds and Inflections.* Rev. ed. Edited by Albert H. Marckwardt. Ann Arbor, Mich.: G. Wahr, 1951.

Moorman, Charles. *Editing the Middle English Manuscript.* Jackson: Univ. Press of Mississippi, 1975.

Mossé, Fernand. *A Handbook of Middle English.* Translated by James A. Walker. Baltimore: Johns Hopkins Univ. Press, 1950.

Muscatine, Charles. *Chaucer and the French Tradition.* Berkeley: Univ. of California Press, 1957.

Niles, John D. *Beowulf: The Poem and Its Tradition.* Cambridge, Mass.: Harvard Univ. Press, 1983.

Owen, Charles A., Jr. "The Crucial Passages in Five of the *Canterbury Tales:* A Study in Irony and Symbol." *Journal of English and Germanic Philology* 52 (1953): 294–311.

Patterson, Lee. *Negotiating the Past.* Madison: Univ. of Wisconsin Press, 1987.

Payne, Robert O. *The Key of Remembrance: A Study of Chaucer's Poetics.* New Haven: Yale Univ. Press, 1963.

Pearsall, Derek, ed. *Manuscripts and Readers in Fifteenth-Century England: The Literary Implications of Manuscript Study.* Cambridge: Brewer, 1983.

Peck, Russell A. "Public Dreams and Private Myths: Perspective in Middle English Literature." *PMLA* 90(1975): 461–68.

Penninger, Frieda E. *English Drama to 1660 (excluding Shakespeare): A Guide to Information Sources.* Detroit: Gale, 1976.

Pickering, Frederick. *Literature and Art in the Middle Ages.* Coral Gables: Univ. of Miami Press, 1970.

Plummer, Charles, ed. *Two of the Anglo-Saxon Chronicles Parallel, with Supplementary Extracts from the Others . . . on the Basis of an Edition by John Earle.* 2 vols. Oxford: Clarendon, 1892–99.

Pope, John Collins, ed. *The Homilies of Aelfric: A Supplementary Collection.* Early English Text Society, vol. 259. London: Oxford Univ. Press, 1967.

———. *The Rhythm of Beowulf.* Rev. ed. New Haven: Yale University Press, 1966.

———, ed. *Seven Old English Poems.* Indianapolis: Bobbs-Merrill, 1966.

Pratt, Robert A., ed. *The Tales of Canterbury.* Boston: Houghton Mifflin, 1974.

Quinn, William A., and Audrey S. Hall. *Jongleur: A Modified Theory of Oral Improvisation and Its Effects on the Performance and Transmission of Middle English Romance.* Washington, D.C.: Univ. Press of America, 1982.

Quirk, Randolph, and C. L. Wrenn. *An Old English Grammar.* 2d ed. London: Methuen, 1958.

Raw, Barbara C. *The Art and Background of Old English Poetry.* London: Arnold 1979.

Rice, Joanne A. *Middle English Romance: An Annotated Bibliography, 1955–1985.* New York: Garland, 1987.

Roberts, Lawrence D., ed. *Approaches to Nature in the Middle Ages*. Binghamton, N.Y.: Binghamton Center for Medieval and Early Renaissance Studies, 1982.

Robertson, D. W., Jr. "Historical Criticism." In *English Institute Essays, 1950*. Edited by Alan S. Downer. New York: Columbia Univ. Press, 1951.

————. *A Preface to Chaucer: Studies in Medieval Perspectives*. Princeton: Princeton Univ. Press, 1967.

Rose, David L., ed. *New Perspectives on Chaucer*. Norman, Okla.: Pilgrim, 1981.

Rowland, Beryl, ed. *A Companion to Chaucer Studies*. Rev. ed. Toronto: Oxford Univ. Press, 1979.

Ruggiers, Paul G. *Editing Chaucer: The Great Tradition*. Norman, Okla.: Pilgrim, 1981.

Russell, Jeffrey B. *Lucifer: The Devil in the Middle Ages*. Ithaca, N.Y.: Cornell Univ. Press, 1984.

Scattergood, V. J., and J. W. Sherborne, eds. *English Court Culture in the Later Middle Ages*. With an introduction by J. A. Burrow. New York: St. Martin's, 1983.

Schrader, Richard J. *God's Handiwork: Images of Women in Early Germanic Literature*. Westport, Conn.: Greenwood, 1983.

Scribanoff, Susan. "Taking the Gold out of Egypt: The Art of Reading as a Woman." In Elizabeth A. Flynn and Patrocinio P. Schweikert, eds., *Gender and Reading: Essays on Readers, Texts, and Contexts*. Baltimore: Johns Hopkins Univ. Press, 1986.

Shoaf, R. A. *Dante, Chaucer, and the Currency of the Word: Money, Images, and Reference in Late Medieval Poetry*. Norman, Okla.: Pilgrim, 1983.

————. *The Poem as Green Girdle: Commercium in Sir Gawain and the Green Knight*. Gainesville: Univ. Press of Florida, 1984.

Skeat, Walter William, ed. *Aelfric's Lives of Saints*. Early English Text Society, vols. 76, 82, 94, 114. London: N. Trübner, 1881–1900.

Stafford, Pauline. *Queens, Concubines and Dowagers: The King's Wife in the Early Middle Ages*. Athens: Univ. of Georgia Press, 1983.

Stenton, F. M. *Anglo-Saxon England*. 3d ed. Oxford: Clarendon, 1971.

Sweet, Henry, ed. *King Alfred's Orosius*. Early English Text Society, vol. 79. London: N. Trübner, 1883.

Szarmach, Paul E., ed. *Sources of Anglo-Saxon Culture*. Kalamazoo, Mich.: Medieval Institute of Western Michigan Univ. 1986.

Theiner, Paul. "Robertsonianism and the Idea of Literary History." *Studies in Medieval Culture* 6/7 (1976): 207–16.

Utley, Francis L. "Robertsonianism Redivivus." *Romance Philology* 19 (1965): 250–60.

Vance, Eugene. "Mervelous Signals: Poetics, Sign Theory, and Politics in Chaucer's *Troilus*." *New Literary History* 10 (1979): 292–337.

A Variorum Edition of the Works of Geoffrey Chaucer. Norman: Univ. of Oklahoma Press, 1979–.

Wasserman, Julian N., and Robert J. Blanch, eds. *Chaucer in the Eighties*. Syracuse: Syracuse Univ. Press, 1986.

Wetherbee, Winthrop P. *Chaucer and the Poets: An Essay on Troilus and Criseyde.* Ithaca, N.Y.: Cornell Univ. Press, 1984.

Whitelock, Dorothy, ed. *Sermo Lupi ad Anglos.* 3d ed. New York: Appleton-Century-Crofts, 1966.

Woods, J. Douglas, and David A. E. Pelteret, eds. *The Anglo-Saxons: Synthesis and Achievement.* Waterloo, Ont.: Wilfrid Laurier Univ. Press, 1985.

Wrenn, Charles Leslie, ed. *Beowulf, with the Finnesburg Fragment.* 3d ed., fully revised by Whitney F. Bolton. London: Harrap, 1973.

————. "On the Continuity of Old English Poetry." *Anglia* 76 (1958): 41–59.

Zacher, Christian K. *Curiosity and Pilgrimage: The Literature of Discovery in Fourteenth-Century England.* Baltimore: Johns Hopkins Univ. Press, 1976.

ल्ॐ 9 लॐ

Latin Philosophies of the Middle Ages

EDWARD A. SYNAN

HREE COMMUNITIES, distinguished by their faiths, cultivated philosophy during the middle ages in western Europe: Jewish,
Christian, and Islamic. Thanks to the erudition of the Greek
Fathers of the Church and to the relative stability of the Roman Empire
in the east, Greek-speaking oriental Christians preserved a philosophical
tradition without a break from antiquity until the end of the Middle Ages.
When Constantinople fell to Islamic armies in A.D. 1453, Byzantine refu-
gees to the West were ready to supply their hosts with the texts of ancient
Greek philosophy, in particular, with all the Dialogues of Plato, as well
as with instruction in their language. Both were received with an enthusiasm that bears witness to how little influence of a direct sort had been
exerted by those sources on Latin-speaking scholars. In contrast, key works
of Augustine and of Aquinas had been translated into Greek during the
thirteenth and fourteenth centuries (cf. Valoriani and Rackl).

The fact that the three philosophizing communities were specified by
their respective faiths establishes a truth so important that it can hardly
be exaggerated. Synagogue, church, and mosque produced sages who
thought the philosophical traditions of Greece and Rome both precious
and incomplete; despite passionate opposition in all three camps, scholars
were eager not only to recover or to preserve the accomplishments of ancient pagan philosophy, but also to correct and to extend that wisdom.

Jewish and Islamic philosophers, for reasons that are both cultural
and geographical, were often in advance of Latin Christians in this enter-

314

prise. Philo (ca. 20 B.C.–ca. A.D. 50) was an Alexandrian Jew who is credited with having made the first attempt to coordinate Scripture and Greek philosophy within a single rational theology (cf. Wolfson). Saadia Gaon (fl. tenth century A.D.) combined Jewish faith with an expurgated Platonism and Aristotelianism; the Jewish poet, Judah ha-Levi (A.D. 1080–1140) used the resources of philosophy to impugn what he counted the pretensions of philosophers.

Philosophy's role in Islam was contested bitterly during the eleventh Christian century by "Asharite" theologians, but thanks to Muslim initiatives, Greek philosophical materials began to appear first in Latin translations of Arabic versions, not directly from Greek. This was the principal channel for the works of Aristotle, except for the *Categories* and *On Interpretation,* which had long been known through versions by Boethius, to reach Latin scholars. Only later were translations made directly from Greek originals, a project in which the great names are those of Robert Grosseteste (ca. 1175–1253) and the Dominican, William of Moerbeke (ca. 1215–1286).

Jewish authors habitually wrote their philosophical works in Arabic rather than in Hebrew, and this misled their Christian readers as to their identity. Solomon Ibn Gabirol (ca. 1020–ca. 1050), the "Avicebron" or "Avicembrol" of the Latins, was thought by William of Auvergne (ca. 1180–1249) to have been an Arab from the period before Mohammed and thus to have been a Christian; Giordano Bruno (ca. 1548–1600) judged him to have been a Muslim. Gabirol was correctly identified as a Jew only in the nineteenth century by Solomon Munk. Throughout the Middle Ages, Gabirol's influential *Fons vitae* was generally taken to have been a Muslim contribution; it was widely cited to buttress two philosophical positions: universal hylomorphism and the plurality of substantial forms. The well-known *Guide for the Perplexed* by Rabbi Moses ben Maimon (1135–1204) and the little-known *Duties of Hearts* by Baḥya Ibn Paḳuda (fl. 1050–1100), although written in Arabic, were recognized as Jewish works. Conflicts within Islam over the role of philosophy engaged notable Muslim scholars on both sides: Al-Kindi (d. 875) and Al-Farabi (ca. 870–ca. 950) supported the use of philosophy, but Al-Ashari (873–935) and Al-Ghazzali (1058–1111) opposed it. The most important of all Islamic writers in the eyes of the Latins were Ibn Sina, "Avicenna" (980–1037), and Ibn Rushd, "Averroës" (1126–98), this last given the honorific title "the Commentator" in recognition of his magistral phrase-by-phrase commentaries on the difficult texts of Aristotle. Both Avicenna and Averroës exercised significant influence on Christian thinkers, Thomas Aquinas (ca. 1225–74) and John Duns Scotus (ca. 1266–1308) included.

Muslim arguments against philosophy were known in the Latin world through the works of scholars who supported philosophy. Moses ben Maimon reported and decried Asharite "occasionalism" in his *Guide,* and Averroës answered Al-Ghazzali's *Incoherence of Philosophy* with an *Incoherence of the Incoherence* and, more positively, with his *Harmony* (cf. Hourani). Peter Abelard (1079–1142) illumined this enduring medieval crisis by representing a Jew, a Muslim philosopher, and a Christian in debate on the ultimate goal of human existence, the summum bonum, with himself as referee (cf. Thomas; Payer). The Jew had his Hebrew Scriptures, the Christian both the Old and the New Testaments, whereas the Muslim had no resource but human reason: he was austerely "philosophical."

Some of this is echoed in medieval literature. Dante was persuaded that he knew exactly where to locate, in the world to come, "Aristotle, the Master of those who know" and "Averroës, who made the great Commentary." Chaucer was following King Alfred and anticipating Queen Elizabeth I when he translated some texts of the philosophizing Christian, Boethius (ca. 480–524), from Latin into English; Boethius counted as a major "authority" for Christian writers throughout and beyond the Middle Ages (cf. Patch). A king of Cyprus received from Brother Thomas Aquinas advice suitable for a Latin monarch who was organizing a new kingdom in a crusading age; the advice was thoroughly Christian, but permeated with Aristotelian political conceptions (cf. Phelan-Eschmann). A grasp of medieval philosophizing is thus an important auxiliary for those who wish to master the literature or the political life of medieval culture in the west.

Here will be set out briefly the course that research into medieval philosophy has taken; second, the situation within which that research proceeds at present will be examined; last, some desiderata will be noted.

Medieval academics generally provided only the most opaque testimony to what contemporaries were doing, the identity of friends and foes alike masked by the phrase "certain ones say" (*quidam dicunt*). A rare exception is the twelfth-century English humanist, John of Salisbury (ca. 1115–80), with his reliable, eye-witness accounts of debates on a number of philosophical issues in the Parisian schools (cf. Webb). Somewhat later Godfrey of Saint-Victor (ca. 1130, d. after 1194) reported on the same milieu in his *Fons philosophiae* (cf. Michaud-Quantin; Synan), but his verses are intended to amuse rather than to inform. For medieval scholars the "history of philosophy" was the history of ancient philosophy, an enterprise for which they possessed neither the documentation nor the necessary techniques. The paradigmatic instance is Walter Burley's (ca. 1275–after 1344) *On the Life and the Way of Life of Ancient Philosophers and Poets,* an anecdotal collage in the tradition of, and likely in dependence upon, the *Speculum doctrinale* by Vincent of Beauvais (ca. 1190-1264). The use of philosophy of pagan origins by theologians was defended by Thomas Aquinas in his study on the *De trinitate* of Boethius (2, 3, To 5; cf. Maurer, 50) by evoking the gospel miracle at Cana (John 2:1-11): the "water of philosophy" is changed into the "wine of theology." His contemporary, Bonaventure (ca. 1220-74), retorted in *Conferences on the Hexaemeron* (3, 7), by reversing this image: the "wine of theology" ought not to be diluted with the "water of philosophy." Despite Bonaventure's opposition (and he spoke for an influential block) most medieval philosophical materials are to be found in the theologians' writing, his own by no means excluded. Still, there is notable work by "arts masters" that is free from theological overtones, especially by Siger of Brabant (ca. 1235-ca. 82) and by four Danish *artistae:* John, Simon, Martin, and Boethius, all "of Dacia" (cf. editions under these names). Their urbane analyses and developments of Aristotelian grammatical, logical, and epistemological problems announce future advances (cf. *Cambridge History of Later Medieval Philosophy*).

A deluge of mainly "peripatetic" works, for the first time in Latin translation, nourished a new philosophical problematic from the mid-twelfth century forward to replace the Platonic-Plotinian dominance which the prestige of Augustine had imposed upon philosophical activity in the West. This led inevitably to new analyses of sensation and of abstractive knowledge, to a new interest in the life sciences, and to a major development of ethical and political theory as well as to a fresh conception of the science of nature in general and, finally, to metaphysics as a science of being precisely "as being." That these had their common source in Aristotle (cf. *Aristoteles latinus*) did not entail a monolithic philosophy on the part of medievals. Not only was there a rear guard of ultimately Platonist inspiration but fighting under the standard of Augustine; Aristotle's conceptions and terminology were the inspiration of diametrically opposed positions, all of them documented from his works. The Cistercian Alan of Lille (ca. 1128-1203) remarked on this practice that "Authority has a nose of wax: It can be twisted in different directions" (*On Catholic Faith* 1:30; *PL* 210.333).

All of these characteristics of medieval philosophizing have contributed to the difficulty researchers encounter in attempting to recover the results of those centuries-long struggles to understand ourselves and our world. The invention of printing did less than might have been expected to make the philosophies of the period available. Although a dramatically widened channel of transmission, printing functioned also as an effective censorship. Erudite printer-editors decided which books ought to be printed; market demand and their own humanism dictated their decisions. One value of Hain's *Catalogus* is its dispassionate witness to which medieval authors seemed worth printing before A.D. 1500. The Christian authors are theologians who used the "water" of philosophy; not unexpectedly, Thomas Aquinas leads with 215 editions, Augustine followed with 168 printings, Bonaventure received 113, Boethius 78; Albert the Great was given 45, John Duns Scotus 41, Giles of Rome 37, Ockham 18, Alexander of Hales 4, and John of Salisbury 1. Avicenna was more widely esteemed than Averroës: The first had 25 printings and the second only 4.

As for the anti-scholastic bias of the humanists, among whom the editor-printers functioned as unofficial censors, for in an age of printed books, manuscripts could not survive, most humanists depised most scholastics. There were, however, some signal exceptions. Marsiglio Ficino (1433–99) was in important ways a Thomist (cf. Collins) and Pico della Mirandola (1463–94) made good use of Henry of Ghent (d. 1293) despite his dedication to humanist ideals (cf. Dulles). No scholastic discipline was more despised by devotees of the "good literature" of antiquity than was medieval logic. To humanists, that logic seemed unnecessarily complex, barbarous in expression, and fatuous in its concerns. Peter Ramus (1515–72) rejected the medieval heritage in logic and offered in its place a new and simpler logic that he felt would be better suited to the aspirations of his time; in ours that logic is little more than a curiosity (cf. de la Ramée; Ong). John of Saint Thomas (1589–1644) composed an immense scholastic *Logica* that is now receiving renewed attention.

Until a certain "Protestant scholasticism" (cf. Petersen, Armstrong, Beardslee, Ritschl) attended the imperfect religious settlements within seventeenth-century Christendom, scholastic philosophy faced a credally grounded opposition from the reformers as well as the culturally inspired opposition from the humanists, Catholic and Protestant alike. Apart from such resistance to philosophy as cultivated during the Middle Ages, there was the perennial reluctance of those named by Gilson "the Tertullian family" (cf. Gilson, *Reason and Revelation,* 10) who were anxious lest they be deceived "through philosophy and empty fallacy" (Col. 2:8) in the words of the Apostle.

In any case, philosophical minds of the first order, F. Bacon (1561–1626), R. Descartes (1596–1650), B. Spinoza (1632–77), J. Locke (1632–1714), G. Berkeley (1685–1753), and D. Hume (1711–76), for all their diversity, were at one in aspiring to new philosophical beginnings; the medieval past, they were persuaded, had little to say to them. The extensive learning of G. W. Leibniz (1646–1716) included a serious knowledge of scholasticism, but it would be fatuous to ignore how little the expositor of monads and of the logical calculus had in common with "the usual scholastic philosophy" from which Leibniz felt he had "liberated" himself.

Scholasticism perdured within seventeenth-century universities if not outside them (cf. Costello) and historical surveys that included medieval philosophy were composed, especially by German university professors, during the seventeenth and eighteenth centuries; these would provide a grounding for the great nineteenth-century pioneer historians of medieval philosophy, notably Cousin and Hauréau who are discussed below. Here and there a medieval philosophical work maintained itself: Ockham's *Summa totius logicae* was reprinted at Oxford in 1665, and there is reason to think that Hume knew some Ockhamist positions; in 1616, a collection of significant texts by Abelard was printed in Paris (cf. Amboise).

In another direction, foundations for modern research in medieval philosophy were laid by J. Mabillon (1632–1707); this Benedictine renewed and rendered scientific the disciplines of paleography and diplomatics in order to meet challenges posed to the traditions of his order by the Jesuit "Bollandists," chief among them J. Bolland (1596–1665) and D. Papebroch (1628–1714); Mabillon's fellow Benedictines in the Congregation of Saint Maur, the "Maurists," issued texts of Church Fathers and of medieval Christian writers in imposing quantity and of high quality (cf. Shook). The Maurists were responsible for the first twelve volumes of the *Histoire littéraire de la France*. In Italy, L. A. Muratori (1672–1750) separated historical wheat from legendary chaff, notably in his *Rerum Italicarum scriptores*. Members of the nobility, or prospering members of the middle class climbing into the ranks of the aristocracy, were concerned with the medieval history of the caste to which they belonged or aspired to join. Knighthood, Gothic architecture, and troubadours captured their attention (cf. Gossman). Clerics appealed to history in the ecclesiological controversies that raged around the *Augustinus* of C. O. Jansen (1585–1638).

Although these interests did not include medieval philosophy, they did forward the development of historiographical techniques, and their accumulation of materials made the recovery of some medieval philosophy possible for later generations. In addition to the survival of medieval speculation within Catholic religious houses, the formidable medieval erudition of Francesco Suarez, S.J. (1548–1617) had its repercussions on a whole series of influential Protestant philosophers: G. W. Leibniz (already mentioned), C. Wolff (1679–1754), and A. G. Baumgarten (1714–62). This was the tradition that formed the pre-critical Immanuel Kant (1724–1804); its dogmas naturally form the prime target of the "critical philosophy" of Kant's maturity.

There was to be a revival of medieval philosophy and, although there were many motives for it, none of them was specifically philosophical in character. One major impulse was the hope of protecting the moral and political welfare of the human community. On the eve of the French Revolution, the Archbishop and Count of Lyons, Antoine de Malvin de Montazet (1712–88) provided a preface for a manual of philosophy he had commissioned for the use of both lay students and seminarians in his diocese; in excellent humanist Latin, he explained why he had done so:

> For what is more necessary in these baleful times (*luctuosis his temporibus*) than to make provision "lest anyone deceive" our unwary youth "through philosophy and empty fallacy" (Col. 2:8); this assumes every form, uses all the allurements of pleasure and of talent, in order that, like a thief, it might insinuate itself into our minds. Everywhere there has burgeoned a sorry crop of sophists who, clubbing together their resources, have determined on this: That they would destroy all principles of faith and morals. . . . (Cf. *Institutiones philosophicae.*)

The Archbishop-Count needed a philosophy suitable for members of a Christian society under a threat he by no means exaggerated, for he wrote in 1782, just a decade before the Terror. A comparable concern on the part of Pope Leo XIII (b. 1810, Pope 1878–1903) would inspire his more successful revival of medieval thought as will be seen.

When the revolution and the Napoleonic aftermath had run their course, no region of Europe had suffered more than had the Germanies in those upheavals. Only four years after Waterloo, however, the "Society for Opening the Sources of German Mediaeval History" was inaugurated at Frankfort with the support of the Kaiser of Austria, kings, princes, and the free cities of Germany. By 1826, the first folio volume of the *Monumenta Germaniae Historica* came from the press, and the series continues to this day. Many a document published in the *Monumenta* contributes to our study of medieval philosophy, but the intention of its founders was to recover evidence of the epic German past.

Although France had provided the focal point for the revolutions that swept away the remnants of feudal institutions all over Europe, Frenchmen remained conscious of a patriotic stake in exploiting a medieval heritage of which philosophy was no small part. France produced brilliant pioneers in the scientific study of the history of medieval philosophy: V. Cousin (1792–1867), J. M. Gerando (1772–1842), and C. de Remusat (1797–1875). Cousin played a major role in establishing two currents of scholarship: the edition of original texts from manuscript and the interpretation of philosophical movements. in 1826 Cousin produced his *Fragments philosophiques* and in 1828 conducted a course in the history of philosophy; medieval philosophy was a feature of both. His Abelard edition was, in his own words, "a task at once patriotic and philosophical" (cf. Cousin, *Ouvrages inédits*, vi), "patriotic" because "scholasticism belongs to France" (ibid., i). Nowhere is the French conviction that medieval philosophy was a French affair any clearer than it is in the terms set down in 1845 by the "Academy for Moral and Political Sciences" to guide contestants in a competition for the best "critical examination of scholastic philosophy" (cf. Hauréau, *De la philosophie, i,* ii). These limited the field to France, especially to the University of Paris, and urged contestants to stay as far from theology as "the intimate bond" between that discipline and philosophy in the Middle Ages would permit. Barthélemy Hauréau won the competition in 1848 with the text of a book that was published in 1850, two volumes under the title *De la philosophie scolastique,* and expanded by 1872 as three volumes with a new title: *Histoire de la philosophie scolastique.* Hauréau had predecessors, whom he cited in his 1848 effort with disconcerting brevity. Those trailbreakers deserve the full citation provided below in the bibliography. Like Cousin, Hauréau from the beginning included transcriptions of texts from manuscript and was to become a curator who could produce a six-volume *Notices et extraits de quelques manuscrits latins de la bibliothèque nationale,* as well as a handwritten index: *Initia operum scriptorum latinorum medii potissimum aevi ex codicibus manuscriptis et libris impressis alphabetice digessit B.H.* in eight volumes.

Cousin and Hauréau set the lines along which work in the philosophy of the Middle Ages has since proceeded, the recovery and interpretation of texts. While philosophy is not theology, theological goals continued to stimulate work in philosophy, not always to the satisfaction of the official Church. F. R. de Lamennais (1782–1845) made extravagant claims for the papacy, but died outside the Church; L. Bautain (1796–1867) was thought to have exalted faith at the expense of reason and was repeatedly asked to sign statements of his orthodoxy; A. Bonnety (1798–1879) edited the *Annales de la philosophie chrétienne,* but was required to answer inquiries on his evaluation of Bonaventure and Thomas Aquinas.

In contrast to these scholars who were considered to have diminished philosophical reason were others who were adjudged to subordinate faith to reason; thus, G. Hermes (1775–1831), A. Günther (1783–1863), G. C. Ubaghs (1800–75), and even A. Rosmini-Serbati (1797–1855) were all considered to have introduced philosophical positions incompatible with faith. The atmosphere in the mid-century, when religious figures were searching for a philosophical ground in an atmosphere that was daily more hostile is vividly conveyed by the words of I.-M. Crémieux (1796–1880) in the Chamber of Deputies at Paris after a Bishop had impugned the secularized University:

> The honorable member who has spoken last now accuses the generation reared by the University of corrupting France and of having prepared the "Days of 1848." I beg him to tell the Chamber by whom was the generation reared that corrupted the 18th century and produced '93? This University did not then exist; there was no "monopoly" then, or if there was one, it was in favor of the clergy . . . the generation that went forth from your hands produced '93! If this University does no better than you did, she will never do worse. Leave off accusing her; the anathemas you hurl at her fall first upon yourselves! (Cf. *Annales de philosophie chrétienne* [1871], 365.)

Against this background some philosophy professors began to hope that society might be renewed through recourse to medieval thought, above all to that of Aquinas. Their movement was to generate a major revival of interest in the philosophy (and theology) of the Middle Ages. One such professor was Joseph Pecci (1807–90), whose brother Joachim (1810–1903) was to become Pope Leo XIII, and his encyclical letter, *Aeterni Patris,* was to signal the birth of a medieval and Thomist revival. The Pope founded the "Leonine Commission" and charged it with the edition of the works of Aquinas in an ambitious format. This project still continues and the volumes of the last few decades are notable for their impeccable scholarship. In another direction, Pope Leo supported the work of D. Mercier (1851–1926) at the Catholic University of Louvain (Leuven) where serious efforts were made by Mercier to correlate medieval speculation with the science of our time. Meanwhile, on a less ambitious scale, the Leonine revival promoted the publication of the *Opera omnia* of a number of medieval figures: Aquinas, Albert the Great, Bonaventure, Duns Scotus, Peter Lombard, and Alexander of Hales. Most of these are reprints of earlier editions, but in the cases of Scotus, Albert, and lately, William of Ockham along with figures from his circle, new editions are appearing worthy to take their place beside the Leonine edition of Aquinas.

Parallel to the publishing of texts is the steady growth in the number of learned journals devoted, at least in part, to medieval philosophy. The *Revue néoscolastique* (1 [1894]: 8) could already cite the *Accademia Romana di San Tommaso, Divus Thomas* (Piacenza), *Annales de philosophie chrétienne, Jahrbuch für Philosophie und speculative Theologie, Philosophisches Jahrbuch, Revue Thomiste,* and the *Archiv für Geschichte der*

Philosophie. To these, the twentieth century has added the *Archivum Franciscanum Historicum* (1908), *La Ciencia Tomista* (1910), another *Divus Thomas* (1914), formerly published at Vienna and Berlin, and since 1923 at Freiburg, Switzerland (in 1969 this was replaced by the *Rassegna di Letteratura Tomistica*), the *Angelicum* (1924), *The Modern Schoolman* (1925), *Archives d'histoire doctrinale et littéraire du moyen âge* (1926), *Scholastik* (1926), *The New Scholasticism* (1927), *Archivum Fratrum Praedicatorum* (1930), *The Thomist* (1939), *Tijdschrift voor Filosofie* (1939), *Aquinas* (1958), and *Vivarium* (1963). To these may be added the *Bibliothèque de l'école des chartes* (1839), *Analecta Bollandiana* (1882) and the *Revue Bénédictine* (1884).

The eight decades that intervened between *Aeterni Patris* and the Second Vatican Council (1962–65) can be understood within the Catholic Church as an epoch of "Leonine Thomism." By 1925 cis-Atlantic medievalists founded the Medieval Academy of America and the next year their journal, *Speculum*. G. B. Phelan (1892–1965), a Louvain graduate, and E. Gilson (1884–1978) helped in founding the Institute of Mediaeval Studies at Toronto in 1929; in 1939 this became the Pontifical Institute and began publication of its annual, *Mediaeval Studies*. The Institut Saint Thomas d'Aquin, founded at Ottawa, has become the Institut d'études médiévales at the University of Montreal. J. Maritain (1882–1973) lectured on the Toronto staff.

Exceptions to this prevalence of Catholic scholars and institutions are striking. In 1939 Bertrand Russell found the staff of the University of Chicago "incredibly learned, especially as regards medieval philosophy," and he thought he had observed an attempt by R. M. Hutchins, no Catholic, "to force neo-Thomism on the philosophical faculty" there (cf. Russell, *Autobiography* 2:246).

Required courses in philosophy at Church-related Catholic colleges and universities made the study of medieval philosophy a programmed mass movement. Many experienced this as a servitude to obsolete norms and as a source of alienation from the present. A resentment, previously all but unexpressed, burst suddenly on the Second Vatican Council's 123d General Congregation on November 16, 1964. From that date forward, access to medieval philosophy ceased to be an objective of general educational policy in Catholic institutions and became instead a research interest in a new intellectual context. The intrinsic value of the great medieval masters, to name a few, Scotus, Abelard, Bonaventure, Ockham, Aquinas, Walter Burley, guarantees their survival outside the setting of imposed academic programs.

A constant in our access to medieval philosophy is that the thing can be done only through the application of historical techniques. Yet research in the philosophy of any period is not merely historical work. It would be unpardonably simplistic to claim that the historical concerns of such scholars as Mandonnet, Grabmann, Gilson, Chenu, Pegis, and Bourke, have entailed doctrinal renunciations on their part. "Scotism" or "Thomism" existed in the intellects of Duns and Aquinas, temporally and culturally conditioned, advancing in identifiable stages from first promise to maturity. If we are to profit from their views on reality, we must submit to the norms of historical exegesis. The center of gravity may well be located where the research worker chooses. He is free to do philosophy, so to speak, in the mode of history or history in the mode of philosophy; he can renounce completely neither discipline.

Like every activity in our time, medieval studies, philosophy included, has been modified seriously by technological developments. Conspicuous among these for a long time has been photography, especially in the form of microfilming, which has made useful access to European manuscript collections relatively cheap and easy. In addition to the microfilming of limited selections of material, the Pius XII Library at Saint Louis University has undertaken the photographing of whole sections of the Vatican Library. An effort begun in 1964 by Saint John's University (Collegeville, Minn.) to record on film monastic holdings has amassed a formidable collection of manuscripts, starting with those of Austrian monasteries; the Medieval Institute of the University of Notre Dame has microfilmed the holdings of the Cathedral Chapter of Monza and of the Ambrosiana at Milan.

For scholars whose principal competence is in fields other than philosophy, a reliable survey of the period remains an invaluable guide. E. Gilson's *History of Christian Philosophy in the Middle Ages* supports an illuminating account with an astonishingly extensive documentation; from its first appearance in 1863–68 the *Grundriss der Geschichte der Philosophie von Thales auf bis die Gegenwart* by R. Ueberweg has been kept abreast of current research by a series of editors, M. Heinze, K. Praechter, and for the medieval volume, B. Geyer. A. A. Maurer has provided a shorter survey that is eminently suitable for teaching. Only a medieval Latin version can reveal to our time how the Greek philosophers appeared to their medieval readers. Hence, the "Latin Aristotle" (*Aristoteles latinus*), begun in 1939 and still appearing, as well as medieval Latin versions of the few Dialogues of Plato known to the Middle Ages, *Timaeus, Meno,* and *Phaedo,* are indispensable. The *Corpus Platonicum Medii Aevi* is providing critical editions of the medieval corpus. Meanwhile, a general bibliography of philosophical publications pertaining to all periods, begun by the editors of the *Revue néoscolastique de philosophie* (from 1946, *Revue philosophique de Louvain*) as a quarterly supplement, has become an annual volume, entitled the *Répertoire bibliographique de philosophie* since 1949. This invaluable research instrument monitors all important journals and provides a cross-indexed listing of books, articles, and even of book reviews. Augustine and Aquinas by their importance and by their extensive literary production have required and received special attention. For Augustine, two publications are proceeding to supplant those of the past (Dekkers, *Clavis;* Van Bavel, *Répertoire bibliographique;* Sciacca, *Augustinus;* Nebreda, *Bibliographia Augustiniana*); these are the *Augustine Bibliography / Fichier Augustinienne* and a *Catalogus verborum.* For Aquinas, works by Mandonnet, Destrez, Grabmann, Bourke, and Eschmann on bibliography are now supplemented by a series of concordances that have recorded by computer every word within the clause or sentence in which it occurs, a massive (fifty-volume) publication by R. Busa with the collaboration of IBM.

Finally, many pressing desiderata offer scope to researchers in medieval philosophy. One such area is formal logic, for in medieval universities this discipline presided over the methodology of all other disciplines. Carried on in "natural language," owing to an inadequate calculus, the logical discourse of the scholastics was repugnant to humanist sensibilities and largely lost. It is heartening to note that this basic discipline is now being recovered, and experts in the logic of our time, without relinquishing modern advances, have no small respect for the subtle and ingenious constructions of the Middle Ages in logic (cf. *The Cambridge History of Later Medieval Philosophy*).

A second such area is that of the philosophical analysis of language. If Wittgenstein thought Augustine's treatment of language too narrowly based upon the way in which the Bishop of Hippo thought we learn the use of nouns (cf. Wittgenstein, *Philosophical Investigations,* 2) he could hardly have urged the same stricture against the *modistae* of the thirteenth century. Noam Chomsky's work (cf. *Cartesian Linguistics*) evokes the innate ideas ambiguously defended by Descartes, but the premier medievalist of our time, E. Gilson, became a medievalist and a Thomist in the course of investigating the medieval sources of Descartes.

A third area in which we have a right to ask for the collaboration of medievalists is that of ethics and politics. A society that has produced two world wars with only nineteen years between them, nuclear weapons, and abortion on demand, manifests an understandable interest in the possibility that medieval "natural law" theories may yet be viable, a project on which natural law philosophers are currently debating in rigorous terms: Veatch,

Hittinger, Schultz, Grisez, Finnis, Boyle. The *Natural Law Forum* published by the Law School of the University of Notre Dame offers an illustration of how ethical dialogue with thinkers of the Middle Ages can interest men and women of our time. A tradition as old at least as Plato and Aristotle makes political theory the natural prolongation of ethics. A certain austerity of motive must be added to an eagerness in responding to these challenges. In the end, scholarship is a human activity, answerable to the medieval ideal of "upright reason" as the work of people whose freedom is totally grounded in their rationality and so subject to moral evaluation. The goal of research in the philosophy of the Middle Ages can only be to recover with precision and to interpret with fidelity the wealth that medieval thinkers have bequeathed to their posterity, which is our world.

BIBLIOGRAPHY

Instruments of Research: General

Bulletin de théologie ancienne et médiévale I. Louvain: Abbaye de César, 1929–32. This useful bibliographical survey, although explicitly theological, includes material for research in medieval philosophy; it has grown out of the *Recherches de théologie ancienne et médiévale,* published under the same auspices since 1929.

Répertoire bibliographique de philosophie. Louvain: Société philosophique de Louvain, 1949–. Publié sous les auspices de l'Institut International de Philosophie avec le patronage de l'UNESCO, 2 février 1949. This annual, extremely full survey continues the *Répertoire bibliographique,* formerly published as a supplement to the *Revue néoscolastique de philosophie* from 1934 and, from 1946, to the successor of that journal, the *Revue philosophique de Louvain.*

Augustine

Bibliographica Augustiniana, seu operum collectio quae divi Augustini vitam et doctrinam quadantenus exponunt. E. Nebreda. Rome: Cuore di Maria, 1928.
Concordantiae Avgvstinianae . . . Edited by F. David Lenfant. Paris: S & G. Crumoisy, 1656–65. Vol. 1, 1656; vol. 2, 1665.
Catalogus verborum, Corpus Christianorum. Eindhoven; Pays-bas. Vol. 1 (1976), *In evangelium Ioannis,* #36; vol. 2 (1978), *Enarrationes in psalmos 1–50,* #38; vol. 3 (1980), *Enarrationes in psalmos 51–100,* #39; vol. 4 (1981), *Enarrationes in psalmos 101–150,* #40; vol. 5 (1981), *De trinitate,* #50, 50A; vol. 6 (1982),

Confessionum XIII, #27; vol 7 (1984), *De civitate dei,* #47, 48; vol. 8 (1985), *Sermones de vetere testamento,* #41; vol. 9 (1987), *Quaestiones Hept., Locutiones Hept., 8 Quaestiones ex vetere testamento,* #33.
Clavis patrum latinorum. 2d ed. Bruges: C. Beyaert, 1961.
Répertoire bibliographique de saint Augustin, 1950–1960. T. Van Bavel and F. Van Der Zande. The Hague: M. Nijhoff; Steenbruges: Abbatia sancti Petri, 1963.

Thomas Aquinas

Bulletin Thomiste 1. Montreal: Institut d'études médiévales, 1924. Since 1965 replaced by *Rassegna di Letteratura Tomistica.* Naples: Edizioni Domenicane Italiane, 1969–.
Bibliographie Thomiste. P. Mandonnet and J. Destrez. Le Saulchoir: Bibliothéque Thomiste 1, 1921–.
Thomistic Bibliography, 1920–1940. V. J. Bourke. *The Modern Schoolman,* vol. 21. St. Louis: *The Modern Schoolman,* 1945.
Index Thomisticus. Sancti Thomae Aquinatis operum omnium indices et concordantiae . . . electronico IBM automato usus digessit Robertus Busa. Stuttgart: Fromman-Holzboog, 1974–80. 49 volumes. Completed by a *Clavis indicis.*
"A Catalogue of St. Thomas's Works: Bibliographical Notes." I. T. Eschmann. E. Gilson, *The Christian Philosophy of St. Thomas Aquinas.* Translated by L. K. Shook. New York: Random House, 1956. A lightly modified version of this "Catalogue" is to be found in J. A. Weisheipl, *Friar Thomas d'Aquino,* 355–405. Garden City, N.Y.: Doubleday, 1974.
Die Werke des Hl. Thomas von Aquin. M. Grabmann. *Beiträge zur Geschichte der Philosophie und Theologie des Mittelalters,* vol. 22, pts. 1–2. Texte und Untersuchungen. Münster: Aschendorf, 1931. XXII, Heft 1-2.

Collections

Patrologiae cursus completus. Series latina. 221 vols. Edited by J. P. Migne. Paris: J. P. Migne, 1844–55. Many subsequent reprints. A *Supplementum,* edited by A. Hamman, includes corrections and critical notes. Paris: Garnier, 1958. An indispensable control is P. Glorieux, *Pour revaloriser Migne* (Cahier supplémentaire of *Mélanges de science réligieuse* for 1952), on the authenticity of Migne texts. Lille: Facultés catholiques, 1952.
Corpus christianorum. Series latina. Turnhout: Brepols, 1954–. Editions are "critical" and not restricted to the patristic period.
Corpus scriptorum ecclesiasticorum latinorum. Vienna: Imperial Austrian Academy, 1866. Subsequent volumes have been published at Leipzig and Prague, as well as at Vienna. Editions are "critical" and accompanied by valuable introductions and indices. Referred to informally as "the Vienna *Corpus.*"

Greek Philosophy in the Middle Ages

Corpus Platonicum Medii Aevi. Edited by R. Klibansky. London: Warburg Insti-
tute, 1940–62. Vol. 1 (1940), *Meno,* Henrico Aristippo. Edited by V. Kordeuter
and C. Labowsky. Vol. 2 (1950), *Phaedo,* Henrico Aristippo. Edited by L.
Mineo-Paluello and H. J. Drossart Lulofs. Vol. 3 (1953), *Parmenides,* usque
ad finem primae hypothesis, necnon Procli, *Commentarium in Parmenidem.*
Intreprete Guillelmo de Moerbeka. Edited by R. Klibansky and C. Labowsky.
Vol. 4 (1962), *Timaeus.* A Calcido translatus Commentarioque instructus.
Edited by P. J. Jensen and J. H. Waszink.
Aristoteles latinus. Works by Aristotle, or works closely associated with his writings, form a section of the *Corpus Philosophorum Medii Aevi.* The first volumes describe the manuscript basis for the editions. *Pars prior.* G. Lacombe,
A. Birkenmajer, M. Dulong, Aet. Franceschini. Rome: La Libreria della Stato,
1939. *Pars posterior.* Cambridge: Cambridge Univ. Press, 1955. *Supplementa
altera.* Ed. L. Minio-Paluello. Bruges: Desclée de Brouwer, 1961. From 1957
fascicles have appeared and continue to appear; two mentioned in the text
are *Categoriae vel Praedicamenta.* Tr. Boethii, tr. composita G. de Moerbeka,
lemmata e Simplicii *Commento.* Ps-Augustini *Paraphrasis* Themistiana. Ed.
L. Minio-Paluello, 1961, and *De interpretatione vel Periermenias.* Tr. Boethii;
specimina tranlationum recentiorum. Ed. L. Mino-Paluello. Tr. G. de Moerbeka. Ed. G. Verbeke, 1965.

Medieval Authors

Abelard, Petrus. *PL* 178; also: F. Amboesius (Amboise), *Petri Abaelardi filosofi
et theologi abbatis Rvyensis . . . opera.* Paris: N. Bvon, 1616; V. Cousin,
Ouvrages inédits. Paris: Imprimerie Royale, 1836; modern edition of work
cited in text: R. Thomas, *Petrus Abaelardus. Dialogus inter Philosophum,
Iudaeum et Christianum.* Stuttgart: F. Frommau Verlag, 1970; and an English translation: P. Payer, *Peter Abelard. A Dialogue of a Philosopher with
a Jew, and a Christian.* Toronto: Pontifical Institute of Mediaeval Studies,
1979.
Albert the Great. *Opera omnia.* Edited by A. Borgnet. Paris: Vivès, 1890–99. 38
vols. *Opera omnia.* "Critical edition." Münster: Aschendorff, 1951–.
Alexander of Hales. *Quaestiones disputatae "antequam esset frater."* Quaracchi:
Collegium S. Bonaventurae, 1960; *Magistri Alexandri de Hales glossa in qua-
tuor libros Sententiarum Petri Lombardi.* Quaracchi: Collegium S. Bonaven-
turae, 1951; *Summa theologica.* Quaracchi: Collegium S. Bonaventurae, 1924.
Averroës. G. Hourani, *Averroës: On the Harmony of Religion and Philosophy.*
London: Luzac, 1961.
Boethius, Anicius Manlius. *PL* 63 and 64. For later, more critical editions, see *Cor-
pus christianorum* and Vienna *Corpus.*
Boethius of Dacia. *Boethii Daci opera.* Pt. 1. Edited by G. Sajō. Copenhagen:

G. E. C. Gad, 1972; *Tractatus de aeternitate mundi*. Edited by G. Sajō. Berlin: W. de Gruyter, 1964.

Bonaventure. *Opera omnia*. Quaracchi: Collegium S. Bonaventurae, 1882–1902. 10 vols. A manual edition of his *Sentence* commentary by the same publisher, 1934.

Duns (John Duns Scotus). *Doctoris subtilis, ordinis minorum opera omnia*. 26 vols. Paris: Vivès, 1891–95; *Ioannis Duns Scoti opera omnia*. Vatican City: Commissio Scotistica, 1950–.

Godfrey of Saint-Victor. *Fons philosophiae*. Edited by P. Michaud-Quantin. Namur-Louvain-Lille: Godenne, 1956. English trans. E. A. Synan, *The Fountain of Philosophy*. Toronto: Pontifical Institute of Mediaeval Studies, 1972.

Henry of Ghent. *Doctoris solemnis Magistri Henrici Goethals a Gandavo . . . disputationes quodlibeticae. . . .* Paris: J. B. Ascensio, 1518; *Summae quaestionum ordinariarum. . . .* Paris: J. Badius, 1520; *Magistri Henrici Goethals a Gandavo . . . Summa. . . .* Ferrara: F. Succius, 1646.

John of Dacia. *Joannis de Dacia: Opera*. Edited by A. Otto. 2 vols. Copenhagen: G. E. C. Gad, 1955.

John Duns Scotus (see Duns [John Duns Scotus] above).

John of Saint Thomas. *Ars logica seu de forma et materia ratiocinandi*. Edited by B. Reiser. Rome: Marietti, 1929.

John of Salisbury. *Opera omnia*. Edited by J. A. Giles. Oxford: J. H. Parker, 1848. Reprinted, Leipzig: Zentralantiquariat der Deutschen Demokratischen Republik, 1969; *Metalogicon libri III*. Edited by C. C. I. Webb. Oxford: Clarendon, 1929; English trans. D. D. McGarry. Berkeley: Univ. of California Press, 1955.

Martin of Dacia. *Martini de Dacia opera*. Edited by H. Roos. Copenhagen: G. E. C. Gad, 1961.

Philo. H. A. Wolfson, *Philo*. 2 vols. Cambridge, Mass.: Harvard Univ. Press, 1947.

Ramus. Pierre de la Ramée, *Dialecticae libri duo*. Frankfurt: J. Wechelum, 1588; *The Logike*. London: facsimile: Leeds: Scolar Press, 1574–1966; *The Logike of the Moste Excellent Philosopher P. Ramus Martyr*. Translated by R. MacIlmaine (1574). Edited by C. M. Dinn. Renaissance Editions, vol. 3. Northridge, Calif.: San Fernando Valley State College, 1969.

Siger of Brabant. "Die Impossibilia des Siger von Brabant, eine philosophische Streitschrift aus dem XIII Jahrhundert." Edited by C. Baeumker. In *Beiträge zur Geschichte der Philosophie des Mittelalters*, vol. 2, pt. 6. 1898; *De aeternitate mundi*. Edited by R. Barsotti. Münster: Aschendorff, 1933; *Questions sur la Physique d'Aristote*. Edited by P. Delhaye. Louvain: L'institut supérieur de philosopie, 1941; *Questions sur la métaphysique*. Edited by C. A. Graiff. Louvain: L'institut supérieur de philosophie, 1948; *Ein Kommentar zur Physik des Aristoteles aus der Pariser Artistenfakultät um 1273*. Edited by A. Zimmermann. Berlin: De Gruyter, 1968; *Quaestiones in Metaphysicam*. Edited by W. Dunphy. Louvain-la-neuve: L'institut supérieur de philosophie, 1981.

Simon of Dacia. *Simonis Daci opera*. Edited by A. Ottoe. Copenhagen: G. E. C. Gad. 1963.

Thomas Aquinas. *Opera omnia*. Rome: Commissio Leonina, 1882–. Marked by

valuable introductions, identification of sources, and thorough exploitation
of manuscript base in later volumes; for less impressive, but usable editions,
Opera omnia. Edited by S. Fretté. Paris: Vivēs, 1871–80, 34 vols. and Parma:
P. Fiaccadori, 1862–73, 25 vols.; for the *Summa theologiae* the best available
edition is Ottawa: Commissio Piana, 1953, 5 volumes; for English trans. of
his Commentary on questions 1–4 on the *De trinitate* of Boethius cited in text,
see A. Maurer, *St. Thomas Aquinas. Faith, Reason and Theology*, Toronto:
Pontifical Institute of Mediaeval Studies, 1987. The same translator has presented questions 5 and 6 of Aquinas on Boethius's *De trinitate* as *The Division and Methods of the Sciences*, under the same auspices, 1953; for a trans.
of the *De regno ad regem Cypri* cited in the text, see G. B. Phelan and I. Th.
Eschmann, *St. Thomas Aquinas On Kingship to the King of Cyprus*. Toronto:
Pontifical Institute of Mediaeval Studies, 1949.

Historians: Pioneers

Brucker, J. J. *Historia critica philosophiae a mundi incunabulis ad nostram usque
    aetatem deducta*. 6 vols. Leipzig: Weidemann, 1742–67.
Cousin, V. *Ouvrages inédits d'Abélard*. Paris: Imprimerie Royale, 1836.
Hauréau, B. *Notices et extraits de quelques manuscrits latins de la bibliothèque
    nationale*. Paris: Klincksieck, 1890–93. Still useful instrument.
———. *Initia operum scriptorum latinorum medii potissimum aevi ex codicibus
    manuscriptis et libris impressis alphabetice digessit B.H.* 8 vols. Turnhout:
    Brepols, n.d. Left unpublished by its author, now available in anastatic repro-
    duction from copy made for the Apostolic Vatican Library.
———. *De la philosophie scolastique*. 2 vols. Paris: Pagnerre, 1850. Revised as
    Histoire de la philosophie scolastique. 3 vols. Paris: Durandet Pedone-Lauriel,
    1872.
Rosenmüller, J. G. De christianae theologiae origine liber. Leipzig: Klaubarthia,
    1786.
Schmoelders, A. *Documenta philosophiae Arabum*. Paris: Firmin-Didot, 1842.
Tennemann, W. G. *Geschichte der Philosophie*. 11 vols. Leipzig: J. A. Barth,
    1798–1819.
Thomasius, J. *Dissertatio de doctoribus scholasticis latinis*. N.P., N.D.
Tribbechov, A. *De doctoribus scholasticis, ex corrupta per eos divinarum huma-
    narumque rerum scientia liber singularis*. Giesse: Vellstein, 1653.

Modern

Armstrong, B. G. *Calvinism and the Amyraut Heresy: Protestant Scholasticism
    and Humanism in Seventeenth-Century France*. Madison: Univ. of Wiscon-
    sin Press, 1969.
Beardslee, J. W. *Reformed Dogmatics*. New York: Oxford Univ. Press, 1965.

Boyle, J. "Aquinas and Prescriptive Ethics." In *Proceedings of the American Catholic Philosophical Association* 49(1975): 82–95.

The Cambridge History of Later Medieval Philosophy. Edited by N. Kretzmann, A. Kenny, and J. Pinborg. Cambridge: Cambridge Univ. Press, 1982.

Chomsky, N. *Cartesian Linguistics: A Chapter in the History of Rationalist Thought.* New York: Harper & Row, 1966.

Collins, A. B. *The Secular is Sacred: Platonism and Thomism in Marsilio Ficino's Platonic Theology.* The Hague: M. Nijhoff, 1974.

Costello, W. T. *The Scholastic Curriculum at Early 17th-Century Cambridge.* Cambridge, Mass.: Harvard Univ. Press, 1958.

Dulles, A. *Princeps Concordiae: Pico della Mirandola and the Scholastic Tradition.* Cambridge, Mass.: Harvard Univ. Press, 1941.

Finnis, J. *Natural Law and Natural Rights.* Oxford: Clarendon Press, 1980.

―――. *Fundamentals of Ethics.* Washington: Georgetown Univ. Press, 1983.

Finnis, J., and G. Grisez. "The Basic Principles of Natural Law: A Reply to Ralph McInerny." *American Journal of Jurisprudence* 26(1981): 21–31.

Gilson, E. *Reason and Revelation in the Middle Ages.* New York: Scribner, 1950.

―――. *History of Christian Philosophy in the Middle Ages.* New York: Random House, 1955.

Gossman, L. *Medievalism and the Ideologies of the Enlightenment: The World and the Work of La Curne de Sainte-Palaye.* Baltimore: Johns Hopkins Univ. Press, 1968.

Grisez, G. "The First Principle of Practical Reason: A Commentary on the *Summa Theologiae,* I-IIae, Q. 94, A. 2." *Natural Law Forum* 10 (1965): 168–201.

―――. *Way of the Lord Jesus.* Vol. 1, *Christian Moral Principles.* Chicago: Franciscan Herald Press, 1983.

Hain, L. F. T. *Repertorium bibliographicum . . . usque ad annum MD typis expressi. . . .* Reprinted, Milan: Gölich, 1948. Several publications have brought this work up to date: W. A. Copinger, *Supplementum.* Reprinted, Milan: Gölich, 1950; D. Reichling, *Appendices ad Hainii-Copingeri repertorium bibliographicum.* Münster: Rosenthal, 1905–11; D. Reichling, *Supplementum.* Münster: Theissing, 1914.

Hittinger, R. *A Critique of the New Natural Law Theory.* Notre Dame: Univ. of Notre Dame Press, 1987.

Hourani, G. (See under Averroës above)

Institutiones philosophicae ("Philosophy of Lyons"). Anonymous, but known to have been the work of a J. Valla. Lyons: Remondinianis, 1783–.

Maurer, A. A. *Medieval Philosophy.* New York: Random House, 1962; 2d ed., Toronto: Pontifical Institute of Mediaeval Studies, 1982. For translations of Commentary by Thomas Aquinas on the *De trinitate* by Boethius, see under Thomas Aquinas above).

McInerny, R. "The Principles of Natural Law." *American Journal of Jurisprudence* 25(1980): 1–15.

Ong, W. J. *Ramus. Method and Decay of the Dialogue: From the Art of Discourse to the Art of Reason.* Cambridge, Mass.: Harvard Univ. Press, 1958.

Patch, H. R. *The Tradition of Boethius.* New York: Oxford Univ. Press, 1935.

Payer, P. (For translation of the *Dialogue,* see above, under Abelard)

Petersen, P. von. *Geschichte der Aristotelischen Philosophie im protestantischen Deutschland.* Leipzig: F. Meiner, 1921.

Phelan-Eschmann. (See *On Kingship,* under Thomas Aquinas above)

Rackl, M. "Demetrios Kydones als Verteidiger und Uebersetzer des heiligen Thomas von Aquin." Sonderabdruck aus *Der Katholik* 1 (1915): 21–40. Mainz:

——. "Die ungedruckte Verteidigungsschrift des Demetrios Kydones fuer Thomas von Aquin gegen Neilos Kabasilas" *Divus Thomas* 7:303–17. Vienna: N.p. 1920.

——. Die griechischen Augustinus-uebersetzungen." In *Miscellanea Francesco Ehrle,* 1–38. Rome: Bibliotheca Apostolica Vaticana, 1924.

Ritschl, O. *Dogmengeschichte des Protestantismus.* Leipzig: Hinrichs, 1908–27.

Russell, B. *The Autobiography of Bertrand Russell, 1914–1944.* 2 vols. Toronto: McClelland-Stewart, 1968.

Schultz, J. L. "Is-Ought: Prescribing and a Present Controversy." *Thomist* 49(1): 1–23 (1985).

——. "Thomist Metaethics and a Present Controversy." *Thomist* 52(1): 40–62 (1988).

Shook, L. K. "The Nature and Value of Medieval Studies" In *Studies in Medieval Culture,* 9–20. Series 7, no. 2. Edited by J. R. Sommerfeldt.

Synan, E. A. (See under Godfrey of Saint-Victor above)

Thomas, R. (See *Dialogus,* under Abelard above)

Ueberweg, F. *Grundriss der Geschichte der Philosophie von Thales bis auf die Gegenwart.* Berlin: 1863–68.

Valorani, S. "Massimo Planude traduttore di S. Agostino." In *Atti VIII° Congresso Studi Bizantini* 1:234ff. Rome: 1953.

Vatican II Council Daybook. Session 3, 267ff. Washington: National Catholic Welfare Conference, 1965.

Veatch, H. Review of J. Finnis, *Natural Law and Natural Rights. American Journal of Jurisprudence* 26 (1981): 247–259.

——. Review of R. Hittinger, *A Critique of New Natural Law Theory. New Scholasticism* 62(3): 353–65 (1988).

Webb, C. C. I (See under John of Salisbury above)

Wittgenstein, L. *Philosophical Investigations.* Translated by G. E. M. Anscombe. New York: Macmillan, 1953.

Wolfson, H. A. (See above, under Philo)

⇙ 10 ⇘

Medieval Law

KENNETH PENNINGTON

LTHOUGH LAW IS A TECHNICAL DISCIPLINE and yields its secrets only grudgingly, a medievalist may learn much about medieval society from legal institutions. Laws, legal doctrine, court procedures, and testimony of witnesses in court reveal a society's structure, its ethical concerns, its values, and, to some extent, its ideals. The extraordinary variety of legal systems in the Middle Ages make medieval law a complex subject. Primitive, customary codes regulated a society in which, at the same time, sophisticated, learned systems were taught at the universities. Further, secular law and ecclesiastical law (also called "canon law") jostled each other over jurisdictional rights in every community. From the time of the Investiture Controversy in the eleventh century, each European society had to work out an arrangement with the Church that recognized her jurisdictional rights. Canon law courts became courts of first instance for many disputes that would be adjudicated in secular courts today. Ecclesiastical judges heard cases dealing with marriage, divorce, dowries, wills, and all matters involving the clergy. Secular judges handled criminal cases, contracts, property and also, in different places and different times, contested the jurisdictional rights of canon law. Consequently in the high Middle Ages every jurisdiction had two competing legal systems: one regulated by customary law and secular judges, and the other administered by clerics with its highest court in Rome.

This chapter will discuss three different types of law: secular, Roman, and canon law. In the early Middle Ages customary law largely replaced the law of Rome in the Germanic kingdoms that were carved out of the provinces of the old Roman Empire. At first the Germanic kings established two separate legal systems for their subjects: one for Romans and the other for Germans. Gradually the two groups merged, and by the ninth century territorial rather than personal law prevailed in western Europe. Germanic law formed the foundation of the secular law of the emerging national monarchies.

At the end of the eleventh century a unique event in legal history changed the course of European law. Scholars began to teach the law of the ancient Romans at Bologna. The Romans had a complex and sophisticated legal system. The Emperor Justinian had ordered a codification of Roman law in the sixth century, and this codification, the *Corpus iuris civilis,* provided the material for teaching Roman law in the eleventh century. The impact that Roman law had on secular and ecclesiastical law during the twelfth century was profound. It provided doctrines governing all aspects of law: family law, contracts, rules of procedure, and, in some respects most importantly, a juristic model of a strong monarchical constitutional system. Justinian became eponymous for legislator and codifier. His codification was mined for precious metals that were used to shape and temper European law.

Shortly after the revival of Roman law at Bologna, a teacher named Gratian compiled a book of canon law. His book, which subsequent generations called the *Decretum,* established canon law as an academic discipline. By the end of the twelfth century, Roman and canon law studies flourished at Bologna and elsewhere. The doctrine of canon law was dependent upon Roman law models, and, increasingly, Roman lawyers had to look to canon law to understand the current state of the law in those areas governed by canonical norms.

I. GERMANIC CUSTOMARY LAW AND
THE EVOLUTION OF SECULAR LAW

In the first century A.D. the Roman historian Tacitus described the laws of the ancient Germanic peoples, but by the time he wrote, the Germans had already become Romanized. Legal historians no longer believe that we can clearly separate Germanic from Roman practices. In spite of this justified caution, we can see a dramatic transformation of the legal system of the western provinces of the Empire after ca. A.D. 450. As the Ostrogoths, Visigoths, Franks, and other Germanic tribes built their kingdoms on the carcass of the Empire, they had to provide codes for their Germanic and Roman subjects. The Germans had no written codes or compilations of legal practices. They had a customary legal system that depended on the memory of the folk — in practice the elders — to establish the content of the law. Because of its primitiveness, the study of Germanic law has profited from comparing it to the legal systems of other primitive peoples studied by anthropologists.

The first Germanic compilations of law were promulgated in Germanic kingdoms closest to the Mediterranean and the center of the old empire. The first was most likely the *Edictum Theodorici,* issued by a Visigothic king, Theodoric II, ca. 458. A slightly later Visigothic king, Euric (ca. 466–485) promulgated a code in ca. 475 that is only partially preserved. Both of these compilations were strongly influenced by Roman law.

The sixth and seventh centuries produced a large number of Germanic legal compilations. The Visigoths, Ostrogoths, Burgundians, Franks, Frisians, Saxons, Lombards, and other tribes issued compilations of laws that for the most part deserve the title "written customary legal systems." The rulers who promulgated these compilations of law were not legislating and did not consider themselves the source of law, but rather they recorded the legal practices of their people. All of these early compilations have been edited in *Leges* volumes of the *Monumenta Germaniae Historica* and a number of them have been translated into English.[1]

The Carolingian period was marked by a more sophisticated legal system, but one still based on the earlier Germanic codes. Charlemagne brought political and, to some degree, legal unity to his realm. His biographer, Einhard, reported that he wanted to reform Frankish law and ordered that the laws of all nations under his jurisdiction should be written down. From the surviving evidence, his efforts were not very successful. However, he did issue a large number of administrative and legislative commands that, because they were divided into chapters, are called "capitularies." These documents regulated secular and ecclesiastical affairs in his kingdom and were promulgated by *missi dominici.* The Capitulary of Herstal (A.D. 779) contained a series of executive orders that mixed ecclesiastical and secular concerns. Charlemagne ordered bishops to be subject to their metropolitans and priests to their bishops, but, within the same capitulary, he regulated the penalties for murderers, robbers, and perjurers. Charlemagne and Louis the Pious promulgated large numbers of capitularies, but this legislative activity came to an end during the reign of Charles the Bald.

The story of how Germanic customary law was transformed into the common laws of the evolving nation states is complex and cannot be told here in any detail. After the disintegration of the Carolingian Empire, law became fragmented in western Europe. With the decentralization of political authority, local lords exercised legal jurisdiction over the inhabitants of their lands. This process of decentralization was more complete in some parts of Europe than in others. Feudalism was the political result, and feudal law regulating the relationships of lords and vassals became an important element of all secular legal systems of the eleventh and twelfth centuries. The chief characteristics of feudal law were the protection of local lords' rights from encroachment by the sovereign and a contractual relationship between monarchs and their vassals. The system of law that arose from these relationships was codified in the eleventh century in northern Italy and was called the *Consuetudines feudorum* or the *Libri feudorum.* The origins of these books are complex. They coalesced around legislation of the German emperors Conrad II (1037) and Lothair II (1136). During the twelfth century two recensions of the *Libri feudorum* evolved. At the end of the twelfth century, legislation of Frederick Barbarossa was added along with other pieces of statute law touching upon feudal law. Pilius was the first jurist to write a learned commentary on the *Libri.* In the middle of the thirteenth century, the author of the Ordinary Gloss to the *Corpus iuris civilis,* Accursius, wrote two commentaries on the *Libri,* the second of which became the standard or Ordinary Gloss (ca. 1227–34). The recension of the compilation that he chose for his second commentary became the vulgate recension over the course of time, and this text of the *Libri,* along with Accursius's gloss, was incorporated into the standard works that were circulated and taught with Justinian's *Corpus iuris civilis* in the schools of law. The *Libri feudorum* were commented on by Baldus de Ubaldis and others and became part of the tradition of learned law.

The evolution of Germanic law into a common-law system can be illustrated by following the development of law in Lombardy. The laws of the Lombard kings of northern Italy from A.D. 643 to 755 were gathered together in *Edictum regum Longobardorum.* To these were added the decrees of Frankish and German emperors. In the first half of the eleventh century, these laws were placed chronologically in a collection entitled the *Liber Papiensis.* Later, this collection was rearranged so that the laws were grouped by subject matter rather than date. The process of reorganization went through several recensions of the text and was not finished until the end of the eleventh century. The final recension of Lombard law was probably made in Pavia and was called the *Lombarda.*

Lombard jurists taught at Pavia, Milan, and Mantua, and, perhaps, also in Bologna. Lombard law went into eclipse in the second half of the twelfth century although its influence can still be seen as late as the fourteenth. The reason for the decline of Lombard law was not the revival of Roman law and the rise of the Bolognese law school. Rather, as the Italian communes became independent they compiled or promulgated their own statutes. The northern Italian city states were the most precocious. Genoa published its first statutes in 1143, Pisa in 1162, Piacenza in 1135. The most prosperous and important city on the Lombard plain, Milan, issued its first known statute in 1170. A compilation of Milanese laws was issued in 1216, the *Liber consuetudinum Mediolani.* This "wave of codification" that swept over the Italian cities in the twelfth and thirteenth centuries eroded the place of Lombard law in northern Italy. The laws of the Italian city-states present the historian with an enormous task. It has been estimated that over 10,000 statutes survive. They are extremely important sources for legal and social history. But they have not yet been systematically analyzed, nor have comparative studies been done to trace their development and filiation.

If we look at secular legal systems north of the Alps, we are struck by two facts. First northern European legal systems are less sophisticated than Italian, and their development is much more difficult to trace because the written evidence is fragmentary until the end of the twelfth century. English law is an exception to the second part of this generalization. More source material for English law exists for the period before ca. 1300 than any other northern European legal system. And, because English constitutional history has proven to be of central importance for the development of representative institutions in the Western and non-Western world, English historians have devoted great energy exploring every nook and cranny of this corner of English legal history.

In large part, English law owes its precociousness, in comparison to other northern legal systems, to the Normans and their conquest of England in 1066. French law comprised a large number of customary law jurisdictions over which the king exercised very little direct control. This remained true until the end of the Middle Ages. In England, on the other hand, William's conquest brought the entire land under his direct jurisdiction. The first result of this can be seen in administrative law. When William surveyed England in 1089 and had the results catalogued in volumes that later came to be called Domesday Book, he wanted to ascertain his rights through a census of his subjects' property, much in the same way that modern bureaucracies establish a value of the property that they wish to tax through assessments. William was succeeded by two extraordinarily competent kings: Henry I (1100–1135) and Henry II (1154–89). They took full advantage of the strong feudal government established by William after the conquest and created institutions and procedures that centralized and unified English law. Henry I was most important for establishing a system of itinerant royal justices who heard pleas in civil and criminal cases. Henry II issued several important pieces of legislation that brought a number of civil and criminal cases into royal courts and through a system of returnable writs inaugurated innovative ways through which his subjects could obtain justice in royal courts. Students of English law can obtain a remarkably detailed picture of English legal practices at the end of Henry's reign through a book called *Glanville*. This work was probably not written by Henry II's justiciar, Ranulf de Glanville, but it describes the writs that had been developed during Henry's reign and also incorporates, if in a rather primitive form, some of the legal learning that was being taught in the schools. The book itself, however, was not a school book, but a practitioner's handbook. One half century later, another anonymous author, in a work that had been long attributed to a royal judge, Henry de Bracton, wrote an even more sophisticated and comprehensive work than Glanville's. These two works of jurisprudence are fundamental for our present understanding of how English common law evolved.

The factors that permitted the English kings to develop a common law for their kingdom did not exist in other parts of northern Europe. French and Germanic law remained fragmented. There were attempts, however, to provide regions of French and German speaking lands with systematic discussions of their customary laws. In the second half of the thirteenth century, Philippe de Beaumanoir wrote a treatise on French customary law of Clermont-en-Beauvaisis, called the *Coutumes de Beauvaisis*. He wrote the tract in French for the use of judges, and discussed procedure, jurisdiction of secular and ecclesiastical courts, inheritance, dowries, crimes, and obligations. He knew some Roman and canon law and used Romano-canonical terms to define some legal concepts. A little earlier (ca. 1225) Eike von Repgow wrote a treatise in German that dealt with customary law in Saxony, the *Sachsenspiegel*. Eike discussed the customary law of the land and feudal law. His treatise had far reaching influence. Over 400 manuscripts exist of various forms of the work. It was adapted for other parts of Germany, translated into Latin, and, in the fourteenth century, was glossed.

Secular law was not an academic discipline during the Middle Ages. Consequently, we have very few commentaries on the law as those of Bracton, Beaumanoir, and von Repgow. The great challenge for the legal historian is to reconstruct the workings and the norms of these system without the help of a learned jurisprudence and, particularly in the twelfth century, without extensive and detailed source material describing cases held in secular courts.

II. THE REVIVAL AND STUDY OF ROMAN LAW

The recovery and study of Roman law in the eleventh and twelfth centuries is a singular event in the history of law. Never before or since had a society turned to a legal system of greater sophistication than that of its own for a model to serve as a source for theoretical and practical applications in its courts. Two factors account for this. First, in their Germanic dress, the Roman Empire and emperor were still living institutions. Secondly, although parts of Justinian's sixth-century codification do not seem to have been known in the early Middle Ages, Roman law had not completely disappeared. The Germanic codes contained substantial borrowings from Roman texts, and Justinian's *Codex* was used throughout the period. The key part of Justinian's codification that was not known was his *Digest*. Justinian's codification had consisted of four parts: the *Institutes,* an introduction to Roman law, the *Codex,* containing imperial legislation from the second to the sixth century, the *Digest,* a compilation of excerpts from the writings of the Roman jurists, and finally, the *Novellae,* a compilation of Justinian's legislation. The *Digest* was of fundamental importance for understanding the intricacies of Roman law. The excerpts from the Roman jurisconsults defined terms, discussed theoretical difficulties, cited court cases, and made the mass of legislation found in the *Codex* understandable and, therefore, usable. Without the *Digest,* Roman law would have had little influence for European legal systems of the Middle Ages.

Jurists regained knowledge of the *Digest* in the second half of the eleventh century. We know little about how the *Digest* was reintroduced into western European legal culture. Manuscripts of the *Digest* were rare. Only one complete manuscript survives from before the twelfth century, the *Codex Florentinus,* formerly the *Codex Pisanus,* of ca. A.D. 600. This manuscript was not the direct source of the vulgate text of the *Digest,* called the *Littera Bononiensis,* that was soon circulating and being taught at Bologna. The format of the Digest and its text eliminate this famous manuscript as the sole source of the *Littera Bononiensis.* The importance and antiquity of the *Codex Florentinus* was, however, already well understood in the twelfth century. We have evidence that the jurists used it to improve the text of *Littera Bononiensis.* Other manuscripts provided the base of the vulgate text that was taught at Bologna, but we shall never know how many or which manuscripts these were.

The medieval *Digest* and *Codex,* like Justinian's codification, are divided into books, the books then subdivided into titles and each title contains subchapters of excerpts of the Roman jurisconsults (*Digest*) or laws

(*Codex*). However, the format of the *Corpus iuris civilis* was quite different from Justinian's codification.[2] The *Digest* was probably not recovered in one piece, and the early teachers of law, called the "glossators" because they glossed the texts, divided the *Digest* into three sections: *Digestum vetus*, book 1, title 1, law 1 to book 24, title 2 (in modern citation, Dig. 1.1.1 to Dig. 24.2), *Infortiatum*, Dig. 24.3 to 38.17, *Digestum novum*, Dig. 39.1 to 50.17. The *Codex* was separated into two parts, books 1 through 9, and books 10 to 12. The other important difference between the medieval and classical text was that the *Novellae* were ordered very differently from Justinian's arrangement. The various titles were placed in nine *collationes* and the entire work was called the *Authenticum*. The medieval and early modern jurists cited the *Digest* with the sign "ff." We do not know why they used this abbreviation. They followed this sign with an abbreviated title, for example, "de manu. que ser. ad uni. pert." (de manumissionibus quae servis ad universitatem pertinentibus imponuntur [Dig. 40.3]), followed by either the abbreviation for lex, l. and a Roman number or the Latin incipit of the law, for example, *l.*iii. or *Nec militi*. The *Codex* was cited by "C." using the same format. Citations to the *Institutes* and the *Authenticum* were signaled by "inst." and "auth." respectively. The most convenient way to verify citations to the entire *Corpus iuris civilis* is to use the index published by Ugo Nicolini and Franca Sinatti d'Amico. One must be careful to distinguish, as do Nicolini and d'Amico, between the medieval vulgate text and Justinian's codification.

Although there is not a complete corcordance, there are a number of reference books that are helpful for finding material in the *Corups iuris civilis*. To find particular words or concepts in the *Digest*, the *Vocabularium iurisprudentiae Romanae* is of great value.[3] A similar work provides the same information for the *Codex*.[4] There is a complete concordance of the *Novellae*.[5] A convenient dictionary of the most important terms used in Roman law is Heumann's *Handlexikon zu den Quellen des roemischen Rechts*.[6] Berger's *Dictionary of Roman Law* is useful for defining terms, but does not give references to where one may find the pertinent material.[7] Justinian's codification of Roman law has been recently translated into English, and this translation replaces Scott's inadequate text.

To understand how medieval jurists understood Justinian's text, scholars must read their glosses and commentaries. The earliest glosses we have are from Irnerius, who taught at Bologna, ca. 1075–1130. He was succeeded in the twelfth century by the four Doctors, Bulgarus, Martinus, Ugo, and Jacobus. The epoch of the "glossators" was concluded by the work of Azo, who composed numerous glosses and a *Summa* on the *Codex* that remained a major text of medieval jurisprudence for at least two centuries, and Accursius (sometimes, but without any foundation, referred to as Franciscus Accursius) who glossed the entire medieval corpus of Roman law. His gloss became the Ordinary Gloss, that is, the gloss that was usually placed in the margins of manuscript copies of the text and the starting point of all discussions of Roman law in the law schools.

The age of the glossators ended with Accursius and was followed by the age of the commentators. This shift was heralded by the Odofredus de Denariis, who wrote an enormous commentary on the *Digest* and by lesser known, but still important figures, like Guido da Suzzara. Odofredus began the tradition of writing long, sometimes prolix, treatises on the various books of the *Corpus iuris civilis*. He was followed by Jacques de Revigny, Pierre de Belleperche, Cinus of Pistoia, and the most prolific commentator of all, Bartolus of Sassoferrato (1314–57). Guido da Suzzara represents another path of development. He wrote *suppletitiones, additiones,* or *appostillae* to the Ordinary Gloss of Accursius. This literary genre flourished in the last half of the thirteenth and first half of the fourteenth centuries. Guido's *additiones* were often placed in the margins of manuscripts that also contained Accursius's gloss and provided a supplement to it.[8] Another important literary genre, the *consilium,* became important in the first half of the fourteenth century. Litigants had consulted lawyers and asked them for their legal opinions since the twelfth century, although we have very few examples from the early period. Oldradus da Ponte, an advocate at the papal curia in Avignon, published a collection of his *consilia* in the 1330s. He started a trend that turned into a flood by the end of the century. The age of the commentators was, by the fifteenth century, replaced by the age of the *consilium.* The jurists collected their *consilia* and published them. They earned money by writing them and fame by publishing their collections. The number of *consilia* that some jurists wrote is staggering. Baldus de Ubaldis wrote over 2,500 *consilia.* If he wrote one a day, he spent over seven years of his life just writing *consilia.* Baldus also revised his *consilia* after he wrote them, and a collection of his *consilia* in the Barberini fond of the Vatican library has many examples of *consilia* revised in his own hand.

The writings of most of these jurists have never been edited in modern times and exist either in early modern printed editions or in manuscripts.[9] In order to study their thought it is necessary to examine the manuscripts of each jurist's work. Recent research has clearly demonstrated that the printed editions of the fifteenth and sixteenth centuries must be checked against the manuscripts when examining the thought of a jurist. These editions are, for the most part, reliable, but they are usually based on late medieval textual traditions that may obscure the chronological development of a jurist's thought. The work of checking texts against manuscripts has been made considerably easier since the publication of Gero Dolezalek's handlist of medieval Roman law manuscripts. Dolezalek compiled a computerized list that arranges the manuscripts according to author, work, incipit, and library. It is an essential tool for anyone who wishes to study medieval Roman law.

III. THE STUDY OF CANON LAW

The revival of Roman law stimulated the systematic study of canon law. The history of canon law can be traced back to the earliest days of the Church. The primitive Church had rules that were based upon the teachings of Christ and the New Testament. These regulations were soon supplemented by the canons of ecclesiastical councils, the writings of the Church fathers like Jerome and Augustine, and, finally, papal decretal letters. Until the twelfth century, there were no formal schools of canon law. The law of the Church was collected by clerics, often with little attention to organization and interpretation. In many collections of early canon law, legislation was not arranged by subject but chronologically. In the eleventh century, several important bishops compiled collections that were arranged according to subject matter. Burchard of Worms (1000–1025) and Ivo of Chartres (1040–1115) composed collections of canon law that span a period of intense interest in ecclesiastical law for intellectual and political reasons. Each collection was divided into books and contained material arranged in very general categories (i.e., marriage, sacraments, etc.).

At some time during the first half of the twelfth century, Gratian, who may have been a monk, began teaching canon law at Bologna. He was not only influenced by the teaching of Roman law, but also by developments in ancillary disciplines, particularly theology and philosophy. Intellectual life in the early twelfth century was characterized by attempts to rationalize and organize knowledge. Gratian's work is a part of this world. He compiled a collection of canons from earlier collections, particularly those of Burchard and Ivo. Although Ivo of Chartres wrote a tract on reconciling contradictory texts, he did not apply this methodology to his collections. Gratian did. He attempted to resolve the contradictions that he found in earlier ecclesiastical laws. He applied the dialectical method of the twelfth-century Schoolmen, exemplified by Abelard's *Sic et Non*. His greatest innovation was to provide a running commentary on the canons (called *dicta*) in which he raised questions about his texts, pointed to contradictions in them, and proposed solutions. He called this work *Concordia discordantium canonum* (Concord of discordant canons), but this cumbersome title was soon replaced by the simple title *Decretum*. Gratian worked on his text over many years and his text betrays signs of additions and incomplete revisions.[10]

Unlike the collections of the eleventh century, Gratian did not divide his work into books. He split his collection into two parts. In all the manuscripts and printed editions, the first part consists of 101 *distinctiones* (abbreviated as either "dist.," "d.," or "di." in the manuscripts). However, some scholars have argued that since Gratian referred to the various sections in the first part of the *Decretum* as *tractatus,* he must not have been responsible for these divisions. The first twenty divisions introduce various types and definitions of law. The remaining twenty-one *distinctiones* of the first part treat ecclesiastical government and clerical discipline. Gratian divided the second half of the *Decretum* into *causae* and subdivided each *causa* into *questiones*. He began each *causa* with a hypothetical problem to which he put a series of questions. The problem and the questions provided the structure of the *causa.* A typical example of his methodology is the beginning of *Causa* 23:

Certain bishops with their flocks committed to them have fallen into heresy. They began to compel neighboring believers by various means to accept heresy. The pope ordered the bishops of the region, who had received civil jurisdiction from the emperor, that they defend the faithful from these heretics. Having received the papal commands, the bishops gathered an army and began to wage war against the heretics . . . Q.1. The first question is whether it is a sin [for clerics] to wage war? Q.2. Secondly, what is a just war? . . . Q.3. Thirdly, should an injury to a companion be repelled by force of arms? Q.4. Is vengeance justified?

Gratian treated each question in turn and collected the relevant legal texts. Often the texts were in conflict, but he clarified or reconciled the contradictions in his *dicta.* Gratian divided the second part of the *Decretum* into thirty-six *causae.* Some of the *causae* treat a single subject, while others, like *Causa* 23, touch upon a variety of problems. Other important areas of law covered in the *causae* are simony (*Causa* 1), procedure (*Causae* 2-7), monks and their discipline (*Causae* 16-20), and marriage (*Causae* 27-36). Two parts of the *Decretum* were not finished by Gratian: a treatise on penance (*De penitentia*) was added to *Causa* 33 after question 2, and a long tract on the sacraments (*De consecratione*) was appended to *Causa* 36. The next generation of canonists who wrote commentaries and glosses on Gratian's *Decretum* cited his work according to its sections. They referred to chapters in the first part as "xxxii. di. [or dist.] c.i." or by the incipit of the chapter, "xxxii. di. Cum sacerdotum." The second part was cited as "C.xxiii. q.v. Principes (c.20)." The modern style of reference is "D.32 c.1" and "C.23 q.1 c.20" respectively. The verification of references to the *Decretum* is made considerably easier by Xaverio Ochoa and Aloisio Diez's index.[11]

The teaching of canon law flourished in the second half of the twelfth century in Italy and northern Europe. Gratian intended that *Decretum* be used for teaching canon law, and it quickly established itself as the basic text for the study of law in the schools. At first the canonists added chapters to Gratian's text (called *paleae*) to supplement it, but soon papal legislation and court decisions (preserved in letters that the canonists named *decretales*) overwhelmed attempts to rely solely on Gratian. The canonists collected these new legislative norms and often added them to manuscripts of the *Decretum*. By the end of the century, unsystematic compilations of decretals had yielded to structured, topically arranged collections.[12] Bernard of Pavia compiled a new collection of decretals, the *Breviarium extravagantium*, later named the *Compilatio prima*, in 1190 or 1191 that established the mode upon which all future collections were based. Bernard divided his collection into five books and subdivided it into titles. Each book covered a major area of law. Between 1190 and 1226, four other major collections were produced. These collections gathered the legislation of Popes Innocent III and Honorius III and earlier papal legislation. The five collections were later called the *Compilationes antiquae*, and the jurists used them in their commentaries and in the classroom as the primary source of contemporary canonical norms and doctrines.[13]

The *Compilationes antiquae* and Gratian's *Decretum* became an unwieldy body of law. There were some contradictory decretals in the *Compilationes*, but, more importantly, judges and lawyers were often frustrated when they looked for specific legislation. Even the pope was annoyed. In 1230, Pope Gregory IX granted a commission to Raymond of Peñafort to unify papal decretal legislation. Raymond shortened, deleted, and edited the decretals in the *Compilationes antiquae*, comparing them with the texts of other collections. He also probably asked Gregory IX for constitutions to explain or clarify points of law that were as of then unresolved. He arranged this mass of legislation in five books following the same organizational plan as had been established by Bernard of Pavia. In 1234, Gregory sent this new collection to Bologna and declared that it superseded all previous collections and should be used exclusively in the schools and courts. This collection was called the *Liber extra* or the *Gregoriana*.[14]

The papacy promulgated almost all the collections of canon law after *Gregoriana*. Pope Innocent IV issued three different recensions (*Novellae*) of his decretals and his decrees from the Council of Lyons (1245). The canonists appended them to the *Gregoriana* but also inserted them under their respective titles in many manuscripts. Between 1234 and 1298, papal decretals circulated in small, private collections as well as in official collections like the *Novellae*. Pope Boniface VIII ordered a new collection of canon law compiled in 1298 that would organize this body of post-*Gregoriana* law. The commission of lawyers followed the same plan as the earlier collections and included many decretals of Boniface VIII. The new collection was called the *Liber sextus*. Twenty years later Pope John XXII arranged a collection of Pope Clement V's decretals and the decrees of the Council of Vienne (1311-12). This collection was known as the *Clementinae*. The *Clementinae* was the last official collection of the Middle Ages. Nevertheless, two other collections became part of the *Corpus iuris canonici*. Zenzelinus de Cassanis compiled a small collection of John XXII's decretals sometime after 1325, and anonymous canonists circulated small collections of *decretales extravagantes* that finally coalesced into a collection called the *Extravagantes communes* in the later Middle Ages. All of these collections, from Gratian to the *Extravagantes communes* were brought together, revised, and edited by a group called the "correctores Romani" and officially issued as the common law of the Church by Pope Gregory XIII in 1582. This official text of the *Corpus iuris canonici* was known as the *Editio Romana*.

The jurists of the Middle Ages cited the collections compiled after Gratian by title and chapter.[15] They referred to Innocent III's famous decree defining the pope's authority to choose the emperor in a disputed election from the *Compilationes antiquae* either as "infra de electione, Venerabilem, lib. iii." or "extra. iii. de electione, Venerabilem," which is in Book one of the Third Compilation (*Compilatio tertia*). The modern citation would be "3 Comp. 1.6.19." When Raymond of Peñafort edited *Venerabilem* and placed it in the *Gregoriana,* the jurists cited it as "extra. de electione, Venerabilem," the modern citation being X 1.6.34 [X = extra]. The change in forms of citation is a sure guide to dating canonistic works to either before or after 1234. The canonists employed the same format for citing decretals the later collections, that is, title, incipit of decretal with an indication (but not always) of the collection. The *Liber sextus* was cited as "sext." or "vi.," the *Clementinae* with the abbreviation "Clem.," and the *Extravagantes Johannis XXII* as "extra. Jo."

The canonists glossed and commented on these collections, and their writings contributed to the creation of medieval jurisprudence. Like the basic texts in Roman law the *Decretum,* Decretals of Gregory IX, and the *Liber sextus* were provided with Ordinary Glosses (Johannes Teutonicus as revised by Bartolomaeus Brixiensis, Bernardus Parmensis, and Johannes Andreae respectively) that were almost always written in the margins of medieval manuscript copies. The canonists also wrote monographic treatises on particular parts of the law, such as on procedure, individual decretals, titles, or testaments, and in the late Middle Ages, turned to the *consilium* as a major vehicle of legal discourse. The *consilia* were intimately connected with the practice of law. Litigants sought legal advice from jurists about cases in which they were involved. The lawyers began to collect the opinions that they wrote. Oldradus da Ponte (died after 1343) was one of the first lawyers to publish a large collection of his *consilia,* many of which he wrote while at the papal curia in Avignon. The best guides to the literature of canon law (Maasen, Fournier and Le Bras, Kuttner, Schulte; see bibliography for details) are all over fifty years old, and a new history is now in progress. A guide to current literature and research can be found in the *Bulletin of Medieval Canon Law,* which contains an annual bibliography, information about manuscripts, and a report on the activity of the Institute of Medieval Canon Law in Berkeley, California.

NOTES

1. See Bibliography following this essay for details.

2. The medieval vulgate text of the *Corpus iuris civilis* has never been edited in modern times. Pietro Torelli began an edition in the 1930s, of which a small part of the *Institutes* with Accursius's Ordinary Gloss was published in 1939: *Accursii Florentini glossa ad Institutiones Iustiniani imperatoris [Liber I]* (Bologna, 1939). The vulgate text was published repeatedly from the beginning of printing in the fifteenth century to the early seventeenth. Almost all these editions also have the Ordinary Gloss of Accursius added to the margins. Theodor Mommsen and Paul Krueger published the modern edition of Justinian's codification with an extensive apparatus of variants in the late nineteenth century: *Digesta Iustiniani Augusti* (Berlin: Weidmann, 1870) and *Codex Iustinianus* (Berlin: Weidmann, 1877). A streamlined version of this edition, including the *Institutes* and *Novellae,* was published in 1872–95 and has been kept in print by many reprint editions.

3. *Vocabularium iurisprudentiae Romanae* (5 vols., Berlin: N.p., 1903–39).

4. Robert Mayr, ed. *Vocabularium Codicis Iustiniani* (2 vols., Prague: N.p., 1923; reprinted, Hildesheim: Georg Olms, 1965).

5. G. G. Archi and A. M. Colombo, eds., *Novellae,* Pars Latina: Legum Iustiniani Imperatoris vocabularium (11 vols., Milan: Cisalpino-La goliardica 1977).

6. H. Heumann, *Handlexikon zu den Quellen des roemischen Rechts,* 9th ed., ed. Emil Seckel (Jena: N.p., 1914).

7. Adolf Berger, *Encyclopedic Dictionary of Roman Law,* Transactions of the American Philosophical Society 43 (Philadelphia: American Philosophical Society, 1953).

8. See, for example, lat. 6201, a manuscript of the *Digest* (Munich: Staatsbibl.).

9. An introduction to these glossators, their successors, and the modern literature can be found in Helmut Coing, *Handbuch der Quellen und Literatur der neueren europäischen Privatrechtsgeschichte,* vol. 1, *Mittelalter* (Munich: Beck, 1973).

10. Gratian's text was printed many times in the fifteenth and sixteenth centuries. The most recent edition is Emil Friedberg, ed., *Corpus iuris canonici: Decretum Magistri Gratiani* (Leipzig: Bernhard Tauchnitz, 1879; reprinted, Graz: Akademische Druck, 1959), vol. 1. Friedberg's text is flawed, but useable.

11. *Indices canonum, titulorum et capitulorum Corporis Iuris Canonici,* Universa Bibliotheca iuris, Subsidia 1 (Rome: Commentarium pro Religiosis, 1964).

12. Charles Duggan, *Twelfth-Century Decretal Collections and their Importance in English History,* University of London Historical Series, 12 (London: Athlone Press, 1963) and Stanley Chodorow and Charles Duggan, *Decretales ineditae saeculi XII,* Monumenta iuris canonici, Series B, Corpus collectionum 4 (Vatican City: Biblioteca Apostolica Vaticana, 1982) are the best guides to this material.

13. Emil Friedberg compiled a register edition of the *Compilationes antiquae* in which he edited the texts not included in Gregory IX's *Liber extra: Quinque compilationes antiquae* (Leipzig: Bernhard Tauchnitz, 1882; reprinted, Graz: Akademische Druck, 1956).

14. Like Gratian's *Decretum,* Gregory's collection was printed in the fifteenth and sixteenth centuries. The most recent edition is Emil Friedberg, ed., *Corpus iuris canonici* (Leipzig: Bernhard Tauchnitz, 1879; reprinted, Graz: Akademische Druck, 1959), vol. 2.

15. Stephan Kuttner has prepared an index to the titles of the medieval canonical collections: *Index titulorum decretalium ex collectionibus tam priuatis quam publicis conscriptus* (Milan: Giuffrè, 1977). Ochoa's index, cited above in note 11, also indexes titles and chapters of the major collections. Friedberg's edition of the *Compilationes antiquae* is the only index to the chapters of those collections.

BIBLIOGRAPHY

This bibliography is a highly selective survey of the standard reference works and the most important recent literature. It is designed to introduce the field to a non-specialist or beginning graduate student.

General Reference Works and Journals

American Journal of Legal History. Philadelphia, 1957–.

Annali di storia del diritto. Milan, 1957–.

Anuario de historia del derecho español. Madrid, 1924–.

Archiv für katholisches Kirchenrecht. Mainz, 1857–.

Bulletin of Medieval Canon Law. Berkeley, 1971–. The Annual Report of the Institute of Medieval Canon Law was published at the back of *Traditio* from 1955–70. The bibliographies cover all aspects of medieval legal history.

Bulletino dell'Istituto di Diritto Romano. Rome, 1897–.

Coing, Helmut, ed. *Handbuch der Quellen und Literatur der neueren europäischen*

Privatrechtsgeschichte. Vol. 1, *Mittelalter (1100–1500): Die gelehrten Rechte und die Gesetzgebung.* Munich: C. H. Beck'sche Verlagsbuchhandlung, 1973. Covers secular, Roman, and canon law. The most important reference work of the last twenty-five years.

Dictionary of the Middle Ages. 12 vols. New York: Scribner, 1982–89. Articles on individual jurists and essays on various legal systems.

Dizionario biografico degli Italiani. 32 vols. Rome: Istituto della Enciclopedia Italiana, 1960–. To "Da Ronco." Many articles on the Italian jurists.

Handwörterbuch zur deutschen Rechtsgeschichte. 3 vols. Berlin: Erich Schmidt, 1964–. A much broader dictionary of law than its title indicates.

Ius Commune. Frankfurt am Main, 1967–.

———. Sonderhefte. 25 vols. Frankfurt am Main: Vittorio Klostermann, 1971–.

Journal of Legal History. London, 1980–.

Law and History Review. Ithaca, 1983–.

Law Quarterly Review. London, 1885–.

Lexikon des Mittelalters. 4 vols. Munich: Artemis Verlag, 1977.

Novissimo Digesto Italiano. 27 vols. Turin: Unione Tipografico-Editrice Torinese, 1957–. A wide-ranging dictionary of legal concepts and terms.

Österreichisches Archiv für Kirchenrecht. Vienna, 1950–.

Revista española de derecho canonico. Madrid, 1946–.

Revue de droit canonique. Strasbourg, 1951–.

Revue historique de droit français et étranger. Paris, 1855–.

Rivista internazionale di diritto comune. Vol. 1. Catania, 1990.

Rivista di storia del diritto italiano. Rome, 1928–.

Studia et documenta historiae et iuris. Rome, 1935–.

Tijdschrift voor Rechtsgeschiedenis. Haarlem, 1918–. Articles in Dutch, English, French, German.

Zeitschrift der Savigny-Stiftung für Rechtsgeschichte. Weimar, Germanistische Abteilung. 1880–. Kanonistische Abteilung. 1911–. Romanistische Abteilung. 1880–.

Secular Law

Sources

Beaumanoir, Philippe de. *Coutumes de Beauvaisis.* Edited by A. Salmon. Collection de textes pour servir à l'enseignement de l'histoire. 2 vols. Paris: A. Picard et fils. 1899–1900. Reprinted, Paris: N.p., 1970.

Bracton, Henry de. *Bracton on the Laws and Customs of England.* Edited and translated by Samuel E. Thorne. 4 vols. Cambridge: Harvard Univ. Press, 1968–77.

Glanville, Ranulf de. *The Treatise on the Laws and Customs of the Realm of England Commonly Called Glanvill.* Edited and translated by George D. G. Hall. London: Nelson, 1965.

Monumenta Germaniae Historica.
Leges (in folio).
    5 vols. Capitularia regum Francorum. Leges Alamanorum, Langobardum, Saxonum. Hannover, 1835–89.
Leges nationum Germanicarum.
    6 vols. Leges Visigothorum, Burgundionum, Saxonum, Thuringorum, Frisionum, Chamavorum, Alamanorum, Longobardorum. Lex Romana Raetica Curiensis, Ribvaria, Salica, Baivariorum. Hannover, 1888–1969.
Capitularia regum Francorum.
    2 vols. Hannover, 1883–97.
Constitutiones et acta publica imperatorum et regum.
    11 vols. Hannover, 1893–1988.
Fontes iuris Germanici antiqui.
    6 vols. Hannover, 1955–74.
Fontes iuris Germanici antiqui in usum scholarum separatim editi.
    14 vols. Hannover, 1869–1989.

Guides and Studies

Bellomo, Manlio. *L'Europa del diritto comune.* 2d ed. Rome: Il Cigno Galilei, 1989. A lucid and comprehensive survey of medieval secular and learned law in the Middle Ages.

Brunner, Heinrich. *Deutsche Rechtsgeschichte.* 2d ed. 2 vols. Edited by C. F. von Schwerin. Leipzig: Duncker und Humblot, 1928. Reprinted, Aalen: Scientia, 1961.

Drew, Katherine Fischer. "Law, German: Early Codes." *Dictionary of the Middle Ages* 7:468–77. New York: Scribner, 1986. Lists English translations of Germanic codes in bibliography.

Giordanengo, Gérard. *Le droit féodal dans les pays de droit écrit: L'exemple de la Provence et du Dauphiné XIIe–début XIVe siècle.* Bibliothèques des Écoles Françaises d'Athènes et de Rome, no. 266. Rome: Ecole Française de Rome, 1988. An excellent survey of feudal law in France.

Kroeschell, Karl. *Deutsche Rechtsgeschichte.* 2 vols. Opladen: Westdeutscher Verlag, 1982.

Milsom, S. F. C. *Historical Foundations of the Common Law.* 2d ed. London: Butterworths, 1981.

Myers, Henry A. "Law, German: Post-Carolingian." *Dictionary of the Middle Ages* 7:477–83. New York: Scribner, 1986.

Pennington, Kenneth. "Law Codes: 1000–1500." *Dictionary of the Middle Ages* 7:425–31. New York: Scribner, 1986.

Pollock, Frederick and Frederic Maitland. *The History of English Law Before the Time of Edward I.* 2d ed. 2 vols. Revised by S. F. C. Milsom. Cambridge: Cambridge Univ. Press, 1968.

Radding, Charles. *The Origins of Medieval Jurisprudence: Pavia and Bologna, 850–1150.* New Haven: Yale Univ. Press, 1988. This is an essay rather than a work based on an analysis of the sources. Radding's thesis is untenable, but he does offer a sketch of Lombard jurisprudence in English.

Reyerson, Kathryn and John Bell Henneman. "Law, French: In South." *Dictionary of the Middle Ages* 7:461–68. New York: Scribner, 1986.

Ruiz, Teofilo F. "Law, Spanish." *Dictionary of the Middle Ages* 7:518–24. New York: Scribner, 1986.

Strayer, Joseph R. "Law, French: In North." *Dictionary of the Middle Ages* 7:457–60. New York: Scribner, 1986.

Van Caenegem, R. C. *The Birth of the English Common Law.* Cambridge: Cambridge Univ. Press, 1973.

Weimar, Peter. "Die Handschriften des Liber feudorum und seiner Glossen." *Rivista internazionale di diritto comune* 1 (1990): 31–98. The most important work on the development of feudal law in the last fifty years. A guide to the sources and commentaries.

Wolf, Armin. "Die Gesetzgebung der entstehenden Territorialstaaten." In *Handbuch der Quellen und Literatur der neueren europäischen Privatrechtsgeschichte.* Vol. 1, *Mittelalter (1100–1500): Die gelehrten Rechte und die Gesetzgebung,* 517–800. Munich: C. H. Beck'sche Verlagsbuchhandlung, 1973. Wolf's essay is of fundamental importance for the creation and codification of law in Western Europe from ca. 1100 to 1500.

Roman Law

Guides and Sources

Coing, Helmut, ed. *Handbuch der Quellen und Literatur der neueren europäischen Privatrechtsgeschichte.* Vol. 1, *Mittelalter (1100–1500): Die gelehrten Rechte und die Gesetzgebung.* Munich: C. H. Beck'sche Verlagsbuchhandlung, 1973. This work is the first comprehensive survey of medieval Roman law since Savigny.

Conrat (Cohn), Max. *Geschichte der Quellen und Literatur des römischen Rechts im früheren Mittelalter.* Leipzig: J. C. Hinrichs 1891. Reprinted, Aalen: Scientia, 1963.

Dolezalek, Gero. *Verzeichnis der Handschriften zum römischen Recht bis 1600.* 4 vols. Frankfurt am Main: Max-Planck-Institut für Europäische Rechtsgeschichte, 1972.

Dolezalek, Gero, and Laurent Mayali. *Repertorium manuscriptorum veterum Codicis Justiniani* 2 vols. Repertorien zur Frühzeit der gelehrten Rechte, Ius Commune, Sonderhefte 23. Frankfurt am Main: Vittoria Klostermann, 1985.

Fowler-Magerl, Linda. *Ordo iudiciorum vel ordo iudiciarius.* Repertorien zur Frühzeit der gelehrten Rechte, Ius Commune, Sonderhefte 19. Frankfurt am Main: Vittorio Klostermann, 1984. A description of the earliest Roman and canon law treatises on procedure. An essential book for understanding how learned law influenced the practice of law in the twelfth century.

Glosse preaccursiane alle Istituzioni: Strato Azzoniano Libro primo. Edited by Severino Caprioli, Victor Crescenzi, et al. Fonti per la Storia d'Italia 107. Rome: Istituto Storico per il Medio Evo, 1984. The first volume of what will be a work of great importance for writing the history of early medieval Roman law.

Savigny, Friedrich Carl von. *Geschichte des römischen Rechts im Mittelalter.* 2d ed. 7 vols. Heidelberg: Bey Mohr und Zimmer, 1850. Reprinted Aalen: Scientia, 1986. Savigny is still the most complete guide to the medieval civilians' biographies and their works.

Scripta anecdota glossatorum. Biblioteca iuridica medii aevi. 3 vols. Bologna: In aedibus Societatis Azzogiudianae 1888–1914. Reprinted, Turin: Forni, 1962.

Studies

Donahue, Charles Jr. "Law, Civil—*Corpus iuris,* Revival and Spread." *Dictionary of the Middle Ages* 7:418–25. New York: Scribner, 1986.

Feenstra, Robert. *Droit savant au moyen âge at sa vulgarisation.* London: Variorum, 1986.

Gouron, André. *Le science du droit dans le Midi de la France au Moyen Age.* London: Variorum Reprints, 1984.

Ius Romanum Medii Aevi. Milan: Giuffrè, 1961–. A large-scale history of the influence of medieval Roman law on European society.

Kantorowicz, Hermann. *Studies in the Glossators of the Roman Law.* Cambridge: Cambridge Univ. Press, 1938. Reissued with addenda and edited by Peter Weimar, Aalen: Scientia Verlag, 1969.

Koschaker, Paul. *Europa und das römische Recht.* 4th ed. Munich: Beck, 1966.

Meijers, Eduard Maurits. *Études d'histoire de droit.* Edited by Robert Feenstra and H. F. W. D. Fischer. 4 vols. Leiden: Universitaire Pers Leiden 1956–66.

Das römische Recht im Mittelalter. Edited by E. J. H. Schrage. Darmstadt: Wissenschaftliche Buchgesellschaft, 1987.

Vinogradoff, Paul. *Roman Law in Medieval Europe.* Oxford: Clarendon Press, 1929. Reprinted with a new foreword by Peter Stein, Cambridge: Speculum historale, 1969. Still one of the most readable surveys of the influence of Roman law in the Middle Ages.

Canon Law

Guides and Sources

Dictionnaire de droit canonique. 7 vols. Paris: Letouzey et Ané, 1935–65.

Fournier, Paul and Gabriel Le Bras. *Histoire des collections canoniques en Occi-*

dent depuis les fausses décrétales jusqu'au Décret de Gratien. 2 vols. Paris: Sirey, 1931–32. Reprinted, Aalen: Scientia, 1972.

Kuttner, Stephan. *Repertorium der Kanonistik (1140–1234): Prodromus corporis glossarum.* Studi e testi 71. Vatican City: Biblioteca Apostolica Vaticana, 1937.

Maassen, Friedrich. *Geschichte der Quellen und der Literatur des canonischen Rechts im Abendlande.* Graz: Leuschner and Lubensky, 1870. Reprinted, Graz: Akademischer Druck, 1956.

Monumenta iuris canonici. Series A: Corpus Glossatorum. 4 vols. Vatican City, 1969–90.

———. Series B. Corpus Collectionum. 7 vols. Vatican City, 1973–88.

Schulte, Johann Friedrich von. *Die Geschichte der Quellen und Literatur des canonischen Rechts.* 3 vols. Stuttgart: Ferdinand Enke, 1875–77. Reprinted, Graz: Akademischer Druck, 1956.

Studies

Kuttner, Stephan. *Gratian and the Schools of Law, 1140–1234.* London: Variorum, 1983.

———. *The History of Ideas and Doctrines of Canon Law in the Middle Ages.* London: Variorum, 1980.

———. *Medieval Councils, Decretals, and Collections of Canon Law.* London: Variorum, 1980.

Fuhrmann, Horst. *Einfluss und Verbreitung der pseudoisidorischen Fälschungen von ihrem Auftauchen bis in die neure Zeit.* 3 vols. Schriften der Monumenta Germaniae Historica 24. Stuttgart: Anton Hiersemann, 1972–74.

Gaudemet, Jean. *La formation de droit canonique médiéval au Moyen Age.* London: Variorum, 1984.

Mordek, Hubert. *Kirchenrecht und Reform im Frankenreich: Die Collectio vetus gallica, die älteste systematische Kanonensammlung des fränkischen Gallien, Studien und Edition.* Beiträge zur Geschichte und Quellenkunde des Mittelalters 1. Berlin: Walter de Gruyter, 1975.

Reynolds, Roger. "Law, Canon: To Gratian." *Dictionary of the Middle Ages* 7:395–413. New York: Scribner, 1986. An excellent survey of early canon law.

Studia Gratiana. 23 vols. Bologna: Apud Institutum iuridicum universitatis studiorum and Libereria Ateneo Salesiano: 1953–78.

Tierney, Brian. *Church Law and Constitutional Thought in the Middle Ages.* London: Variorum, 1979.

Medieval Science and Natural Philosophy

EDWARD GRANT

THE HISTORIOGRAPHY OF MEDIEVAL SCIENCE

 ERIOUS STUDY OF THE HISTORY of medieval science developed almost concurrently with the emergence of the history of science as an independent discipline during the late nineteenth and early twentieth centuries. That it did so is due almost exclusively to the heroic efforts of one scholar: Pierre Duhem (1861–1916) (for biographical and bibliographical data, see Jaki 1984; Gillispie 1970–80, 4:225–33. A gifted French physicist, who published in history and philosophy of science, as well as in physics and chemistry, Duhem sought to show that the expression "medieval science" was not a contradiction in terms. In support of this claim, he wrote fifteen volumes on medieval science between 1902 and 1916, the year of his death (of these, five were published posthumously as part of a ten-volume work; see Duhem 1913–59).

In these volumes, Duhem revealed wholly unexpected scientific developments in obscure and largely unknown medieval Aristotelian commentaries and theological treatises. Indeed, Duhem was often the first to blow away the dust of centuries from manuscript codices that had lain untouched since the late Middle Ages. What he found led him to the startling claim that the Scientific Revolution of the seventeenth century, associated with the glorious names of Nicholas Copernicus, Galileo Galilei, Johannes Kepler, and Isaac Newton, was but an extension and elaboration of physical and cosmological ideas formulated in the fourteenth century, primarily by Parisian masters at the University of Paris. Medieval scholastic authors were now important precursors of Galileo.

Duhem made medieval science a respectable field for research and placed it in the mainstream of scientific development. In so doing, he filled the hiatus that had existed between Greek and early modern science. For the first time, the history of science was provided with a genuine sense of continuity.

Although Duhem, and others whom he influenced, placed considerable emphasis on the subsequent impact of medieval science on seventeenth-century developments, our objective here will be to describe medieval science and natural philosophy in their own terms and in their own contexts without regard to subsequent influence.

Unfortunately, this is not as simple as it sounds. A fundamental problem arises in the seemingly different conceptualizations that characterize medieval science and science since the seventeenth century. It is difficult to avoid the use of modern terms to categorize certain medieval activities that were only given names and identities long after. Historians of medieval science inevitably speak about "geological" or "chemical" or "biological" thought in the Middle Ages, although those sciences received their names and disciplinary identities in the eighteenth and nineteenth centuries. Are historians of medieval science justified in using such anachronistic terms? Is it appropriate to speak of Aristotle's treatises on animals as "biology"? Indeed may we even speak of "Aristotelians" in the Middle Ages, when scholastic authors did not refer to themselves by such a term? Many similar anomalies could be mentioned. In my judgment, the use of such terms seems appropriate, not merely for convenience, but also because they represent similar subject matters common to both the medieval and modern periods.[1]

THE TRANSMISSION OF GRECO-ARABIC SCIENCE
TO THE LATIN WEST

If we conceive the Middle Ages as extending from approximately A.D. 500 to 1500, science on a large and meaningful scale did not intrude into the Latin West until the second half of the twelfth century, when the effort to appropriate Greco-Arabic science by translation into Latin was well underway.

Before that, only a miniscule part of Greek science had been available in Latin. During the early Middle Ages, western Europe subsisted on

a meager scientific fare that had been absorbed into handbooks and encyclopedic treatises associated with the names of Chalcidius, Macrobius,
Martianus Capella, Boethius, Isidore of Seville, Cassiodorus, and the Venerable Bede. The science embedded in these treatises was usually superficial, and frequently inaccurate or contradictory. Nothing illustrates the
sorry state of affairs better than the virtual absence of Euclid's *Elements,*
without which astronomy, optics, and much of mechanics were impossible.
Although a cosmological view of the world was available in Chalcidius's
partial translation of Plato's *Timaeus,* the latter did not of itself provide
a sufficiently detailed natural philosophy with adequate physical and meta-
physical principles.

Despite these enormous handicaps, a group of twelfth-century scholars
trained in a variety of Cathedral schools and including the likes of Ade-
lard of Bath, Bernard Silvester, Thierry of Chartres, William of Conches,
Clarenbaldus of Arras, and others, had begun to interpret natural phenomena, and even biblical texts, with critical objectivity (see Stiefel 1985;
H. Lemay 1977). Whether, if given sufficient time, this bold intellectual
venture would have generated new insights and theories about the physical
world will never be known. The influx of Greco-Arabic science into western Europe had already begun and would soon overwhelm the incipient
rational science that had been gradually evolving within the context of the
old learning.

The new positive attitude toward learning undoubtedly encouraged
Europeans to seek out Arabic and Greek scientific and philosophical texts.
They now behaved much as the Arabs before them. Just as many Arabic
speaking scholars actively sought, rather than passively received, Greek
science and philosophy following the rapid spread of Islam, so also did
Latin scholars of the twelfth century travel to the sources of the new knowledge and actively and vigorously appropriate it.

The achievements of the international brigade of translators that
labored in Spain, Sicily, and northern Italy were truly monumental. Within
a period of approximately 130 years, they made available in Latin much,
if not most, of the cumulative scientific knowledge that had been produced
by the civilizations of Greece and Islam. Among these treasures were the
works of Aristotle and the commentaries of Averroës, which together would
dominate scientific thought for the next 400 years; Euclid's *Elements;* Ptolemy's *Almagest,* the greatest astronomical treatise until the *De revolutioni-
bus* of Copernicus; Alhazen's *Optics,* the *Algebra* of al-Khwarizmi; and
the medical works of Galen, Hippocrates, and Avicenna. Many lesser works
were also rendered into Latin (Lindberg 1978, 52–90; Grant 1974, 35–38).
And if we push into the 1260s and 1270s, we must add the approximately

fifty translations from Greek into Latin by William of Moerbeke, which include nearly all the works of Archimedes and Aristotle, as well as numerous commentaries on the latter's works of Aristotle by such famous Greek commentators as Simplicius, Themistius, Alexander of Aphrodisias, and John Philoponus (Grant 1974, 39–41).

As a direct consequence of the translations, two things occurred that might not otherwise have happened. Firstly, they made available a powerful, comprehensive body of philosophical and scientific literature which provided the fundamental core of the medieval university curriculum. Secondly, the study of that curriculum and the reaction to it generated a vast literature, much of it in the form of commentaries on authoritative texts (especially the natural books of Aristotle). Here, then, was the foundation on which the continuous development of science from the thirteenth century to the present was based. Although much, indeed most, of medieval natural philosophy was rejected by the end of the seventeenth century, the problems it had posed and grappled with constituted much of the agenda for the emerging new anti-scholastic science. In truth, the Scientific Revolution of the seventeenth century is not readily conceivable without the nearly five centuries of medieval thought that preceded.

SCIENCE IN THE MEDIEVAL UNIVERSITIES

During the late Middle Ages, science was essentially a university activity carried on primarily by university teachers and university graduates whose similar backgrounds tended to generate treatises of similar format and structure.[2] To speak of "science in the medieval universities" is to speak of medieval science in general.

To appreciate the range of science and sciences that were taught at medieval universities, it is essential to grasp the division of the faculties at universities such as Paris and Oxford, which were perhaps the most important in Christendom during the thirteenth and fourteenth centuries. The largest and most basic was the arts faculty, which granted the bachelor of arts and master of arts degrees. The former required four years and the latter two additional years. The master of arts degree was a prerequisite for entry into the higher faculties of theology, medicine, and law. Although only medicine, of the three higher faculties, was devoted to the teaching of a particular science, theologians, as we shall see, discussed numerous scientific problems within the context of theology. Their discussions, however, were ultimately based upon the science that was taught in the arts faculty, to which we must now turn (based on Grant 1984).

Science in the Arts Faculty

The Division of Knowledge

Before the twelfth century most works available in the domain of theoretical secular knowledge belonged to one or another of the seven liberal arts, namely, grammar, rhetoric, and dialectic or logic, which formed the *trivium,* and arithmetic, geometry, astronomy, and music, which together comprised the *quadrivium.* With the influx of the works of Aristotle and Greco-Arabic science in the second half of the twelfth century, the primacy of the seven liberal arts ceased as they became pathways, or handmaidens to philosophy (see McInerny in Wagner 1983, 248–72, especially 250–53),[3] which consisted of natural philosophy, metaphysics, and moral philosophy. Of these "three philosophies," as they were usually called (for texts, see Weisheipl 1964, 173–76), the last-named was irrelevant for science. The other two — natural philosophy and metaphysics — plus mathematics made up theoretical knowledge as Aristotle and his scholastic followers conceived it.[4] Of these domains of knowledge, natural philosophy treated of motion and change in material bodies; mathematics considered things (lines, surfaces, and solids) that are mobile and immaterial but which are abstracted from material bodies; and metaphysics, sometimes called "first philosophy" or "the divine science," was used to evaluate things that are immobile and immaterial, that is, wholly separated from matter (see Grant 1974, 61–62; Kilwardby 1976, 14). Thus, natural philosophy, or "natural science" as it was often called (Kilwardby 1976, 17, 23, 64), was concerned with the whole spectrum of change that affected bodies, including motion from place to place. Although all three subdivisions of theoretical knowledge were represented in the curriculum of medieval universities, metaphysics seems to have been taught as part of natural philosophy (Siraisi 1973, 134; Daly 1961, 79–80) and masters of arts lectured and published in both subjects. Since the mathematical sciences and natural philosophy constituted the core of science in the arts faculty, we shall focus on them.

The Quadrivium or Mathematical Sciences

In its narrower signification, mathematics in the Middle Ages and at the universities was equivalent to the *quadrivium* of the seven liberal arts — that is, arithmetic, geometry, astronomy, and music.[5] The versions of these subjects that were taught in the universities and that were generally available in the late Middle Ages differed greatly in rigor and sophistication from what passed for these subjects in the time of Boethius and the early

Middle Ages. Because Boethius wrote extant treatises on arithmetic and music, there was continuity in these two subjects between the early and late Middle Ages. Perhaps because it was overly philosophical and lacked formal proofs, Boethius's *De arithmetica* remained popular throughout the late Middle Ages (Weisheipl 1964, 170; Masi 1981, 67–80; P. Kibre in Masi 1981, 81–95). It was, however, necessary to supplement it with books 7–9 of Euclid's *Elements,* the propositions of which were exclusively arithmetical and formally demonstrated.[6] There was also a significant practical component to arithmetic, where treatises with names like *Algorismus vulgaris* described and exemplified the four arithmetic operations with whole numbers, while others with names like *Algorismus minutiarum,* or *Algorismus de minutiis,* described the same operations for sexagesimal and vulgar fractions (Grant 1984, 73, 95–96, nn. 23, 24).

Boethius's *De musica* also served as a university text, but was supplemented as theoretical music leaped forward in the fourteenth century with new texts by Philippe de Vitry (1291–1361) and John of Murs (fl. first half of fourteenth century).[7]

Prior to the twelfth century, when the translation of Euclid's *Elements* from Arabic to Latin dramatically altered the situation, geometry does not appear to have been a functional discipline. Only meager fragments survived to serve the *quadrivium.*[8] Although university courses in geometry relied mostly on the first six books of the *Elements,*[9] practical and applied geometry were also emphasized in treatises that were called *Practica geometriae,* wherein methods were described for determining various measurements, such as the heights of objects and the areas and volumes of different figures (see Grant 1974, 180–87; Victor 1979).

Subjects within natural philosophy to which mathematics was applied were grouped under the heading of "middle sciences" (*scientiae mediae*). Classified within this group were the sciences of astronomy, one of the quadrivial sciences which will be considered in the next paragraph, optics, or perspective (*perspectiva*), statics, or the "science of weights" (*scientia de ponderibus*) (Weisheipl 1964, 171) harmonics, the doctrine of the intension and remission of forms, which applied arithmetic and geometry to represent the variation of qualities (see Grant 1972) and engineering, or the "science of devices (*scientia de ingeniis*)."[10]

By comparison to what preceded, astronomy was virtually a new science in the twelfth century when Ptolemy's famous *Almagest* was translated along with a number of Arabic astronomical treatises most of which utilized Ptolemy's work and a few that opposed it.[11] During the Latin Middle Ages, astronomy was intimately linked with astrology. According to Robert Kilwardby, astronomy (*astronomia*) was concerned with the motions, magnitudes, and positions of the celestial bodies and was wholly dependent on mathematics. By contrast, astrology (*astrologia*) was concerned with the powers and forces that emanated from those celestial bodies and the manner in which they affected terrestrial bodies (Kilwardby 1976, 34). Despite the different definitions, Kilwardby observes that, like *scientia* and *sapientia,* the terms *astronomia* and *astrologia* were often used interchangeably.[12]

As described here, astrology was compatible with Aristotle's conviction that the celestial region was the ultimate cause of all physical change in the terrestrial region. But in the tradition deriving from Ptolemy's dominant astrological treatise, *Tetrabiblos* (Ptolemy 1948), known as the *Quadripartitum* in its Latin translation (for Latin versions, see Carmody 1956, 13–14, 18–19) and from numerous Arabic treatises, astrology also claimed that if properly interpreted the stars could provide knowledge about future events in the terrestrial world and about the fate of individual human beings. Some even believed that astral control over the celestial region was total. While such claims were controversial and even contrary to Christian doctrine, judicial and horoscopic, or natal, astrology were sometimes taught at the universities.[13] But greater emphasis was placed on astronomy as embodied in two famous medieval texts: *On the Sphere* (*De sphaera*) by John of Sacrobosco, which provided in four chapters a general cosmological and astronomical sketch of the spherical universe (for text and translation, see Thorndike 1949; for selections, Grant 1974, 442–51) and *The Theory of the Planets* (*Theorica planetarum*), a more technical treatise that not only provided a lengthy list of definitions of astronomical terms but also described the motions of the planets in Ptolemaic terms, that is by means of eccentric orbs and epicycles.[14]

Natural Philosophy

Although the introduction of Aristotelian learning to the University of Paris generated resistance during most of the thirteenth century, Aristotle's natural philosophy was firmly entrenched in the arts curriculum, and formed its core, by 1250. Of the three philosophies mentioned above, "natural philosophy," or "natural science," was the most extensive. It encompassed what were known as Aristotle's "natural books" (*libri naturales*), namely his *Physics, On the Heavens (De caelo), On Generation and Corruption, On the Soul (De anima), Meteorology, The Small Works on Natural Things (Parva naturalia),* and *On Animals (De animalibus).*[15] On the basis of these treatises, natural philosophy, as we saw above, was said to treat of mobile and material bodies (Kilwardby 1976, 14, par. 15; 17, par. 21), or as Domingo Gundisalvo put it, "the matter of natural science is body . . . according to what is subjected to motion and rest and change."[16] Based on the content of the "natural books," natural philosophy included cosmology, matter theory (that is, the theory of elements and compounds),[17] sense perception, and physics in the broad sense of substantial, qualitative, and quantitative change, as well as the motions of bodies from one place to another. It also embraced the study of animate matter in the form of plants and animals. Natural philosophy was thus the study of the principles of change for all animate and inanimate bodies that made up the physical world. Its principles delineated the structure and operation of the physical world.

Questions on Natural Philosophy

As the broadest and most comprehensive discipline for the study of the physical world, natural philosophy consisted of the study of the works of Aristotle mentioned above. Although initially the texts of those works were explained section by section, the teaching masters frequently posed questions at the end of a lecture on the texts they had just explained. The customary treatment of such a question required the presentation of its pros and cons, followed by the master's resolution (see Beaujouan 1963). In this way, each question represented a problem based on a portion of text in a particular work of Aristotle's, but also included the opinions of the teacher as well as the ideas of other commentators, both ancient and modern. Eventually the questions, themselves, became the focal point of a medieval education in natural philosophy. For each book and chapter of every treatise in the Aristotelian corpus of natural philosophy, certain problems, or *questiones* emerged. Thus instead of commenting on each text section by section in sequence, as was done in a typical commentary, the arts masters extracted a series of questions they thought important and discussed them sequentially.[18] Since the *questio* lies at the heart of medieval scholastic method, let us briefly describe the anatomy of a typical question.

In its structured format, the enunciation of the problem or question came first, usually beginning with a phrase such as "let us inquire whether" or simply "whether," as, for example, "whether the earth is spherical," or "whether the earth moves." This was followed by one or more solutions supporting either the negative or affirmative position. If the affirmative position was initially favored, the reader could confidently assume that the author would ultimately adopt the negative position; or conversely, if the negative side appeared first, it could be assumed that the author would subsequently adopt and defend the affirmative side. The initial opinions, which the author would later reject, were called the "principal arguments" (*rationes principales*). Immediately after the enunciation of the principal arguments, the author might explain his understanding of the question, that is, he might further clarify and qualify it or define and explain particular terms in it. Following this, he was ready to present his opinions, usually by way of one or more detailed conclusions or propositions. In order to anticipate objections, he might choose to raise doubts about his own conclusions and subsequently resolve them. At the termination of the question, the master would respond to each of the "principal arguments" enunciated at the outset.

Hundreds of questions drawn from Aristotle's natural books formed the basis of natural science in the medieval university.[19] To a considerable extent, doing medieval scholastic science meant analyzing and evaluating these questions to arrive at the most satisfactory conclusions. Although the number of original thinkers among the medieval masters was not large, many arts masters and theologians contributed *questiones* treatises to an always growing body of scientific literature. The questions encompassed heaven and earth, and ranged over virtually every aspect of celestial and terrestrial operation that was deemed important in the Middle Ages.

By its very nature, the *questio* form encouraged differences of opinion. It was a good vehicle for dispute and argumentation. Medieval scholastics were trained to dispute and therefore often disagreed among themselves. Far from slavish devotion to Aristotle, they were emboldened by the very system within which they were nurtured to arrive at their own conclusions, or at the very least to choose from a minimum of two, and often more, previously distinguished conclusions. The system might have been quite different, had it simply provided them with a conclusion and then merely supplied a rationale and defense of that conclusion.

In principle, one was expected to evaluate arguments critically and by a process of elimination arrive at the truth. Scholastic ingenuity was displayed by introducing subtle distinctions that, upon further development, might yield new opinions on a given question.

Within the framework of these typical questions, medieval teaching masters organized their lecture courses and eventually their publications, which were usually based on revised versions of their lectures. By critical analysis of these questions based upon the substance of Aristotle's texts and available interpretations of them, Aristotle's ideas were explained and frequently altered, sometimes unwittingly. In this way did medieval conceptions about the physical world change.

Science in the Medical Faculty

Of the great decline in the sciences between the fifth to twelfth centuries, medicine had suffered the least. Not only were a small number of Latin translations of Greek texts from the Hippocratic corpus and the works of Galen available, but Latin medical treatises were also written, especially in the ninth century. These treatises were practical in nature, concentrating on diagnosis and therapeutics with virtually no concern for the causes and symptoms of disease. In a word, they ignored the theory of medicine (see Talbot in Lindberg 1978, 392).

The remedy for this deficiency began with the translations of Constantine the African (d. 1085) at Monte Cassino in the eleventh century. But it was not until "the 1230s and 1240s that medical writings permeated with Aristotelian and Arabic modes of thought began to appear" (Talbot in Lindberg 1978, 402). Medicine came now to be thought of as a science (*scientia*) rather than a craft because it had absorbed Aristotelian metaphysics and natural philosophy. It was thus a worthy subject of study for the emerging universities of the thirteenth century, worthy enough to acquire independent status as a higher faculty, a development that acknowledged its reliance on the arts curriculum as an essential component of a medical education.[20] As beneficiaries of Greco-Arabic learning in natural philosophy and medicine, famous medical schools emerged in the thirteenth century at the universities of Paris, Bologna, Montpellier, and Padua. With its status as an independent, higher faculty in the medieval university, medicine achieved professional status and was the first science to do so (see Bullough 1966, 46–73).

Medical education was based upon authoritative texts from Galen, Hippocrates, Avicenna, Averröes, and other Arabic and Jewish medical authors. Just as in the faculty of arts, teachers in the medical faculty often expressed their opinions by way of commentaries or *questiones* on basic texts. But they also composed independent treatises as a great number of extant medical works from the late Middle Ages bears witness (for examples, see McVaugh in Grant 1974, 700–808). A special kind of medical treatise of Italian origin was the *consilium,* which was something akin to a case history. *Consilia* were written by physicians for patients or for study by other physicians and perhaps also for students (on *consilia,* see Lockwood 1951, 44–138; Siraisi 1973, 160–61; Daly 1961, 95).[21]

If medicine gained scientific status this was because as a *scientia* it could derive universal truths by necessity from certain assumed premises. But medicine was also an art (*ars*), which signified that it treated contingent, particular cases that could not yield universal truths. These two divergent and seemingly conflicting aspects of medicine were much discussed by scholastic medical authors.[22] Medicine was also naturally divided into theoretical and practical. The latter, like theoretical medicine, was also taught from textbooks. It was an aspect of medical education in which rules and norms were formulated for application to individual cases each of which seems unique (McVaugh 1987, 310). Thus, the practice (*practica*) of medicine in the sense just described belonged more to theory than to the actual practice of medicine in the sickroom at the bedside of a patient.

Although the integration of natural philosophy and the arts into medicine[23] made the latter more respectable during the thirteenth century, it had, for obvious reasons, a more practical and social side than any of the disciplines with theoretical and practical aspects among the sciences of the *quadrivium*. However theoretical medicine was, it had to be applied ultimately to those who were ill or to those who sought to preserve their health. Recent evidence indicates that both students and professors in medical schools were actively involved in the practice of medicine (McVaugh 1987, 301). At Padua, "despite the emphasis upon the study of Greek and Arab authorities, despite the emphasis upon scholastic analysis of texts, and despite the emphasis upon astrology, the teaching of medicine . . . was in the hands of practicing physicians and largely oriented toward medical practice" (Siraisi 1973, 162). Even the well-known divorce between surgery and medicine was by no means universal. In universities like Paris and Oxford, surgery was excluded from the curriculum because it was viewed as a mere craft, whereas in Italian medical schools like Bologna and Padua surgery was considered a science and therefore included in the curriculum, wherein it was taught by professionals who were accepted as colleagues by the physicians (Talbot in Lindberg 1978, 411; Siraisi 1973, 165–66).

SOME GENERAL FEATURES OF MEDIEVAL SCIENCE

The Doing of Science

The sciences we have briefly described or mentioned made up virtually the whole of medieval science and natural philosophy. Although the *questiones* format of scientific literature has been emphasized here, numerous straightforward treatises were also written, some of which actually included the term *tractatus* in their titles, as *Tractatus de spera* or *Tractatus de proportionibus*. Here, some particular subject was examined in systematic detail. Among such works, a few which have already been mentioned, are the treatises on proportions by Thomas Bradwardine and Nicole Oresme; the treatises on the sphere by Robert Grosseteste and John of Sacrobosco; the *Opus Maius* and *De multiplicatione specierum* of Roger Bacon; the *De iride (On the Rainbow)* of Dietrich of Freiberg; the *Perspectiva* of Witelo, and many others. Composed by university trained scholars, few of these treatises were used as texts, although some were undoubtedly well known in university communities.

Except for the application of medicine to the sick, medieval science was essentially a bookish activity based upon a learned tradition. Although at least one medieval author, Roger Bacon, sought to make experimental science a separate and indispensable discipline for the doing of science (Fisher and Unguru 1971), the concept of experimental science and systematic observation to test hypotheses never formed an integral part of medieval scientific methodology.[24] Laboratory research was unknown because experiments were not thought of as a regular feature of scientific investigation. Medieval natural philosophers reacted to the textual tradition they inherited and remained within it.

Without laboratory research or any sense of regular experimentation, the doing of science during the Middle Ages was overwhelmingly a matter of reacting to a text or a disciplinary tradition embodied in a text. For a medieval master to do science or natural philosophy within the framework of the university system was to present an oral or written analysis of some of the many questions that collectively formed the basis of the medieval view of the physical world.

The Application of Mathematics to Nature

Almost all historians of science would agree that the application of mathematics to physics, that is, the use of mathematics to measure and quantify natural phenomena, especially motion, is a characteristic feature of modern science, one that is associated with the Scientific Revolution of the seventeenth century and most prominently with the names of Galileo and Newton. This breakthrough has been hailed as a dramatic departure from medieval Aristotelian science in which mathematics was conceived as largely inapplicable to natural phenomena. But one must distinguish between what Aristotle may have said and how medieval scholastics interpreted him. Already in the thirteenth century, Robert Grosseteste and Roger Bacon considered the application of mathematics to physics as essential to science (Fisher and Unguru 1971, 371-74; Lindberg 1982, 24-25). During the fourteenth century, the application of mathematics and mathematical modes of thought to problems about natural phenomena became commonplace. Many such applications occurred in areas that represented significant departures from Aristotle's ideas, or expansions of his ideas that he would not have recognized.[25]

But there are vital differences between the way mathematics was applied in the late Middle Ages and in the seventeenth century. When scholastics applied proportionality theory to problems of motion, they never tested the results to see if bodies actually moved in accordance with the mathematical laws they formulated.[26] Moreover the problems treated in the widely used discipline of the intension and remission of forms and qualities were of a hypothetical nature, often described as *secundum imaginationem*. Imaginary situations were conjured in which variable qualities and passions of all kinds — for example, colors, temperatures, sounds, pains, fears, hopes, sorrows, joys, motions, and so on — were assumed to vary. Whether such qualities actually varied in nature in the ways imagined seemed of no concern. Despite the divorce from reality, medieval natural philosophers managed to arrive at important definitions about the variation of qualities that were especially relevant to the motion of bodies. Thus, they defined concepts such as uniform motion, uniformly accelerated motion, and instantaneous motion. From such definitions, they formulated the famous mean speed theorem, which Galileo used as the foundation of his new mechanics, and upon which he did not improve.[27]

The Impact of Theology on Science

The assumption of imaginary conditions, or counterfactuals, was commonplace in medieval natural philosophy. Inferences drawn from such imaginary conditions were rarely applied to nature as a physical reality. Such activities were not confined to the application of measure languages.[28] Fear of theological censure during the thirteenth century encouraged some to frame certain arguments *secundum imaginationem.*

Because they espoused the eternity of the world and seemed to deny the immortality of the soul, among other things, Aristotle's natural books caused considerable turmoil when introduced into the University of Paris in the thirteenth century. In one form or another, Aristotelian natural philosophy lay at the heart of controversies that pitted arts masters against theologians and theologians against theologians. The culmination of these troubles came in 1277, when the bishop of Paris issued his famous – or infamous – condemnation of 219 propositions, quite a number of which affected natural philosophy.[29]

One of the major issues concerned God's absolute power. A number of theses about the physical world that Aristotle showed to be naturally impossible had to be conceded as supernaturally possible to the divine power. Indeed, article 147 proclaimed this very sentiment when it condemned the view that not even God can do what is naturally impossible. For example, Aristotle had argued that it was impossible that more than one world could exist; or that a vacuum could exist; or that new effects could be introduced into the world. After 1277, however, one had to concede that God could, if He wished, create a plurality of worlds, produce vacua anywhere He pleased, or create new effects in the world.

A significant consequence of the frequent appeal to God's absolute power was to encourage the formulation of hypothetical arguments in which God was assumed to produce a supernatural effect that was considered impossible in Aristotle's physics and cosmology. The implications of that naturally impossible effect were then drawn and analyzed. Such hypothetical conditions were frequently assumed in discussions about the possibility of vacua where God was imagined to annihilate all or some of the matter within our world. Many questions, or "thought experiments," were then posed about the behavior of bodies in those empty spaces (for examples, see Grant 1979). Much that was of interest in medieval natural philosophy resulted from inquiries into hypothetical situations.

Societal Influences on Medieval Science

Insofar as the Church attempted to control and guide the development of natural philosophy, as in the Condemnation of 1277, it may have functioned as an external social influence shaping opinions about the physical world. By means of benefices the Church also furnished support to faculty and students, and may thus be said to have indirectly served as a patron of the sciences.[30] Since Church support was channeled through the universities, the latter were the real social, or better, institutional, matrices of medieval science.

Through their faculties, the universities determined the kinds of scientific questions and problems that would occupy scholastic authors and students. Apart from physicians, the Middle Ages did not produce a professional class of scientists. Because science and natural philosophy fell under their jurisdiction, the members of arts faculties were the nearest medieval analog to such a class. Arts masters trained students from diverse backgrounds — nobles, peasants, and burgers — and molded them into a homogeneous intellectual group from which they would recruit their colleagues and successors. Scholastic training compelled all to operate within a certain framework based largely on the *questio,* which changed hardly at all over the centuries. Indeed, the questions treated and the responses given often seem strikingly similar. And yet, the questions and the responses were by no means static. Authors who chose to write on a particular Aristotelian treatise rarely treated the very same questions, and often enough differed in their conclusions. But the format remained impersonal, so that one could no more determine the social class of a scholastic author who had written questions on Aristotle's natural books than one could determine the social background of a modern physicist from a scholarly article or book.

Except for the university and the Church, operating through the university, no other meaningful social influences appear to have affected medieval science and natural philosophy. Despite significant political, religious, and economic changes in Europe during the thirteenth to fifteenth centuries, the format and content of an arts education remained remarkably constant. The scholastic *questio* reigned supreme, with virtually no change in its structure and content.

The Manuscript Basis of Medieval Science

Before the advent of printing in the middle of the fifteenth century, medieval science depended for its existence on handwritten texts, and therefore unavoidably suffered all the concomitant uncertainties of such a medium of preservation and dissemination. Reliance on manuscripts meant that versions of the same treatise in Paris and Oxford might well differ, perhaps in significant ways. Often essential diagrams and figures in mathematical and astronomical works were omitted in some manuscripts, or only partially included. Even when included, scribal errors could reduce or destroy the utility of a diagram. Errors abounded in scientific texts, as is readily apparent by an examination of variant readings in modern editions.

From our vantage point, we can see how difficult it must have been to do science in the Middle Ages. Knowledge was as likely to disappear as to be acquired. An enormous effort was required simply to preserve the status quo or occasionally to restore texts that had been inherited from Greco-Arabic sources.[31] Although we may be unable to measure the detri-

mental effects on medieval science that followed solely from dependence
on a manuscript tradition, we may rightly judge that they were enormous.
It is not a mere coincidence that the Scientific Revolution began shortly
after the introduction of printing in Europe.

CONCLUSION

Because popular opinion has often portrayed the Middle Ages as a period
virtually devoid of science and often openly hostile to it, it is surprising,
if not astonishing, to learn that for centuries the education of legions of
medieval university students was essentially a study of the science of the
day and was thus concerned with the structure and operation of the physical world. Whether or not they pursued an academic career, university-
educated individuals were probably well versed in the prevalent theories
and interpretations of contemporary science, a claim that cannot be made
for modern society.

What was transmitted from generation to generation of students and
scholars during the late Middle Ages was the Greco-Arabic scientific heritage made available by the translators of the twelfth and thirteenth centuries. In this regard, medieval scholastics served to preserve a rich legacy
of learning. But the medieval contribution was not merely passive and
preservative. The Middle Ages witnessed the creation of an intellectual environment that promoted the study of science and natural philosophy.
Within this environment, significant and praiseworthy contributions were
made that greatly expanded the Greco-Arabic scientific corpus.

The existence of an atmosphere conducive to scientific and philosophical creativity was possible in no small measure because the Church and
its theologians encouraged rather than opposed these activities. For despite occasional appearances to the contrary, as in the Condemnation of
1277 and the unfortunate case of Galileo, the Church and its theologians were keenly interested in science and natural philosophy and made
significant contributions to it. The names of Roger Bacon, Albertus
Magnus, Thomas Aquinas, Thomas Bradwardine, Dietrich of Freiberg,
and Nicole Oresme bear eloquent testimony to this claim. What might have
been a devastating split between natural philosophy and theology, with
the latter dominating and controlling the former, did not occur. The tensions that developed between science and theology cannot overshadow
the fact that for the most part they survived independently but interacted
fruitfully.

Centuries of analysis, evaluation, and criticism had also altered the scientific inheritance and produced significant additions and alterations. While Aristotle retained his status as the preeminent authority in natural philosophy, his judgments on many subjects and problems were challenged and often abandoned. These challenges to Aristotle and others formed part of the legacy that reached the sixteenth and seventeenth centuries.

Medieval science preserved and expanded the Greco-Arabic scientific heritage. To recognize the significance of late medieval science one has only to realize that a Scientific Revolution would have been improbable if the level of science available to natural philosophers and scientists in the sixteenth and seventeenth centuries had been that of the first half of the twelfth century, prior to the great influx of translations. The Middle Ages presented to the developers of the new science a body of ideas to which they could react. To this extent, the new science may be said to have grown from the old, despite the fact that most of those ideas would be abandoned or repudiated.

NOTES

1. Without such terms, we could not, for example, speak of Newtonian "physics," since Newton, when he wrote in the seventeenth century, did not use the term. Indeed, there was as yet no special discipline of physics.

2. Because alchemy does not appear to have been a university subject, alchemists might prove an exception to this generalization. For summaries of the life and works of a few authors who may not have had university connections, see Gillispie 1970–80, 4:604–13 (Leonardo of Pisa or Fibonacci); 5:360 (Gerard of Brussels); 7:171–79 (Jordanus de Nemore); and 10:532–40 (Peter Peregrinus).

3. Although all the seven liberal arts were represented in the university curriculum, they were not taught under the name of the seven liberal arts, nor was a university education perceived as an education in the seven liberal arts. The influx of Greco-Arabic knowledge into western Europe in the twelfth century had expanded the notion of higher education far beyond the bounds of the seven liberal arts. See Grant 1984, 93–94, n. 9.

4. Aristotle divided knowledge into theoretical, practical, and productive sciences. See Aristotle, *Topics* 6.6.145a and *Metaphysics* 6.1.

5. The term *quadrivium* rarely occurs in university statutes (Kibre 1969, 175).

6. Jordanus de Nemore's early thirteenth-century *Arithmetica,* with its Euclidean format and more than 400 propositions, may also have served as a text. On Jordanus, see Grant in Gillispie 1970–80, 7:171–79.

7. Philippe's name is associated with the *Ars nova* (Sarton 1927–48, 3(1): 742–44), which introduced new musical notations, while John of Murs's treatises considered musical problems mathematically. On the latter and for the titles of his musical treatises, see E. Poulle in Gillispie 1970–80 7:128–33. The extent to which music formed a university subject is little known. At Oxford, it does not appear in the curriculum lists until 1431 (Weisheipl 1964, 171).

For the role of music at Padua, see Siraisi 1973, 94–107. On the impact of natural philosophy on music, see Murdoch, 1976 119–36.

8. For a brief history of the fate of geometry and Euclid's *Elements* in the early Middle Ages, see Menso Folkerts in Masi 1981, 187–209.

9. For a history of the translation of medieval versions of Euclid's *Elements,* see J. E. Murdoch in Gillispie 1970–80, 4:443–48.

10. In his *De divisione philosophiae,* Domingo Gundisalvo (fl. 1140) considers the application of geometry to the measurement of stones by stone masons, for devices that lift things, and even for the making of bows and arrows (see Grant 1974, 76).

11. The extent of Arabic influence on Latin astronomy and astrology can be gauged from Carmody (1956).

12. In *De divisione philosophiae,* Domingo Gundisalvo actually switched their usual meanings, describing astrology as "the science of mobile magnitude which seeks out with searching reason the courses of the stars, their figures, and the relations of the stars both with respect to themselves and with respect to the earth" and astronomy as "the science which describes, according to the belief of men, the courses and position of the stars, for obtaining a knowledge of the times" (Grant 1974, 74, 75).

13. Peter of Abano seems to have taught astrology at the University of Padua around 1300 (Siraisi 1973, 81–89).

14. For Olaf Pedersen's English translation of the *Theorica,* see Grant 1974, 451–65. The *Theorica,* which may have been composed at Paris between 1260 and 1280 (Grant 1974, 451), is extant in hundreds of manuscripts. Sometime between 1261 and 1264, Campanus of Novara produced another popular treatise with the same title. Although far longer and more technical, Campanus's work may also have been used as an astronomy text. For the edition and translation, see Francis S. Benjamin, Jr., and G. J. Toomer, ed. and trans., *Campanus of Novara and Medieval Planetary Theory* (Madison: Univ. of Wisconsin Press, 1971).

15. These are the same books Kilwardby cites (1976, 23–28) in his discussion of the content of natural philosophy. He also adds the pseudo-Aristotelian *Liber vegetabilium,* which is actually the *De plantis* of Nicholas of Damascus. In chaps. 6–10, pp. 15–29, Kilwardby describes natural philosophy.

16. Gundisalvo distinguished eight parts of natural philosophy most of which correspond to one or more of Aristotle's treatises (Grant 1974, 63–64). He omits the *Parva naturalia* but includes two spurious Aristotelian works: the *Book on Minerals (Liber de mineralibus),* which Kilwardby omitted, and *On Plants (De plantis).*

17. Although the elements and compounds bear no real relationship to modern chemical elements and compounds, this part of natural philosophy corresponds to chemistry. Geology would also fall under natural philosophy.

18. Although the selection of questions on a particular Aristotelian treatise would vary from master to master, a surprisingly large number of substantially identical questions appeared between the thirteenth and seventeenth centuries.

19. For typical questions from four of Aristotle's works on natural philosophy by three famous fourteenth century masters, see Grant 1974, 199–210.

20. The impact on medicine of two of the quadrivial arts, music and astrology or astronomy, was considerable. For the influence of music on medicine, see Cosman 1978; for the role of astrology in medicine, see R. Lemay 1976, 200–208.

21. Siraisi (1973, 161) observes that other kinds of medical literature included "medical dictionaries, herbals, and collections of medical recipes."

22. On the division between *scientia* and *ars,* see McVaugh 1987, 308.

23. More than one physician called himself "magistrum in artibus et medicina" (Mc-Vaugh 1987, 308).

24. A few authors did make sustained observations and some performed occasional experiments. For illustrations, see Grant 1974, 368–76 (Peter Peregrinus); 657–81 (Frederick II of Hohenstaufen); 654–57 (Albertus Magnus); 435–41 (Dietrich of Freiberg).

25. John Murdoch (1975) has characterized the different types of mathematical applications as "measure languages."

26. Occasionally someone appealed to experience to refute a theory, as did Thomas Bradwardine in his *Tractatus de proportionibus* (Grant 1974, 298).

27. For a description of the mean speed theorem and a medieval proof, see Grant 1971, 56–58. Unlike his medieval predecessors, Galileo not only organized the medieval definitions into an ordered whole but applied the mean speed theorem to real motions rather than to hypothetical and imaginary variations of qualities. What emerged was the beginning of modern mathematical physics.

28. To an astonishing degree, the measure languages were also applied to a host of problems in theology, including the relations between God and His creatures, such as the concepts of sin, merit, grace, and so on. God was imagined in all manner of situations in which He performed some action that allowed for the application of these various languages of quantification. During the late Middle Ages, theology became a rather quantified subject, which illustrates the extent to which theologians were captivated by the quantitative aspects of natural philosophy in which they had all been trained.

29. There is now a considerable body of literature on the resistance to Aristotelian learning in the thirteenth century, which came to a climax with the Condemnation of 1277. See Wippel 1977; Hisette 1977; Grant 1974, 42–52; and Grant 1979.

30. Monarchs occasionally performed similar services. Thus, Frederick II is said to have subsidized Greek, Arabic, and Latin scholars at his court and in 1377, Charles V of France rewarded Nicole Oresme for his translations from Latin to French of four of Aristotle's works, one of which was the *De caelo,* a significant scientific treatise. Perhaps William of Moerbeke, who, while at the Papal Court in Viterbo, translated many scientific works from Greek into Latin, including most of the works of Aristotle and Archimedes, also received Church support for his activities.

31. For a discussion of this point, see Eisenstein 1979, 2:463–65.

BIBLIOGRAPHY

Beaujouan, Guy. 1963. "Motives and Opportunities for Science in the Medieval Universities." In *Scientific Change: Historical Studies in the Intellectual, Social and Technical Conditions for Scientific Discovery and Technical Invention, from Antiquity to the Present,* edited by A. C. Crombie, 219–36. Symposium on the History of Science, University of Oxford 9–15 July 1961. New York: Basic Books.

Bullough, Vern L. 1966. *The Development of Medicine as a Profession. The Contribution of the Medieval University to Modern Medicine.* Basel: Karger.

Carmody, Francis J. 1956. *Arabic Astronomical and Astrological Sciences in Latin Translation, A Critical Bibliography.* Berkeley: Univ. of California Press.

Clagett, Marshall. 1959. *The Science of Mechanics in the Middle Ages.* Madison: Univ. of Wisconsin Press.

Cosman, Madeleine Pelner. 1978. "Machaut's Medical Musical World." In *Machaut's World: Science and Art in the Fourteenth Century,* edited by Madeleine Pelner Cosman and Bruce Chandler, 1–36. Annals of the New York Academy of Sciences, 314. New York: New York Academy of Sciences.

Crombie, A. C. 1953. *Robert Grosseteste and the Origins of Experimental Science, 1100–1700.* Oxford: Clarendon.

————. 1959. *Medieval and Early Modern Science.* 2d ed. 2 vols. New York: Doubleday. Reprinted, Cambridge, Mass.: Harvard Univ. Press, 1963.

Daly, Lowrie J., S.J. 1961. *The Medieval University, 1200–1400.* With an introduction by Pearl Kibre. New York: Sheed & Ward.

Demaitre, Luke E. 1975. "Theory and Practice in Medical Education at the University of Montpellier in the Thirteenth and Fourteenth Centuries." *Journal of the History of Medicine and Allied Sciences* 30:103–23.

Duhem, Pierre. 1913–59. *Le Système du monde: Histoire des doctrines cosmologiques de Platon à Copernic.* 10 vols. Paris: Hermann.

————. 1985. *Medieval Cosmology: Theories of Infinity, Place, Time, Void, and the Plurality of Worlds.* Edited and translated by Roger Ariew. Chicago: Univ. of Chicago Press.

Eisenstein, Elizabeth L. 1979. *The Printing Press as an Agent of Change. Communications and Cultural Transformations in Early-Modern Europe.* 2 vols. Cambridge: Cambridge Univ. Press. The second volume treats of the impact of printing on science.

Fisher, N. W., and Sabetai Unguru. 1971. "Experimental Science and Mathematics in Roger Bacon's Thought." *Traditio* 28:353–78.

Gillispie, Charles Coulston, ed. 1970–80. *Dictionary of Scientific Biography.* 16 vols. New York: Scribner. Vol. 16 is an index to the whole. Contains hundreds of articles on medieval natural philosophers.

Grant, Edward. 1968. Essay Review of *Nicole Oresme and the Medieval Geometry of Qualities and Motions. A Treatise on the Uniformity and Difformity of Intensities known as 'Tractatus de configurationibus qualitatum et motuum.'* Edited with an introduction, English translation and commentary by Marshall Clagett. Madison: Univ. of Wisconsin Press. Reviewed in *Studies in the History and Philosophy of Science* 3(1972): 167–82.

————. 1971. *Physical Science in the Middle Ages.* New York: John Wiley. Reprinted, Cambridge: Cambridge Univ. Press, 1977.

————, ed. 1974. *A Source Book in Medieval Science.* Cambridge, Mass.: Harvard Univ. Press.

————. 1979. "The Condemnation of 1277, God's Absolute Power, and Physical Thought in the Late Middle Ages." *Viator* 10:211–14.

————. 1984. "Science and the Medieval University." In *Rebirth, Reform and Resilience: Universities in Transition, 1300–1700.* Edited by James M. Kittelson and Pamela J. Transue, 68–102. Columbus: Ohio State Univ. Press.

————. 1986. "Science and Theology in the Middle Ages." In *God and Nature,*

Historical Essays on the Encounter between Christianity and Science, edited by David C. Lindberg and Ronald L. Numbers. Berkeley: Univ. of California Press.

Hisette, Roland. 1977. *Enquête sur les 219 articles condamnés à Paris le 7 Mars 1277.* Louvain: Publication Universitaires; Paris: Vander-Oyez.

Isis Cumulative Bibliography. 1971-82. A Bibliography of the History of Science Formed from Isis Critical Bibliographies 1-90, 1913-1965. 5 vols. Edited by Magda Whitrow. London: Mansell.

Isis Cumulative Bibliography, 1966-1975. 1980-85. A Bibliography of the History of Science Formed from Isis Critical Bibliographies 91-100, indexing literature published from 1965 through 1974. 2 vols. Edited by John Neu. London: Mansell, in conjunction with the History of Science Society.

Jaki, Stanley L. 1984. *Uneasy Genius: The Life and Work of Pierre Duhem.* The Hague: Martinus Nijhoff.

Kibre, Pearl. 1969. "The *Quadrivium* in the Thirteenth Century Universities (with Special Reference to Paris)." In *Arts libéraux et philosophie au moyen âge,* 175-91. Actes du quatrième congrès international de philosophie médiévale, Université de Montréal, Canada, 27 août-2 septembre 1967. Montreal: Institut d'études médiévales; Paris: Librairie philosophique J. Vrin.

Kilwardby, Robert, O.P. 1976. *De ortu scientiarum.* Edited by Albert G. Judy, O.P. Toronto: Published jointly by the British Academy and The Pontifical Institute of Mediaeval Studies.

Kren, Claudia. 1985. *Medieval Science and Technology. A Selected, Annotated Bibliography.* New York: Garland. See especially under "Research Aids," pp. 7-13.

Kretzmann, Norman, Anthony Kenny, and Jan Pinborg, eds. 1982. *The Cambridge History of Later Medieval Philosophy from the Rediscovery of Aristotle to the Disintegration of Scholasticism.* Cambridge: Cambridge Univ. Press.

Lemay, Helen Rodnite. 1977. "Science and Theology at Chartres: The Case of the Supracelestial Waters." *British Journal for the History of Science* 10:226-36.

Lemay, Richard. 1976. "The Teaching of Astronomy in Medieval Universities, Principally at Paris in the 14th Century." *Manuscripta* 20:197-217.

Lindberg, David C. 1976. *Theories of Vision from al-Kindi to Kepler.* Chicago: Univ. of Chicago Press.

———, ed. 1978. *Science in the Middle Ages.* Chicago: Univ. of Chicago Press. Includes articles on translations, philosophy, universities, astronomy, cosmology, motion, statics, optics, mathematics, matter, natural history, and magic.

———. 1982. "On the Applicability of Mathematics to Nature: Roger Bacon and His Predecessors." *British Journal for the History of Science* 15:3-25.

Lockwood, Dean P. 1951. *Ugo Benzi Medieval Philosopher and Physician, 1376-1439.* Chicago: Univ. of Chicago Press.

Maier, Anneliese. 1982. *On the Threshold of Exact Science. Selected Writings of Anneliese Maier on Late Medieval Natural Philosophy.* Edited and translated with an introduction by Steven D. Sargent. Philadelphia: Univ. of Pennsylvania Press.

Masi, Michael, ed. 1981. *Boethius and the Liberal Arts, A Collection of Essays.* Utah Studies in Literature and Linguistics, vol. 18. Berne: Peter Lang.

McLaughlin, Mary Martin. 1977. *Intellectual Freedom and its Limitations in the University of Paris in the Thirteenth and Fourteenth Centuries.* New York: Arno Press. Ph.D. dissertation (Columbia University), 1952.

McVaugh, Michael. 1987. "The Two Faces of a Medical Career: Jordanus de Turre of Montpellier." In *Mathematics and its Applications to Science and Natural Philosophy in the Middle Ages,* edited by Edward Grant and John E. Murdoch, 301–24. Cambridge: Cambridge Univ. Press.

Murdoch, John E. 1975. "From Social into Intellectual Factors: An Aspect of the Unitary Character of Late Medieval Learning." In *The Cultural Context of Medieval Learning,* edited with an introduction by John Emery Murdoch and Edith Dudley Sylla, 271–348. Boston Studies in the Philosophy of Science, 26. Dordrecht: D. Reidel.

———. 1976. "Music and Natural Philosophy: Hitherto Unnoticed *Questiones* by Blasius of Parma." In *Science, Medicine, and the University: 1200–1550. Essays in Honor of Pearl Kibre.* Pt. 1. Special editors, Nancy G. Siraisi and Luke Demaitre. *Manuscripta* 20:119–36.

Ptolemy, 1948. *Tetrabiblos.* Edited and translated into English by F. E. Robbins. Loeb Classical Library. Cambridge, Mass.: Harvard Univ. Press.

Riddle, John M. 1974. "Theory and Practice in Medieval Medicine." *Viator* 5: 157–84.

Sarton, George. 1927–48. *Introduction to the History of Science.* 3 vols. in 5 parts. Baltimore: Williams & Wilkens, for the Carnegie Institution of Washington.

Siraisi, Nancy. 1973. *Arts and Sciences at Padua: The "Studium" of Padua before 1350.* Toronto: Pontifical Institute of Mediaeval Studies.

———. 1981. *Taddeo Alderotti and His Pupils: Two Generations of Italian Medical Learning.* Princeton, N.J.: Princeton Univ. Press, 1981.

Stahl, William H. 1962. *Roman Science: Origins, Development and Influence to the Later Middle Ages.* Madison: Univ. of Wisconsin Press.

Steneck, Nicholas H. 1977. *Science and Creation in the Middle Ages: Henry of Langenstein (d. 1397) on Genesis.* Notre Dame, Ind.: Univ. of Notre Dame Press.

Stiefel, Tina. 1985. *The Intellectual Revolution in Twelfth-Century Europe.* New York: St. Martin's Press.

Thorndike, Lynn. 1923–58. *A History of Magic and Experimental Science.* 8 vols. New York: Columbia Univ. Press.

———. 1949. *The Sphere of Sacrobosco and Its Commentators.* Chicago: Univ. of Chicago Press.

Victor, Stephen, ed. and trans. 1979. *Practical Geometry in the High Middle Ages: Artis cuiuslibet consummatio and the Pratike de geometrie.* Memoirs of the American Philosophical Society, 134. Philadelphia: American Philosophical Society.

Wagner, David L., ed. 1983. *The Seven Liberal Arts in the Middle Ages.* Bloomington: Indiana Univ. Press.

Weisheipl, James A., O.P. 1964. "Curriculum of the Faculty of Arts at Oxford in the early fourteenth century." *Mediaeval Studies* 26:143–85.

———. 1966. "Developments in the Arts Curriculum at Oxford in the Early Fourteenth Century." *Mediaeval Studies,* 28:151–75.

White, Lynn Jr. 1978. *Medieval Religion and Technology: Collected Essays.* University of California at Los Angeles, Publications of the Center for Medieval and Renaissance Studies, 13. Berkeley: Univ. of California Press.

Wippel, John F. 1977. "The Condemnations of 1270 and 1277 at Paris." *Journal of Medieval and Renaissance Studies* 7:169–201.

ᴄᴏ⁄ᴏ 12 ᴏᴄᴏ

Tradition and Innovation in Medieval Art

WAYNE DYNES

ERIOUS STUDY OF MEDIEVAL ART, according to modern criteria of precision and objectivity, began about 150 years ago. Prerequisite for the emergence of the discipline was the establishment of aesthetic pluralism replacing the normative classicism of such earlier art historians as Giorgio Vasari (1511–74) and Johann Joachim Winckelmann (1717–68), who had seen only decadence in the centuries from the fall of antiquity to the rise of the Renaissance.

In his *Handbuch der Kunstgeschichte* of 1842, Franz Kugler, following Hegelian principles, had taken the bold step of highlighting medieval monuments as important and organic parts of the universal history of art. Before this time, they had either been excluded from consideration altogether, or "ghettoized" by being relegated to specialized works. Despite his efforts and those of the compilers of other, more accurate handbooks that were to follow, the fit was not a seamless one, deriving in part from the fact that the evolution of medieval art shows no single, easily graspable pattern after the fashion of classical and Renaissance art. Perhaps in consequence, scholars of medieval art have tended to regard themselves as medievalists as much as historians of art. This dual allegiance was evident in France with the archaeologists Arcisse de Caumont (1801–73) and Eugène-Emmanuel Viollet-le-Duc (1814–79), and in England with the architect and propagandist A. W. N. Pugin (1812–52).

In any event, medieval art studies developed apace in Germany after 1871, sparked by the general prosperity and felt need to support culture. Reflecting the prestige of German models, the first two art history depart-

376

ments established in the United States (Harvard and Princeton, both in the second decade of the present century) were initially dominated by medievalists. In Central Europe, medieval art history, despite many splendid achievements, was always subject to nationalist temptations, a problem that became acute after Hitler's accession to power in 1933. Nazi persecution caused a number of major medieval art scholars, including Adolph Goldschmidt, Walter Horn, Adolf Katzenellenbogen, Richard Krautheimer, and Erwin Panofsky, to emigrate to the United States.

Nonetheless, the great Depression and World War II were not favorable for the field or for scholarship in general. Yet this situation was to be reversed after 1950, when a major revival of medieval art studies in Europe was borne on a flood of confidence and prosperity engendered by successful postwar reconstruction. The birth of the Common Market revived the long-dormant idea of Europe as a single entity, stoking interest in pre-Renaissance roots. America was drawn in through the Marshall Plan, the Atlantic Alliance, Fulbright scholarships, and easy air travel. In 1968 and the years immediately following, disturbances (turmoil in universities, efforts to politicize scholarship) held back growth, but the forward movement resumed, perhaps more strongly than before, in the 1970s. After the war, the religious element had been stressed to compensate for the vacuum of values of the Nazi era. In the 1980s, the computer era par excellence, a new emphasis on social and material data emerged.

Medieval art study continued to lack a "master narrative" — a sequence following the pattern of archaic to classic to baroque, as found in the two adjacent epochs of classical Antiquity and the Renaissance. By way of compensation, medieval art scholars maintained close links with medieval studies as a whole (and latterly, in so far as they are autonomous, Byzantine studies): this dual allegiance to art history and medieval studies has helped to keep the field interdisciplinary. Yet the long apprenticeship, conditioned by the need to master auxiliary sciences like paleography and sigillography, has made the field relatively atheoretical, and recording and marshalling of data continue to predominate over interpretation.

THE GREAT EXHIBITIONS

A salient feature of the postwar period was the fashion for huge, comprehensive exhibitions of historic art treasures which began to be held in most major European cities. These shows initially displayed works that had been kept in storage during the war prior to being reinstalled in their old quarters, or, as frequently happened, in settings refurbished after the damage

inflicted by hostilities. A great impression was made by the big shows organized in a spirit of international cooperation by the Council of Europe.
Several of these—real "blockbusters"—were devoted to the Middle Ages:
Romanesque Art, Barcelona, 1961; Art around 1400, Vienna, 1962; Byzantine Art, Athens, 1964; The Age of Charlemagne, Aachen, 1965; Gothic
Europe, Paris, 1968. Other large exhibitions have featured the art of particular regions in the Middle Ages, as the Mosan region (Liège, Paris,
Amsterdam, 1951–52); North Germany (Essen, 1956); Champagne (Paris,
1959); the Rhine-Meuse area (Cologne, 1972). England has benefited from
a particularly distinguished series: The Golden Age of Anglo-Saxon Art,
1984; Romanesque Art, 1984; Age of Chivalry, 1986. Yet others were devoted to particular categories of art production, for example, manuscripts
(Rome, 1953–54); Paris, 1954, 1955, 1958); church treasures (Cologne, 1985);
reliquaries (Paris, 1965); stained glass (Paris, 1953). There has been some
emulation of the vogue for great exhibitions in North America: Medieval
France, Cleveland, 1967; The Twelfth Century, Providence, 1969; The Year
1200, New York, 1970; Age of Spirituality, New York, 1979. In some instances, these exhibitions seemed to catch some current of the mood of
the times and consequently become enveloped in a great penumbra of publications. Sometimes this discussion was deliberately stimulated by the
scheduling of scholarly congresses to coincide with the exhibitions, the acts
of which were then published. Generally, the catalogues of these exhibitions are themselves solid pieces of work, and with their relatively low
price and up-to-date information have formed the foundation of many a
student's private library. In the mid-seventies the great exhibitions seemed
threatened. With the general increase of art prices in the market, insur-
ance costs soared. Moreover, fears that some fragile objects would suffer
deterioration in the course of these migrations have proved only too real—
though with increasing pollution pieces could deteriorate rapidly even in
situ. The appeal of the great exhibitions both to the general public and
to the scholarly world remained enormous, and means of financing of new
ventures were found. Indeed, some believed that institutions such as the
Metropolitan Museum of Art may have become too dependent on an ever-
changing roster of new events.

CORPUS PROJECTS

Another feature of recent years has been the founding or refounding of
important corpus projects, oftentimes assured now by a team of collabo-

rators rather than individual great scholars. Among these are the Carolingian miniature project (now being continued by Florentine Mütherich after the death of the original author, Wilhelm Koehler), the comparable publication of Ottonian miniatures of the Cologne school by Peter Bloch and Hermann Schnitzler, and the new *Repertorium* of early Christian sarcophagi edited by Friedrich Wilhelm Deichmann. In Italy the *Corpus della scultura altomedievale* recorded pre-Romanesque sculpture region by region, and the *Corpus of Anglo-Saxon Stone Sculpture in England* in England has begun to perform a similar service for England. By common consent, however, the *Corpus Vitrearum Medii Aevi,* a multivolume country-by-country inventory of stained glass sponsored by the Union Académique Internationale, is the greatest undertaking of this kind; it has revolutionized the study of medieval stained glass. The primary virtues of today's corpus publications are sobriety and objectivity, though they tend to lack the subtlety of argument and analysis that distinguishes some of the older achievements.

In the field of architecture, a phenomenon paralleling the renewal of corpus ventures for the figural arts is the resurgence of monographic inventories of historical monuments of particular regions and cities. This tradition originally sprang up around the turn of the century in the German-speaking countries (the various German Kunstdenkmäler series, the *Österreichische Kunsttopographie,* and the *Kunstdenkmäler der Schweiz*). These monographs often contain much information for the medievalist, both for religious and secular architecture, and the newer volumes record war damage and reconstruction. Since the war these older undertakings have been resumed vigorously, and in Germany an astonishing production of new series began for Bavaria, Berlin, the German East, Fulda, Hamburg, Lower Saxony, the Rhineland, the Rhine-Palatinate, Rosenheim, and Schleswig-Holstein.

Regrettably, initiative for inventories of historical monuments has been spotty in other countries. In the Netherlands, by exception, a series modeled on the German example proceeds apace. In Italy, however, two similar series were allowed to lapse with World War II. In England, the Royal Commission on Historical Monuments (active since 1910) is bringing out a series of well-executed inventory volumes arranged by county, but progress is slow, so that it is often more convenient to refer to the volumes of Sir Nikolaus Pevsner's *Buildings of England.* Modeled on the famous German *Handbuch der Deutschen Kunstdenkmäler* of Georg Dehio, Pevsner's entries are often quite explicit, the treatments on medieval cathedrals amounting to monographs in miniature. Cataloguing of Spanish monuments has been under way since 1915, Portuguese ones since 1947.

PERIODICALS

In the history of art, as in other scholarly fields, much of the valuable material is published in periodicals, and it is to these that the student must turn to "take the pulse" of the field. In art history the postwar years have seen a bewildering proliferation of new periodicals — monthly, quarterly, biannual and annual. Leading scholars are showing a tendency to spread their material among a number of outlets, especially the new ones, partly to help them get established and partly in hopes of reaching new circles of readers. Most of these periodicals are covered in the annual roundups of bibliography of the *Répertoire d'Art et d'Archéologie* and the *RILA (Répertoire International de la Littérature de l'Art)*. These two merged in 1991 as the *Bibliography of the History of Art*. The student, however, must be ever watchful for the appearance of new periodicals since they may contain important new material. Periodicals devoted exclusively to medieval art are few: *Arte Medievale, Cahiers Archéologiques, Dumbarton Oaks Papers,* and *Gesta* are the only ones that spring immediately to mind, but noteworthy articles often appear in such organs as the *Art Bulletin, Bolletino d'Arte, Bulletin Monumental, Burlington Magazine, Gazette des Beaux-Arts, Journal of the Warburg and Courtauld Institutes, Revue de l'Art, Scriptorium, Zeitschrift für Kunstgeschichte,* and *Zeitschrift des deutschen Vereins für Kunstwissenschaft*. Articles on medieval art also appear from time to time in a wide array of general medieval periodicals; here, it must suffice to mention *Cahiers de Civilisation Médiévale, Frühmittelalterliche Studien, Römische Quartalschrift,* and *Speculum*. Especially valuable in view of the current dispersed patterns of the publication are the articles on the state of the question appearing in the *Art Bulletin,* the *Zeitschrift für Kunstgeschichte,* and occasionally in general medievalist journals.

ICONOGRAPHY

The period since the end of World War II has seen a gratifying increase of interest in the field of iconography and symbolism. The founding of the Princeton Index of Christian Art with its over 500,000 cards, heralding a systematic approach to the subject, took place as early as 1917. It is now more readily accessible, however, thanks to the establishment of up-to-date copies in other locations: the Vatican, Utrecht (Rijksuniversiteit), Washington, D.C. (Dumbarton Oaks), and Los Angeles (University of California). While there have been a number of truly outstanding monographs on iconographical themes, some of them illuminating links with Antiquity on the one hand and the Renaissance on the other, the material is generally presented in the form of articles, and is mostly easily accessible through multivolume reference works such as Louis Réau's *Iconographie de l'art chrétien,* now somewhat antiquated, and the excellent *Lexikon der christlichen Ikonographie.* In very general terms, the motivation of much of the current crop of iconographical research seems both negative and positive — negative in the desire to escape the formalistic concerns that have so long dominated art historical research, and positive in an effort to get closer to the wellsprings of medieval life from which the works developed. Collaboration with other medievalists whose field is not art history is a frequently expressed desideratum.

ILLUMINATED MANUSCRIPTS

A medium where iconography is often extremely important, illuminated manuscripts have in the last few years attracted the attention of an increasing number of scholars, especially those just entering the field. In the United States and England at any rate probably a majority of the gifted young medievalists writing dissertations in the last decade have chosen illuminated manuscripts as their subject. Excellent monographic publications on schools and individual manuscripts have either appeared or are on the way. The pacesetter is the magisterial *Survey of Manuscript Illumination in the British Isles,* begun in 1978 by J. J. G. Alexander, and including volumes by Alexander, C. M. Kauffmann, Nigel Morgan, Lucy Freeman Sandler, and Elzbieta Temple.

There are several reasons for this groundswell of interest. One is the attraction of what appears to be, relatively speaking, virgin territory, since many important illuminated manuscripts, especially of the Romanesque and Gothic periods, have never been adequately published. Moreover, their condition is generally vastly superior to that of works in other media. Colors are unfaded, surfaces unbattered, and the original context of the paintings generally unchanged. Finally, the study of manuscripts invites the interdisciplinary interests already noted as active for those scholars pursuing iconographic research. The student of illuminated manuscripts is often plunged into the study of calendars, liturgy, and textual recension. In general, one feels that one is being led closer to the original spiritual context of the work by this method than by the usual way of treating, say, some isolated panel painting or historiated capital in a museum.

NEW GEOGRAPHICAL PERSPECTIVES

Improved travel facilities have made possible a shifting of geographical foci. Despite all the attendant political difficulties, this has been most evident in the direction of attention to the art of the eastern Mediterranean. This means, first and foremost, Byzantium. The patient uncovering and restoration of the mosaics of the Istanbul churches of the Hagia Sophia and Kahrie Camii begun by American scholars in the 1930s has been followed more recently by unexpected new finds. Armenia and Georgia have attracted interest both within and outside those ancient lands. On Mount Sinai, spectacular icons were carefully studied by the Princeton-Alexandria Universities Expedition, the results being published by Kurt Weitzmann and others. In the Balkans, reviving national feeling and a desire to encourage tourism has fostered extensive restoration and study of Christian monuments by scholars in Yugoslavia, Bulgaria, and Romania. In western Europe also, improved economic conditions and a general sense of curiosity have stimulated interest in areas too often considered peripheral, including Spain, Ireland, and the Viking Lands.

HANDBOOKS AND PICTURE BOOKS

Educational expansion since World War II has served to stimulate publishers in the creation of a new series of handbooks and picture books of all kinds. Handbooks are sought by teachers, both as an aid to classroom instruction and as a way of "listening in" on the progress of areas of research adjacent to their own. It cannot be said, unfortunately, that the situation is as good for the Middle Ages as for other periods of the history of art. The most prestigious series of handbooks is the Pelican History of Art, launched in 1953 by Sir Nikolaus Pevsner, with volumes on the Middle Ages by John Beckwith, C. R. Dodwell, Peter Lasko, Richard Krautheimer, Margaret Rickert, and Geoffrey Webb. In Germany the old Propyläen Kunstgeschichte has been revived, with well-produced medieval volumes by Beat Brenk, Hermann Fillitz, Otto von Simson, and Wolfgang Friedrich Volbach (with Jacqueline Lafontaine-Dosogne). Some volumes of the French series Arts du Monde have appeared in English, but the full conspectus is available only in French. In its more limited field, Viktor Lazarev's *Storia della pittura bizantina* is an exemplary achievement. One should mention, also, two valuable multivolume histories of art for countries that have often been neglected: *Ars Hispaniae* and the *Oxford History of English Art,* edited by T. S. R. Boase.

Another current trend due to publishers' initiatives is represented by the flood of picture books released in several languages simultaneously under cooperative publishing schemes ("coffee-table books"). Collaboration of several publishers brings costs down, permitting more and better plates, including color. These books are often laid out according to a tripartite formula pioneered by the Phaidon Press in England: a belletristic introduction that avoids technicalities and is addressed to the general reader, a hefty sheaf of plates, and finally a scholarly catalog with bibliography. Although the plate selections are sometimes too strong on flashy details at the expense of whole works, they have diffused a great deal of visual material that was formerly difficult of access. Unfortunately, it cannot be claimed that technical problems of color reproduction have been solved, as readers comparing color plates of the same work in volumes issued by two different publishers will discover to their dismay. In some cases these books offer new syntheses by scholars at the top of their profession (e.g., Otto Demus, Jean Porcher, and Willibald Sauerländer).

Still in the area of response to publishers' initiatives are the luxurious facsimiles of illuminated manuscripts. The texts joined to the facsimiles are often summary, but a few make a real contribution to knowledge. After World War II, this field of publication was launched by the Urs Graf firm in Switzerland which, concentrating on early medieval codices, managed to achieve an unusually high standard of accuracy of reproduction. More recently, facsimiles of Carolingian, Ottonian, and Gothic manuscripts have begun to appear from other sources. In a few cases, as in the admirable Gothic illuminated manuscripts published by George Braziller, prices have been kept within the reach of middle-class purchasers; in others the sky seems to be the limit. Now a frustrating situation seems to be developing in which a great variety of new facsimiles are being announced (some of them, incidentally, containing scholarly commentary of real value), but so expensive as to be out of reach of even many specialized libraries.

PERIODIZATION

This question has been neglected in recent years, a neglect that is connected with an overall trend toward cautious positivism and a distrust of ambitious generalizations. The periodization conundrum encountered at the very outset is of course the demarcation of the Middle Ages from classical antiquity. When does medieval art begin? Does it evolve gradually and smoothly out of the ancient matrix, or are there sudden shifts and breaks? Many medieval art historians have been able to avoid grappling with these problems because of their concern with later eras, the Romanesque and the Gothic. Conversely, some scholars of early Christian art could sidestep the problem by simply treating their area as the last phase of the ancient cycle. Toward the end of the nineteenth century, two Viennese scholars, Alois Riegl and Josef Strzygowski, addressed themselves to this question, reaching conclusions that were startlingly different. Riegl stressed the elements of continuity, asserting that late antique art was an organic development of ancient art and that it led on logically to medieval art proper and even to later European art. His was a grandiose vision. So was Strzygowski's, but he was more impressed by discontinuities. He felt, moreover, that Early Christian art came into being not through endogenesis, that is, through the working out of factors previously latent *within* the ancient matrix, but by exogenesis, through the aggressive incursion of new trends stemming from the Near East, from Syria, Armenia, and Iran. Unfortunately, archaeological finds from these countries have not, on the whole, seemed to bear out Strzygowski's claim, his own diligent activity in the field notwithstanding, and the "Romanist" camp has been able to mount a strong counterattack. In recent years a new theory has come to be widely accepted which offers a kind of compromise between the endogenetic and exogenetic approaches. This is that late Antique and early Christian art result from the legitimization of plebeian currents previously outside the pale of high-class Greco-Roman art. These currents were active in the provinces, particularly the non-Greek ones (Ernst Kitzinger's "subantique" trend), as well as in the popular art of the urban proletariat. Thus, the ethnographic perspective of the earlier debate is replaced by one of social stratification. According to this view, medieval art arose from popular sources in a way analogous to the rise of the Romance languages from the humble soil of Vulgar Latin (already documented at Pompeii prior to A.D. 79). The proponents of this view do not insist that it is necessarily the whole story. In fact quite recently, renewed attention has been focused on the Eastern caravan cities of Hatra, Dura Europos, and Palmyra. Thus, exogenesis may have to be considered as at least a contributing factor, and Strzygowski may be partially vindicated after all. In any event, it is clear that there can be no satisfactory solution to what at first appears a straightforward question — When did medieval art begin? — until the strengths of the various motivating factors are fully assessed.

Outside the late Antique period other problems of periodization present themselves. Some periods are seen, for example, to overlap others more extensively than we had thought. In some parts of Europe, the Romanesque style still flourished until the middle of the thirteenth century, when the central regions were already mutating into late Gothic. In the Carolingian period we have become increasingly aware of the persistence of pre-Renaissance "Merovingian" currents up to and even beyond the year 800.

Apart from the matter of overlappings and prolongations, there is the phenomenon of conscious reversion to a previous era, generally classical Antiquity or some phase thereof. This is the "Renaissance" syndrome, and as examples one may mention (in a list that is far from exhaustive) the Theodosian, Heraclian, Macedonian, Paleologan, Carolingian, Ottonian, Mosan, and Provençal "Renaissances." A different approach is that of Kurt Weitzmann of Princeton University. Working with great patience and tenacity, Weitzmann has tried to formulate as accurately as possible the rules governing the transmission of classical formulas and themes, especially for Byzantine art. At least for Byzantium, Weitzmann seems to be suggesting that classical Antiquity never really ended.

Then, too, there is the problem of the relative autonomy of the various style periods. For some time it has been clear that in the history of art the Ottonian period does not enjoy quite the same independent status as its predecessor, the Carolingian age. Ottonian art was confined mainly to Germany, the Low Countries, and eastern France, contrasting with a contemporary southern European style sometimes termed the First Romanesque. Is Ottonian then perhaps in its different way also to be regarded as a preparatory stage of Romanesque? It should be evident that this is not merely a pedantic quibble concerning the arrangement of chronological pigeonholes, for the solution of the problem adopted will necessarily condition the way in which we define the inner essence of specific Ottonian art objects.

Finally, there is the problem of the end of the Middle Ages. For teaching purposes, it is often the custom to begin courses in the Italian Renaissance with Cimabue and Giotto, that is, around 1280. In Flanders, the Renaissance is held to begin only later, around 1410. Yet there are medievalizing artists active in both Italy (Sassetta, Giovanni di Paolo) and Flanders (Gerard David, Bosch) well beyond 1410, and in painting, at any rate, fifteenth-century Flanders seems paradoxically more precocious than Italy. The most astonishing case of stylistic longevity is that in some areas of Europe (England and Germany) Gothic architecture continues through the seventeenth century and occasionally even beyond, so that the Gothic survival almost meets the Gothic revival. It is customary to deal with such persistences by labeling them *retardataire,* but some are beginning to wonder whether this handy adjective really meets the bill.

PROBLEMS OF DATING

Related to and encapsulated within the general problem of periodization
is the narrower one of assigning specific dates to individual art objects.
In some periods, such as the Gothic and Carolingian, we feel relatively
confident about dating. Some fixed points are supplied by documents and
other objective criteria, and the thus dated monuments serve in turn as
points of attachment for others which are clearly allied to them. In the
early Christian period as a whole, and in the ensuing early medieval period in Italy there are, however, very few fixed dates. Attempts to fix the
chronology of the Great Palace mosaic in Constantinople, the stucco figures at Cividale, and the Castelseprio frescoes range over several centuries.
Discrepancies of this magnitude are, to say the least, unsettling. Moreover,
the inability to place these important monuments in a general evolutionary pattern points to a fundamental inadequacy in our present develop-
mental schemata, which are perhaps too linear and simplistic, making
insufficient allowance for the "epicycles" of history, the revivals and survivals of earlier traits. In any case, it is clear that at least some factual
questions regarding dating could be resolved by the application of radiocarbon and other scientific techniques; use of these for medieval objects
is just beginning.

REGIONS

Complementary to the various questions of temporal division, which have
been discussed above, is the matter of the articulation of regions in space,
self-contained groupings of monuments that possess a local character patent enough to persist over a substantial period of time. As in the case
of periodization, the theory behind the articulation of art regions (*Kunst-
landschaften*), or artistic chorography, to revive an old term, has been neglected in recent decades. One apparent reason for this is the interference
of contemporary nationalistic drives: the period leading up to World War
II saw an intense preoccupation with the territorial integrity of the nation-
state, and a consequent playing down of regional identity. Since the war,
however, Europe has seen movements in the direction of supranational-
ism. Both these trends alike serve to obscure the fact that often it is the
region that is the natural unit in the Middle Ages. Only in Byzantium was
a central government sufficiently powerful and stable to efface, at least in
part, the centrifugal impulses of local particularism. Sometimes very nar-

rowly based *campanilismo,* or the "parish-pump" attitude, definitely predominates. Attempts to define clearly the boundaries of individual regions encounter the difficulty that political circumscriptions do not (in contrast with modern times) mesh well with ecclesiastical provinces, nor do either of these match linguistic units held together by consciousness of sharing a common dialect. Moreover, the artistic groups of monuments that have been discerned may not agree in their distribution with any of the former units.

In France, for example, the attempt to establish a regional scheme for Romanesque architecture, the "school system," goes back to the time of Arcisse de Caumont, who in his *Abécédaire* (1850–53) distinguished seven schools. His ideas were revised by Anthyme de Saint-Paul (who reduced the list to five) and by Jules Quicherat (who again increased the number of schools to eight). In the twentieth century, this school system in all its variations was subjected to fundamental criticisms by Eugene Lefèvre-Pontalis and others. Yet something survives from the wreck and in some neighboring areas, such as the Mosan region of eastern Belgium and Catalonia, art historians have been working happily within the framework of the regional concept for some time.

Studies of Gothic architecture have reinforced the primacy of North France centered on the Ile-de-France, though interpretations differ. Jean Bony has analyzed the development of early and high Gothic buildings primarily in aesthetic terms, while Kimpel and Suckale stress construction, economics, and political emblematics.

In Italy, a strong sense of regional identity (whose formation is in part rooted in the circumstances of the Roman conquest and in part in the inescapable facts of geography) has persisted into our own day. There are, of course, plenty of monographs on the architecture, painting, and sculpture of the later medieval regions of Italy, but no adequate synthesis of the regional preferences of the Italian regions. Armenia has long been stressed by eminent scholars of that extraction, while quite recently Cappadocia has come into its own with several substantial monographs, while Syria, Ethiopia, and Coptic Egypt are also receiving renewed attention.

Perhaps the best results in applying a regional approach have occurred in the field of illuminated manuscripts. At least up to the Romanesque period, certain powerful monastic houses succeeded in developing and maintaining art traditions of a pronouncedly individual character. The present system of Carolingian schools of manuscript illumination was adumbrated a century ago. A little later a comparable classification for Ottonian manuscripts was worked out. More recently this school approach has been fruitfully extended to Romanesque manuscripts in such outstanding monographs as those of J. J. A. Alexander, Knut Berg, Hugo Buch-thal, C. R. Dodwell, D. Gaborit-Chopin, and Edward Garrison. Here again, however, some difficulties present themselves. The late Wilhelm Koehler has shown that two quite different schools flourished side by side in Carolingian Aachen in the early years of the ninth century. The status of the Reichenau school of Ottonian manuscript illumination remains problematic.

TEXT AND PICTURE

The relation between text and picture calls for study on several planes. Serious editing of original texts on art historical techniques began in England in the mid-nineteenth century with work by Sir Charles Eastlake and Mary P. Merrifield. The interest in this type of material spread to the Continent and became firmly established in Vienna after 1871 with the founding in that year of Rudolf von Eitelberger's and Albert Ilg's *Quellen-schriften für Kunstgeschichte und Kunsttechnik des Mittelalters und der Neuzeit*. This series provided editions not only of original treatises, but also general collections of excerpts from medieval texts (chronicles, diaries, poems) as they relate to art. Recently an effort has been undertaken to make art history sources available in English translations to a larger public in the Prentice-Hall Sources and Documents in the History of Art series, edited by H. W. Janson. A thoroughgoing examination of texts concerning Gothic architecture, many of them post-medieval, has been provided in Paul Frankl's 1960 masterwork, *The Gothic*.

The field of the encounter between text and picture is, of course, most completely exemplified in illuminated manuscripts, and the standard works on this subject contain much scattered material that is of value. Yet for the historiated initial, perhaps the most intense zone of interaction between text and picture, there still remains no adequate survey of the whole development. Broad parallels between literature and art of various eras are often asserted, and literary historians have from time to time sought to investigate these in programmatic enquiries of such topics as the "Romanesque lyric" and "Flamboyant drama," but such links have in general attracted little attention from their art historian confreres. As regards the methodological questions posed by such work, much food for thought is provided in the challenging book by Frederick P. Pickering.

A special area of contact between art and literature is the influence of the tradition of scriptural exegesis on pictorial representation. Already in early Christian times one finds instances of the introduction of features not mentioned in the Scriptural source but derived from some noncanonical work or commentary. This factor of extrascriptural sources is important also in the Jewish elements found in early Christian depictions. While Jewish pictorial art did exist in late Antiquity, it is too seldom realized that Jewish elements may have made their way into Christian images not by way of a previously existing stock of Jewish illustration, but directly from Jewish texts or oral legends available to the artists and their patrons. In the case of typological interpretations, where an effort is made to pair New Testament persons and events with their Old Testament prefigurations, a curious time lag is seen in the reception of this principle into art. Although typology was a prominent feature of textual exegesis since the time of Origen in the third century of our era, it did not really become prominent in art until after 1200, in such compilations as the *Bible Moralisée* and the *Biblia Pauperum.*

SECULAR ASPECTS

Although some aspects of religious influence on medieval art are not fully clarified, there is little danger of the role of the religious factor as a whole being slighted. A noninitiate glancing at modern works of synthesis might be tempted to assume that the cathedrals and monasteries, with their great treasures, arose out of an empty landscape. As yet we know little of medieval town planning, though the brilliant study of Wolfgang Braunfels (1966) showed that Tuscan civic authorities employed a kind of zoning policy to shape the development of the urban fabric according to aesthetic principles; the oft-noted harmony of medieval cities in Italy is thus frequently a matter of conscious design, not accident. A variety of other sources for the understanding of medieval cities could be tapped, including air photography. The admirable collection of city models kept in the Musée des Plans Reliefs in Paris awaits full study. Contemporary interest in "architecture without architects" has stirred some interest in vernacular traditions, especially Mediterranean stone-vaulted houses of the *trullo* type (though they are often very hard to date), and Walter Horn has investigated various aspects of medieval wood structures, but the truth is that we know next to nothing about the dwellings in which most medieval people lived. The situation is, of course, better for the upper reaches of the social ladder. For palaces, however, much evidence has been obliterated or altered past hope of recovery. As every traveler knows, Europe retains a vast patrimony of castles; serious research into these is now getting under way.

One specialized field of secular art, the study of regalia and attributes of state in general, is flourishing. This area of research owes its existence almost entirely to the efforts of Percy Ernst Schramm and his pupils. These scholars consider not only the material side of the question but are concerned with the actual use of the objects in coronations and other rites of state, as well as the essential underpinnings of royal and papal ideology.

ART AND LIFE

We conclude with what is perhaps the most fundamental question of all: the relation of medieval art objects to their actual situation in medieval life, their *Sitz-im-Leben* (to borrow a useful term from German theology). Any attempt to reach a solution to this multifaceted problem comes directly up against an attitude cherished by many art historians, the more tenaciously held perhaps because rarely consciously avowed: the tendency to segregate the art object from other aspects of human concern, removing it to a sphere of self-contained perfection. This displacement of the art object into an ontologically numinous realm is now beginning to evoke notice and self-examination on the part of some younger art historians. We can illustrate this situation first by turning to buildings. A moment ago we alluded to the tendency to concentrate on notable monumental religious structures in contrast to the humbler buildings surrounding them. Then there is the question of the life function of the church building itself. Too often these monuments are treated simply as "vieilles usines desaffectées de Dieu," in T. S. Eliot's phrase. Any development of proper insight into an ecclesiastical building's original role as a functioning entity must begin with the liturgy — no simple problem when it is realized that the historical evolution of the liturgy is extremely complex with many local variants, and there are many lacunae in our knowledge of it. Severe problems are posed in this regard by buildings that are destroyed, secularized, or de-Christianized (as in Islamic countries). Even in buildings with no interruption of tradition, as the Gothic cathedrals of western Europe, there is the neglected question of such important features as rood screens, most of which have been removed in modern times. How did these affect the worshipper's perception of space and his habits of movement through the building? With a better understanding of factors such as these it may be possible to discover that some building features, hitherto regarded as arbitrary or accidental in origin, have a functional rationale. A scholarly congress held at the Metropolitan Museum in spring 1972 on the cloister (proceedings in *Gesta* 12, 1973) revealed how much is still to be learned about this key feature of medieval monasteries.

The matter of the liturgical and devotional use of buildings is linked to the whole question of folk piety, the vast complex of everyday usages in religion existing alongside, and sometimes even in competition with official orthodoxy. The cult of relics and reliquaries requires much more study than it has received, as do the artistic reflections of the lives of the saints. Sermons and vernacular writings contain a mass of material which could be brought to bear on medieval art. In the case of *drôleries* in medieval manuscripts a valuable beginning has been made in interpreting them along these lines by Lilian M. C. Randall, to whom in any case we are indebted for a valuable indexed collection of the material. More attention needs to be devoted to the artistic reflections of relations with heterodox groups in the Middle Ages, the heretics, and the Jews. Recently work has begun on sculptural *obscaena* (J. Andersen; A. Weir and J. Jerman).

Within the sphere of the relationship to medieval life, a large field concerns the working procedure of architects and artists. Much ink has been spilt in what appears to be a vain attempt to uncover some arcane, cabbalistic significance in the proportional relationships evident in medieval buildings. But our sources do convey information about the actual means of designing and constructing buildings, and this data is receiving attention from François Bucher, John Fitchen, and others. As has been mentioned above, we do know the names of a good many individual artists working in the Middle Ages, and something can be learned of them, especially of their social situation. We also know something of their actual working conditions in their studios and *chantiers,* thanks in part to actual representations they have left behind of themselves at work. All this knowledge needs, however, to be sifted and coordinated with the general picture of crafts and technology in the Middle Ages.

In the foregoing pages, some criticism has been made regarding areas in which art historians seem neglectful of opportunities to advance our knowledge. In fairness, however, it must be admitted that much evidence, sometimes whole categories of evidence, has been lost, and there are some aspects of medieval art about which we can never expect to be more than sketchily informed. In other instances formidable obstacles of methodology, technique, and political restrictions need to be overcome before further progress can be achieved. All in all, the historiography of medieval art can take pride in accumulating an impressive mass of information, generally accessible in research tools of proven reliability. This work, it must be remembered, was achieved in the face of various prejudices against medieval art, prejudices whose effects still linger in some quarters even today.

BIBLIOGRAPHY

Limitations of space require that this bibliography be highly selective. Emphasis is on standard works and recent monographs and exhibition catalogues, especially those with extensive bibliographies affording access to other studies.

Abbot Suger and St. Denis. Edited by Paula Lieber Gerson. New York: Metropolitan Museum of Art, 1986.

Age of Chivalry: Art in Plantagenet England 1200–1400. London: Royal Academy of Arts, 1987. Exhibition catalogue.

Age of Spirituality. New York: Metropolitan Museum of Art, 1979. Exhibition catalogue.

Age of Spirituality. Edited by Kurt Weitzmann. New York: Metropolitan Museum of Art, 1980.

Alexander, Jonathan J. G. *Insular Manuscripts, 6th to 9th Century.* London: Harvey Miller, 1978.

———. *Norman Illumination at Mont St. Michel, 966–1100.* Oxford: Clarendon, 1970.

Andersen, Jørgen. *Witch on the Wall: Medieval Erotic Sculpture in the British Isles.* Copenhagen: Rosenkilde and Bagger, 1977.

Architektur des Mittelalters: Funktion und Gestalt. Edited by Friedrich Möbius and Ernst Schubert. Weimar: Hermann Bohlaus Nachfolger, 1980.

Armi, C. Edson. *Masons and Sculptors in Romanesque Burgundy: The New Aesthetic of Cluny III.* 2 vols. Univ. Park: Pennsylvania State Univ. Press, 1983.

Art and Architecture of the Crusader States. Edited by H. W. Hazard. A History of the Crusades, vol. 4. Madison: Univ. of Wisconsin Press, 1977.

Arte románica. Barcelona; N.p., 1961. Exhibition catalogue.

Art of the Courts: France and England from 1259 to 1328. 2 vols. Ottawa: National Museum of Canada, 1972.

Avril, François. *Manuscript Painting at the Court of France.* New York: George Braziller, 1978.

Badawy, Alexander. *Coptic Art and Archaeology: The Art of the Christian Egyptians from the Late Antique to the Middle Ages.* Cambridge, Mass.: MIT Press, 1978.

Barnes, Carl. *Villard de Honnecourt: The Artist and His Drawings.* Boston: G. K. Hall, 1982.

Baxandall, Michael. *The Limewood Sculptures of Renaissance Germany.* New Haven: Yale Univ. Press, 1980.

Beckwith, John. *Early Christian and Byzantine Art.* London: Penguin, 1970.

Belting, Hans. *Das Bild und sein Publikum im Mittelalter.* Berlin: Mann, 1981.

Berg, Knut. *Studies in Tuscan Twelfth-Century Illumination.* Oslo: Universitets-forlaget, 1968.

Białostocki, Jan. "Late Gothic: Disagreements about the Concept." *Journal of the British Archaeological Association* 29 (1966): 76–105.

Bloch, Herbert. *Montecassino in the Middle Ages.* 3 vols. Cambridge, Mass.: Harvard Univ. Press, 1986.

Bloch, Peter, and Hermann Schnitzler. *Die ottonische Kölner Malerschule.* 2 vols. Düsseldorf: Schwann, 1967.

Blumenkranz, Bernhard. *Juden und Judentum in der mittelalterlichen Kunst.* Stuttgart: Kohlhammer, 1965.

Boase, T. S. R. *English Art, 1100–1216.* Oxford: Clarendon, 1953.

Bonne, Jean-Claude. *L'art roman de face et de profil: Le tympan de Conques.* Paris: Le Sycomore, 1984.

Bony, Jean. *French Gothic Architecture of the 12th and 13th Centuries.* Berkeley: Univ. of California Press, 1983.

Boüard, Michel de. *Manuel d'archéologie médiévale: De la fouille à l'histoire.* Paris: SEDES, 1975.

Branner, Robert. *Burgundian Gothic Architecture.* London: Zwemmer, 1960.

———. *The Cathedral of Bourges and Its Place in Gothic Architecture.* London: Zwemmer, 1988. With additional material by Shirley Prager Branner and Jean Bony.

———. *Manuscript Painting in Paris during the Reign of St. Louis.* Berkeley: Univ. of California Press, 1977.

———. *St. Louis and the Court Style in Gothic Architecture.* London: Zwemmer, 1965.

Braunfels, Wolfgang. *Mittelalterliche Stadtbaukunst in der Toskana.* 3d ed. Berlin: Mann, 1966.

———. *Die Welt der Karolinger und ihre Kunst.* Munich: Callwey, 1968.

Brenk, Beat. *Spätantike und frühes Christentum.* Berlin: Propyläen, 1977.

———. *Tradition und Neuerung in der christlichen Kunst des ersten Jahrhunderts.* Vienna: Wiener Byzantinische Studien, 1966.

Bruce-Mitford, R. S., et al. *The Sutton Hoo Burial.* London: British Museum, 1975–.

Bucher, François. *Architector: The Lodge Books and Sketchbooks of Medieval Architects.* New York: Abaris, 1977.

Buchthal, Hugo. *Miniature Painting in the Latin Kingdom of Jerusalem.* Oxford: Oxford Univ. Press, 1957.

———. *Historia Troiana: Studies in the History of Medieval Secular Illustration.* London: Warburg Institute, 1971.

Cabanot, Jean. *Les débuts de la sculpture romane dans le Sud-Ouest de la France.* Paris: Picard, 1985.

Cahn, Walter. *Romanesque Bible Illumination.* Ithaca, N.Y.: Cornell Univ. Press, 1982.

——. *The Romanesque Wooden Doors of Auvergne.* New York: New York Univ. Press, 1974.

Cahn, Walter, and Linda Seidel. *Romanesque Sculpture in American Collections.* New York: Burt Franklin, 1979-.

Calkins, Robert G. *Illuminated Books of the Middle Ages.* Ithaca, N.Y.: Cornell Univ. Press, 1983.

Camille, Michael. *The Gothic Idol: Ideology and Image-Making in Medieval Art.* Cambridge: Cambridge Univ. Press, 1989.

Caviness, Madeline. *The Early Stained Glass of Canterbury Cathedral.* Princeton: Princeton Univ. Press, 1977.

——. *Stained Glass Before 1540: An Annotated Bibliography.* Boston: G. K. Hall, 1983.

Colvin, Howard. *A History of the King's Works.* London: Her Majesty's Stationery Office, 1963-.

Cormack, Robin. *Writing in Gold.* London: George Philip, 1985.

Conant, Kenneth. *Carolingian and Romanesque Architecture.* 2d ed. London: Penguin, 1978.

——. *Cluny: Les églises et la maison du chef d'ordre.* Macon: Protat, 1968.

Corpus della Scultura Altomedievale. Spoleto: Centro Italiano di Studi sull'Alto Medioevo, 1959-.

Corpus der mittelalterlichen Wandmalereien Österreichs. Vienna: Österreichische Akademie der Wissenschaften, 1983-.

Corpus of Anglo-Saxon Stone Sculpture in England. Edited by Rosemary Cramp. Oxford: Oxford Univ. Press, 1984-.

Corpus Vitrearum Medii Aevi. N.p., 1956-.

Crosby, Sumner. *The Royal Abbey of St. Denis from its Beginnings to the Death of Suger, 475-1151.* Edited and completed by Pamela Z. Blum. New Haven: Yale Univ. Press, 1987.

Ćurčić, Slobodan. *Art and Architecture in the Balkans: An Annotated Bibliography.* Boston:. G. K. Hall, 1984.

Debidour, V.-H. *Le bestiaire sculpté du moyen âge en France.* Paris: Arthaud, 1961.

Deichmann, Friedrich Wilhelm. *Einführung in die christliche Archäologie.* Darmstadt: Wissenschaftliche Buchgesellschaft, 1983.

——. *Ravenna: Hauptstadt des spätantiken Abendlandes.* 3 vols. in 6. Wiesbaden: Franz Steiner, 1958-88.

Deichmann, Friedrich Wilhelm, and Giovanni Bovini. *Repertorium der christlichantiken Sarkophage.* Vol. 1. Wiesbaden: Franz Steiner, 1967.

De Hamel, Christopher. *A History of Illuminated Manuscripts.* Boston: Godine, 1986.

Demus, Otto. *Byzantine Art and the West.* New York: New York Univ. Press, 1970.

——. *Byzantine Mosaic Decoration.* Boston: Boston Book and Art Shop, 1955.

——. *The Mosaics of San Marco in Venice.* 3 vols. Chicago: Univ. of Chicago Press, 1984.

——. *Romanesque Mural Painting.* New York: Abrams, 1970.

Deshman, Robert. *Anglo-Saxon and Anglo-Scandinavian Art: An Annotated Bibliography.* Boston: G. K. Hall, 1984.

Dodwell, Charles Reginald. *Anglo-Saxon Art: A New Perspective.* Ithaca, N.Y.: Cornell Univ. Press, 1982.

————. *Painting in Europe, 800–1200.* London: Penguin, 1971.

Dumbarton Oaks Bibliographies Based on Byzantinische Zeitschrift. Edited by Jelisaveta S. Allen. London: Mansell, 1973–.

Dynes, Wayne R. "The Middle Ages in the West." In *Encyclopedia of World Art* 16:103–16. New York: McGraw-Hill, 1983.

Egbert, Virginia W. *The Medieval Artist at Work.* Princeton: Princeton Univ. Press, 1967.

English Romanesque Art, 1066–1200. London: Hayward Gallery, 1984. Exhibition catalogue.

Das erste Jahrhundert. Edited by Viktor H. Elbern. 3 vols. Düsseldorf: Schwann, 1962.

Europäische Kunst um 1400. Vienna: Kunsthistorisches Museum, 1962. Exhibition catalogue.

L'Europe Gothique, XIIe–XIVe siècles. Paris: Musée du Louvre, 1968. Exhibition catalogue.

Les fastes du gothique: Le siècle de Charles V. Paris: Musées Nationaux, 1981. Exhibition catalogue.

Fernie, Eric. *The Architecture of the Anglo-Saxons.* London: Batsford, 1983.

Fillitz, Hermann. *Das Mittelalter.* Vol. 1. Berlin: Propyläen, 1969.

Fitchen, John. *The Construction of Gothic Cathedrals.* Oxford: Oxford Univ. Press, 1961.

Focillon, Henri. *Art of the West in the Middle Ages.* 2 vols. New York: Phaidon, 1963. English version of work first published in French in 1938.

Folda, Jaroslav. *Crusader Manuscript Illumination at St. Jean d'Acre, 1275–1291.* Princeton: Princeton Univ. Press, 1976.

Forsyth, Ilene. *The Throne of Wisdom.* Princeton: Princeton Univ. Press, 1972.

Forsyth, William H. *The Entombment of Christ: French Sculptures of the Fifteenth and Sixteenth Centuries.* Cambridge, Mass.: Harvard Univ. Press, 1970.

Francovich, Geza de. *Persia, Siria, Bisanzio e il medioevo artistico europeo.* Naples: Liguori, 1984.

Frankl, Paul. *Gothic Architecture.* London: Penguin, 1962.

————. *The Gothic: Literary Sources and Interpretations through Eight Centuries.* Princeton: Princeton Univ. Press, 1960.

Gaborit-Chopin, Danielle. *La décoration des manuscrits à Saint-Martial de Limoges et en Limousin du IXe au XIIe siècle.* Paris: Droz, 1969.

————. *Ivoires du moyen âge.* Fribourg: Office du Livre, 1978.

Garrison, E. B. *Studies in the History of Mediaeval Italian Painting.* 4 vols. Florence: N.p., 1953–56.

Gauthier, Marie-Madeleine. *Les émaux du moyen âge.* Fribourg: Office du Livre, 1972.

Glass, Dorothy F. *Italian Romanesque Sculpture: An Annotated Bibliography.* Boston: G. K. Hall, 1983.

Golden Age of Anglo-Saxon Art, The. London: British Museum, 1984. Exhibition catalogue.

Goldschmidt, Adolph. *Die Elfenbeinskulpturen.* 4 vols. Berlin: Cassirer, 1914–26.

Grabar, André. *Early Christian Art.* New York: Braziller, 1967.

———. *The Golden Age of Justinian.* New York: Braziller, 1966.

———. *Martyrium.* 3 vols. Paris: College de France, 1943–46.

Grodecki, Louis. *L'architecture ottonienne.* Paris: A. Colin, 1958.

———. *Le Moyen âge retrouvé: de l'an mil à l'an 1200.* Paris: Flammarion, 1986.

———. *Le vitrail roman.* Fribourg: Office du Livre, 1977.

———, and Catherine Brissac. *Le vitrail gothique au XIIIᵉ siècle.* Fribourg: Office du Livre, 1984.

Gutmann, Joseph. *Hebrew Manuscript Painting.* New York: Braziller, 1978.

Harvey, John. *English Medieval Architects: A Biographical Dictionary Down to 1550.* Rev. ed. Gloucester: Alan Sutton, 1987.

Heitz, Carol. *L'architecture religieuse carolingienne.* Paris: Picard, 1980.

Henry, Françoise. *Irish Art.* 3 vols. Ithaca, N.Y.: Cornell Univ. Press, 1965–70.

Horn, Walter, and Ernest Born. *The Plan of St. Gall.* 3 vols. Berkeley: University of California Press, 1979.

Hubert, Jean, Jean Porcher, and Wolfgang Friedrich Volbach. *The Carolingian Renaissance.* New York: Braziller, 1969.

———. *Europe of the Invasions, 300–750 A.D.* New York: Braziller, 1969.

The International Style: The Arts in Europe around 1400. Baltimore: Walters Art Gallery, 1962. Exhibition catalogue.

Kaiser Karl IV. Nuremberg: Germanisches Nationalmuseum, 1978. Exhibition catalogue.

Karl der Grosse: Lebenswerk und Nachwirkung. Edited by Wolfgang Braunfels and others. 5 vols. Düsseldorf: Schwann, 1965–68.

Karl der Grosse: Werk und Wirkung. Aachen: N.p., 1975. Exhibition catalogue.

Katzenellenbogen, Adolf. *The Sculptural Programs of Chartres Cathedral.* Baltimore: Johns Hopkins Univ. Press, 1959.

Kauffmann, C. M. *Romanesque Manuscripts, 1066–1190.* Oxford: Harvey Miller, 1975.

Kemp, Wolfgang. *Sermo corporeus: Die Erzählung der mittelalterlichen Glasfenster.* Munich: N.p., 1987.

Kessler, Herbert. *The Illustrated Bibles from Tours.* Princeton: Princeton Univ. Press, 1977.

———. "On the State of Medieval Art History." *Art Bulletin* 70(1988): 166–87.

Kimpel, Dieter, and Robert Suckale. *Die gotische Architektur in Frankreich, 1130–1270.* Munich: Hirmer, 1985.

Kitzinger, Ernst. *Byzantine Art in the Making.* Cambridge, Mass.: Harvard Univ. Press, 1977.

———. *Medieval Art in the British Museum.* London: British Museum, 1955.

Koehler, Wilhelm. *Die Karolingischen Miniaturen.* Berlin: Cassirer, 1930–.

Kraus, Henry. *Gold Was the Mortar: The Economics of Cathedral Building.* London: Routledge, 1979.

Krautheimer, Richard. *Early Christian and Byzantine Architecture.* 3d ed. London: Penguin, 1987.

———. *Studies in Early Christian, Medieval and Renaissance Art.* New York: New York Univ. Press, 1969.

Kubach, Erich, and Albert Verbeek. *Romanische Baukunst an Rhein und Maas: Katalog der vorromanischen und romanischen Denkmäler.* 3 vols. Berlin: Deutscher Verlag für Kunstwissenschaft, 1976.

Kunst und Kultur im Weserraum, 800–1600. 2 vols. Münster: Aschendorf, 1967.

Lanfranco e Wiligelmo: Il Duomo di Modena. Modena: Panini, 1984.

Lasko, Peter. *Ars Sacra, 800–1200.* London: Penguin, 1972.

Lazarev, Victor. *Storia della pittura bizantina.* Turin: Einaudi, 1967.

Leedy, Walter C., Jr. *Fan Vaulting: A Study of Form, Technology, and Meaning.* Santa Monica, Calif.: Arts + Architecture Press, 1980.

Leroy, Jules. *Les manuscrits coptes et coptes-arabes illustrés.* Paris: P. Geuthner, 1974.

———. *Les manuscrits syriaques à peintures conservés dans les bibliothèques d'Europe et d'Orient.* 2 vols. Paris: P. Geuthner, 1964.

Lewis, Suzanne. *The Art of Matthew Paris in the Chronica Majora.* Berkeley: Univ. of California Press, 1987.

Lexikon der christlichen Ikonographie. Edited by Engelbert Kirschbaum. 8 vols. Freiburg: Herder, 1968–76.

Lord, Carla. *Royal French Patronage of Art in the Fourteenth Century: An Annotated Bibliography.* Boston: G. K. Hall, 1985.

Lyman, Thomas W., and Daniel Smartt. *French Romanesque Sculpture: An Annotated Bibliography.* Boston: G. K. Hall, 1987.

Mâle, Emile. *Religious Art in France.* Edited by Harry Bober. Princeton: Princeton Univ. Press, 1978–.

Marrow, James. *Passion Iconography in Northern European Art of the Late Middle Ages and Early Renaissance.* Kortrijk: Van Ghemmert, 1979.

Masterpieces of Tapestry from the Fourteenth to the Sixteenth Century. New York: Metropolitan Museum of Art, 1973. Exhibition catalogue.

Matthiae, Guglielmo. *Mosaici medievali delle chiese di Roma.* 2 vols. Rome: Istituto Poligrafico dello Stato, 1967.

———. *Pittura romana del medioevo.* 2 vols. Rome: Fratelli Palombi, 1965–66.

Meiss, Millard. *French Painting in the Time of Jean de Berry.* 3 vols. in 5. New York: Braziller, 1967–74.

Mende, Ursula. *Die Bronzetüren des Mittelalters.* Munich: Hirmer, 1983.

Monumenta Annonis: Köln und Siegburg: Weltbild und Kunst im hohen Mittelalter. Cologne: Schnüttgen Museum, 1975. Exhibition catalogue.

Morgan, Nigel. *Early Gothic Manuscripts.* 2 vols. Oxford: Harvey Miller, 1982–87.

Müller, Theodor. *Sculpture in the Netherlands, Germany, France, Spain, 1400–1500.* London: Penguin, 1966.

Murray, Stephen. *Building Troyes Cathedral: The Late Gothic Campaigns.* Bloomington: Indiana Univ. Press, 1987.

Mussat, André. *Le style gothique de l'ouest de la France (12ᵉ-13ᵉ siècles)*. Paris: Picard, 1963.

Nees, Lawrence. *From Justinian to Charlemagne: European Art, 565-787: An Annotated Bibliography*. Boston: G. K. Hall, 1985.

Nicholaus e l'arte del suo tempo. 3 vols. Ferrara: Corbo, 1985.

Nordenfalk, Carl. *Celtic and Anglo-Saxon Painting*. New York: Braziller, 1977.

———. *Die spätantiken Zierbuchstaben*. 2 vols. Stockholm: N.p., 1970.

Nuit des Temps, La. La Pierre-qui-Vire: Zodiaque, 1958–.

Ohlgren, Thomas H. *Insular and Anglo-Saxon Illuminated Manuscripts: An Iconographic Catalogue c. A.D. 625 to 1100*. New York: Garland, 1986.

Ornamenta ecclesiae. 3 vols. Cologne: Schnüttgen Museum, 1985. Exhibition catalogue.

Oswald, Friedrich, Leo Schaefer, and Hans Rudolf Sennhauser. *Vorromanische Kirchenbauten*. Munich: Prestel, 1971.

Pächt, Otto. *Book Illumination in the Middle Ages*. London: Harvey Miller, 1987.

Palol, Pedro de, and Max Hirmer. *Early Medieval Art in Spain*. New York: Abrams, 1966.

Panofsky, Erwin. *Abbot Suger on the Abbey Church of St. Denis and Its Art Treasures*. 2d ed., revised by Gerda Panofsky-Soergel. Princeton: Princeton Univ. Press, 1979.

Die Parler und der Schöne Stil, 1350-1400: Europäische Kunst unter den Luxemburgern. 3 vols. Cologne: Schnüttgen Museum, 1978. Exhibition catalogue.

Paysage monumental de la France autour de l'an mil. Edited by Xavier Barral i Altet. Paris: Picard, 1987.

Pevsner, Nikolaus. *The Buildings of England*. 46 vols. London: Penguin, 1951-74.

Pickering, F. P. *Literature and Art in the Middle Ages*. London: Macmillan, 1970.

Porcher, Jean. *Medieval French Miniatures*. New York: Abrams, 1959.

Randall, Lillian M. C. *Images in the Margins of Gothic Manuscripts*. Berkeley: Univ. of California Press, 1966.

Regensburger Buchmalerei: Von frühkarolingischer Zeit bis zum Ausgang des Mittelalters. Munich: Bayerische Staatsbibliothek, 1987.

The Renaissance of the Twelfth Century. Edited by Stephen K. Scher. Providence: Rhode Island School of Design, 1969. Exhibition catalogue.

Rhein und Maas: Kunst Kultur, 800-1400. 2 vols. Cologne: Schnüttgen Museum, 1972-73. Exhibition catalogue.

Rickert, Margaret. *Painting in Britain: The Middle Ages*. 2d ed. London: Penguin, 1965.

Riegl, Alois. *Late Roman Art Industry*. Translated by Rolf Winkes. Rome: Giorgio Bretschneider, 1985.

Ringbom, Sixten. *Icon to Narrative: The Rise of the Dramatic Close-Up in Fifteenth-Century Devotional Painting*. 2d ed. Doornspijk, Netherlands: Davaco, 1984.

Ross, D. J. A. *Illustrated Medieval Alexander Books in Germany and the Netherlands*. Cambridge: Cambridge Univ. Press, 1971.

Salvini, Roberto. *Wiligelmo e le origini della scultura romanica*. Milan: Aldo Martello, 1956.

Sandler, Lucy Freeman. *Gothic Manuscripts, 1285–1385.* 2 vols. Oxford: Harvey Miller, 1985.

Sapin, Christian. *La Bourgogne préromane.* Paris: Picard, 1986.

Sauerländer, Willibald. *Gothic Sculpture in France, 1140–1270.* New York: Abrams, 1973.

————. *Von Sens bis Strasbourg.* Berlin: De Gruyter, 1966.

Schapiro, Meyer. *Late Antique, Early Christian and Mediaeval Art.* New York: Braziller, 1979.

————. *The Parma Ildefonsus.* New York: New York Univ. Press, 1964.

————. *Romanesque Art.* New York: Braziller, 1977.

Scheller, R. W. *A Survey of Medieval Model Books.* Haarlem: N.p., F. Bohn, 1963.

Schramm, Percy Ernst. *Herrschaftszeichen und Staatssymbolik.* 3 vols. Stuttgart: Hiersemann, 1954–56.

Secular Spirit, The: Life and Art in the Middle Ages. Edited by Thomas Hoving. New York: The Cloisters, 1975.

Sears, Elizabeth. *The Ages of Man: Medieval Interpretations of the Life Cycle.* Princeton: Princeton Univ. Press, 1986.

Seidel, Linda. *Songs of Glory.* Chicago: Univ. of Chicago Press, 1981.

Simson, Otto von. *The Gothic Cathedral.* 2d ed. New York: N.p., 1962.

————. *Das Mittelalter.* Vol. 2. Berlin: Propyläen, 1972.

Sinding-Larsen, Staale. *Iconography and Ritual: A Study of Analytical Perspectives.* Oslo: Universitetsforlaget, 1984.

Stoddard, Whitney. *Monastery and Cathedral in France.* Middletown, Conn.: Wesleyan Univ. Press, 1966.

————. *The Sculptors of the West Portals of Chartres Cathedral.* New York: Norton, 1987.

Stubblebine, James. *Dugento Painting: An Annotated Bibliography.* Boston: G. K. Hall, 1983.

Swarzennski, Hanns. *Monuments of Romanesque Art.* 2d ed. Chicago: Univ. of Chicago Press, 1967.

Taylor, H. M., and J. Taylor. *Anglo-Saxon Architecture.* 3 vols. Cambridge: Cambridge Univ. Press, 1965–78.

Temple, Elzbieta. *Anglo-Saxon Manuscripts 900–1066.* Oxford: Harvey Miller, 1976.

Thérel, Marie Louise. *Le triomphe de la Vierge Eglise: Sources historiques, littéraires et iconographiques.* Paris: CNRS, 1984.

Treasures from Medieval France. Cleveland: Cleveland Museum of Art, 1967. Exhibition catalogue.

Vergnolle, Eliane. *St.-Benoît-sur-Loire et la sculpture du XIe siècle.* Paris: Picard, 1985.

Viollet-le-Duc, Eugène-Emmanuel. *Dictionnaire raisonné de l'architecture française du XIe au XVIe siècle.* 10 vols. Paris: Bance, 1854–68.

Volbach, Wolfgang Friedrich. *Elfenbeinskulpturen der Spätantike und des frühen Mittelalters.* 3d ed. Mainz: Von Zabern, 1976.

Volbach, Wolfgang Friedrich, and Jacqueline Lafontaine-Dosogne. *Byzanz und der christliche Osten.* Berlin: Propyläen, 1968.

Webb, Geoffrey. *Architecture in Britain: The Middle Ages.* 2d ed. London: Penguin, 1966.

Weir, Anthony, and James Jerman. *Images of Lust: Sexual Carvings on Medieval Churches.* London: Batsford, 1986.

Wietzmann, Kurt. *Illuminations in Roll and Codex.* Princeton: Princeton Univ. Press, 1947.

————. *The Monastery of St. Catherine's at Mount Sinai: The Icons.* Princeton: Princeton Univ. Press, 1976.

————. *Studies in Classical and Byzantine Manuscript Illumination.* Chicago: Univ. of Chicago Press, 1971.

Werner, Martin. *Insular Art: An Annotated Bibliography.* Boston: G. K. Hall, 1984.

Wesenberg, Rudolf, *Frühe mittelalterliche Bildwerke: Die Schulen Rheinischer Skulptur und ihre Ausstrahlung.* Düsseldorf: Schwann. 1972.

Wieck, Roger S. *Time Sanctified: The Book of Hours in Medieval Art and Life.* New York: Braziller, 1988.

Williams, John. *Early Spanish Manuscript Illumination.* New York: Braziller, 1977.

Wilson, David M. *Anglo-Saxon Art from the Seventh Century to the Norman Conquest.* London: Thames and Hudson, 1984.

Wilson, David M., and Ole Klindt-Jensen. *Viking Art.* London: Routledge, 1966.

Wormald, Francis. *Collected Writings.* Oxford: Oxford Univ. Press, 1984–.

Year 1200, The: A Symposium. Edited by Jeffrey Hoffeld. New York: Metropolitan Museum of Art, 1975.

Zarnecki, George. *Art of the Medieval World.* Englewood Cliffs, N.J.: Prentice-Hall, 1975.

Die Zeit der Staufer. 5 vols. Stuttgart: Württembergisches Landesmuseum, 1977.

13

Medieval Music in Perspective

THEODORE KARP

ORKING WITH DOCUMENTS of bygone ages, the historian faces problems that are loosely comparable to those of the paleontologist who seeks to transform in the mind's eye a fragmentary skeleton into an image of a living creature and the environment in which it flourished. The specific problems to be encountered in each of the various disciplines are of course to a large extent individual, and it is only natural that these play a major role in shaping both the objectives and the working methods of each discipline. In seeking to summarize the methodology and accomplishments of musicologists treating medieval music, it may be useful to begin by reviewing their special problems, even though many fundamental points may seem obvious.

Music, like dance and drama, is an art that exists in time. The music historian does not have direct access to the artistic productions of past centuries. Nor are the equivalent of surviving paintings, sculptures, and buildings available that furnish the point of departure for the art historian, however ravaged by time these may be. Certainly oral tradition played a major role in the transmission of medieval music. Nevertheless, without notation, a musical work within a nontraditional culture could have only a brief life expectancy. For such music to achieve greater permanence, its patterns of sound had to be fixed as visual patterns, which could be reconverted into sound at later date.

Certain points concerning this dual process must be kept in mind. In the first place, not all of the essential features of a composition are necessarily committed to notation. In the Middle Ages and Renaissance, for example, the sharps and flats that might change the pitch of essential tones were often left to the understanding of the performers, sometimes with dubious results. Not only do modern scholars frequently disagree concerning those accidentals that must be supplied by the editor (*musica ficta*), but we may still read scornful remarks concerning mistakes made in performance by medieval and Renaissance musicians. With regard to much music written before 1200, modern scholars strongly disagree on the vital issue of whether or not the notation indicates rhythm. And if one is not able to establish a rhythmic profile with security, then the harmonic structure of polyphonic composition in which the voices are not synchronized in a note-against-note relationship is also open to question. The musicologist's task then becomes one of major reconstruction, comparable perhaps to the creation of drawings illustrating the early, destroyed basilica of St. Peter's at Rome. It is not at all surprising to find that different reconstructions of the same piece, whether committed to paper or brought to life in performance, vary in fundamental ways. We are also in the dark concerning vital aspects of ornamentation and instrumentation in medieval music.

In the second place, with the exception of a small number of recently created computer compositions, no musical notation has ever been devised that is capable of defining all of the nuances that are essential to a musical performance. In the same manner, the text of a play that survives does not indicate the speech rhythms and inflections, the pacing or the details of acting, the costumes, stage properties, or even the nature of the stage envisioned by the dramatist. Yet all of these factors must be taken into consideration, just as one must take into consideration tempo, articulation, accentuation, instrumentation, improvisation, and even room acoustics, if one is to bring to life either a play or a composition in a performance that is faithful to the spirit of the original. We are only slowly coming to grips with the complex of problems involved in the performance of medieval music, and our attitudes toward the solution of these problems has changed to such an extent since the first production of long-playing records that in reviewing a discography issued in 1964, Andrew Hughes could justly caution that "many of the older discs . . . do not present performances acceptable by more recent standards and opinions about how the music should sound."[1]

Finally, the details of musical notation have undergone vast and fundamental transformations over the course of the centuries. Some early works that would be of extraordinary historical interest — including laments on the death of Charlemagne and his son, Hugo of St. Quentin, and early settings of Virgil and Horace—cannot be deciphered at all, since the notation in which they survive does not indicate either pitch or rhythm. It is understandable, therefore, that the basic point of departure for studies of medieval music—apart from the discovery and description of surviving sources—lies in the efforts to solve the problems of notation and to make the music available in the most accurate and easily understandable form.

In order to appreciate the accomplishments of musicologists treating medieval music, it is helpful to remember that musicology is one of the younger of the humanistic disciplines. There were, of course, antiquarians of various periods who probed into the history of music, including the music of the Middle Ages and Renaissance. But even these were active at a later period than their counterparts in other disciplines. Especially important were the contributions in the late eighteenth century of the Prince-Abbot of St. Blasien, Martin Gerbert, who wrote a history of sacred music, *De cantu et musica sacra* (1774), and who provided the basis for much further work in medieval music through this epochal edition of theoretical treatises, *Scriptores ecclesiastici de musica* (1784). Noteworthy contemporaries included such others as Jean Benjamin de La Borde, Charles Burney, John Hawkins, and Johann Nikolaus Forkel, who each treated medieval music in the course of their general music histories. While these men command respect for their pioneering efforts, and while their views of more recent music are of considerable historical importance, their approach to medieval music was prejudiced and their knowledge extremely limited. The historians active during the Enlightenment viewed earlier periods of European culture as mere stepping-stones in the path toward the perfection reached by their age. Hence, they could not examine medieval music with sympathetic minds: ". . . great perfection cannot be expected in the music of Europe during the Middle Ages, when the Goths, Vandals, Huns, Germans, Franks, and Gauls, whose ideas were savage, and language harsh and insolent, have seized on its most fertile provinces."[2] More important, very little medieval music was known then, not even enough to qualify as the tip of the iceberg. Much of this was in the realm of trouvère song, and, by means of insipid harmonizations and arbitrary rhythmic interpretations, these pieces were usually converted to a form that was at least compatible with eighteenth-century practice. Another handful of musical examples and excerpts was culled from theoretical treatises, and it was these treatises that furnished the main avenue of approach.

The situation improved slightly during the first half of the nineteenth century with the issuance of *Musica Antiqua* (1812?), an anthology prepared by John Stafford Smith, and with the further work of François-Joseph Fétis and Raphael Georg Kieswetter. But striking change occurred only after mid-century, through the efforts of August Wilhelm Ambros and Charles Edmond de Coussemaker. The latter not only continued the work of Gerbert with his *Scriptorum de musica medii aevi novam seriem a Gerbertina alteram* (1874–76), but provided important access to various repertoires of the twelfth and thirteenth centuries in transcriptions that accompanied such works as *Histoire de l'harmonie au moyen âge* (1852), *Drames liturgiques du moyen âge* (1860), *Les Harmonistes des XIIe et XIIIe siècles* (1865), *L'Art harmonique aux XIIe et XIIIe siècles* (1865), and *Oeuvres complètes d'Adam de la Halle* (1872).

Nevertheless, the establishment of musicology as a rigorous discipline supported by a sizable community of scholars scarcely antedates the turn of the twentieth century. Among the outstanding medievalists of the first generation were Friedrich Ludwig, Peter Wagner, Johannes Wolf, Hugo Riemann, Pierre Aubry, Théodore Gérold, Dom André Mocquereau, André Pirro, Jean Baptiste Beck, Walter Frere, Harry Ellis Woolridge, and Henry Marriot Bannister. Some of the better work done by these men is still of current value and lies at the foundation for more recent studies.

The upsurge of interest in medieval music continued in the years preceding World War II, and was best exemplified in the work of scholars such as Higini Anglès, Heinrich Besseler, Yvonne Rokseth, and Gustave Reese. The rapid expansion witnessed by other humanistic disciplines following that war held true also in musicology. On the one hand, we have multiplied many times over our fund of knowledge and revised many basic concepts; on the other, the tasks facing the young discipline have been sufficiently numerous and varied that we only now are beginning to replace such fundamental works as the editions of Gerbert and Coussemaker with modern ones based on the comparison of all surviving readings.

The dramatic growth in all aspects of scholarly investigation of music has brought home the need for bibliographic control over the wealth of material produced during the recent past. A broad, though selective, survey of the secondary literature has been provided by Andrew Hughes in *Medieval Music, the Sixth Liberal Art* (rev. ed., 1980). Useful capsule comments are provided for approximately 2,000 items, organized into workable categories. More detailed summaries of 50–200 words are available for material published since 1967, the date of inception of the *Répertoire International de Littérature Musicale* (*RILM*). This quarterly publication is a cooperative effort sponsored by the International Musicology Society, the International Association of Music Libraries, and the American Council of Learned Societies. It covers the entire field of music, including material of interdisciplinary interest. The abstracts are prepared largely by the individual authors, and reasonable completeness of coverage is overseen by numerous area editors. Other general bibliographic works dealing with music that antedate *RILM* include the *Music Index* (1949–) and the *Bibliographie des Musikschrifttums* (1936–), edited by Wolfgang Schmieder. Persons seeking modern scholarly editions of medieval music may wish to consult either Sydney Robinson Charles's *A Handbook of Music and Music Literature in Sets and Series* or Anna Heyer's *Historical Sets, Collected Editions and Monuments of Music.*

As a youthful discipline, it is not surprising that many of musicology's basic methods were adapted from older disciplines such as philology, history, and art history. The brevity of our tradition also makes itself felt in various other ways. The discipline has not been much given to self-examination with regard to either the philosophy of history or approaches to the writing of history. Most publications dealing with this area are concerned with general problems, and touch on questions of medieval music only briefly, if at all. One of the early major efforts was Warren Dwight Allen's *Philosophies of Music History* (1939). More recent are the essays by Arthur Mendel, "Evidence and Explanation";[3] Leo Treitler, "On Historical Criticism"[4] and "The Present as History";[5] and Donald Grout, "Current Historiography and Music History."[6]

Interest in problems of periodization has been relatively minor. Since the earliest substantial sources do not antedate the late ninth century, and since the discipline, as a whole, tends to focus strongly on European developments, questions of transition from the music of Antiquity to that of the Middle Ages have occupied comparatively few musicologists. A natural dividing point in musical style, marked by changes in both repertoire and notation, occurred ca. 1300. The polyphony before that time belongs to the *Ars antiqua,* while that following falls under the heading of the *Ars nova.* Despite significant changes in the treatment of rhythm, the underlying principles of harmony and formal structure in fourteenth-century music are generally considered to be medieval. There is little agreement regarding the primary style characteristic or combination of characteristics that are to be taken as the hallmark of Renaissance musical style — simplification of rhythm, increased use of the imperfect consonances (thirds and sixths) relative to the perfect consonances (unisons, fifths, and octaves), or the unification of the different strands of the polyphonic web by means of imitation. Most scholars tend to place the boundary between the Middle Ages and Renaissance variously between the years 1425 and 1475.[7] Some, however, have written in terms of an "Early Renaissance," referring to some portion of the fourteenth century. In his book, *Humanism in Italian Musical Thought,*[8] Claude Palisca calls for a much broader approach to the conception of "Renaissance" in music, and seeks to define this period in terms of intellectual concepts. It is likely that under the impetus of this study there will be fresh interest among musicologists in defining the boundaries between medieval and Renaissance music.

Although the need for studies that relate music to broad humanistic and sociological concepts was stressed decades ago by scholars such as Curt Sachs, scholars have been slow to follow his lead.[9] Two slim volumes, *Il Medievo* 1 and 2,[10] by Giulio Cattin and F. Alberto Gallo respectively, give more than average consideration to interrelationships between music and other disciplines. Some information concerning the role of music in medieval society may be found in several older histories, including those of Gérold and Reese, and in smaller, specialized studies. More recently a major series, *Man and Music*,[11] has been undertaken to improve the previous imbalance. James McKinnon edits a volume of essays, *Ancient and Medieval Music*, while Iain Fenlon edits a counterpart, *The Renaissance*. There have been two major works on medieval music education[12] and some smaller essays. Scholars such as Abert and Schrade have inquired into the role of music in the writings of such important figures as Boethius, John Scotus Erigena, and St. Augustine. John Stevens has provided a broad overview of a controversial subject in his *Words and Music: Song, Narrative, Dance and Drama, 1050–1350*,[13] and there has been a general upsurge of interest in the interrelationship between text and music in many smaller studies and in more general works.

There is an active and growing interest in the collection and interpretation of iconographical evidence relating to medieval music. Emmanuel Winternitz's "The Visual Arts as a Source for the Historian of Music"[14] may be cited as a general guide to problems of interpretation. The standard one-volume anthology of pictorial materials concerning music — Georg Kinsky's *Geschichte der Musik in Bildern* — is in process of being superseded by a large series begun by Heinrich Besseler and Max Schneider, *Musikgeschichte in Bildern.* Some fascicles of volume 3, which deals with medieval and Renaissance music, have already appeared. In addition, a number of histories are beautifully illustrated; unfortunately, it is necessary to add that some of the more handsome ones are not uniformly reliable with regard to text. Scholars have begun increasingly to use art historical evidence in connection with musicological problems, as in Rebecca Baltzer's "Thirteenth-century Illuminated Miniatures and the Date of the Florence Manuscript."[15]

To demonstrate part of the range of broader approaches to problems of medieval music, we might cite such studies as Manfred Bukofzer's "Speculative Thinking in Medieval Music,"[16] Nino Pirrotta's imaginative "Dante Musicus: Gothicism, Scholasticism, and Music,"[17] and Leo Treitler's

"Homer and Gregory."[18] And there is much that the medievalist can gain from similar studies that focus primarily on the Renaissance, such as the thought-provoking studies of Edward Lowinsky, "The Concept of Physical and Musical Space in the Renaissance."[19] and "The Goddess Fortuna in Music."[20] Many technical characteristics of medieval music are translatable into more general concepts. Consonance and dissonance are equatable to stability and instability. Problems of formal organization — repetition of units, variation, balance, and symmetry — are common to several arts. The musicologist, too, must deal with closed and open-ended forms. It is to be hoped that a greater amount of interest will be evinced in investigating the degree of correlation existing among the medieval approaches to comparable problems in different arts.

During the first three quarters of this century, the mainstream of musicological activity sought to make accessible the musical monuments themselves and to investigate their technical characteristics. This remains an important ongoing activity. Therefore, the main portion of this chapter will concern itself with bibliographies of source materials, facsimile editions, handbooks on notation, principles of edition, performance practice, and recordings. The achievements and needs of individual areas will then be taken up in succession.

A comprehensive survey of musical source materials is in process of being issued in the *Répertoire International des Sources Musicales* (*RISM*), also made possible through the cooperation of the International Musicology Society and the International Association of Music Libraries. The series will eventually cover all sources of music and music theory through the end of the eighteenth century. Several volumes dealing with various kinds of medieval and early Renaissance music have appeared over the past decade, but others still remain to be published. The volumes are each prepared under the direction of a leading specialist in the field, but vary considerably in the depth of information provided. Those that present detailed lists of contents for individual manuscripts may often be consulted profitably by scholars in related disciplines such as philology and liturgiology. These volumes not only indicate the location of sources, but also furnish useful bibliographical information concerning discussion of the sources and partial or complete editions or their contents.

In addition to *RISM,* there are a number of guides to specific genres of source materials. Manuscripts bearing on the Mass are catalogued and their musical interrelationships explored in the two volumes of *Le graduel romain* that have thus far appeared. A more detailed accounting of manuscripts for the Office has been provided by Dom René Hesbert in his *Corpus Antiphonalium Officii* (6 vols.). Other important guides cover the fields of organum, clausula, conductus, motet, and polyphonic music of the Trecento.[21] Lastly, catalogues are available for the musical holdings of a sizable number of major libraries. These and other useful reference tools are listed in Vincent Duckles's *Music Reference and Research Materials* (4th ed. by Michael Keller, 1988).

In general, our command over surviving source material seems reasonably comprehensive. We may hope for important new discoveries of small scope, such as reported in Kenneth Levy's "A Dominican Organum Duplum"[22] and K. D. Hartzell's "An Eleventh-century English Missal Fragment in the British Library."[23] And opportunities for fascinating detective work, exemplified by Margaret Bent's "A Lost English Choir Book of the Fifteenth Century"[24] will not be entirely lacking. However, the likelihood of discoveries of large scope is not great. The best hope for such finds lies in little-explored holdings on the Iberian peninsula and in central and eastern European countries.

Since primary sources of medieval music are widely scattered and are rarely immediately accessible, the availability of several important manuscripts of medieval music and complete facsimile editions is extremely helpful. In the realm of Gregorian chant, the the series *Paléographie musicale,* issued by the monks of Solesmes, is invaluable, and there are individual issues of other important codices. Sections of manuscripts devoted to proses and sequences are being issued in facsimile by Dom René Hesbert. A large segment of secular and nonliturgical monophony—the songs of the troubadours, trouvères, and minnesingers, the *laude* and *cantigas*—has likewise been made available. The most important sources of twelfth- and thirteenth-century polyphony—organum, *conductus, clausula,* and motet—have been published in facsimile, several in monumental editions of great importance. We are less well supplied with published reproductions of fourteenth-century sources, but there are facsimiles available of *Le Roman de Fauvel,* the Machaut Mass, and various sources of Italian secular polyphony.

However fundamental is the access to original sources, and however useful the availability of facsimile editions, the materials contained therein remain unusable to those not intimately familiar with the various medieval systems of musical notation. The basic principles of several of these systems have been set forth in books by Johannes Wolf,[25] Willi Apel,[26] and Carl Parrish,[27] and still a broader survey of notational concepts is offered by Jacques Chailley.[28] More specialized studies—for example, of Gregorian notation and of certain aspects of the notation of early polyphony—are also available. While the handbooks mentioned serve as useful introductions to the subject, they are now too old to provide access to recent advances made in the more controversial fields of chant interpretation and early polyphony. *Palaeographie der Musik,* a series under the editorship of Wulf Arlt, provides a more up-to-date account of various monophonic notations. Two more volumes, dealing with polyphonic notations and notations after A.D. 1600 were announced, but have not appeared in more than a decade.

The element of uncertain interpretation must be kept in mind in dealing with modern editions of medieval (especially early medieval) music. There are several problems in the preparation of these editions. Should the original notation be modernized or not? If modernized, to what extent and in what manner? If multiple sources survive, how should these be taken into account?

Given the fact that medieval notations are understood thoroughly by comparatively few knowledgeable musicians and still fewer nonmusicians, an affirmative answer to the first of these questions might seem a foregone conclusion. Actually, however, the matter is still under debate. In the first place, it would seem that a number of editors seeking to present authoritative, scholarly editions are extremely wary of allowing personal interpretations to enter — perhaps indistinguishably — into the presentation of the musical text. Since, as has been previously indicated, many medieval notations do not supply us with as much information about music as is needed for performance, there is no way in which these notations can be fully converted into modern forms without a major element of personal interpretation. And this interpretation cannot be treated as the equivalent of historical fact. The major issue of debate, however, concerns a rather different point. In the opinion of scholars such as Thrasybulos Georgiades, the musical thought of a composer is inextricably bound up with the notation in which the thought is recorded, and any alteration of the original notation thus constitutes a falsification of the musical thought itself. Depending upon the nature of the original notation, editors adhering to this premise may present pseudofacsimiles of the manuscripts, or, while retaining the original note forms, they may superimpose in a score voice parts that in the manuscripts were written on different parts of the page. Even prior to the formulation of Georgiades' theories, there were editions in which the original note values were retained, although the note forms were converted into machine-reproducible equivalents and the compound symbols containing two or more notes were subdivided into individual components.

Although the desire to offer scientifically accurate texts, uncontaminated by the conclusions of the editor, is laudable, the policy nevertheless results in editions that are not understandable to the nonspecialist. Furthermore, it deprives the user of the most valuable contribution that the editor has to offer, a detailed account of his own perceptions, reached after prolonged familiarity with the subject. The opposite to Georgiades' philosophy is ably presented by Ewald Jammers in "Interpretationsfragen mittelalterlicher Musik."[29]

Generally, editors offer at least partial modernizations of the original notation. In the early years of the twentieth century, the changes were often limited to the substitution of modern note forms for those of the original, while retaining the original values. In more recent editions, the original note values are usually subdivided, either to a greater or lesser extent, in order that they might conform more closely with modern notational practices. The reason for this may be put simply as follows. In the early thirteenth century, there was terminology for only two note values. The briefer of these was so rapid that it could be subdivided into no more than two or three ornamental tones, which were at first unnamed. As these ornamental tones were used in greater profusion and as their musical functions became more basic, the tempo was gradually relaxed. Because of the slowing of tempo, fast ornamentation then had to be expressed by means of newer values that were subdivisions of the old ones. This process was repeated several times from the thirteenth through the seventeenth centuries, with the result that the original short value, the breve, is now twice as long as the longest value normally employed in modern notation, that is, the whole note — or, in late thirteenth-century terms, the semibreve.

Since there is no universally observed standard for the division of values, the nonspecialist must take into account the fact that different modern symbols may be used to represent the same medieval symbol, and that these normally have identical, or nearly identical, significance. (This situation may be encountered even within a volume of transcriptions by one editor.) While early editions generally employ minimal subdivision, realization that ready comprehensibility calls for a reduction of values that will produce a visual impression in terms of tempo that is akin to the impression produced by the notation employed in standard concert fare increased markedly in editions issued following World War II. At the same time, the old clefs previously employed have been discarded in favor of the ones most commonly used in the nineteenth and twentieth centuries. It is likely that the employment of editions in which note values were not sufficiently reduced was responsible for many of the overly slow, distorted performances of medieval music that occurred even after 1950.

With regard to the editing of music that survives in multiple sources, there was a tendency early in the century to seek to restore the hypothetical "original" by means of a conflation. Now we tend to question whether such objectives are indeed appropriate to the material at hand. The present practice is normally to adhere to the readings of the most accurate identifiable source unless evidence shows that certain emendations are mandatory. A broad overview of the complex of problems involved in the preparation of musical editions is available in the articles, "Editing," by Howard Mayer Brown[30] and "Editionstechnik," by Hans Albrecht.[31]

The accomplishments of musicologists in the realm of editions of medieval music have been substantial. To be sure, there are significant portions of the chant repertoire and of secular monophony that remain unedited, although partly available in facsimile. But we are quite well supplied with scholarly editions of medieval polyphony. Broadly speaking, we are nearing the end of what might be regarded as a "first generation" of editions and are preparing to enter into a second. It will undoubtedly be possible to improve materially on the accuracy of editions of music composed prior to 1300. Editions of music composed after that date will be less affected. Even there, changes will be forthcoming based on greater sensitivity to editorial problems, on concordances not known at earlier date and on improved knowledge of certain notational practices.

Although the majority of medieval polyphony and a substantial amount of monophony are available for performance, the field of early performance practice is still youthful. Older general studies, such as Robert Haas's *Aufführungspraxis,*[32] and Thurston Dart's more modest book, *The Interpretation of Music,* provide only slender information concerning medieval music. More concentrated treatment is to be found in Timothy McGee, *Medieval and Renaissance Music: A Performer's Guide,* and in Christopher Page, *Voices and Instruments of the Middle Ages: Instrumental Practice and Songs in France, 1100–1300.* An important group of essays, *Studies in the Performance of Late Mediaeval Music,* has been edited by Stanley Boorman. Two new journals, the *Basler Jahrbuch für historische Musikpraxis* and *Performance Practice Review,* though not restricted to any one period, are adding to our knowledge of practical music-making in the Middle Ages and Renaissance, and material of interest may be gleaned from the longer-established periodical, *Early Music.* Two general bibliographies of the field are available: *Performance Practice,* by Mary Vinquist and Neal Zaslaw, and a similarly titled work by Roland Jackson. Current materials are indexed in the *Basler Jahrbuch.*

Perhaps the most important of the results of musicological scholarship are the recordings that have appeared in both increasing quantity and increasing quality since about 1965. A truly wide range of musical experience is now available to all medievalists. A recommendation to become acquainted with these musical treasures cannot be urged too strongly. Even though recordings go out of print rather quickly, a second index, *Medieval and Renaissance Music on Long-Playing Records,* compiled by James

Coover and Richard Colvig—issues in 1973—is still of use, particularly at institutions with extensive phonograph record archives. Although the pioneering ensembles, the Pro Musica Antiqua and the New York Pro Musica Antiqua, as well as the later Early Music Consort of London are now defunct, their place is being filled by a rapidly growing number of excellent groups. Among the better-informed, more challenging directors of the period, 1975–90, are Thomas Binkley, Alexander Blachly, John Blackley, Mark Brown, Grayston Burgess, René Clemencic, Joel Cohen, László Dobszay, Paul Hilliard, Michael Morrow and John Beckett, Christopher Page, Andrew Parrott, Marcel Pérès, Alejandro Planchart, Konrad Ruhland, Mary Springfels, and Denis Stevens. Until such time as a newer discography may be issued, it may be possible to keep up with more recent recordings of medieval music either through the American listing of *Notes,* the journal of the Music Library Association, or through the European listings of *Early Music.*

On the whole, the mainstream of medieval music is represented by music of French origin, even though there are periods in which Italian and English contributions—each having individualistic style traits—are of equal importance. Again speaking in very general terms, the discipline as a whole has been shaped to a considerable extent by the work of German scholars and scholars educated in the German tradition. Understandably, scholars of other nationalities have been particularly instrumental in the investigation of their individual national heritages. Nevertheless, it is not practical to discuss the accomplishments of the discipline in terms of the idiosyncracies of "national schools." Therefore, the remainder of the chapter will summarize very briefly the state of affairs in selected areas of research into medieval music.

Chant studies constitute one of the oldest and most complex fields of musicological investigation. The complexity arises from the vastness of the material, the need for a thorough understanding of both the liturgy and the music, the scarcity of reliable documentation for the first millennium A.D., and the problems of interpreting verbal texts that to us are equivocal in meaning. Still other problems arise owing to the differences between the objectives of various scholars. A great deal of present knowledge of Western chant in particular rests on the work of Benedictines from the Abbey of Solesmes. Prior to the Second Vatican Council, their main objective was the restoration of Gregorian chant to its "original state," following a period of several centuries during which the well-intentioned but nevertheless mutilated versions of Medicean chant had served the liturgy. Unfortunately, modern liturgical considerations and historical considerations are not fully compatible. No chant repertoire was created at any one time or in any one place. Furthermore, the liturgical situation has changed since the Middle Ages. Many old feasts of the Sanctorale have been dropped and new ones have been instituted. As a result, modern chant books do not, on the one hand, contain the full medieval repertory of any given time, while, on the other, they present, without any distinguishing marks, modern compositions for feasts of recent origin.

Partly on the basis of modern chant books, and partly on the basis of various medieval sources, a broad overview of the field has been constructed. The most comprehensive summary remains that of Peter Wagner, *Einführung in die gregorianischen Melodien* (latest eds., 1911-21), while Willi Apel's, *Gregorian Chant* (1958), provides a more compact survey of the field. Traditional problems have included the interpretation of notation (including rhythmic implications), analysis of form, and modal classification. While numerous analytical problems remain — for example, a better understanding of the role of melodic formulae is still to be sought — our grasp of fundamentals of melodic construction appears to be on a higher level than our knowledge of historical development.

The presumed role of Pope Gregory I in the codification of the texts and melodies for the Mass Proper, which appeared unshakeable through the first half of this century, has come under stronger and stronger questioning, and is no longer held to be true by most scholars. A search for the origins of the later medieval forms of these melodies — whether they be Roman or Frankish — will continue to occupy both musicologists and liturgists for some time to come. This question is intertwined to some extent with a search for the origins of Western musical notation and with the attempt to gain a better understanding of the processes and accuracy of the oral transmission of liturgical melodies. Even if the results of such probes remain largely speculative, our understanding of the later development of chant remains to be put on a firmer footing. Thanks to the publication of the *Antiphonale missarum sextuplex* by Dom René Hesbert, we know which texts were employed in the Mass Proper prior to the time of the earliest surviving major musical codices. While there is an extensive study of many manuscript versions of the gradual, *Justus et palma,* from the ninth through the seventeenth centuries,[33] there are not yet counterparts for other chants and classes of chant. Gregorianists have gained some knowledge of the nature of variants that may occur in the transmission of individual melodies, and samples of these variants are given as the basis for the manuscript genealogies proposed in *Le graduel romain.* However, we do not yet have text-critical studies which would enable us to trace the growth of chant repertoires in various parts of Europe. Our knowledge of the medieval repertoire is improving, thanks in part to the volumes thus far issued of the *Monumenta Monodica Medii Aevi* and to the individual volumes devoted to the study of different sections of the Mass Ordinary. But a full understanding of changes in repertoire and in musical style will not be achieved until we acquire a better chronological outline for the growth of chant repertoire during the ninth–fourteenth centuries.

The field of paraliturgical chant (including tropes, sequences, *prosulae,* etc.) has also witnessed a rethinking of many basic positions during the third quarter of this century. Early studies in the field were conducted primarily from the philological and liturgical points of view, resulting in the valuable text editions of *Analecta Hymnica.* Editions of the music, itself, are in shorter supply, although their number has increased markedly during the past decades. During the same time, we have come to appreciate that, in attempting to draw order from an inherently chaotic field, earlier scholars tended to obliterate distinctions among different types of works that were drawn in the Middle Ages and are still valid now. A tighter use of terminology has been advocated. There is also a renewed search for the origins of the various practices. While some have sought to draw attention to the importance of the musical aspects of these forms, others have demonstrated links of poetic technique to the creations of late Antiquity and the early Middle Ages. Still more remains to be done in the investigation of the relative roles of text and music in the creation of the various paraliturgical forms of the Middle Ages and in the investigation of the significance of the different kinds of changes undergone in the transmission of such works.

Secular monophony in the vernacular constitutes another area of music historical research that both possesses a longer than average tradition and is interdisciplinary in nature. But even though transcriptions of trouvère songs were published as early as the mid-eighteenth century, our coverage of this area remains somewhat spotty and rife with controversy. Two complete transcriptions of troubadour melodies have been published by Friedrich Gennrich[34] and Hendrik van der Werf.[35] And there are complete facsimiles and transcriptions of individual manuscripts of the trouvères, the minnesingers, the *cantigas,* and the *laude.* But the latter editions are seldom the equivalent of the critical edition of the texts that have been prepared by philologists. While the variants in the transmission of liturgical melodies are often restricted in number and scope, the variants in the transmission of secular monophony, particulary the works of the trouvères and troubadours, seem more numerous and more far-reaching. In order to assess the melodic tradition for most chansons it is necessary to have available an account of all manuscript readings of the music. It is only recently that editions, such as those prepared by Hendrik van der Werf,[36] have begun to address this need. The aforementioned variants furnish one of the basic problems still under debate: the nature of the transmission of the melodies. To what extent do the recorded melodies reflect the personal knowledge of the scribes? To what extent do they reflect written materials available to the scribes, who might have copied or edited them without prior knowledge of the melodies? Was there purely oral transmission, purely written transmission, or a combination of both? Related to this problem is one of assessing the nature of the musical aesthetic that permitted such variants, and placed limits on them. The nature of the interrelationship between text and music in secular monophony is also in need of further exploration. To what extent did the poem determine the form, melodic shape, and rhythm of the melody? There is much more information available concerning the poetic craftsmanship of the troubadours, trouvères, and minnesingers than there is concerning the musical craftsmanship of these men.

The area of rhythmic interpretation is a particularly thorny one. Rhythm is indicated in the notation of only a small percentage of surviving melodies. During the first decade of this century, Aubry, Beck, and Ludwig each advanced theories to the effect that the rhythm of secular monophony was governed in its entirety by the modal patterns employed in the polyphony of the late twelfth and thirteenth centuries. Each theory adduced a different body of evidence, and each employed a different form of reasoning. Unfortunately, acrimonious dispute arose over the question of priority of authorship and so clouded the issues involved that these were not debated fully. Instead scholars in succeeding years began to attempt refinements of the theory before its bases and validity were fully investigated. Cautions concerning the acceptance of the theory were voiced decades ago and opposition has increased during the past several years. The rhythmic modes are a series of patterns that are comparable to (but not all identical with) classical meters, and both proponents and opponents of the modal theory seem to imply that the rhythm of the poetry should be mirrored in the rhythm of the music. Much closer scrutiny ought to be given to the validity and limitations of such an assumption. In this matter, there have been brief references to current styles of performance of Mediterranean folksong, and suggestions have been made concerning the possibility of a continuous tradition. This avenue is yet to be fully explored.

Closer cooperation with ethnomusicologists and musical anthropologists would be useful also in the investigation of the roots of European polyphony. Perhaps because polyphony has been developed to a far greater extent in the European tradition than in any other, and perhaps because of a natural interest in, and bias in favor of, one's own heritage, there has been a tendency to focus on evidence from European sources in seeking to understand early European polyphony. Yet there are several points of similarity between the earliest European polyphony and that still practiced today in other areas, including regions of the Near East. Many musical instruments employed in medieval Europe came from the Near East, and it would appear improbable that Crusaders brought home such instruments, while remaining completely indifferent to and unaffected by Near Eastern music. A strong argument in favor of Eastern influence has been furnished by Alexander Ringer.[37]

The investigation of cross-currents of influence, often a treacherous undertaking, has been begun in many areas of study of medieval music, and research in this direction will likely continue to expand. The subject of Byzantine influence on Western chant is being explored slowly but steadily. The influence of Arabian music (as produced in Spain) on the troubadours and trouvères is still in the process of being evaluated. There is need for the elucidation of musical currents within Europe — for example, those between the polyphony of Aquitania and that of the Ile-de-France in the mid-twelfth century, that of French polyphony on Italian polyphony of the late fourteenth century. Such studies may provide salutary antidotes to the threatened compartmentalization of knowledge.

In the field of early European polyphony, there are many knotty problems other than those involved in the search for origins. Documents antedating A.D. 1100 are few in number and do not form a reliable continuum. The deciphering of pitches is problematic in some, while others have evaded transcription entirely. Theoretical writings constitute one main source of information, but the theorists are not often interested in providing details of early practices. Furthermore, it is by no means assured that the theorists are discussing the most recent practices of their day. The treatise ascribed variously to John Cotton and John of Affighem seems, for example, to be roughly contemporaneous with the oldest polyphony from the St. Martial circle, ca. 1100. Yet the latter is far more sophisticated than the level illustrated by the theorist's musical examples.

The two earliest repertoires of polyphony whose pitches can be read with complete or reasonable certainty are those associated with the centers of St. Martial (Limoges) and Santiago de Compostela. Disagreement prevails concerning the dating of these repertoires, though there is a tendency to place most compositions prior to 1150. Lack of knowledge concerning rhythm constitutes an acute embarrassment here, because many compositions have several notes in the upper voice to one in the lower, or have groups of differing numbers of notes against each other. There is no methodological agreement regarding appropriate methods of dealing with this problem. In many instances, transcriptions are provided without indication of rhythm. Yet no music can be performed without some form of rhythm. Prominent questions that are debated include the following. Was the rhythm of the music determined primarily by the rhythm of text declamation? Was instrumental performance a significant factor in the rhythmic style of the day? To what extent were consonance and dissonance governing forces in musical composition and performance?

Still more basic questions are these. Was the notation fully consistent — that is, was the same solution expected for all appearances of a given figure? Or was the notation only systematic — that is, did the same solution obtain only in the same context? Can we hope to find a corpus of fact that can serve to unravel these problems, or must we base our conclusions on one or more working hypotheses? If the latter, are there means for evaluating contrasting results? Lastly, to what extent are comparisons with repertoires of slightly later times and other geographic provenances valid? Despite the handicaps posed by notational uncertainties, considerable progress has been made in the past decades concerning the treatment of melodic and formal elements in these repertoires.

Questions concerning rhythm still plague scholars dealing with the next important repertoire, that centered about Notre Dame de Paris. The first major master was Leonin (ca. 1135?–ca. 1205?), followed a generation later by Perotin (fl. 1190–1205). Here we begin to reach more certain ground. Parts of this repertoire accord closely with the rhythmic systems described by mid-thirteenth-century theorists and can be transcribed accurately. Unfortunately, passages not obviously covered by theorists' rules are to be found side by side with passages of clear notation in many works. Thus, we debate whether there was one, overall guiding principle of rhythmic style, or whether the works were based on the contrast of opposing rhythmic principles. We still question whether we are in danger of applying, retrospectively, principles that had not yet come into existence. Since the first clear evidence of modal rhythm occurs in the works of Leonin, we debate whether it was he who devised this system[38] — basing his conception of St. Augustine's *De musica* — or whether the system developed gradually and even unconsciously. Apart from the matter of rhythmic interpretation, there are two subjects of particular concern with regard to the Notre Dame organa for two voices. Increasingly we are exploring the manner in which many of these works are put together, utilizing both standard fragments and longer sections that are shared by two or more works. Secondly, we are interested in documenting in greater detail the transmission of these works. The organa were not preserved unchanged; rather entire sections in the older, more rhapsodic style were replaced by newer sections of tighter construction.

Evidence has been brought forth to indicate that not all of "Notre Dame polyphony" was created at Notre Dame de Paris, but that some contributions may stem from other important Parisian churches. It is known that polyphony flourished at other twelfth-century centers, but thus far few musical monuments have been discovered. The subject of peripheral musical centers of the thirteenth–seventeenth centuries, which often cultivated archaic styles, is gradually being taken up by a greater number of scholars. Compositions notated during the fifteenth–seventeenth centuries from outlying areas such as central and eastern Europe and Iceland may occasionally be comparable to works of the tenth–thirteenth centuries from France and Italy. It would even appear that an unbroken tradition in the performance of medieval polyphony existed in Cividale del Friuli until the advent of World War II.

Returning to the mainstream of development, to the thirteenth-century French motet, we finally reach firm ground with respect to the interpretation of notation. Most of the music is available in modern edition. Several of the larger, more recent studies of the genre are devoted primarily to statistical surveys of technical features, but broader stylistic questions have been dealt with as well. Under normal circumstances, medieval polyphony was created in layers, one complete voice at a time. The motet composer, for example, generally began by selecting a preexistent melody (most often a chant melisma) as the basis for his work. This was normally laid out in some predetermined rhythmic pattern. Usually the preexistent material was repeated one or more times in order to provide the desired length. Then one or more upper voices were added in turn. Because of this method of construction, it was possible to add, subtract, or replace voice parts almost at will. There are works that survive in three parts in some manuscripts, and in four in others. There are works that employ the same nucleus of two bottom parts, but with different third parts. This method of construction is quite different from that employed in the composition of most familiar music from the concert repertoire, in which the interaction of the various lines with each other is envisaged from the beginning. Thus, questions of the aesthetic comprehension and evaluation of such works have been raised from time to time. Actually, the motet of this period would serve well to extend the parallels drawn in Panofsky's study, *Gothic Architecture and Scholasticism*. The organization of the motet tenor corresponds to his main observation concerning the increasing organization of knowledge and the systematic division of space, while the phrasing of the *triplum* serves to resolve the *sic et non* situation arising from the independent phrasing of the tenor and *motetus*. In certain ways, this kind of parallelism can be seen to extend to the end of the fourteenth century, the late style of the closing years being termed the *ars subtilior* by some.

The main repertoires of the fourteenth century are also fairly easily accessible. Occasionally there are some unexpected problems. It was not known until fairly recently that there was a tradition from the twelfth to the fourteenth century of notating polyphonic parts as if they were separate monophonic works. Consequently, in the two collected editions of the music of Machaut, one or more works are presented as monophonic that are in actual fact polyphonic.[39] And there are occasional, other needs for the correction of available transcriptions in instances of rhythmic complexity. But, on the whole, we are reasonably well served. Names of a few composers of polyphony active before the fourteenth century are known, and a handful of pieces are ascribed, but it is only during the fourteenth century that the general veil of anonymity is lifted. In France, Philippe de Vitry and Guillaume de Machaut are the two main figures prior to the last quarter of the century. Machaut appears as such a dominant figure — owing in part to the number of manuscripts devoted to his works — that one of the problems facing scholars dealing with fourteenth-century French music is the acquisition of a balanced perspective of the period as a whole. This kind of problem is less acute in dealing with the music of the Trecento, even though Francesco Landini appears there as the dominant figure. We are better informed concerning a sizeable number of Landini's predecessors, contemporaries, and successors. However, the striking efflorescence of secular polyphony in fourteenth-century Italy continues to astound the modern scholar because our knowledge of Italian music-making in the thirteenth century remains sketchy. Consequently, we continue to search for more information regarding early Italian polyphony. And the Trecento compositions are examined from the standpoint of structure in order to determine whether their construction will provide clues regarding the wellsprings of this music.

A few medieval compositions can be dated with relative accuracy. There are some that set texts referring to specific persons or events, and this is a help. The number of such compositions increases somewhat in the early fifteenth century, and one source of this period assigns specific dates to a number of works. We know of few mentions in medieval and early Renaissance chronicles of works that can be securely identified. The proportion of datable pieces remains small. Given that we are much interested in the development of the styles of great masters, questions of chronology and of stylistic evolution loom larger as we know more about the identities of the composers. Efforts have been made toward chronologies of the thirteenth-century motet, but more important are the attempts of providing chronologies for the works of fourteenth- and fifteenth-century composers. Occasionally a composer — such as Dufay — lived at a period when significant changes in notational technique followed in close succession. Thus, a chronology of his oeuvre could be reached on the basis of the technical features of the notation.[40] (The method has been applied to the works of Dufay, but not yet to those of his more important contemporaries.) More often, we are dependent upon various aspects of structural analysis, as in studies of the works of Machaut and Landini.[41] As our command of the various medieval repertoires increases, it is to be expected that refinements in analytical techniques will be employed in the establishing of criteria for the evaluation of authenticity of attribution and date of composition. The broad outlines of the history of medieval music have been sketched. We are now in the process of seeking greater refinement.

NOTES

1. Andrew Hughes, *Medieval Music: The Sixth Liberal Art* (Toronto: Univ. of Toronto Press, 1974), 12.

2. Charles Burney, *A General History of Music* (London: N.p., 1782), vol. 2, chap. 2, par. 4 (cited after edition by Frank Mercer, reprinted New York: Dover, 1957, 457).

3. Arthur Mendel, "Evidence and Explanation," in *International Musicological Society: Report of the Eighth Congress, New York* 2 (1961): 3–18.

4. Leo Treitler, "On Historical Criticism," *The Musical Quarterly* 53 (1976): 188–205.

5. Treitler, "The Present as History," *Perspectives of New Music* 7 (1969): 1–58.

6. Donald Grout, "Current Historiography and Music History," in *Studies in Music History: Essays for Olive Strunk,* ed. Harold Powers (Princeton: Princeton Univ. Press, 1968), 23–40.

7. Early in this century some cultural historians, interpreting too literally the concept of the Renaissance as a rebirth of interest is classical Antiquity, sought to place the beginning of the musical Renaissance ca. 1600 — that is, coinciding with the birth of opera. Even apart from the fact that humanism was an important force in music throughout the sixteenth century, such periodization is totally untenable. Mention of this old error, long since ignored by music historians, may not be amiss in view of the fact that some misconceptions seem to lead charmed lives, recurring long after they seemed to have been safely interred.

8. Claude Palisca, *Humanism in Italian Musical Thought* (New Haven: Yale Univ. Press, 1985).

9. We are somewhat better equipped with regard to interdisciplinary studies in Renaissance music, thanks in part to the impetus provided by scholars such as Edward Lowinsky.

10. Giulio Catlin, *Il Medievo* 1, and F. Alberto Gallo, *Il Medievo* 2 (Edizioni di Torino: Turin, 1979, 1977). Vol. 1 trans. Steven Botterill and Vol. 2 trans. Karen Eales as *Music of the Middle Ages* 1 and 2 (Cambridge: Cambridge Univ. Press, 1984, 1985).

11. Man and Music, Stanley Sadie, general ed. (New York: Prentice Hall, 1990).

12. Cf. Nan C. Carpenter, *Music in the Medieval and Renaissance Universities* (Norman: Univ. of Oklahoma Press, 1958), and Joseph Smits van Weasberghe, *School en Muziek in de Middeleeuwen* (Amsterdam: Uitgeversnaatschapij, 1949).

13. John Stevens, *Words and Music: Song, Narrative, Dance and Drama, 1050-1350* (Cambridge: Cambridge Univ. Press, 1986).

14. Emmanuel Winternitz, "The Visual Arts as a Source for the Historian of Music," in *International Musicological Society: Report of the Eighth Congress, New York, 1961* 1: 109-20.

15. Rebecca Baltzer, "Thirteenth-Century Illuminated Miniatures and the Date of the Florence Manuscript," *Journal of the American Musicological Society* 25 (1972): 1-18.

16. Manfred Bukofzer, "Speculative Thinking in Medieval Music," *Speculum* 17 (1942): 165-80.

17. Nino Pirrotta, "Dante Musicus: Gothicism, Scholasticism, and Music," *Speculum* 43 (1968): 245-57.

18. Leo Treitler, "Homer and Gregory," *The Musical Quarterly* 60 (1974): 333-72.

19. Edward Lowinsky, "The Concept of Physical and Musical Space in the Renaissance," in *Papers Read by Members of the American Musicological Society, 1941* (N.p., 1946), 57-84.

20. Lowinsky, "The Goddess Fortuna in Music," *The Musical Quarterly* 29 (1943): 45-71.

21. Cf. Bibliography, music bibliographies dealing mainly with primary materials (specialized).

22. Kenneth Levy, "A Dominican Organum Duplum," *Journal of the American Musicological Society* 27 (1974): 183-211.

23. K. D. Hartzell, "An Eleventh-Century English Missal Fragment in the British Library," *Anglo-Saxon England* 20 (1989): 45-97.

24. Margaret Bent, "A Lost English Choir Book of the Fifteenth Century," in *International Musicological Society: Report of the Eleventh Congress, Copenhagen, 1972* 1:257-62.

25. Johannes Wolf, *Handbuch der Notationskunde,* 2 vols. (Leipzig: Breitkopf and Härtel, 1913), 1,919.

26. Willi Apel, *The Notation of Polyphonic Music, 900-1600,* 5th ed. (Cambridge, Mass.: Medieval Academy of America, 1961).

27. Carl Parrish, *The Notation of Medieval Music* (London: Faber, 1958).

28. Jacques Chailley, *La musique et le signe* (Lausanne: Guilde du disque, 1967).

29. Ewald Jammers, "Interpretationsfragen mittelalterlicher Musik," *Archiv für Musikwissenschaft* 14 (1957): 230-52. Cf. also Thurston Dart, *The Interpretation of Music* (London: Hutchinson, 1954).

30. Howard Mayer Brown, "Editing," in *The New Grove Dictionary of Music and Musicians,* ed. Stanley Sadie (London: Macmillan, 1980) 5:839-48.

31. Hans Albrecht, "Editionstechnik," in *Die Musik in Geschichte and Gegenwart,* ed. Friedrich Blume (Kassel: Bärenreiter, 1949-), vol. 3, cols. 1109-46.

32. Robert Haas, *Aufführungspraxis,* 1 vol. of *Handbuch der Musikwissenschaft,* ed. Ernst Bücken (Potsdam: Akademie Verlagsgesellschaft Athenaion, 1931).

33. *Paléographie musicale,* ed. Dom André Mocquereau, ser. 1, vols. 2-3, 1891-93.

34. Friedrich Gennrich, *Der Musikalische Nachlass der Troubadours* (Summa Musicae Medii Aevi, vol. 3; cf. also vols. 4 and 15).

35. Hendrik van der Werf, *The Extant Troubadour Melodies,* texts ed. Gerald A. Bond (Rochester, N.Y.: Privately published, 1984).

36. Van der Werf, *The Chansons of the Troubadours and Trouvères* (Utrecht: Oosthoek, 1972).

37. Alexander Ringer, "Eastern Elements in Medieval Polyphony," *Studies in Medieval Culture* 2 (1966): 75-83.

38. Thesis proposed by William Waite, *The Rhythm of Twelfth-Century Polyphony* (New Haven: Yale Univ. Press, 1954).

39. Cf. Richard Hoppin, "An Unrecognized Polyphonic Lai of Machaut," *Musica Disciplina* 12 (1958): 93–104; Margaret Hasselman and Thomas Walker, "More Hidden Polyphony in a Machaut MS," *Musica Disciplina* 24 (1970): 7–16; Sarah Fuller, "Hidden Polyphony — A Reappraisal," *Journal of the American Musicological Society* 24 (1971): 169–92.

40. Charles Hamm, *A Chronology of the Works of Guillaume Dufay Based on a Study of Mansural Practice* (Princeton: Princeton Univ. Press, 1964).

41. Gilbert Reaney, "A Chronology of the Ballades, Rondeaus and Virelais Set to Music by Guillaume de Machaut" and "Towards a Chronology of Machaut's Musical Works," *Musica Disciplina* 6 (1952): 33–38, and 21 (1967): 87–96; Ursula Günther, "Chronologie und Stil der Kompositionen Guillaume de Machauts," *Acta Musicologica* 35 (1963): 96–114; Kurt von Fischer, "Ein Versuch zur Chronologie von Landinis Werken," *Musica Disciplina* 20 (1966): 31–46.

BIBLIOGRAPHY

Bibliographies of Music

Music Bibliographies Dealing Mainly with Secondary Materials

FOCUSING ON MEDIEVAL MUSIC

Hughes, Andrew. *Medieval Music: The Sixth Liberal Art*. Toronto Medieval Bibliographies 4. Rev. ed. Toronto: Univ. of Toronto Press, 1980.
Smits van Waesberghe, Joseph. "Das gegenwärtige Geschichtsbild der mittelalterlichen Musik." *Kirchenmusikalisches Jahrbuch* 46(1962): Cumulative index in vol. 53 (1969).

GENERAL MUSIC BIBLIOGRAPHIES

Bibliographie des Musikschrifttums. Edited by Kurt Taut and Georg Karstädt, 1936–39; Wolfgang Schmieder, 1950–. Leipzig: Hofmeister, 1936–.
International Inventory of Music Literature. RILM Abstracts of Music Literature. *Répertoire International de la Littérature Musicale*. New York: International RILM Center, 1967–. *The Music Index*. Detroit: Information Service, 1949–.

SPECIALIZED MUSIC BIBLIOGRAPHIES

Charles, Sydney Robinson. *A Handbook of Music and Music Literature in Sets and Series*. New York: The Free Press, 1972.
———, and Julie Woodward. "Editions, historical." In *The New Grove Dictionary of Music and Musicians* 5:848–69.

Coover, James, and Richard Colvig. *Medieval and Renaissance Music on Long-playing Records: Supplement, 1962–1971.* Detroit Studies in Music Bibliography 26.

Duckles, Vincent, and Michael Keller. *Music Reference and Research Materials.* 4th ed. New York: Schirmer Books, 1988.

Hagopian, Viola. *Italian Ars Nova Music: A Bibliographic Guide to Modern Editions and Related Literature.* University of California Publications in Music 7. Berkeley: Univ. of California Press, 1964.

Heyer, Anna Harriet. *Historical Sets, Collected Editions, and Monuments of Music.* 3d ed. Chicago: American Library Association, 1980.

Jackson, Roland. *Performance Practice, Medieval to Contemporary, A Bibliographic Guide.* Music Research and Information Guides 9. New York: Garland, 1988.

Schmieder, Wolfgang. "Denkmäler der Tonkunst." In *Die Musik in Geschichte und Gegenwart* 3:164–92.

Sendry, Alfred. *A Bibliography of Jewish Music.* New York: Columbia Univ. Press, 1951.

Vinquist, Mary, and Neal Zaslaw, eds. *Performance Practice: A Bibliography.* New York: Norton, 1971.

Music Bibliographies Dealing Mainly with Primary Materials

GENERAL

International Inventory of Musical Sources. *RISM* (*Répertoire International des Sources Musicales*). Munich: G. Henle, 1960–. Series B, topical volumes.
   3:1. Joseph Smits van Waesberghe, Pieter Fischer, and Christian Maas, eds., *The Theory of Music from the Carolingian Era up to 1400.* 1961.
   3:2. Pieter Fischer, ed. *The Theory of Music from the Carolingian Era up to 1400. Italy.* 1968.
   4:1. Gilbert Reaney, ed. *Manuscripts of Polyphonic Music, 11th–early 14th century.* 1966.
   4:2. Gilbert Reaney, ed. *Manuscripts of Polyphonic Music (c. 1320–1400).* 1969.
   4:3–4. Kurt von Fischer and Max Lütolf, eds. *Handschriften mit mehrstimmiger Musik des 14. 15. und 16. Jahrhunderts.* 1972.
   5:1. Heinrich Husmann, ed. *Tropen- und Sequenzenhandschriften.* 1964.
   9:2. Israel Adler, ed. *Hebrew Writings Concerning Music in Manuscripts and Printed Books from Geonic Times up to 1800.* 1975.

SPECIALIZED

Anderson, Gordon. "Notre Dame and Related Conductus: A Catalogue Raisonné." *Miscellanea Musicologica* 6(1972): 153–229; 7(1973): 1–81.

Besseler, Heinrich. "Studien zur Musik des Mittelalters." *Archiv für Musikwissenschaft* 7(1925): 167–252; 8(1927): 137–258.

Fischer, Kurt von. *Studien zur italienischen Musik des Trecento und frühen Quattrocento.* Bern: P. Haupt, 1956.

Gennrich, Friedrich. *Bibliographie der ältesten französischen und lateinischen Motetten.* Summa Musicae Medii Aevi 2. Darmstadt: Privately published, 1957.

———. *Der musikalische Nachlass der Troubadours: Kommentar.* Summa Musicae Medii Aevi 4. Darmstadt: privately published, 1960.

Le graduel romain. Edited by the Monks of Solesmes. Vol. 2, *Les Sources;* vol. 4, *Le Texte neumatique* (all that is published). Solesmes: Abbey of St. Pierre, 1957, 1960.

Gröninger, Eduard. *Repertoire-Untersuchungen zum mehrstimmigen Notre Dame-Conductus.* Regensburg: Bosse, 1939.

Linker, Robert White. *Music of the Minnesinger and Early Meistersinger.* Chapel Hill: Univ. of North Carolina Press, 1962.

Ludwig, Friedrich. "Die Quellen der Motetten ältesten Stils." *Archiv für Musikwissenschaft* 5(1923): 185–22, 273–315. Summa Musicae Medii Aevi 7, edited by Friedrich Gennrich. Langen bei Frankfurt: privately published, 1961.

———, ed. *Repertorium organorum recentioris et motetorum vetustissimi stili.* Vol. 1, pt. 1, Halle: Niemeyer, 1910. 2d ed., expanded, with preface by Luther Dittmer, Musicological Studies 7. Brooklyn: Institute of Mediaeval Music, 1964; Vol. 1, pt. 2; vol. 2, Musicological Studies 26, 17. Brooklyn: Institute of Mediaeval Music, 1978, 1972. Portions of vol. 1, pt. 2 and vol. 2 issued by Friedrich Gennrich, Summa Musicae Medii Aevi 7, 8. Langen bei Frankfurt: Privately published, 1961. 1962.

Pillet, Alfred; and Carstens, Henry. *Bibliographie der Troubadours.* Halle: Niemeyer, 1933.

Raynaud, Gaston. *Bibliographie des chansonniers français des XIIIe et XIVe siècles.* 2 vols. Paris: F. Vieweg, 1884.

Spanke, Hans. *G. Raynauds Bibliographie des altfranzösischen Liedes.* Leiden: Brill, 1955.

Encyclopedias and Dictionaries

Multivolume Works Incorporating Results of Original Research

The New Grove Dictionary of Music and Musicians. Edited by Stanley Sadie. 20 vols. London: Macmillan, 1980.

Handwörterbuch der musikalischen Terminologie. Edited by Hans Heinrich Eggebrecht. Wiesbaden: F. Steiner. 1972–.

Die Musik in Geschichte und Gegenwart. Edited by Friedrich Blume. 17 vols. Kassel: Bärenreiter, 1949–67. Supplement, 1969–86.

Shorter Reference Works

Baker's Biographical Dictionary of Musicians. 7th ed. Edited by Nicolas Slonimsky. New York: Schirmer, 1984.
The New Harvard Dictionary of Music. Edited by Don Randel. Cambridge, Mass.: Belknap Press of Harvard Univ. Press, 1986.
Riemann, Hugo. *Musik Lexikon.* 12th ed. Edited by Wilibald Gurlitt. 3 vols. Mainz: B. Schott's Söhne, 1959–67. Supplement, 2 vols., edited by Carl Dahlhaus, 1972–75.

Histories of Music

Multivolume Works and Series with Individual Volumes Treating Medieval Music

Bücken, Ernst, ed. *Handbuch der Musikwissenschaft.* 13 vols. in 9. Wildpark-Potsdam:
Akademische Verlagsgesellschaft Athenaion, 1927–21.
Besseler, Heinrich. *Die Musik des Mittelalters und der Renaissance,* 1931.
Haas, Robert. *Aufführungspraxis der Musik.* 1931.
Sachs, Curt. *Die Musik der Antike.* 1928.
Ursprung, Otto. *Die katholische Kirchenmusik.* 1931.
Harman, Alec, and Wilfrid Mellers. *Man and His Music.* 4 vols. London: Rockliff, 1957–59. reissued in 1 vol. in 1962. Vol. 1, *Medieval and Early Renaissance,* 1958.
Man and Music. 4 vols. Englewood Cliffs, N.J.: Prentice-Hall, 1989–90.
McKinnon, James, ed. *Ancient and Medieval Music.* 1990.
Fenlon, Iain, ed. *The Renaissance.* 1989.
The New Oxford History of Music. 10 vols. London: Oxford Univ. Press, 1954–86.
1. *Ancient and Oriental Music.* Edited by Egon Wellesz, 1957.
2. *Early Medieval Music up to 1300.* 2d ed., edited by Richard Crocker and David Hiley, 1990.
3. *Ars Nova and the Renaissance* (1300–1540). Edited by Anselm Hughes and Gerald Abraham, 1960.
The Norton History of Music Series. 7 vols. New York: Norton, 1940–.
Sachs, Curt. *The Rise of Music in the Ancient World, East and West,* 1943.
Reese, Gustave. *Music in the Middle Ages,* 1940.
———. *Music in the Renaissance,* rev. ed., 1959.
The Prentice-Hall History of Music Series. Englewood Cliffs, N.J.: Prentice-Hall, 1965–89.
Brown, Howard Mayer. *Music in the Renaissance.* 1976.
Yudkin, Jeremy. *Music in Medieval Europe.* 1989.
Robertson, Alec, and Stevens, Denis, eds. *The Pelican History of Music.* 3 vols. Harmondsworth, Middlesex: Penguin Books, 1960–69. Vol. 1, *Ancient Forms to Polyphony,* 1960.

Sternfeld, Fredrick William, ed. Praeger History of Western Music. New York: Praeger, 1973–. Vol. 1, Music from the Middle Ages to the Renaissance. 1973.

Individual Volumes Devoted to Medieval Music and General Music Histories with Significant Chapters on Medieval Music

Adler, Guido, ed. Handbuch der Musikgeschichte. 2 vols. 2d ed. Berlin-Wilmersdorf: H. Keller, 1930.

Cattin, Giulio. Il Medievo 1. Turin: Edizioni di Torino, 1979. English translation by Steven Botterill, Music of the Middle Ages 1. Cambridge: Cambridge Univ. Press, 1984.

Chailley, Jacques. Histoire musicale du moyen âge. 2d ed. Paris: Presses universitaires de France, 1969.

Crocker, Richard. A History of Musical Style. New York: McGraw-Hill, 1966.

Gallo, F. Alberto. Il Medievo 2. Turin: Edizioni di Torino, 1977. English translation by Karen Eales, Music of the Middle Ages 2. Cambridge: Cambridge Univ. Press, 1985.

Gérold, Théodore. La musique au moyen âge. Paris: Champion, 1932.

―――. Histoire de la musique des origines à la fin du XIVᵉ siècle. Paris: Renouard, 1936.

Lang, Paul Henry. Music in Western Civilization. New York: Norton, 1941.

Pirro, André. Histoire de la musique de la fin du XIVᵉ siècle à la fin du XVIᵉ. Paris: Renouard, 1940.

Anthologies

Anthology of Music (original German edition, Das Musikwerk). 47 vols. and index. Edited by Karl Gustav Fellerer. Cologne: Arno Volk Verlag: Philadelphia: Theodore Presser, 1960–76.

2. Gennrich, Friedrich, ed. Troubadours, Trouvères, Minnesang, and Meistergesang, 1960.

9. Husmann, Heinrich, ed. Medieval Polyphony, 1962.

13. Wellesz, Egon, ed. The Music of the Byzantine Church, 1959.

18. Tack, Franz, ed. Gregorian Chant, 1960.

30. Schmidt-Görg, Joseph, ed. History of the Mass, 1968.

47. Hüschen, Heinrich, ed. The Motet, 1975.

Davison, Archibald T., and Willi Apel, eds. Historical Anthology of Music. Vol. 1, Oriental, Medieval and Renaissance Music. Rev. ed. Cambridge, Mass.: Harvard Univ. Press, 1949.

Fuller, Sarah, ed. The European Musical Heritage, 800–1750. New York: Knopf, 1987.

Marrocco, W. Thomas, and Nicholas Sandon, eds. The Oxford Anthology of Music: Medieval Music. London: Oxford Univ. Press, 1977.

Parrish, Carl, ed. A Treasury of Early Music. New York: Norton, 1958.

————, and John F. Ohl, eds. *Masterpieces of Music Before 1750*. New York: Norton, 1951.

Schering, Arnold, ed. *Geschichte der Musik in Beispielen*. Leipzig: Breitkopf & Härtel, 1931. Reprinted, New York: Broude Brothers, 1950.

Iconographies

Kinsky, Georg, ed. *Geschichte der Musik in Bildern*. Leipzig: Breitkopf & Härtel, 1929. French ed., *Album Musical*. Paris: Delagrave, 1930. English eds., *A History of Music in Pictures*. 1930, 1937, 1951.

Komma, Karl Michael, ed. *Musikgeschichte in Bildern*. Stuttgart: Alfred Kröner, 1961.

Lang, Paul Henry, and Otto Bettmann, eds. *A Pictorial History of Music*. New York: Norton, 1960.

Musikgeschichte in Bildern. Founded by Heinrich Besseler and Max Schneider, present editor, Werner Bachmann. 28 vols. issued thus far. Leipzig: Deutscher Verlag für Musik, 1961–.

    2:5. Günter Fleischhauer, ed. *Etrurien und Rom*. 1965.

    3:2. Henry George Farmer, ed. *Islam*. 1966.

    3:3. Joseph Smits van Waesberghe, ed. *Musikerziehung*, 1969.

    3:4. Bruno Stäblein, ed. *Schriftbild der einstimmigen Musik*. 1975.

    3:5. Henrich Besseler and Peter Gülke, eds. *Schriftbild der mehrstimmigen Musik*. N.d.

    3:8. Edmund A. Bowles, ed. *Musikleben im 15. Jahrhundert*. 1977.

Medieval Musical Theory

Histories and Anthologies of Excerpts

Riemann, Hugo. *Geschichte der Musiktheorie im IX.–XIX. Jahrhundert* (History of Music Theory: Books I.II, Polyphonic Theory to the 16th Century). 2d ed. Berlin: Max Hesse, 1920. Books I and II translated and edited by Raymond H. Haggh. Lincoln: Univ. of Nebraska Press, 1962.

Strunk, Oliver. *Source Readings in Music History*. New York: Norton, 1950.

Tello, Francisco. *Estudios de Historia de la Tearia musicale*. Madrid: Consejo Superior de Investigaciones Cientificas, 1962.

Collections of Treatises

Corpus scriptorum de musica. 34 vols. issued thus far. Rome: American Institute of Musicology, 1950–. Various editors.

Coussemaker, Edmond de. *Scriptorum de Musica Medii Aevi*. 4 vols. Paris: Durand,

1864–76. Reprinted, Milan: Bollettino Bibliografico Musicale, 1931; Hildesheim: G. Olms, 1963.

Eggebrecht, Hans Heinrich, and Friedrich Zaminer. *Ad organum faciendum: Lehrschriften der Mehrstimmigkeit in nachguidonischer Zeit.* Mainz: B. Schott's Söhne, 1970.

Erlanger, Randolphe d'. *La musique arabe.* 6 vols. Paris: Geuthner, 1930–59.

Gerbert, Martin. *Scriptores ecclesiastici de musica sacra potissimum.* 3 vols. St. Blasien, 1784. Reprinted, Milan: Bollettino Bibliografice Musicale, 1931; Hildesheim: G. Olms, 1963.

Notation

Apel, Willi. *The Notation of Polyphonic Music, 900–1600.* 5th ed. Cambridge, Mass.: Medieval Academy of America, 1961.

Arlt, Wulf, ed. *Palaeographie der Musik.* Cologne: Arno Volk-Verlag & Hans Gerig, 1973–79.

  1:1. Wulf Arlt. *Einleitung,* 1979.

  1:2. Max Haas. *Byzantinische und Slavische Notationen,* 1973.

  1:3. Solange Corbin. *Die Neumen,* 1977.

  1.4. Ewald Jammers. *Aufzeichnungsweisen der einstimmigen ausserliturgischen Musik des Mittelalters,* 1975.

Parrish, Carl. *The Notation of Medieval Music.* London: Faber, 1958.

Suñol, Dom Grégorie. *Introduction à la paléographie musicale grégorienne.* Paris: Tournai, Desclée, 1935.

Wolf, Johannes. *Handbuch der Notationskunde.* 2 vols. Kleine Handbücher der Musikgeschichte nach Gattungen, 8. Leipzig: Breitkopf & Härtel, 1913, 1919. Reprinted, Hildesheim: Olms, 1963.

Monographs and Editions with Major Volumes of Commentary

Abert, Hermann. *Die Musikanschauung des Mittelalters.* Halle: Niemeyer, 1905. Reprinted, Tutzing: Schneider, 1964.

Anglès, Higini. *El Còdex musical de las Huelgas.* 3 vols. Biblioteca de Catalunya, Publicacions del Department de Música 6. Barcelona: Institut d'Estudis Catalans, 1931.

————. *Historia de la música medieval en Navarra.* Diputación Foral de Navarra, Institución Príncipe de Viana. Pamplona: N.p., 1970.

————. *La Música a Catalunya fins al segle XII.* Biblioteca de Catalunya, Publicacions del Department de Música 10. Barcelona: Institut d'Estudis Catalans, 1935.

————. *La música de las Cantigas de Santa Maria del Rey Alfonso el Sabio.* 3 vols. Barcelona: Biblioteca Central, 1943–64.

Apel, Willi. *Gregorian Chant.* Bloomington: Univ. of Indiana Press, 1958.

Apfel, Ernst. *Studien zur Satztechnik der mittelalterlichen englischen Musik.* 2 vols. Abhandlungen der Heidelberger Akademie der Wissenschaften, Philosophisch-historische Klasse. Heidelberg: Carl Winter Universitätsverlag, 1959.

Auda, Antoine. *Les modes at les tons de la musique et spécialement de la musique médievale.* Académie royale des sciences, des lettres et des beaux-arts de Belgique: Classe de beaux-arts. Mémoires, series 3, vol. 1. Brussels: Palais des Académies, 1931. Reprinted, Hildesheim: Georg Olms, 1979.

Batka, Richard. *Geschichte der Musik in Böhmen.* Vol. 1, *Böhmen unter deutschem Einfluß 900-1333.* Prague: Dürerverlag, 1906.

Bent, Margaret. *Dunstaple.* Oxford Studies of Composers 17. London: Oxford Univ. Press, 1981.

Bukofzer, Manfred F. *Geschichte des englischen Diskants and des Fauxbourdons nach den theoretischen Quellen.* Strasbourg: Heitz, 1936.

——. *Studies in Medieval and Renaissance Music.* New York: Norton, 1950.

Carpenter, Nan C., *Music in the Medieval and Renaissance Universities.* Norman: Univ. of Oklahoma Press, 1958.

Chailley, Jacques. *L'École musicale de Saint Martial jusqu'à la fin du XIᵉ siècle.* Paris: Les Livres essentials, 1960.

Clercx-Lejeune, Suzanne. *Johannes Ciconia: Un musicien liégeois et son temps.* 2 vols. Académie royale de Belgique, Classe des beaux-arts. Mémoires, series 2, vol. 10. Brussels: Palais des Académies, 1960.

Corbin, Solange. *L'Église à la conquête de sa musique.* Paris: Gallimard, 1960.

——. *Essai sur la musique religieuse portugaise au moyen âge.* Collection portugaise, 8. Paris: Les Belles lettres, 1952.

Crane, Frederick. *Extant Medieval Musical Instruments.* Iowa City: Univ. of Iowa Press, 1972.

Dannemann, Erna. *Die spätgotische Musiktradition in Frankreich und Burgund vor dem Auftreten Dufays.* Strasbourg: Heitz, 1936.

Evans, Paul. *The Early Trope Repertory of Saint Martial de Limoges.* Princeton Studies in Music 2. Princeton: Princeton Univ. Press, 1970.

Farmer, Henry G. *A History of Arabian Music to the XIIIth Century.* London: Luzac, 1929. Reprinted, 1967.

——. *Historical Facts for the Arabian Musical Influence.* London: Reeves, 1930. Reprinted, Hildesheim: Olms, 1970.

Fellerer, Karl Gustav, ed. *Geschichte der katholischen Kirchenmusik.* Vol. 1, *Von den Anfängen bis zum Tridentium.* Kassel: Bärenreiter Verlag, 1972-.

Flotzinger, Rudolf. *Der Discantus-satz im Magnus liber und seine Nachfolge.* Wiener musikwissenschaftliche Beiträge 8. Vienna, Harmann Böhlaus Nachf., 1969.

Gamberini, Leopoldo. *Le Parola e la musica nell' antichità.* Historiae musicae cultores, Biblioteca, 15. Florence: Olschki, 1961.

Gennrich, Friedrich. *Grundriß einer Formenlehre des mittelalterlichen Liedes.* Halle: Niemeyer, 1932; reprinted Tübingen, 1970.

Harrison, Frank Lloyd. *Music in Medieval Britain.* London: Routledge, 1958.

Holschneider, Andreas. *Die Organa von Winchester.* Hildesheim: Olms, 1968.

Jammers, Ewald. *Anfänge der abendländischen Musik.* Strasbourg: Heitz, 1955.

————. *Musik in Byzanz, im päpstlichen Rom und in Frankreich.* Abhandlungen der Heidelberger Akademie der Wissenschaften, Philosophisch-historische Klasse. Heidelberg: Carl Winter Universitätsverlag, 1962.

Kippenberg, Burkhard. *Der Rhythmus im Minnesang.* Münchner Texte und Untersuchungen zur deutschen Literatur des Mittelalters, 3. Munich: Beck, 1962.

López-Calo, José. *La Música medieval en Galicia.* Corunna: Fundación "Pedro Barrie de la Maza, Conde de Fenosa," 1982.

Lütolf, Max. *Die mehrstimmigen Ordinarium Missae-Sätze.* 2 vols. Bern: Haupt, 1970.

Machabey, Armand. *Genèse de la tonalité classique des origines au XVᵉ siècle.* Paris: Richard-Masse, 1955.

————. *Guillaume de Machaut, 130?-1377.* 2 vols. Paris: Richard-Masse, 1955.

Maillard, Jean. *Évolution et esthétique du lai lyrique.* Paris: Centre de documentation universitaire, 1963.

McGee, Timothy. *Medieval and Renaissance Music: A Performer's Guide.* Toronto: Univ. of Toronto Press, 1985.

Montagu, Jeremy. *The World of Medieval and Renaissance Musical Instruments.* Woodstock, N.Y.: Overlook Press, 1976.

Moser, Hans Joachim. *Geschichte der deutchen Musik.* Vol. 1, *Von den Anfängen bis zum Beginn des Dreißigjährigen Krieges.* 4th ed. Stuttgart: Cotta, 1926.

Munrow, David. *Instruments of the Middle Ages and Renaissance.* London: Oxford Univ. Press, 1976.

Page, Christopher. *Voices and Instruments of the Middle Ages: Instrumental Practice and Songs in France, 1100-1300.* Berkeley, Univ. of California Press, 1986.

Pietzsch, Gerhard W. *Die Klassifikation der Musik von Boethius bis Ugolino.* Studien zur Geschichte der Musik-Theorie im Mittelalter. Halle: Niemeyer, 1929.

Quasten, Johannes. *Musik und Gesang in den Kulten der heidnischen Antike und Christlichen Frühzeit.* Liturgiegeschichtliche Quellen und Forschungen 25. Münster: Aschendorff, 1930.

Reaney, Gilbert. *Guillaume de Machaut.* Oxford Studies of Composers 9. London: Oxford Univ. Press, 1971.

Rokseth, Yvonne. *Polyphonies du XIIIᵉ siècle: Le MS H.196 de la Faculté de Médicine de Montpellier.* Paris: Oiseau-Lyre, 1935-39.

Sachs, Curt. *The History of Musical Instruments.* New York: Norton, 1940.

Seagrave, Barbara G., and Wesley Thomas. *The Songs of the Minnesingers.* Urbana: Univ. of Illinois Press, 1966.

Sesini, Ugo. *Poesia e musica nella latinità cristiana dall'III al X secolo,* ed. Giuseppe Vecchi. Nuevo Biblioteca Italiana 6. Turin: Società editrice internazionale, 1949.

Smits van Waesberghe, Joseph. *Muziekgeschiedenis der Middeleeuwen.* 2 vols. Nederlandsche Muziekhistorische en Muziekpaedagogische Studiën. Series A. Tilburg: W. Bergmans, 1939, 1942.

————. *School in Muziek in de Middeleeuwen; De muziekdidactiek van de vroegen middeleeuwen.* Amsterdam: Uitgeversnaatschapij, 1949.

Smoldon, William L. *The Music of the Medieval Church Dramas.* London: Oxford Univ. Press, 1980.

Stevens, John. *Words and Music in the Middle Ages: Song, Narrative, Dance and Drama, 1050–1350.* Cambridge: Cambridge Univ. Press, 1986.

Strohm, Reinhard. *Music in Late Medieval Bruges.* Oxford: Oxford Univ. Press, 1985.

Van der Werf, Hendrik. *The Chansons of the Troubadors and Trouvères.* Utrecht: Oosthoek, 1972.

Velimirovic, Milos. *Byzantine Elements in Early Slavic Chant: The Hirmologion.* Monumenta Musicae Byzantinae, Subsidia, 4. Copenhagen: Munksgaard, 1960.

Wagner, Peter. *Einführung in die gregorianischen Melodien.* 3 vols. Leipzig: Breitkopf & Härtel, 1911–21. Reprinted, Hildesheim: Olms, 1962. Vol. 1, *Introduction to the Gregorian Melodies.* Translated by Agnes Orme and E. G. P. Wyatt. London: The Plainsong and Mediaeval Music Society, 1901.

Waite, William G. *The Rhythm of Twelfth-Century Polyphony.* Yale Studies in the History of Music 2. New Haven: Yale Univ. Press, 1954.

Wellesz, Egon. *Eastern Elements in Western Chant.* Monumenta Musicae Byzantine, Subsidia, 2. Oxford: Oxford Univ. Press, 1947.

———. *A History of Byzantine Music and Hymnography.* 2d ed. Oxford: Clarendon, 1961.

Werner, Eric. *The Sacred Bridge.* 2 vols. London: Dobson, 1959; New York: Ktav Publishing House, 1984.

Whitehill, Walter M., Dom German Prado, Jesús Carro García. *Liber Sancti Jacobi: Codex Calixtinus.* 3 vols. Santiago de Compostela: Consejo superior de investigaciones cientificas, Instituto P. Sarmiento de estudios gallegos, 1944.

Index

For references to authors and titles cited in the text, see the bibliographies at the end of chapters.

433

Medieval Studies: An Introduction, Second Edition
was composed in 10 on 12 Times Roman on Digital Compugraphic equipment
by Metricomp,
with display type in Libra by Dix Type, Inc.;
printed by sheet-fed offset on 60-pound Natural Smooth,
Smyth-sewn and bound over binder's boards in Holliston Roxite B
and notch bound with paper covers printed in 2 colors
by Braun-Brumfield, Inc.;
and published by

Syracuse University Press
Syracuse, New York 13244-5160